GREGG
Typewriting for Colleges

SECOND CANADIAN EDITION

Complete Course

Alan C. Lloyd, Ph.D.
Director, Gregg Typing Instructional Service
Gregg Division, McGraw-Hill Book Company

John L. Rowe, Ed.D.
Chairman, Department of Business Education
College of Education, University of North Dakota

Fred E. Winger, Ed.D.
Professor of Secretarial Science and Business
Education, Oregon State University

Revised by

Janet H. Stevenson
Assistant Professor, Secretarial and Administrative
Studies, The University of Western Ontario

McGRAW-HILL RYERSON LIMITED

Toronto   Montreal   New York   St. Louis   San Francisco   Auckland
Bogota   Düsseldorf   Johannesburg   London   Madrid   Mexico
New Delhi   Panama   Paris   Sao Paulo   Singapore   Sydney   Tokyo

Copyright © McGraw-Hill Ryerson Limited, 1978
Copyright © McGraw-Hill Company of Canada Limited, 1971
Copyright © McGraw-Hill, Inc. 1964, 1957

Canadian Cataloguing in Publication Data

Lloyd, Alan C., 1915-
  Gregg typewriting for colleges: complete course

Includes the basic and intensive courses.
ISBN 0-07-082615-3

1. Typewriting. I. Rowe, John L., 1914-
II. Winger, Fred E., 1912- III. Stevenson,
Janet H., 1939- IV. Title.

Z49.L7 1978   652.3   C77-001644-8

 2345678910 D 7654321098

Printed and bound in Canada

CONTENTS

INDEX

OVERVIEW

This book focuses on three goals—

Gregg Typewriting for Colleges, Canadian Edition, has been developed, tested, and published—

A. To help you become a rapid, accurate touch operator of the typewriter.
B. To make you proficient in the production of letters, reports, tables, documents, forms, and manuscripts.
C. To help you master the rules that govern word division, paragraphing, correspondence courtesies, and similar typewriting technicalities.

Millions of trainees achieved these goals via the preceding edition of this book. To help you achieve them, too, but even more quickly and easily, this edition features a number of notable aids:

A. To help you become a skillful typist

solely on skill boosting, and every lesson contains some drills for sustaining and extending your skill.

1. *Selective Practice.* You will learn how to analyze and select drills so that you may (a) focus mainly on those that will help *you* most and (b) practice them in the way that will most surely help *you.*
2. *Massed Drill.* Skill comes from drill. This book contains more drills than any other book of similar length. More than a fourth of the lessons concentrate
3. *Copy Control.* Your drill needs will change as you improve; to be sure the drills are right for you at each stage, every drill and exercise has been controlled for word length, vocabulary, repetition, and other factors basic to rapid growth.

B. To help you become a production expert

step in each area of production begins with studying, then copying, an annotated model. This book has more models than any similar book.

4. *Power Cycles.* You will learn to use your typing power even while you increase it, for this book is organized in a spiral. After the introductory first Part, each Part is a 25-lesson cycle:

   6 lessons on skill extension
   6 lessons on correspondence typing
   6 lessons on tables or business forms
   6 lessons on manuscripts and reports
   1 lesson that is a test on the others

   Each cycle boosts your typing power and then gives you production assignments geared to your new level of power.
5. *Picture-Page Approach.* So that you may develop full understanding of production typing, every new
6. *Production Count.* The production exercises are accompanied by a special "production word count" that will enable you to use identical material for both building skill and applying it—a procedure that will enable you to attain much higher production rates and to achieve them much sooner.
7. *Practical Procedures.* The typing shortcuts introduced in the first edition and now standard in all books are continued; and new ones are provided for letter placement, postal coding, ZIP-coding, metrication, balance-lining, and error-absorbing.

C. To help you master typing technicalities

8. *Learning Guides.* Pioneering in the direction of programmed instruction, this book introduces in its companion workbooks "Learning Guides" that you will use in your typewriter (making a "teaching machine" of it). By providing instant confirmation of your answers to questions, the Learning Guides will give you greater mastery, faster. These aids cover such technical areas as margin determination, word division, number expression, footnoting, punctuating, and related areas that the informed typist is expected to master.
9. *Copy Editing.* Most rules about technicalities are presented, also, in intensive summaries that you will reproduce as reports (and keep for permanent reference!) and then apply to the kinds of unedited material with which most typists work.   **THE AUTHORS**

1 THE TYPEWRITER • THE ALPHABET
AND THE NUMBER KEYS

Parts you need to know
for the first lessons

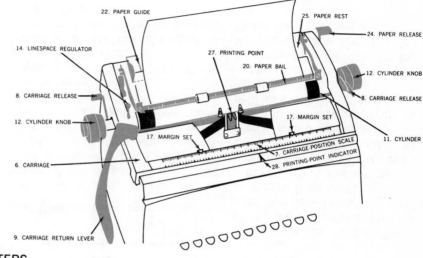

22. PAPER GUIDE
25. PAPER REST
24. PAPER RELEASE
14. LINESPACE REGULATOR
27. PRINTING POINT
20. PAPER BAIL
12. CYLINDER KNOB
8. CARRIAGE RELEASE
8. CARRIAGE RELEASE
12. CYLINDER KNOB
17. MARGIN SET
17. MARGIN SET
11. CYLINDER
7. CARRIAGE-POSITION SCALE
6. CARRIAGE
28. PRINTING-POINT INDICATOR
9. CARRIAGE RETURN LEVER

REFERENCE • MANUAL TYPEWRITERS

Parts you need to know
for the first lessons

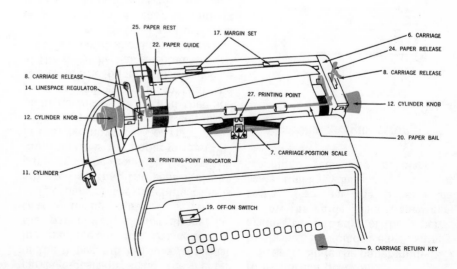

25. PAPER REST
17. MARGIN SET
6. CARRIAGE
22. PAPER GUIDE
24. PAPER RELEASE
8. CARRIAGE RELEASE
8. CARRIAGE RELEASE
14. LINESPACE REGULATOR
27. PRINTING POINT
12. CYLINDER KNOB
12. CYLINDER KNOB
20. PAPER BAIL
28. PRINTING-POINT INDICATOR
7. CARRIAGE-POSITION SCALE
11. CYLINDER
19. OFF-ON SWITCH
9. CARRIAGE RETURN KEY

REFERENCE • ELECTRIC TYPEWRITERS

5

C. HORIZONTAL SPACING

1. Counting the spaces

Each time a key or the space bar is tapped, the carriage (6) moves one space to the left. Each tap moves the carriage exactly one space. Each space is the same size.

Remember: Typewriters space uniformly, as though printing on graph paper.

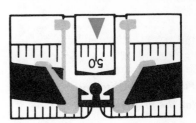

The spaces can be counted. Every typewriter has a carriage-position scale (7) that marks off the spaces. The scale numbers every fifth or tenth space, too, so that the typist may know the number of each space across the carriage.

Every machine has some kind of arrowhead, line, or other marker, called the printing-point indicator (28), that points to the space on the scale at which the carriage is positioned and at which the machine is ready to print. When the carriage is at the 50th space, for example, the marker points at 50.

2. Finding the center space

A typist is expected to center what he types—that is, he arranges what appears on each side of the paper. Such centering requires the typist

to know at what point on the carriage-position scale the center of the paper will fall and to adjust his machine so that the center of the paper will always appear at that centering point.

The part of the machine that is adjusted so that the center of the paper will be consistently at the same point is the paper guide (22). It may be moved left or right.

The typist selects the centering point he wishes to use and then adjusts the paper guide so that the center of the paper will always be at the point he has selected.

Which point should be selected? *Recommended: 50.* This number is easy to remember, easy to find on the carriage-position scale, and easy to add to and subtract from in planning margin settings. *Remember: For efficiency, adjust the paper guide so that the center of the paper will fall at 50.*

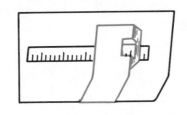

3. Adjusting the paper guide

To adjust the paper guide so the center of the paper will always be at 50 [or whatever point may be selected], seven steps are involved. They need to be taken only once; after that, the typist *knows* where the guide belongs and does not need to repeat the steps.

STEP 1. Set the carriage at 50 [or other selected point].

STEP 2. At the top of a sheet of paper, mark the center by a pencil mark or by a crease.

STEP 3. Insert the paper.

STEP 4. Depress the paper release (24), so the paper will be loose and can be slid left or right.

STEP 5. Keeping the paper straight, slide it left or right until the center crease or mark is squarely at the printing point (27).

STEP 6. Restore the paper release to its normal position.

STEP 7. Slide the paper guide (22) to bring its blade edge snugly against the left edge of the paper. Now the guide is positioned correctly. Note on the paper-guide scale *exactly* where you have set the guide; remember the place.

4. Planning margin settings

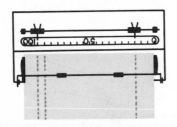

STEP 1. Determine what length of writing line is to be used. The line length for drills is given in the lesson headings. For example, LINE: 40 means "set margins for a 40-space line." The line length for letters, reports, and other work is something to be learned as an aspect of producing such work [see Index, page iv].

STEP 2. Plan the setting for the left margin stop. From the center of the paper, *subtract* half the desired line length and set the stop at the resulting number.

STEP 3. Plan the setting for the right margin stop. To the center of the paper, *add* half the desired line length *plus 5 extra spaces* [to provide for the warning signal of the bell] and set the stop at the resulting number.

EXAMPLE: Settings for a 40-space line would be $50-20=30$ for the left margin stop and $50+20+5=75$ for the right margin stop.

COMMON MARGIN SETTINGS
(With the Paper Centered at 50)

LINE DESIRED	LEFT MARGIN STOP AT	RIGHT MARGIN STOP AT
40 spaces	$50-20=30$	$50+20+5=75$
50 spaces	$50-25=25$	$50+25+5=80$
60 spaces	$50-30=20$	$50+30+5=85$
70 spaces	$50-35=15$	$50+35+5=90$

5. Setting the margin stops

Procedures vary for different makes and models of typewriters.

SPRING-SET MACHINES. Royals, Smith-Coronas, and some R. C. Allens have a margin-set key (17) at each end of the carriage. To set the left stop: Press the left margin-set key, move the carriage to the desired scale point,

and release the set key. To set the right stop: Press right margin-set key, move carriage to desired scale point, and release set key.

HAND-SET MACHINES. The margin stops (18) of Olivettis, IBM Selectrics, Remingtons, and some R. C. Allens are adjustable by hand, without use of a set key. Adjust each margin stop separately: Press

down the top of the margin stop, slide the stop left or right to desired scale point, and release stop.

HOOK-ON MACHINES. Electric Olivettis, standard IBMs, and some Remingtons have hook-on margin stops. To set the left margin

stop: Move the carriage to the left margin, hook onto the left margin stop by holding down firmly the margin-set key (17) on the keyboard, move the carriage to the desired scale point, and release the set key. To set the right margin stop: Move the carriage to the right margin, hook onto the right stop by holding down firmly the set key (same key you used for left margin), move carriage to desired scale point, and release margin-set key.

6. a) Pica and elite spacing

Typewriters are usually equipped with either of two sizes of type: pica [pronounced *pie*-ka] and elite [pronounced ay-*leet*].

Pica type, the larger, prints 10 letters to an inch; elite prints 12 letters to an inch. On standard P4 typing paper, 21.5 cm wide, a

pica machine can type 85 characters; and an elite machine can type 102 characters.

To determine whether a machine is pica or elite, type a series of periods and compare them with the ones printed here: (10 pitch)

• • • • • • • • • • (10 pitch)

• • • • • • • • • • • • (12 pitch)

To convert pica strokes into the elite equivalent, refer to the following table:

Line length	Strokes (or spaces)		
Line length	40	50	60
Pica	40	50	60
Elite	50	60	70

6. b) SI (Metric) spacing information

Because of Canada's decision to convert to the international metric system, SI, paper sizes are no longer given in inches; instead they appear in centimetres and/or millimetres. Therefore, instead of specifying an inch line for a typing exercise, this text specifies the line length in strokes. For example, line 40 = 40 strokes (pica).

In metric terms, 10 pica strokes fill 2.54 cm of space; 12 elite strokes fill 2.54 cm of space. On standard business size metric paper, P4, which is 21.5 cm wide, a pica machine can type $21.5 \div 2.54 = 8.5 \times 10$ strokes = 85 strokes; and an elite machine can type $8.5 \times 12 = 102$ strokes.

7. Indenting with the tabulator

For use in indenting paragraphs and other operations in which the typist wishes to spring the carriage to an assigned point without repeatedly striking the space bar, all machines have a "tabulator" mechanism. It has three controls on, or slightly above, the keyboard:

TAB-SET KEY is used to set a pin, known as a "tab stop," at the point where it is desired that the carriage stop automatically.

TAB-CLEAR KEY is used to clear, or eliminate, an individual tab stop that was previously set. Some machines have an ALL-CLEAR KEY to eliminate simultaneously all stops that are already set.

TAB KEY OR BAR is used to free the carriage from its regular spac-

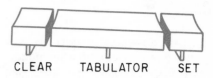

ing so that it may spring to the point where a tab stop is set.

The use of these controls is illustrated by the steps involved in preparing for paragraph indenting:

STEP 1. Confirm margin settings.

STEP 2. Clear any tab stops already set: Press the all-clear key or move the carriage to the right margin and then return it while pressing the clear key.

STEP 3. Set a tab stop at the point to which the carriage is to spring: Space in from the margin (standard indention: 5 spaces) and press the tab-set key.

STEP 4. Test the setting: draw the carriage back to the margin; then firmly press the tab bar or key. The carriage should hop to the point where the stop is set.

8. Centering a word or line

To center a word or group of words (title of an essay, for example), three steps are involved:

STEP 1. Set the carriage at the centering point.

STEP 2. Say *in pairs* the strokes (letters *and* spaces) in the material to be centered, depressing the backspacer (3) once for each pair of strokes. If an odd, leftover letter remains after calling the pairs, do *not* backspace for it.

STEP 3. Beginning at the point to which the carriage has been backspaced, type the material; it will be centered horizontally.

If several lines are to be centered, centering the carriage for each line is simplified by setting a tab stop at the center. The typist then tabulates (indents) to that point instead of positioning the carriage manually.

D. VERTICAL SPACING

9. Controlling the spacing

The amount of blank space between lines of typing is controlled by the linespace regulator (14), which may be set at "1" for single spacing and which provides no space between typed lines; at "2" for double spacing, which provides one blank line between lines of typing; and at "3" for triple spacing, which provides two blank lines between lines of typing. Examples:

```
single         single         single
——————         ——————         double
double         ——————         ——————
               triple         triple
```

Some machines also have 1½ spacing (midway between single and double) and 2½ spacing (midway between double and triple); but on such machines, most work is typed in standard single and double spacing.

10. Inserting extra blank lines

To leave extra space between lines of typing, advance the paper one line more than the number of lines that are to be left blank. For example, to leave a blank line between two sets of drills, advance

```
fff fff jjj jjj fff fff jj jj jj j
fff fff jjj jjj fff fff jj jj jj j
fff fff jjj jjj fff fff jj jj jj j

ddd ddd kkk kkk ddd kkk dd kk dd k
ddd ddd kkk kkk ddd kkk dd kk dd k
ddd ddd kkk kkk ddd kkk dd kk dd k
```

the paper two lines (by returning the carriage twice instead of once), one to be the blank line and one to be the next line on which to type.

Remember: Always advance the paper one more line than the number of lines to be left blank.

11. Centering material vertically

P4 paper (standard business size, 28 cm long) provides 66 possible lines of space to a page. To center lines within these 66 lines:

STEP 1. Count the lines (including blank ones) the material fills.

STEP 2. Subtract the number of lines needed from the 66 available [or from 33, on a half sheet (P5)].

STEP 3. Divide the remainder by 2 (count a fraction as a whole) to get the number of the line, counting from the top, on which to begin.

[NOTE: For material to look centered, the bottom margin should be a little wider than the top one; the three steps above provide for this desirable difference.]

EXAMPLE. A 21-line display would be $66-21=45$; and $45 \div 2 = 22\frac{1}{2}$ or 23, the line on which to begin. This provides a top margin of 22 lines and a bottom one of 23 lines.

Sometimes the instructions are to "Leave 2.5 cm space." Most machines provide 6 lines of space to 2.5 cm. To leave 6 blank lines, advance the paper 7 lines—6 for the blank 2.5 cm and 1 to reach the line of typing.

```
cm/mm
       Line 1
  1
       Line 2
       Line 3
  2
       Line 4
       Line 5
       Line 6
```

The typist must always be aware of the spacing for which his typewriter is set. Advancing the paper three lines when the machine is set for single spacing, for example, simply requires three carriage returns. But advancing the paper the same three lines when the machine is set for double spacing requires a single carriage return (two lines) and one line turned up by hand.

This book occasionally displays an arrow and a number to signal how many lines to advance the paper, to solve a special arrangement problem. An ↓3 arrow-3, for example, does not mean to leave three blank lines but to leave two blank lines by advancing the paper three lines.

E. CARE OF THE TYPEWRITER

12. Keeping a machine in trim

DAILY CARE. Brush the printing faces of the typebars. Dust inside the machine with a long-handled brush. Wipe adjacent desk surfaces and under the machine. Keep machine covered when not in use.

WEEKLY CARE. Using a cloth moistened with oil, wipe the rails on which the carriage moves.

BIWEEKLY CARE. Using a cloth dampened with alcohol, wipe the cylinder (11) and paper-bail rolls (21).

CONSTANT CARE. Return carriage briskly but without a bang! Untangle jammed keys carefully—never pull typebars, lest they be bent.

13. Putting on a new ribbon

STEP 1. Before removing the old ribbon, note how it is threaded and which of these winding arrangements is used to approach the spool:

FRONT OUTSIDE   FRONT INSIDE

FRONT TOP

STEP 2. Then practice each phase of the ribbon change—lift out a spool, put it back; unthread the carrier, rethread it; and so on.

STEP 3. Wind the old ribbon on one spool; detach the end, noting how it was hooked to the spool. Discard old spool and ribbon.

STEP 4. Fasten end of the new ribbon on the empty spool. Place both spools in their sockets.

STEP 5. Thread the new ribbon into place. (Depressing the shift lock makes it easier to thread the ribbon through the carrier.) Check that the ribbon reverses properly.

F. STEPS WHEN PREPARING TO TYPE

1. Arrange the table

Machine, even with front of table. Book at right, turned and tilted. Extra paper, left of machine.

2. Check the paper guide

Paper guide should be adjusted so center of paper will be at 50. Review §8 on page 6.

3. Set the linespace regulator

Instructions at the start of each lesson say whether to set machine for single or double linespacing.

4. Set the margin stops

LINE: 40

Instructions at the start of each lesson state for what line length you are to set the margins. Review §4, page 6; and §5, page 7.

5. Move paper bail away

So the paper bail will not interfere with the paper insertion, pull the bail toward you. (If it will not pull forward on your typewriter, lift the bail straight upright.)

6. Grasp and insert paper

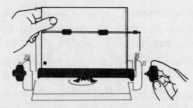

Left hand grasps paper and puts it behind cylinder, against paper guide. Right hand turns cylinder knob, to draw paper into machine. Turn up about 10 cm (24 lines) of paper.

7. Straighten the paper

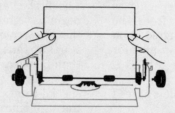

The left side of the paper should align, top and bottom, at the paper guide. If the alignment is not correct, loosen paper (use paper release) and straighten it.

8. Reset the paper bail

Adjust rolls to divide paper approximately into thirds; then place the bail snugly against the paper.

9. Provide for top margin

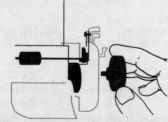

If preparing to type drills: Turn paper down (use cylinder knob) until only two lines or so of paper shows above the top of the bail.

If preparing for production work: Before resetting paper bail, turn paper down until its top edge is even with aligning scale (1) and then advance the paper for the assigned depth of top margin. *Then* reset the paper bail in clamping position.

10. Check typing posture

Head erect, turned to face the book

Back straight, elbows relaxed

Body centered opposite J key, leaning forward

Feet apart and firmly set

11. Check hand position

Position finger tips on home keys:
Left hand on A S D and F
Right hand on J K L and Semicolon

ON MANUAL MACHINE, curve fingers *tightly* (as though to pull an iron bar) and let them rest lightly *on* home keys, without pressure.

ON ELECTRIC MACHINE, curve fingers *slightly* and hold them as close to home keys as you can without quite touching them (as though they were too hot to touch).

Rules For Typewriting Contests

The following rules are given for the convenience of teachers and students who wish to observe contest rules in marking papers or in conducting competitions. *These are the rules commonly used in calculating scores on employment tests.* The rules are based on those issued by the late James N. Kimball, official judge of the International Typewriting Contests for 25 years.

Rules for correcting papers

1. General Rule. Every word (including its following punctuation and spacing) omitted, inserted, misspelled, or changed in any way from the test copy must be penalized. BUT NOTE: Only *one* error may be charged against any one word.

2. Errors in Printed Copy. Any error in the printed test copy may be copied exactly or corrected.

3. Punctuation and Horizontal Spacing. A word that is otherwise correct must be marked as an error if its following punctuation mark or spacing is omitted, incorrectly made, or changed from the copy. NOTE: Contest authorities should agree upon definite rules for sequence of punctuation and for spacing and describe them in detail. Require each contestant's work to be consistent.

4. Erasing. Erasing is not allowed, unless agreed upon prior to a specific test.

5. Transposition. Any transposition in any word or group of characters constitutes an error. Single words or groups of words that are transposed are penalized one error for the transposition plus one error for each mistake in the transposed matter.

6. Rewritten Matter. Rewritten words, groups of words, or characters are charged one error for the rewriting, plus an error for each mistake in the rewritten matter.

7. Last Word. An error made in the last word typed, whether the word is completed or not, must be charged.

8. Crowding, Piling, and Misspacing. No word shall occupy other than its proper number of spaces. If a portion of one character overlaps a portion of another character or extends into the space between words so that it would overlap a portion of any character that might be in that space, an error is charged.

9. Word Division. A word incorrectly divided at the end of a line is penalized. NOTE: Contest authorities should identify acceptable guides.

10. Faulty Shifting and Lightly Struck Characters. Unless the complete character is discernible, an error is charged.

11. Left-Hand Margin and Paragraph Indention. The first character on all lines, except those that begin paragraphs, must appear at the same point on the line scale—at the left margin. Each line not starting thus and each paragraph indented other than 5 spaces will constitute errors.

12. Short and Long Lines. Except when using special copy designed and declared for shorter lines, the last character typed on each line (other than the last line of a paragraph or of the test) must rest on some space between the 61st and 76th, inclusive, considering the left margin as space No. 1. Every shorter or longer line is an error.

13. Short Pages. Any page, except the last, containing fewer than 33 lines (on 33 cm paper) or 27 lines (on P4 paper) is a short page and constitutes an error.

14. Line Spacing. Double spacing is required. Each line irregularly spaced is penalized one error.

15. Cut Characters. If any part of a character or a word is cut off at the edge of the paper, it is charged as an error.

16. Other Questions. Interpretations of the rules and any question not described in them shall be subject to final decision by the contest manager.

Calculation of test results

17. Gross Strokes. Strokes are counted correctly by considering the entire copy as having been typed in *one continuous line.* Each character or space in such a line counts as one stroke.

18. Gross Words. The total gross words are the total gross strokes typed, divided by 5. Do not add strokes in repeated matter or subtract strokes in omitted matter. NOTE: The count given with most test copy is the cumulative gross word count (strokes ÷ 5).

19. Penalty. For each error charged under these rules, *10 words* must be deducted from the gross words.

20. Net Words. After deducting the penalty from the gross words, the remainder represents the *total net words.* The typist's *net rate* (words a minute—wam) is computed by dividing the total net words by the number of minutes of typing. Fractions of .500 or less are discarded; fractions over .500 are credited to the next whole number.

EXAMPLE: A typist writes 5808 gross strokes with 8 errors in 15 minutes—

$5808 \div 5 = 1161.6$ or 1162 gross words

8 (errors) $\times 10 = 80$ (penalty)

$1162 - 80 = 1082$ net words

$1082 \div 15$ (minutes) $= 72.1$ net words a minute

Home Keys

Space Bar ... Right thumb

1-A. With all fingers held
motionless in the home
position, poise your right
thumb well above the space
bar. Now sharply tap the
space bar in its center—
bounce your thumb off it.
Repeat until you hear the
margin bell ring.

1-A. Practice striking the space bar

Space once [TAP THE SPACE BAR ONCE] . . . twice [TAP THE
SPACE BAR TWICE] . . . once . . . once . . . twice . . . once . . .
twice . . . once . . . twice . . . twice . . . once . . . once . . . Repeat

1-B. Practice returning the carriage

1-B. Practice returning
the carriage (including
getting your hand back to
home position) until you
can do so with confidence
and without raising your
eyes from the book. Then
repeat the drill until you
can return the carriage
without raising your eyes
from the printed words.

MANUAL MACHINE. In one continuous sweep of the left hand, (a) place the forefinger and next two fingers against the return lever; (b) *flip* the lever with a toss of the wrist, returning the carriage to the margin; and (c) dart your left hand back to its home-key position.

ELECTRIC MACHINE. In a quick, stabbing motion, (a) extend the little finger of your right hand to the adjacent carriage-return key; (b) lightly flick—press—the return key, causing the carriage to return automatically; and (c) *zip* the finger back to its home-key position.

Space once . . . twice . . . once . . . twice . . . Ready to return
[MOVE HAND TO RETURN LEVER OR FINGER TO RETURN KEY]
—Carriage! [RETURN IT] . . . Home! [FINGERS ON HOME KEYS] . . . Repeat

1-C. Practice striking the forefinger keys

1-C. Using the right-hand
thumb and the forefingers
(with all other fingers
kept in home position),
type these three lines ex-
perimentally to determine
how much force is needed
to make each key print
clearly and cleanly. On a
manual machine, use a
very sharp, "biting" stroke;
on an electric machine,
just "tap" the keys lightly.

Left forefinger on *F* key⎫
Right thumb on space bar⎭   fff fff ff ff f f ff ff f f

Right forefinger on *J* key⎫
Right thumb on space bar⎭   jjj jjj jj jj j j jj jj j j

Left forefinger on *F* key⎫
Right forefinger on *J* key⎬   fff jjj ff jj f j ff jj f j
Right thumb on space bar⎭

Spacing: double
Paragraphs: tab 5
Line: 70 (lines
   will align)
SI: 1.49—fairly
   difficult

| 1 | 2 | 3 | 4 | 5 | 6 | 7 | 8 | 9 | 10 | 11 | 12 | 13 | 14 |

    As long as the memory of man goes back, the people living in the   14
British Isles have thought of the English Channel as a veritable moat   28
that kept enemy invaders from their shores; and the enemy thought the   42
same. Half the conquerors of Europe have floundered in their efforts   56
to ford the 48 km or so of turbulent water that make the Channel.   70

    So for whole centuries the British have thwarted every proposal,   84
rejected every plan, denied all consideration of any of the ideas for   98
building a bridge over the Channel or constructing a tunnel under it.   112
It is said that some Britons still shudder when a historian refers to   126
the plans that Napoleon was shaping for tunneling to England in 1802.   141

    But the age of airplanes and missiles has dried up the moat, you   155
might say, so that the Channel is just a nuisance that handicaps both   169
the British and their neighbors in both trade and vacation ambitions.   183
All concerned want to build an easy route across the Channel, and the   197
number of speculators who are anxious to make a fortune by financing,   211
through stock purchases, the construction of a bridge or a tunnel has   225
no limit; the argument is not about "whether" but only about "which."   239

    At the moment the odds seem to favor a "chunnel," as the channel   253
tunnel is called in Britain; but there is room for debate. Those who   267
prefer a bridge, possibly one made on anchored pontoons, point up the   281
economy of such construction; a tunnel would cost infinitely more, of   295
course. Those who favor the tunnel, however, point out the hazard of   309
the weather and scornfully claim that one earnest Channel storm would   323
spread the bridge over or under the whole North Sea; whereas, there'd   337
be no weather in a tunnel but only a steady stream of toll dividends.   351

    Many fine engineers have given great study to the tunnel design.   365
It is envisioned as no scant mining shaft but rather as a multilevel,   379
gigantic tube that would carry trains and trucks and automobiles both   393
directions in their own lanes. One plan calls for having automobiles   407
ride piggyback on trains built for the purpose; this would be faster,   421
they say, and a lot safer. It would sure cut down on the collisions!   436

    The point of leapfrogging the Channel is only in part the factor   450
of time; a bridge or tunnel would reduce the trip only from about two   464
hours to forty or so minutes. The big thing is the facility; ferries can   478
carry only a thousand autos a day, but a bridge or a tunnel could carry   492
three thousand vehicles each way across the Channel every hour!   506

| 1 | 2 | 3 | 4 | 5 | 6 | 7 | 8 | 9 | 10 | 11 | 12 | 13 | 14 |

A S D F   J K L ;

SPACE BAR

Space Bar ... Right thumb

1-D. Use forefingers on F and J keys. Keep other fingers motionless in home position. Tap the space bar with the thumb of your right hand.

1-D. Practice the F and J keys

1
```
fff fff jjj jjj fff jjj ff jj ff jj f j
fff fff jjj jjj fff jjj ff jj ff jj f j
fff fff jjj jjj fff jjj ff jj ff jj f j
```

Leave a blank line (return carriage twice) before you start a new drill.

1-E. Use second fingers. The forefingers may rise slightly; other fingers should remain motionless in their home positions.

1-E. Practice the D and K keys

2
```
ddd ddd kkk kkk ddd kkk dd kk dd kk d k
ddd ddd kkk kkk ddd kkk dd kk dd kk d k
ddd ddd kkk kkk ddd kkk dd kk dd kk d k
```

1-F. Use third fingers. Little fingers should be kept anchored in their home position. Your other fingers may rise slightly.

1-F. Practice the S and L keys

3
```
sss sss lll lll sss lll ss ll ss ll s l
sss sss lll lll sss lll ss ll ss ll s l
sss sss lll lll sss lll ss ll ss ll s l
```

Return the carriage without looking up.

1-G. Use fourth fingers. Keep forefingers anchored in home position. Other fingers may rise slightly.

1-G. Practice the A and ; keys

4
```
aaa aaa ;;; ;;; aaa ;;; aa ;; aa ;; a ;
aaa aaa ;;; ;;; aaa ;;; aa ;; aa ;; a ;
aaa aaa ;;; ;;; aaa ;;; aa ;; aa ;; a ;
```

1-H. Note the pattern of each drill line; then type lines 5-7 two times each (plus an extra time if the line is difficult for you).

1-H. Build some words

5
```
aaa ddd add add|aaa lll all all|add all
```

6
```
aaa sss kkk ask|jjj aaa lll jal|ask jal
```

7
```
ddd aaa ddd dad|lll aaa ddd lad|dad lad
```

1-I. Notice the change in the drill pattern here from that in lines 5-7; then type lines 8-10 two or three times each.

1-I. Build a few longer words

8
```
a as ask asks asks; f fa fal fall falls
```

9
```
a al ala alas alas; f fl fla flas flask
```

10
```
a ad add adds adds; s sa sal sala salad
```

1-J. Type line 11 twice. GOAL: To finish both of the copies in 1 minute.

1-J. Measure your progress

11
```
a sad fad; a lass falls; dad asks a lad
```

Space once after semicolon.

Manuscript 82
2-PAGE REPORT
WITH FOOTNOTES

Paper: workbook 445-446
Spacing: double
Line: 6 inches, centered
Grade: as marked on copy,
for 30 minutes' work

LESSON

224

Report Test

MAKING CORRECTIONS
By (Your Name)

There is no such thing as a perfect typist; so we must all learn to correct mistakes. This report is intended as a guide for making corrections. It is a digest of information to be found in books by Rowe[1] and by Gavin and Hutchinson.[2]

TECHNIQUE 1: ERASING

A. Be sure your hands and eraser are clean. (To clean an eraser, rub it briskly on paper or on fine-grained sandpaper.)

B. Move the carriage as far as possible to one side so that erasure crumbs cannot fall into the machine.

C. Roll the paper so that the error to be corrected is on top of the cylinder. Hold the paper firmly by pressing it against the cylinder with the tips of your fingers.

D. Erase with light, short, circular motions, blowing very lightly to keep the dust out of the machine. *(Grade: D)*

E. Return the paper to writing position and type the correction. Tap the key lightly. Tap it repeatedly until the corrected letter is as dark as the other letters on the page.

---

1. John L. Rowe, *et al., Gregg Typing, 191 Series, Book One* (Toronto: McGraw-Hill, 1965), page 129.

2. Ruth E. Gavin and William A. Sabin, *Reference Manual for Stenographers and Typists*, Canadian Edition (Toronto: McGraw-Hill Ryerson, 1970).

TECHNIQUE 2: REALIGNING *(Grade: C)*

If an error is detected after the paper has been removed, erase the error and reinsert the paper for typing a correction:

A. Insert the paper and roll it up so that the line on which the correction is to be made is above the aligning scale.

B. Depress the paper release and adjust the paper so that (1) the line is straight, (2) the line is the same distance above the scale as in normal typing, and (3) the white lines on the scale point exactly to the center of the letter i or l.

C. Set the carriage at the point of correction. *(Grade: B)*

D. Type the correction very, very lightly—so lightly that you can barely see it—to check the accuracy of your aligning.

E. Improve the aligning, if necessary.

TECHNIQUE 3: WORD SHIFTING

When an extra letter is to be typed in a correction, the whole word is erased and retyped a half space to the left of its original position. If one less letter is to be typed, the word is erased and retyped a half space to the right.

Shifting the word may be accomplished by moving the paper or by holding the carriage in half-space position as each letter is typed. Rowe[3] suggests using the backspace key to hold the carriage in half position. The carriage can also be held by hand or, on some machines, by holding down the space bar.

---

3. Rowe, *op. cit.*, page 129. *(Grade: A)*

LINE: 40
SPACING: SINGLE
GOAL: CONTROL E, U,
     G, AND RIGHT SHIFT
STRESS: KEEPING
     FEET FLAT ON FLOOR

New Keys

On charts like this, keys
already practiced appear
in color. New keys to be
mastered in the lesson are
shown in black and white.

2-A. Type lines 1 and 2
twice each. Leave 1 blank
line (return the carriage
twice) after the second
copy of each of the lines.

2-A. Review the keys you know

1 fff jjj ddd kkk sss lll aaa ;;; fff jjj

2 sss aaa ddd sad sad aaa sss kkk ask ask

2-B. Use D-finger. Try the
ded reach (keep A-finger
in home position, to guide
D-finger back after it has
struck E key); then type
lines 3-6 three times.

2-B. Practice the E key

3 ddd ded eee ddd ded eee ddd ded eee ded

4 ded see see ded fee fee ded lee lee ded

5 ded led led ded fed fed ded fee fee ded

6 ded sea sea ded elk elk ded elf elf ded

Dotted lines are
to spotlight the
reach-path you
are practicing.

2-C. Use J-finger. Try the
juj reach (keep Sem-L-K-
fingers in home position,
to guide J-finger back
after striking U key); type
lines 7-10 three times.
Speed up on repetitions.

2-C. Practice the U key

7 jjj juj uuu jjj juj uuu jjj juj uuu juj

8 juj dud dud juj due due juj sue sue juj

9 juj us; us; juj use use juj uke uke juj

10 juj due due juj sue sue juj use use juj

2-D. Use F-finger. Try the
fgf reach (keep your A-S-D
fingers at home; move only
the F-finger); then type
lines 11-14 three times.

2-D. Practice the G key

11 fff fgf ggg fff fgf ggg fff fgf ggg fgf

12 fgf lag lag fgf jag jag fgf sag sag fgf

13 fgf dug dug fgf lug lug fgf jug jug fgf

14 fgf leg leg fgf keg keg fgf egg egg fgf

2-E. To capitalize any
letter that is on the left
half of the keyboard:

(1) Keeping J-finger home,
press and hold down right
shift key with Sem-finger.

(2) Strike the letter key.

(3) Release the shift key
and return all fingers to
their home-key position.

Type lines 15-18 three
or more times each.

2-E. Practice the right SHIFT key

15 ;;; A;; A;; ;;; S;; S;; ;;; D;; D;; ;;;

16 ;;; Ask Ask ;;; Alf Alf ;;; Ada Ada ;;;

17 ;;; See See ;;; Sal Sal ;;; Del Del ;;;

18 ;;; Elk Elk ;;; Fae Fae ;;; Gae Gae ;;;

STANDARD REFERENCE BOOKS

Information	*Source Book* (*Title*)
Almanac	McGraw-Hill Directory & Almanac of Canada
Books	Canadian Books in Print
Business	Canadian Business Handbook
Credit	Dun & Bradstreet Reference Book
Finance	Dun & Bradstreet Reference Book
Government	Directory of Municipal Governments
Hotels	Wrigley's Hotel Directory
Industry	Canadian Trade Index
People	The Canadian Who's Who
Postal	Canadian Postal Guide

NAMES OF THE MONTHS IN FOUR LANGUAGES
(Note the Capitalization)

ENGLISH: January, February, March, April, May, June, July, August, September, October, November, December. **FRENCH:** janvier, février, mars, avril, mai, juin, juillet, août, septembre, octobre, novembre, décembre. **GERMAN:** Januar, Februar, Marz, April, Mai, Juni, Juli, August, September, Oktober, November, Dezember. **SPANISH:** enero, febrero, marzo, abril, mayo, junio, julio, agosto, septiembre, octubre, noviembre, diciembre.

COMPARATIVE EARNINGS STATEMENT
(Years Ending December 31)

Item	Last Year	This Year
Operating Revenues	$65 605 838	$81 960 327
Operating Charges	53 283 067	61 011 682
Net Income before Taxes	$12 322 771	$20 948 645
Federal and State Taxes	3 207 610	6 960 400
NET INCOME	$9 115 161	$13 988 245

INVENTORY OF OFFICE EQUIPMENT
Toronto Office, August 31 *today & year*

ITEMS	Good	Fair	Poor	TOTAL
Chairs, Executive	2	8	4	14
Chairs, Guest	10 ~~12~~	8 ~~10~~	8 ~~3~~	25
Chairs, Stenographic	8 ~~9~~	7 ~~8~~	13 ~~11~~	28
Desks	10	20 ~~24~~	13 ~~8~~	43 ~~42~~
Electric Fans	4 ~~5~~	7 ~~9~~	4 ~~1~~	15
Files, 3-Drawer	8 ~~6~~	0	0	8 ~~6~~
Files, 4-Drawer	24	11	12	47
Mimeograph Machines	1 ~~2~~	2 ~~1~~	0	3

2-F. Note the pattern of each line; then type lines 19-21 twice each. Speed up and sustain an even pace on the repetitions.

2-F. Build some word families

19 Dell fell jell ell; fads gads lads dads

20 Flag slag skag lag; fuse uses used use;

21 Gale kale sale ale; full dull gull lull

2-G. Type line 22 twice. GOAL: To finish both of the copies in 1 minute.

2-G. Measure your progress

22 Sue fed a sad lad a salad; Ask a judge;

LINE: 40
SPACING: SINGLE
GOAL: CONTROL R, PERIOD, H, AND LEFT SHIFT
STRESS: BOUNCE-OFF SPACE-BAR STROKES

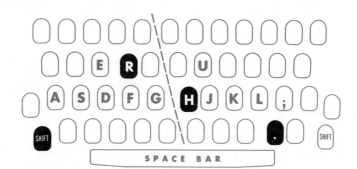

New Keys

3-A. Type lines 1 and 2 twice—evenly and rapidly.

3-A. Review the keys you know

1 aaa ;;; sss lll ddd kkk fff jjj aaa ;;;

2 ded led fed fgf leg keg juj jug lug dug

3-B. Use F-finger. Try the frf reach (keep the A-S-D-fingers at home; move only the F-finger); then type lines 3-6 three times. You should be able to type each of the lines rapidly.

3-B. Practice the R key

3 fff frf rrr fff frf rrr fff frf rrr frf

4 frf fur fur frf far far frf jar jar frf

5 frf err err frf ere ere frf are are frf

6 frf red red frf rug rug frf rag rag frf

3-C. Use L-finger. Try the l.l reach (keep Sem-finger anchored in home position, to guide L-finger back); then type lines 7-10 three times. Keep arms still!

3-C. Practice the . key

7 lll l.l ... lll l.l ... lll l.l ... l.l

8 l.l dr. dr. l.l sr. sr. l.l fr. fr. l.l

9 l.l Dr. Dr. l.l Sr. Sr. l.l Fr. Fr. l.l

10 Dad fed us. See us. See Al. Ask Red.

Space once after a period following an abbreviation, and twice after a period at end of sentence.

Forms Test

Paper: workbook 439

Form 90

VOUCHER CHECK

Voucher cheque No. 240, to Edward L. Hastings, 835 Lakeshore Boulevard East, Toronto, Ontario, M4M 1B3 for $53.67 in payment of travel expenses on trip to Calgary on the sixth of last month.

Paper: workbook 439

Form 91

RECEIPT

Receipt for $98.75, paid on account, by Mrs. Esther K. Stouffer.

Paper: workbook 439

Form 92

PROMISSORY NOTE

Note No. 273: Alexander Wilson promises to pay the sum of $500 at The Provincial Bank of Canada to the order of the International Supply Company, Inc., within 30 days. Be sure Mr. Wilson's name is typed beneath the line for his signature.

Paper: workbook 440

Form 93

PURCHASE REQUISITION

Mr. Hazleton requisitions (No. AD-8-H) 10 new venetian blinds (green metal, with white tapes), to measure 0.9 m by 2.1 m, to replace those now in the Advertising Department offices. The blinds are needed next Monday. Mr. Gibson approves the requisition.

Paper: workbook 440

Form 94

PURCHASE ORDER

Mr. W. P. Busk authorizes the purchases of the blinds for Mr. Hazleton from Martin Miller & Sons, 58 Broadview Avenue, Toronto, Ontario M4M 2E4. Each blind (Cat. No. 392-WG-7) costs $10.00. The purchase order is No. J-18803.

Paper: workbook 441

Form 95

TELEGRAM

Fred T. Dixon, of Martin Miller & Sons, wires W. P. Busk, Purchasing Manager, International Supply Company, Inc., 8325 de l'Acadie Boulevard, Montréal, Québec H3N 2W5. "Delivery your order J-18803 delayed ten days because size of blinds is irregular."

Paper: workbook 441

Form 96

INVOICE

Martin Miller & Sons sends invoice No. 3013 for Mr. Hazleton's blinds, at $10 each, less 2% in the net amount for payment within 30 days, plus delivery charges (by railway express) of $8.68. The invoice is addressed (and delivery is the same) to the International Supply Company, Inc., 8325 de l'Acadie Boulevard, Montréal, Québec H3N 2W5. There was no salesman involved in the transaction for which this invoice is the bill.

Tables Test

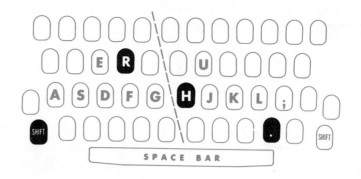

SPACE BAR

If you forget where a key is located, fight off the temptation to look at your fingers; look at this keyboard chart instead.

CAUTION! It is natural to make typing errors at this stage. It is better to risk some errors than to slow down, or break rhythm, or look away from the line you are copying. Sail right in and type every line vigorously!

3-D. Use J-finger. Try the jhj reach (anchor K-L-Sem fingers in home position); then race through lines 11-14 three times each.

3-D. Practice the H key

11   jjj jhj hhh jjj jhj hhh jjj jhj hhh jhj

12   jhj had had jhj hag hag jhj has has jhj

13   jhj he; he; jhj she she jhj her her jhj

14   jhj ash ash jhj hue hue jhj hug hug jhj

SMOOTHLY!

3-E. To capitalize any letter that is on the right half of the keyboard:

(1) Keeping F-finger home, press and hold down left shift key with A-finger.

(2) Strike the letter key.

(3) Release the shift key and return all fingers to their home key position.

Type lines 15-18 three or more times each.

3-E. Practice the left SHIFT key

15   aaa Jaa Jaa aaa Kaa Kaa aaa Laa Laa aaa

16   aaa Jed Jed aaa Lea Lea aaa Hal Hal aaa

17   aaa Her Her aaa Has Has aaa Had Had aaa

18   aaa Use Use aaa Led Led aaa Les Les aaa

3-F. Analyze pattern of each line; then type it twice. GOAL: To finish both copies of line 22 in 1 minute. Keep eyes very firmly on copy. Can you?

3-F. Measure your progress

19   Hear dear gear ear; hues rues sues dues

20   Hare dare fare are; reed reel reek reef

21   Rash sash hash ash; Jake lake fake sake

22   Jed has a glue jar; Alf has a red desk.

3-G. This routine should be followed at the end of each practice period— but note: your instructor may not wish you to cover the machine at the end of each period during the day.

3-G. Clean up your table

1. Remove your paper: depress paper-release lever (24); draw out paper; release the lever.

2. Place bail (20) against cylinder (11).

3. Center the carriage: holding the right cylinder knob (12), press carriage release (8); move carriage to middle; release the lever.

4. Cover the typewriter; put away your work.

Letter Test

Scoring 30 Minutes' Production Output	
4 mailable . . . . A	2 mailable C
3 mailable . . . . B	1 mailable . . . . D

Letter 116
FULL-BLOCKED LETTER

Paper: P4, workbook page 435
Production words: 334
SI: 1.48—fairly difficult

The letter below is from John R. Powell, training director. Type it in full-blocked form. Address it to Herbert ("Dear Herb:") J. Mullen, 521 Brander Drive West, Edmonton, Alberta T6H 4V4.

Letter 117
BLOCKED LETTER

Paper: official size,
workbook page 436
Production words: 291
SI: 1.48—fairly difficult*

Retype the letter, this time addressing it to L. Richard Shields, personnel manager, Scott-Williams Company, 1657 Dorchester Blvd. West, Montréal, P.Q. H3B 1T4. Omit paragraph 3 and arrange the three items in paragraph 2 as an enumeration.

Letter 118
SEMIBLOCKED LETTER

Paper: P5, workbook page 437
Production words: 221
SI: 1.58—difficult

Retype the letter, omitting paragraphs 2 and 3 but inserting a subject line, *Some Ideas, Please!* Address: Mrs. Eunice F. Markham, executive secretary, Legal Secretaries Association, 20-11th Avenue, Regina, Saskatchewan S4P 0J4. A carbon copy is to go to Mr. Kling.

Letter 119
BLOCKED LETTER

Paper: P5 workbook page 438
Production words: 157
SI: 1.58—difficult

Use only paragraph 4, divided into three paragraphs. Address the letter to Executives Association, 4 Third Avenue West, Vancouver, British Columbia V5Y 3T8. *Attention Training Director.* After the word *observance*, add the phrase *of Secretary's Day.*

(1) you will be interested to learn...i   7
am sure...that one of the groups to which   15
i belong...the national personnel club...   23
will soon take steps to boost the Secretary's   32
Day sponsored each spring by the national   41
secretaries association...   46

(2) we feel that this special day is most   54
worthwhile and that our support of it will   63
achieve several goals: first...it is sure to   72
give us a chance to publicize the merits of   81
office work in general and of the secretarial   90
career in particular...secondly...the pub-   98
licity should attract the interest of more   107
bright young men and women to this career   115
field...thirdly...the publicity may revive   124
ambition in our present staffs...   130

(3) the npc thinks so highly of the value   139
of this observance that...as a part of the   147

| 1 | 2 | 3 | 4 | 5 | 6 | 7 | 8 |

campaign...member firms will be asked to   155
show an orchid and a statement of tribute   164
to secretaries in advertisements that are   172
scheduled to appear on that day...april 27   181
...this request will be for both the local   189
and national levels...   193

(4) as a member of a special committee   201
for my chapter of npc...i'm looking for   209
things we can ask local firms to do to boost   218
the observance...do you have any sugges-   226
tions...the best that our committee has   234
come up with yet is to suggest that em-   241
ployers give their secretaries a gift of candy   251
or flowers or perhaps take them to lunch...   259
but we know that a great many employers   267
would be unreceptive to this sort of per-   275
sonal gesture...if you have any suggestions   284
...we should be grateful to have them.   292

| 1 | 2 | 3 | 4 | 5 | 6 | 7 | 8 |

New Keys

LINE: 40
SPACING: SINGLE
GOAL: CONTROL I,
O, AND T
STRESS: KEEPING A-
AND SEM-FINGERS
ANCHORED AT HOME

SPACE BAR

4-A. Type lines 1 and 2
twice each, stressing an
even and rapid pace.

4-A. Review the keys you know

1   aaa ;;; sss lll ddd kkk fff jjj fgf jhj

2   a;a ded l.l frf juj fgf jhj a;a Les Sue

4-B. Use K-finger. Try the
kik reach (keep Sem- and
L-fingers anchored on the
home keys, grazing but not
pressing them); then type
lines 3-6 three times.

4-B. Practice the I key

3   kkk kik iii kkk kik iii kkk kik iii kik

4   kik air air kik fir fir kik sir sir kik

5   kik kid kid kik did did kik rid rid kik

6   kik dig dig kik jig jig kik rig rig kik

4-C. Use L-finger. Try the
lol reach (keep J-finger
or Sem-finger, whichever
is easier for you, in the
home position); then type
lines 7-10 three times.

4-C. Practice the O key

7   lll lol ooo lll lol ooo lll lol ooo lol

8   lol log log lol jog jog lol dog dog lol

9   lol off off lol odd odd lol old old lol

10   lol oar oar lol our our lol oil oil lol

4-D. Use F-finger. Try the
ftf reach (keep the A-S-D-
fingers at home); then
type lines 11-14 three
times each. Return the
carriage without looking
up even once as you do so.

4-D. Practice the T key

11   fff ftf ttt fff ftf ttt fff ftf ttt ftf

12   ftf aft aft ftf its its ftf hat hat ftf

13   ftf too too ftf toe toe ftf the the ftf

14   ftf let let ftf lot lot ftf got got ftf

4-E. Analyze the pattern
of each line; then type
lines 15-18 twice each,
without hesitating and
without looking up once.

4-E. Build skill on word families

15   to toe tog tot too; it sit fit hit kit;

16   ut jut hut rut out; ot got rot lot hot;

17   ig fig dig rig jig; et let jet set get;

18   at sat hat fat eat; ir ire sir fir air;

Unit 36. Final Tests

Could you do a typist's work, hold down a typist's job? Do you know enough; have you skill enough? This unit contains six tests to help answer these questions—to answer them *now*, while you still have time in which to fill in any gaps you unveil.

You are allotted the time of seven lessons (Lessons 219-225) in which to preview and take the six tests. This schedule permits one period (Lesson 219) in which to preview the tests and to verify any details of which you are uncertain, plus one period for each of the six tests to be taken.

You are encouraged to preview, to study, *even to practice* these tests before you take them. Reason: If the tests are to succeed in measuring your capacity as an office typist, you should be just as familiar with the vocabulary, arrangement patterns, phrasing of directions, and so on, as the office typist is familiar with these characteristics of the work. But note: do not use or mark your workbook pages for the tests until you take the tests officially, under your instructor's direction.

The production tests may be taken in either of two ways, as your instructor may direct.

1. Your instructor may time you for exactly 30 minutes, permitting you to correct a reasonable number of errors; then you proofread your work and grade it (standards are given with each test) on the quantity of acceptable work you have produced.

2. Your instructor may permit you as much time as you need (within reason!) to complete all the assignments in a test, *without* correcting errors; then you would proofread your work, grade *each page* of work on the basis of the penalty-point table below, and then average the page grades to arrive at a mark for that test. The grading table:

> **Deduct 3 points for each major error (wrong top margin, line length, linespacing, form, etc.).**
>
> **Deduct 2 points for each minor error (each instance of incorrect blocking, aligning, centering, indenting, pivoting, and similar technicalities.**
>
> **Deduct 1 point for each typographical error.**
>
> **Grade the total penalty points of each page:**
>
> | 10 | 9 | 8 | 7 | 6 | 5 | 4 | 3 | 2 | 1 | 0 |
> |----|---|---|---|---|---|---|---|---|---|---|
> | D | D | D | C | C | C | B | B | A | A | A |

A 120-question test covering general typing information (word division, typing terminology, language usage, error detection, etc.) is provided on workbook pages 431-434. Detach these pages and bring them to class. Fill in the answers under the supervision of your instructor when directed to do so.

Note that office typists do not have time to ponder answers to the kind of questions that are included in this test, nor do they have an opportunity to change their minds. To simulate the same conditions, (1) you are to complete all 120 questions in 30 minutes, maximum time; and (2) you are not to

erase on this test—each page of questions has been printed with fine dots so that (as on a bank cheque) any mark or erasure will be seen immediately.

When you preview this test, therefore, be very careful not to place any marks on the test pages, for you will not be able to remove any marks.

Checking your answers against the list provided to your instructor, grade your work on the number of incorrect answers (use the same scale as in the panel above): 10-9-8 incorrect answers, *D;* 7-6-5 incorrect answers, *C;* 4-3 incorrect answers, *B;* and 2-1-0 incorrect answers, *A.*

4-F. Learn how errors are marked and counted

The red (shue) is (his,) It is a good (fit .)
The red shoe is his. It is a good fit.

All of us (l ke) Sue; she has (good) taste.
All of us like Sue; she has good taste.

Ask^ to (to) see that all of (get us) to go.
Ask (Al) to see that all of us (fgrt)to go.

As indicated in the examples above, *count it an error* when—

1. Any stroke is incorrect.
2. The punctuation, if any, after a word is incorrect or is omitted.
3. The spacing after a word or after its punctuation is incorrect.
4. Any stroke is so light that it does not show clearly.
5. A stroke is made over another.

6. A word is omitted.
7. A word is repeated.
8. Words are transposed.
9. A direction about spacing, indenting, etc., is violated.
10. A word contains a capital that does not print completely.

Note that (11) only one error is charged to any one word, no matter how many errors it may contain.

4-G. Build skill on short sentences

19 The red shoe is his. It is a good fit.

20 All of us like Sue; she has good taste.

21 Ask Al to see that all of us get to go.

4-H. Check your progress

22 Joe fell off a ladder; he hurt his leg.
He asked Dr. Todd to take a look at it.

LESSON

5

Review

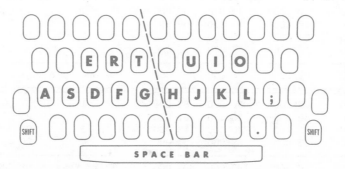

5-A. Review the keys you know

1 aaa sss ddd fff fgf jhj jjj kkk lll ;;;

2 ded lol frf kik ftf juj fgf jhj ded l.l

3 Alf Sue Del Flo Gae Joe Kit Lil Ted Her

Paper: plain, full
Carbons: file only
Review: page 150
Spacing: double

The material in 217-B, including the centered sub-headings, is the revision to which Mr. Fairbanks referred in his letter to Mr. Spooner. Type this material on a 50-character line, identifying it as pages 14 and 15. Use 3-space paragraph indentions.

Paper: workbook 429

1. To spooner & moran...ltd....156 northern avenue...thunder bay...ontario...for $100 in payment of consultation fee for november...per agreement of may 1.

2. To mr. tracy r spooner...same address ...for $85.10 in payment of traveling expenses to toronto...per memorandum received from him on december 6.

Table 81

RULED 2-PAGE TABLE

Paper: plain, full
Carbons: two

"This table," says Mr. Fairbanks as he gives you the two-page table shown below, "is so important that I want it typed more attractively. Please retype it with normal spacing between the columns and a full space above and below each horizontal ruled line. Arrange it on two, face-to-face pages. And put today's date somewhere on it, too."

SALES ESTIMATES OF
Eastern Division

Quarter	Toronto	Ottawa	New York	Totals
1	12 000	8 000	10 000	30 000
2	14 000	12 000	15 000	41 000
3	18 000	15 000	15 000	48 000
4	20 000	12 000	12 000	44 000
First Year	64 000	47 000	52 000	163 000
1	20 000	12 000	15 000	47 000
2	24 000	18 000	24 000	66 000
3	30 000	24 000	32 000	86 000
4	33 000	27 000	35 000	95 000
Second Year	107 000	81 000	106 000	294 000
1	30 000	25 000	30 000	85 000
2	36 000	30 000	35 000	101 000
3	42 000	36 000	40 000	118 000
4	40 000	25 000	38 000	103 000
Third Year	148 000	116 000	143 000	407 000
THREE YEARS	319 000	244 000	301 000	864 000

PREFABRICATED HOUSES
Western Division

Quarter	Vancouver	Edmonton	Totals	NATIONAL TOTALS
1	7 000	5 000	12 000	42 000
2	10 000	8 000	18 000	59 000
3	12 000	12 500	24 500	72 500
4	10 000	10 000	20 000	64 000
First Year	39 000	35 500	74 500	237 500
1	12 000	10 000	22 000	69 000
2	15 000	11 000	26 000	92 000
3	20 000	12 000	32 000	118 000
4	20 000	10 000	30 000	125 000
Second Year	67 000	43 000	110 000	404 000
1	17 000	10 000	27 000	112 000
2	20 000	12 500	32 500	133 500
3	25 000	15 000	40 000	158 000
4	20 000	12 500	32 500	135 500
Third Year	82 000	50 000	132 000	539 000
THREE YEARS	188 000	128 500	316 500	1 180 500

5-B. Strengthen control of the home-row keys

5-B. Note the pattern (one letter changes from word to word in each group); then type lines 4-8 two times. Speed up and keep a steady, smooth pace on each of the repetitions.

4 Ada ade are art aft |;;; to; so; do; go;
5 Sal sat set sit sir |Lou lot log lug lag
6 Dee due dug dog dig |Kit elk ilk irk ark
7 Fil fir far fur for |Joe jog jag jug jig
8 Go; got get gat gag |Hal hat hit hut hot

5-C. Strengthen control of the other keys you know

5-C. The pattern is like that in 5-B. Type lines 9-12 two times, increasing your speed but keeping the pace steady as you repeat each of the drill lines.

9   Ira ire irk ilk ill |Tat hat oat eat fat
10 Rue rug rut rot rod |Era ere err ear eat
11 Our oar oat out oft |1.1 Jr. Sr. Dr. Fr.
12 Ted tee toe tie the |Usa use uke ute ure

5-D. Learn how typing speed is measured

5-D. It is helpful to time some of your efforts, so that you may know exactly how rapidly you can type.

If you record your error score and your speed score in each lesson, you can note your progress. Such scores also tell you if you should press more for accuracy improvement or if you should press more for an increase in speed.

1. Type for an exact number of minutes while someone times you.

2. Find how many words you typed. Every 5 strokes count as 1 word, as marked off by the horizontal scales and, in paragraph copy, as cumulatively totaled after each line. The first example below contains $(8+8+4=)$ 20 words. The second example contains $(24+4=)$ 28 words.

3. Divide the words typed by the minutes typed. If you type 28 words in 2 minutes, for example, you type $(28÷2=)$ 14 *wam* (words a minute); or in 1 minute, $(28÷1=)$ 28 *wam*; or in ½ minute, $(28÷.5=)$ 56 *wam*.

```
Ask Ted or Louis to go out to see Kirk.
Ask Ted or Louis to go out to see Kirk.
Ask Ted or Louis to
1 | 2 | 3 | 4 | 5 | 6 | 7 | 8
```
Compare with line 15.

```
The goal for this task is to do it just
as fast as is safe.  Look out for a lot
of errors if too great a rush is tried.
The goal for this
1 | 2 | 3 | 4 | 5 | 6 | 7 | 8
```
Compare with paragraph 16.

5-E. Build skill on sentences

5-E. Type lines 13-15 two times (or take a 1-minute writing on each line, so that you can figure your typing speed); then mark and count your errors.

13 The girls tried to get out to the lake.
14 Gail has a fur; her dad got it for her.
15 Ask Ted or Louis to go out to see Kirk.

    1 | 2 | 3 | 4 | 5 | 6 | 7 | 8   = 5-stroke words

5-F. Build skill on a paragraph

CUMULATIVE WORDS

5-F. Type this paragraph twice (or take three 1-minute writings on it); then circle any errors.

16 The goal for this task is to do it just   8
    as fast as is safe. Look out for a lot   16
    of errors if too great a rush is tried.   24

    1 | 2 | 3 | 4 | 5 | 6 | 7 | 8

5-G. Measure your progress

5-G. Type the paragraph two times. GOAL: To type it once in 1-minute.

17 The three of us took a good ride out to   8
    the lake to fish. Jake got us a trout.   16

    1 | 2 | 3 | 4 | 5 | 6 | 7 | 8

Assume the date is DECEMBER 10. You work for Mr. Fairbanks, of International, in Toronto. He prefers blocked letter style and this closing arrangement:

```
Sincerely yours,

INTERNATIONAL ENGINEERING
AND CONSTRUCTION COMPANY


Richard Ellington Fairbanks
Executive Vice-President
```

Letter 114
2-PAGE, BLOCKED

Paper: workbook 425
Carbons: file, 1 cc, 2 bcc
SI 1.67—difficult

mr duncan j pomeroy...secretary...east- 15
ern association of architects...1000 ch. 23
cote st-antoine...montréal...québec H3Y 30
2K7.

we appreciate very much the interest in 44
our plans for developing prefabricated 52
homes expressed by your letter of inquiry 60
...we certainly have no objection to your 68
publishing in *the eastern architect* any com- 84
mentary you wish about our plans... 91

as i intimated to you some time ago, we 100
have no idea whatsoever of displacing 107
architects by this process of building low- 116
and medium-priced homes...our prefabri- 124
cated materials are in a form that permits 132
of infinite variation...especially for interior 142
construction...sufficient leeway exists in 150
the choice of materials for the exterior of 159
homes to enable an architect to construct 168
two homes of the same materials side by 176
side...yet with enough difference in ap- 183
pearance to satisfy most homeowners...as 191
a matter of fact...we are counting on archi- 200
tects to help us avoid the sameness that is 209
the bane of the prefabricating industry. 217

within the next two or three months... 225
we expect to issue a booklet prepared espe- 234
cially for architects...it is being prepared 243
with the counsel of tracy r spooner...whom 251
i believe you know...once the publication 260
date of the booklet is firmed...we shall 268

take space in your and other trade journals 277
to announce its availability. 283

if there are more particulars you may 291
wish spelled out...i should be happy to tell 300
you what you wish...perhaps you would 308
prefer to write to mr spooner...whose ad- 343
dress is below...since he is the one person 351
who is completely familiar with the tech- 359
nical nature of our plans. 365

cc mr tracy r spooner...spooner & mo- 410
ran...ltd....156 northern avenue...thun- 417
der bay...ontario P7C 2V5...bcc TTJ. 435
and RBW.

Letter 115
BLOCKED LETTER

Paper: workbook 427
Carbons: file, 2 bcc
SI 1.50—fairly difficult

dear tracy...*spooner, that is*...a letter i 33
have just received from duncan pomeroy 41
indicates that "the cat is out of the bag" 49
and that word has got around about our 57
prefab plans...this is what he wrote: 65

the ominous news that your organ- 73
ization is planning to enter and develop 82
the prefabrication field has come to my 91
attention...can you tell me whether 100
it is true? 102

if it is true...can you tell me any- 112
thing about the scope and nature of 120
your plans...for release to *the eastern 134
architect* magazine? 142

i think...tracy...that it would be wise 150
for you to write to him without waiting 158
for him to write to you...give him enough 167
information to stir his curiosity and per- 175
haps to stimulate some degree of enthusi- 183
asm...if you do write to him...be kind 190
enough to send me carbons of your letters 199
...will you...please? 203

ps i have gone over part one of your ar- 257
ticle series and think it is wonderful...i 266
felt...however...that page 14 and the first 274
part of page 15 were a bit negative...i am 283
enclosing for your consideration a revision 292
of that portion of your manuscript. 317

Clinic Review

LINE: 40
SPACING: SINGLE
GOAL: INCREASE
  KEYBOARD CONTROL
STRESS: KEEPING
  EYES ON COPY

6-A. Type lines 1-3 twice each, with a blank line after each repetition. The lines are very easy; get off to a racing start!

6-A. Review the keys you know

1 aaa ;;; sss lll ddd kkk fff jjj ggg hhh
2 lol ded kik frf juj ftf jhj fgf l.l aaa
3 a d e f g h i j k l o r s t u . ; a d e

6-B. Measure your control of keys

6-B. To reveal weaknesses, type straight through lines 4-7 once. Press for speed and do not look up. Each key you know is used at least eight times here.

4 self jail late just good felt dogs joke
5 huge took dust jade tiff hulk flag jigs
6 tuft jerk high furl drag judo ajar kite
7 lake fork held risk hair fish jugs hard

EYES ON
THE COPY!

6-C. Reinforce your skill selectively

6-C. Proofread your copy of lines 4-7 very carefully and make a list of all the letters typed incorrectly. Then, take these steps:

(1) Note the four letters you incorrectly typed most often. Then, in lines 8-22, find the drills for the four letters and type each of the drills twice.

(2) Then type lines 8-22 straight through once, but pause to rest briefly after typing lines 12 and 17.

(3) Finally, retype lines 4-7 as a retest. You should do much better this time.

8 aa alas aa ajar aa area aa gala aa data
9 dd deed dd died dd dude dd duds dd dead
10 ee seek ee free ee feel ee flee ee edge
11 ff ruff ff gaff ff doff ff guff ff huff
12 gg eggs gg flag gg gags gg gift gg grog

13 hh high hh hush hh hath hh hoot hh hash
14 ii idea ii irks ii ills ii idol ii idle
15 jj jell jj joss jj just jj jolt jj jilt
16 kk kale kk kill kk silk kk disk kk talk
17 ll loll ll doll ll lilt ll sell ll lull

18 oo food oo hood oo odor oo door oo oleo
19 rr roar rr errs rr rare rr risk rr rear
20 ss sees ss sits ss sirs ss toss ss sets
21 tt trot tt taut tt tuft tt that tt test
22 uu used uu dull uu uses uu full uu true

6-D. Measure your progress

6-D. Type the complete sentence twice. GOAL: To finish the sentence easily in 1 minute or less.

WORDS

23 Jud is to go to the edge of the lake to   8
    see if the old oak tree is still there.   16

    1 | 2 | 3 | 4 | 5 | 6 | 7 | 8

LINE: 60
TAB: 5
SPACING: DOUBLE
DRILLS: THREE TIMES
GOAL: DO AN HOUR'S
  WORK IN AN HOUR!
STRESS: USABLE COPY
  ON FIRST ATTEMPT

217-A. Three copies of
each paragraph, or a
1-minute writing on
each and a 2-minute
writing on the group.
Repeat in Lesson 218.

217-A. Tune up on these easy review lines

1   One way the man can get the job and get the pay for it   12
is to show that he can do the work as well as we can do it.   24

2   Margie filled four or five dozen jars with jam, sealed   36
them with liquid wax, and packed them away on a back shelf.   48

3   We were told that the answer to question 10 on page 56   60
was to be found on pages 28, 39, or 47; I couldn't find it.   72

  1 | 2 | 3 | 4 | 5 | 6 | 7 | 8 | 9 | 10 | 11 | 12

217-B. Sustain your skill on production copy

217-B. Change margins
to 70 spaces, plus a
tab-5 indention (lines
should align at right).

How long should it take
you to type these 322
words of straight copy?
At 40 wam, about 8 or
so minutes; at 50, an
estimated 6 minutes; at
60, about 5 minutes.
Test your power:

Type the selection,
pausing to correct any
errors you are conscious
of making; and then
compute your speed.

Or, take two 7-minute
writings, with rests
after each minute in
the first writing but
none in the second.

SI 1.44—average

4 One of the factors that encourage those who work in the field of   14
prefabricates is the increasing interest that architects are showing.   28
Suddenly, many of the best are responding to the challenge of prefab.   43

Illustrious Origins

The past reluctance of some architects to use prefabricates is a   57
perplexing thing, for prefabs are as Canadian as is Canadian history.   71

The first prefab on this continent, we believe, was a log cabin.   85
Consider: For a log cabin, trees of a uniform size had to be located   99
and cut down; and then the logs had to be trimmed to a uniform length   113
and girth. Only when uniform units were ready did building commence.   127

Or if you reject that instance, then think of "house raising" of a   142
slightly later day. The walls of a house were built on the ground, and   156
then the men of the community together raised the walls and bound   169
them together; and the jeering that exploded when two of the prebuilt   183
walls did not adjoin evenly has a sturdy echo that still rings today.   197

Canadian? Indeed, there are some who say that the first man who   211
made a mold in which to press straw and clay and so evolve a brick is   225
the person to whom the whole industry of prefabs should offer homage.   240

The Enduring Shadow

The prejudice against prefabs finds its main root, I believe, in the   254
long rows of callously identical houses that were the curse of so many   269
mill and mining towns at the turn of the century and in too many of   282
the housing developments spawned in support of the war industries.   296
I think that all of us rebelled against the dull sameness and against   310
some of the shoddy pretenses of distinction which some builders used.   324

  1 | 2 | 3 | 4 | 5 | 6 | 7 | 8 | 9 | 10 | 11 | 12 | 13 | 14

Manuscript 81

MAGAZINE ARTICLE
See page 337

217/218-C. Apply your skill to an integrated typing project

New Keys

LINE: 40
SPACING: SINGLE
GOAL: CONTROL COMMA,
C, M, AND COLON
STRESS: KEEPING
WRISTS CLOSE
TOGETHER

7-A. Type lines 1 and 2 twice, leaving a blank line between each of the pairs. Keep your fingers going!

7-A. Review the keys you know

1   if it is; to go to; or to us; or if it.

2   Joe is; Kit is; Let us; For Al; His dog

7-B. Use K-finger. Try the k,k reach (keep Sem- and L-fingers at home; curl K-finger, to ease reach to Comma key). Then, type lines 3-6 three times.

7-B. Practice the , key

3   kkk k,k ,,, kkk k,k ,,, kkk k,k ,,, k,k

4   k,k as, as, k,k is, is, k,k us, us, k,k

5   k,k to, to, k,k do, do, k,k so, so, k,k

6   k,k of, of, k,k if, if, k,k it, it, k,k

7-C. Use D-finger. Try the dcd reach (keep your A- and S-fingers anchored on home keys; curl D-finger, to make reach to C easier). Then type lines 7-10 three or more times each.

7-C. Practice the C key

7   ddd dcd ccc ddd dcd ccc ddd dcd ccc dcd

8   dcd cad cad dcd cod cod dcd cud cud dcd

9   dcd ice ice dcd ace ace dcd act act dcd

10 dcd cue cue dcd cut cut dcd cur cur dcd

7-D. Can you complete a copy of the sentence in 1 minute? Type it twice, concentrating on the C's.

Note: 1 space after Comma.

7-D. Measure your progress

WORDS

11 Get Carol, Charles, or Cathie to act as   8

a guide; the others are to check coats.   16

    1 | 2 | 3 | 4 | 5 | 6 | 7 | 8

7-E. Use J-finger. Try the jmj reach (keep K-L-Sem-fingers anchored at home). Type lines 12-15 three times each, speeding up on each of the repetitions.

7-E. Practice the M key

12 jjj jmj mmm jjj jmj mmm jjj jmj mmm jmj

13 jmj jam jam jmj ham ham jmj him him jmj

14 jmj mar mar jmj mat mat jmj mad mad jmj

15 jmj sum sum jmj gum gum jmj hum hum jmj

pects them to score their papers by the 'net' method that is explained in this bulletin. Please type enough copies to have a carbon for each young lady. We will use your original copy as a guide for having the bulletin duplicated. You can almost copy this line for line."

"May I make a copy for myself?" you ask.

"Certainly, if you wish," he replies.

4 + 1 file

SCORING THE TESTS

TYPING TESTS / 2

printed

You copy simple essay material from a ∧leaflet for the 10 minutes. You listen for the warning bell; you do not copy line for line as the material is printed. You use a 70-space line and double spacing. *You indent the paragraphs 5 spaces.*

Scoring ~~involves~~ *takes* four steps. First, you proofread the work and ∧circle the errors. Second, you find the total number of words typed. Third, from that total you subtract 10 for each error. Fourth, you divide what is left by 10 (the number of minutes) to get your "net" words a minute. ~~This is your score~~.

Idea: Find your "net" 10-minute rate; use page 278.

For example, in 10 minutes you type 575 words and ~~you~~ make 5 errors. You subtract 50 from 575, to get 525; and you divide the 525 by 10, ~~(minutes)~~ to get 52.5 net words a minute as your score. In effect, you lose 1 wam for each error. Accuracy pays⊙

PREPPING FOR THE TEST

Don't make the mistake of practicing 10-minute writings one after anothe . If you do, you will get tired and ~~simply~~ drill yourself in ~~typing with~~ poor posture, poor stroking, etc. Instead, take one 10-minute writing a day, preceding this practice by short writings in which you get the feel of a pace that you can manage to sustain for 10 minutes. *(for five or six days)*

Don't make the mistake of pushing for speed. If you do, you invite errors; at ~~fifty~~ *50* strokes each, they cost ~~you~~ too much.

Do practice changing the paper quickly. With practice, you can get it down to 2 or 3 seconds.

Do sharpen your proofreading. A paper with ~~even just one~~ *an* unmarked error is likely to stamp you as unreliable and to end in the wastebasket, along with all your application papers⊙

If you can type ∧at a net rate of 50.0 or ~~more~~ *higher* for 10 minutes, let us know. We will test you to confirm your score and arrange for your placement interview and ~~official~~ test ~~by the employer~~.

—Richard E. Longley

WHAT TO DO RIGHT NOW

December 9, 19—

3
5
19
39
65
77
95
108
120
134
154
167
180
192
216
218
222
260
276
286
303
316
321
353
364
393
400
423
436
448
469
482
489
497
502

Final Page of a Manuscript Typed in News-Bulletin Form

7-F. The Colon (:) is the shift of Sem. Practice ;:; several times, keeping the J-K-L fingers anchored on home keys. Type lines 16-19 three times each.

Note: 1 space after Period used with an abbreviation; 2 spaces after the Colon.

7-F. Practice the :️ key

16 ;;; ;:; ::: ;;; ;:; ::: ;;; ;:; ::: ;:;

17 Dear Al: Dear Jo: Dear Lu: Dear Sir:

18 Mr. Em: Dr. Doe: Miss Ree: Mrs. Mor:

19 To Mr. Ulm: To Mrs. Ulm: To Miss Ulm:

7-G. Type each note twice. GOAL: To finish note 20 or 21 in 1 minute or less and both notes in 2 minutes.

7-G. Measure your progress

WORDS

20 Dear Mack: I heard that Carl, Jack, or   8
    Cedric might come to see our last game.   16

21 Dear Harold: Either Cora or Jack is to   24
    go home for the game. Dick is too ill.   32

    1 | 2 | 3 | 4 | 5 | 6 | 7 | 8

LINE: 40
SPACING: SINGLE
GOAL: CONTROL W, Y, V, AND N
STRESS: KEEPING ARMS MOTIONLESS

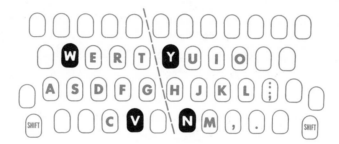

8-A. Type lines 1-2 twice. Keep wrists quiet and type with sharp, biting strokes.

8-A. Review the keys you know

1 aaa ;;; sss lll ddd kkk fff jjj fgf jhj

2 lol ded kik frf juj ftf jmj dcd k,k l.l

8-B. Use S-finger. Try the sws reach (anchor either A- or F-finger at home—which is easier for you?). Type lines 3-6 three times.

8-B. Practice the W key

3 sss sws www sss sws www sss sws www sws

4 sws sow sow sws sew sew sws saw saw sws

5 sws low low sws mow mow sws wow wow sws

6 sws we, we, sws who who sws was was sws

Dotted lines are to spotlight the reach you are practicing.

8-C. Use J-finger. Try the jyj reach (anchor K-L-Sem-fingers at home); note angle of the reach to J key. Type lines 7-10 three times, without pauses.

8-C. Practice the Y key

7 jjj jyj yyy jjj jyj yyy jjj jyj yyy jyj

8 jyj sly sly jyj shy shy jyj sky sky jyj

9 jyj yes yes jyj yet yet jyj you you jyj

10 jyj jay jay jyj way way jyj may may jyj

Paper: plain, full
Copies: five
SI: 1.54—fairly hard

"We must have a copy of this bulletin, which I have just finished, for each of the four young ladies we are sending to Mr. Fudenske," says Mr. Stevens. "He always tests applicants; and when he does, he ex-

"Block center": center longest line, set tab, align other lines at tab.

TAKING TEN—MINUTE TYPEWRITING TESTS   21
    22

Fred C. Stevens   38
Stevens Secretarial Service,   46
Oshawa, Ontario L2W 2X7   54
December 9, 19—   58

BULLETIN TO CLIENTS   63

A large East Coast firm, extending its operations to the west, is open-   79
ing a district office in Oshawa next month. Needed: about 325   97
office workers within three months.   121

To attract top-drawer ~~superior~~ talent, the firm ~~plans to~~ will pay 5 to 10   134
per cent above present rates in this city. So: There will be   152
stiff competition for these ~~attractive~~ positions.   175
    177
    178

CAUTION

Applicants for typing positions in most ~~of our~~ Oshawa   190
firms are given a qualifying test. Usual base: #60 words a min-   210
ute, 5 minutes, 3 or fewer errors, better of 2 efforts.   221

But the new office, to get a better staff in ~~exchange~~ return for   234
better pay, plans to use a competitive test, not a qualifying   254
test. The test will be for 10 minutes. Speed will be charged   266
50 strokes (10 words) for each error. Those who make the top   288
scores will get ~~the~~ first consideration for the jobs.   317

If you hope to land one of these ~~superior~~ better jobs, learn how   334
to take and to score a ~~ten~~ 10-minute typewriting test: 352
    354
    357

TAKING THE TEST

You start 9 or 10 lines from the top of the paper. You stop typing about 2.5   374
cm or so from the bottom of the sheet, change paper quickly, and   387
continue on another sheet.   393

(To speed up paper change: Make a double crease about 3.75 cm   407
from the bottom of the paper; your typing will sound a lot   420
different when you reach the creases. Do not use the paper bail.   431
Use two sheets of paper; when you remove the two, ~~shove~~ move them   443
straight back across the top of the cylinder and reinsert both,   456
bringing the clean paper up in ~~the~~ front.)   467

First Page of a Manuscript Typed in News-Bulletin Form

By curling your finger under whenever reaching downward, like d-to-c and j-to-m, you can make such reaches without moving your hands at all. Result: accuracy; greater speed.

Spacing reminder: Space once after a comma, semicolon, or a period following an abbreviation.

Space twice after a sentence and after a colon.

8-D. Type this note twice, concentrating on the W's and Y's. GOAL: To finish a copy in 1 minute or less.

8-D. Measure your progress

WORDS

11   Dear Mary: We wish you would tell Judy   8

      how to get her team to work like yours.   16

      1 | 2 | 3 | 4 | 5 | 6 | 7 | 8

8-E. Typists who keep their wrists low and hold their right thumb well above the space bar make few spacing errors. The thumb should be bent so that its tip points toward and nearly touches the B key.

8-E. Check your space-bar technique

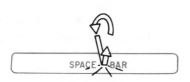

SPACE-BAR

Q: Sometimes I leave out a space. Sometimes I get extra spaces. What am I doing wrong?

A: Probably letting your thumb rest on the space bar or your palm lean on the machine. Hold your thumb well above the bar, so you can get a sharp, *bounce-off* space stroke.

8-F. Use F-finger. Try the fvf reach (keep the A-S-D-fingers anchored at home). Then type lines 12-15 three times. Can you make the fvf reach without moving any finger except the F?

8-F. Practice the V key

12   fff fvf vvv fff fvf vvv fff fvf vvv fvf

13   fvf vie vie fvf vim vim fvf via via fvf

14   fvf vet vet fvf vat vat fvf eve eve fvf

15   fvf velvet, fvf valves, fvf vividly fvf

8-G. Use J-finger. Try the jnj reach (K-L-Sem-fingers should be anchored in home position). Type lines 16-19 three times. Move only J-finger as you reach for the N key. Speed up on each of the repetitions.

8-G. Practice the N key

16   jjj jnj nnn jjj jnj nnn jjj jnj nnn jnj

17   jnj nun nun jnj run run jnj sun sun jnj

18   jnj not not jnj now now jnj nor nor jnj

19   jnj and and jnj one one jnj can can jnj

8-H. Measure your control of all keys that you have learned so far by typing each note at least twice. GOAL: To finish each note in 1 minute or less and to finish both in 2 minutes.

8-H. Measure your progress

WORDS

20   Dear Vic: When we see Jay, we will ask   8

      him to give Wally a list of five names.   16

21   Dear Roy: I may have to see Amy today;   24

      if so, I will try to run over at seven.   32

      1 | 2 | 3 | 4 | 5 | 6 | 7 | 8

We have testing and training facilities, as well as an extensive file 339
of qualified applicants ready to begin work. If you will send us your 353
job roster and your authorization, we shall embark at once upon the 367
recruitment of your staff. Indeed, if you wish, we would be pleased 381
to fly a member of our staff to your office in order that precise in- 394
structions about your employment needs and policies could be given 407
us. 408

| 1 | 2 | 3 | 4 | 5 | 6 | 7 | 8 | 9 | 10 | 11 | 12 | 13 | 14 |

215/216-C. Apply your skill to an integrated typing project

Assume the date is <u>DECEMBER 9</u>. You work for Fred C. Stevens, owner-manager of Stevens Secretarial Service, in Oshawa, Ontario. He prefers the standard *modified* blocked letter arrangement.

Letter 113
2-PAGE, BLOCKED

Paper: workbook 417
Carbons: 1 bcc, 1 file
Review: page 203
SI: 1.51—fairly difficult

"First," says Mr. Stevens, giving you the letter in 215-B, "this letter to Mr. J. Harrison Law, Director of Personnel, Matthews and Carter, Ltd., Cactus Road, Dartmouth, Nova Scotia. Will you, also, send a bcc copy to Bob (that is, Robert L.) Foods, at the Chamber of Commerce, with the note: *Wouldn't it be wonderful IF*."

Form 83
FILL-IN RECORD

Paper: workbook 419
Spacing: double

"Here is the record [below] of the tests that Catherine Quincy gave today," says Mr. Stevens. "Please type it on a clean sheet for the files."

Forms 84-87
INTRODUCTION CARDS

Paper: workbook 421-424

"There are two openings at Perry-Willis," says Mr. Stevens. "Let's send the four women who typed 60 and better over tomorrow for interviews by Frank Fudenske. Schedule them alphabetically, the first at 9:30, then one every 30 minutes after that."

Table 80
ORIGINAL TABLE

Paper: plain, full
Carbons: file only

"Prepare for the first applicant to take to Mr. Fudenske, but in a sealed envelope, the *List of Applicants from Stevens Secretarial Service To Be Interviewed December 10*," says Mr. Stevens.

"Arrange them in the sequence of their appointments, of course; and indicate the *Hour*, the *Name*, and *10-Minute Typing Score*. You know, even though the scores were made on straight paragraph copy, they are pretty good, aren't they? I wonder, now, are their scores better than *yours* would be?"

	APPLICANT	TYPEWRITING			TRANSCRIPTION			FILING			
No.	Name	Mins	Gross	Error	Mins	Speed	Rate	Alph	Num	Subj	Geog
1291	Marotsky, Alice Anne	10	63	2	3	100	31	Yes	No	Yes	Yes
1292	Beemes, Norma Jean	10	48	9	—	—	—	Yes	No	No	No
1293	Tannen, Roger L.	10	61	3	—	—	—	Yes	No	Yes	Yes
1294	Priness, Mary Agnes	10	67	0	3	120	30	Yes	Yes	Yes	Yes
1295	Korbin, Betty C.	10	62	3	3	100	19	Yes	No	Yes	No
1296	Belham, Ruth P.	10	66	1	3	120	28	Yes	No	No	Yes

Administrator

Catherine

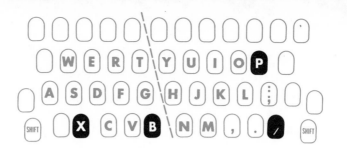

New Keys

LINE: 40
SPACING: SINGLE
GOAL: CONTROL X, P,
   B, AND DIAGONAL
STRESS: KEEPING
   ELBOWS IN

9-A. Type lines 1-2 twice each, trying to double your speed on each repetition. Leave a blank line between each pair of drill lines.

9-A. Review the keys you know

1   led vet ice due kit rim jay aft fan jam
2   for how joy fog cod sow gum jug sum log

9-B. Use S-finger. Try the sxs reach (keep A-finger or F-finger anchored in home position, whichever is easier for you). Then type lines 3-6 three times. Speed up on repetitions.

9-B. Practice the X key

3   sss sxs xxx sss sxs xxx sss sxs xxx sxs
4   sxs six six sxs nix nix sxs fix fix sxs
5   sxs wax wax sxs tax tax sxs lax lax sxs
6   sxs fox fox sxs sox sox sxs axe axe sxs

9-C. Use Sem-finger. Try the ;p; reach (anchor your J-K-L-fingers close to the home keys and keep elbows in, motionless). Then type lines 7-10 three times.

9-C. Practice the P key

7   ; ; ; ;p; ppp ; ; ; ;p; ppp ; ; ; ;p; ppp ;p;
8   ;p; lap lap ;p; nap nap ;p; map map ;p;
9   ;p; pin pin ;p; pen pen ;p; pan pan ;p;
10 ;p; pox pox ;p; pot pot ;p; put put ;p;

9-D. Type the note twice. GOAL: A copy in 1 minute. Concentrate on P's and X's.

9-D. Measure your progress

WORDS

11 Dear Rex: Please pay Max for the sixty   8
    papers I lost; I can pay you next week.   16

    1 | 2 | 3 | 4 | 5 | 6 | 7 | 8

9-E. Use F-finger. Try the fbf reach, keeping your A- and S-fingers at home (D-finger, too, if you can!). Type lines 12-15 three or more times. Speeding up?

9-E. Practice the B key

12 fff fbf bbb fff fbf bbb fff fbf bbb fbf
13 fbf fob fob fbf job job fbf rob rob fbf
14 fbf bud bud fbf but but fbf bug bug fbf
15 fbf be, be, fbf box box fbf by, by, fbf

9-F. Use Sem-finger. Try the ;/; reach (keep your J-finger at home—and your K-L-fingers, too, if you can). Type lines 16 and 17 three times. Gradually speed up on repetitions.

9-F. Practice the / (diagonal) key

16 ; ; ; ;/; /// ; ; ; ;/; /// ; ; ; ;/; /// ;/;
17 ;/; his/her ;/; him/her ;/; we/they ;/;

LINE: 60
TAB: 5
SPACING: DOUBLE
DRILLS: THREE TIMES
GOAL: DO AN HOUR'S
   WORK IN AN HOUR!
STRESS: CLEAN COPY

215-A. Three copies of each paragraph, or a 1-minute writing on each and a 2-minute writing on the group.

215-A. Tune up on these easy review lines

1   The old log was too big for the saw the men had found,   12
and the oak was too much for the axe the men had with them.   24

2   When he worked as agent for a jazz band, Dixie had one   36
battle after another. He proved to be quite lucky in most.   48

3   The answers ranged from 1910 to 1956, but most writers   60
picked out 1928, 1939, and 1947 as the most critical years.   72

   1 | 2 | 3 | 4 | 5 | 6 | 7 | 8 | 9 | 10 | 11 | 12

215-B. Sustain your skill on production copy

215-B. Confirm margins and tab stop (the lines should always align).

How long should it take you to type this letter body of 408 words? At 40 wam, about 10 or so minutes; at 50, about 8; at 60, less than 7. Make this a test situation:

Type the entire body (it continues on page 332), pausing to correct any errors you know that you make; and then compute your "output" speed.

Or, take two 7-minute writings, with rests after each minute in the first writing but with no rests in the second.

SI 1.48—fairly difficult

4   Dear Mr. Law: Thank you for your letter of December 5 and the   14
exciting news that it contains. The thought that a famous firm such   27
as Matthews and Carter may establish headquarters in Oshawa is   40
a most welcome one; you may be sure that all services of the com-   53
munity stand ready to help you.   60

You may also be sure that most of the employees needed for your   74
new installation will be available locally. There is no lack of trained   88
talent for your office staff, for the local schools and colleges have strong   104
and popular programs of office training. Indeed, there is even a surplus   118
in the office labor force, one that is so strong that leaders here have   133
been concerned about the number who have been going to Toronto,   146
and elsewhere, in their search for office work.   156

There is also a strong force of skilled technicians to man your plant.   171
As you are undoubtedly aware, the foundry, steel, and other heavy   185
industries have long maintained huge installations here in Oshawa,   198
a fact that has led schools to offer wide, effective programs of training   213
for industry.   216

Moreover, the automating of most plants has created an excess   229
supply of skilled labor. In their responsibility to the community,   243
local firms have tried to spread employment, principally by reducing   256
the number of turns a week that the men report for work. These firms   270
would welcome an employer who would share the labor force and so   283
bolster our economy.   288

This agency is concerned solely with the recruiting of office em-   302
ployees. If you so authorize us, we should gladly undertake the task   316
of assembling the office force you need.   [Turn page.]   324

   1 | 2 | 3 | 4 | 5 | 6 | 7 | 8 | 9 | 10 | 11 | 12 | 13 | 14

Letter 115

2-PAGE, BLOCKED
See page 332

9-F, continued. Type lines 18-19 three times. Keep elbows in close and eyes on the copy at all times.

9-F. Practice the ⟋ (diagonal) key, continued

18 Two kinds of current: the a/c and d/c.

19 There is no charge.   Mark the bill n/c.

9-G. Measure your control of keys you have practiced so far by typing each of the notes twice. GOAL: A copy of note 20 or 21 in 1 minute and a copy of both notes in 2 minutes.

9-G. Measure your progress

WORDS

20 Dear Bill: We will plan on your taking   8
   five or six boys to the game on Friday.   16

21 Dear Pat: My car may be in the garage;   24
   so I will get Jack to bring those boys.   32

   1 | 2 | 3 | 4 | 5 | 6 | 7 | 8

LINE: 40
SPACING: SINGLE
GOAL: CONTROL ?, Z, Q, AND HYPHEN
STRESS: KEEPING ELBOWS IN

LESSON

10

New Keys

10-A. Type lines 1, 2, 3 twice, both times as evenly and unhesitantly as though keeping time to music.

10-A. Review the keys you know

1 ask lad met sue jam dig rub hog sir boy

2 fog the jet six ice cup gum now via sow

3 Rex Ned Von Kay Alf Joe Con Jan Gay Pam

10-B. The Question Mark is shift of the Diagonal, controlled by Sem-finger. Practice the ;/; and ;?; reaches. Then type lines 4-7 three or more times.

10-B. Practice the ? key

4 ;;; ;/; ;/?; ;??; ;;; ;/; ;/?; ;??; ;?;

5 ;/; ;?; who? who? ;/; ;?; how? how? ;?;

6 ;/; ;?; why? why? ;/; ;?; you? you? ;?;

7 ;?; Who is there? ;?; Will you see? ;?;

10-C. Use A-finger. Try the aza reach (keep F-finger at home; curve A-finger tightly, to make the reach to Z easy). Type lines 8-11 three times, keeping your elbows motionless.

10-C. Practice the Z key

8 aaa aza zzz aaa aza zzz aaa aza zzz aza

9 aza zip zip aza zig zig aza zag zag aza

10 aza zoo zoo aza zed zed aza zee zee aza

11 aza buzzers aza zestful aza dizzily aza

between columns, thus providing ample room for the vertical lines you will need to draw; and to leave one blank line of space at each point where you will need to draw a horizontal ruled line.

Table 79

LONG BOXED TABLE

Paper: P5 size,
Carbons: enough for all
attending conference

"At our conference," says Mr. Gibbs, "I want to propose that we group our districts in a different way, making six districts instead of four. The six districts would be—" He gives you a slip:

Dist. 1		#2		#3	
Alberta	7	N.S	12	Manitoba	26
B.C.	16	N.B	12	Ontario	10
Sask.	10	Quebec	12		36
Yukon	3		36		
	36				

#4		#5		#6	
P.E.I	9	Ariz.	7	Kansas	12
Nfld	22	Cal.	13	Neb.	10
	31	Wyo.	7	N.D.	6
			27	S.D.	5
					33

"Now, type another table, *arranged exactly like that last one*, but grouping the states as I have shown on this listing. Let's call this table *Proposed District Organization*. You can copy all the 1960, 1970, and 1977 data off the first table."

Letters 111-112

BLOCKED LETTERS

Paper: P5 size,
workbook page 415
Copies: you decide

dr edward h swensen...school of business ...utah state university...logan...utah ...84321...i shall be at the hotel utah in salt lake city on december 13...14...and 15...is there any possibility that you and mrs swensen could drive down to have dinner with me on december 12...please drop a line to me at the hotel to let me know. 15 22 36 44 53 61 70 98

mr kenneth fairpoint...president... fairpoint & greeves...1200 timpanogos avenue...salt lake city 84102...by a wonderful stroke of luck...i shall be in salt lake 14 21 36 45

city on december 14 and...therefore... will be able to attend your dinner and reception for senator martin...thank you very much for inviting me...please express my appreciation...also...to mrs fairpoint. 52 61 69 78 106

Manuscript 79

TRIP ITINERARY

Paper: plain, full
Copies: three

itinerary ... december 13-15 ... tuesday ...december 13...07:00 depart san francisco on united air lines 352...09:29 arrive salt lake city ... 10:15 check in hotel utah and confirm facilities for conference; arrange lunch in suite...12:00 luncheon in suite to open conference; distribute agenda and discuss it in broad terms...13:30 begin discussion of topic one..."dealerships"...idea: see whether edward vargen...salt lake city dealer... would join this part of the discussion... 17:00 adjourn for the day...18:30 open for dinner with dr and mrs swensen... utah state university...if they accept the invitation. 28 36 43 53 62 70 80 89 98 107 116 124 132 140 150 152

wednesday...december 14...09:00 breakfast in suite...10:00 resume conference...probably start topic two..."district organization"...distribute copies of "proposed organization"...12:30 lunch in suite...14:00 resume conference...try to wind up "organization"...17:00 adjourn for the day...18:30 dinner at home of kenneth fairpoint...president of fairpoint & greeves. 162 170 179 188 196 203 211 218 225 233

thursday ... december 15 ... 09:00 breakfast with mr prince in suite...10:00 resume conference...probably start topic three..."incentive pay"...12:00 end of conference...13:30 lunch with mr vargen if he wishes ... 17:00 limousine to salt lake city airport...18:05 depart salt lake city on western airlines 75 ... 18:35 arrive san francisco ... met by mrs gibbs. 243 251 259 268 277 288 299 306 314

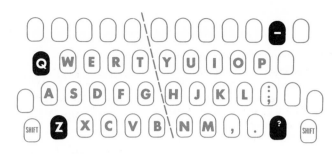

Note in 10-H that Hyphen is typed without a space when used as follows:

(1) To indicate any word division (as in line 21).

(2) To join words in a compound (as in line 22).

(3) To indicate a dash, which is made with two hyphens (as in line 23).

10-D. Type the note twice. GOAL: A copy in 1 minute.

10-D. Measure your progress

WORDS

12   Dear Blaze: Would you and/or Buzz like   8
      to hear our new jazz records? Tonight?   16

      1 | 2 | 3 | 4 | 5 | 6 | 7 | 8

10-E. Check your elbow control

Q: Is it all right to swing out the elbows for keys like Q, -, and Z?
A: No. If you do, your hands will be out of position for striking the next keys. REMEMBER: Keep your elbows in close, hanging loosely by your sides. Keep your shoulders down and your fingers well curved.

10-F. Use Sem finger. Try ;-; reach, keeping the J-finger at home. Your K-L-fingers spread and rock forward as Sem-finger straightens for long reach to Hyphen. Then type lines 13-16 three times each.

10-F. Practice the ▬ (hyphen) key

13   ;;; ;p; ;p-; ;--; ;;; ;p; ;p-; ;--; ;-;
14   ;p- ;-; blue-gray ;p- ;-; one-third ;-;
15   ;p- ;-; one-fifth ;p- ;-; part-time ;-;
16   ;p- ;-; left-hand ;p- ;-; one-sixth ;-;

10-G. Use A-finger. Try the aqa reach (keep your F-finger anchored and lift your D-S-fingers only slightly; A-finger stays curled). Then type lines 17-20 three times each.

10-G. Practice the ▣ key

17   aaa aqa aqqa aqqa aaa aqa aqqa aqqa aqa
18   aqa aqa quit quit aqa aqa quip quip aqa
19   aqa aqa quiz quiz aqa aqa quay quay aqa
20   aqa quick quickly aqa quiet quietly aqa

10-H. Type each note twice. GOAL: A copy of each note in 1 minute and a copy of any two in 2 minutes.

If time permits, take a 2-minute timing: begin with the first note and type straight through the others as far as you can get in 2 minutes. Proofread your work carefully. Do errors indicate that you need special practice typing?

10-H. Measure your progress

WORDS

21   Dear Jacqueline: Do you know the equa-   8
      tion Mr. Zelt quoted? Is it a new one?   16

22   Dear Zoe: My family is planning for an   24
      eight-day trip to Zion Park next month.   32

23   Dear Buzz: Was the quiz--the one about   40
      the mazes--very hard? Were you amazed?   48

      1 | 2 | 3 | 4 | 5 | 6 | 7 | 8

Assume the date is DECEMBER 8. You are secretary to Mr. J. T. Gibbs, general manager of Western Corporation, with the headquarters in San Francisco and with branch offices in Portland, Denver, and Vancouver. The president of the firm, Paul V. Prince, has asked Mr. Gibbs to set up a conference, and it is with this that you will be busy. Mr. Gibbs prefers standard blocked letter form and this closing to his letters:

```
                    Cordially yours,


                    John T. Gibbs
                    General Manager
```

Forms 79-82

TELEGRAMS

Paper: workbook 411, 413
Note that one is a full-rate telegram and three are night letters

"Send a telegram for me," says Mr. Gibbs, "to the Hotel Utah." He continues speaking and dictating as indicated in 213-B, page 328. He adds, "Make a folder for me to take on this conference trip; include copies of *everything* in it."

Manuscript 78

MEETING AGENDA

Paper: plain, full
Carbons: enough for all attending conference

agenda...salt lake city management con- 28
ference...december 13-15...topic one: the 54
dealership development program...ques- 60
tion 1...are new dealerships developing on 70
the schedule made at our sun valley meet- 80
ing...question 2...do the previous esti- 87
mates for 1970 look good...what is the 96
substantiating evidence...question 3...is 104
it time to move eastward to the next tier of 113
districts...quebec to louisiana...question 122
4...are dealers gratified with their present 131
rate and amount of compensation... 140

topic two: the district organization 150
...question 1...are our present districts 158
too large for good supervision by the dis- 168
trict managers...question 2...would the 175
company interest be served best by adding 184
assistant managers or by creating more 193
districts, each with its own district man- 204

ager...question 3...if we have more dis- 211
tricts, how would the regions be grouped 221
in the new plan of organization... 227

topic 3: incentive pay for field repre- 238
sentatives...question 1...in general...how 246
much of an increase in compensation is 256
needed to attract top personnel...question 263
2...is it better to provide an increase in 272
base salary or to provide for incentive com- 283
pensation... 285

Table 78

LONG BOXED TABLE

Paper: plain, full
Carbons: enough for all attending conference

DISTRICT ORGANIZATION
Western Corporation

District	Areas	Number of Dealerships 1960	1970	1977
1	Alberta	0	4	7
	British Columbia	2	5	16
	Saskatchewan	1	4	10
	Yukon	0	1	3
	TOTAL	3	14	36
2	Manitoba	12	18	26
	Quebec	4	8	12
	Ontario	3	7	10
	Nova Scotia	3	7	12
	New Brunswick	4	8	12
	TOTAL	26	48	72
3	Newfoundland	4	8	13
	P.E.I.	3	7	13
	Gaspé	0	3	6
	Labrador	0	2	5
	Northwest Ter.	2	4	7
	St. Lawrence	0	3	5
	TOTAL	9	27	49
4	Arizona	2	4	7
	Nebraska	4	6	12
	Oklahoma	0	4	9
	Texas	0	14	22
	TOTAL	6	28	50

"Please type this, including the figures I have added for 1977," says Mr. Gibbs, "but spread it so it will look good on a full sheet of paper." You plan carefully: You decide to leave the standard six spaces

Review

LINE: 40
SPACING: SINGLE
GOAL: STRENGTHEN
   CONTROL
STRESS: SHARP,
   BOUNCE-OFF STROKES

11-A. Type each line twice. Stress sharp, even strokes.

11-A. Review the alphabet keys

1 kit lid mad net vie why yet zoo aim tax
2 bow fit hug icy jig orb pit quo sir use

11-B. Type each line twice, followed by a blank line (return carriage twice).

If you break rhythm, look up, or jam keys on second typing of any line, type that line once more.

Try to maintain a very even, steady pace and to keep your arms and wrists almost motionless—to make reaches FINGER motions, not arm motions.

The dotted lines remind you of the reach-path that you are practicing.

11-B. Build accuracy on reach-stroke words

3 aza azure aza amaze ;/? ball? ;/? hall?   Downward reaches
4 sxs taxes sxs sixes l.l mall. l.l call.
5 dcd coded dcd decoy k,k mask, k,k bank,
6 fvf favor fvf fives jmj major jmj James

7 fbf abaft fbf fable jnj joins jnj junks   Inward reaches
8 fgf fight fgf flags jhj rajah jhj John;
9 ftf after ftf swift jyj delay jyj enjoy

10 aqa quail aqa quake ;p; prop; ;p; shop;   Upward reaches
11 sws sweet sws swipe lol loose lol slope
12 ded deeds ded delay kik skill kik kilts
13 frf fresh frf fruit juj judge juj juror

11-C. Apply the directions given for 11-B, above.

The vertical lines guide your eyes for grouping the words in phrases. Do not pause when you reach any words in phrases; do not pause when you reach any vertical line.

Lines 14-24 are extremely easy, so easy that you run the risk of jamming keys unless you strike them very sharply. If typebars do jam, untangle them very carefully—never yank!

11-C. Build speed on phrase sequences

14 if he |if he |if he is |if he is |if he is   Twos
15 is to |is to |he is to |he is to |he is to
16 to go |to go |is to go |is to go |is to go
17 or do |or do |or do so |or do so |or do so

18 and for |and for |and for the |and for the   Threes
19 got the |got the |and got the |and got the
20 has had |has had |has had the |has had the
21 the man |the man |the man may |the man may

22 with them |with them both |with them both   Fours
23 will have |will have them |will have them
24 came from |came from them |came from them

        1 | 2 | 3 | 4 | 5 | 6 | 7 | 8

Unit 35. Secretarial Projects

213-A. Three copies of each paragraph; or a 1-minute writing on each and a 2-minute writing on the group.

Repeat in Lesson 214.

213-A. Tune up on these easy review lines

1　　The two men had the boy get out the old red box.　Then　12
the men put the key in the box and had the boy put it back.　24

2　　Vic took from their waxy bags the dozen or so jugs you　36
had purchased in Iraq; we thought they were very beautiful.　48

3　　There were a lot of 10¢ and 28¢ items for sale, but it　60
seemed that those for 39¢ or 47¢ or 56¢ were put out first.　72

  1　|　2　|　3　|　4　|　5　|　6　|　7　|　8　|　9　|　10　|　11　|　12

213-B. Make errorless copy of each paragraph or take two 5-minute writings, with rests after the minutes in the first writing but no rests in the second.

GOAL: 60 or more words a minute with two or fewer typing mistakes.

SI 1.39—normal

213-B. Sustain your skill on production copy

4　　Please send a telegram for me, J. T. Gibbs of Western　12
Corporation, to the Hotel Utah.　It is on Temple Avenue, in　24
Salt Lake City.　Say "Please reserve a suite of three rooms　36
plus three single rooms for December 13 through 15.　Please　48
wire confirmation."　Oh, can you cut that down to 15 words?　60

5　　Now send a telegram to our branch manager in Portland,　72
Oregon.　He is Mr. F. I. Beauchamp, and the address for him　84
is our office at 800 Fourth Street West.　Say, "Paul Prince　96
has called meeting of branch managers at Hotel Utah in Salt　108
Lake City for noon, December 13, through noon, December 15.　120
Your room has been reserved.　Bring full data on dealership　132
plans for your territory."　That message is a night letter.　144

6　　Now we must send a similar night letter to our manager　156
in Denver.　He is Bob Ferris, and his address is our office　168
in the Brown Palace Hotel.　The message is exactly the same　180
as the one I gave you to send to Mr. Beauchamp.　Have that?　192

7　　One more night letter, then we are through.　It is for　204
the manager of our office in Vancouver, but right now he is　216
away on vacation.　Well, we can reach him in Houston, where　228
he is visiting some relatives.　Send the following message,　240
please, to Gerald T. Foster, care of Mr. Tellman Foster, at　252
3928 Ruskin Street, in Houston:　"Regret to break into your　264
vacation, but Paul Prince" and so on.　Thank you very much.　276

  1　|　2　|　3　|　4　|　5　|　6　|　7　|　8　|　9　|　10　|　11　|　12

Forms 79-82

TELEGRAMS
See page 329

Setting a tab stop:
1. Clear machine.
2. Space in 5 from left margin setting.
3. Press "tab set."
4. Test setting.

Word-count credit: The word counts in this book credit you 1 word (5 strokes) for each of the indentions and each of the EXTRA carriage returns you must make in timings.

11-D. Learn how to indicate a new paragraph

When a paragraph is double spaced, indent the first word 5 spaces. Use the tabulator for this indention. Review (page 7) the steps for using the tabulator mechanism.

When a paragraph is single spaced, precede it with 1 blank line. The first word may be either indented 5 spaces or blocked at the margin. Summary of possibilities:

```
Dear Mr. Hale:

     I do appreciate very much

your help in tracking down the

list of customers in Alberta.

     If there is ever a chance

that I can repay the favor, do

give me a chance to do so.
```

Double spaced, indented

```
Dear Mr. Hale:

     I do appreciate very much
your help in tracking down the
list of customers in Alberta.

     If there is ever a chance
that I can repay the favor, do
give me a chance to do so.

     I think that your company
will be rather pleased to know
that your bid got our order.
```

Single spaced, indented

```
Dear Mr. Hale:

I do appreciate very much your
help in tracking down the list
of customers in Alberta.

If there is ever a chance that
I can repay the favor, do give
me a chance to do so.

I think that your company will
be rather pleased to know that
your bid got our order.
```

Single spaced, blocked

11-E. Three steps:
1. Measure your skill; type a double-spaced copy and proofread it.

2. Improve your skill: If you made 5 or more errors in 11-E, repeat 11-B once; but if you made 4 or fewer errors, then repeat 11-C once.

3. Test your skill: Retype the letter once. GOAL: A complete copy in 2 minutes or less.

11-E. Boost and measure your progress

WORDS

Dear Mr. Jackson:	4
5➤ Our club is quite grateful to you,	12
sir, for what you have done to help us.	20
5➤ In the next few days we shall send	28
you a gift, very small in size but very	36
big in what it means.	40

1 | 2 | 3 | 4 | 5 | 6 | 7 | 8

LINE: 40
TAB: 5
SPACING: SINGLE
GOAL: REVIEW KEYS;
   CORRECT WEAKNESSES
STRESS: EYES ON COPY

12-A. Type each of these lines twice. Eyes on copy!

12-B. Measure your skill and then increase it:

1. Using double spacing and tab-5 indention, type and proofread a copy of 12-B. Count your errors.

2. If you make 5 or more errors, type lines 4-12 (page 27) twice each and lines 13-21 once each.

3. If you make 4 or fewer errors, type lines 4-12 (page 27) once each and lines 13-21 twice each.

LESSON 12

Clinic Review

12-A. Review the alphabet keys

1 move back quit pond girl waxy fish jazz
2 vows joke foxy quiz calm drab nigh tops

12-B. Measure your keyboard control

WORDS

3 My dear Mr. Baker:	4
5➤ I had to stop in the office on the	12
sixth floor today; I saw Mr. Jay there.	20
He told me he had changed his mind	28
and does not plan to give a quiz at the	36
end of the course.	40

1 | 2 | 3 | 4 | 5 | 6 | 7 | 8

3. our local borough council passed an ordinance in february against unnecessary noise in general and noise from faulty mufflers in particular...as a result...we have enjoyed some added business.

These are the figures:

ANALYSIS OF MUFFLER SALES		
Period Ending November 30, 19—		
	This Year	Same Period
Make	To Date	Last Year
Buick	162	190
Chevrolet	278	264
Chrysler	193	167
Ford	315	290
Mercury	198	173
Plymouth	246	237
Pontiac	192	168
Studebaker	131	102
Oldsmobile	201	139
TOTALS	1 916	1 730

part four: miscellaneous matters...this month...mr vance...there are two matters about which i should like your opinion:

1. until recently there was a small coffee shop adjacent to our store...where customers often went while waiting for us to install seat covers...seat belts...or mufflers...now the customers stand around and impatiently wait as they watch every move of our men...might we have permission to install a coffee and candy canteen... we would put it at the garage entrance... around back...and maintain it exclusively for waiting customers and our staff.

2. i have been dismayed at the dismal ...even macabre...nature of our promotion for the wonderful corey roll-up seat belt...i think we would sell a great many more of these belts if our advertisements were cheerier...to illustrate what i mean ...i enclose a sample...if you feel it has any merit...would you pass it along to the appropriate agency...please?

respectfully submitted...and so on.

20
29
37
46
52
74
96
116
124
147
153
160
165
171
178
185
191
198
215
244
252
260
270
278
287
294
302
310
318
327
335
343
351
361
367
376
384
419
428
436
444
450
495

Paper: plain, full
Review: pages 305, 306

Manuscript 76
ADVERTISING DISPLAY

Giving you the display below, Mr. Horne says, "This is the 'sample' to which I referred. Please type it as attractively as you can."

5cm × 2.5cm

BUTTONS...

2" × 1" picture of a child's hand pushing down the button of a door lock.

'n' BELTS...

2" × 1" picture of a child fastening a Corey seat belt around himself.

COREY ROLL-UP SEAT BELTS
Aren't seat belts wonderful! They make driving so much safer. At least, they do when they are as sturdily web-anchored as those strain-tested

COREY ROLL-UP SEAT BELTS
And aren't you glad that someone perfected that idea of having the belts "drawn in" by a button spring! It keeps the seat straps out of your way when you don't want them, but right in reach when you do. And the handiest belts of all are

COREY ROLL-UP SEAT BELTS

Paper: plain, half sheet
Arrangement: you decide
Review: pages 305, 306

Manuscript 77
BULLETIN DISPLAY

"Finally," says Mr. Horne, "prepare a bulletin announcement to say—" and he dictates:

to the staff...in order that you may make your holiday plans...i am pleased to tell you that...in view of the fact that both christmas and new year's day fall on sunday this year ...our store will close at 17:00 on saturday and remain closed until 09:00 on tuesday morning...let me add the best wishes of the corey stores and of myself for the holiday season...my name.

UNIT 34   N. H, Man   LESSON 212
Fort. Pierce Branch

327

12-C. Using single spacing, type each line twice if you made 5 or more errors in 12-B, but only once if you made 4 or fewer typing errors in 12-B (page 26).

The drills are designed to help you keep your wrists and arms almost motionless (most of the words bring your fingers back to their home-key positions).

Any time you want a drill to sharpen stroking, turn to this page and retype lines 6, 9, and 12.

12-C. Build accuracy on tight motions

4	calls backs chalk flax mass balk baa zag	Rows 1&2
5	glass flask shall slag dash glad ask all	Row 2
6	equal plush yells risk owls wish oil was	Rows 2&3
7	bands smash naval jabs sank ball cad bag	Rows 1&2
8	flags flash halls sash alas gala sag ash	Row 2
9	usual heels pulls talk desk poll rag ail	Rows 2&3
10	lacks gnash banks mask sank labs van bad	Rows 1&2
11	slags slash salad flag lash shag lag has	Row 2
12	toils speak swish rush yolk wail era old	Rows 2&3

12-D. Using single spacing, type each line twice if you made 4 or fewer errors in 12-B, but only once if you made 5 or more errors in 12-B (on page 26).

Do not pause when you come to the vertical lines —they are simply guides to help you read the copy by grouping words for you.

12-D. Build speed on phrase sequences

13	if it |if it |if it is |if it is |if it is	Twos
14	or if |or if |or if it |or if it |or if it	
15	if we |if we |if we do |if we do |if we do	
16	are not |are not |are not yet |are not yet	Threes
17	ask him |ask him |ask him for |ask him for	
18	get the |get the |get the one |get the one	
19	they said |they said that |they said that	Fours
20	with this |with this form |with this form	
21	they wish |they wish that |they wish that	

```
1 | 2 | 3 | 4 | 5 | 6 | 7 | 8
```

12-E. Set tab stops at the points indicated on the scale; using the tab by touch, type lines 22-23 three times. Don't look up!

12-E. Sharpen proficiency in tab-indenting

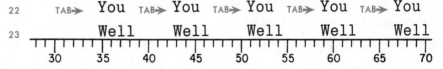

```
22  TAB➤ You  TAB➤ You  TAB➤ You  TAB➤ You  TAB➤ You
23       Well     Well     Well     Well     Well
        30    35    40    45    50    55    60    65    70
```

12-F. To measure progress, type 12-F twice. Use a tab-5 indention and double spacing. GOAL: A complete copy in 2 minutes or less, with 4 or fewer errors.

Remember to tab-indent the paragraphs without looking up from the book once.

12-F. Measure your progress

WORDS

24	Dear Mr. Lovejoy:	4
	5➤ You asked me to try to get you two	12
	tickets for the next World Series.	19
	Well, sir, I was quite lucky.	26
	Two prize seats are yours, back of	34
	third base, for the opener.	40

```
1 | 2 | 3 | 4 | 5 | 6 | 7 | 8
```

Assume the date is DECEMBER 3. You work for Norton Horne, manager of the Fort Pierce, Ontario, store of the Corey chain of stores. He expects you to type these few tasks in about an hour. He prefers semiblocked letter style with this closing arrangement:

Sincerely yours,

C O R E Y ,   I N C .

Norton Horne, Manager
Fort Pierce Branch

Letter 110

SEMIBLOCKED LETTER

Paper: workbook 405
SI: 1.47—fairly hard
Review: bcc, page 247
Carbons: you decide

"This letter," says Mr. Horne, "is in answer to one we received today from the sales manager of the *Fort Pierce Daily Press*." He continues speaking and dictates the letter, as in 211-C, page 325.

Form 78

Tables 75-77

INTERBRANCH REPORT

Paper: workbook 407-410
If you lack workbook forms, type report as a four-page semiblocked letter; use the ruled form for the tables

4 page memo

Dec. 3

Re:

monthly report to john p jamieson...district sales manager...corey stores inc... 155 lakeshore boulevard west...toronto ontario M8V 1C1...financial summary ...i am pleased to report a net profit of 3500 dollars, a gain of 300 dollars over the corresponding figure for last year... this gain of 8.6 percent is especially good in view of the fact that we had two fewer merchandising days this year. *bottom half*   13 / 21 / 28 / 57 / 67 / 73 / 81 / 89 / 97 / 105

no rules

SUMMARY OF OPERATIONS
Month Ending November 30 19--

Item	This Year	Last Year
Total Sales	$24 600	$23 800
Mdse cost	− 6 500	− 6 300
Gross profit	$18 100	$17 500
Fixed expenses	− 14 600	− 14 300
Net before taxes	$ 3 500	$ 3 200

125 / 147 / 166 / 190 / 200 / 220 / 229 / 230 / 250

Merchandise

part two: staff performance...members of the sales staff averaged 3 280 dollars sales during the month...which is an average 53 dollars higher than last month and accounts for the increase in sales...mr brody and mr rheems continue in their race for first place...with mr rheems still ahead for the year but mr brody passing him slightly for the month...note particularly that mr holman...who joined our staff only two weeks ago...got off to an excellent start.   285 / 293 / 301 / 308 / 350 / 358 / 366 / 375 / 383 / 390 / 398 / 402

bottom half

ANALYSIS OF SALES PERFORMANCE
Period Ending November 30, 19--

Name	Month	Year to Date	
Brody, J.B.	$3750	$39 200	
Dodds, Edward	3 150	33 175	
Holman, William	1 500	1 500	a
Jackson, Thomas	2 780	31 250	
Lewis, Frank T.	3 225	30 685	
Norris, Parker	3 320	12 940	b
Rheems, Jorge	3 700	40 350	
Klein, Robert	3 175	32 600	
TOTALS	$24 600	$221 700	
a. from 11/14	b. from 9/1		

425 / 441 / 462 / 486 / 495 / 506 / 515 / 524 / 534 / 544 / 554 / 573 / 592

part three: directed analysis...in accordance with the directive in your staff bulletin dated november 21...i have made a study to compare sales of mufflers for the makes we carried in stock both this year and last...the analysis indicates that we have sold 186 more this year than last... which is almost one a day...for a 10.8 percent increase...i would attribute this gratifying increase to three causes: 618 / 626 / 634 / 643 / 652 / 660 / 668 / 676 / 685 / 691

1. we have included display reference to our muffler installation service in all advertisements...along with the specific makes of cars we can serve without delay.   701 / 710 / 718 / 726

2. we now have a competitor within half a block...he advertises...also...and so motorists come to both stores to "shop" ...because our prices are lower...we gain.   736 / 744 / 752 / 760

Unit 3. Skill Development

LINE: 50
TAB: 5
SPACING: SINGLE
GOAL: LEARN TO
CENTER HORIZONTALLY
STRESS: TOUCH
CONTROL

13-A. Type each line twice, as smoothly as you can.

13-A. Review the alphabet keys

1   back dent high joke melt hope quiz rust vows foxy

2   Jack Dave Ruth John Mell Hope Quen Russ Vera Ford

13-B. To select practice goals, type and proofread a copy. Use single spacing and a tab-5 indention.

Note that the word count credits you with 1 word (5 strokes) for each extra carriage return (for the blank line before each of the paragraphs) and for each paragraph indention.

13-B. Measure and improve your keyboard control

                  WORDS

3   Jeff King: 2

      The next time you are out this way, try   12
to drop in at our plant.   17

      We are quite worried about our accident   27
rate and hope you will help us look over the   36
hazards to our men.   40

  1 | 2 | 3 | 4 | 5 | 6 | 7 | 8 | 9

13-C. To boost accuracy, type lines 4-7 three times if you made 5 or more errors in 13-B, but each line twice if you made 4 or fewer errors. Keep your hands from bouncing!

13-C. Build accuracy on one-hand words

4   wade join free milk fact look face hull dare hill

5   fare jump stew link wave pull vase hoop rate pink

6   best mill east pony raft hulk ease puny fast lump

7   date only test pump afar oily fads upon draw poll

13-D. To increase speed, type lines 8-11 three times if you made 4 or fewer errors in 13-B, but each line twice if you made 5 or more errors. Always tap keys sharply, to keep the typebars from jamming.

13-D. Build speed on alternate-hand words

8   chapel bushel endow angle they lend for the it is

9   profit formal bugle right work duty vow rib or if

10   height dismay their gland than when owl pan do so

11   handle mangle handy giant coal mend lay cut ox of

13-E. To synchronize the capital-shift motions and eliminate "flying caps," type lines 12-13 three or more times each. Increase speed on repetitions.

13-E. Increase efficiency in capitalizing

12   Drew Earl Evan Carl Fred June Kirk Lois Jill Lola

13   Cora Dick Bill Rita Anne Paul Jane Hank Nate Irma

13-F. To boost and to measure your skill, type 13-F twice, line for line. GOAL: A complete copy in 2 minutes or less, with 4 or fewer typing errors.

13-F. Measure your progress

                  WORDS

14   Miss Gray: 2

      As soon as you can, please find out for   12
us the exact steps in the new Ozite process.   21

      What I have read about it seems to show   31
it may be just what we require for our work.   40

  1 | 2 | 3 | 4 | 5 | 6 | 7 | 8 | 9

211-A. Three copies of
each paragraph; or a
1-minute writing on
each, plus a 2-minute
writing on the group.

211-A. Tune up on these review lines

1 When will Miss Hall come from the bank with that cash?   12
They said that the young lady left the bank some while ago.   24

2 The log jam broke up with a quiver and crash after the   36
logger used his oversize ax to hack and slash the key logs.   48

3 We were ahead 39 to 28 at the half, but then the other   60
team ran up 10 straight and then finally took us, 56 to 47.   72

    1 | 2 | 3 | 4 | 5 | 6 | 7 | 8 | 9 | 10 | 11 | 12

211-B. Type to your need.

ACCURACY: Lines 4-5
as a paragraph four or
more times; then lines
6-7 as a paragraph two
or more times.

SPEED: Each line three
consecutive times.

211-B. Sharpen skill by selective preview practice

4 unauthorized manifestly, appreciate immediate December June
5 advertising, responsible repetition attention contract West
    1 | 2 | 3 | 4 | 5 | 6 | 7 | 8 | 9 | 10 | 11 | 12
6 feel that will note ask you one of for it but it and not to
7 to one of the to pay if you to our to the do not we had not

211-C. Confirm margins
are for 60-space line
(lines will align if you
observe bell correctly).

Type one complete copy
or take two 5-minute
writings, with rests
after each minute in
the first writing but
no rests in the second.

GOAL: 60 or more words
a minute with no more
than 2 typing mistakes.

SI 1.39—normal

211-C. Sustain skill on production copy

	C	D
This letter is in answer to one we received today from the sales	14	9
manager of the Fort Pierce Daily Press. We reach him at Post	26	17
Office Box 882 in Fort Pierce, Ontario. He has repeated one of our	40	24
ads without our telling him to, and now he wants us to pay for it.	54	..
Well, we're not going to do so.	60	..
Dear Sir: I am returning for correction the statement you	73	39
mailed to this office on December 1. If you will refer to our space	87	54
contract, dated June 19 of this year, you will note that you are	100	67
authorized to run our advertisements only according to the exact	113	80
schedule we provide on the first day of each month. We provided	126	93
you such a schedule last month.	132	100
Although we appreciate the value of extra advertising, we do	146	114
not feel that we are responsible for the unauthorized repetition	159	127
on November 21 of the display we had run the day previous.	171	139
Manifestly, it is not our fault that the display was repeated in	184	152
error. We ask you for a revised statement, and we assure you we	197	167
shall give it our immediate attention.	205	175
Sincerely yours, and so on, and send a blind carbon of that to	218	204
Mr. John Jamieson, in Toronto. On his copy, please add a	230	222
comment: "You told me this would happen, and it has; I really	242	234
think, however, that the error was an honest one."	252	244

    1 | 2 | 3 | 4 | 5 | 6 | 7 | 8 | 9 | 10 | 11 | 12

Letter 111

SEMIBLOCKED LETTER
See page 326

To center words across the page:

1. Set the carriage at the center point of the paper.

2. Find the backspace key in the upper left or right of the keyboard. This key is ordinarily controlled by the nearest little finger; but, *on a manual machine,* it is better to use the *thumb* on the backspace key *when using it for centering.*

3. Say the letters and spaces of the words in pairs, pressing and releasing the backspace key one time after you say each pair of strokes.

Caution: You will often have a letter left over after calling the pairs; do *not* backspace for this letter.

4. Type the words. They should appear in the middle of the paper.

PRACTICE. Center these names.

Ralph Tolberts
Helen Debolt
Kathryn Robinson
Mary Lee Busch
Joseph F. Bentley
John Thomas Philbertson, Jr.

Check: The letter "B" lines up.

Shortcut to save time in centering the carriage: Before you begin to backspace, set the stop at the centering point; then you can tabulate to that point to center the carriage.

If you correctly center the names in the exercise, the letter B in each name will align vertically.

LINE: 50
TAB: 5 AND CENTER
SPACING: SINGLE
GOAL: LEARN TO CENTER HORIZONTALLY
STRESS: TOUCH CONTROL

LESSON

14

Skill Drive

14-A. Type each line twice; keep eyes on the copy.

14-A. Review the alphabet keys

1 tab vow lag zip fox ham bed irk joy quo act an so

2 jobs vary zone flax lone milk crew quit digs help

14-B. To define practice goals, type and proofread a copy of this letter.

Note that you must tab twice in succession to reach the center, where you begin the name "Jeff King." The double tab—make it without looking up!—counts as 2 words.

14-B. Measure and improve your keyboard control

	WORDS
3 Mr. Queen:	2
	3
Thank you for inviting me to stop in at	12
your plant. I expect to be able to do so on	21
Monday and will do my best to see what risks	30
or hazards I can detect.	35
	36
➡TAB ➡TAB Jeff King	40

1 | 2 | 3 | 4 | 5 | 6 | 7 | 8 | 9

14-C. To boost accuracy, type lines 4-7 three times each if you made 5 or more errors in 14-B, but twice each if you made 4 or less typing errors in 14-B.

14-C. Build accuracy on double-letter words

4 grammarian succeeds powwows apples radii burr add

5 assistants quitters vacuums suffer guess ebbs baa

6 bookkeeper withhold flivver jammed dizzy eggs inn

7 staggering possible process supper fluff been odd

14-D. To increase speed, type lines 8-11 three or more times each if you had 4 or fewer errors in 14-B, but twice each if you had 5 or more errors in 14-B.

14-D. Build speed on phrase sequences

8 to see |to see |to see him |to see him |to see him at

9 are you |are you free |are you free |are you free to

10 to show |to show us |show us their |to show us their

11 have been |been able |have been able |have been able

1 | 2 | 3 | 4 | 5 | 6 | 7 | 8 | 9 | 10

the broadcast; so make enough carbons! On each person's copy, underscore *his* cues in colored pencil, as I marked the 'Husband' cue lines."

"Do I mark the 'sound' and 'music' cue lines, also?" you ask Mr. Lawrence.

"Yes, please do," he replies.

Manuscript 75

RADIO SCRIPT

	CHQM & CBU	6
	Station Break Commercial	23
	KINLEY ELECTRONICS COMPANY	41
	Saturday, December 6, 19——	58
	7:29–7:30 P.M. CST	72
		73
SOUND	CLATTER OF DISHES BEING WASHED.	82
<u>HUSBAND</u>	HUMMING...STOPS HUMMING AND SPEAKS SOLICITOUSLY. Darling,	97
	you take care of those hands of yours! The old boy doesn't	110
	mind doing ~~up those~~ dishes. Matter of fact, might show you	121
	a thing or two!	126
WIFE	*Thanks, Dear. I don't like to ask you!*	136
MUSIC	SPRIGHTLY VERSION OF "PRISONER'S SONG"...STAB...UP...UNDER.	151
ANNCR	Good old Jonesy. It's Saturday, and this businessman is at	166
	home. Doesn't mind doing the dishes. Not at all!	178
MUSIC	SWEEP IN, SLIGHTLY SLOWER "PRISONER'S SONG"...FADE OUT.	192
<u>HUSBAND</u>	Hands still bad, Trudie? ~~Well,~~ *Okay,* I'll do ~~the dishes.~~ *them*	205
SOUND	CLATTER OF DISHES BEING WASHED.	214
ANNCR	Good old Jonesy! He's a trooper! He doesn't mind doing the	229
	dishes...once in a while. But, day after day?	240
MUSIC	SWEEP IN WITH HEAVY, SLOW "PRISONER'S SONG"...FADE OUT.	254
<u>HUSBAND</u>	Honest to goodness, Tru, the boys in the office are accusing	270
	me of having dishpan hands!	276
WIFE	You know, Dear, they are starting to look like mine.	290
<u>HUSBAND</u>	Didn't anyone ever invent a machine for this job?	303
ANNCR	BREAKS IN. You bet someone did, Mr. Jones! It's the famous	319
	Kinley dishwasher—Kinley! Mr. Jones...Mr. Jones?	350
WIFE	He's gone. To the Kinley dealer. *I hope!*	362
MUSIC	SWELL IN WITH SWING VERSION OF "PRISONER'S SONG"... *STAB* ~~FADE~~ OUT.	377

SOUND   BANG OF A DOOR AND RUNNING FEET.
ANNCR   CALLING ANXIOUSLY.

14-E. To sharpen your carriage returns, type each word on a separate line; repeat the drill, this time indenting each word 5 spaces. If your machine is manual, type line 13 before line 12.

14-F. To increase and to measure your typing skill, type this letter twice.

GOAL: A complete copy in 2 minutes or less, with 4 or fewer typing errors.

Remember to double-tab to the name of the writer.

14-G. Centering and "all capping" are two display techniques that all typists use. If you type the lines correctly, the letter E will align vertically. Use the tab to recenter the carriage; double space.

14-E. Increase efficiency in returning carriage

12 will bill Jake Joan Mark Kaye Dell Sara Rita They

13 pour miss Dana Walt Bill Ford Miss Jory Mrs. Lane

14-F. Measure your progress

WORDS

14 Mr. Glenn: 2

                                                                     3

    I have been able to make a date for the   12
man from the Ozite firm to show us their new   21
process. Are you free to see him at a quar-   30
ter to four next Monday?   35

                                                                    36

➤TAB ➤TAB   Jane Gray   40

1 | 2 | 3 | 4 | 5 | 6 | 7 | 8 | 9

14-G. learn to type all capitals

To type all the letters of a word or group of words in capitals:

    1. Press the shift lock. It is above one or both shift keys.

    2. Type the word or words.

    3. Release the lock by touching the opposite shift key.

    CAUTION. Do not forget to release the lock whenever a stroke that cannot be typed in capitals (a hyphen, for example) appears among the capitalized letters. Why?

    PRACTICE. Center horizontally:

A Report by Earl Carr on the
OZITE PROCESS
Newly Developed by the
OZITE-PARKER CORPORATION
of Toronto, Ontario

LESSON

15

Skill Drive

LINE: 50
TAB: 5 AND CENTER
SPACING: SINGLE
GOAL: IMPROVE SKILL AND CENTERING
STRESS: TOUCH CONTROL

15-A. Each line twice, with almost perfect rhythm.

15-B. To pinpoint your practice goals, type and proofread a copy of 15-B.

Remember to double-tab to the signature position.

If you do complete this letter in 2 minutes, what is your average speed?

15-A. Review the alphabet keys

1 ply jam keg cot big her fox sat zoo que vied know

2 many spur wove back quit hazy deft exit high jolt

15-B. Measure and improve your keyboard control

WORDS

3 Dear Dean Case: 3

                                                                     4

    I wish to express my thanks now for the   13
time you gave me on Thursday. I realize how   22
busy you are, sir; and I am grateful for the   31
quarter hour that you gave me.   37

                                                                    38

                                    Jay White   42

1 | 2 | 3 | 4 | 5 | 6 | 7 | 8 | 9

Assume the date is DECEMBER 2. You work for A. T. Lawrence, advertising manager of Kinley Electronics Company, of Vancouver. He expects you to accomplish the following tasks in about an hour. He uses P5 14 cm x 21.5 cm stationery. He prefers the full-blocked arrangement and this closing arrangement in letters:

```
Sincerely yours,

Advertising Manager
Kinley Electronics
```

Form 75
Manuscript 74
NEWS RELEASE

Paper: workbook 399
Review: pages 147, 148
Material: page 322
Arrangement: you decide
SI: 1.45—fairly difficult

Giving you the material in 209-B, page 322, Mr. Lawrence says, "Please arrange this copy as a news release. Note that it is dated December 16, not today. Send the news release—"

Form 76
Table 74
MEMO INCLUDING A DICTATED TABLE

Paper: workbook 401
Table: decide whether to
    type it separately or
    in the memorandum
SI: 1.58—difficult

"—to our Executive Vice-President, Mark B. 14
Kinley, along with this memorandum." 28

i am enclosing for your approval a copy 36
of the news release we plan to issue at 44
the december 16 r/t congress...we will 52
take immediate steps to have the release 60
processed...something that will require a 68
week or so...as soon as we have your ap- 76
proval...the campaign...as i have worked 85
it up with pratt & wilson...includes the 93
following schedule or calendar: 99
date dec 10 responsibility mr gershwin 159
advertising plates to trade magazines 170
date dec 11 responsibility miss bonner 176
bulk mailing of circulars to dealers 186
date dec 12...mr young..."what's up at 195
kinley" news teaser to the wire services 207
date dec 13...miss bonner...mailing of 217
picture mats and "hold for action" note 229
to all newspapers with TV news columns 238

date dec 15...mr young..."sneak pre- 247
view" for vancouver newspapermen 255
date dec 16...my job...the big news 264
conference at the r/t congress 278
you will be pleased to know...also... 299
that we have changed the commercial in 307
the dishwasher campaign as you suggested. 331

Form 77
TELEGRAM

Paper: workbook 403

richard k young...pratt & wilson...inc 30
...418 south dearborn street...toronto... 37
ontario...cancel script for saturday...de- 47
cember 6...new script mailed today will 55
require same personnel and sound effects. 75

Letter 109
FULL-BLOCKED LETTER

Paper: workbook 401
SI: 1.54—difficult

"Now this letter to confirm that telegram," says Mr. Lawrence. He dictates:

dear mr young...in confirmation of the 37
telegram i sent you today...a copy of 44
which is attached...i am enclosing the new 53
script for use on chqm and the net in the 61
december 6 try-out...although the possi- 70
bility of changing the script is one that 78
you had forecast...i suspect that you will 86
be relieved to know that the changes are 95
modest and the personnel the same...mark 103
kinley thought the original script was a 111
bit implausible and suggested the changes 120
...if there are any difficulties with the 129
studio...do not hesitate to phone me. 157

Manuscript 75
RADIO SCRIPT

Paper: plain, full
Caution: study directions
    very, very carefully
SI: 1.48—fairly difficult

Giving you the script shown on the next page, Mr. Lawrence says, "In addition to a file copy, we shall need a copy of this for each of the participants in

15-C. Build accuracy on double-reach words

15-C. To strengthen your accuracy, type lines 4-7 three times if you made 5 or more errors in 15-B, but twice each if you made 4 or fewer mistakes.

4 gr groan grown growl grope grape grade graze gray
5 hu hurry hurts hubby hush, hunts hulks human hull
6 rt smart heart chart start quart darts apart cart
7 my enemy hammy Sammy dummy rummy gummy tummy army

15-D. Build speed on rock-reach words

15-D. To speed up your key stroking, type lines 8-11 twice each if you made 5 or more errors in 15-B, but three times if you made 4 or fewer typing errors.

8 at plate crate orate float that flat neat pat hat
9 ly dully fully sully silly July only lily sly fly
10 ag again snags flags stage cage crag slag jag lag
11 py happy nippy wispy pylon copy pyro pyre pyx spy

15-E. Increase efficiency in using space bar

15-E. To develop sharper space-bar strokes, type lines 12-14 three times— once very slowly and then twice more, to pick up a faster and faster stroke.

12 b c d e f g h i j k l m n o p q r s t u v w x y z
13 We are to go to the shop as soon as we can do so.
14 He tried . . . tried very hard . . . but he lost.

15-F. Measure your progress

15-F. To increase and to measure your skill, type this letter twice. GOAL: A copy in 2 minutes or less, with 4 or fewer errors.

WORDS

15 Dear Vic: 2
                                                     3

    Our group will meet at a quarter to six   12
on Monday to plan the kind and size of proj-   21
ect the club will do this year. I hope that   30
you will plan to be there with us.   37
                                                     38

                        Bob Grant   42

     1 | 2 | 3 | 4 | 5 | 6 | 7 | 8 | 9

15-G. Learn to center vertically

15-G. There are 66 lines on a full sheet of paper. There are 33 lines on a half sheet.

If you have not already done so, study the section on "Vertical Spacing" on page 8.

PROBLEMS. On what line of a *full* page of paper would you begin typing to center: (*a*) 26 single-spaced lines? (*b*) 25 single-spaced lines? (*c*) 12 double-spaced lines?

On what line of a *half* page would you begin typing to center: (*d*) 21 single-spaced lines? (*e*) 18 single-spaced lines? (*f*) 12 double-spaced lines? (*g*) 8 triple-spaced lines?

PRACTICE. Center this display on a half sheet of paper. Center each line horizontally. Use double spacing.

"CENTER" CHECK: To see whether you correctly center the work vertically, fold the paper, top to bottom, and make a crease across the center. The crease should come close to the point indicated by the arrow. Does it?

16   The Next Meeting of

17   THE WOODLAWN BUSINESS CLUB

18   Will Be Held
     CENTER→

19   OCTOBER SIX :: THREE-THIRTY :: ROOM NINE

20   Members Only

LINE: 60
TAB: 5
SPACING: DOUBLE
DRILLS: THREE TIMES
GOAL: DO AN HOUR'S
  WORK IN AN HOUR!
STRESS: COMPLETELY
  MAILABLE WORK

209-A. Three copies of each paragraph, or a 1-minute writing on each and a 2-minute writing on the group.

209-A. Tune up on these review lines

1   When they send Miss Hall over with cash from the bank,   12
make very sure that they have paid what they owed our firm.   24

2   Jim acquired poor typing habits because he was so lazy   36
that he never faced up to the extra work that was required.   48

3   It's one thing to pay $10 or $28 for a jacket, but $39   60
or $47 or $56 is too much to pay for a light spring topper.   72

    1 | 2 | 3 | 4 | 5 | 6 | 7 | 8 | 9 | 10 | 11 | 12

209-B. Adjust margins to 55-space line.

Type one complete copy or take two 5-minute writings, with rests after each minute in the first writing but no rests in the second.

GOAL: 60 or more words a minute with two or fewer typing mistakes.

SI 1.44—normal

209-B. Sustain your skill on production copy

KINLEY DEVELOPS MIRROR TV   15

                                                              16
    VANCOUVER, Dec. 16—Would you like your TV screen   27
the size of a bedroom mirror? One which was only 8 cm   38
in depth? One that really IS a mirror when the TV set   49
is not turned on? One that you can hang above a piano   60
in the living room, or over a chest of drawers in your   71
bedroom, or on the wall of the family playroom or den?   82

    Well, you can have it. It is here. It is great.   93
You put it where you want it, like hanging a painting.   104

    Today the Kinley Electronics Company unveiled its   115
spectacular new TV Mirror in a news conference here in   126
Vancouver in conjunction with the opening of the Radio   137
and Television Congress, meeting at the Hotel Denkler.   148

    "It's the biggest development since the invention   159
of color television," said Paul Kinley, KEC president,   170
as he commented upon the research behind the new sets.   181

    The TV Mirror is composed of two units. One, the   192
size of a small end table, contains the basic receiver   203
of the set. It may be placed anywhere, even in a dif-   214
ferent room. It connects to the second unit, which is   225
the mirror screen, by a slim wire cable. The "screen"   236
really is a mirror. At its base is the Kinley cathode   247
tube, core of the new development. The tube is shaped   258
like a fluorescent light and is as long as the mirror.   269
It projects onto the mirror the pictures received from   280
the other unit. Speakers are mounted at both sides of   291
the mirror, which has "touch controls" along its base.   302

    Price of the Kinley TV Mirror will be competitive   313
with standard color TV sets. Sets in a broad range of   324
sizes and decor will be displayed by dealers tomorrow.   335

    1 | 2 | 3 | 4 | 5 | 6 | 7 | 8 | 9 | 10 | 11

Form 75
Manuscript 74
NEWS RELEASE
See page 323
Review: pages 147-148

147-48
News Release

UNIT 34   LESSONS 209-210

LINE: 50
TAB: CENTER
SPACING: SINGLE
GOAL: EXTEND
    CENTERING SKILL
STRESS: TOUCH
    CONTROL

16-A. Type each line twice; use very sharp strokes.

16-B. To target practice goals, type and proofread a copy on a 40-space line.

16-C-D. To reinforce skill, type lines 4-7 three times each and lines 8-11 twice each if you made 5 or more errors in 16-B; but if you made 4 or fewer errors, then type lines 4-7 twice each and lines 8-11 three times each. Eyes on copy!

16-E. To improve your touch control of the shift lock and release, type lines 12-13 three times.

16-F. To improve and to measure your skill, type two copies on a 40-space line. GOAL: A complete copy in 2 minutes (start with carriage centered) with 4 or fewer mistakes.

Remember to tab-indent to the center to position the name of the writer.

16-A. Review the alphabet keys

1   the lap vex bag ask wig car jet qua fed zoo no my

2   silk whim quiz five lock jade oxen cafe type brig

16-B. Measure and improve your keyboard control

WORDS

3   CARL VANCE   6

will explain the unique new Ozite chalk   15
process in the Board Room at three next   23
Friday. All those who wish to hear his·   31
talk are free to plan to do so.   37

TAB➤   Kane Glenn, Jr.   42

        1 | 2 | 3 | 4 | 5 | 6 | 7 | 8

16-C. Build accuracy on double-stroke words

4   sw sweep sweet sweat swear swap swat swab swim sw

5   lo loose lords longs lower loaf load lore love lo

6   de delay demon dense delve deny desk deal dent de

7   ki kinds kilts kitty kings kits kite kick kiln ki

16-D. Build speed on alternate-hand words

8   such they hand half soap held mane naps dusk amen

9   firm clan diem when pair with down roam curl girl

10   rich hang clay wish paid lake land fork fuel make

11   duty coal clam disk fish cork dock flap duel cozy

16-E. Increase efficiency in using the shift lock

12   The TWO men from HILL—AGE want two MORE meetings.

13   Get ANOTHER jar of HI—SPEED, the SHINE—UP powder.

16-F. Measure your progress

WORDS

14   WE REGRET   6

to tell you that Carl Vance was injured   15
quite badly when a box of Ozite blew up   23
in his car en route to see us. We will   31
not plan a new meeting date.   37

TAB➤   Kane Glenn, Jr.   42

        1 | 2 | 3 | 4 | 5 | 6 | 7 | 8

Table 73
REVISED RULED TABLE
See page 320

William Blake & Sons Company

O V E R D U E   A C C O U N T S

~~October 31, 19—~~ November 30, 19—

Account	30 Days Overdue	60 Days Overdue	Total Overdue
Mr. Harry Pepper, Treasurer Consumers' Cooperative Assn. 312 Monroe Avenue South Saskatoon, Saskatchewan S7N 1J9	$1210.45 ~1210.45~		$1210.45
~Mr. R.N. Maxwell, Manager Marine Association of Canada 322 Arcade Building Pine Falls, New Brunswick E2Z 3X6~		~$ 68.75~	~68.75~
Mrs. Mark E. Smythe, Manager The Farmers League of Women 616 Great Northern Street Sault Ste. Marie, Ontario P6B 4Z9	294.75	~1130.60~ 294.75	~1425.35~ 294.75
~Mr. M.M. Zimmerman, Manager Consumers' Exchange, Inc. 217 United Farmers Building Winnipeg, Manitoba R7B 1S7~	~1704.90~		~1704.90~
~Miss Evangeline C. Springer Manager, Elkhart Association 3197 Portage Avenue, Bathurst, New Brunswick E8V 4S3~	~811.38~	~438.44~	~1249.82~
Miss Ella Q. Wilcox, Manager National Cooperative Assn. 314 Patterson Avenue Kelowna, British Columbia V1Y 5C4	162.75 ~149.68~		162.75 ~149.68~
TOTALS	~$4171.16~ 1388.48 ?	~$1637.79~ 1505.20 ?	~$5808.95~ 2793.68 ?
Mr. James T. Beckman, Mgr. Dartmouth Citizens' League 6 Woodland Avenue Dartmouth, Nova Scotia B3A 3J5	$ 1125.73		1125.73

16-G. Learn to center paragraph copy

Announcements to be circulated among a staff or posted on a bulletin board are usually centered both vertically *and* horizontally.

1. Vertical centering is by steps you know: (*a*) Count the lines the display will fill, (*b*) subtract them from the lines available on the paper, and (*c*) split the difference. To center the single-spaced display in 16-F on a half sheet, for example: $33-8=25$; and $25 \div 2 = 12\frac{1}{2}$, or 13, the line where typing begins.

2. Horizontal centering: To determine where to set the left margin stop, select an average-length line and backspace from the middle of the paper enough to center that line.

PRACTICE 1. Center on a P5 sheet the announcement in 16-B. Use *single* spacing. Leave 1 blank line before and after the body of the display.

PRACTICE 2. Center on a P4 sheet the announcement in 16-F. Use *double* spacing. Leave 2 blank lines before and after the body of the display.

Skill Drive

LINE: 50
TAB: CENTER
SPACING: SINGLE
GOAL: EXTEND SKILL
STRESS: ARM CONTROL

17-A. Type lines 1 and 2 twice, with smooth-as-music rhythm each time.

17-A. Review the alphabet keys

1 joy irk quo ham bed lag fox zip vow bat act no so

2 zone vary jobs help quit digs crew milk lone flax

17-B. To increase skill and to target your practice goals, type and proofread a copy of this letter. Try to finish it in 2 minutes.

17-B. Measure and improve your keyboard control

WORDS

3 Dear Mr. Vance: 3

4

We are glad to learn that you have recovered   13
from the explosion and will be in to see us.   22
However, our interest in Ozite cannot be re-   31
vived by all the eloquence in the world.   39

40

TAB ➤   Kane Glenn, Jr.   44

   1 | 2 | 3 | 4 | 5 | 6 | 7 | 8 | 9

17-C. Boost your accuracy by typing lines 4-7 three times each if you made 5 or more errors in 17-B or twice each if you made only 4 or fewer errors.

17-C. Build accuracy on outside reaches

4 az blaze amaze craze fazed lazy daze gaze haze az

5 l; nail; bail; fail; mail; ail; oil; ill; all; l;

6 qa quart quack quail quake quay quad aqua Iraq qa

7 op opera opens chops slope hope mope stop shop op

17-D. Increase speed by typing lines 8-11 three times each if you made 4 or fewer errors in 17-B or twice each if you made 5 or more typing errors.

17-D. Build speed on different phrase rhythms

8 he did| he and| he put| he may| he saw| he got| he told

9 can he| may he| and he| for he| did he| say he| for him

10 he will| he says| he gave| he said| he took| he is the

11 when he| that he| wish he| sure he| then he| for he is

Assume the date is DECEMBER 1. You work for Layne I. Collyer, assistant manager of the Credit Department of William Blake & Sons Company. Before beginning any of the work in this one-hour project, review all of it so you may determine how many carbons to make of each task. Looking in the files, you see that Mr. Collyer prefers blocked letter style and this closing arrangement:

Yours sincerely,

center WILLIAM BLAKE & SONS COMPANY

should be underscored
Assistant Manager
Credit Department

Layne I. Collyer/urs

Table 72
REVISED RULED TABLE

Giving you the revised table on the next page, Mr. Collyer says, "I have brought up to date our list of overdue accounts. Please type the list with a file copy and a working copy for next month's report."

You notice that he did not compute the new totals figures. You will do this.

Form 74
INTEROFFICE MEMO

Paper: workbook 389
SI: 1.51—fairly difficult

"Send the original of the table to Mr. Busk—that is William P. Busk, the credit manager—on the eighth floor," says Mr. Collyer, "with this memorandum."

i have attached the december 1 listing 38
of overdue accounts...you will be pleased 47
to note that the number is down to four 55
...the lowest we have had for some time... 63

you will be interested to note...also 71
...that consumers' exchange has finally 79
squared away its account...a letter from 87
the firm explained that the recent election of 96
new officers led to litigation in which the 105
exchange's treasury was tied up for three 113
months...now that that matter is cleared 122
...the exchange has moved swiftly to meet 130
its obligations... 133

there is only one new account on the 142
overdue list...it is that of the dartmouth 150

citizens' league...i was surprised to see 159
this...for they have always paid their 166
bills promptly in the past... 172

we shall dispatch the usual notices to 181
all the current overdue accounts. 196

Letters 105-108
BLOCKED FORM LETTERS

Paper: workbook 391 ff.
Enclosure: Manus. 73
SI: 1.57—difficult

"Next," says Mr. Collyer, "as soon as that memo is on its way to Mr. Busk, please send a copy of the credit-policy statement [Manuscript 73, page 319] and this letter to each of the overdue accounts."

your account shows a balance of (*insert* 41
the correct amount)...which is now (*insert* 46
the correct number days, written in figures) 47
days overdue... 50

you are undoubtedly aware that...with 58
the exception of such organizations as the 67
one you represent...our terms are cash 74
only...our splendid service and low prices 83
are based on our ability to dispense with 91
an expensive credit and accounting organi- 100
zation... 101

we appreciate that many associations 110
like yours find they must extend credit 118
to their members...since our position and 126
policies are so well known...however... 134
we feel that you should have made some 142
arrangement to liquidate this account 149
within the usual 30-day period... 156

(*Insert this next paragraph only in the* ··
"*60 days overdue*" *letters.*) since your ac- 159
count is now more than 60 days overdue 167
...we are compelled to call your attention 175
to our policy of shipping c.o.d. any goods 184
you may order in the future until you remit 193
the (*insert the balance due*) that is now so 199
long overdue... 202

we hope that you will find some way to 210
clear up this matter shortly...in the mean- 219
time...we shall continue to serve you both 227
promptly and well. 287

17-E. To increase your concentration power: Omitting the word "no" wherever it occurs, type each line twice. All lines should end up at exactly the same point.

12 is if it in no at ax as am ah aw ad no by my me no
13 pa ma ha no ok oh or ow ox of on no el em et en no
14 be me he we re no us up pi no do so lo ho go to no

17-F. Measure your progress

17-F. To encourage and to measure your skill, type this letter twice. GOAL: A complete copy in 2 minutes or less, with 4 or fewer typing errors in your copy.

		WORDS
15	Dear Mr. Vance:	3
		4
	I admit that I am quite impressed by the way	13
	you refuse to give up on Ozite. You are one	22
	exceptional salesman. How would you like to	31
	join OUR staff and sell OUR products?	39
		40
	Kane Glenn, Jr.	44

    1 | 2 | 3 | 4 | 5 | 6 | 7 | 8 | 9

17-G. Learn to block-center a group of lines

Centering a block of lines is much like centering a paragraph. The difference:

To center a block, you center the longest line in the block; but to center a paragraph, you center the average full line instead of the longest line. The difference may matter.

Could each line in a list be centered individually? Yes, but doing so takes about three times as long as it does to block-center the same group of lines.

When several lines or words are to be listed, center them as a block: NOTE: Centre a title first. Then block-center as follows: (a) Pick the longest item; (b) backspace to center that item and set the margin stop at the point to which you backspace; and (c) type the list, with each word beginning at the margin stop.

PRACTICE 1. Block-center the adjacent display on a half sheet of paper. Use single spacing. Leave 2 blank lines below the title.

PRACTICE 2. Block-center the adjacent display on a full sheet of paper. Use double spacing. Leave 2 blank lines below the title.

```
METHODS OF DISPLAY TYPING

   Aligning
   Block Centering
   Blocking
   Capitalizing
   Extra Spacing
   Horizontal Centering
   Indenting
   Pivoting
   Spread Centering
   Typing All Capitals
   Underscoring
```

LINE: 50
TAB: 5 AND CENTER
SPACING: SINGLE
GOAL: INCREASE SKILL
STRESS: TOUCH
   CONTROL

18-A. Review the alphabet keys

18-A. Type lines 1-3 two times, as smoothly as you can each time. Set a good pace on easy line 1; then try to sustain it on the harder lines that follow.

1 pox him beg jot zip via sin ask fed cry qua lo we
2 part view frog next dime just quit cabs yolk haze
3 Quickly pick up the box with five dozen gum jars.

    1 | 2 | 3 | 4 | 5 | 6 | 7 | 8 | 9 | 10

LINE: 60
TAB: 5
SPACING: DOUBLE
DRILLS: THREE OR MORE
GOAL: DO AN HOUR'S
WORK IN AN HOUR!
STRESS: MAILABLE,
COMPLETE WORK

207-A. Three copies of each paragraph, or a 1-minute writing on each and a 2-minute writing on the group.

207-A. Tune up on these review lines

1   They said that they will have paid what they owed when   12
they send over Miss Hall with some more cash from the bank.   24

2   I know that Mr. Bank became a florist, specializing in   36
violets and jonquils; he moves about sixty dozen every day.   48

3   The firm used to be at 25 Jackson Street; but now it's   60
moved to 394 Westgate Street, which is near Bayview Avenue.   72

1 | 2 | 3 | 4 | 5 | 6 | 7 | 8 | 9 | 10 | 11 | 12

207-B. Confirm margins for 60-space line (the lines will align).

Type one complete copy with all corrections made; save your paper for reference use when you type Manuscript 73.

Or, take two 5-minute writings, with rests after each minute in the first writing but with no rests in the second. GOAL: 60 or more words a minute with two or fewer typing mistakes.

SI 1.51—fairly difficult

207-B. Sustain your skill on production copy

4 <u>Credit Policy</u>   8

    The firm of (Wm.) Blake & Sons was founded ~~about~~ *MORE THAN* a quar-   22
ter century ago on the worthy principal of giving ~~our cus-~~   32
~~tomers~~ the maximum quality and service with *THE* minimum cost.   43
Through the years, this principle has brought growth and   55
success to the ~~company~~ *FIRM* and satisfaction to its ~~whole~~ great   65
family of customers.   69

    Basic to the factor of minimum cost, of course, is the need   82
for keeping down the ~~collection costs for~~ *(COST OF COLLECTING)* the moneys due   93
the firm for its goods and service. William Blake & sons,   105
therefore, has always held to a policy of cash dealing with   117
~~with~~ all its customers. Some 80 per cent of these *CUSTOMERS* send   129
payment with their orders; Most of the remaining 20 per   140
cent remit within seven days after receiving delivery.   152

no ¶ It is an uncommon thing for William Blake & Sons to   162
request payment.   167

    An exception to the *CREDIT* policy has been made in the case of   179
co-operative organizations because the officers of these   191
groups may have to hold payment until the expenditure is   202
approved at a group meeting, ~~and so~~ a period of 30 days   212
CREDIT ~~grace~~ has been and is allowed such accounts. New orders   224
received from them when they are in arrears, however, may be   236
shipped only C.O.D. or on receipt of cash with ~~the new~~   245
order. (It's) unjust to our great family of *CASH* customers   257
to raise the prices ~~to them~~ and thus to require them, ~~in~~   267
~~effect~~ to subsidize the ~~extension of~~ credit to others.   274

    James Blake, president   289

TODAY'S DATE   *on same line*   293

1 | 2 | 3 | 4 | 5 | 6 | 7 | 8 | 9 | 10 | 11 | 12

Manuscript 73
CENTERED DISPLAY
Paper: plain, full
Carbons: Enclosures,
  Letters 107-110
Line: 60
Spacing: double
SI: 1.51—fairly difficult

18-B. To define practice goals, type and proofread a copy. Remember to tab once for the paragraph indentation and twice for the writer's signature.

18-B. Measure and improve your keyboard control

4 Dear Miss Queen: 3

     It was kind of you to correct the index   13
to our club handbook for us. The job needed   22
to be done. All the men realize what a fine   31
task you did and are very grateful.   38
                                                                    39
                  Paul J. West   44

`1 | 2 | 3 | 4 | 5 | 6 | 7 | 8 | 9`

18-C. To boost accuracy, type lines 5-8 three times each if you made 5 or more errors in 18-B, but only twice each if you made 4 or fewer errors in 18-B.

18-C. Build accuracy on alphabetic word lines

5 five high worm quid back lazy boys axle join port
6 mink dove taxi jump bowl size figs hour quit clay
7 silk daze hymn upon text rave flag wick aqua jobs
8 band gave rest quip lazy joke from axis what race

18-D. To boost your speed, type lines 9-12 three times each if you made 4 or less errors in 18-B, but twice each if you made 5 or more typing errors in 18-B.

18-D. Build speed on alternate-hand words

9   work such them city dial hand pans maid held pays
10 both than make with keys duel soap form half dusk
11 when mane town maps form lake roam dorm lamb then
12 down firm turn duty auto wish goal paid half rush

18-E. To improve your control of the hyphen, type lines 13 and 14 two times each—by touch!

18-E. Increase efficiency in the hyphen reach

13 The blue-green mat is the most up-to-date design.
14 The shadow--that of a man, I believe--faded away.

18-F. To increase and to measure your skill, type this note twice. GOAL: A complete copy, with 4 or fewer errors, in 2 minutes or less. How many times will you use the tab?

18-F. Measure your progress

15 Dear Miss Queen: 3
                                                                    4
     The men in the club believe they should   13
extend more than just thanks to you for fix-   22
ing the index for us. So, by way of a bonus   31
prize, a little gift is on its way.   38
                                                                    39
                  Paul J. West   44

`1 | 2 | 3 | 4 | 5 | 6 | 7 | 8 | 9`

The shortcut method of centering works because it is really the same as the regular method—except for saying "space" after each letter (or space between the words) to make a pair of strokes for which you then backspace one time. If you do the practice exercises correctly, the letter E aligns vertically.

18-G. Learn to center spread-out words

To spread words for extra display impact, leave 1 space between letters and 3 spaces between words. To center a spread line, use the standard backspace-centering method (13-G) *or use this shortcut:* From the center, backspace once for each space *except the last* that the line would occupy if it were *not* spread out.

PRACTICE 1. Using the standard method, spread-center these lines.
PRACTICE 2. Using the shortcut method, spread-center these lines.

A T T E N T I O N
S P E C I A L
S U P P E R   M E N U
T H E   E N D

206-A. Repeat 205-A for a quick tuneup

206-B. Measure your skill on weighted technical copy

206-B. Steps to follow:

STEP 1. Make one copy of paragraph 13 without pausing or looking up.

STEP 2. Proofread very carefully. If you erred on a $, ", or ', place a check mark beside the appropriate paragraph following (14, 15, 16).

STEP 3. Type paragraphs 14, 15, and 16 twice each plus once more if you checkmarked it.

STEP 4. Finally, repeat paragraph 13 until you have an errorless copy.

13   "Okay," says Sergeant; "whose money is this?" He   11
counts it out, "$10, $28, $39, $47, $56. Wow!" Bob's   22
face "reds up" a bit, but we're "mum." Sergeant says,   33
"Well, if it ain't nobody's, it's mine!" That's that.   44

   1 | 2 | 3 | 4 | 5 | 6 | 7 | 8 | 9 | 10 | 11

14   Joe cleared $10 on Monday, $28 on Tuesday, $39 on   11   55
Wednesday, $47 on Thursday, and $56 on Friday morning.   22   66

15   How do you "start" a "timed writing"? Some call,   11   77
"Three, two, one, type"; others call, "Ready? Begin."   22   88

16   It's Joe's dog we see, blinkin' at us and yawnin'   11   99
in the sun. Joe's dog! That means Joe's around, too!   22   110

   1 | 2 | 3 | 4 | 5 | 6 | 7 | 8 | 9 | 10 | 11

206-C. Measure your skill on more weighted technical copy

17   When I checked Invoice #3829 from Dubbs & Miller,   11   121
I saw it was discounted 28% only for the first 10# and   22   132
then 39% for the rest. Invoice #3928 from Coe & Clark   33   143
was right: 28%, the first 100#; and 39% for the rest.   44   154

   1 | 2 | 3 | 4 | 5 | 6 | 7 | 8 | 9 | 10 | 11

206-C. As in 206-B.

18   We find 10% discounts common, but those of 28% or   11   165
39% are just as irregular as discounts of 47% and 56%.   22   176

19   You sent them 10# of #10, 28# of #28, 39# of #39,   11   187
47# of #47, and 56# of #56, to total at 180# of candy.   22   198

20   I did business with Hall & Hill until Hall & Hill   11   209
were merged with Karen & Kole, or was it Kole & Karen?   22   220

   1 | 2 | 3 | 4 | 5 | 6 | 7 | 8 | 9 | 10 | 11

206-D. Measure your skill on more weighted technical copy

21   In summary, <u>our</u> analysis of the 30 vacancies gave   12   232
(1) 10 stenographers, 20 typists; (2) 10 women, 8 men,   23   243
12 either men or women; and (3) 10 with <u>no</u> experience,   35   255
9 <u>with</u> experience, plus 11 <u>with or without</u> experience.   54   274

   1 | 2 | 3 | 4 | 5 | 6 | 7 | 8 | 9 | 10 | 11

206-D. As in 206-B.

22   We need someone who can (a) sell at the counters,   11   285
(b) arrange window displays, and (c) keep sales books.   22   296

23   <u>First</u>, take the crate apart; <u>second</u>, remove scale   15   311
from wrappings; and <u>last</u>, mount the legs on the scale.   28   324

   1 | 2 | 3 | 4 | 5 | 6 | 7 | 8 | 9 | 10 | 11

206-E. Make a complete copy of the typewriting on this page or take a 5-minute writing on it.

206-E. Measure your sustained skill on technical copy

LINE: 50
SPACING: SINGLE
GOAL: CONTROL 1, 2, 3, AND 4
STRESS: ANCHOR KEYS

Unit 4. The Number Keys

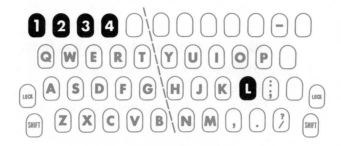

Some machines have a "1" key on the top row, which is controlled by A-finger.

On other typewriters, the small letter L is used as the "1" and is controlled by L-finger, of course.

19-A. Type each line twice. Set a fast pace on line 1; hold the pace on line 2.

19-A. Review the alphabet keys

1 Few men can say the lazy boy can run his car far.

2 John will keep the six dogs very quiet this week.

19-B. If you have a 1 key on your machine, control it with A-finger (keep F-finger anchored). If not, use the small letter L as the 1. Type lines 3-5 three or more times each.

19-B. Practice the **1** key

3 aqla aqla alla alla alal alal all 111 and 111,111

4 11 arts 11 axes 11 aims 11 alms 11 aces 1.11 1:11

5 We need 11 pairs of size 11 shoes for the 11 men.

19-C. Use S-finger. Try the sw2s reach (keep your F-finger at home). Type lines 6-8 three times.

19-C. Practice the **2** key

6 sw2s sw2s s22s s22s s2s2 s2s2 all 222 and 112,122

7 22 sons 22 sums 22 seas 22 sips 22 suns 2.22 2:22

8 The 12 men and the 22 boys played 122 full games.

19-D. Type lines 9-10 two times. GOAL: A complete copy of both lines in 1 minute, with eyes kept on copy and with no errors.

19-D. Measure your progress

9 Of the 122 who paid, only 11 or 12 were children.

10 About 112 caught the 12:12 train on Track No. 21.

    1 | 2 | 3 | 4 | 5 | 6 | 7 | 8 | 9 | 10

19-E. Use D-finger. Try the de3d reach (keep your A- or F-finger at home—which is easier?). Type lines 11-13 three times.

19-E. Practice the **3** key

11 de3d de3d d33d d33d d3d3 d3d3 all 333 and 123,123

12 33 dads 33 dips 33 dues 33 dots 33 dogs 3.13 3:13

13 Did the 3 men catch 31 or 33 fish in the 13 days?

19-F. Use F-finger. Try the fr4f reach (keep your A-finger at home). Type lines 14-16 three times.

19-F. Practice the **4** key

14 fr4f fr4f f44f f44f f4f4 f4f4 all 444 and 123,441

15 44 furs 44 fins 44 fish 44 fell 44 flew 4.14 4:14

16 The 44 boys lost only 14 of their 144 golf games.

LINE: 60
TAB: 5
SPACING: DRILLS SINGLE,
 PARAGRAPHS DOUBLE
DRILLS: THREE OR MORE
GOAL: STRENGTHEN
 NUMBER CONTROLS
STRESS: TYPE BY TOUCH!

205-A. Race through the three drills three times without pausing, without looking up even once. Repeat in Lesson 206.

205-B. Type four copies, being sure that at least one is error free. GOAL: A copy per minute.

SI 1.29—fairly easy IF you know your numbers

205-C. Three times each. Type slowly on the first copy and seek to speed up on every repetition. Do not type the underscores.

205-D. Type another copy of 205-B and then three copies of paragraph 8; be sure at least one copy is completely error free.

SI 1.30—fairly easy IF you know your numbers

205-E. Three times each. Speed up on repetitions.

205-F. Type one copy of 205-B and of 205-D and then two copies of this. Be sure one copy of this is error free. Remember: Keep eyes on the copy!

SI 1.30—fairly easy IF you know your numbers

205-A. Tune up on these review lines

1 Both of the men paid us for the visit to the island chapel.
2 Roxanne won eight major prizes equal to your seven cheques.
3 If it isn't on pages 10, 28, or 39, look on pages 47 or 56.

205-B. Measure your skill on technical material

4 At the start of the 1900's, gliding had become quite a hobby. Orville and Wilbur Wright built and flew gliders in 1900, 1901, and 1902; their biplane glider set all kinds of records in 1902. In 1903, they built a motor and propellor for their glider and, on December 17 of that year, flew it.

205-C. Increase number fluency via "we 23" drills

5 we 23 24 25 you 697 698 699 tow 592 593 594 rut 475 476 477
6 or 94 95 96 wit 285 286 287 wry 246 247 248 tri 548 549 550
7 to 59 60 61 rye 463 464 465 wet 235 236 237 pry 046 047 048

205-D. Measure your skill again on technical material

8 Orville made the first of four successful flights that day; it was for 36 m and lasted 12 s. Wilbur was the pilot on the last and longest flight; it lasted 59 s, and he flew 255 m from the upskid to the downskid marks. Thus, December 17, 1903, is the birthdate of all airplanes.

205-E. Increase number fluency on number-sequence sentences

9 They have their main offices on 17th, 18th, or 19th Street.
10 Lt. Coe was at sea during 1941, 1942, 1943, 1944, and 1945.
11 The firm did well in 1955 and 1956 but not in 1957 or 1958.

205-F. Measure your skill again on technical material

12 During 1904 and 1905, the Wrights constructed many new planes; and they flew a craft for 38 minutes in 1905. They were then awarded patents, in 1906, and won the interest of the War Department, which requested bids in 1907, looked at models in 1908, and gave them their first contract in 1909.

19-G. Measure your progress

17 1. Of the 43 persons attending, 34 placed orders.

18 2. The orders of the 34 came to about 112 pounds.

19 3. Of the 34 persons, 12 ordered 2 or more boxes.

20 4. About 12 of the 34 asked us to ship the candy.

  1 | 2 | 3 | 4 | 5 | 6 | 7 | 8 | 9 | 10

LESSON

20

Number Review

LINE: 50
TAB: 5 AND CENTER
SPACING: SINGLE
GOAL: INCREASE
    CONTROL OF 1, 2,
    3, AND 4
STRESS: TOUCH
    CONTROL

20-A. Review the keys you know

20-A. Type lines 1-3 two times; then repeat line 3 until you can type it without pausing once.

1 Joe and the six new men may now quit for the day.

2 Eve will come back when they play that maze game.

3 To get 111, add up 1 and 11 and 22 and 33 and 44.

20-B. Measure and improve your keyboard control   WORDS

20-B. To improve and test your control of numbers you now know, type a copy, line for line and double spaced, and proofread it.

Use the tab for indenting and positioning the name of the writer. Remember: each use of the tabulator is counted as 1 word.

4 Dear Mr. Quigley: 4

     If we could get the six crews in train-   13

ing by May 3 or 4 instead of June 1 or 2, we   22

might have a chance to take first prize this   31

year. Does May 3 or 4 seem to be too early?   40

                         Ed Steele   44

  1 | 2 | 3 | 4 | 5 | 6 | 7 | 8 | 9

20-C. Build accuracy on the number keys

20-C-D-E. To improve skill, type lines 5-13 (continuing on page 38) twice each.

Then repeat twice more each one of the following:

(a) Lines 5-7 if you made any number error in 20-B.

(b) Lines 8-10 if you made more than 4 errors in 20-B.

(c) Lines 11-13 if you made no figure errors and had 4 or fewer errors in 20-B.

5 May 11 and 12, May 12 and 13, then May 13 and 14.

6 May 21 and 22, May 22 and 23, then May 23 and 24.

7 May 11 and 22, May 12 and 23, then May 13 and 24.

20-D. Build accuracy on the alphabet keys

8 prize might quite jury deft loan back fix saw eve

9 exact dozen quart evil upon whom jack say beg fun

10 every seize equip echo bang next walk job mud for

204-A. Repeat 203-A for a quick tuneup

204-B. Inventory your present skill on difficult copy

204-B. Type the last three paragraphs, page 315; or take a 5-minute writing on them. GOAL: 50 or more wam with 2 or fewer mistakes. If you make more than two errors, your goal is ACCURACY; if you make fewer, then your goal should be SPEED.

204-C. Improve stroking on 3-letter word endings

25 ING speaking thinking getting sending meeting typing having
26 AGE mortgage coverage package postage average garage damage
27 ITY priority activity quality ability charity rarity parity

28 UAL punctual habitual gradual unusual factual actual annual
29 EST interest greatest highest largest nearest finest nicest
30 IFY identify simplify clarify specify qualify modify notify

204-C-D. Type to goal determined in 204-B.

ACCURACY: Type each three-line group, as a paragraph, three times.

SPEED: Type each line three consecutive times.

31 BLE probable portable visible capable taxable enable double
32 IAL material official initial special cordial burial social
33 FUL faithful grateful tactful fearful careful sinful useful
    1 | 2 | 3 | 4 | 5 | 6 | 7 | 8 | 9 | 10 | 11 | 12

204-D. Improve stroking on 4-letter word endings

34 TENT penitents competent impotent penitent existent content
35 ABLE honorable insurable payables portable syllable capable
36 IBLE invisible inedibles credible sensible possible visible

37 TION education objection deletion fraction relation section
38 TION exemption rejection question position notation mention
39 TION condition dictation creation ambition adoption station

40 MENT apartment implement pavement basement tenement torment
41 MENT deferment equipment judgment shipment document element
42 MENT allotment sentiment argument sediment bailment ailment

43 TIAL essential impartial initials partials official initial
44 TIVE defective executive relative positive elective festive
45 TURE departure miniature immature puncture fracture fixture
    1 | 2 | 3 | 4 | 5 | 6 | 7 | 8 | 9 | 10 | 11 | 12

204-E. Regain stride on very easy sentences

204-E. Take a series of 1-minute writings to regain peak fluency.

ACCURACY: Use the three-line groups as a solid paragraph.

SPEED: Take each timing on a separate line.

SI 1.00—very easy

46 It is a shame that you did not buy some of the stock today.
47 The form they sent you is a good one and will help our job.
48 They both think the man should spend more time at his work.
    1 | 2 | 3 | 4 | 5 | 6 | 7 | 8 | 9 | 10 | 11 | 12
49 The time from six to nine is the right one for such a plan.
50 We do not wish to have as much stock as you ask us to take.
51 Both of them paid more than they should have for a new car.

204-F. Repeat 204-B to measure your progress

20-E. Build speed on alternate-hand words

20-E. Note directions on page 37. Try to hold your typing at a steady pace, though words get longer.

11 it for map fuel they pane wish forms panel chapel
12 of aid but also body form hand spend works visual
13 by men she paid vial then odor visit handy usurps

20-F. Measure your progress

WORDS

20-F. To bolster and to measure your typing skill (on numbers particularly), type the letter twice, line for line and double spaced. GOAL: A complete copy in 2 minutes or less, with 4 or fewer errors.

14 Dear Ed: 2

     I think that May 3 or 4 is a bit early,   11
but perhaps the six crews could begin indoor   20
work then and strike the water about May 21,   29
22, or 23. The prize idea sounds very good.   38

             J. Fred Quigley   43

LINE: 50
TAB: 5 AND CENTER
SPACING: SINGLE
GOAL: CONTROL 7,
8, 9, AND 0
STRESS: TOUCH
CONTROL

21-A. Review the keys you know

21-A. Type lines twice; speed up on second copy.

1 Zoe can pay you the new tax but may ask for help.
2 Only four boys got done when Joel gave that quiz.
3 To get 123, add up 1 and 44 and 23 and 34 and 21.

21-B. Practice the 7 key

21-B. Use J-finger. Try the ju7j reach (L-Sem-fingers anchored); type lines 4-6 three times. Note use of / in making a fraction (in line 5).

4 ju7j ju7j j77j j77j j7j7 j7j7 you 777 for 123,477
5 77 jugs 77 jars 77 jigs 77 jets 77 jogs 7/17 7:17
6 On June 7, the 7 men left Camp 7 on the 7:17 bus.

21-C. Practice the 8 key

21-C. Use K-finger. Try the ki8k reach (with Sem-finger anchored); type lines 7-9 three times. Note no space after the period between small-letter initials (in line 9).

7 ki8k ki8k k88k k88k k8k8 k8k8 irk 888 for 123,478
8 88 kits 88 keys 88 kids 88 inks 88 inns 8/18 8:18
9 Train No. 188 departs at 11:18 a.m. or 12:18 p.m.

21-D. Measure your progress

21-D. Type each line twice. GOAL: A complete copy of both lines in 1 minute or less, without looking up.

10 Of the 178 who paid, only 37 or 38 were children.
11 About 187 caught the 12:47 train on Track No. 18.

1 | 2 | 3 | 4 | 5 | 6 | 7 | 8 | 9 | 10

LINE: 70
SPACING: DOUBLE
TAB: 5
SI: 1.57—difficult

The paper used for paper currency is just about the most precise 14
product of the whole paper industry. You can hardly believe what the 28
Treasury Department requires. The paper has to be so very tough that 42
it's next to impossible to tear it, it has to weigh a certain amount, it must 58
be only the right size, and its quality must be so definitely superior that 73
it cannot possibly be duplicated. That's asking a lot! 84

In Canada, one outstanding paper company has held the contract 98
for manufacturing this special paper for nearly a century. The other 112
firms try to compete for the current order, but the standards for the 126
paper are so high that other manufacturers cannot meet them. You can 140
get some insight into the manufacturing problem when you realize that 154
this paper has to be able to withstand 4000 foldings and unfoldings. 168
Even so, a new one-dollar bill is expected to last only about a year; the 183
monthly wear-out rate in Canada today is 175 million dollars. 196

Currency paper is produced in sheets rather than in rolls. Each 210
sheet permits the printing of 32 bills. Once approved, the paper for 224
a new shipment is escorted to Ottawa, where it is guarded no less 238
carefully before the printing operation than after it. Even the mill that 253
produces the special paper is under surveillance 24 hours a day. 266

1 | 2 | 3 | 4 | 5 | 6 | 7 | 8 | 9 | 10 | 11 | 12 | 13 | 14

LINE: 70
SPACING: DOUBLE
TAB: 5
SI: 1.64—very difficult

Only the finest materials go into the making of currency papers. 14 280
The percentage of rag content is extraordinarily high, and the fibers 28 294
used are not from old, discarded, junk-style rags but are exclusively 42 308
new cotton and linen cuttings from cloth mills and tailor industries. 56 322
Among the fibers are unique red and blue ones that are characteristic 70 336
of American currency; these, by law, cannot be used in any other paper. 84 350

The actual production process is quite interesting, based mostly on 99 365
the original Chinese formula for paper making, although cotton and 112 378
linen have replaced the silk the Chinese used. The secret formula of the 127 393
Chinese was guarded closely for centuries and did not arrive here until 141 407
1690. The ancient manufacturers would recognize the steps that the 155 421
paper undergoes, but they would be amazed at the huge boilers and 168 434
giant mixing vats and tremendous drying cylinders we are using today. 182 448

The newest money in circulation in the U.S.A. is the new Federal 196 462
Reserve series, which augments the Silver Certificate series that has 210 476
been in dominance since 1943. Behind the new issuance lies the great 224 490
demand for more currency for everyday use by the swelling population, 238 504
on the one hand, in the face of diminishing silver stocks and growing 252 518
prices for it, on the other hand. The bullion released by the recent 266 532
Federal Reserve series will thus be available for new silver coinage. 280 546

1 | 2 | 3 | 4 | 5 | 6 | 7 | 8 | 9 | 10 | 11 | 12 | 13 | 14

21-E. Use L-finger. Try the lo9l reach (keep the J-finger anchored). Type lines 12-14 three times. In line 13, note use of / in making a fraction.

21-E. Practice the 9 key

12 lo9l lo9l 1991 1991 1919 1919 all 999 for 234,789
13 99 lots 99 lids 99 laws 99 logs 99 less 9/19 9:19
14 In 1919, there were 199 men in each of 19 lodges.

21-F. Use Sem-finger. Try the ;p0; reach (J-finger anchored). Type lines 15-17 three times each. In line 17, note spacing between capital letters.

21-F. Practice the 0 key

15 ;p0; ;p0; ;00; ;00; ;0;0 ;0;0 dip 000 for 347,890
16 10 pegs 10 pins 10 play 10 paid 10 push 1/10 1:10
17 Meet them at 10:00 A. M. or 1:00 P. M. for lunch.

21-G. To increase and to measure your skill (on the numbers particularly), type the letter twice, line for line and double spaced. GOAL: A complete copy in 2 minutes or less, with 4 or fewer errors.

21-G. Measure your progress

WORDS

18 Dear Mr. Quigley: 4

        I have arranged for the six crews to do   13
indoor drills from May 4 until May 17 or 18,   22
with May 19 or 20 for hitting the lake; they   31
will be ready for the prize meet on July 23.   40

                        Ed Steele   44

    1 | 2 | 3 | 4 | 5 | 6 | 7 | 8 | 9

21-H. This assignment is optional but worth doing, for it reviews four things that are required in the test on pages 44 and 45:

(1) Spread centering.
(2) Horizontal centering.
(3) Vertical centering.
(4) Block centering (if you are wise and do not center names individually).

Center this announcement on a half sheet of paper; use single spacing. Leave 2 blank lines under the all-capitals title.

21-H. Optional review of centering

19   A N N O U N C E M E N T

The Annual Banquet of The Business Club
will be held on December 10 at 19:00 in
the Silver Room of the Queens Hotel.

Tickets are four dollars each and may be
CENTER→obtained from these committee members:

                John King, Chairman
                  Maxwell Gilbert
                Holly Anne Parker

Reservations should be made on or before
November 24. Members are urged to make
their reservations as early as possible.

LINE: 60
TAB: 5
SPACING: DRILLS, SIN-
GLE; PARAGRAPHS,
DOUBLE
DRILLS: THREE TIMES
GOAL: BOOST SKILL
STRESS: STEADY PACE

203-A. Type each line in
"pyramid" style, like:
Their
Their firm
Their firm is

203-B. Type the first
three paragraphs, page
315, or take a 5-minute
timed writing on them.

GOAL: 50 words a
minute, 0-1-2 errors.

If you make more than
two errors, your goal
in Lesson 203 must be
for accuracy; fewer,
the goal is speed.

203-C-D-E. Type to the
goal found in 203-B.

ACCURACY: Each three-
line group three times
as though a paragraph.

SPEED: Each line three
consecutive times.

SUGGESTION: These
drills will be easy if
you type very smoothly.
Do not press for speed;
let the repetitions and
downhill momentum bring
a speed upsurge to you.

203-A. Tune up on these review lines

Their firm is paid to visit the towns for the eighth audit.
Five extra—bright boys could work now to pass a major quiz.
We looked at Models 2810, 2839, 2847, and 2856 at the shop.
1 | 2 | 3 | 4 | 5 | 6 | 7 | 8 | 9 | 10 | 11 | 12

203-B. Inventory your present skill

203-C. Improve stroking on 2-letter word beginnings

RE request regards receipt record really rebate refer react
AL almonds already altered alloys almost always allow album
DE deposit details depends demand decide deduct delay defer

EX expense explain express excess expect except extra exact
UN unusual untried unknown unpaid unless unable until under
IM improve imagine impress import impose impact imbue imply
1 | 2 | 3 | 4 | 5 | 6 | 7 | 8 | 9 | 10 | 11 | 12

203-D. Improve stroking on 3-letter word beginnings

COM complete commence compete company comment common coming
PRO progress provided project produce proceed proper profit
SUB subtract sublease sublime subways subject submit sublet

OUT outcomes outright outlook outline outside output outfit
CAN canteens canopies candies candles canvass cannot candid
PRE prepared previous precede premium prevent prepay prefer

SUR surfaces surmount surpass surplus survive surtax survey
PER perspire personal persist perfect perhaps person permit
CEN centered censured century central censure census center

DIS district distance discuss dislike display disown dispel
SUP supplied supplant suppers suppose support supple supply
CON contract consider conduct contain concern concur confer
1 | 2 | 3 | 4 | 5 | 6 | 7 | 8 | 9 | 10 | 11 | 12

203-E. Improve stroking on 4-letter word beginnings

WITH withdrew withdraw withers without withal wither within
POST postpone postmark postman postage posted postal poster
FORE forebear foremost forearm foreman forest foredo forego
1 | 2 | 3 | 4 | 5 | 6 | 7 | 8 | 9 | 10 | 11 | 12

203-F. Repeat 203-B to mark your progress

UNIT 33

LESSONS 203-204

LINE: 50
TAB: 5 AND CENTER
SPACING: SINGLE
GOAL: INCREASE
CONTROL OF 7, 8,
9, AND 0
STRESS: TOUCH
CONTROL; CORRECT
POSTURE

22-A. Type each line twice; then repeat once more if you break rhythm on any line. Sitting properly?

22-B. To inventory your controls (particularly of numbers), type a double-spaced copy; proofread it.

Before starting, locate the three points where you use the tabulator—by touch!

22-C-D-E. To improve skill, type lines 5-16 twice each. Then repeat twice more one of the following:

(a) Lines 5-7 if you made any figure error in 22-B.

(b) Lines 8-11 if you made more than 4 errors in 22-B.

(c) Lines 12-16 if you made no figure errors and had 4 or fewer errors in 22-B.

Do you find it difficult to concentrate? Then, try this: Retype lines 12-16, typing the words in reverse order —last word, next-to-last, etc. Makes you alert!

22-A. Review the keys you know

1 Mel and his boy may get our back pay for one day.
2 That next quiz will have just five more new jobs.
3 The 23 men and 40 boys ate 90 apples and 78 pies.

22-B. Measure and improve your keyboard control

WORDS

4 Dear Jim: 2

It may be November 27 or 28 before I am   11

sure of the exact number of dinners to order   20

for the banquet. The size of the group will   29

be between 190 and 200, I believe, as it was   38

last year.   40

John King   44

1 | 2 | 3 | 4 | 5 | 6 | 7 | 8 | 9

22-C. Build accuracy on the number keys

5 November 27, 28, 29, or 30 and December 13 or 14.
6 Look for Invoices No. 3900, 3977, 3988, and 3999.
7 We must read pages 171–178, 181–189, and 191–200.

22-D. Build accuracy on one-hand words

8 aware imply extra holy acre loom case hip bad ill
9 great union trade polo gave kink save joy car you
10 refer knoll after milk draw only safe non age mum
11 grade jolly exact upon area join data ink tax him

22-E. Build speed on alternate-hand words

12 an cot due city form gown idle their firms social
13 is fit got keys mane risk work goals audit profit
14 us hem bit yams duty fuel sign fight usual bushel
15 do jam key busy with down them gowns widow formal
16 if own sue born span diem town theme shame lament

202-D. Improve stroking on horizontal reaches

39   attends purse agree water lunge save puff army once put ate
40   attempt slate lunch about ounce late page able purr ago wag
41   hollows blade gaily trace trail hope talk game ball ram pat
42   barging upper basal frail value gale shop hoop hump tan gas

202-E. Repeat 202-B to mark your improvement

202-F. Now set a record on this smooth, easy copy

1 | 2 | 3 | 4 | 5 | 6 | 7 | 8 | 9 | 10

43   The first and quickest step to take, for the   10
person who wants to win the title of The Pest, is   20
to become the ear of the head of the office. Run   30
to him or her with any bit of news; he or she may   40
not seem grateful, and it is hardly surprising to   50
learn that your fellow workers will be unhappy to   60
have you do this. But there is no doubt that they   70
will know who you are. This is a sure method for   80
becoming well known, even if not very well liked.   90

44   Another big, sure step, and it is not a very   100
hard one for most of us, is to become the one who   110
knows all the answers, right or wrong. If you do   120
not know an answer, invent one. Don't hold back;   130
speak up. When a group in the office is talking,   140
barge in and have your say. There is probably no   150
better way to break up office cliques and prevent   160
wasteful use of office time. It also keeps other   170
folks from talking about you, something that they   180
will be prone to do if you take this simple step.   190

45   A third step that you can take if you desire   200
more direct action in winning the title is to ask   210
for help from all the others. Make it clear your   220
work load is heavier than that of the others, and   230
much more important, too, and that the least they   240
can do is lend a hand. Now, you cannot make much   250
headway in this realm unless you persist; plan to   260
grab at least two helpers a day. And watch them,   270
too, so you can be sure to criticize what they do   280
for you. They will concede your title very soon.   290

46   There are, of course, many other tricks that   300
one can do to become The Pest. You can always be   310
late, you can make mistakes and pass the blame on   320
to others, you can wear strange clothing and talk   330
about it a lot, you can tell others to make phone   340
calls for you, and so on; but the truly effective   350
steps are the three outlined above. And when you   360
have won the title, cherish it; for, you will not   370
be there long enough to make very much use of it.   380

1 | 2 | 3 | 4 | 5 | 6 | 7 | 8 | 9 | 10

202-D. As in 202-C. Don't let your hands move—keep the little fingers well anchored.

202-F. Use single spacing, a 50-space line, and tab-5 indention for paragraphs.

Type one fluent copy with no pauses except a brief rest after each paragraph. Or, take two 5-minute writings, the first with a rest after each minute and the second solidly.

Strive for near-perfect rhythm and error-free copy.

SI 1.22—easy

CAUTION: It is very easy to lose your place in single-spaced material like this; pay strict attention to the copy.

22-F. Measure your progress

18   Dear John: 2

     Mr. Blazer tells me that we can have up   11
to December 7 for an exact count on the ban-   20
quet, with final figures on December 8. Can   29
we, I hope, push sales over the 200 mark to,   38
say, about 210?   41

                Jim   44

1 | 2 | 3 | 4 | 5 | 6 | 7 | 8 | 9

22-F. To increase and to measure your skill, type this letter twice. GOAL: A copy in 2 minutes, with 4 or fewer typing errors. It is permissible to practice any troublesome words between timings.

LINE: 50
SPACING: SINGLE
GOAL: CONTROL ½, ¼, 5, AND 6
STRESS: TOUCH CONTROL

LESSON

23

Number Keys

23-A. Review the keys you know

23-A. Type each line twice; then repeat once more if you falter (break rhythm, lose place in copy, stall) in the second typing.

1   Max did not run for our team but did get his cup.

2   Jack told them that your last quiz was very hard.

3   Adding 13 and 43 and 10 and 78 and 90 totals 234.

23-B. Practice the ½ key

*23-B. Use Sem-finger. Try the ;½; reach (with your J-finger anchored and the other fingers spreading). Type lines 4-6 three times.

4   ;$\frac{1}{2}\frac{1}{2}$; ;$\frac{1}{2}\frac{1}{2}$; ;$\frac{1}{2}$;$\frac{1}{2}$;$\frac{1}{2}$;$\frac{1}{2}$ $\frac{1}{2}$ pay; $\frac{1}{2}$ page; $\frac{1}{2}$ hour; $\frac{1}{2}$ week

5   Yes, 4 is $\frac{1}{2}$ of 8, $4\frac{1}{2}$ is $\frac{1}{2}$ of 9, and 7 is $\frac{1}{2}$ of 14.

6   He worked $10\frac{1}{2}$ hours in May and $11\frac{1}{2}$ hours in June.

23-C. Practice the ¼ key

*23-C. The ¼ is shift of ½ and is controlled by Sem-finger. Try the ;½ ¼; reach. Then type lines 7-9 three times, steadily not rapidly.

7   ;$\frac{1}{2}\frac{1}{4}$; ;$\frac{1}{2}\frac{1}{4}$; ;$\frac{1}{4}$;$\frac{1}{4}$;$\frac{1}{4}$;$\frac{1}{4}$ $\frac{1}{4}$ pay; $\frac{1}{4}$ page; $\frac{1}{4}$ hour; $\frac{1}{4}$ week

8   Yes, 2 is $\frac{1}{4}$ of 8, $2\frac{1}{4}$ is $\frac{1}{4}$ of 9, and 7 is $\frac{1}{4}$ of 28.

9   We gave $\frac{1}{2}$ to him and $\frac{1}{4}$ to her; I got the other $\frac{1}{4}$.

23-D. Measure your progress

*23-D. Type the sentences twice each—once straight through and once with this GOAL: To finish each of the sentences in 1 minute, with no number errors.

*NOTE: If your machine does not have a ½-¼ key, you must construct the fractions (see note at top of page 42).

10   Please order 10 more of size $10\frac{1}{2}$, 28 more of size
$28\frac{1}{2}$, 39 more of size $39\frac{1}{2}$, and 4 more of size $47\frac{1}{2}$.

11   Then ask for 10 more of size $10\frac{1}{4}$, 28 more of size
$28\frac{1}{4}$, 39 more of size $39\frac{1}{4}$, and 7 more of size $47\frac{1}{4}$.

1 | 2 | 3 | 4 | 5 | 6 | 7 | 8 | 9 | 10

201-F. Measure your skill on one-hand-loaded text

23 Once upon a time, it was a treat to look upon the vast herds of 14
skinny cattle that lanky cowboys, feet in stirrups and seat in saddle, 28
drove off the grasslands to the market. The great drives were uphill 42
going, likely, and were a test of man and beast. The cattle were far 56
from the plump breed we enjoy now; but the reward for millions of 69
steers was raw cash, cash pumped willy-nilly East to West. In my 82
opinion, only by the drives of wild, jumpy steers did the West grow. 96

  1 | 2 | 3 | 4 | 5 | 6 | 7 | 8 | 9 | 10 | 11 | 12 | 13 | 14

201-G. Improve stroking on one-hand words

24 after area are imply hulk hip freed best bet jumpy join ink
25 craft card car kinky kiln joy defer date dad lumpy noun lip
26 extra ease ear milky mink mum farce gave set nylon upon kin
27 great fare get onion lion oil react read red pupil yolk ply
28 state save web phony only him waste were few union p.m. mop

29 seated pinion better uphill treats hominy crate lymph after
30 aware pylon grade knoll exact plump deter holly water mommy
31 acre holy base jump case kink draw lily edge mill fact noon
32 age hum bad ill car nip err ohm fad pun gas yon sew hop vex
33 at on as no we in be my ad up ax un ex ho de pi re oh be no

201-H. Repeat 201-F to mark your improvement

202-A. Repeat 201-A for a quick tune-up

202-B. Measure your skill on long-reach-loaded text

34 The cultivation of our coffee requires limitless care, and five pains- 15
taking years are required to develop a mature product. The snowy 28
and fragrant blossoms turn into red and green cherries; they cannot be 42
harvested by machinery. The beans are the pits from the coffee 55
cherries. Approximately 2000 of these are necessary for 448 g of 69
roasted coffee. Beans require a long drying process before they are 83
hulled, graded, and shipped out to be tested, blended, and roasted. 96

  1 | 2 | 3 | 4 | 5 | 6 | 7 | 8 | 9 | 10 | 11 | 12 | 13 | 14

202-C. Improve stroking on vertical reaches

35 borrow chance enemy bran boat bore mush mutt cue may but my
36 models creams noisy veer note crow vest bent mix cry vow be
37 axioms lesson gowns poem webs room iron town web pin won on
38 loaned convex items next oxen owns pins upon ebb ton one in

NOTE in line 14:
In a mixed number, leave 1 space between the whole number and the fraction when the fraction is made with a diagonal. If one fraction must be made with a diagonal, use a diagonal with all fractions that are in the same sentence.

23-E. Use F-finger. Try the f5f reach (with the A-finger anchored); type lines 12-14 three times. See note above concerning fractions in line 14.

23-E. Practice the **5** key

12 f55f f55f f5f5 f5f5 5 falls 5 fires 5 folks 5 red

13 55 fell 55 find 55 fewer 55 fix 55 fuss 5/55 5:55

14 The answer to No. 155 is either 55 1/2 or 55 2/5.

23-F. Use J-finger. Try the jy6j reach (with Sem-finger at home); then type lines 15-17 three times. Can you make reach to 6 without moving your arm?

23-F. Practice the **6** key

15 jy6j jy6j j66j j6j6 6 jays 6 jumps 6 jugs 6 jades

16 66 join 66 jump 66 more 66 must 66 have 1/66 1:16

17 We shall need 36 pencils or 6 pens for the 6 men.

23-G. Type a complete copy with this GOAL: To finish in 2 minutes or less, with no number errors and not more than 4 other errors. Then center a copy on a half sheet of paper.

23-G. Measure your progress

WORDS

18 WAYS TO DISPLAY TYPING   5

1. Aligning   8

2. Block Centering   12

NOTE: When you type any enumeration, the periods after the numbers must line up. The typist must remember to check whether the enumeration includes two-digit numbers. To type two-digit numbers: (a) return carriage, (b) press and release the margin release key on the top left or right of the keyboard, (c) back-space once, (d) type the two-digit number. Repeat for EACH two-digit number.

To align the periods press margin release and backspace once. Repeat for line 11.

3. Blocking   15

4. Capitalizing   18

5. Extra Spacing   22

6. Horizontal Centering   27

7. Indenting   30

8. Pivoting   32

9. Spread Centering   36

10. Typing All Capitals   41

11. Underscoring   44

NOTE: If there are several lines beginning with two-digit numbers, move the left margin one space to the left to save time.

LINE: 50
TAB: 5 AND CENTER
SPACING: SINGLE
GOAL: INCREASE
      NUMBER CONTROL
STRESS: KEY-STROKE
      PRECISION

LESSON

24

Number Review

24-A. Type each line twice. You should easily finish each line in ½ minute.

24-A. Review the keys you know

1 She may quit her job the day you get her new car.

2 Buzz will pack your five bags when her taxi goes.

3 I dialed rooms 10, 28, and 39; he rang 47 and 56.

1 | 2 | 3 | 4 | 5 | 6 | 7 | 8 | 9 | 10

Unit 33. Skill Development

LINE: 60
TAB: 5
SPACING: DRILLS, SIN-
GLE; PARAGRAPHS,
DOUBLE
DRILLS: THREE TIMES
GOAL: BOOST SKILL
STRESS: LEVEL HANDS

201-A. Type each line in "pyramid" style, like:
The
The chairman
The chairman of

201-A. Tune up on these review lines

1 The chairman of the panel paid us for a visit to the dorms.
2 Zeke buys exquisite jewels and gives them for a prize copy.
3 For 2 for 23 for 234 for 2345 for 6 for 67 for 678 for 7890
   1 | 2 | 3 | 4 | 5 | 6 | 7 | 8 | 9 | 10 | 11 | 12

201-B. Type one copy. If you stall, circle the word.

If you make more than one error, your goal must be for accuracy; one or no error, the goal is speed.

SI 1.53—rough, tough, and alphabetic!

201-B. Measure your skill on double-letter-loaded text

4 All sorts of goods, needs, and supplies are offered in vending ma-   14
chines. A traveler buys sweet-smelling perfumes, a toothbrush and   27
toothpaste, hairdressing, and other common traveling needs. Such   40
supplies as books, booklets, writing paper, boxes of cards, puzzles,   54
and hobby goods help pass a few hours. Hungry people have access to   68
all manner of food matter. One buys apples, coffee, eggs, jellies, bot-   82
tles of liquids, butter, rolls, berries, cheeses, and allied foods.   96
  1 | 2 | 3 | 4 | 5 | 6 | 7 | 8 | 9 | 10 | 11 | 12 | 13 | 14

201-C-D. Type to goal you ascertained in 201-B.

ACCURACY: Each group of lines as a paragraph at least three steady times.

SPEED: Each individual line three or more times.

If the drill is for any letter you missed or on which you paused in 201-B, type the line two or three extra times.

201-C. Improve stroking on double-letter words

5   EE veneered between upkeep seems green breed been sees feel
6   OO overlook foolish cooler looks goods flood pool soon good
7   SS possible express excess dress asset class toss pass miss
8   LL followed million fellow spell hilly drill mill full ball
9   TT attempts matters bitter attic witty putty mutt putt mitt
10 FF effected differs effort stuff offer cliff miff buff cuff
11 MM commands commerce immense grammar mammoth hammers common
12 CC accepted accuracy accused success account accents occurs
13 PP happened equipped appeals dropped clipper support apples
14 ZZ dazzling puzzling puzzles fizzled muzzles fuzzily nuzzle
15 BB pebbling cribbage cabbage cribbed jobbers ribbons abbeys
16 NN connects channels manners pennies annexed annuals canned
17 GG suggests struggle begging baggage logging diggers bigger
18 OO moonshot bloodily coolant toolbox schools boodles stools
19 RR surround borrowed stirred correct arrived borrows errors

201-D. If you can be timed, take 1-minute writings on each line (speed) or the group of lines (accuracy) rather than as directed in "201-C-D" preceding.

201-D. Regain stride on alternate-hand speed sentences

20 The eight men may make their bid for the big fight by then.
21 Hang the fur cowls by the big chair; then sit down with us.
22 The men paid us for six pans, but did they pay us for soap?
   1 | 2 | 3 | 4 | 5 | 6 | 7 | 8 | 9 | 10 | 11 | 12

Errorless copy, please!

201-E. Repeat 201-B to mark your improvement

24-B. Measure and improve your keyboard control

4 Dear Jim: 2

As of December 3, our ticket sales come   11
to 187. Holly Anne has 14 or 15 requests on   20
hand, and Max has 6 or 7 more. These add up   29
to 207 or 209. The 210 victory goal will be   38
realized.   40

John King   44

1 | 2 | 3 | 4 | 5 | 6 | 7 | 8 | 9

24-C. Build accuracy on the number keys

5 The total of 10, 28, 39, 47, and 56 is about 180.
6 Now, please total 10 and 28 and 39 and 47 and 56.
7 The sum of 10, 28, 39, 47, and 56 is exactly 180.

24-D. Build accuracy on alphabetic word lines

8 only view drag back taxi jump left helm size quip
9 hazy quit junk very flax grab clip spot weed mane
10 next bowl limp zero vice hunk good quay from just

24-E. Build speed on fluent, rhythmic phrases

11 have firm |goal will |for you |add our |as of |up to a
12 sure wish |make this |and has |did you |or if |to be a
13 have sold |when they |ask the |you get |if it |is to a

24-F. Measure your progress

14 Dear Jim: 2

We have sold 194 tickets and have firm,   11
extra requests for 15, to total 209. I sure   20
wish we could tell Mr. Blazer to make up the   29
210 you wished. Say, Chum, did you get YOUR   38
tickets?   40

John King   44

1 | 2 | 3 | 4 | 5 | 6 | 7 | 8 | 9

24-G. Review centering

15 ADMIT ONE
16 To the Annual Banquet of
17 THE BUSINESS CLUB
18 December 10, 197-, at 19:00
19 SILVER ROOM : : QUEENS HOTEL

9 SKILL BUILDING • SECRETARIAL
PROJECTS • INVENTORY TESTS

Progress Test on Part One

Test 1

The group of us stood by the small twig fire   10

and wished we could be dry, even if just for five   20

minutes. Max pushed a wet stick into the flames;   30

it squeaked and sizzled and then started smoking.   40

    With a yell of dismay, we jumped back from a   50

gust of smoke. Max stood there, quietly laughing   60

at us. I looked at the heavy clouds; they seemed   70

to promise that the drizzle would last all night.   80

  1 | 2 | 3 | 4 | 5 | 6 | 7 | 8 | 9 | 10

Dear Jim: 2

    Now that the banquet is all over and all the   12

money is in, let me report: 18

    1. Max Gilbert sold 87 tickets.   26

    2. Holly Anne Parker sold 56 tickets.   34

    3. I sold 76 tickets, including the one that   44

you almost forgot to buy.   50

    4. Altogether we sold 219 tickets.   58

    I am sure that you take as much pride in the   68

record we set as my committee does.   76

          John King   80

  1 | 2 | 3 | 4 | 5 | 6 | 7 | 8 | 9 | 10

If preferred, Tests 8-B, 8-C, and 8-D may by typed completely (maximum time: 15 minutes for each) and be graded on this penalty scale.

PENALTY SCALE

—3 for each major error (top margin, line length, line-spacing, general correctness of form, etc.)
—2 for each minor error (blocking, aligning, centering, indenting, etc., of individual parts of the job)
—1 for each typographical error

GRADING SCALE

0-1 PENALTY . . . . A
2-3 PENALTY . . . . B
4-6 PENALTY C
7-8 PENALTY . . . . D

Test 8-C
Letter 104
TIMED WRITING ON DICTATED LETTER

Paper: workbook 385
Style: blocked
Grade: panel above or page 308 box
Body: 245 words
SI: 1.35—easy-normal

Test 8-D
Table 71
TIMED WRITING ON DICTATED TABLE

Paper: workbook 386
Style: ruled table
Grade: panel above or page 308 box
Start: plan made and machine adjusted

james e flaherty. . .392 hathway street. . .	16
wawanesa. . .manitoba.. dear jim. . .	24
i am more than delighted to learn of	33
your quick recovery from your accident	41
. . .it does not seem possible that you are	49
ready to come back to work already. . .but	57
. . .of course. . .i am extremely happy that	64
you are. . .i hope that you will not overdo	73
things at the start. . .take it easy for a	81
while. . .jim. . .please do not try to step	89
back into full harness right away. . .	96
i suspect that the visit to harding-hill	105
company will be the first thing you will	113
wish to confirm. . .i found mr thompson. . .	121
our contact at harding-hill. . .to be a very	130
congenial man who really knows what the	138
score is. . .he was promoted up from the	145
ranks. . .he has been an operator of most	153
kinds of office machines and is now in	161
charge of the mailroom production work	169
for his firm. . .he knows exactly what he	177
wants and how he will use whatever equip-	185
ment is purchased for him. . .	191
mr thompson is almost certain to requi-	199
sition a battery of eight or nine of our	208
model 19's. . .but he also wants a folder	215
that will handle a special paper stock. . .	224
the factory is now completing this spe-	231
cial folder and will have it in your hands	240
within a week. . .i have been told. . .	247
if you can. . .jim. . .write him two or	254
three days before you call to see him. . .	262
and when you do. . .tell him that you will	270
be bringing the special folding machine	278
for which he asked. . .cordially *and so*	290
on. . .theodore wilson. . .sales manager	301

This is table 16, "secretarial impact on	28
supply purchases," compiled by you. . .	34
we will have the rank of each item, the	52
name of the item, and its percent.	82
rank 1 is carbon paper, 60%	90
rank 2 is typewriter ribbons, 59%	97
rank 3 is erasers, 55%	103
rank 4 is filing materials, 53%	109
rank 5 is typewriter cleaners, 50%	118
rank 6 is typewriting paper, 49%	124
rank 7 is electric typewriters, 48%	132
rank 8 is manual typewriters, 47%	139
rank 9 is posture chairs, 46%	146
rank 10 is desk staplers, 45%	152
rank 11 is writing ink, 43%	158
rank 12 is duplicating stencils, 41%	165
rank 13 is duplicating masters, 40%	173
rank 14 is copyholders, 39%	178
rank 15 is desk pen sets, 38%	184
rank 16 is dictation notebooks, 37%	192
rank 17 is boxed paper clips, 36%	199
rank 18 is boxed ball pencils, 34%	208
rank 19 is office desks, 32%	214
rank 20 is dictation machines, 31%	221
rank 21 is engagement calendars, 30%	230
rank 22 is scissors, blades, 29%	236
rank 23 is postal meters, 28%	242
rank 24 is duplicating machines, 27%	250
rank 25 is boxed lead pencils, 26%	257
rank 26 is adding machines, 24%	263
rank 27 is filing cabinets, 22%	269
rank 28 is photocopy equipment, 16%	277
. . . . .Average is 34%	293

PENALTY SCALE

—3 for each major error (top margin, line length, line-spacing, general correctness of form, etc.)
—2 for each minor error (blocking, aligning, centering, indenting, etc., of individual parts of the job)
—1 for each typographical error

GRADING SCALE

0-1 PENALTY . . . . A
2-3 PENALTY . . . . B
4-6 PENALTY C
7-8 PENALTY . . . . D

If preferred, Tests 1-B, 1-C, and 1-D may each be centered on a page (time: 10 minutes each) and then checked for penalties (Penalty Scale); the total penalty then graded on the Grading Scale.

Test 1-C

2-MINUTE WRITING, GROUP CENTERING
Paper: workbook page 22; or plain
Line: clear out
Tab: center
Spacing: single
Start: carriage centered
Grade: box below
SI: 1.65—difficult

2-MINUTE SPEED WITHIN 4 ERRORS*

40-up wam . . . . . . A
35-39 wam . . . . . . B
25-34 wam C
20-24 wam . . . . . . D

* If more than 4 errors are made, compute the speed on what is typed before the fifth error.

Test 1-D

2-MINUTE WRITING, LINE CENTERING
Paper: workbook page 22; or plain
Line: clear out
Tab: center (for recentering carriage for each line)
Spacing: double
Centering: each line separately
Start: carriage centered
Grade: box above
SI: 1.67—difficult

TYPEWRITING DISPLAY TECHNIQUES

CENTER→

1. Align lines
2. Block lines
3. Capitalize words
4. Center a group of lines
5. Center horizontally
6. Center vertically
7. Indent paragraphs
8. Pivot from margin
9. Spread and center
10. Type in all capitals
11. Underscore
12. Use extra spacings

18
19
20
33
36
40
46
51
55
59
64
68
73
76
81

TRAINEES

Richard I. Edwards

Alvin Dwight Smith

Quintin Dark

CENTER→ Aloysius Witt

Henry Ira Brown

Dominic Wirt

J. Gilbert

Emil Lisle Park

5
6
18
30
38
47
58
66
73
83

Check: The letter "i" lines up.

PART ONE TEST

LESSON 25

45

Progress Test on Part Eight

Training Bulletin 23:   THE TELEPHONE

When a customer or other friend of the company reaches one of us 14
on the telephone, we are the company to that caller. If we are quick 28
to answer the phone, the company seems wide awake. If we are 40
helpful and sympathetic, the company seems to be that way, too. If 54
our voice is zestful, if our manner is friendly, the caller will associate 69
such cheerfulness and friendliness with the whole company. These 82
examples are obvious. The reverse is also obvious, is it not? 95

Anything that we can do, therefore, to improve our techniques of 109
telephoning will be to the good. The purpose of this bulletin is not 123
to criticize any department or person but simply to review some basic 137
things that make a difference in the image we create with the public. 151

WHEN WE ANSWER   1. We Are Prompt.

As already intimated, few things are quite as critical as is the 165
promptness of our picking up the phone when it rings. It should be a 179
general rule that we answer between the first and second ring, surely 193
before the third. This means that all of us should make arrangements 207
with someone to answer our phone when we are not there. 219

2. We Identify Ourselves.

The first words we speak are also keenly significant. We should 233
express a word of greeting appropriate to the hour of the day and 246
add a word or two that will assure the caller that he has the right 259
party or department. A secretary says, "Good morning, Mr. 271
Wilson's office; Miss Smith speaking. May I help you?" If she then 285
connects the call to Mr. Wilson, he says, "Good morning; Mr. 297
Wilson speaking," or "Good morning; this is George Wilson." A call 311
to a department should bring the reply, "Good morning, Credit 323
Department; Miss Hall speaking. May I help you?" The person who 335
simply says, "Hello," doesn't play fair! 344

3. We Smile As We Speak.

There is a middle ground we should seek between being too sugary 358
and too crisp. The middle ground seems to come best if we smile 371
when we reach for the phone and hold the smile as we express our 384
greeting. It is very hard, thank goodness, to smile and grumble 397
simultaneously. 400

4. We Really Try to Help.

When someone calls us, it is for a reason; if we can satisfy his 414
purpose, he is indebted and impressed and grateful. We serve 428
company interest best if, within the limits of our authority, we try 440
our best to help him fulfill his purpose. 448

1 | 2 | 3 | 4 | 5 | 6 | 7 | 8 | 9 | 10 | 11 | 12 | 13

Right-column word counts: 8-B / 8-A 22, 36, 50, 62, 76, 91, 104, 117, 131, 145, 159, 173, 186, 200, 214, 228, 242, 254, 269, 283, 296, 309, 321, 335, 347, 361, 373, 385, 394, 408, 422, 435, 448, 461, 464, 479, 493, 507, 519, 527

2 SKILL BUILDING • BASIC LETTERS, TABLES, AND MANUSCRIPTS

Table 69
DICTATED TABLE

Paper: full, plain
Carbons: file only
Style: ruled form

[handwritten: no more than 3 corrections]

The material you have been typing [pages 299-305] has been for Miss Priscilla Trotter, director of training. She dictates a table to you, which is to be an enclosure for the next letter.

[handwritten: Ruled Table]

Entitle this table "Distribution of Training Time," subtitled "Portland Products Company." We have three columns, to be headed "Activity," "Hours," and "Percent." Ready? 18 / 29 / 33 / 48 / 50

Correspondence, 40 hours, 28.6%. Skill building, 30 hours, 21.4%. Tabulation, 25 hours, 17.8%. Reports, 23 hours, 16.5%. Forms, 15 hours, 10.7%. Company policies, 5 hours, 3.5%. Display typing, 2 hours, 1.5%. Totals, 140 hours, 100.0% 67 / 77 / 84 / 93 / 101 / 128

Letter 102
2-PAGE LETTER, DICTATED; BLOCKED

Paper: workbook 377
Carbons: file only
Review: page 203
Body: 291 words
SI: 1.46—fairly hard

"This letter," says Miss Trotter, "is a reply to one from Miss Jane T. Brown, Department of Personnel, Martin Miller & Sons, 58 Broadview Street, Toronto, Ontario M4M 2E4. Ready for dictation? 4 / 15 / 24 / 34

[handwritten: Dear]

We feel very much flattered by your inquiry about some of the details of our training program for new members of our office staff... I am pleased to reply to your questions... *Please center a heading, "1. Time Allotment"*... our program for new office employees lasts for four weeks of 35 hours each, giving us a total of 140 hours for the program. The hours are distributed as indicated on the enclosed table... *paragraph* ...you will wish to note that the program is for persons who have already had basic training in school. The program is focused on orienting the new worker to our (*underscore "our"*) policies... for example... you 42 / 51 / 59 / 67 / 78 / 94 / 102 / 120 / 129 / 136 / 145 / 153 / 162 / 170 / 176

[handwritten: follows; insert table]

know that there are dozens of ways to arrange letters... In our program we deal only with the one (*underscored*) way we (*underscored*) arrange our (*underscored*) letters... *Center a heading, "2. Display Typing"* ... 184 / 192 / 198 / 204 / 223

Yes, we do give much attention to display typing... Of the 140 hours, we schedule 2 hours for what might be considered art (*quote "art"*) typing... We teach newcomers to justify lines and to construct large letters. Few new employees know how these are done... *paragraph* ... 232 / 240 / 248 / 253 / 261 / 269 / 273

You may wonder why we give this much attention to artyping (*quote "artyping"*) ...the answer is simple: many of our employees are typists, and we find that they give more attention to announcements when they are embellished with signs of real typing craft. Also, our firm makes great use of duplicated advertisements... these, too, get more attention when they are given deft art touches... *paragraph*... I am enclosing for your interest two of our current training bulletins that deal with display typing, as well as a sample of the kind of attractive displays we post on the bulletin boards in our offices and lounges... You would be surprised by some of the fine work that our typists are able to create. *Fine. Please enumerate the four enclosures.* 282 / 287 / 294 / 303 / 311 / 319 / 327 / 335 / 342 / 349 / 382 / 390 / 398 / 407 / 416 / 424 / 432 / 439 / 451

[handwritten: Yours sincerely; 2 current training Bulletins, 1 Display sample]

Letter 103
Table 70
LETTER WITH TABLE

Paper: workbook 379
Carbons: file only
Body: 317 words
SI: 1.47—fairly hard

Looking at your work, Miss Trotter says, "It seems foolish—especially for a training director!—to put the table on a separate page when it is short enough to fit in the letter. Please retype the letter and insert the table—without the title and subtitle, of course—after the second paragraph. Change the lead-in to *hours are distributed as follows*." With a grin, she adds, "Now that will change the enclosure listing, too, won't it?"

LINE: 50
TAB: 5
SPACING: SINGLE
GOAL: INCREASE SKILL
STRESS: WRISTS LOW,
    FINGERS CURVED

Unit 5. Skill Development

26-A. Ripple through lines 1-3, typing each at least twice. Use these lines as the warmup for Lesson 27.

26-A. Tune up on these easy lines

1 a; sl a;sl dk a;sldk fj a;sldkfj gh a;sldkfjgh a;

2 and the in so do to is it if ox or go do by an am

3 work wish they lazy quit cove oak six jam pay own

26-B. Measure and improve your keyboard control

WORDS

26-B. To define your goal for Lesson 26, type and proofread a double-spaced copy of this paragraph. If you make 4 or fewer errors, your goal is SPEED; but if you make more than 4, your goal must be ACCURACY.

SI 1.19—easy copy*

4   Typing skill grows best in two steps: First 10
the typist drills on copy that is so easy that he 20
is sure to type at a good speed and with very few 30
errors; in this way he gets the feel of typing at 40
a better pace. Then he must seek to hold the new 50
rate as he works on copy that, while not hard, is 60
not easy. In this book the booster step is taken 70
in the first unit of the four units in each part, 80
and the second is taken in the other three units. 90

  1 | 2 | 3 | 4 | 5 | 6 | 7 | 8 | 9 | 10

*NOTE: SI (the syllabic intensity—average number of syllables per word) indicates the approximate difficulty of the copy:

SI 1.00-1.15 . . . very easy
SI 1.15-1.25 . . . . easy
SI 1.25-1.35 . . fairly easy
SI 1.35-1.45 . . . . . normal
SI 1.45-1.55 . . . fairly hard
SI 1.55-up . . . . . . difficult

26-C. Improve skill on patterned word drills

26-C. Target on your goal.

ACCURACY: Type lines 5-7 three times each and lines 8-11 two times each.

SPEED: Type lines 5-7 two times each and lines 8-11 three times each.

5 po po post pour poem pore port pods pout poll pot

6 as as asks ashy task mask dash lash last past ash

7 oi oi toil soil boil coil foil coin join loin oil

8 th th thou thud thug thus than them they then the

9 fo fo fore folk fold fort foam fork form fowl for

10 sl sl slat slow sled slot slag slay slap slam sly

11 bu bu bulb bulk burr buff busy bury burn bush bud

26-D. Improve skill on patterned sentence drills

26-D. Target on your goal.

ACCURACY: Type lines 12-14 three times each and lines 15-18 two times each.

SPEED: Type lines 12-14 two times each and lines 15-18 three times each.

12 Quietly pack more new boxes with five dozen jugs.

13 Quietly pick up the box with five dozen gum jars.

14 Quickly pack the box with five dozen modern jugs.

  1 | 2 | 3 | 4 | 5 | 6 | 7 | 8 | 9 | 10

15 It is their duty to pay for the six fuel signals.

16 He is busy with the big social but may come down.

17 The form she got for them may work also for this.

18 She may go to the city for a visit with the girl.

Manuscript 70

LETTERED DISPLAY

Paper: plain
Carbons: file
Spacing: optional
Style: as shown

The most useful form of artistic lettering in display typing
is the style shown in the alphabet below. It is constructed
of small m's, arrayed with half spacing. The easiest way to
make such letters is to type
all the m's that will appear   machine to half-line spacing
on the regular single-spaced   so you may insert the needed
lines. Next, you adjust the   parts of each letter. Thus:

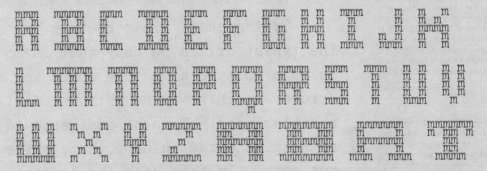

Manuscript 71

LETTERED AND
JUSTIFIED DISPLAY

Paper: plain
Carbons: file

**Be sure to justify
all the lines!**

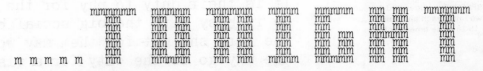

Members of the Portland Products Company Chorale will meet,

speak, sing, recite, enact, and in general have a wonderful

time this evening at eight o'clock in the auditorium. New#

members are welcome. There are no dues. All you need is##

a standard speaking voice. Come one, come all! Have fun##

26-E. Improve skill on special paragraph copy

19   As soon as you know that you are to go up to   10
the camp, be sure to tell me so that I can plan a   20
trip up there, too. I would like to be with you,   30
if I can, when it is time to cast the first line.   40

    1 | 2 | 3 | 4 | 5 | 6 | 7 | 8 | 9 | 10

20   There is one sure way that we can get from a   10
job what we should like to get, and that is to be   20
sure to look in the job for some of the things we   30
know that we can do well and like to do that way.   40

    1 | 2 | 3 | 4 | 5 | 6 | 7 | 8 | 9 | 10

21   The path that goes past our house is the one   10
that goes down to the lake. The fish down there,   20
they say, are so quick to bite that you must hide   30
in a bush or climb a tree when you bait the hook.   40

26-F. Make an interim progress check

27-A. Learn to respond to the margin bell

Sometimes you cannot copy material line for line, but must yourself decide where to end lines. To help you in making line-ending decisions without looking up from your copy, your machine has a bell that rings when the carriage is 7 or 8 spaces from the right margin stop. For example, if you wish lines to end at 75 and have therefore set the margin stop at 80, the bell rings when the carriage reaches 72 or 73, to warn you that the carriage is only 2 or 3 spaces from 75. When the bell rings, plan to end the line as near the desired ending point as you conveniently can (preferably without dividing a word). If your typewriter gives a 3-space warning, for example, here are typical line-ending decisions you would face and make:

DESIRED ENDING	RETURN CARRIAGE AFTER TYPING
BELL ↓ LOCK ↓	
I now realize these	*realize*
Somehow, we must be	*we*
The possibility she	*possibility*
He is philosophical	*philo-*

27-B. Improve skill on patterned word drills

22   qu qu quote quilt quill quart quip quiz quad quit
23   up up upper group croup super coup soup cups upon
24   cr cr cruel crown cross crush crux crib crow crop
25   um um crumb flume strum humid dumb jump chum drum

26   oo oo stood floor crook proof book soon good look
27   ss ss gross issue guess cross loss boss less miss
28   ll ll shall skill stall droll will full sell tell
29   ee ee speed sheer trees creed need been feel keep

198-C. Adjust machine for double spacing, 70-space line (lines will align), and a tab-5 indention.

In Lesson 198, type the first paragraph three times with no more than one error in each copy or until you have a copy that is errorless. Type the second paragraph in this way in Lesson 199.

SI 1.28—easy-normal

198-C. Boost skill on alphabetic paragraphs

₇ Once in a while a typist has a task that is important enough for   14
one to take extraordinary pains to make it look professional. When   28
that occasion comes up, the typist who can make every line end evenly   42
with the others and can design big display letters to use in headings   56
will have a truly big jump over other typists. Such specialized   70
skills require a bit of practice, but they are easy and fun after you   84
have got the knack of them. They are not skills for a beginner; they   98
demand that the typist be a true master of the machine and its parts.   112

₈ When you wish to justify a group of lines (that is, make all the   126
lines end at the same point), you start by typing a first draft. You   140
set the margins for the length of line you want to fill; and then you   154
type the material, making every line come as close as you can to your   168
desired point of line ending. In general, it is better to have lines   182
too short than to have them too long. Scrutinize the draft carefully   196
and note exactly how many spaces have to be saved or inserted to   209
make the lines end evenly; most typists fill out the lines with the   223
number sign, to show how many spaces will be needed. Finally you   236
retype the copy, making all the adjustments you need—if you miss   249
one, look out!   252

1 | 2 | 3 | 4 | 5 | 6 | 7 | 8 | 9 | 10 | 11 | 12 | 13 | 14

198/199-D. Apply your skill to display production

Training Bulletin 21:   LINE JUSTIFYING   23

25

When there is occasion to give material special display, try   37
the artistic touch of line justifying; here is how to do it: 49

50

Manuscript 69

JUSTIFIED DISPLAY
Paper: plain, full
Carbons: file
Spacing: optional
Style: as shown

To justify lines (that is, to make them end evenly),### two steps are required: 63/76/87

1. Type the copy, ending## each line as near to the de-sired ending point as you### can. Except for paragraph## endings, fill in short lines with # signs to show how#### many spaces each line needs.   99/112/124/137/150/162/175

2. Type the final draft,## inserting all the necessary# spaces to spread the lines.# Scatter the spaces so that## they do not occur together.   188/200/213/226/238

To justify lines (that is, to make them end evenly), two steps are required:

1. Type the copy, ending each line as near to the de-sired ending point as you can. Except for paragraph endings, fill in short lines with # signs to show how many spaces each line needs.

2. Type the final draft, inserting all the necessary spaces to spread the lines. Scatter the spaces so that they do not occur together.

239

This technique would not be used in correspondence but would   252
be very fine in typewritten announcements or advertisements.   264

27-C. Improve skill on patterned sentence drills

30 I was quite crushed when he had to quit the crew.
31 Lum was quoted saying it was dumb to crib a quiz.
32 My group went to the quad and got quarts of soup.
33 His chum jumped across a flume by the upper crib.

    1 | 2 | 3 | 4 | 5 | 6 | 7 | 8 | 9 | 10

34 Dee will collect all the needed bookkeeping fees.
35 Ross needs a better broom for glossing the floor.
36 Bess will miss her book and will need to call us.
37 Bill took three weeks to sell all his good books.

27-D. Target on your goal.

ACCURACY: Lines 38-41, three times; 42-45, twice.

SPEED: Lines 38-41, two times; 42-45, three times.

One-hand words:

Troublesome words:

Troublesome words:

Double letters:

Speed phrases:

Speed phrases:

Speed phrases:

Alternate-hand words:

27-D. Improve skill on preview words and phrases

38 million feed are you eat few on we no at in be up
39 excellence present, typists realize powder typing
40 although, invention fingers learned beaten though
41 classroom million offices dollars shall pill feed

42 those who|pick up|stop at|able to|come to|that no
43 know that|glad to|nice to|more in|take to|kind of
44 stop to|if you|to pay|no one|is not|to eat|we did
45 handy such they rich rush did pay box to do so if

27-E. Measure your progress in sustained writing

WORDS

46 If you would like to become a rich person in   10
a rush, just invent some kind of pill or tonic or   20
powder a typist could take to double his skill in   30
typing. Do you realize that there are about nine   40
million typists in offices and some three million   50
more in classrooms who would be glad to pay a few   60
dollars for such a quick route to excellence? It   70
is so. It is nice to know that no one has beaten   80
you to the invention yet; although, come to think   90
about it, it would be handy to be able to stop at   100
a shop and pick up a box of words a minute, would   110
it not? For the present, though, just like those   120
who learned to type before we did, we shall drill   130
and drill our fingers until at last they learn to   140
eat up the word meals that our eyes feed to them.   150

    1 | 2 | 3 | 4 | 5 | 6 | 7 | 8 | 9 | 10

IDEA: Type 27-E as a 5-minute timed writing and record your scores on the timed-writing scoreboard on workbook page 47. If you complete the copy before the 5 minutes are up, start it over.

SI 1.21—easy copy

```
;'; ''' ;'; Al's car isn't as new as he'd like us to think!    13

;'" """ ;"; "Welcome home," I said.   "When did you arrive?"    31

k8* *** k*k The asterisk (*) is on the 8 on some electrics.    50

j6¢ ¢¢¢ j¢j Jim bought 14 for 5¢, 21 for 6¢, and 18 for 7¢.    68

s2@ @@@ s@s The gloves sell @ 26¢ a pair, not @ 62¢ a pair.    86
```

22. POWER DRILLS. Repeat each of these lines until you can do so   100
without one pause or one error.   107

```
Jack quietly moved up front and seized the big cask of wax.    125

Jinx gave back the prize money she won for her quaint doll.    143

Ask her for the big rig she had the two men get out for us.    161

Jan got the forms for the firm and may also work with them.    179
```

A FINAL SUGGESTION   189

Some typists expect their speed to soar the moment they begin to   208
work on an electric machine. Please note that your speed will *not*   223
soar. It might creep up slightly, but not much. It is like having a new   237
pair of fine shoes: you have to break them in; then you can walk more   251
comfortably and with less fatigue, but your habits of walking will   264
probably keep you from walking faster than you did before.   276

It takes about three days on an electric before the manual typist   291
is fully at home with the new machine. On the first of these three   305
days, aim for about half your former speed; on the second day,   319
for about three-fourths your speed; on the third day, get back to   332
your normal pace. *Then* perhaps you can speed up a bit!   343

If you use the same
space-savers you did
on pages 299 and 300,
you will complete
"Bulletin 20" fully
in three typed pages.

LINE: 60
SPACING: SINGLE
DRILLS: THREE TIMES
GOAL: TO LEARN ABOUT
    DISPLAY ARTYPING
STRESS: EVEN STROKING

198-A. Each line three
times or a 1-minute
timed writing on it.
Repeat in Lesson 199.

198-A. Tune up on these review lines

```
1   Both the town and city may make the firm fix both big oaks.
2   Roxie picked off the amazing yellow jonquils by the cavern.
3   She lost cheques #10, #28, #39, #47, and #56 along the way.
    1 | 2 | 3 | 4 | 5 | 6 | 7 | 8 | 9 | 10 | 11 | 12
```

198-B. Type to your need.
ACCURACY: The three
lines as a paragraph
three or more times.
SPEED: Each three times.

198-B. Regain full skill on preview words

```
4   extraordinary important headings justify squeeze pains look
5   professional carefully indicate occasion finally other jump
6   specialized scrutinize inserted material require draft long
```

Skill Drive

LINE: 50
TAB: 5
SPACING: SINGLE
DRILLS: TWICE OR MORE
GOAL: INCREASE SKILL
STRESS: POSTURE

28-A. Type each line twice. Don't sag on the numbers! Use these lines for the warmup in Lesson 29, too.

28-A. Tune up on these review lines

1 a;sldkfjghfjdksla; a;sldkfjghfjdksla;sldkfjghfjdk
2 cab yet fed zoo ask jig not lax him row eve quips
3 Read pages 10–28, then pages 39–47, then page 56.

28-B. To define your goal for Lesson 28, type and proofread a double-spaced copy of this paragraph. If you make 4 or fewer errors, your goal is SPEED; but if you make more than 4, your goal is ACCURACY.

SI 1.23—easy copy

28-B. Measure and improve your keyboard control

WORDS

4 The oceans of the world are huge; they cover   10
more than 70 percent of its surface and, in a few   20
spots, are so deep that a mountain the size of an   30
Everest would be lost in them. The oceans play a   40
major role in shaping the weather. They serve as   50
a source of food, as an exciting playground, as a   60
means of travel. The oceans touch on the life of   70
each of us, and frequently at that. Yet, in some   80
regards, man knows more about the distant planets   90
than he does about the seas that lie at his feet.   100

   1 | 2 | 3 | 4 | 5 | 6 | 7 | 8 | 9 | 10

28-C. Target on your goal.

ACCURACY: Lines 5-8, three times; 9-12, twice.

SPEED: Lines 5-8 two times; 9-12, three times.

28-C. Improve skill on patterned word drills

5 op op open hope rope lope crop flop stop shop top
6 sa sa same sail sank sang salt safe sash sane say
7 ew ew blew flew slew view crew brew drew stew hew
8 ly ly only duly ably lily oily ally July illy fly
9 di di dish disk dire dine dime dial dice dirk did
10 le le lend lent leap lean left lest leak less led
11 co co cork coat cone come colt corn coal coke cot
12 na na name nail nape nays navy naps snap gnaw nab

28-D. Target on your goal.

ACCURACY: Lines 13-15, three times; 16-19, twice.

SPEED: Lines 13-15, two times; 16-19, three times.

28-D. Improve skill on patterned sentence drills

13 Joe quietly picked six razors from the woven bag.
14 The quick brown fox jumps over all the lazy dogs.
15 Jack Farmer was quite vexed by such lazy plowing.
   1 | 2 | 3 | 4 | 5 | 6 | 7 | 8 | 9 | 10
16 He may go to the club and work with the chairman.
17 The man may endow the chapel with an ivory panel.
18 She is apt to laugh when I go to the city social.
19 Eight of the girls do wish to go to the big lake.

For extra practice, have someone time your work; then take a series of 1-minute timings until you achieve your GOAL:

ACCURACY: Line 13 typed three times in 1 minute or less; Lines 13-15 typed once in 1 minute or less, with 2 or fewer mistakes.

SPEED: Line 16 finished four times in 1 minute or less; lines 16-19 typed in 1 minute or less, with 2 or fewer typing errors.

Leave a blank half-space above each line of drill and a full blank line after each set of drills. Use tab-5 on each drill.

```
aa ;; ss ll dd kk ff jj gg hh ff jj dd kk ss ll aa ;; ss ll      13
aqqa ;pp; swws lool deed kiik frrf juuj fttf jyyj fggf jhhj      31
azza ;//; sxxs l..l dccd k,,k fvvf jmmj fbbf jnnj fghj jhgf      49
```

15. SPACING. Get the thumb off the space bar quickly. Keep your   64
wrists low. Emphasize a straight, sharp, up-and-down tap stroke. Do   78
not let your thumb swerve inward or outward.   87

```
z y x w v u t s r q p o n m l k j i h g f e d c b a ; : , .      105
a b c d e f g h i j k l m n o p q r s t u v w x y z . , / ?      123
```

16. CARRIAGE OR CARRIER RETURN. After each of these words,   136
return the carriage or carrier by a single quick jab of the little finger.   151

```
waist seize farms exits stirs shall silky doily quick whist     169
payer minor order hunts handy leash moron pearl match knock     187
```

17. CAPITALS. Get every letter squarely on the line of writing. Hold   202
the shift key down long enough—but not too long. In the last line,   216
capitalize each letter separately; do not use the shift lock.   228

```
aAa bBb cCc dDd eEe fFf gGg hHh iIi jJj kKk lLl mMm nNn oOo     246
pPp qQq rRr sSs tTt uUu vVv wWw xXx yYy zZz ;:; ,,, ... ;/?     265
Fran Dale Carl Stan Drew Bess Anne Cora Ruth Vick Alan Dora     283
Lyle Jinx Lisa Nora Linc Mina Jack Hall Nate Hank Jane Paul     301
A NEIGHBOR MAY WISH TO MAKE A VISIT TO THE CHAPELS WITH US.     319
```

18. TAB CONTROL. Clear any stops that may already be set and set   333
new ones 13, 28, 38, and 50 spaces from the left margin.   344

Leave 6 spaces between these "columns."

```
Abcdefg        Hijklmnop        Qrst        Uvwxyz        Alphabets    362
Toronto        Kitchener        Fogo        Munich        Fort York    380
Atlanta        Vancouver        Lima        London        Lone Pine    398
```

19. REPEAT UNDERSCORE. Use the same tab stops as in No. 18.   412
Avoid "running over" with the repeat underscore. You will need to   426
look at the paper as you do this practice with the repeat underscore.   440

```
Calgary        Penticton        Rome        Moscow        Baltimore    472
___            ____             ___         ____          _____      490
```

20. BACKSPACER AND SHIFT LOCK. Clear the tab stops from No. 19   503
and set a new stop at the center. Center each of these lines; if you do   518
so correctly, the letter E should align.   526

Leave 4 spaces between these groups of words.

```
Come One     Come ALL     To the Finest     Junior-Senior Ball    545
```

21. NEW KEYS. Type the drills appropriate for the key relocations   560
on your new machine.   564

Hermes Electric

Olympia Electric

28-E. Improve skill on special paragraph copy

20 With a whoop and a shout, the gang rushed to   10
the truck and piled in, just the way your dad and   20
I and our friends did a score of years back, when   30
each fall of snow would bring out the old sleigh.   40

1 | 2 | 3 | 4 | 5 | 6 | 7 | 8 | 9 | 10

21 It is said that we can see the soul of a man   10
in the books that he keeps in his own room, and I   20
think that this is so. They show what he dreams,   30
what he likes to think of, and where his mind is.   40

1 | 2 | 3 | 4 | 5 | 6 | 7 | 8 | 9 | 10

22 When I was a child, it was a grand old tree;   10
but it was hit by a bolt from the sky which split   20
it, and then the rain and snow and wind got in to   30
strip it down to the rough, old trunk we now see.   40

28-F. Make an interim progress check

29-A. Learn when NOT to divide words

1. Don't divide if you can get within 3 strokes, plus or minus, of a desired margin without dividing.

2. Don't divide any word with fewer than 6 strokes (but a 5-letter word followed by a punctuation mark may be divided, such as *six- ty*, or *uni- fy*; or *mix- er!*).

3. Don't divide a word pronounced as one syllable, like *shipped*.

4. Don't divide a contraction, like *couldn't*, *shouldn't*, *mustn't*.

5. Don't divide an abbreviation, like UNESCO or U. S. N. R.

6. Don't divide a word unless you can leave at least a 2-letter syllable (and hyphen) on the upper line, e.g., around.

7. Don't divide a word unless you can carry at least 3 strokes (the third may be a punctuation mark) to the next line, e.g., teacher.

8. Don't divide a number unless it fills 10 or more spaces.

NOTE. These rules are for typists, not printers. Because their lines must end evenly, printers use a different set of word-division rules.

29-B. Improve skill on patterned word drills

23 rt rt short court inert forth port hurt fort dirt
24 ou ou could bough tough touch bout sour rout ours
25 af af chafe shaft after draft safe cafe deaf raft
26 in in train incur pains inner rain find gain inch

27 bb bb blabber rubber bubble babble abbot abbey bb
28 mm mm trimmed summer gummed dimmer rummy dummy mm
29 tt tt buttons kitten bottle gotten ditto petty tt
30 pp pp shopper happen pepper supper apple upper pp

IBM Selectric has a

printing head instead of
type bars and carriage.

Adler Electric

Facit Electric

1. How to release the carriage (or carrier) by hand so that you may reposition it; practice moving it back and forth. 14 25

2. How to know at what point the carriage (or carrier) is now set; move the carriage to 40, to 75, and so on, noting where the space scale, the print-point indicator, and so on, are located. 39 52 64

3. How to adjust the paper guide; set it to center your paper at 50 or 60 or some other point that is easy to find and remember. 78 91

4. How to set the margin stops; set them for a 60-space line. 105

5. How to adjust the spacing; set it for single spacing. 117

6. How to adjust the ribbon; set for the top, black, position. 131

STAGE TWO: THE NEW 141

Because the typewriter is electric, it has some parts you do not have on a manual. Locate and use these parts: 161 169

7. *The pressure regulator* adjusts the impact of the typebars on the paper; move it from lowest to highest, then back to midway. 193 205

8. *The carbon impression regulator* moves the cylinder back to provide room for thick carbon packs; adjust the regulator across its full range and then set it at its lowest (forward) position. 231 246 257

9. *The power switch* turns the motor on and off; turn it on. 277

10. *The space bar* may have two positions: a shallow one for normal spacing and a deep one for continuous spacing. Try both a heavy and a light stroke on your space bar—any difference? 296 310 320

11. *The carriage or carrier return* is an oversize key at the right side of the keyboard (if there is one on the left side, too, ignore it). It is controlled by the little finger of the right hand. This key, too, may have two positions: a shallow one for a single return, a deep one for repeated returns. Test yours. 347 362 376 390 396

12. Most electrics have some "repeat keys" that continue to repeat their function so long as you hold them depressed. Check your machine for a repeat space bar, a repeat carriage or carrier return, a repeat underscore, and a repeat backspace key. 411 425 439 447

13. Confirm whether your machine has relocated its apostrophe, quotation, underscore, cent, per, and asterisk keys. 460 471

STAGE THREE: BUILD CONTROL 482

The thing to avoid in becoming used to your electric machine is any effort to press for speed in the first hour of using it. Instead, type each of the following drill lines three or more times. 502 517 527

14. STROKING. Use short *tap* strokes, just miniatures of the firm strokes you use on a manual. Keep hands in home position, but *above*, not *on*, the home keys. Say "and" to yourself before each key stroke. 542 556 570

29-C. Target on your goal.

ACCURACY: Lines 31-32, three times; 33-34, twice.

SPEED: Lines 31-32, two times; 33-34, three times.

29-C. Improve skill on patterned sentence drills

31 I doubt that a train could gain one hour in four.
32 The staff quit after your craft was safe in port.
   1 | 2 | 3 | 4 | 5 | 6 | 7 | 8 | 9 | 10
33 Mr. Abbott has written that he is getting better.
34 The yellow bottle was crammed in a supply closet.

29-D. Improve skill on special paragraph copy

29-D. Use double spacing, a 50-space line, and a tab-5 indention. Make a complete copy of this material, trying to finish it within 4 or fewer minutes and with 4 or fewer errors. Proofread your copy and then repeat for either:

ACCURACY: Type straight through the copy twice.

SPEED: Type two copies of each paragraph.

SI 1.00—very easy

WORDS

35   The need for food, which the sea gives up to those who   12
have both the stout heart and the sheer strength it takes to   24
fight for it, has led to new thought of what is to be found   36
in the dark deeps.   40

36   Far down in the silt in the beds of the sea, there are big   53
fields of ore; and lakes of oil are trapped in the thick folds of   66
rock that crust the world and serve as the strong shell of our   79
globe.   80

37   And in the sea, too, are the things that the streams of the   93
earth have squeezed from the soil, gouged from their banks,   106
and dragged on for miles through hill and vale to sink at   117
last in the sea.   120
   1 | 2 | 3 | 4 | 5 | 6 | 7 | 8 | 9 | 10 | 11 | 12

29-E. Improve skill on preview words

29-E. Target on your goal.

ACCURACY: Line 38, three times; 39, twice.

SPEED: Line 38, twice; 39, three times.

38 streams indeed on great in start up reefs no seas
39 naught island field their then map own men got to

29-F. Measure your skill in sustained writing

29-F. To measure your skill achievement, type a copy, using a 50-space line and double spacing, and alertly listening for the bell.

GOAL: To complete these two alphabetic paragraphs in 5 minutes or less, with 4 or fewer errors. All Lines should end evenly.

SI 1.24—easy copy

WORDS

40   Men have long traveled the seas without much knowledge   12
of them. They made a few charts of the coastal bays and is-   24
lands, but they knew naught of currents and depths. Indeed,   36
one of the first to explore this field of science was the very   48
amazing Benjamin Franklin, who asked sailors a great many   60
questions and then put their answers on a map, to fashion the   72
first crude chart of the Gulf Stream.   80

41   In the years that followed this start, other inquirers have   93
mapped the sea streams. But ocean science as men now know   105
it got its start when the submarine came on the scene. Since   117
then, mapping currents and reefs and depths has led the   128
experts through a maze of research that is judged just as   140
urgent as what other men are doing up in the sky.   150
   1 | 2 | 3 | 4 | 5 | 6 | 7 | 8 | 9 | 10 | 11 | 12

LINE: 60
SPACING: SINGLE
DRILLS: THREE TIMES
GOAL: LEARN ABOUT
   ELECTRICS
STRESS: CONTINUITY

196-A. Each line three
times or a 1-minute
timed writing on it.
Repeat in Lesson 197.

196-A. Tune up on these easy review lines

1 A neighbor may wish to make a visit to the chapels with us.
2 Jack quietly moved up front and seized the big cask of wax.
3 The different log lengths were 10", 28", 39", 47", and 56".

   1 | 2 | 3 | 4 | 5 | 6 | 7 | 8 | 9 | 10 | 11 | 12

196-B. Adjust margins
for 65-space line; set
for tab-5 indention.
Allow 6-line top margin
and plan for 3-line
to 6-line bottom margin.

Read the copy and note
where you will need to
half-space. This is to
be arranged in space-
saver style, as you used
on pages 299 and 300.

If possible, start by
taking a 5-minute timing
on this page, then con-
tinue the manuscript.

SI, this page 1.62—difficult

196-B. Apply skill to sustained production

Training Bulletin 20: ELECTRIC TYPING   23

GENERAL PURPOSE   32

The purpose of this bulletin is to provide help and guidance for   51
manual typists who convert to the use of electric typewriters. As 65
in the rest of the business community, several of our machines   78
are already electric; we look forward to a complete transfer away 92
from the manual machine within a relatively short time.   102

GENERAL ORIENTATION   112

Several kinds of electric typewriters are manufactured in Canada 131
and the U.S.A. They are the IBM, Remington, Royal, Smith-Corona, 144
and the Olivetti-Underwood. Imported from Europe are the Adler,   157
the Facit, and the Olympia.   163

Two manufacturers produce machines with proportional spacing   176
(that is, the machines allow more space for wide letters and less space 191
for narrow letters); these machines are the IBM "Executive" model 204
and the Underwood "Raphael" model.   211

Illustrations: standard
American electrics, pages
4-5; "Selectric" and the
European, pages 302-303.

One manufacturer also produces a machine, the IBM "Selectric"   224
model, with no typebars and no carriage. It has a "printing head" the 239
size and shape of a golf ball that whirls and tilts to strike the paper. 253
The printing head is mounted in a carrier that spaces across the paper. 268
Except that one returns the carrier instead of a carriage, the machine 282
is operated like most other electrics.   290

The Smith-Corona electric is available in three sizes: the full-size 305
"400" model, a portable, and a mid-size "250" model.   316

When you receive your machine, orient yourself to it in three   329
stages: find the known; find the new; then build control.   341

STAGE ONE: THE KNOWN   351

All machines must have certain basic controls. Start on your new 371
machine by learning the controls for these operations: 382

   1 | 2 | 3 | 4 | 5 | 6 | 7 | 8 | 9 | 10 | 11 | 12 | 13 | 14

Manuscript 68

LONG MANUSCRIPT IN
SPACE-SAVER FORM
Paper: plain, full
Carbons: one, for
   you to retain
Line: 65
Style: page 299-300
Spacing: single with
   half-space blanks

Skill Drive

30-A. Type each line twice (extra drill on line 3?). Repeat in Lesson 31, too.

30-A. Tune up on these review lines

1 asdfghjkl; asdfghjkl; asdfghjkl; asdfghjkl; asdfg
2 jag ask new zip ray six cob vim led for his quite
3 Order 10 red, 28 tan, 39 blue, 47 gray, 56 white.

30-B. To define your goal for Lesson 30, type and proofread a copy of this letter (reset margins for a 40-space line).

(a) Your goal is NUMBERS if you mistype any of the numbers in the paragraph.

(b) If you made no number errors and had 4 or fewer other errors, your goal in Lesson 30 is SPEED.

(c) If you made no number errors and had 5 or more other errors, your goal in Lesson 30 is ACCURACY.

SI 1.19—easy (if you know your numbers!)

30-B. Measure and improve your keyboard control

                                       WORDS

4   Dear Mr. Keezer: 4

                                         5

5   It is a pleasure to hear from you after 13
    so long a time. I guess it was back in 21
    October, 1975, that you last wrote. 28

                                        29

6   Yes, the club still meets once a month; 37
    our next meeting will be on Friday, the 45
    24th. There will be about 17 or 18 who 53
    attend; it would be quite a happy event 61
    if you could join us. 66

                                        67

7   I shall be driving to this next meeting 75
    and would be more than pleased to drive 83
    by your office and pick you up at, say, 91
    5:30 or 5:45. Shall I do so? 97

                                        98

8   Cordially yours, 103

    1 | 2 | 3 | 4 | 5 | 6 | 7 | 8

30-C-D. To increase skill, type lines 9-20 twice each and repeat twice more whichever fits your goal—

NUMBERS: Lines 9-11.
ACCURACY: Lines 13-16.
SPEED: Lines 17-20.

NOTE: In lines 9-12, the words and numbers appear in pairs: each word and following number are typed with the same fingers and in the same sequence. Such drills, called "we-23 drills," are especially good for developing your number-typing fluency.

30-C. Improve skill on patterned number drills

9   we 23 you 697 two 529 rip 480 wore 2943 pipe 0803
10 it 85 yet 635 put 075 rut 475 pity 0856 wiry 2846
11 or 94 wet 235 our 974 eye 363 your 6974 type 5603
12 up 70 tie 583 pit 085 owe 923 tory 5946 pier 0834

30-D. Improve skill on patterned word drills

13 ef ef chief brief cleft grief chef deft left beef
14 ok ok choke broke stoke poker book took joke coke
15 ar ar arrow heart clear charm harm year mare tear
16 lu lu glued lurid blunt clues flue lurk blue plum

17 fi fi first field fined final firm fish fist five
18 je je jeans jelly jeers jewel jerk jest jeep jets
19 sh sh shall crash blush shave ship dash rush bush
20 oz oz dozed froze dozen ozone ooze doze doz. cozy

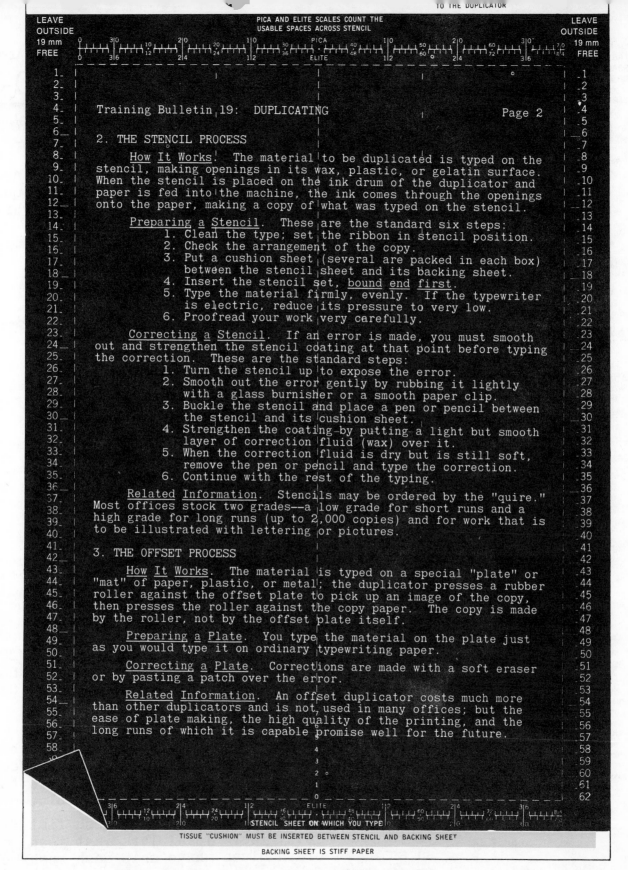

TO THE DUPLICATOR

PICA AND ELITE SCALES COUNT THE
USABLE SPACES ACROSS STENCIL

LEAVE
OUTSIDE
19 mm
FREE

LEAVE
OUTSIDE
19 mm
FREE

Training Bulletin 19: DUPLICATING   Page 2

2. THE STENCIL PROCESS

How It Works. The material to be duplicated is typed on the
stencil, making openings in its wax, plastic, or gelatin surface.
When the stencil is placed on the ink drum of the duplicator and
paper is fed into the machine, the ink comes through the openings
onto the paper, making a copy of what was typed on the stencil.

Preparing a Stencil. These are the standard six steps:
1. Clean the type; set the ribbon in stencil position.
2. Check the arrangement of the copy.
3. Put a cushion sheet (several are packed in each box)
   between the stencil sheet and its backing sheet.
4. Insert the stencil set, bound end first.
5. Type the material firmly, evenly. If the typewriter
   is electric, reduce its pressure to very low.
6. Proofread your work very carefully.

Correcting a Stencil. If an error is made, you must smooth
out and strengthen the stencil coating at that point before typing
the correction. These are the standard steps:
1. Turn the stencil up to expose the error.
2. Smooth out the error gently by rubbing it lightly
   with a glass burnisher or a smooth paper clip.
3. Buckle the stencil and place a pen or pencil between
   the stencil and its cushion sheet.
4. Strengthen the coating by putting a light but smooth
   layer of correction fluid (wax) over it.
5. When the correction fluid is dry but is still soft,
   remove the pen or pencil and type the correction.
6. Continue with the rest of the typing.

Related Information. Stencils may be ordered by the "quire."
Most offices stock two grades--a low grade for short runs and a
high grade for long runs (up to 2,000 copies) and for work that is
to be illustrated with lettering or pictures.

3. THE OFFSET PROCESS

How It Works. The material is typed on a special "plate" or
"mat" of paper, plastic, or metal; the duplicator presses a rubber
roller against the offset plate to pick up an image of the copy,
then presses the roller against the copy paper. The copy is made
by the roller, not by the offset plate itself.

Preparing a Plate. You type the material on the plate just
as you would type it on ordinary typewriting paper.

Correcting a Plate. Corrections are made with a soft eraser
or by pasting a patch over the error.

Related Information. An offset duplicator costs much more
than other duplicators and is not used in many offices; but the
ease of plate making, the high quality of the printing, and the
long runs of which it is capable promise well for the future.

STENCIL SHEET ON WHICH YOU TYPE

TISSUE "CUSHION" MUST BE INSERTED BETWEEN STENCIL AND BACKING SHEET

BACKING SHEET IS STIFF PAPER

Manuscript 67: Space-Saver Arrangement (Pica) on a Duplicating Stencil

30-E. Type each paragraph once; repeat twice more whichever paragraph fits your improvement goal—

NUMBERS: Paragraph 21.

ACCURACY: Paragraph 22.

SPEED: Paragraph 23.

SI 1.00—very easy (if you have touch control and can respond instantly to the sound of the margin bell.)

30-F. To confirm your goal for Lesson 30 and to set your goal for Lesson 31, retype the 30-B letter. Use the same guides (30-B) to define your goal for the practice in Lesson 31.

31-A. Besides studying the six rules here (continued from 29-A, page 51), use the Learning Guide (pages 29-30 in the workbook) to reinforce your knowledge of the word-division rules.

The only intricate rule is rule 13. As a suggestion, make it your own private rule never to "lop off" a -ble ending; either finish the word at the risk of an overlong line or divide it at some other point.

31-B-C. To increase skill, type lines 24-35 (see page 55, too) twice each. Then repeat twice more those lines that fit your goal—

ACCURACY: Lines 24-27.

SPEED: Lines 28-31.

NUMBERS: Lines 32-35.

30-E. Improve skill on special paragraph copy

WORDS

21   We won the game by a score of 32 to 28. The strange thing   13
is that we hoped to win by 15 or 16 points, and at times we   25
led by 10, by 9, and by 7 points; but we won the cup by just   37
4 thin points.   (All the numerals)   40

    1 | 2 | 3 | 4 | 5 | 6 | 7 | 8 | 9 | 10 | 11 | 12

22   When Mr. Bruce said we would have a quiz, we thought he   12
meant a brief one; but, sad to say, it turned out to have six   25
parts and took at least an hour to write. I got done just as   37
the bell rang.   (All the letters)   40

    1 | 2 | 3 | 4 | 5 | 6 | 7 | 8 | 9 | 10 | 11 | 12

23   If the two men are to get paid for their day off next week,   13
they will have to ask one of us to sign on their time slips to   26
show on the slip that the day off is one for which they are to   38
be paid.   (Common words)   40

30-F. Make an interim progress check

31-A. Learn how to divide words correctly

9. Divide only between whole syllables. If uncertain about syllabic structure, consult a dictionary. Examples: *prod- uct*, not *pro- duct* and *knowl- edge*, not *know- ledge*.

10. Divide near the middle of the word if there is an option. Thus: *pictur- esque*, not *pic- turesque*.

11. Divide after, not within, any prefix. (A prefix is a combination of letters put before a root word to change meaning; thus, in *foreman*, *fore-* is the prefix and *-man* is the root. Common prefixes include *anti-*, *ante-*, *be-*, *con-*, *de-*, *ex-*, *fore-*, *in-*, *intro-*, etc.) You may write *intro- duce*, but not *in- troduce*.

12. Divide before, not within, a suffix. (A suffix is a combination of letters put after a root word to change meaning; thus, in *leading*, the root is *lead-* and the suffix is *-ing*. Common suffixes include *-able*, *-fully*, *-ible*, *-icle*, *-ing*, *-sion*, *-tion*, *-tive*, etc.) You may write *wonder- fully*, but not *wonderful- ly*.

13. Divide after a one-letter syllable in the middle of a word *unless the syllable is part of a suffix*. Thus: *sepa- rate*, not *sep- arate*. But: *vis- ible*, not *visi- ble*.

14. When two strongly-accented vowels appear together, divide between them (even though the second may be a one-letter syllable). Thus: *radi- ator*, not *radia- tor*.

31-B. Improve skill on patterned word drills

24   be be below berth bench bells bent belt lobe tube
25   no no noble north known snort snow none know note
26   ag ag again stage pages brags slag flag agog rage
27   pu pu punch purge purse putty pure puts push punt

28   ic ic icing stick which quick rich nice pica tick
29   em em ember remit tempt lemon gems memo hems stem
30   os os those gloss hosts whose lost most post pose
31   wh wh while whale wheel white what when whim whip

ORIGINAL ON WHICH YOU TYPE

INSERT THIS OPEN END,
NOT THE BOUND END

Training Bulletin 19:   DUPLICATING ↓2½   11
                                                           17
GENERAL POLICY ↓1½   27

As recommended in most books on office procedure, it is our   40
policy to <u>duplicate copies by stencil when 200 or more are needed</u>   69
<u>or when the copies are to be sent outside our office</u> and to use   89
the spirit process on all other occasions. This office does not 102
have an offset duplicator (but it is discussed in this bulletin). ↓2   117
                                                                  118
1. THE SPIRIT PROCESS ↓1½   127

<u>How It Works</u>. A "master" is made on a sheet of coated paper   145
against which is placed a sheet of special carbon (it contains a 158
reproducing dye). The coated paper and carbon sheet are fastened 171
at the bottom and called a "master set." Typing on the master   184
set creates a carbon copy on the reverse side of the master.   196
When the master is put on the duplicator, the machine dampens   210
the copy paper with a chemical fluid, which is the "spirit," then 223
presses the damp paper against the dye on the back of the master. 236
Some of the dye transfers to the paper, making a copy on it. ↓1½ 254

<u>Preparing the Master</u>. Six steps are involved. They are: 279
    1. Clean the typewriter type.   287
    2. Check the arrangement of the material.   297
    3. Remove the protective packing sheet from the set.   310
    4. Insert the master set, <u>open end first</u>.   326
    5. Type the material firmly, evenly. If the typewriter   340
       is electric, reduce its pressure to very low.   352
    6. Proofread your typing with great care.   362

<u>Correcting a Master</u>. Making a correction is just a matter of 387
removing the carbon of the error and replacing it with the carbon 400
of the correction, a process that can be executed in many ways.   413
    To correct a simple typing error: 421
    1. Roll the paper up and bend the master back to expose   434
       the carbon of the error.   442
    2. Using a knife or dull razor, lightly scrape off the   455
       carbon containing the error.   464
    3. Place a slip of unused carbon (cut from a top corner)   477
       at the point where the correction is to be typed.   490
    4. Roll the paper back to typing position and type the   503
       correction. It appears on the front as a strikeover.   517
    5. Remove the carbon slip; then continue typing.   529

<u>Related Information</u>. Reproducing carbon is available in red, 554
green, blue, black, and purple colors. Of these, only the purple 567
serves for long runs (up to 200) of vivid copies, which explains 580
why most spirit copies one sees are purple. The other colors are 593
used for illustrating, ruling, and other special art effects.   606
When writing, drawing, or tracing on a master, use a ball pen   619
with a very fine tip or a hard, sharp pencil.   627

PERFORATION PERMITS YOU TO DETACH CARBON EASILY
WHEN READY TO PUT THE MASTER ON THE DUPLICATOR

Manuscript 66: Space-Saver Arrangement (Pica) on a Spirit Duplicating Master

31-C. See the directions on the preceding page.

31-C. Improve skill on patterned number sentences

32 The sum of 10 and 28 and 39 and 47 and 56 is 180.
33 I need 10 of Blue 28, 39 of White 47, and 56 Red.
34 Add up 10 and 28 and 39 and 47 and 56 to get 180.
35 Ship it May 10 to 2938 West 47 Street, Newark 56.

1 | 2 | 3 | 4 | 5 | 6 | 7 | 8 | 9 | 10

31-D. Improve skill on special paragraph copy

31-D. For more practice in responding to the bell and making correct line-ending decisions without taking your eyes off the copy, type a double-spaced copy of each paragraph (use a 50-space line and a tab-5 indention). Then repeat twice more the paragraph that targets your goal—

SPEED: Paragraph 36.
ACCURACY: Paragraph 38.
NUMBERS: Paragraph 38.

SI 1.07—very easy

Update SI: Leave a full space between a number and a symbol. Type the symbols in lower case.

See: Typing Style Guide for SI and Metric Symbols, p. 117.

WORDS

36 The wheel is a great help to man, and he who thought of it   13
in the first place should have deep thanks from all of us. But   26
it now looks a bit as though the end of the wheel may well   37
be in sight.   (SI 1.00)   40

37 Come to take the place of a wheel is what is called an air   53
cushion. You get in your car. You switch on a fan, and it   65
pushes air under the car; the car lifts up, and now you are   77
off the ground.   (SI 1.09)   80

38 You turn on the next jet, and air shoves you forward. Off   93
you go, getting up to a speed of 112 km/h in a minute or so   105
and whizzing with equal ease over road or field or marsh   118
or stream.   (SI 1.14)   120

1 | 2 | 3 | 4 | 5 | 6 | 7 | 8 | 9 | 10 | 11 | 12

31-E. Improve skill on preview words

31-E. Target on your goal.

ACCURACY: Lines 39-40, three times; 41-42, twice.

SPEED: Lines 39-40, two times; 41-42, three times.

39 adjustable hydrofoils stabilize waterbug exciting
40 faster waters jump bear look fast hull test 70 80
41 world giant shape work lake when rush down air go
42 one is use of and to on and on to our as it in an

31-F. Measure your skill in sustained writing

31-F. To measure your skill achievement, type a copy, using a 50-space line and double spacing and alertly listening for the bell.

GOAL: To complete these two alphabetic paragraphs in 5 minutes or less, with 4 or fewer errors. Lines should end evenly, without need for dividing words.

SI 1.24—easy

WORDS

43 A new kind of work boat has come to our lake and coastal   12
waters. It looks like any small boat when it glides along slowly   26
and lazily. But when it jumps up its speed in quiet water,   38
it rises on stilts to skim above the water, for all the world   50
like a giant waterbug, except that this one roars as it scoots on   63
and on at 112 to 128 km/h.   68

44 This new boat required two special points of design. One   81
is the use of adjustable fins, known as hydrofoils, to lift and to   94
stabilize the boat. The other is the shape of the hull, which is   107
made to trap air under it in an air cushion that lifts the boat   120
so that it can go faster and bear bigger loads while taking less   133
water. This is exciting, for the boat is seen as a kind of truck   146
that will rush heavy loads up and down even shallow rivers.   158

1 | 2 | 3 | 4 | 5 | 6 | 7 | 8 | 9 | 10 | 11 | 12

Unit 32. Manuscripts

194-A. Tune up on these easy review lines

194-A. Each line three times or a 1-minute timed writing on it. Repeat in Lesson 195.

1   When they got to the lake, the men paid for the oak panels.
2   Joe quietly picked six razor blades from the old woven bag.
3   Did he move from 1028 39th Street or from 4756 39th Street?
    1 | 2 | 3 | 4 | 5 | 6 | 7 | 8 | 9 | 10 | 11 | 12

194-B. Learn to half-space vertically

194-B. See whether you can produce this:

$\frac{1}{2}$ 1 $1\frac{1}{2}$

mmm	mmm	mmm
mmm		
mmm	mmm	mmm
mmm		
mmm	mmm	mmm
mmm		
mmm	mmm	mmm

To delete half a line of space: [1] press the variable spacer (button in left cylinder knob) as you [2] turn down the paper *half a line* (until the tops of the short letters disappear under the aligning scale); then [3] release the variable spacer and [4] return the carriage as usual.

194-C. Sustain skill on manuscript production copy

194-C. Confirm machine settings: 60-space line, tab-5; change to double spacing. Lines align.

Type two copies (one in Lesson 194, one in 195) or take two 5-minute writings, the first with 10-second rests after each minute, the second solidly, without rests.

SI 1.27—fairly easy

4   When a report must be duplicated so that copies may be given to   14
many persons or departments, the typist must study its length so he   27
can decide how many "space savers" to use.   36
     There are dozens of ways to save space. You might use single   50
spacing. You might use run-in headings instead of a style that calls   64
for headings on separate lines. You might leave only one blank line   77
where you would otherwise provide two, and only half a blank line, or   91
perhaps none at all, at points where you would usually leave one.   105
Paragraphs could be indented less than five spaces, and the margins   119
could be cut a half inch to get more, and longer, lines on the page.   132
     Why bother? Well, a great deal more than space itself is saved. The   147
report will take fewer stencils, less paper, and less time for running   161
and collating the copies; postage will be less for the mailed copies;   175
less file space will be used in the files of all concerned. A great deal is   191
saved! It will be saved, that is, if the typist saves a whole page and not   206
just a fraction of a page; cutting a report of five pages to four and a   220
half does not save much paper, does it?   228
    1 | 2 | 3 | 4 | 5 | 6 | 7 | 8 | 9 | 10 | 11 | 12 | 13 | 14

Manuscript 65

EXPERIMENTATION
Paper: 2, plain
Line: 60
Copies: 2
Copy 1: 1½ spacing
Copy 2: 2½ spacing
Title: Space Savers
By-Line: yours

194/195-D. Apply skill to manuscript production

After typing the two forms of Manuscript 65 to master the technique of half-spacing, type Manuscripts 66 and 67 in the space-saver form shown, *using a 65-stroke line*. If possible, type Manuscript 66 on a spirit master and Manuscript 67 on a stencil, using the techniques they describe.

Unit 6. Correspondence

LINE: 50
TAB: CENTER
SPACING: SINGLE
DRILLS: TWICE OR MORE
GOAL: START LETTER
    PRODUCTION
STRESS: ALERTNESS TO
    DETAILS

32-A. Tune up on these review lines

32-A. Type each line twice. Hold on lines 2 and 3 the pace you set on line 1. Repeat in Lesson 33.

1   The new man did not get pay for the day he had off.

2   g H i J k L m N o P q R s T u V w X y Z a B c D e F

3   10 28 39 47 56 we 23 or 94 tip 580 you 697 rue 473.

32-B. Learn how to "pivot"

32-B. Pivoting is an important technique you will use in positioning the date line of letters, as a glance at pages 57 and 58 will show you.

To pivot a line (make it *end* at a preselected point):

STEP 1. Set the carriage at the first space *after* that point.

STEP 2. Backspace once for each space the typed line will occupy.

STEP 3. Type the line; the final stroke will be in the desired space.

In timed writings, each stroke of pivoted copy counts as 3 strokes.

PRACTICE. Pivot these lines so that each ends at 70 on the scale.

Richard Montrose   Use your name;
Period 4   class period;
October 16, 197-   today's date.

32-C. Learn three symbol keys you will need today

32-C. NEW KEYS.

Parentheses are the shift of the 9 and 0 keys, controlled respectively by the L- and Sem-fingers.

Ampersand (&), meaning "and," is the shift of the 7 key, controlled by the J-finger. Type lines 4-9 two times each.

4   191 1(1 191 1(1 and ;0; ;); ;0; ;); (1) (10) (11)

5   The captain (John, that is) caught the long pass.

6   Bob is (1) tall, (2) dark, and (3) very handsome.

7   They need (a) six invoices and (b) six envelopes.

8   j7j j&j j7j j&j Jones & Sons buy from Brown & Co.

9   Write to Dodd & Co., Hess & Park, and Wold & Son.

32-D. Build skill for production power

32-D. Type the letter once, trying to finish it within 3 minutes, with 4 or fewer errors; or take a 3-minute writing on it to see whether you can hold on this production copy the best pace you developed in Unit 5.

The letter is shown in elite type (12 spaces to an inch), so you may contrast it with the pica type (10 spaces to an inch) in the drill lines above it.

SI 1.31—fairly easy

10 Dear Mr. Jones: 3
                                                            4
    It was a real pleasure to receive your order this   14
    morning, for it has been too long (six months, at   24
    least) since we have had one from Jones & Frazer.   34
                                                            35
    The goods that you requested are in stock and are   45
    scheduled to be delivered to you (we have our own   55
    truck now) in the morning or at noon, October 23.   65
                                                            66
    Thanks again, Mr. Jones, for your order. We hope   76
    that it will mark the renewal of frequent service   86
    to our old friends and customers, Jones & Frazer.   96
                                                            97
                    Yours truly,   100

    1 | 2 | 3 | 4 | 5 | 6 | 7 | 8 | 9 | 10

```
          IMPORTANT EMPLOYMENT ANNIVERSARIES
                  Week of February 16

      Employee          Department       Date        Year

                        Toronto Branch
   Mr. Ulysses Hunter    Warehouse      February 16   10th
   Mr. Norton McCall     Mail Sales     February 20   15th
   Miss Georgia Tyrone   Accounting     February 18   10th
   Miss Helen T. Ki      Advertising    February 19   10th

                        Halifax Branch
   Mr. Stephen Kloss     Jewelry        February 17   10th
   Miss Margaret Carte   Personnel      February 20   10th
```

Horizontal rules are used to subdivide a ruled table.

Table 67	Paper: plain, full
	Carbons: file and 3
ABSTRACTED TABLE	Special: clip table draft
	to typewritten table

Mr. Hildreth says, "Each week our computer tells us which employees will be observing their tenth and fifteenth anniversaries the following week. Here is the report for the week of the fourteenth."

```
ANNIVS 10 & 15 WEEK 14TH 20TH INCL

ARTMAN JOAN — TOR — PERSNL — 14TH — 15
DODDS ALICE — CAL — ACCTG — 17TH — 10
EASTMAN HAROLD — HAL — WAREHS — 15TH — 10
FRENCH BENJ F — TOR — BLDG — 16TH — 10
JORDAN WM — HAL — EXEC — 18TH — 15
JUSTIN FAITH — TOR — DRUGS — 19TH — 10
MANN BITHA W — HAL — JEWELRY — 16TH — 15
MASSEY EDNA L — CAL — RETAIL — 16TH — 10
STRUTH O D — HAL — ADVER — 20TH — 10
TOLBER RICHARD — CAL — WAREHS — 19TH — 15
```

Computer data is usually highly abbreviated.

"You notice," he continues, "that it includes the employee's name, the branch and department where he works, the date of the anniversary, and whether the anniversary is the tenth or fifteenth. Please make three copies of the data, typed in proper, *un-abbreviated* form, *and subdivided by branches*, for us to send to our branch managers."

Letter 100	Paper: plain, full
	Carbons: file and 3
DICTATED MEMO	Enclosure: Table 62

"Now please prepare the following memo for our Director of Personnel, Mr. Dixon, to send to *Branch Managers*. Use my initials in the reference line."

Subject…employment anniversaries…week of june 14…we are pleased to send you on the enclosed page the usual data about employee anniversaries for next week…the list is shorter this year…i believe…than it was a year ago and a great deal shorter than the last two or three lists we sent to you…you will wish to note that personnel bulletin no. 17-J concerning proper observance of anniversaries becomes effective with this group of celebrants… russell p dixon.

Table 68	Paper: plain, full
Letter 101	Carbons: file only
MEMO CONTAINING AN ABSTRACTED TABLE	

"Our next task," says Mr. Hildreth, "is to send this same information to the editor of the *News Bulletin*, our employees' paper. So take a memo, please:"

i am pleased to provide you with the data about the employees whose tenth and fifteenth anniversaries will be observed next week…

Insert the table, please, but arrange it with the Fifteenth Year people first, followed by the Tenth Year people.

there are two newsworthy aspects in this release above and beyond the usual credit and honor to the employees named…first…the fifteen-year people are the first to benefit by the new policy of awarding an extra week's vacation to these employees…and secondly…bill jordan …i mean william jordan…assistant manager of the halifax office…whose fifteenth anniversary is to be observed…was a war hero who received the victoria cross in world war ii…the human-interest side of that honor might enable you to build quite a story in connection with his fifteen years with the company.

"Is this memorandum from you or from Mr. Dixon?" you ask. "From me," he replies, "in my role of Personnel Statistician."

32-E. Learn to identify the basic parts of a business letter

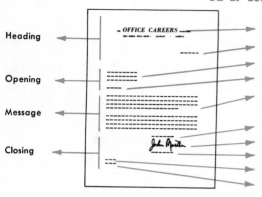

Heading

Opening

Message

Closing

Letterhead . . . printed name and address of the company.

*Date line . . . month, day, and year the letter is written.

Inside address . . . address of the party to whom you are writing.

Salutation . . . opening greeting, such as "Dear Ms. Smith."

Body . . . text of the letter, usually single spaced, with 1 blank line between the paragraphs.

Complimentary closing . . . closing farewell, such as "Yours truly."

Signature . . . handwritten signature of the writer.

Writer's identification . . . the typed name, or title, or both.

Reference symbols . . . initials of dictator and/or typist.

Enclosure reminder . . . used if something accompanies letter.

*Numeric Dating (see p. 200) — year, month, day.

32-F. Learn the steps in producing a business letter

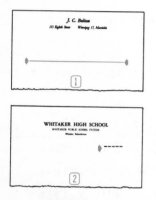

STEP 1. Insert paper. Estimate number of words in *body* of letter and set appropriate margins:

WORDS			LENGTH OF WRITING LINE STROKES
Under	**100**	**(short)**	.... **40 pica, 50 elite**
100 -	**200**	**(average)**	.... **50 pica, 60 elite**
Above	**200**	**(long)**	.... **60 pica, 70 elite**

STEP 2. Type *today's date* on line 15. Estimate position, or pivot, so date will end at margin.

STEP 3. Drop down 5 lines and type the inside address; continue through the letter, leaving 1 blank line before the salutation, each paragraph, and the complimentary closing. After typing the compli-

mentary closing, *pause to judge the placement.* If the letter appears to be well placed (bottom margin will be a little wider than the side margins), finish it: drop 4 lines and type the signer's identification; then drop 2 more lines and type the reference initials. BUT:

STEP 4A. If the letter is *high,* spread the closing lines: allow extra space for the signature (up to 6 blank lines) and before typing the initials (up to 4 blank lines). OR:

STEP 4B. If the letter is *low,* condense the closing lines: allow less signature space (as few as 2 blank lines) and, if necessary, raise the initials (may be level with the identification line).

32/33-G. Practice the production of business letters

GOAL: To finish each letter, pages 58-59, within 4 errors and 5 minutes from the time the paper is at the date line and the carriage is at the margin, ready for you to backspace-pivot the date. Use workbook letterheads or plain paper on which you crease a

line 9 lines from the top to represent a letterhead's depth. Note whether each letter is shown in the type size you have on your machine; if the size is different, you must set margins correctly and listen carefully for the warning bell.

LINE: 60
TAB: 5
SPACING: SINGLE
DRILLS: THREE TIMES
GOAL: HANDLE TABLES
LIKE A SECRETARY
STRESS: SUSTAINED
PRODUCTION

192-A. Type lines 2-3 in cadence with someone who sets a good but steady pace on line 1. Repeat in Lesson 193.

192-B. Adjust machine for double spacing; confirm 60-space line (lines are aligned) and the tab-5.

Read each paragraph very closely, looking for any words that you remember have been troublesome; practice these words by typing a line of each. Then type each paragraph until you have produced a copy with 1 or 0 errors.

SI 1.32—fluently easy

Alternate plan: Take two 5-minute writings, the first with a rest after each minute, the second with no rest whatsoever.

NOTE: The solution here is the one you will use in Lessons 192 and 193.

192-A. Tune up on these review lines

1 Why did the man say the box was for him and was not for me?
2 Five or six big jet planes zoomed quickly by the new tower.
3 He gave us 10% plus 28% for 39%. He gave them 47% for 56%.
   1 | 2 | 3 | 4 | 5 | 6 | 7 | 8 | 9 | 10 | 11 | 12

192-B. Regain full stride on easy alphabetic paragraphs

4 There is an old, old saying to the general effect that 12
there is more than one way to skin a cat. It is difficult, 24
indeed, to imagine any kind of work where the adage applies 36
more truly than in typewriting. Think, for example, of the 48
many ways to set up a letter. Think of tables; you can fix 60
them up with rules or without rules. Think of reports; you 72
can type them with wide margins or thin ones, equal ones or 84
odd sizes. Just think of all the options that you can use! 96
   1 | 2 | 3 | 4 | 5 | 6 | 7 | 8 | 9 | 10 | 11 | 12

5 Now, some typists lament the options. They wish there 108
were just one way to do each different thing, not realizing 120
that each option was invented to solve some unique problem; 132
thus, knowing the options gives you a kit of ways to settle 144
most problems. For example, suppose you have a letter with 156
a table in it; and suppose further that it is a very wicked 168
table—too wide to stay within the letter margins, perhaps; 180
or so long it spoils the letter placement. What do you do? 192
   1 | 2 | 3 | 4 | 5 | 6 | 7 | 8 | 9 | 10 | 11 | 12

6 The obvious thing to do, of course, is to lift out the 204
table and type it on a separate sheet as an enclosure; then 216
you say "on the enclosed table" or something like that when 228
you come to the spot where the table should be. Or, if you 240
wish, you can squeeze the columns together, putting four or 252
two spaces between them instead of six. And you can always 264
inject a subtitle that might save space, too, or change the 276
phrasing of your column headings. Yes, options are useful! 288

192/193-C. Apply skill to secretarial production

BLOCKED LETTER STYLE

Some Persons Call This the "Modified Block Style"

Letter 1

BLOCKED LETTER
Shown: in pica
Body: 90 words
Line: 40
Tab: center
Date: today's,
  on line 15
Paper: letterhead
SI: 1.31—fairly
  easy

UPDATE:
Use numeric dating 19—
10 15 Year (space) month
(space) day. See p. 200
for more about numeric
dating and for a copy of
the simple chart to help
you adjust the production
count for numeric dating.

UPDATE:
See pp. 90, 93, and 100
about Canadian postal
codes.

Standard
punctuation:
colon after
salutation,
comma after
closing line.

If the dictator's name is
typed under his signature,
type only your initials
(instead of URS). If his
name is not typed, type
his initials, a colon, and
your initials as shown here.

October 15, 19--▼ 5

Mr. Alexander F. Jones
Jones & Frazer Company
Government Road West
Kirkland Lake, Ontario
P2N 2C9

Dear Mr. Jones:

When we talked at the Kiwanis meeting last
Tuesday, I promised to send you a letter
in blocked form. Well, sir, here it is.

All lines begin at the left margin except
the date (it is typed at the right margin)
and the principal closing lines (they are
begun at the center). The typist usually
sets a tab stop at the center to use when
he/she positions the closing lines.

If there is anything else that you would
like me to explain, I should be pleased
to try to do so.

                    Cordially yours,▼ 4 or 5

                    Training Director

HIS:URS

12
13
14
15
16
21
25
30
34
35
36
39
40
49
59
66
67
75
84
92
100
109
115
116
125
133
136
137
142
143
144
145
149
150
151

If you take a timed writing on
production copy and end with an
incomplete line, count 1 word
credit for each 5 strokes and
for each use of the tabulator
in that final incomplete line.

Business Letter in Blocked Style

Table 12

WHERE OUR EMPLOYEES WENT FOR VACATIONS
AND WHAT THEY SPENT EACH DAY AWAY

(Summer, 19—)

Place	Percent Employees	Daily Expense
Metropolitan city	38%	$14.00
Seaside resort	32%	19.00
Mountain resort	23%	11.50
Motor trip	20%	14.00
Lake resort	9%	12.50
Miscellaneous	18%*	11.75
AVERAGES	23%	$13.80

* That is, 18 percent of employees collec-
tively had other kinds of vacations.

Summary of Guides for Arranging a Ruled Table

25. Department D has 19 often, 10 sometimes, 4 never, to total 33. Department E has 13 often, 9 sometimes, 3 never, for a total of 25. Department F has 20 often, 4 sometimes, and 10 never, to total 34. The column totals are 98 often, 70 sometimes, 34 never, and 200 as the final total.

Table 65
DICTATED TABLE

Paper: plain, full
Carbons: file, draft
Special: clip the written
table to the typed one

Table 2 is entitled, in two lines, *Do Our Supervisors Recommend That a Coffee Break Be Authorized?* Again, five columns, to be headed *Dept., Yes, Indifferent, No, Total.* Department A scores 2 - 1 - 1 - 4. Department B scores 4 - 1 - 0 - 5. Department C scores 4 - 0 - 0 - 4. Department D scores 3 - 0 - 0 - 3. Department E, 3 - 0 - 1 - 4. Department F scores 3 - 1 - 1 - 5. The bottom totals are 19 yes, 3 indifferent, 3 no, for a grand total of 25.

Table 66
DICTATED TABLE

Paper: plain, full
Carbons: file, draft
Special: clip the written
table to the typed one

Table 3 is entitled, in two lines, *What 382 Large Firms Have Found Upon Introducing Coffee Breaks, Serviced by a Caterer.* There are four columns; head them *Question, Yes, Perhaps,* and *No.* The question *Has it been popular?* scored 95% yes, 3% perhaps, 2% no. The question *Has it improved morale?* got 80% yes, 15% perhaps, 5% no. The question *Has it reduced tardiness?* got 72% yes, 18% perhaps, 10% no. The question *Has it saved time?* got 60% yes, 30% perhaps, 10% no. The question *Has it been convenient?* got 60% yes, 25% perhaps, 15% no. The question *Has it been inexpensive?* got 50% yes, 0% perhaps, 50% no. The question *Has it reduced absenteeism?* got 40% yes, 36% perhaps, 24% no. Question *Would you recommend it?* got 80% yes, 12% perhaps, 8% no. There are no total figures at the bottom.

October 16, 19—— ▼ 5   12
                              16
Mr. Paul J. Thorne   20
Thorne & Clark, Ltd.   24
596 Nottingham Avenue   28
Winnipeg, Manitoba *M13*   32
R2K 2C5   33
                              34
Dear Mr. Thorne: 37
                              38
Mr. Wilcox and I are glad to approve the layouts   48
and the artwork for the two ads. We believe you   58
have done a fine job.   62
                              63
We shall need to check the wording of the copy very   74
closely, of course. (Ever since that trouble last   84
year, we have been very wary about using the super-   94
lative degree.)   97
                              98
I should like to have a conference with you about   108
the ads next Monday. Will you plan to be here at   118
noon and have lunch with me? This would save time 129
for both of us.   132
                              133
                  Sincerely yours, ▼ 4 or 5   137
                              140
                  Benjamin I. Foster   145
                  Sales Manager   149
                              150
URS   151

3 Inch line   *Full open*

block 2-point

Current date ▼ ? | Miss Lee Anne Smith | Apartment   23
14-C | 1206 158 Street | Edmonton, Alberta | T5R 2B3   35
Dear Ms. Smith: 39

We were pleased to receive the letter in which you asked   50
whether we might have any vacancy for which you could apply. 63

In about two weeks, we shall have open a position for an ac- 75
countant who would do tax work and cost breakdowns. Would   87
you be able to do the work of this position?   96

If you would like us to consider you for this fine opening,   109
please call Miss Wells (my assistant); she will arrange for your 122
interview and a review of your credentials. | Very cordially   139
yours, ▼ ? | Frank L. Tressler | Director of Personnel | *Initials*   152

semi-block closed

Current date ▼ ? | [Type the letter in 32-D, page 56, using the inside address and closing lines that appear on page 58. The total production word count is 145 words.]

Table 60
ORIGINAL TABLE

Paper: plain, full
Carbons: file, draft
Special: make new tally,
 type it as a table,
 clip tally to table

Mr. Hildreth says, "Here's the first of three reports to prepare for Mr. Dixon. This one reports the *monthly* employment record of *each branch*. I made a tally—" He shows you this tally:

NUMBER OF NEW EMPLOYEES
(By Month and Branch)
January 1 Through May 30

Month	Tor	Hal	Cal	Total
Jan	III	II	II	7
Feb	III	III	I	7
Mar	IIII III	I	I	10
Apr	I	II	IIII	8
May	III	II	II	8
Total	19 ⊗	11 ⊗	10	40

"—but it is incorrect; Toronto, I know, should be 18, not 19. Please do it over and type it."

"No memo?" you ask.

"No," he replies. "Center the table on a page."

Table 61
ORIGINAL TABLE

Paper: plain, full
Carbons: file, draft
Special: make tally, type it,
 clip tally to the table

"The next job is easier but requires your making another tally," says Mr. Hildreth. "Mr. Dixon wants the score on the respective numbers of men and women employed by each branch. You'll have four columns: *Branch, Men, Women,* and *Total*."

You ask, "Center it on the page?" Yes. The tally sheet you draft shapes up like this:

NUMBER OF NEW EMPLOYEES
(By Branch and Sex)
January 1 Through May 30

Branch	Men	Women	Total
Tor			
Hal			
Cal			
Total			

Table 62
ORIGINAL TABLE

Paper: plain, full
Carbons: file, draft
Special: work on draft
 of Table 56; attach
 it to Table 57

"Next," says Mr. Hildreth, "type again that same table [Table 56], but convert it to percents. For example, the Toronto tally is 12 - 6. In percentages, that would be 66.7% and 33.3%. You won't need a totals *column*, of course, although you *will* need a totals line at the bottom."

Table 63
ORIGINAL TABLE

Paper: plain, full
Carbons: file, draft
Special: make the tally,
 type it, attach tally
 to the typed table

"Now, for the last table in this series," says Mr. Hildreth, "prepare for Mr. Dixon an analysis by *departments* and *branches*. You will have five columns: *Department, Toronto, Halifax, Calgary,* and *Total*. You'll have to tally the scores.

You say, "Let's see: The title will be *Number of New Employees* with two subtitles, (*By Departments and Branches*) and *January 1 Through May 30*. Right?"

"Right."

Table 64
DICTATED TABLE

Paper: plain, full
Carbons: file, draft
Special: clip your written
 table to the one you type

As you finish Table 58, Mr. Hildreth says, "Now we are starting a new project, an investigation I have been making for Mr. Dixon. My report consists of three tables; you'll find them interesting."

He gives you the table shown at the top of the next page. "This is the *form* I wish you to use," he says. "Ruled. Double spaced. Columns a half inch [six spaces] apart. One of the three titles will go on a single line, but the other two will take two lines, as shown in this sample table."

You make a note to study the sample table *very* closely; you are *not* to type *it*. Mr. Hildreth begins to dictate the first table:

Table 1 is entitled *Do Our Employees Take a Coffee Break?* It has five columns, to be headed *Dept., Often, Sometimes, Never,* and *Total*. Department A has 12 often, 18 sometimes, 3 never, to total 33. Department B has 18 often, 21 sometimes, 11 never, to total 50. Department C has 16 often, 6 sometimes, 3 never, to total

LINE: 50
TAB: CENTER
SPACING: SINGLE
DRILLS: TWICE OR MORE
GOAL: LEARN ', ", AND !
STRESS: EVEN TYPE
IMPRESSIONS.

34-A. Type each line twice.
In line 2, keep capitals
on the line. In line 3,
speed up slowly! Repeat
these lines in Lesson 35.

34-B. Type each line twice.

Manual   Electric

MANUAL: Apostrophe is the
shift of 8 key. Quotation
mark is shift of 2 key.
Omit lines 4E and 7E.

ELECTRIC: Apostrophe is
the key beside Sem key,
controlled by Sem-finger.
Quotation mark is shift of
the Apostrophe key. Omit
drill lines 4M and 7M.

NOTE: Exclamation point in
line 4 is typed this way:
(1) Period.
(2) Backspace.
(3) Apostrophe.

34-C. Reinforce your study
of the rules by doing the
Learning Guide exercises
on workbook pages 45-46.

34-D. Set margins for a
55-space line, so that you
can copy line for line.

Type the letter once; try
to finish it in 3 minutes,
with 4 or fewer errors.

OR, take a 3-minute timing
to see if you can type the
letter at a record rate.

Hold a steady pace when
you type the apostrophes,
the quotation marks, and
the parentheses. Can you?

SI 1.37—normal

34-A. Tune up on these review lines

1 Why did the new man get no pay for his one day off?

2 j K l M n O p Q r S t U v W x Y z A b C d E f G h I

3 we (23) up (70) to (59) or (94) it (85) your (6974)

34-B. Practice two symbol keys you will need today

4M k8k k'k k8k k'k It's John's job to get Dad's car.

4E ;'; ''' ;'; ''' It's John's job to get Dad's car.

5 We can't find Johnny's cap. Help us look for it!

6 A dog's bark isn't as bad as his growl, I'm told.

7M s2s s"s s2s s"s "Well," he said. "Hello, again."

7E ;'; ;"; ;'; ;"; "Well," he said. "Hello, again."

8 Joe "hurried"; so did I. He "mewed": "Who, me?"

9 I called, "Help!" Did he "beg"? How he "cried"!

34-C. Learn about quotation mark sequences

Rules to remember about punctuation sequences at the end of a quotation:

1. A quotation mark is typed *after* a comma or period, but *before* a colon or a semicolon. *Always.*

2. A quotation mark is typed *after* a question mark or exclamation mark *if the quotation asks a question or makes an exclamation;* otherwise, the quotation mark is typed *before* the question mark or exclamation mark.

Find an example of each possible punctuation sequence in lines 7, 8, and 9 above.

34-D. Build skill on production power practice

10 Dear Mr. Wood: 3
                                                         4
I should like to authorize you to sublet the apartment 15
for the months of December and January. I shall leave 26
here on the last day of November, and I expect to move 37
back in on or about the first of February.   46
                                                         47
To protect all the "belongings," I request that a bond 58
be posted (but I'm sure you'll have no trouble on this 69
score, Mr. Wood).   72
                                                         73
Please feel free to bring people to see the apartment, 84
Mr. Wood, any time you have someone who wishes to look 95
at it; I don't need to be there, you know!   104

  1 | 2 | 3 | 4 | 5 | 6 | 7 | 8 | 9 | 10 | 11

LINE: 60, THEN 70
SPACING: SINGLE
DRILLS: THREE TIMES
GOAL: EDIT TABLES
 LIKE A SECRETARY
STRESS: PLANNING
 BEFORE TYPING

190-A. Type lines 2-3 in cadence with someone who sets a good pace on easy line 1, if you can. Repeat in Lesson 191.

190-A. Tune up on these review lines

1 Joe and Bob did not get the day off but got the pay for it.

2 Jane gave my excited boy quite a prize for his clever work.

3 He asked for 47% and 56% but instead got 10%, 28%, and 39%.

    1 | 2 | 3 | 4 | 5 | 6 | 7 | 8 | 9 | 10 | 11 | 12

190-B. Type to your need.

ACCURACY: Type lines 4-6 four times as a paragraph and then lines 7-9 two times as a paragraph.

SPEED: Type each line three consecutive times.

190-B. Improve skill by selective preview practice

4 parentheses horizontal designing feasible titles nouns data

5 expedients, mentioning subtitles majority reader "all" kept

6 indifferent frequently adjective vertical column equal trim

    1 | 2 | 3 | 4 | 5 | 6 | 7 | 8 | 9 | 10 | 11 | 12

7 came from used most both the one more but not has to an aid

8 date line trim down they are the size aid for are in or the

9 also used they must line for and your use the out of to any

190-C. Adjust machine for double spacing, 70-space line (lines will align), and tab-5 indention.

In Lesson 190, type the first paragraph three times with no more than one error in each or until you have a copy that is errorless. In Lesson 191, similarly do the second paragraph.

SI 1.38—normal

190-C. Build skill on alphabetic paragraphs

10 One more guide well worth mentioning as an aid for designing new   14
tables concerns headings. There are three kinds of them: titles and   28
subtitles and column headings. Every tabulation has to have a title,   42
of course; but not all tables justify both the others. Use the other   56
two as expedients to trim down the size of a table or make it clearer   70
for your reader. The subtitle is used most frequently as a date line   84
for a table. It is also used, with parentheses, to explain where the   98
data came from or what units of measure are used, like: "All figures   112
are hundreds of litres" or "All figures are in millions of dollars."   126

    1 | 2 | 3 | 4 | 5 | 6 | 7 | 8 | 9 | 10 | 11 | 12 | 13 | 14

11 Column headings are, of course, the most useful expedients; they   140
are frequently the chief part of the table. They must be kept brief,   154
concise, and clear. A group of such headings should be, if possible,   168
phrased in similar terms—don't use nouns for some and adjectives for   182
others unless there is no other way out of the problem. If feasible,   196
keep equal headings to the same number of lines; but if some are long   210
and some are short, at least make sure that all end on the same line.   224
What about rules? The majority of firms like horizontal rules, which   238
make any table look better, but are indifferent about vertical lines.   252

Alternate plan: Take two 5-minute writings, the first with a rest after each minute, the second with no rest whatsoever.

MINIMUM GOAL: to complete the paragraphs in 5 or fewer minutes with 2 or fewer errors.

190/191. Apply skill to unarranged tables

See how many of the letters below and on page 62 you can produce in the time allotted for typing Lessons 34-35. Type the letters on *plain* paper.

GOAL: To finish each letter (*a*) with 4 or fewer errors and (*b*) within 5 minutes, counting from the time when the paper is inserted to line 13 (where the return address should be begun) and the carriage is at the margin, ready for you to backspace-pivot the longest line of the return address. Read Letter 5 before typing it.

Pivot first line; when you return carriage for other two lines, draw it back only to this same starting point. (If using an electric, set a tab stop to use in repositioning carriage to this point.)

Letter 5

BLOCKED LETTER
Shown: in elite
Body: 89 words
Line: 40
Tab: center
Paper: plain
Start: line 13, so
  date will fall
  on line 15
SI: 1.30—fairly easy

```
                              38 South Park Drive          13
                              Ottawa, Ontario K1B 3A8       20
                              October 17, 19—  ▼ 5          24
                                                            25
                                                            26
                                                            27
                                                            28
      Mr. Edward Whitman                                    31
      Smith & Whitman, Ltd.                                 35
      560 Front Street West                                 40
      Toronto, Ontario                                      44
      M5V 1C6                                               46
                                                            47
      Dear Mr. Whitman:                                     51
                                                            52
      This letter shows how to use the "blocked style" in  62
      one's personal business letters, typed on ordinary    73
      plain paper.                                          75
                                                            76
      You should type your address in two lines above the   87
      date, with the number and street on the first line    97
      and the city, province, and postal code on the second; 107
      start these two lines and the date at the point       117
      reached by pivoting for the longest line.             125
                                                            126
      You must always be sure to type your name below the   137
      space where you will sign the letter.                 144
                                                            145
                              Yours sincerely,  ▼ 4 or 5    150

                                                            153

                              J. Henry Hale                 156
```

Use no reference initials in letters that you type for yourself.

Personal Business Letter in Blocked Style

Table 56

See page 291

NEW EMPLOYERS—ALL BRANCHES

January 1 Through May 30

Name	Branch	Dept.	Position	Date
Adams, Yvonne	Calgary	Music	Clerk	Jan 20
Allison, Allan	Toronto	Advertising	Layouts	Mar 10
Baker, Alexander	Toronto	Drugs	Buyer	Mar 12
Boer, Willard	Halifax	Drugs	Clerk	Apr 2
Brown, Jerome	Toronto	Boy's Wear	Buyer	Jan 18
Burton, Frederick	Calgary	Executive	Asst Mgr	Jan 2
Chinnock, Susan	Halifax	Executive	Secy	Apr 19
Counts, Edward	Toronto	Advertising	Photog	May 27
Doyle, Richard	Halifax	Off Eqt	Salesman	May 15
Drury, Caroline	Toronto	Jewelry	Clerk	Feb 8
Edwards, John	Toronto	Off Eqt	Salesman	Mar 10
Everett, Polly	Halifax	Shipping	Steno	Jan 18
Farmer, Paul S.	Halifax	Furniture	Buyer	Jan 25
Farmer, Ralph	Halifax	Furniture	Clerk	Feb 8
Esuark, Ruthetta	Toronto	Personnel	Director	Mar 18
Fein, Henrietta	Toronto	Boys' Wear	Asst Buyer	May 16
French, Mary	Toronto	Jewlry	Buyer	May 23
Gordon, Howard	Halifax	Advertising	Writer	Apr 19
Graham, Ruppert	Toronto	Drugs	Clerk	Mar 25
Hamilton, Wilma	Calgary	Boys' Wear	Buyer	Feb 1
Harper, Jerry	Toronto	Off Eqt	Asst Mgr	Mar 17
Harrison, Joe	Toronto	Building	Porter	Feb 15
Jones, Jeremiah	Halifax	Executive	Steno Secy	Apr 12
Kenwood, Martin	Toronto	Shipping	Wrapper	Apr 19
Kliptok, Virginia	Halifax	Mail Sales	Supervisor	May 18
Llewelyn, Inez	Calgary	Mail Sales	Asst Mgr	Apr 25
Morrison, Joanne	Halifax	Building	Elev Op	Feb 8
Norton, Willard	Calgary	Shipping	Supervisor	Mar 19
Olivia, Sarah	Calgary	Personnel	Recep	May 15
Parker, Josephine	Toronto	Accounting	Clerk	Jan 2
Potter, Alice	Calgary	Drugs	Clerk	May 29
Quincy, Jason	Calgary	Mail Sales	Clerk	Apr 2
Rawlson, Robert	Halifax	Building	Porter	Feb 8
Reilly, Patrick	Halifax	Executive	Vice-Pres	Mar 15
Rowe, Howard	Calgary	Accounting	Asst Mgr	Apr 12
Sullivan, Anne	Toronto	Furniture	Asst Buyer	Feb 3
Stone, Freeman	Toronto	Accounting	Clerk	Jan 2
Rarranti, Angelo	Toronto	Personnel	Interviews	Mar 11
Tomlinson, Bertha	Calgary	Shipping	Steno	May 18
Wilhelms, Francis	Toronto	Music	Buyer	Mar 25

38 South Park Drive   13
Ottawa, Ontario K1B 3A8   19
Current date ↓5   23
   27
   38

Type this heading (on lines 13, 14, and 15) for these four letters.

Letter 6

BLOCKED LETTER
Shown: unarranged
Body: 86 words
Paper: plain
Line: 40
Tab: center
SI: 1.36—normal

Mr. John Green, Editor | Home Living | 316 Raynor Avenue   47
| Victoria, British Columbia V9A 3A4 | Dear Mr. Green: 49

   The last time we met, you said, "Let me know whenever you   62
get a unique idea for a different kind of magazine article."   74

   In about three weeks, I shall leave for a two-month trip   87
through France and England. Would you like an article on   98
places where Canadians abroad can get a meal (or at least a   110
cup of coffee!) to their taste?   117

   What day next week could we have lunch to talk over the   129
idea or a much better one that you might have? | Cordially   143
yours, ↓4 or 5 | J. Henry Hale   150

Letter 7

BLOCKED LETTER
Body: 91 words
Paper: plain
SI: 1.28—fairly
easy

Foreign Department | Bank of Nova Scotia | 16 Highland   37
Avenue | Windsor, Ontario N3A 2S7 | Gentlemen: 45

   I have read that you have "a new plan" for issuing letters of   58
credit to persons who take a trip to a nation in which your   70
firm has a branch office.   76

   I shall leave in about three weeks for a long trip through   89
France and England. I shall be gone nine weeks or more,   100
spending nearly all my time in Paris and in London.   111

   If you have branches in these cities, I should be pleased to   124
learn all the details of your new plan. Might I hear from you   136
soon? | Yours very truly, ↓4 or 5 | J. Henry Hale   150

Letter 8

BLOCKED LETTER
Body: 83 words
Paper: plain
SI: 1.31—fairly
easy

Customer Service Agent | Trans World Airlines | Kennedy   37
Airport | Jamaica, NY   11430, U.S.A. | Dear Sir: 46

   I wish to fly to Paris, then to London, then back to New   58
York. Do you have any tourist-rate flights for such a trip?   71

   If you do, please let me have complete information about the   84
flight schedules, the fare, the luggage weight permitted, and   96
the steps I must take to get the passport that I shall need.   109

   If you do not have "tourist flights" this season, please let   122
me know which airline does have them; I shall be most grateful   134
for your advice. | Yours very truly, ↓? | J. Henry Hale   150

Letter 9

BLOCKED LETTER
Body: 96 words
Paper: plain
SI: 1.37—normal

Mr. George Wood, Manager | Colfax & Mills Agency | 77   36
South Drive | Perth, Ontario K1B 3B5 | Dear Mr. Wood: 48

   The body of this letter is given as 34-D, page 60.   Cordially   152
yours, ↓? | J. Henry Hale   162

senior statistician in Personnel. Most of his work is compiling data for company executives. Your work is to type the data (which may be in his writing, or be in rough draft, or be dictated to you) as tables within memos or as tables centered on full pages and accompanied by memos. You use only the ruled form for tables (review page 139). Always make a file carbon and one spare to use in drafting an additional problem.

Table 56
RULED TABLE

Paper: plain, full
Carbons: 4 or 5 to use
in subsequent tasks

Mr. Hildreth gives you the rough draft shown on the next page. "Please type this," he says. "Make several carbons for us to use."

"Why so many copies, Mr. Hildreth?" you ask.

"Well," he replies, "we have to prepare a number of reports that consist of parts of this master table. It will be easier for us if we have copies we can use as work sheets—we can simply cross out what we *don't* use and then copy what is left."

You study the job, noting:

1. The page looks crowded. You decide to put just 4 spaces between the columns. Grouping the lines in 5-line groups will help, too.

2. The year was overlooked; you will add it.

3. Unpunctuated abbreviations are shown; this is satisfactory on the work sheet you are to prepare but would not be satisfactory for reports to be sent to anyone outside the Personnel Department.

Table 57
Memo
Letter 97
MEMO CONTAINING AN
ABSTRACTED TABLE

Paper: plain, full
Carbons: file, draft
Special: group names
in 4-name groups
Special: clip the marked
worksheet to your work

"Evangeline Prescott is president of the company Women's Club," says Mr. Hildreth. "She has asked for a list of the women who have joined the company since January 1. Please prepare a table of the *names*, *branches*, and *departments* for her."

You realize this will be easy. You will use a copy of Table 56, crossing off the last two columns and all the lines about the men. Then you will type what is left as the table. There will be 16 names, which group handily in 4-name groups.

To evangeline prescott...billing department ...(president...women's club)...*from me*, john hildreth...personnel department...*dated today, of course...subject*...names of new women employees...last week...miss prescott...you asked for the names of the women who have joined the company since january 1...here are the names: *Insert the table here, then wind up:* please note that this table overlaps a similar one that we sent to you two months ago...have a good year!

Table 58
Memo
Letter 98
MEMO CONTAINING AN
ABSTRACTED TABLE

Paper: plain, full
Carbons: file, draft
Special: group names
Special: clip the marked
worksheet to your work

"Let's make the same kind of report for the Men's Club," says Mr. Hildreth, "even though the request has not yet come in. The name of the president is George Montgomery, in accounting. The memo—"

someone in the men's club always asks for a list of the spring crop of new men employees along about this time...george...but this time i am beating you to it! here it is:

Table 59
Memo
Letter 99
MEMO CONTAINING AN
ABSTRACTED TABLE

Paper: plain, full
Carbons: file, draft
Special: group names
Special: clip the marked
worksheet to your work

"Please make a copy of all parts of the master table concerning employees who joined our staff on *April 1 or later,*" says Mr. Hildreth, "for us to send to Mr. Dixon, Director of Personnel, in this memo:"

we are pleased to provide you...mr dixon... the identification of the 16 employees who have joined the staff since april 1...you will wish to note that the disproportionately large number in calgary is due to the expansion of the retail facilities there...*The table; since it is to someone within the same department, you may use the abbreviated form*...if there are other data you would like to have, we should be very much pleased to provide them.

Letter Review

LINE: 50
TAB: 5 AND CENTER
SPACING: SINGLE
DRILLS: TWICE OR MORE
GOAL: INCREASED
 PRODUCTION POWER
STRESS: EVEN STROKES

36-A. Type lines 1-3 two or more times, as evenly as though typing to music. Repeat them in Lesson 37.

36-A. Tune up on these review lines

1 The men may go to the city or the island with us.
2 a A ; : s S l L d D k K f F j J g G h H / ? , , .
3 "we" 23 "our" 974 "rut" 475 "pit" 085 "type" 5603

36-B. Type each line twice, as smoothly and evenly as a clock ticking. Pause and check your work after each repetition; if you made any error or if you recall faltering, repeat the line.

Manual typists omit 4E and 6-E; electric typists omit drill lines 4M and 6M.

36-B. Reinforce control of the symbol keys

4M ki8' ki8' ki8' ki8' It's Richard's car, isn't it!
4E ;''; ;''; ;''; ;''; It's Richard's car, isn't it!
5   ju7& ju7& ju7& ju7& He works for the T. Eaton Co.
6M sw2" sw2" sw2" sw2" "So," he said, "Here we are!"
6E ;'"; ;'"; ;'"; ;'"; "So," he said, "Here we are!"
7   lo9(lo9(;p0) ;p0) He is (a) short and (b) slim.

36-C. Type each paragraph once. GOAL: To finish both paragraphs in 2 minutes, with 3 or fewer errors.

Repeat paragraph 8 twice if you made more than 3 errors; repeat paragraph 9 if you had fewer than 3.

SI 1.12/1.06—both easy

36-C. Improve skill on special paragraph copy

8   The next time I have a note to type, I shall   10
make sure I use paper that is just the right size   20
and quality; I know that both of these do matter.   30
9   Bob has such fine work habits that he may be   40
one of the first to get his work done. If so, it   50
is then his duty to ask for some more work to do.   60

   1 | 2 | 3 | 4 | 5 | 6 | 7 | 8 | 9 | 10

36-D. Take these steps in practicing this selection:

(1) Read the article and compare what it says with the letter on page 64.

(2) Scan the copy once more, selecting and typing from two to four times any word you wish in each line.

(3) Type a double-spaced copy, trying to finish it in 5 minutes or less, with 4 or fewer errors. OR, take a 5-minute timing on it and record your score.

SI 1.42—normal

36-D. Measure your skill in sustained writing

10   Now and then the typist must write a message   10
for which a standard business letter may not seem   20
adequate. One would not wish a "commercial" look   30
for a letter of condolence, for example, which an   40
employer might send to a customer or for a letter   50
of thanks or regret that a typist might write for   60
himself. The form that is used on such occasions   70
is the one that is known as "formal" arrangement.   80
    To make a letter "formal," the typist writes   90
the inside address at the end of the letter. The   100
writer's name may or may not be typed beneath the   110
signature; the absence of a typed name means that   120
the writer is claiming to be a personal friend of   130
the addressee, and so the name is typed when that   140
claim should not be made or would be presumptive.   150
    The models that follow contrast the "formal"   160
design with two of the standard business designs.   170

Unit 31. Tabulation

188-A. See whether you can type difficult lines 2 and 3 in cadence with someone who sets a fast pace on easy line 1! Repeat in Lesson 189.

188-A. Tune up on these review lines

1 The two men got the big saw and cut the old oak log for us.

2 Professor Charlton was quite vexed by Jimmy's buzzing talk.

3 My answers are: 10%, 28%, 39%, 47%, and 56%; what are his?

   1 | 2 | 3 | 4 | 5 | 6 | 7 | 8 | 9 | 10 | 11 | 12

188-B. Type to your need.

ACCURACY: Type lines 4-6 four times as a paragraph and lines 7-9 two times as a solid paragraph.

SPEED: Type each line three consecutive times.

188-B. Improve skill by selective preview practice

4 surrounding considered experience mystery series often felt

5 information tabulation adjusting, exactly that's table size

6 interesting emphasize, unarranged version guides typed down

   1 | 2 | 3 | 4 | 5 | 6 | 7 | 8 | 9 | 10 | 11 | 12

7 long time this kind know why has been for the out of is one

8 read over take time when you the most you can air of do not

9 felt that look like that you not hard try the one of is not

188-C. Build skill on alphabetic paragraphs

188-C. Adjust machine for double spacing, 70-space line (lines will align), and tab-5 indention.

In Lesson 188, type the first paragraph three times with no more than one error in each or until you have one copy that is errorless. In Lesson 189, similarly do the second paragraph.

SI 1.33—easy-normal

10 For a long time there has been an air of mystery surrounding the   14
most interesting aspect of typing: designing a table from unarranged   28
information. I do not know why this should be considered hard. Yes,   42
this kind of work takes time; but I should like to emphasize the fact   56
that planning is not hard. It takes a little experience, that's all.   70
Nine times out of ten, the grouping of the data is quite obvious when   84
you read over the information; for the tenth instance, the files will   98
probably have a precise model that you can follow. I have often felt   112
that planning a table is not as hard as adjusting the machine for it.   126

   1 | 2 | 3 | 4 | 5 | 6 | 7 | 8 | 9 | 10 | 11 | 12 | 13 | 14

11 There are several guides that could be kept in mind when you are   140
planning a table. The first guide: If the table is one of a series, then   155
it should be made to look and read exactly like the others; this applies   170
not only to tables in a report or thesis but equally to those that you   184
type in business, where most tabulations are just the newest version   198
of the tables you typed last month. The second guide: Where you can,   212
make a table longer than it is wide; try to make its general size in the   227
same shape as the sheet of paper. A third guide: If you can, get the   241
totals figures typed down at the bottoms of the columns.   252

Alternate plan: Take two 5-minute writings, the first with a rest after each minute and then the second without a rest.

MINIMUM GOAL: To complete the paragraphs in 5 or fewer minutes with 2 or fewer errors.

188/189-D. Apply skill to statistical tabulation

36/37-E. Produce a summary of letter basics

Using plain paper or workbook pages 47-50, produce a letter summary: on page 47, center a copy of 36-D (double spaced); on pages 48, 49, and 50, produce three copies of the letter below, in these arrangements:

ASSIGNMENTS	ARRANGEMENTS	SPECIAL INSTRUCTIONS	WORDS
Letter 10	Blocked form, formal (personal) display	Arrange as shown, with inside address below the signature.	152
Letter 11	Blocked form, personal-business arrangement	Type inside address above salutation in arrangement shown on page 61.	147
Letter 12	Blocked form, standard business arrangement	Omit return address; type inside address above salutation; add initials.	142

Letter 10
BLOCKED LETTER
Shown: in elite
Body: 89 words
Tab: center
Line: 40
SI: 1.34—fairly easy

5 Frank Street 10
Winnipeg, Manitoba R3N 1W1 16
October 20, 19—— ▼ 5 20

24

Dear Doctor Brown: 28

29

Thank you very, very much for giving me so much of 39
your time yesterday morning. I did follow up your 49
suggestion; and, I am happy to report, I got the 59
position for which you recommended me. I begin my 69
work this coming Friday, at three. 77

78

Getting this weekend job means that I shall be able 88
to go on with my program and, at the same time, get 98
experience that should prove a help in my studies 108
and my career. I do not know how I can thank you 118
enough. 120

121

Respectfully yours, ▼ 4 or 5 126

127

128

129

George C. Mills ▼ 2 to 5 133

137

The typed signature is usually omitted in letters between persons who know each other well. The inside address may be raised or lowered to give visual balance to the letter.

Dr. Lee K. Brown 141
Institute of Commerce 145
26 Fifth Avenue East 149
Flin Flon, Manitoba 152
R8A 0Z4 153

Formal Letter in Blocked Style

```
To:       Theodore Wilson, Sales
From:     Jay Trayne, Advertising
Date:     October 14, 19—
Subject:  Conference on Publicity for Portland Folder

          Thanks to your suggestion, Ted, we will hold a staff
meeting to discuss publicity possibilities for the Folder:

          1.  We will meet next Monday, 9:30 to 11:00, in the
Fourth Floor conference room.  My entire staff will be there.

          2.  An agenda for the discussion is attached.
          We are delighted that you suggested having this con-
ference and even happier to know that you can attend it.
                                            J. T.

CJW
Enclosure:  Agenda
```

A Style of Interoffice Memo Typed on Plain Paper

Letter 95 DICTATED MEMO	Paper: plain, full Line: 60 Tab: 10 Carbons: file only SI: 1.42—normal

First, a memo to jay trayne *in* advertising 7
on specimen letter for the trade journals... 30
after our staff conference about means of 40
getting the folder mentioned in more news 49
columns...i drafted a sample letter...a 56
copy is attached...i should like your re- 64
actions: (1) would such a letter get the re- 75
sults for which we hope...namely...a 82
picture and a news report? (2) you are the 93
advertising man whom the magazine is 100
eager to please...accordingly...would it 108
be better if such a letter were signed by you 118
...not by me? (3) if we send review clippings 129
...an editor might think our folder is not 137
"news" any longer...therefore...would it 144
be better *not* to send the clippings? if you 155
will think the matter through and then see 164
me about it...maybe we can get the snow- 172
ball rolling!...*Now for the*— 183

Letter 96 DICTATED LETTER	Paper: plain, full Carbons: file only Body: 149 + display SI: 1.39—easy-normal

—*sample letter we mention in the memo. Just* ..
draft it, please, on plain paper to journal of 10
office supplies...375 sixth street east... 18

saskatoon...saskatchewan 57 H1 B9...atten- 26
tion new products editor...as i have received 38
each recent issue of the *journal of office sup-* 56
plies...i have looked closely for some men- 66
tion of the new portland folding machine 74
in your column about new products...to 82
this point...alas,...no mention of it has 90
been made...when i was wondering why 97
it has not been mentioned...i realized that 106
we may not have sent you the material you 114
would need for the column...therefore...i 122
am sending you: (1) a large photograph of 132
the machine (2) a brochure that tells how it 142
works (3) copies of the photographs that 151
we used in the brochure (4) some clippings 162
from other reviews...if there is any other 171
aid we can provide...i should be happy to 179
send it...or...if you would like to see a 187
demonstration of the way the machine 195
works...i should be most happy to arrange 203
one for your office. 227

I think Jay will like that!

Forms 72-73 DICTATED TELEGRAMS	Forms: workbook 375 Carbons (plain): file Review: page 109

Telegram, please to the general manager *of* 22
our factory at 5720 gable street in toronto 35
...how much advance notice would you 42
require to deliver 500 model 19 folders to 51
burlington? 67

Day letter to that fellow thompson *up in* 24
winnipeg [Letter 88]: our representative 46
...james flaherty...was injured in auto 54
accident en route winnipeg will be laid 62
up at least a month...may i send one mod- 70
el 19 portland folder for your trial use...i 79
will gamble that it will pay for itself so 88
quickly that you will decide to keep it. 110

Unit 7. Tabulation

38-A. Type lines 1-3 two times. Repeat in Lesson 39.

38-A. Tune up on these review lines

1 They will wish this plan done over one more time.
2 We vexed Jack by quietly helping a dozen farmers.
3 "Is the room 28' 10" long or is it 39' 10" long?"

38-B. Type each line twice (manual typists omit 10E; electric typists omit 10M).

Number/pounds sign is the shift of the 3 key. Percent sign is the shift of the 5 key.

Underscore* is shift of the 6 key (manual) or of the hyphen key (electric).

38-B. Practice three symbol keys you will need soon

4   d3d d#d d3d d#d d3#d Order #3 needs 13# of nails.
5   Pack them in lots of 10#, 28#, 39#, 47#, and 56#.
6   Give orders #10, #28, #39, #47, and #56 to Frank.
7   f5f f%f f5f f%f f5%f We want 5% and 15% and 155%.
8   Try to get a 4.5% stock or some 5% bonds for her.
9   She wanted 15% interest, but I would pay only 5%.
10M j6j j_j j6j j_j He did say he would not ask Paul.
10E ;-; ;_; ;-; ;_; He did say he would not ask Paul.
11 I have not read that new book, Paying for Supper.
12 Remember, he is not to help us solve the problem.

38-C. Each line: Backspace to center the line; set the left margin at the point to which you backspace; then type the line three times.

In lines 15 and 16, allow 6 spaces between words; set tab stops to help align the words when line is repeated.

38-C. Review horizontal centering

13   South Prince Albert, Saskatchewan
14   Petrified Forest National Park
15   Oldsmobiles   6→   Cadillacs
16   Coffee   6→   Milk   6→   Tea

38-D. See whether you can type both paragraphs in 4 minutes or less, with 4 or fewer typing mistakes.

SI 1.30—fairly easy

38-D. Build sustained skill on paragraph copy

17   One of the more challenging kinds of work in   10
the office is that of typing data in column form.   20
Known as tabulation, this kind of typing requires   34*
more thought and judgment than do other tasks and   44
so is a welcome break from routine kinds of work.   54

When you stop to analyze how a table is pro-   65
duced, you will see that it is mostly a matter of   75
centering. You pick out the longest item in each   85
column, then back up from the middle of the paper   95
enough to center all those items and to leave six   105
blank spaces between them. You set tab stops, to   115
make it easy to line up the items in each column.   125

   1 | 2 | 3 | 4 | 5 | 6 | 7 | 8 | 9 | 10

* Underscore solidly (line 11) unless each word is to be stressed separately (as in line 12). Type the words to be underscored, backspace (if 5 or fewer strokes) or draw the carriage back by hand, and then underscore.

Word count includes triple credit for all underscored material in timed writings.

LINE: 60
TAB: 3, 6
SPACING: SINGLE
DRILLS: THREE TIMES
GOAL: EDIT AND TYPE
    LIKE A SECRETARY
STRESS: SMOOTH-AS-
    MUSIC RHYTHM

186-A. Type lines 2-3 in cadence with someone who sets a good pace on the first line, if possible. Repeat in Lesson 185.

186-A. Tune up on these review lines

1 When your boys must win, then they find that they know how.

2 The very next question emphasized the growing lack of jobs.

3 They give discounts of $10\frac{1}{2}$, $28\frac{1}{4}$, $39\frac{1}{2}$, $47\frac{1}{4}$, and $56\frac{1}{2}$ percent.

   1 | 2 | 3 | 4 | 5 | 6 | 7 | 8 | 9 | 10 | 11 | 12

186-B. Type the lines slowly to pinpoint any awkward parts; practice those parts. Then type each line three times.

186-B. Sustain rhythm on difficult preview words

4 conjunction expressions semicolon paragraph events left out

5 explanation independent connected separate clauses hire him

6 enumeration commodities adverbial contains between save $5.

186-C. Type a complete copy or take two timed writings for 5 minutes, the first with 10-second rests after the minutes and the second with no rests during the effort.

Be sure to leave a blank line before each rule.

SI 1.42—normal

186-C. Sustain full pace on technical copy

1. Use the semicolon to separate two independent clauses if   12
   there isn't any conjunction between them: 22
   a. There may be a big crowd; we can handle it all right.   34
   b. He tried hard for the order; his best was not enough.   47

2. Use the semicolon between two independent clauses if the   60
   clauses are connected by adverbial connectives: 71
   a. We need a new man; however, we must not hire him yet.   83
   b. They did not write us; therefore, it is not my fault.   96

3. Use the semicolon between two independent clauses if the   109
   first clause contains one or more commas: 118
   a. Yes, we lost it, Mr. Smith; but we really tried hard.   131
   b. We had one until March, 1964; and then it was stolen.   144

4. Use the semicolon before any term that introduces an ex-   156
   planation or enumeration; a comma comes after that term: 169
   a. We picked three men; namely, Frank, Lloyd, and Blake.   182
   b. It is a good bargain; that is, you can save $5 on it.   194

5. Use the semicolon to set off groups of items, like names   207
   and addresses, dates and events, commodities and prices,   220
   persons and offices, and so on, if they're in a sentence   232
   form; use the comma to separate the items within groups: 245
   a. The new officers are Ralph Haynes, president; William   257
     Brown, treasurer; and Clyde Hall, secretary.   268
   b. New members of the team include Mr. Frost, East Lynn;   280
     Mr. White, West Lynn; and Mr. Keene, Partch.   291

   1 | 2 | 3 | 4 | 5 | 6 | 7 | 8 | 9 | 10 | 11 | 12

NOTE: To reinforce your control of these rules, which you must apply in lessons 186 and 187, do the Learning Guide on workbook pages 373-374.

186/187-D. Apply skill to communication production

38-E. Learn to identify the basic parts of a table

- *Title* . . . identifies table; is centered and typed in all capitals.
- *Subtitle* . . . gives more information about table; is centered a double space below title, with principal words capitalized; is not always used; may be arranged on more than one line (if more, the lines are single spaced).
- *Column heads* . . . tell what is in columns; are centered above columns; are preceded by 2 blank lines and followed by 1 blank line.
- *Body* . . . consists of the columns; is centered horizontally, usually with 6 spaces between columns; is commonly single spaced, but may be double spaced or arranged with lines in groups that facilitate horizontal reading of the table.
- *Column* . . . is a listing in a table, including the column head; is considered as wide as the longest item in the column (body *or* head); word columns align at left; number columns align at right.

38-F. Learn basic steps in arranging a simple table

PRELIMINARY STEP. CLEAR THE MACHINE:

Eliminate all tab stops that may already be set and move margin stops to ends of the carriage.

STEP 1. SELECT THE "KEY LINE":

It consists of the longest item in each column, plus 6 spaces for each between-column open area.

STEP 2. SET LEFT MARGIN STOP:

From the middle of the paper, backspace to center the key line; set left margin stop at the point to which you backspace. The backspace-centering is easiest if you backspace for the blank areas first— simply backspace 3 times (half of 6 spaces) for each blank area—and *then* backspace for the pairs of letters in all the longest items combined.

STEP 3. SET TAB STOPS:

Using the space bar, space across the paper to set a tab stop at the start of each new column.

STEP 4. COMPUTE TOP MARGIN AND INSERT PAPER:

Figure the top margin necessary to center the table vertically. Insert the paper to the appropriate starting line and center the carriage.

Now you are ready to type the table. You back-space-center the title and type it in all capitals, drop down 3 lines, and type the body of the table. To avoid confusion in spacing after heading lines, leave

the machine set for single spacing until you are ready to type the body; *then* adjust for double spacing.

PRACTICE 1. Type this short table, centering it in double spacing on a half sheet. Can you complete it correctly in 5 or fewer minutes?

STEP

1   sentence¹²³⁴⁵⁶though¹²³⁴⁵⁶tables

2

3

4

TABULATING ↓3

Always	type	tables
line	after	line
as	though	you
were	typing	one
sentence	like	this.

38/39-G. Practice the production of simple tables

GOAL: To finish each table on page 67 in 6 minutes (3 for making machine adjustments and 3 for typing the table) or less, with *no* arrangement errors and with not more than 3 typographical errors.

For each table, use a full sheet of plain paper. Type the title in all capitals and follow it with 2 blank lines. Double space the body. Tabulate from column to column wholly by *touch* control.

When you type any table as a timed writing, note (1) that you start with the carriage centered, ready to backspace-center the title; (2) that you triple space and start over if you finish the copy before time is called; and (3) that the word count credits you with 1 word for each use of the tabulator (as, between columns) and each extra carriage return (as, after a heading line).

Type another sample double card for me, please. Use the same two addresses that you typed on the first double card, but arrange the message to say: 70

dear dealer...you will be pleased to 78 know that the new model portland folding 97 machine...concerning which you have re- 104 ceived a number of announcements in the 112 past few weeks...has come off the assem- 120 bly line...has been introduced with great 128 [*please put "great" in all-caps*] success at the 131 vancouver show of business machines... 142 and is now ready [*please put "now ready" in* 145 *all-caps*] for prompt delivery...please re- 151 turn the attached card to let us know how 160 many to deliver to you...delivery will be 168 made within two weeks after we receive 176 your card...portland products company 186 [*in all-caps, clear to the right, please*]...

Then arrange the return message like the other one, except that the message between the salutation and the address lines should be: Send _____ portland folding machines to 199 us...on our usual credit terms...at the ad- 207 dress below *and use a colon after "address."* 255

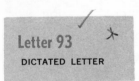

60

Letter 93	Paper: plain, full
DICTATED LETTER	Carbons: you decide
	Body: 190 + display
	SI: 1.39—normal
	Review: page 170

Please make this letter attractive. We may eventually duplicate it, so please use plain paper and center our name and address at the top. Address it: to all office managers who 61 worry about costs in handling mailings 69 dear friends... 73

this letter was printed on a duplicator, 82 ...folded by a folding machine,...placed 90 in its envelope by an inserting machine,... 98

and then sealed and stamped by a mailing 106 machine... each of the machines did its 114 part in preparing this mailing,...which is 122 of 7,500 pieces,...in an hour or less... a real 131 accomplishment, that!... can you do as 138 well with your staff and equipment? 146

if your answer is "no, i cannot," 154 then it is time to take a look at 161 the line of portland machines. 168

the newest member of the portland line 176 of mailing machines is the portland fold- 185 er,...which will fold any paper that can 193 be run through a duplicating machine,... 201 it can give you 1, 2, 3, or 4 folds on any 210 sheet of paper from 10 cm to 23 cm wide 218 and from 10 cm to 35 cm long...you 227 ought to see how fast it works! 230

there's an idea: see how fast the 238 portland folder works! write us to 246 arrange a demonstration for you. 253

and when your friendly portland man is 262 there for the demonstration,...ask him for 270 more details about the whole line of port- 278 land machines. *Use the company signature* 294 *and my name and title, please.* 306

mr lester d brinks...c/o mr tauro kimoto 16 ...post office box 20...miyakojima, osaka 24 ...japan...this is just a quick report,... 36 mr brinks...to let you know that the port- 45 land folder is off to a wonderful start... 54 taking top honors at the vancouver show 62 ...the campaign in the trade journals is a 71 great success...just as you predicted... 78 we are working now on the direct-mail 86 plans...copies of which are enclosed for 94 your interest...all of us hope you are en- 103 joying your visit with mr kimoto,...to 111 whom i hope you will give my regards,... 118 and his family... we are looking forward to 127 your return. *Oh, leave my title off this one.* 147

Table 1 ✓

3-COLUMN TABLE
Paper: P4
Spacing: double
Tab stops: 2

CENTER→
(See page 31)

TRANSPORTATION TERMS ↓3

			12
			13
airline	collision	dunnage	14
automobile	commutation	embargo	21
backhaul	compartments	excursion	30
baggage	consignee	f.o.b.	38
boxcar	consignor	freightage	45
carload	demurrage	gondola	53
carrier	destination	hangars	60
coastwise	drayage	helicopter	68
			76

automobile₁₂₃₄₅₆compartments₁₂₃₄₅₆freightage ←Key Line

Table 2 ✓

4-COLUMN TABLE

CENTER→

TRANSPORTATION TERMS ↓3

				12
				13
airline	carrier	consignor	excursion	14
				24
automobile	coastwise	demurrage	f.o.b.	35
backhaul	collision	destination	freightage	46
baggage	commutation	drayage	gondola	56
boxcar	compartments	dunnage	hangars	67
carload	consignee	embargo	helicopter	77

automobile₁₂₃₄₅₆compartments₁₂₃₄₅₆destination₁₂₃₄₅₆freightage ←Key

Table 3 ✓

3-COLUMN TABLE

CENTER→

Note in column 2 that the % sign is always repeated.

AVAILABLE BOND ISSUES ↓₂

			13
			14
			15
Vancouver, City of	5.0%	25 years	23
Trois Rivières, City of	4.5%	18 years	33
Québec, Province of	4.8%	20 years	41
Lethbridge, City of	5.0%	25 years	52
Cumberland, School District of	4.8%	20 years	71
Charlottetown, City of	4.7%	19 years	80

Cumberland, School District of₁₂₃₄₅₆5.0%₁₂₃₄₅₆25 years ←Key

P. 283.

184/185-C. Apply skill to correspondence production

Letter 90

DICTATED LETTER

Paper: workbook 367
Carbons: file, 1 cc
Body: 156 + display
SI: 1.27—easy

mr. james l. marsh, young & gaul co. ltd., 37 fifty-first street, portage-la-prairie, manitoba R1N 2Z3. *Oh, in this project, make a copy of everything for Mr. Brinks. Subject line:* drafts of mailing pieces.

here are the drafts...about which i phoned you today...of the mailing pieces for the next campaign: (1) the postal card you developed and which...with apologies to the author...i have revised...it would do the job on our mailing to List B...(2) my own design for another postal card...which

16
23
25
41
51
59
67
77
87
96
106
114

is based on yours...of course...i think that it would be right for mailing to the new list c...(3) a display letter...which is based on the one we used when we brought out the new duplicator...to mail with a circular to the master list a...what I like about all three pieces is that they can be prepared on our own machines...a fact that will save us both time and money...i think...however ...we should test each of the pieces before we nail them down...do you agree...if so ...how soon do we start? *That's it.* comp

124
134
144
153
163
172
181
190
198
206
214
242

Letter 91

DOUBLE POSTAL CARD

Card: workbook 369
Carbons (plain paper): file and Mr. Brinks
Material: below

60

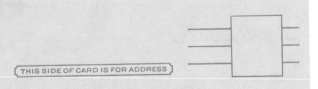

Dear ^Mr. Stationer:

Two weeks ago the great/new Portland Folder ^ing Machine was ~~introduced~~ unveiled ^at the business machines show in Vancouver. It was an ~~instantaneous~~ success—the hit ^of these of the show! If you would like one or more ^machines on consignment, we could deliver an order to you within ~~two or~~ three weeks. Be the first in your community with this ^timesaver! Just fill in the ^card (attached) and return it to us. ACT NOW!

wonderful

        PORTLAND PRODUCTS COMPANY)→||

            center top ↕ and bottom

THIS SIDE OF CARD IS FOR ADDRESS

        Mr. Theodore Wilson
        Sales Manager
        Portland Products Company
        3 27th Avenue
        Brandon, Manitoba R7B 2E1

THIS SIDE OF CARD IS FOR ADDRESS

→ Manager, Stahl's Stationery
→ 352 West Eighth Avenue
→ Kamloops, British Columbia

Dear Mr. Wilson: the   my

YES! I want to be ^first in ~~this~~ community to show—~~AND~~ SELL—your new folding machine!

Send _____ machines on^consignment to:

Address:

Signed: _____   ~~Authorized Signature~~

FRONT SIDE: MESSAGE AND RETURN ADDRESS

Double Postal Card

BACK SIDE: ORIGINAL ADDRESS AND REPLY

UNIT 30   LESSONS 184-185   286

LINE: 50
TAB: 5
SPACING: SINGLE
DRILLS: TWICE OR MORE
GOAL: LEARN TO USE
   COLUMN HEADINGS
STRESS: TOUCH
   CONTROL

40-A. Type each line two times. Repeat in Lesson 41.

40-B. Type each line twice (manual typists omit lines 7E and 10E; electric typists omit lines 7M and 10M).

Dollar sign ($) is shift of 4 key (manual and electric).

MANUAL   ELECTRIC

Cent (¢) key is beside Sem on a manual machine or the shift of 6 on an electric.

Per (or "at") sign is shift of ¢ key (manual) or shift of 2 key (electric).

40-C. Two ways to reinforce the information given here:

(1) Use the Learning Guide on workbook pages 53-54.

(2) Study each column in the tables on pages 69-70.

Then center each column head above the longest item in its column.

40-D. After slow, arduous drills like those above, it is always wise for you to type something easy "to get back in stride." So:

(1) Preview by practicing any one word in each line.

(2) Type the paragraph twice. On the second copy, see if you can finish it in 3 or fewer minutes, with not more than 3 typing errors.

SI 1.21—easy

40-A. Tune up on these review lines

1 He may go by bus to visit the firm on the island.
2 Jack Mixbye had a powerful zest for quiet living.
3 Orders #10 and #28 made up over 39% of the total.

40-B. Practice three symbol keys you need soon

4 f4f f$f f4f f$f f4$f Pay $4 or $14 or $41 or $44.
5 Buy him the gift for $4 or $5, not for $9 or $10.
6 May thought that $14 was about $4 or $5 too much.

7M ;;; ;¢; ;;; ;¢j ;¢j Pay up to 16¢ or 16½¢ or 17¢.
7E j6j j¢j j6j j¢; j¢; Pay up to 16¢ or 16½¢ or 17¢.
8 We got 6 orders at 16¢, 6 at 16½¢, and 12 at 17¢.
9 Prices were 10¢, 28¢, 39¢, 47¢, and 56¢ per item.

10M ;¢; ;¢@ ;@; ;¢; ;@; We got 12 @ 16¢ and 12 @ 19¢.
10E s2s s2@ s@s s2s s@s We got 12 @ 16¢ and 12 @ 19¢.
11 Order 12 boxes @ 86¢ and another 12 boxes at 87¢.
12 Try to get 10 @ 28¢, 39 @ 47¢, and 56 @ 56¢ each.

40-C. Learn to center a heading above a column

To center a heading over its column, (*a*) note the difference between the length of the heading and the length of the longest item in its column; then (*b*) divide the difference by 2, ignoring fractions, to find how much to indent the shorter line from the start of the longer line. Example:

Juniors12345   12Juniors345
Alice Weller   Alice Weller

If the column includes a $ sign, it may be counted or ignored, whichever makes the centering easier. Example:

Amount   Amount
$100 $75

40-D. Renew typing fluency on this easy material

13 If you would like to cut down the errors you 10
make, check first on your posture. It is amazing 20
how much the way you sit alters the way you type. 30
Control is what you have when each finger goes up 40
and down the same path, exactly the same path, to 50
jab the key or keys assigned to it; if you change 60
posture, so that the angle of the path is not the 70
same, then the finger gets off the path and makes 80
an error. The majority of mistakes can be traced 90
to moments when you squirmed in your seat, or let 100
your wrists or shoulders sag, or did something to 110
change the pathway your fingers expected to take. 120

1 | 2 | 3 | 4 | 5 | 6 | 7 | 8 | 9 | 10

LINE: 60
TAB: 3
SPACING: SINGLE
DRILLS: THREE TIMES
GOAL: EDIT AND TYPE
LIKE A SECRETARY
STRESS: CLEAR-CARBON
STROKING

184-A. Type lines 2 and 3 in cadence with someone who sets a pace on the first line, if possible. Repeat in Lesson 185.

184-A. Tune up on these review lines

1 They will have much that they must save when they sell out.
2 Six or seven quickly jumped off with Frank for a big pizza.
3 The postage dues this week are .10, .28, .39, .47, and .56.

1 | 2 | 3 | 4 | 5 | 6 | 7 | 8 | 9 | 10 | 11 | 12

184-B. Sustain your pace on technical copy

184-B. Type a complete copy or take two timed writings for 5 minutes, the first with 10-second rests after the minutes and the second with no rests in the effort.

Be sure to leave a blank line before each rule.

SI 1.27—easy

1. Use a comma before a conjunction in a compound sentence: 12
   The store will open today, and we expect a big crowd.   24
   We have worked here for a week, but we are resigning.   36

2. Use a comma before a conjunction that connects the final   49
   two parts of a series of words, phrases, or clauses: 61
   Should Doctor Smith go by plane, by train, or by car?   73
   You took first place, Joe got second, and I got last.   85

3. Use a comma to set off a dependent clause or long phrase   98
   that precedes the main clause of a sentence: 108
   If you have a good record, you will get a better job.   120
   In answer to your request, we are sending a new list.   132

4. Use a comma to set off a nonrestrictive clause (one that   145
   gives facts about the antecedent but that can be omitted   157
   without changing the meaning of the main clause):   169
   Mr. French, whom you met today, is a credit customer.   181
   Her fine gold watch, which was a gift, has been lost.   193

5. Use a comma to set off also a nonrestrictive participial   206
   phrase, which may or may not start the sentence: 217
   Being her close friend, Jan would not talk about her.   229
   Ralph quit that job, believing that it had no future.   241

6. Use a comma to set off a word, phrase, or clause that is   254
   parenthetic (not needed for the sense of the sentence):   266
   We may find we must, therefore, mail them their bill.   278
   Both of us, as you might guess, were pleased with it.   290

7. Use a comma to set off a word, phrase, or clause that is   303
   introductory to the main part of the sentence: 314
   Of course, there is still a chance to get that order.   326
   If you wish, we can get a man to take it over to you.   338

8. Use a comma to set off expressions that are in contrast: 351
   It was Smith, not Stern, who got us the big contract.   363

9. Use a comma to set off a word, phrase, or clause that is   376
   in apposition to other words, phrases, or clauses: 387
   Last June, the month of our annual sale, we did well.   399
   The new rule, that we get Saturdays off, now applies.   411

1 | 2 | 3 | 4 | 5 | 6 | 7 | 8 | 9 | 10 | 11 | 12

NOTE: To reinforce your control of these rules, which you must apply in Lessons 184 and 185, do the Learning Guide on workbook pages 365-366.

A table with column heads is produced almost like simpler tables (as described on page 66):

STEP 1. Select the key line (but note: the longest item in a column may be the column head; if so, the column head is used in the key line).

STEP 2. Backspace-center to set left margin.

STEP 3. Space across to set column tab stops.

STEP 4. Compute top margin and insert paper.

But you must pause *between Steps 3 and 4* to note how many spaces to indent each column head from the start of its column (or, if the column head is wider than its column, to note how many spaces to indent the column from the start of the head). Writing lightly, pencil in each indention reminder, right on the problem copy, so you cannot possibly forget to make each indention. As you type the table and reach the point where each reminder applies, space in accordingly. Study this table:

Table 4

3-COLUMN TABLE
Paper: P4
Spacing: double
Tab stops: 2

ACE BOX COMPANY

Branch	Manager	Years with the Company
Scarborough	Irwin F. Massey	12
Calgary	Earl Lane Simpson	10
Regina	Richard Miller, Jr.	15
Windsor	Gertrude Slattery	7
Medicine Hat	Robert Wellerton	13
Acton	Harold H. O'Brian	24

Scarborough123456Richard Miller, Jr.123456the Company

THIS TABLE ILLUSTRATES THE FOLLOWING TECHNICALITIES

A. TITLE: Centered, typed in all capitals.

B. COLUMN HEADS: Centered, underscored, capitalized, preceded by 2 blank lines, followed by 1 blank line.

C. ANNOTATIONS: Typist marks on problem copy his reminders of indentions for centering.

D. TWO-LINE COLUMN HEAD: Aligned with other headings at bottom, underscored completely (both lines) and solidly, preceded by 1 blank line if it "clears" the title (by 2 blank lines if it fell under title).

E. TAB SHIFT: When typist reaches start of a narrow column, he clears the heading tab stop and sets a stop at point appropriate to center the column.

F. LINESPACING: Typist uses single spacing through headings; shifts to double spacing for body.

G. NUMBERS: Always aligned at right side; typist spaces in to align shorter number.

40/41-G. Practice production of tables with column heads

GOAL: To produce Tables 4-7 in 6 minutes each (3 for setting margin and tab stops, 3 for typing the table) or less, with *no* arrangement errors and with not more than 3 typographical errors. Center each table on a full sheet, the body double spaced.

When you type any table as a timed writing, note that the word count credits you with 5 strokes (1 word) for each use of the tabulator, each clearing and each resetting of a tab stop, each extra carriage return, and each linespace adjustment. As in other kinds of copy, material that must be underscored or centered is given a triple count.

i am beginning to wonder whether there 96
might be someone in that office who, for 105
reasons of his own, is *deliberately* tampering 114
with the equipment. the last two times you 123
visited mm&s, remember, you noted that 130
the motor governors on both the duplicator 139
and the postal meter had been tampered 147
with and "cleaned." i simply cannot believe 156
that the same thing could go wrong with 164
each of the five pieces of equipment that 172
we have installed. 176

in any case, gene, if you cannot find the 186
answer when you see them again, please 193
yank out the installation and replace it; 202
itemize the whole cost of doing this and 210
send it to me as a charge for special serv- 219
ices, which i shall have credited to your 227
account. we would rather take a loss on 235
this department than jeopardize our con- 243
siderable volume with the rest of mm&s. 251

Cordially yours and so on; oh, add a post- 270
script, please: i would like us to exhibit in 272
the toronto business show, gene, but the 281
prices are wholly out of line. i have written 290
to kling (carbon copy is enclosed) in the 298
hope we can pressure him into a more real- 307
istic view of the situation. want to follow 316
up for us? 328

Letter 88

DICTATED LETTER

Paper: workbook 361
Carbons: file, Letter 89
Body: 153
SI: 1.57—difficult

mr. thomas j. simmons, martin miller & 8
sons, 58 broadview avenue, toronto, on- 15
tario M4M 2E4 with a carbon to gene. 22

thank you for your letter about the un- 30
satisfactory service that you are getting 39
from your portland duplicator. i am deeply 47
concerned about the situation and am ask- 55
ing our toronto dealer, mr. gordon, to see 64
you about it. 67

this latest breakdown is the fifth you 76
have had with as many machines, isn't it? 84

how annoying it must be to you! we are, 93
naturally, disturbed about this record; we 101
have had a few machines get out of order 109
before, but we have never had so many col- 118
lapse in one installation. most of our cus- 126
tomers have never had even one service 134
call, let alone any need for the replacement 143
of our equipment. moreover, no other in- 151
stallation has ever had the drum of the 159
duplicator "run backwards," as you said 167
was the case this time. 172

i am writing to mr. gordon, giving him full 182
authority to settle the matter. your friends 191
in this company appreciate your patience. 200
That ought to do it! 221

Letter 89

DICTATED LETTER

Paper: workbook 363
Carbons: file, Letter 89
Body: 119 + display
SI: 1.59—difficult

toronto business show ltd., attention mr. 14
kenneth w. kling, national trust building, 18
7 heath street, toronto, ontario M2L 1Z3. 37

we appreciate very much your invitation 46
to exhibit in the business show you will 54
sponsor next month. we have read your 62
prospectus with interest but, for the fol- 70
lowing reasons, have decided not to reserve 79
space for an exhibit: (1) your space rates 90
are much higher than for shows that draw 99
much larger crowds. (2) your conference 109
activities are to be held away from the ex- 119
hibit hall, thus drawing away prospective 128
viewers. (3) the innumerable extra fees for 139
labor and facilities, which are a part of the 149
flat exhibit fee in other shows, have priced 159
your space beyond its value, in our opinion. 169
if there occurs a basic change in the admin- 179
istration of these three items, we may be 187
interested. 190

Remember to make a "bcc" for gene. Add 206
this note on his copy: what we really object 229
to, gene, is the third item. If they corrected 239
that, we'd be interested.—TW *Be sure that* 245
note is on the file, too.

Table 5

3-COLUMN TABLE
Paper: full sheet
Spacing: double
Tab stops: 2

THE MOST FREQUENTLY USED METRIC UNITS

Quantity	Unit	Symbol
Length	metre*	M
Mass	kilogram*	kg
Temperature	degree Celsius	°C
Time	second*	s
Volume	litre	L

CENTER→

*Also SI base units

47
55
60
68
75

Table 6 ✓

3-COLUMN TABLE

UPDATE SI:
Use a space, not a comma,
between groups of 3
digits to the left and right
of the decimal marker.
Example: 53 000.214 956.
The space is unnecessary
if there are only 4 digits.
See: Typing Style Guide
for SI and Metric Symbols,
p. 117
Note the two places where
tab stops should be reset.

Note that $ sign is not
repeated, but that space
is left as though it were.

YEARBOOK BIDS ↓2

November 3, 19— ↓3

Company	Quantity and Rate	Amount ↓2
Atlas Printing	2000 @ $1.50	$3000
Haber & Haber	2500 @ 1.40	3500
Jackson, Inc.	2000 @ 1.35	2700
Phillips Printing	2000 @ 1.38	2760
Rogers & Sons	2500 @ 1.30	3250

8
9
20
22
43
44
57
68
77
86
95

Table 7

3-COLUMN TABLE

DUTY ROSTER, OCTOBER 24 ↓?

Watch	Officer of the Deck	Junior Officer of the Deck ↓?
0000	Lt Martin	Ens Hughes
0400	Lcdr Greene	Ens Shaw
0800	Lt Foster	Ltjg Carews
1200	Ltjg Young	Ens Krell
1600	Lt Martin	Ens Hughes
2000	Lcdr Greene	Ens Shaw

14
16
33
52
53
61
69
76
83
90
97

* Count assumes the four
make-ready steps (page 66)
are taken: stops set,
paper inserted to starting
line, carriage centered, etc.

UNIT 7

LESSONS 40-41

You work for Theodore Wilson, sales manager, Portland Products Company. He prefers blocked letter form. He dictates the following letters, expecting you—when necessary—to paragraph them (page 207), capitalize them (page 282), and provide correct salutations and closings (page 208) and the appropriate carbons and annotations.

Letter 85
DICTATED LETTER

Paper: workbook 355
Carbons: file only
Body: 185 words
SI: 1.44—normal

This letter is to my (friend) Jim Flaherty. That's james e. flaherty, at 392 hathway street, wawanesa, manitoba 5 16 25

as you will see from the letter i am enclosing, we have a strong prospect in the harding-hill corporation, in winnipeg. your itinerary indicates that you will be in winnipeg about the end of next week. could you get there a day or two ahead of schedule and give the firm some time? i am particularly anxious to land this deal because, if i may judge by the number of h-h circulars that come to my desk, this prospect will need not one but several of the machines. 34 43 52 60 69 77 86 94 112 120 128 130

i checked on the weight of paper stock that h-h is using; it varies, but none of it is too heavy for our machine. h-h has apparently standardized on No. 10 envelopes and two folds. it would be good strategy to have the machine ready. 139 148 156 164 173 178

i should not bother to go into the mechanics of the machine's operation, if i were you, jim. i think this customer is interested in only one thing: economy. i suspect that this is the line to follow. let me know whether you visit the company, jim, and how you make out. 187 195 204 212 220 228 233

cordially yours, theodore wilson, sales manager, *and so on.* 247 252

Letter 86
DICTATED LETTER

Paper: workbook 357
Carbons: file, letter 87
Body: 140 words
SI: 1.46—fairly hard

Now, this is the letter I was telling Jim about. It's to marvin j. thompson, production manager, harding-hill corporation, 1067 south assiniboine street, winnipeg manitoba R3J 0A9. 15 22 30 37

we appreciate very much your inquiry about our new folding machine. i assure you that it will fold all the standard sizes of paper used in duplicating machines. as a matter of fact, it will fold papers as small as 10 cm² and as large as 22 cm by 35 cm. 45 54 63 71 81 90

our representative for this province, mr. james e. flaherty, to whom i am sending a copy of this letter, will be in your city in about ten days. i believe that he will be able to stop in to see you when he arrives in winnipeg. he has a model of the folding machine and can let you see for yourself how efficient it is. 99 107 117 126 134 143 151 156

i am enclosing literature about the new machine. if there is any other help i can give, mr. thompson, please let me know. 165 173 202

Letter 87
DICTATED LETTER

Paper: workbook 359
Carbons: file only
Body and PS: 251
SI: 1.47—fairly hard

This letter is to eugene r. gordon, 818 rhodes-hart building, 12 conway avenue, toronto, ontario M4M 1K5. dear gene. 13 21 31

we seem to be having another tussle with your friend simmons at martin miller & sons, as you can tell from the enclosed copy of my current letter to him. i don't know why we have had so much trouble with the installation in his department. do you have any thoughts on the subject? [CONTINUED] 40 48 57 65 74 83 89

Review

LINE: 60
TAB: 5
SPACING: DOUBLE
DRILLS: TWICE OR MORE
GOAL: REFRESH SKILL
AND REVIEW LETTERS,
TABLES

42-A. Type each line twice, hitting the keys sharply. Repeat lines in Lesson 43.

42-B. Type paragraph 9 once, within 2 minutes; proofread the copy. Then:

(1) If you made more than 3 errors, type lines 4-5 three times each; then type 6-7 two times each.

(2) If you made 3 or fewer errors, type lines 4-5 two times each; then type lines 6-7 three times each.

42-C. First, scan your copy to satisfy your curiosity about it. Second, practice three or four times each any ONE word in each line.

Then, center a copy on a full sheet OR take two 5-minute writings. GOAL: 35 or more words a minute, with 4 or fewer errors.

SI 1.35—near normal

42-A. Tune up on these review lines

1 She may make the girls do the theme for their eighth panel.
2 Poor Jack was vexed about my long and quite hazy falsehood.
3 We bought the $47 bracelet for $28 and the $56 pin for $39.

42-B. Improve skill on patterned sentence drills

4 Zoe was given pay for that queer black box of jade markers.
5 Kay reviewed the subject before giving Max and Paul a quiz.
    1 | 2 | 3 | 4 | 5 | 6 | 7 | 8 | 9 | 10 | 11 | 12
6 He paid for the world maps and then cut them for the girls.
7 When may Mr. Melvor make the sights for the six new rifles?

42-C. Measure and build your sustained typing skill

8 For more than a year now, it has been my pleasure each   12
morning to study the window of a fine jewelry store that is   24
located at the corner where I get my bus. I arrive there a   36
little before eight each morning and have six or seven min-   48
utes to wait before the bus is due. While I wait for it, I   60
study the big display of clocks in the window; it is really   72
quite something to see, with clocks of all sizes and kinds.   84
There are several timepieces that always amaze me. You see   96
no moving parts whatsoever, just the oval faces and pointed   108
hands, somehow suspended in the front corner of the window.   120
9 I have never seen so many clocks in different sizes or   132
shapes as appear there in the display at the jewelry store.   144
You see shelves of small, squatty alarm clocks and two rows   156
of small, slim china clocks shaped exactly like spires of a   168
church. There is a very big display of wrist watches, too.   180
10 One particular clock (a sign explains) is wound by the   192
changes in the weather. That one dumbfounds me, and I have   204
some very real doubts about it. Deep inside I nurture some   216
quiet little prayers that the expert who built that job for   228
us lazy folks must, surely, have put a winding key in some-   240
where as insurance on days when the weather stays the same.   252
    1 | 2 | 3 | 4 | 5 | 6 | 7 | 8 | 9 | 10 | 11 | 12

SUGGESTION: When you are typing line after line of steady copy, concentrate on evenness instead of pushing hard for speed.

A high speed score comes from not losing time. The most common speed cutters are losing the place (from looking up) in the copy and key jams.

LINE: 60
TAB: 5
SPACING: DRILLS SINGLE, PARAGRAPHS DOUBLE
DRILLS: THREE TIMES
GOAL: EDIT AND TYPE SECRETARIAL LETTERS
STRESS: GOOD POSTURE, VIGOROUS STROKING

182-A. If you can, type lines 2 and 3 in cadence with someone who sets a pace by typing line 1. Repeat in Lesson 183.

182-B. Type to your need.

ACCURACY: Lines 4-7 as a paragraph, three times.

SPEED: Each line three times consecutively.

182-C. One errorless copy of each paragraph or two 5-minute writings—one with a 10-second rest after each minute and one without such rests.

GOAL: To complete the selection within two errors and five minutes.

SI 1.42—normal

182-D. To reinforce your control of these rules review page 151 and then do the Learning Guide on workbook pages 353-354.

UNIT 30

182-A. Tune up on these review lines

1 Many find that they must have more cash when they dine out.
2 Zeke quietly placed five new jumping beans in the gray box.
3 We need the discount signs for 10%, 28%, 39%, 47%, and 56%.

   1 | 2 | 3 | 4 | 5 | 6 | 7 | 8 | 9 | 10 | 11 | 12

182-B. Sharpen skill on an alphabetic preview

4 AA aims BB been CC capital DD said EE needed FF for GG gaps
5 HH whom II bit JJ major KK clerk LL skill MM most NN carbon
6 OO ought PP proper QQ quickly RR rules SS secretary TT that
7 UU must VV have WW knowledge XX exception YY likely ZZ hazy

182-C. Hold your best pace on normal paragraph copy

8   As has been said before, the man who dictates a letter must decide 14
when he must send out a letter and what he must say in it. He leaves 28
to his secretary, whom he employs for this purpose, the details of 42
typing the letter, deciding on the carbon copies needed, and so on. 56
Among the "and so on" items is the responsibility for editing the 69
letter so it is proper in language, in punctuation, and in use of capitals. 84

  This means that the typist who aims at the secretarial desk must 98
know the rules that concern these matters. It is important that one 112
know them, for the skill in applying such rules is one of the two things 126
that distinguish a secretary from a clerk typist. (The other factor is 141
the knowledge of shorthand.) Most persons have gaps in their control 155
of the laws of writing; let us be sure that you are the exception. 168

  Of all the categories of rules that you ought to know, the first one 183
is the set of rules about using capitals. It may also be the most im- 197
portant set; for while a businessman may be a bit hazy about the 210
distinction between a comma and a semicolor., he is likely to be 223
familiar with all the major proprieties of capitals. He will spot your 237
oversights more quickly in this regard than in others. So, know the 251
rules! 252

   1 | 2 | 3 | 4 | 5 | 6 | 7 | 8 | 9 | 10 | 11 | 12 | 13 | 14

182-D. Review the business uses of capitals

In business letters, capitalize—
1. The start of any sentence.
2. Personal titles (like *Miss*).
3. Business titles *preceding* names and in addresses and signatures.

4. Names of persons, places, companies, and trade-named products.
5. First and all major words in attention and subject lines, salutations, and titles of publications.

42/43-D. Speed up production of letters and tables

Letters 13-14. Review letter typing, pages 57-58; then type Letters 13-14 on workbook letterheads (or plain paper with a line or crease 9 lines from the top, to represent a letterhead). GOAL: To finish each letter in 5 minutes or less, with 4 or fewer errors.

Tables 8-9. Review table typing, pages 66-70; then center these two tables on P4 sheets. Use double spacing for the bodies; arrange the columns 6 spaces apart. GOAL: To finish each table in 6 minutes (2-3 for adjustments, 3-4 for typing) with 3 or fewer errors.

Letter 13

BLOCKED LETTER
Paper: letterhead
Body: 90 words
Line: 40
Tab: center
SI: 1.37—normal

NOTE: When something is to be mailed with a letter, type "Enclosure" below your initials as a reminder.

Date Miss Florence Stahl Apartment 12-C 659 Lakeshore Drive Surrey, BC V3J 5E5 Dear Miss Stahl:	24 / 36

Thank you for the recent letter in which you asked about the plays for which you might still be able to obtain tickets for a show in the first week of December. — 48 / 61 / 69

We are enclosing a list of such plays. — 78

If you wish us to reserve seats for you, please let us know within the next week. It is necessary for you to make a deposit of $1 on each ticket you wish to reserve; we will then hold the ticket or tickets until 24 hours prior to curtain time. Yours sincerely, John Clark Williams Ticket Reservations URS Enclosure — 91 / 104 / 117 / 131 / 148 / 150

Letter 14

BLOCKED LETTER

Date Mr. John R. Jackson Park Hotel 120 King Street Truro, Nova Scotia B3B 1C9 Dear Mr. Jackson: — 24 / 36

[*Repeat the body and closing of the letter above.*] — 150

Table 8

3-COLUMN TABLE
Paper: full sheet
Spacing: double

THEATER TICKETS AVAILABLE — 15
For Week of December 3 — 31

Play	Star	Price Range	
Shadowed Rainbow	Nancy Reeves	$2.40 to $6.80	62
Seventh Son	Gloria Langley	2.20 to 7.50	75
Inherit a Plew	Paul Montrose	2.20 to 8.80	85
Holly Ann, Dear	Ross Willard	4.40 to 8.80	96
Comedy of Errors	Victor Bennett	1.60 to 4.40	107
Regretfully So	Janis Prellis	2.20 to 5.50	117

(49)

Table 9

4-COLUMN TABLE
Paper: full sheet
Spacing: double

SUMMARY OF ORDERS — 10
Received on November 18 — 26

Cat. Item	Quantity and Rate	Billing	Company	
376	160 boxes @ 42¢	$67.20	Phelps, Ltd.	71
376	200 boxes @ 42¢	84.00	Harris & Sons	84
394	100 units @ 37¢	37.00	Dale-Acme	94
416	144 boxes @ 46¢	66.24	Stephens Bros.	105
739	100 reams @ 71¢	71.00	The Bay	116

(30 / 55)

181-B. Without looking up or pausing even once, type one double-spaced copy. As you proofread, put a light checkmark beside the drill below for each key that you have typed incorrectly.

181-B. Inventory your present symbol-typing skill

18   Invoice #3311 was addressed to Smith & Hart, Inc. (now   12

Hart & Sons, Ltd.) and was for 1000# of #12 filings (15.5%   24

steel) @ 11¢ a pound, for a total of $110.00, _less_ discount   38

(5% on _whole_ 100's); so the "amount due" _is_ $105.00. Their   53

credit is "good" as Smith & Hart but "poor" as Hart & Sons.   65

1 | 2 | 3 | 4 | 5 | 6 | 7 | 8 | 9 | 10 | 11 | 12

181-C. Each line three times, plus another time if you missed the key when you typed 181-B.

181-C. Improve control of the #, $, %, () and & keys

19 dd ## Box #333 contained 3.3# of blue labels, the #33 size.

20 jj && We get Lord & Howe ties at Swiss & Sons or Cole & Co.

21 ff $$ The suit cost $75; the shoes, $20; and the coat, $90.

22 ll ((;;)) He looked for (10), (28), (39), (47), and (56).

23 ff %% She says that 5% of 5% is .25%, but 10% of 10% is 1%.

1 | 2 | 3 | 4 | 5 | 6 | 7 | 8 | 9 | 10 | 11 | 12

181-D. Repeat 181-B to confirm your progress

181-E. Each line three times, plus another time if you missed the key when you typed 181-D.

181-E. Improve control of the ¢, @, ", ', and __ keys

24 ;; ¢¢ jj ¢¢ The pamphlets cost 10¢, 28¢, 39¢, 47¢, and 56¢.

25 ;; @@ ss @@ Please order 100 @ 28¢, 39 @ 47¢, and 10 @ 56¢.

26 kk '' ;; '' It's Tim's or Bob's cap; it's not Vi's or Jo's!

27 ss "" ;; "" "Average" is "good" but "superior" is "better."

28 jj __ ;; __ They are _not_ to know what _cherchez la femme_ is!

1 | 2 | 3 | 4 | 5 | 6 | 7 | 8 | 9 | 10 | 11 | 12

181-F. Repeat 181-B to confirm your progress

181-G. If you made any number-key error when typing 181-B-D-F, type 29-31 three times as a paragraph; otherwise, type each line three times consecutively.

181-G. Regain fluency with pair-pattern sentences

29 They assigned us Rooms 10, 28, 39, 47, and 56 for seminars.

30 Put Group 10 in Room 28, Group 39 in 47, the others in 156.

31 Check lockers 10, 28, and 39 for books numbered 56 and 147.

1 | 2 | 3 | 4 | 5 | 6 | 7 | 8 | 9 | 10 | 11 | 12

181-H. Repeat 181-B to confirm your progress

181-I. Type three rapid copies at full stride. If time permits, take a wrap-up 5-minute writing on the page 278 copy.

SI 1.36—easy-normal

181-I. Regain full stride on an alphabetic paragraph

32   Did you ever wait for a bus in a big station and spend   12

your time watching other people? Some quietly relax. Some   24

visit with friends or doze. Some pass the time just watch-   36

ing others. A great many go over to the magazine stand and   48

look sideways at the daring covers of books they won't buy.   60

1 | 2 | 3 | 4 | 5 | 6 | 7 | 8 | 9 | 10 | 11 | 12

Unit 8. Manuscripts

44-A. Tune up on these review lines

44-A. Type each line twice. Repeat them in Lesson 45.

1 They paid for the pen and the box, so I paid for the chair.
2 Pack my five boxes in with the dozen jugs of brown lacquer.
3 I phoned rooms 10, 28, 39, and 47 before he phoned room 56.

44-B. Practice the rest of the symbol keys

44-B. Each line twice. If necessary, construct the symbols that you need.

1. Exclamation. If your machine has a top-row *1* key, ! is its shift. Use A-finger to drill *ala!* with F-finger anchored. If you have no *1* key, make the ! by typing a period, backspacing, and typing an apostrophe.

4 alala ala!a a!a!a Vote for Jones! Vote for Jones! Hurrah!
5 They counted the seconds: Five! Four! Three! Two! One!

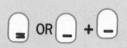

2. Equals. Some machines have = key at the top right of the keyboard, controlled by Sem-finger: ;=;=;. On other machines, make = by typing a hyphen, backspacing, and typing another hyphen with the cylinder turned up slightly.

6 ;=; ;=; ;=; F = 25, A = 30, S = 40, E = 45 (for 3 minutes).

3. Plus. On machines with = key, + is shift of =. Drill: ;=;+;. On other machines, make + by typing a hyphen, backspacing, and intersecting the hyphen with an apostrophe or diagonal (whichever gives the better result).

7 ;=; ;+; ;+; He said to total a + b, then b + c, then c + d.
8 if a + b = 25 and b + c = 45, could a = 10, b = 15, c = 30?

4. Asterisk. The asterisk (*) is the shift of either the hyphen (drill: ;-;*;) or of the 8 key (drill: *k8k*k*), depending on the make of machine.

9 John Wilson* used an asterisk (*) in a number of footnotes.

44-C. Regain fluency on easy paragraph material

44-C. To get back in full stride and maybe pick up some extra speed, type each paragraph twice. Or, even better, make two attempts to finish each paragraph in 2 minutes or less within 3 errors, followed by a 5-minute writing in which you set a new speed record (but do it within 4 errors!).

SI 1.00—very easy

10   All through the lunch hour, we sat there and played an   12
old quiz game that Mike had found in a box of junk that his   24
dad had thrown out. The game was a lot of fun, too; but we   36
got tired of that, of course. The rain kept on. Dave came   48
up with a game he had found in some old book; we tried this   60
one for a while, too. We were glad to see the sun at last.   72

   1 | 2 | 3 | 4 | 5 | 6 | 7 | 8 | 9 | 10 | 11 | 12

11   Once in a blue moon, it is good to get up at the crack   12
of dawn and watch the world wake up. You see the sun break   24
through the shades and mist of night and gleam on the drops   36
of dew that weigh down the leaves and the grass; and as you   48
look, the leaves lift up and the grass turns straight while   60
the dew fades and dries in the first soft breath of breeze.   72

LINE: 60
SPACING: DOUBLE FOR (B), OTHERS SINGLE
DRILLS: THREE OR MORE
GOAL: STRENGTHEN TOP-ROW CONTROLS
STRESS: EYES ON COPY

180-A. Race through each drill three times without pausing and without looking up. Repeat in Lesson 181.

180-A. Tune up on these review lines

1 They may wish to work with the social chairman of the firm.
2 Kay bought five or six cans to award as equal major prizes.
3 Type 1 and 2 and 3 and 4 and 5 and 6 and 7 and 8   [Continue to 50]
   1 | 2 | 3 | 4 | 5 | 6 | 7 | 8 | 9 | 10 | 11 | 12

180-B. Without looking up or pausing even once, type one double-spaced copy. As you proofread, put a light checkmark beside the drill below for each key that you have typed incorrectly.

180-B. Inventory your present number-typing skill

4 7601 2702 2603 6804 2805 4906 1607 7308 3809 8010 4711 9512

8013 2914 7815 5016 9617 6718 5719 3620 1821 1922 9823 4624

9425 1926 9827 4028 9029 5630 8531 8932 9633 8334 7035 2936

6737 4838 6439 2040 6941 3042 7543 8744 5945 9146 5847 8348

6349 9750 6151 8652 7253 1054 1755 3756 7457 6258 7959 6760
   1 | 2 | 3 | 4 | 5 | 6 | 7 | 8 | 9 | 10 | 11 | 12

180-C. Each line three times, plus another time if you missed the key when you typed 180-B.

180-C. Improve control on number keys 1-5

5 aa 11 The 11 teams from 11 schools had 11 games in 11 days.
6 ss 22 I sold 22 cars in 22 days to 22 people from 22 towns.
7 dd 33 The 33 groups sent 33 books to the 33 men in tier 33.
8 ff 44 Seat 44 in row 44 was 44 rows up and 44 seats inward.
9 ff 55 Car 55 traveled 55 laps in 55 minutes and 55 seconds.
   1 | 2 | 3 | 4 | 5 | 6 | 7 | 8 | 9 | 10 | 11 | 12

180-D. Repeat 180-B to confirm your progress

180-E. Each line three times, plus another time if you missed the key when you typed 180-D.

180-E. Improve control on number keys 6-0

10 jj 66 Route 66 is 66 miles west of 66th Street on U. S. 66.
11 jj 77 The 77 workers in Plant 77 average 77 dollars weekly.
12 kk 88 The 88 teams from District 88 won the first 88 games.
13 ll 99 The 99th division handles 99 items for 99 cents each.
14 ;; 00 If you add 00 or 000 or 0000 to 00, you still have 0.
   1 | 2 | 3 | 4 | 5 | 6 | 7 | 8 | 9 | 10 | 11 | 12

180-F. Repeat 180-B to confirm your progress

180-G. If you made any error in 180-F, type 15-17 three times as a paragraph; otherwise, type each line three times consecutively.

180-G. Increase fluency by typing "we 23" drills

15 we 23 24 25 toe 593 594 595 owe 923 924 925 rye 463 464 465
16 ty 56 57 58 pry 046 047 048 try 546 547 548 toy 596 597 598
17 it 85 86 87 wit 285 286 287 pit 085 086 087 out 975 976 977
   1 | 2 | 3 | 4 | 5 | 6 | 7 | 8 | 9 | 10 | 11 | 12

180-H. Repeat 180-B to confirm your progress

44-D. Learn to identify the basic parts of a short manuscript

- *Title* . . . identifies manuscript; is centered and typed in all capitals.
- *Subtitle* . . . tells more about manuscript; is centered a double space below title, with first and principal words capitalized; may require more than one line (single spaced).
- *By-line* . . . "By" and name of author; may be single spaced with subtitle lines or may be displayed separately, preceded by 1 blank line.
- *Body* . . . separated from heading by 2 blank lines; 5-space indentions.
- *Subheading* . . . principal subdivision; centered and underscored, with first and principal words capitalized; preceded by 2 blank lines.
- *Sideheading* . . . important subdivision; may be underscored capital and small letters, but usually all caps; preceded by 2 blank lines.
- *Balance line* . . . something (date, reference, etc.) added at bottom to stretch manuscript when it is too short or too high on the page.

44-E. Learn basic procedures in positioning short manuscripts

MECHANICAL OPERATIONS

Tab stops. Always set two—one for the standard 5-space paragraph indention and one for use in repositioning the carriage for centering lines.

Spacing. As when typing tabulations, set the machine for single spacing until you begin the body.

Extraspacing. To leave one additional blank line when the machine is set for double spacing, turn up the paper one line by hand (turn the right cylinder knob) *before* returning the carriage.

Bottom guard. Typists usually pencil two very light lines (later erased) near the bottom of the paper: one to mark where the last line of typing could go and a cautionary signal an inch higher. Or, they use a *visual guide*—a sheet on which the four margins are ruled; placed under the paper on which you will type, the ruled lines show through to guide you visually in margin observance. Your workbook has a visual guide to use in this unit.

Placement plans. The two common ways of positioning material are *by centering* and *by formula*.

1. PLACEMENT BY CENTERING

The final typing of a short manuscript is usually a *retyping* of a preliminary draft; with the draft at hand for use as the basis of figuring, the typist can readily center it just as one centers any block of lines: One counts lines and computes the appropriate top margin, then selects an *average full-length line* and backspace-centers this line to determine where to set the margins.

2. PLACEMENT BY FORMULA

When a manuscript is composed directly at the machine or when the preliminary draft is inadequate for centering (if written by hand, for example), the typist follows this formula:

Top margin, 12 lines (start on line 13).

Line length and spacing depend on the amount of material in the manuscript:

```
Under 200 words: line 50; double space
200 - 300 words: line 60; double space
Above 300 words: line 60; single  space
```

Bottom margin, 12 lines when line 50 is used, 9 lines when line 60 is used. *If the copy is too long*, continue it on another page or retype it higher on the page. *If the copy is too short* (too high on the page), type a "balance line" (date, assignment number, etc.) near the bottom to give the page proper balance.

44/45-F. Practice the production of short manuscripts

GOAL: To finish each manuscript on pages 75-76 in 10 minutes (3-4 for studying the problem and making machine adjustments, 6-7 for typing the work) or less, with *no* arrangement errors, and with not more than 4 typographical errors.

Note that each manuscript is to be typed twice: first by formula, *including a balance line* about 12 lines from the bottom, with the use of the visual guides, workbook pages 59-60; and then by centering, *without a balance line*, using your first copy for figuring the centering adjustments. Use plain paper and appropriate line length and spacing.

The word count credits you fully for all centering, indenting, and other required operations.

179-B. Inventory your present skill

179-C. Improve skill via selective practice

28 McMann member mimic madam hammy maim memo mums harm mom May
29 Norton ninety noons linen ninth neon none nine nuns one Nan
30 Olivio orator odors polio solos onto oboe polo oleo too Ona
31 Pepper people poppy pipes paper prop pulp pipe pups pop Pat
32 Quincy quoted equip query quart quad quiz quit aqua quo Que

    1 | 2 | 3 | 4 | 5 | 6 | 7 | 8 | 9 | 10 | 11 | 12

33 problem lament curls visit tight dusk sigh idle map fit eye
34 torment wieldy bugle shake handy gown bury worm sob ham fog
35 auditor bushel ivory widow shelf lane pane worn tie lap oak
36 apricot social fight chair spend risk half snap box foe aid

179-D. Improve skill via more selective practice

37 Reigor repair refer recur error purr rare roar rear err Ron
38 Sister senses suits sizes sales sees sirs uses says sis Sue
39 Tootle traits trout truth total tent trot that tact tot Ted
40 Ushers unused usurp usury usual true unto upon unit but Una
41 Velvet vivify verve vivid valve vote view have very vow Van

    1 | 2 | 3 | 4 | 5 | 6 | 7 | 8 | 9 | 10 | 11 | 12

42 ancient theory world shame laugh paid when turn lay row sit
43 chapels visual shape panel eight soap rush body bid pen key
44 antique eighty giant blame right form worn lame dog cow due
45 visitor profit title throw their with both them fur rod sir

179-E. Improve skill via still more selective practice

46 Wislow window which where widow whew what when with owe Wes
47 Xavier deluxe proxy exact toxin exit text next taxi fix Tex
48 Youngs yearly slyly study shyly your duty year city fly You
49 Zinzer puzzle dozen dizzy dozed zone zero jazz lazy zip Zoe

    1 | 2 | 3 | 4 | 5 | 6 | 7 | 8 | 9 | 10 | 11 | 12

50 turkeys mantle docks rocks blend lair tidy sock rye jam hay
51 sleighs pajama soaps autos turns cork duel urns bit fig tub
52 dismays icicle tucks dog's toxic alto idle jamb fox pry woe
53 bushels enrich virus roams socks also firm name rug sow cue

179-F. Speed up your spacebar stroke

54 hand duck kept torn name ends slow wish held disk keys soft
55 tool look keen nook keep peer room mood deer roll loop pool
56 let two one end dry yet the elf for rim may yes sit tug gem

    1 | 2 | 3 | 4 | 5 | 6 | 7 | 8 | 9 | 10 | 11 | 12

179-G. Repeat 179-B to confirm your progress

NOTE: Substitute your teacher's
name for "Mr. Strang" and your
name for "Jean L. Worth."

ONE-PAGE REPORTS   ←TITLE   10

                                                          11

A Report to Mr. Strang   ←SUBTITLE   26
By Jean L. Worth ↓3   ←BY-LINE   38

                                                          40

This report is designed to show how a one-page   51

report should be arranged. ↓3   57

                                                          58

SIDEHEADING→ HEADINGS   60

Business asks that a report be identified by a   70

heading (what, to whom, by whom) and by sideheadings   81

that classify the contents at a glance.   89

                                                          90

MARGINS AND SPACING   94

The top margin is 12 lines (but can be less).   104

The common line lengths are: 110

Under 200 words: line 50, double spaced   121

200 - 300 words: line 60, double spaced   130

Above 300 words: line 60, single spaced   140

                                                          142

BALANCE LINE   145

If a report is so short that it looks high on   155

the page, the typist writes something (date, for in-   166

stance) 12 lines from the bottom at either margin. ↓?   176

                                                          177

BALANCE LINE→ November 15, 19--   180

   1 | 2 | 3 | 4 | 5 | 6 | 7 | 8 | 9 | 10

One-Page Report with Sideheadings

1 | 2 | 3 | 4 | 5 | 6 | 7 | 8 | 9 | 10 | 11 | 12 | 13 | 14

The annual vacation is one outing to which families look forward   14
all year long. Most families plan for a week or two or more for this   28
big affair. The youngsters hardly realize, of course, how many exact   42
plans have to be made—how cash for the sojourn must be set aside and   56
frozen there, how the wardrobe of each member of the family has to be   70
designed for the minimum space per suitcase, and other such problems.   84

And problems they are, and they must be settled; but whether the   98
problems are fun or troublesome to solve depends on how a family goes   112
about them. Our family tackles the plans together, with the juvenile   126
members pulling an oar with the rest of us; you would be quite amazed   140
at the soundness of most of their suggestions, and it is mighty smart   154
to hear the ideas expressed before the vacation instead of during it.   168

The first step is picking the dates for the excursion, something   182
that is not much of a problem to wage earners. If you have a cottage   196
and a boat waiting for you, deciding where to go is not a tough deal,   210
either. It's the options that make vacation planning hard, you know.   224
Then you have to contemplate the kind of junket you'll take, the size   238
of your luggage load, and a hundred or two questions along that line.   252

1 | 2 | 3 | 4 | 5 | 6 | 7 | 8 | 9 | 10 | 11 | 12 | 13 | 14

There are some of us who seize this one chance a year to get new   14 266
experience. We go to a different part of the country, or we make the 28 280
journey by some different means of transportation, or we rough it the 42 294
camping way instead of living in hotel luxury. Thus, you see, option 56 308
there is; and this means discussion, a few squabbles, and finally The 70 322
Great Decision. After that, we enjoy a gradually growing excitement. 84 336

Two summers ago our family followed one of the historical trails   98 350
and took our chances on lodging; that was some experience, a new one, 112 364
all right. It is amazing how suddenly there aren't any motels except 126 378
ones that have just one bank vault left. The next summer we equipped 140 392
ourselves with camping gear; this was an experience, too, in which we 154 406
never did learn the basic thing in camping: how to cook in the rain. 168 420

So this summer, the family council has decided, we will take our   182 434
comfort with us: we are going to rent a trailer. We shall scorn the 196 448
hotels and motels and camping sites. We shall laugh at the rain. We 210 462
shall be cozy, living as poshly as a railroad czar. We shall drive a 224 476
thousand—mile jaunt up the coast, stopping as long as we wish at each 238 490
quaint or beautiful place we see. If only I can keep it on the road! 252 504

1 | 2 | 3 | 4 | 5 | 6 | 7 | 8 | 9 | 10 | 11 | 12 | 13 | 14

Manuscript 3
Manuscript 4

ONE-PAGE REPORT
Shown: in elite
Body: 137 words
SI: 1.34—fairly easy
Copies: 2 (directions,
page 74)

CHANGING THE LENGTH   12
                                                        13
A Report to Mr. Strang   28
By Jean L. Worth   40
                                                        42

    It is possible for the typist to make a report look long   55
or look short. It is a matter of using headings that do or   67
do not take extra space.   72
                                                                     73

TO STRETCH A REPORT   77

    To make a report look long, the typist may use sidehead-   89
ings or centered subheadings. Each of these occupies a line,   102
is preceded by two blank lines, and is followed by one blank   114
line—four lines in all.   119
                                                                     120

TO CONDENSE A REPORT   124

    To make a report look short, the typist will change to   136
"paragraph headings," which take no extra space at all, as   148
shown in these two: 152

PARAGRAPH →   <u>Point 1</u>. Paragraph headings are indented the same five   167
HEADINGS
spaces as other paragraphs.   173

→   <u>Point 2</u>. To make them stand out clearly, such headings   188
are underscored.   192

                November 16, 19—   197

1 | 2 | 3 | 4 | 5 | 6 | 7 | 8 | 9 | 10 | 11 | 12

One-Page Report with Paragraph Headings

LINE: 60
SPACING: DRILLS
  SINGLE, PARAGRAPHS
  DOUBLE
DRILLS: THREE OR
  MORE
GOAL: BOOST SKILL FOR
  FIVE MINUTES
STRESS: EVEN CADENCE,
  STEADY INCREASE

178-A. Each line three times or for a minute. Repeat in Lesson 179.

178-B. Adjust machine to double spacing, 70-space line, tab-5 indention. Copy the first three paragraphs on page 278.

If you make more than 2 errors, your goal for Lesson 178 is accuracy; 2 or fewer, then speed.

178-C-D-E. Type exactly for the goal determined by your 178-B results.

ACCURACY: The four alphabetic-control lines as a paragraph three times plus once more if the letters drilled on include one you missed when you typed 178-B; then type the alternate-hand lines two times as an easy paragraph.

SPEED: Each alphabetic-control line twice, then each alternate-hand line four consecutive times.

178-A. Tune up on these review lines

1   If he and Al go to town, they may visit with the neighbors.
2   Judge Flynn was very much puzzled by Alex's quick thinking.
3   Type 7 and 14 and 21 and 28 and 35 and 42 and 49 [Continue to 100]
      1 | 2 | 3 | 4 | 5 | 6 | 7 | 8 | 9 | 10 | 11 | 12

178-B. Inventory your present skill

178-C. Improve skill via selective practice

4   Addams banana salad mania again alas data aqua saga any Ada
5   Bobbit bubble bobby bible abbey blob blab balm barb bib Bob
6   Church cancel check chuck click city nice each came can Cas
7   Druids deduct deeds daddy dried duds dude dyed adds did Don
      1 | 2 | 3 | 4 | 5 | 6 | 7 | 8 | 9 | 10 | 11 | 12
8   neighbor socials icicle burnt audit neigh malt slap and dig
9   quantity divisor quench amend slang title vial coal for the
10 chairman rituals height shape cycle visor mane dusk she own
11 downtown bushels ensign rocks whale throb curl diem big did

178-D. Improve skill via more selective practice

12 Elders degree level every exert ease else even edge fee Eve
13 French buffer fluff fifty fifth cuff tiff muff fife oft Flo
14 Grange groggy aging going gauge gags gang agog eggs ago Gus
15 Heathe hurrah harsh humph hunch hush hath hash high had Hal
      1 | 2 | 3 | 4 | 5 | 6 | 7 | 8 | 9 | 10 | 11 | 12
16 ornament element shaken forks laity quake clan dial but man
17 rhapsody suspend thrown works rifle soaks turn such may cut
18 problems visible author angle theme sighs pair soak got six
19 fieldmen ensigns handle shape vigor field tock disk fix end

178-E. Improve skill via still more selective practice

20 Inslip invite visit limit livid hide bite item five irk Ida
21 Jaguar jacket major enjoy judge join jury ajar just job Joe
22 Kelley kicker knock knack khaki milk know kick kink ask Kim
23 Leslie little local loyal lilac tall lilt loll lily all Les
      1 | 2 | 3 | 4 | 5 | 6 | 7 | 8 | 9 | 10 | 11 | 12
24 vigoroso enamels turkey forms turns dorms girl tick hem nap
25 sorority bicycle dismal sight throw elbow lame cozy pay men
26 rifleman signals island slept usual gowns dusk wish icy wit
27 Manfield sleighs chapel rigid signs ducks iris owls bow pan

178-F. Repeat 178-B to confirm your progress

PROFESSIONAL TIP:

To keep drill repetition from becoming monotonous, give your mind something to think about: make a game of seeing how evenly you can type. Keep saying "Smoothly, smoothly!" to yourself, as you type.

LINE: 60
TAB: 5
SPACING: SINGLE
DRILLS: TWICE OR MORE
GOAL: TYPE
ENUMERATIONS BY
TABULAR TOUCH
STRESS: EYES ON COPY

46-A. Each line two or more times. Repeat in Lesson 47.

46-B. Type an experimental copy of each example; then, each three times on a line.

"times":
"equals":
"minus":
"divided by":
"plus":
"degrees":
superior figures:
inferior figures:
military "zero":
"brackets":
roman numerals:

46-C. Type each line two times; then type all lines straight through once more.

OR, take five consecutive 1-minute writings (that is, a 5-minute writing with a 10-second rest after every minute); and then take one unbroken 5-minute writing (but with each minute called off so you can see if you are keeping up with the pace set previously).

GOAL: To set new speed record within 4 errors.

SI 1.00—very easy

46-A. Tune up on these review lines

1 Pamela works for us but may wish to work for the city firm.
2 Paul said Buzz and Jack might quit five or six weeks early.
3 If you add 10, 28, 39, 47, and 56, the total should be 180.

46-B. Learn to construct special characters

4 What is 2 x 2? ....expressed by small letter x.
5 12 x 12 = 144. ...two hyphens, one below the other (*turn roll by hand*).
6 106 - 14 = 92. ....a single hyphen or a raised underscore.
7 144 ÷ 12 = 12. ....hyphen intersected by the colon.
8 92 + 14 = 106. ....hyphen intersected by one or more apostrophes.
9 Freeze at 0°C. ....small letter o, raised slightly (*turn roll by hand*).
10 4^3 x 5^2 = 39^a. ....type number or letter above line (*turn roll by hand*).
11 H_2O is liquid. ....type number or letter below line (*turn roll by hand*).
12 Leave at 18∅∅. ....0, intersected by a diagonal.
13 He /Williams/. ....diagonals, with underscores facing inside.
14 Chapter XLVII. ....capitals of I, V, X, L, C, and M.

46-C. Renew typing fluency on these speed sentences

15 When can we two men find time to see those four firms? 11
16 I do not seem to have done my share at the old school. 22
17 He may call him back and ask him to work with us soon. 33
18 Both the men we met on the street came here to see us. 44
19 We should ask him to come to the club for a golf game. 55
20 One rich man said he would come down here if he could. 66
21 It is time for us and the right men to leave for town. 77
22 I could make it to class if I could get back by eight. 88
23 Both of us would like to roam by the side of the lake. 99
24 I was to have been there at one, but got there at two. 110
25 We might get the stuff out on time if we work all day. 121
26 One of them should be here to help you with the sales. 132
27 You ought to pay the sales tax by cheque on the ninth. 143
28 How much do you plan to pay me for the desk and chair? 154

177-C. Improve control on one-hand-run preview words

30 multiplying standard targets letter starts think loose junk
31 sarcastic millions sandbags ponders create quill wages case
32 excellent protested formula success revamp idiom frank only

    1 | 2 | 3 | 4 | 5 | 6 | 7 | 8 | 9 | 10 | 11 | 12

177-D. Improve control on preview words on rows 2 and 3

33 qualities judged really tailor tossed adjust wages high out
34 protested spiral target dipped itself squirt prior halt use
35 writers stirred whether effort people dilute first read how

177-E. Improve control on preview words stressing row 1

36 excellent ancient having mixes began lack than lamb dab an,
37 exciting obvious dozens; pains alas, land make lick can am,
38 exchange really, revamps dizzy basic back curb each man and

    1 | 2 | 3 | 4 | 5 | 6 | 7 | 8 | 9 | 10 | 11 | 12

177-F. Improve control on alternate-hand-run preview words

39 qualities problem handle, mighty when firm with both men if
40 onslaught produce ancient chaos, they halt such than did do
41 quantity eloquent whether might, turn them work lend bit of

177-G. Sharpen attention on a concentration paragraph

42 D—ar Mr. W—lliams: I sh—ll b— pl—as—d to h—lp y—u and 12
yo—r st—ff s—t up a n—w f—ling syst—m. As y—u kn—w, I h—v— 24
b——n d—ing m—ch —f th—s k—nd —f w—rk r—c—ntly. If y—u w—ll 36
not—fy m— wh—n to b—g—n, I sh—ll b— th—r—. C—rd——lly y——rs 48

    1 | 2 | 3 | 4 | 5 | 6 | 7 | 8 | 9 | 10 | 11 | 12

177-H. Now inventory your skill again!

43 There is no obvious way to halt the onslaught of trite letters. If 15
you have dozens to produce in the hour, you do not tailor them; you 28
squirt them out of a formula gun. You do not have time to review 41
and revamp, to chop out boastful words and replace them with proud 55
ones, to dilute the sugar with a bit of frank honesty, to toss in an 69
eloquent turn of words in place of the standard idioms, or to curb or 83
adjust an ironic expression that proves more sarcastic than witty. 96
Still, wouldn't it be exciting if each writer did take time and pains to 111
write one excellent, inspired letter each day? The injection of such a 125
letter from each of the millions of correspondents might at least revive 140
the ancient qualities. 144

    1 | 2 | 3 | 4 | 5 | 6 | 7 | 8 | 9 | 10 | 11 | 12 | 13 | 14

177-C-D. For your goal:

ACCURACY: Type 177-C three times and 177-D two times, typing the lines in paragraph form.

SPEED: Type each line of 177-C twice and each line of 177-D three times.

This drill is especially good as a remedy for the typist who jams keys!

177-E-F. For your goal:

ACCURACY: Type 177-E three times and 177-F two times, typing the lines in paragraph form.

SPEED: Type each line of 177-E twice, each line of 177-F three times.

177-G. Filling in all the missing vowels (and don't mark the book!), type two copies. GOAL: To finish a copy without an error in 1 minute or less time.

177-H. Measure your growth by typing this paragraph in the same way you typed 176-B and 176-G. GOAL: To finish the copy within 3 minutes and 1 error.

SI 1.34—normal and fully alphabetic

Using plain paper or workbook pages 61-64, type Manuscripts 5-8 as a four-page project to illustrate forms of enumerations. GOAL: To complete each manuscript in 10 minutes (3-4 to prepare for the assignment; 6-7 to produce it) or less, with *no* arrangement errors and 4 or fewer other errors.

Manuscript 5

ONE-PAGE REPORT
Paper: full sheet
Plan: by formula
Body: 117 words
SI: 1.45—high
  normal

ENUMERATIONS | A Report to Mr. Strang | By Jean L. Worth |	34

ENUMERATIONS │ A Report to Mr. Strang │ By Jean L. Worth │ 34
An enumeration is a series of steps or items whose exact sequence is shown by numbers, letters, alphabetic arrangement, or other means. 50 / 62 / 65

FOUR STYLES │ Style 1 is illustrated by this and the following three paragraphs. 81 / 85

Style 2 is one in which numbers or letters are typed at the margin, with all other copy indented in one tabular step of either three or four spaces. 101 / 114 / 120

Style 3 is the outline form in which the copy is typed in tabular steps of four spaces each. 135 / 142

Style 4 is the kind used in book and article listings: alphabetic by last name of first author. 159 / 166

SPACING │ Any of the four styles may be arranged either in single or in double spacing. │ Balance line? 179 / 190

LISTED ENUMERATIONS

12
13
14

Manuscript 6

ENUMERATION
Paper: full sheet
Plan: center an
  exact copy
SI: 1.41—normal

1. Any series of numbered items may be classified as an "enumeration"; to most persons, however, the word means a displayed listing like this one, with numbers standing out at the left. 24 / 34 / 44 / 54 / 55

2. The numbers are typed at the margin. The word copy is aligned after the period and space that follow the number. A tab stop is set to help align the "run over" lines of copy. 65 / 76 / 86 / 95 / 96

CENTER→

3. If most items take one line or less, they are single spaced with no blank lines left between them; one space follows the period. 106 / 116 / 124 / 125

4. If most listed items fill more than one line, all are single spaced with one blank line left between items; two spaces follow the period. 135 / 146 / 156 / 157

These are the basic rules; they are not applied to the unique displays of listings.

5. The periods must align. When the figures run to 10 or more, the typist must use the margin release key and backspace before typing a two-digit number. 167 / 177 / 188 / 190

1 │ 2 │ 3 │ 4 │ 5 │ 6 │ 7 │ 8 │ 9 │ 10

ACCURACY: Each group of lines, as a paragraph, three evenly paced times.

SPEED: Each line three rapid, consecutive times.

176-E. Improve control on adjacent-stroke preview words

14 UI linguistic UI squirt UI quills XC excellent XC exciting,
15 OP proportion OP people OP chop PO oppose PO ponder PO upon
16 AS sarcastic AS phrasing AS phrases AS basic AS case AS has
17 RT courtesy RT effort RT squirt RT effort RT start RT short
   1 | 2 | 3 | 4 | 5 | 6 | 7 | 8 | 9 | 10 | 11 | 12
18 IO injection IO proportion IO obvious IO millions IO idioms
19 ER shorter ER writer ER ponder ER expert ER wonder ER every
20 OU courtesy OU could OU proud OU hour OU your OU out OU our
21 RE create RE great RE fired RE read RE sure RE more RE core

176-F. Regain stride on very easy material

176-F. Type three times, double spaced; or take three 1-minute writings.

GOAL: To finish the copy in 1 minute without error.

SI 1.00—very easy

22 Pride in work is one thing that will make you like the   12
job you have now. To work so well that you can be proud of   24
what you do and what you turn out, you have to have all the   36
skill that you can use in the job. If you do not have what   48
it takes, you will not do work in which you can take pride.   60
   1 | 2 | 3 | 4 | 5 | 6 | 7 | 8 | 9 | 10 | 11 | 12

176-G. Now inventory your skill again

176-G. To mark progress and set your goal for Lesson 177, follow the same directions you did when you typed 176-B.

SI 1.39—normal and fully alphabetic

23 The core of the problem, one suspects, is the quantity of mail that   15
an office must handle. Mail has a clear habit of multiplying itself. It all   30
starts when a firm targets a broadside to stir up some more business;   44
back come replies, and these evoke replies in turn. And while the ex-   58
change of letters goes on, some zealot, stirred up by the success, if   72
such it be judged, of his prior effort, lets loose with new broadsides,   86
to start new spirals that overlap the first one and create a dizzy chaos   101
that makes the firm use lackluster letters as so many sandbags on the   115
dikes of correspondence. The man who protested that he didn't have   128
time to compose a shorter letter seems to have crystalized the basic   142
problem.   144
   1 | 2 | 3 | 4 | 5 | 6 | 7 | 8 | 9 | 10 | 11 | 12 | 13 | 14

177-A. Tune up by repeating 176-A

177-B. Improve control on opposite-finger preview words

177-B. Type to your goal, defined by 176-G score.

ACCURACY: Each group of lines, as a paragraph, three vigorous times.

SPEED: Each line three times individually.

24 OW flow ow slow ow now ow how WO wonders wo worked wo would
25 GH onslaught gh mighty gh light gh high NG change ng having
26 IC sarcastic ic ironic ic basic UR further ur turns ur sure
   1 | 2 | 3 | 4 | 5 | 6 | 7 | 8 | 9 | 10 | 11 | 12
27 TH whether th there th think th them th that th with th the
28 NT investments nt eloquently nt quantity nt ancient nt want
29 DI directions di dilute di didn't di idioms di dikes di did

line 19

Manuscript 7

OUTLINE
Paper: full sheet
Plan: center an
   exact copy
SI: 1.44—normal

double space

CENTER→

Many typists follow this
simple rule: Double space
all lines in an outline
except "run over" lines.

TYPING AN OUTLINE

I.   MARGINS

    A. Set margin stops to center the average full
        line, allowing for the first roman numeral.
    B. Center the outline vertically. ↓3

II. INDENTIONS ↓2

    A. Steps are indented 4 spaces each.
       1. Set several tab stops 4 spaces apart.
       2. Indent similar parts in similar steps.
    B. Guide letters or numbers precede the steps.
       1. Follow each guide with a period.
       2. Space twice after the period.
    C. For roman numerals that take more than one
        space, use the margin release and backspace
        from the left margin stop.

III. SPACING

    A. Put 2 blank lines before an all-caps line.
    B. Put 1 blank line after an all-caps line.
    C. Single or double space all the other lines,
        but be consistent in which you use.

	10
	12
	15
	16
	26
	37
	46
	48
	52
	53
	62
	73
	83
	94
	104
	113
	123
	134
	142
	144
	148
	149
	160
	170
	181
	190

—19—

line 13

Manuscript 8

BIBLIOGRAPHY
Paper: full sheet
Plan: center an
   exact copy
SI: 1.41—normal

BIBLIOGRAPHY ↓3

A. Books ↓2

Book by 1 author   Ames, James Hill. The Colonials, Rebels. Boston:
      indent 5 → Cole Press, 1962.

Book by 2 authors   Barr, Ruth L.; and Max H. Blaine. Background of
   Indent 5 → The Flag. New York: McGraw-Hill, 1963. *{single space} {double space between}*

Government publication   U. S. Bureau of the Census. Eighteenth Census of
     the United States, 1960. Washington:
     Government Printing Office, 1961. ↓3

B. Magazine Articles

Article by 1 author   Huges, Anne Mae. "Paul Revere, Man on a Horse,"
     Newsweek, August 12, 1963, pp. 16-17.

Article by 3 authors   Krell, John F., Lee Ki Chan, and Anne F. Wilbert.
     "John Adams Said So", Journal of History,
     June, 1962, pp. 216-232.

Article with volume number   McCrae, June M. "Business Letter Writing".
     Journal of Communication, XXI (1977),
     196-210.

	7
	9
	16
	36
	41
	57
	70
	89
	104
	112
	114
	126
	137
	150
	161
	177
	184
	194
	202
	205

Unit 29. Skill Development

LINE: 60
TAB: 5
SPACING: DRILLS SINGLE,
  PARAGRAPHS DOUBLE
DRILLS: THREE TIMES
GOAL: BOOST SKILL FOR
  THREE MINUTES
STRESS: EVEN PACING,
  VIGOROUS STROKES

176-A. Tune up on these review lines

176-A. Each line three
times, or a half-minute
timing on each line.
Repeat in Lesson 177

1 Ken did pay for half the ham, but they paid for the turkey.
2 The day her film took a prize box, Jacqueline was very gay.
3 Type 3 and 6 and 9 and 12 and 15 and 18 and 21   [Continue to 60]
     1 | 2 | 3 | 4 | 5 | 6 | 7 | 8 | 9 | 10 | 11 | 12

176-B. Inventory your present skill

176-B. Confirm 60-space
line, 5-tab indention,
and double spacing. The
lines should align.

To determine your goal
for this lesson, take a
3-minute writing or type
one copy (GOAL: Complete
a copy within 3 minutes
and within 1 or 0 error).

If you make 1 or 0 error,
your goal is speed. If
you make 2 or more errors,
your goal is accuracy.

SI 1.34—normal and
fully alphabetic

4 When you think of how many letters are tossed into the nation's   14
mailbags each day and how many people compose them and read   26
them over, you would guess that by now we would be a nation of   38
mighty expert letter writers. Alas, such isn't the case at all. In spite of   54
high wages, great investments of time, the use of fine machines, and   68
the frenzied efforts of our better writers, a high proportion of our   82
letters are just linguistic junk. You cannot help but wonder whether a   96
bit of the lovely phrasing of olden days came, really, from the slowness   111
of the ancient scribe who worked with a quill. Having time to ponder   125
every nuance as he dipped his pen, he mixed a flow of his personal   138
courtesy with the flow of ink.   144
     1 | 2 | 3 | 4 | 5 | 6 | 7 | 8 | 9 | 10 | 11 | 12 | 13 | 14

176-C. Improve control on double-letter preview words

176-C. Type to your goal.

ACCURACY: The lines as
a paragraph, three times.

SPEED: Each line three
times, individually.

5 correspondents really, letters effort guess dizzy will seem
6 excellent slowness millions tossed cannot dipped still toss
7 correspondence stirred success office loose quill witty all
     1 | 2 | 3 | 4 | 5 | 6 | 7 | 8 | 9 | 10 | 11 | 12

176-D. Improve control on double-stroke preview words

176-D. Type to your goal.

ACCURACY: Lines 8-10 as
a paragraph, three times;
lines 11-13 as paragraph,
two slow-but-even times.

SPEED: Lines 8-10 twice
each; lines 11-13 three
speed-pickup times each.

8   MU multiply MU formula MU much MU must FR frenzied FR frank
9   EC suspects EC injection CE excellent CE success CE offices
10 JU adjust JU judge JU junk NU nuance UN junk UN gun NY many
     1 | 2 | 3 | 4 | 5 | 6 | 7 | 8 | 9 | 10 | 11 | 12
11 RR courtesy RT effort RT squirt RT expert RT short RT start
12 LO eloquent LO slowness LO tailor LO loose LO flow OL olden
13 ED frenzied ED worked ED tossed ED judged ED mixed ED fired

LINE: 60
TAB: 4 AND CENTER
SPACING: SINGLE
DRILLS: TWICE OR MORE
GOAL: REVIEW LETTERS,
  TABLES, MANUSCRIPTS
STRESS: ALERTNESS

48-A. Lines twice—or more if you falter! Repeat the lines in Lesson 49, too.

48-A. Tune up on these review lines

1 When did he go to the city and pay them for the world maps?

2 Max had a zest for quiet living and placed work before joy.

3 At 39:00 & 28:00 & 47:00 & 56:00 & 10:00 & (THEME) (ANNCR:)

48-B. Lines twice. Speed up on each repetition. To build confidence in number control, force yourself to keep your eyes on the copy!

48-B. Improve control of the number keys

4 we 23 or 94 to 59 up 70 ye 63 it 85 re 43 ow 92 pi 08 et 35

5 wee 233 you 697 try 546 pet 035 wit 285 our 974 tee 533 533

6 weep 2330 true 5473 wore 2943 type 5603 wipe 2803 purr 0744

7 wet 235 tie 583 out 975 yet 635 ore 943 pup 070 tot 595 595

48-C. Make an exact, line-for-line copy of the letter, without pausing or raising your eyes a single time.

Or, take a 5-minute writing on it; start with carriage at right margin, ready to pivot today's date. If you finish before time is called, double space and start over (begin with date).

GOAL: A copy in 5 minutes, with 4 or fewer errors.

48-C. Sustain your skill in production typing

Current date	12
Mr. Wayne F. Potter	20
Potter & Vince, Ltd.	24
148 Beaverbrook Court	28
Scarborough, Ontario M1C 3A9	34
Dear Wayne:	37

We are pleased to approve your campaign plan for the next   50
radio series, but with the following two changes: 60

1. We wish to strengthen the commercial at the end of the   73
    tenth broadcast. We are enclosing a proposed revision.   85

2. We wish to drop the two Alberta stations from the plan,   98
    for we have no dealer in those areas. The revised list   110
    of stations is also enclosed.   117

Please let me know when you have received this note. I   129
shall be eager to hear what you have to say about the new   141
script!   143

                    Sincerely yours,   149

                                        152

                    Paul Ness Trent   157

urs   159
2 Enclosures   162

Letter 15

**BLOCKED LETTER
WITH ENUMERATION**
Paper: letterhead
Tab: 4 and center
Line: 40
  (not as shown!)
Body: 92 words
SI: 1.33—fairly
  easy

When a letter has more than one enclosure, use correct number and "Enclosures."

48/49-D. Speed up production of a letter and enclosure

Review letter typing, pages 57-58, then type Letter 15 on a workbook letterhead page. Review tabulation, pages 66-70; then type Table 10 on a full sheet of plain paper. Review enumerations, pages 78-79; then type Manuscript 9 on a full sheet, too.

GOAL: To complete each assignment within 4 errors and 5 minutes from when the paper is inserted.

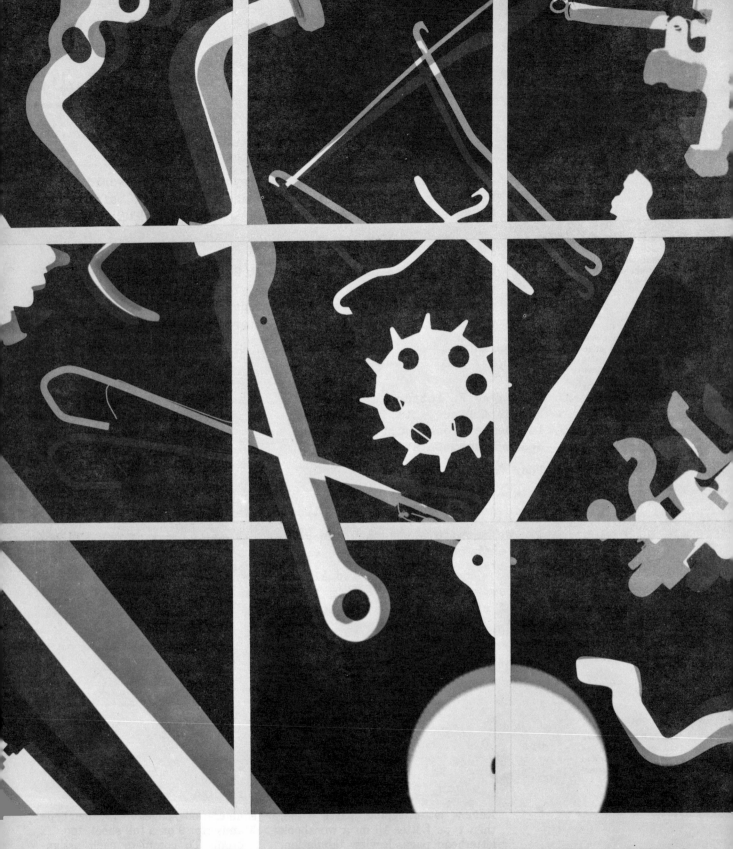

8 SKILL BUILDING • DICTATED LETTERS
UNARRANGED TABLES • REPORTS

THE MONARCH CAMPAIGN (REVISED)
First Quarter, 19——

Station	City	A. M.	P. M.
CFPL	Brandon	07:15	18:30
CHFM	Cornwall	07:30	19:00
CFMB	Hamilton	06:59	19:30
CKX	Kingston	07:20	19:30
CKSB	Burlington	07:00	19:45
CFBC	Montreal	07:30	19:15
CJOB	St. Boniface	06:45	18:45
CHWK	Saint John	07:00	18:55
CKOM	Sarnia	07:45	18:45
CFRN	Saskatoon	07:00	19:15
CFML	Sherbrooke	06:55	19:05
CKLC	Winnipeg	07:00	19:00

CENTER➤

Leaving a blank line after every three lines makes it easier to read a long table.

The numbers along the right margin: 32, 34, 51, 62, 69, 77, 85, 93, 101, 110, 118, 126, 134, 142, 149

SCRIPT 10 (REVISED)

Music	(Theme)	
Anncr	Your typing tip for today—	
Music	(Up and fade on theme)	
Anncr	—from Monarch, the Portable for today!	
Music	(Up and fade into . . .)	
Mary	Ralph, get out the Monarch for me, will you?	
Ralph	Sure, honey. (Sound) Here he is, Monnie,	
	good old Monnie. (Sound of opening case)	
Mary	Hey, don't take the machine out of the case!	
	Just unhook the cover!	
Ralph	Hey yourself! You SHOULD take any portable	
	out of its case when you want to type!	
Anncr	Ralph is right, Mary. Never leave your port-	
	able in its carrying case. Remember:	
	"To keep a portable from starting to skid,	
	Take it out of the case and out of the lid!"	
Music	(Theme)	

CENTER➤

The numbers along the right margin: 12, 13, 16, 24, 31, 41, 48, 60, 70, 80, 91, 97, 108, 117, 128, 137, 146, 156, 160

A script is an enumeration by cues, isn't it! Options: (1) The "cue" name at the ... caps, ...owed ...erial ...y be ...aps.

272

LESSON 49

81

RADIO STATION CKCW   5

1740 Redthorne Avenue   12

Fredericton, New Brunswick   19

E3B 2M1

                    October 23, 19—   36

                                               44

Dr. Graham J. Goodman   50
Head, Department of Speech   55
Mount Allison University   60
Sackville, New Brunswick   66
                                               67

Dear Doctor Goodman: 72
                                               73

I am pleased to tell you that our Montreal office has sent me   85
the official word that our network will be happy to sponsor   97
the appearance of William Newhouse as a speaker at your next   109
workshop for news broadcasters. This is the message: 120
                                               121

    Mr. Newhouse will be available to you and to the   133
    University from May 3 through May 7. There will   143
    be no expense to the University; we are pleased to   155
    sponsor him as a service of the network. We are   165
    sure that Mr. Newhouse will wish the full details   176
    about the part he is to play in the program, how   177
    many talks he is to prepare and give, whether he   188
    will be housed on campus, and so on, just as soon   199
    as these matters are settled.   206
                                               207

I believe, Doctor Goodman, that it would now be appropriate   219
for you to write directly to Mr. Newhouse and give him as many 231
details as you can. If the schedule is not yet fixed, you may 244
wish to note that Mr. Newhouse has Sunday broadcasts before   256
and after your program; so he is certain to be grateful if you 269
can stage him late on Monday and early on Friday.   279
                                               280

If there is any way in which I can help with arrangements or   292
equipment for your workshop, please let me know.   302
                                               303

                    Cordially yours,   308

                                               317

                    Director, Department of   324
                    Service and Public Relations   332
EJLambert:TEK   Radio Station C K C W   339

Blocked Letter with Quotation Paragraph, Three-Line
Signer's Identification, and Signer's Name in Reference Position

PART SEVEN TEST   LESSON 175

Progress Test on Part Two

Test 2

Test 2-A

5-MINUTE WRITING
ON PARAGRAPHS
Paper: workbook
  page 71; or plain
Line: 60
Tab: paragraph
Spacing: double
Start: machine set,
  carriage at margin
Grade: box below
SI: 1.34—fairly easy

So you like to hike the trail, do you, and camp in the | 12
woods and fish in the lakes and cook over open fires! Then | 24
you are one of legions who have that idea. It's been esti- | 36
mated that some five million families took such a "four for | 48
the price of one" vacation last summer. The national parks | 60
themselves had a total of more than thirty million campers. | 72

One of the things that surprise us all over again each | 84
year is the variety of shelters that vacation campers bring | 96
with them, ranging from a simple pup tent to a big imported | 108
camping trailer. The most popular type of tent is probably | 120
the umbrella tent, with its four corner poles; at least, we | 132
see more of this kind than of any other kind. The umbrella | 144
comes in two sizes, the 10 by 10 for four people and the 12 | 156
by 12 for five people. It is easy to put up and even looks | 168
nice, for it has a canopy that serves to roof a front porch | 180
or kitchen for you. It is usually equipped with a floor of | 192
canvas and screens for door and windows. [START OVER] | 200

1 | 2 | 3 | 4 | 5 | 6 | 7 | 8 | 9 | 10 | 11 | 12

5-MINUTE SPEED
WITHIN 4 ERRORS*

40-up wam	A
35-39 wam	B
25-34 wam	C
20-24 wam	D

* If more than 4 errors
are made, compute the
speed on what is typed
before the fifth error.

CARE OF THE MACHINE

| | 12 |
| | 14 |

1. Daily: Clean the type faces by brushing them | 24
   with a stiff brush or by using some commercial | 34
   product made for the purpose. | 41

2. Daily: Dust the machine carefully, using a | 52
   long-handled brush to whisk out the inside and | 62
   a soft cloth to wipe off the outside. | 71

3. Daily: Wipe off the desk, being sure to wipe | 82
   under the machine as well as around it. | 91

4. Daily: Keep machine covered when not in use. | 102

5. Weekly: Wipe the carriage rails with a soft | 113
   cloth that has been dampened in oil. Do not | 123
   put oil directly on any part of the machine. | 133

6. Monthly: Wipe the cylinder with a soft cloth | 144
   that has been dampened in alcohol. [START OVER] | 152

1 | 2 | 3 | 4 | 5 | 6 | 7 | 8 | 9 | 10

Test 2-B
(Manuscript 10)

5-MINUTE WRITING
ON AN ENUMERATION
Paper: workbook
  page 72; or plain
Center exact copy
Tab: for overruns
Start: machine set,
  carriage centered
Grade: box above
SI: 1.31—fairly easy

PART TWO TEST

Paper: workbook 348
Style: a bound page
Grade: box, page 270;
or panel, page 233

Test 7-B

Manuscript 64

Table 55

5-MINUTE WRITING ON PRINTED MANUSCRIPT

SECRETARIAL DUTIES   Page 38

Table 43
How Secretaries Influence Purchases

Item	Percent	Rank
Adding machines	24%	10
Calculating machines	17%	11
Copyholders	39%	5
Desk pen sets	38%	6
Desk staplers	45%	4
Dictation machines	31%	8
Duplicating machines	27%	9
Electric typewriters	48%	1
Manual typewriters	47%	2
Office desks	32%	7
Posture chairs	46%	3
Photocopy equipment	16%	12
Average	34%	—

16
39
51
60
72
80
87
94
100
107
114
122
129
138
144
151
158
170
176
188

The secretarial influence in purchases of desk and office equipment should be recognized by salesmen. As shown by the figures in Table 43, above, a third of the secretaries say they influence the brand selection in purchases of the items listed.

The editor of the magazine made an interesting comment in her editorial remarks about the survey: ". . . apparently the employers trust their secretaries' judgment more in those things that secretaries themselves will use (45.5 percent) than in the things that will need to be shared with others on the office staff (21.0 percent)."[12]

199
207
215
223
232
241
249
256
265
274
282
291
300
310

12. Sally Browne, "A Survey Told Us So," *Modern Secretary*, Volume 59, No. 11 (July, 1964), page 19.

328
342

Test 7-C

Form 71

5-MINUTE WRITING ON FILL-IN CARDS

Paper: workbook 349
Data: abstract from
following narrative
Grade: box, page 270;
or panel, page 233

CARD 1. Robert F. Buckner, of 889 West Bend Street, Scarborough, Ontario, applied yesterday for a job as accountant but was turned down because your company would not pay the $9000 a year he requested. Born on May 1, 1932, Mr. Buckner graduated from Carleton University (Ottawa) in 1954 and from Woodbridge (Ont.) Senior High School in 1950. Since 1963 he has worked as an accountant with H.H. Harris Ltd., at $9200 a year. Prior to that, he worked from 1959 until 1963 for the Toronto Transit Commission as an accountant at $7600 a year; and from 1954 to 1959 for Winco Company as a junior accountant at $6800 a year. Note: He has a standing offer to join our staff at $9500 a year.

9
15
24
34
39
49
60
77
85
89
96
103
109
117
129

CARD 2. Harriet B. Stewart, of 177 Rymer Street, Scarborough, applied yesterday for a stenographic job. She asked $105 a week, but there was no vacancy. She was born July 12, 1945, and attended Howe High School, in Picton, graduating in 1962. She has worked as a stenographer at $95 a week for the Jackson Company since June, 1963; and prior to that was a receptionist at the same company at $80 in 1962 and 1963. Note: Miss Stewart should be contacted for the next vacancy.

8
15
30
41
56
71
79
82
89
95
100

If preferred, Tests 2-B, 2-C, and 2-D may each be centered on a page (time: 10 minutes each) and then checked for penalties (Penalty Scale); the total penalty then graded on the Grading Scale.

PENALTY SCALE

—3 for each major error (top margin, line length, line-spacing, general correctness of form, etc.)
—2 for each minor error (blocking, aligning, centering, indenting, etc., of individual parts of the job)
—1 for each typographical error

GRADING SCALE

0-1 PENALTY	A
2-3 PENALTY	B
4-6 PENALTY	C
7-8 PENALTY	D

Test 2-C
Table 11

5-MINUTE WRITING ON A TABULATION
Paper: workbook page 73; or plain
Center the table
Spacing: double
Start: machine set, carriage centered
Grade: box below

5-MINUTE SPEED WITHIN 4 ERRORS*

40-up wam	A
35-39 wam	B
25-34 wam	C
20-24 wam	D

* If more than 4 errors are made, compute the speed on what is typed before the fifth error.

Test 2-D
Letter 16

5-MINUTE WRITING ON A LETTER
Paper: workbook page 74; or plain
Style: blocked
Tabs: center, 4
Start: machine set, carriage ready to pivot the date
Caution: use correct line and spacing; need initials and enclosure note
Body: 98 words
Grading: box above
SI: 1.36—normal

BASIC RATING PLAN FOR TIMED WRITINGS
Five Minutes Within Four Errors

Speeds	Lesson 25	Lesson 50	Lesson 75	
15–19 wam	Fair	Under Par	Under Par	22
20–24 wam	Average	Fair	Under Par	43
25–29 wam	Average	Average	Fair	69
30–34 wam	Superior	Average	Average	81
35–39 wam	Excellent	Superior	Average	90
40–44 wam	Excellent	Excellent	Superior	99
45–49 wam	Excellent	Excellent	Excellent	109
50–up wam	Excellent	Excellent	Excellent	120

[START OVER]

1 | 2 | 3 | 4 | 5 | 6 | 7 | 8 | 9 | 10 | 11

Today's date

Mr. Carl S. Norman   12
The Norman Press, Ltd.   20
306 Prince Albert Road   24
Dartmouth, Nova Scotia B2Y 1N2   28
Dear Mr. Norman: 34
   39

Please let us know what you would charge to print the   51
two displays that I enclose. Details of these two jobs   62
are as follows: 65

1. We require 5000 copies of each job.   75

2. The table should be set in type styles suitable for   88
display in a dark green ink on a light green card,   99
15 cm by 10 cm.   103

3. The listing would be set in a similar type size and   116
displayed in dark brown ink on a buff or a tan card,   126
15 cm by 10 cm.   131

We would ask for assurance that the cards could be de-   143
livered before January 3.   148

Yours truly,   154

Dexter K. Lynch   162

Closing lines   166

[START OVER]

1 | 2 | 3 | 4 | 5 | 6 | 7 | 8 | 9 | 10 | 11

Progress Test on Part Seven

Test 7

Test 7-A

TIMED WRITING ON
PARAGRAPH COPY
Paper: workbook 347
Line: 70 spaces
Tab: paragraph 5
Spacing: single
Length: 5 min. (2)
   or 10 min. (1)
Grade: box below
SI: 1.37—easy-normal

| 1 | 2 | 3 | 4 | 5 | 6 | 7 | 8 | 9 | 10 | 11 | 12 | 13 | 14 |

Of all the skills that people wish they had, the skill of typing ranks   15
first. Just about every person who knows that you can type has said   29
to you that he wishes that he, too, knew how to type; the person who is   43
a skilled typist is the envy of all his friends. One evidence that typing   58
is so popular is shown by the fact that more persons take courses in   72
typing than in anything else (except English, that is; but then,   85
English is a required course). Today it is not just the office trainee   100
who learns to type, although he must, of course; but everyone else   113
seems to be taking the course, too. I visited a college a short time ago   128
and found that the school had just taken a poll to find what purpose   142
the students had in mind when they signed up for typing. You might   155
be amazed at one finding of this poll: enrolled for the typing course   169
was at least one student from every department in the college!   182

It is natural to marvel and to wonder why so many persons desire   197
this skill. The answer is that almost all careers in modern life now   211
involve the use of much paper and require that you be able to express   225
yourself, whether what you wish to report is a new plan for packaging   239
snow, a new scheme for a sales campaign, a history of jazz, a formula   253
for splitting the atom, or a news account of life in Quebec. And the   267
simple truth is that what you write has to be typed. No editor worth   281
his salt would look at a penned manuscript these days; and the modern   295
employer would be aghast if one of his assistants handed him any note   309
of more than a dozen words that was handwritten; he wants them   322
typed!   323

The simple truth is that the typewriter has become an instrument   338
that is used in a great many trades. These would, of course, include   352
the office jobs of a thousand and one kinds, not only secretarial and   366
clerical posts but also the creative ones of editors and writers, and   380
so on. In addition, there are many positions in which the ability to   394
type is a plus value that helps a person meet competition. The field   408
salesman who can type his own reports is preferred to one who cannot.   422
The dental assistant who can type is preferred to one who cannot. An   436
assistant in a physics lab who can type the lab reports is preferred,   450
of course, to one who cannot. We seem to have approached a time   463
when just about everyone had jolly well better become an efficient   477
typist.   478

| 1 | 2 | 3 | 4 | 5 | 6 | 7 | 8 | 9 | 10 | 11 | 12 | 13 | 14 |

**5-MINUTE SPEED
WITHIN 2 ERRORS**

**10-MINUTE SPEED
WITHIN 5 ERRORS**

55-up	. . . .	A
50-54	. . . .	B
40-49	. . . .	C
35-39	. . . .	D

If you make excessive
errors, base speed on
what you type prior to
first excessive error

3

POSTAL CODE • METRIC GUIDE
SKILL BUILDING • CARDS AND LETTER
DISPLAY • FORMS • REPORTS

TABLE OF CONTENTS

Design for a Table of Contents

CORRESPONDENCE MANUAL

Prepared by
Charles R. Perkins

Center in
upper half

TYPEWRITING III

Miss Mary Bowers, Instructor
School of Business
October 10, 19—

Center in
lower half

Design for a Cover Page

Cards in visible index overlap
(names show at bottom) and
flip up to reveal recorded data.

Stevens,		Patrick	A. (Dr.)
LAST NAME		FIRST NAME	MIDDLE NAME OR INITIAL

1.
2. Address: 19 Meadow Road
3. Brantford, Ontario N3R 3K9
4.
5. Post: Brantford
6. Initiation: September 22, 19--
7. Service: Navy (Medical Corps)
8. Rank: Commander
9. Years Service: $3\frac{1}{2}$
10. Occupation: Physician
11.

LAST NAME	FIRST NAME	MIDDLE NAME OR INITIAL
Stevens,	Patrick	A. (Dr.)

TYPIST PLEASE NOTE: THIS SCALE CORRESPONDS TO PICA SPACING. If your machine is elite, use the other side of this card. Set the paper guide so that the scale on your machine corresponds to the spacing on this scale. Set the left margin stop at the first arrow and tab stops at the other arrows. Fold back or remove this stub after typing card.

Index Card for a Visible-Index File

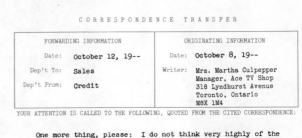

CORRESPONDENCE TRANSFER

FORWARDING INFORMATION

Date: October 12, 19--

Dep't To: Sales

Dep't From: Credit

ORIGINATING INFORMATION

Date: October 8, 19--

Writer: Mrs. Martha Culpepper
Manager, Ace TV Shop
318 Lyndhurst Avenue
Toronto, Ontario
M8X 1M4

YOUR ATTENTION IS CALLED TO THE FOLLOWING, QUOTED FROM THE CITED CORRESPONDENCE:

One more thing, please: I do not think very highly of the
new window-display pieces that you sent us this fall. They
are drab and faded. They do not "pull in the customers
right off the street," as you had said they would. With
better support from your advertising department, maybe my
store could sell some JK sets and get some money to pay the
bill you have been sending me twice a week!

Correspondence Transfer Form

1. Transfer from Sales to Advertising a copy of paragraph 2, letter 77, page 245.

2. Transfer from E. R. Bigler, Accounting, to John Fleshman, Credit Union, a copy of paragraph 3, Letter 85, page 258.

Unit 9. Skill Development

LINE: 60
TAB: 5
SPACING: SINGLE
DRILLS: THREE TIMES
        EACH
GOAL: TO BOOST BOTH
        SPEED AND CONTROL
STRESS: CORRECT
        POSTURE

51-A. Ripple through lines 1-3 three times each. Try to keep your palms low, but not touching the machine. Repeat in Lesson 52, too.

51-A. Tune up on these easy lines

1 duel rich town pale odor name melt lamb kept cork irks hang
2 Inez says Jack played a very quiet game of bridge with Rex.
3 Did the Halls move to 1028 39th Street or 3947 56th Street?

51-B. To define practice needs, type a double-spaced copy and then proofread it carefully. GOAL: To finish it in 3 minutes or less.

Should you make 4 or more typing errors, your goal in Lesson 51 is ACCURACY.

Should you make 3 or fewer typing errors, it is SPEED.

51-B. Measure and improve your skill

4 If you ever get a chance to observe the technique of a   12
truly expert typist, listen to the sound of the typing. It   24
is certain to have a steady flow that seems to waver within   36
a span of a dozen words a minute. When the going is rough,   48
which is to say that the copy is difficult, one drops to an   60
easy pace, which sounds like a jog trot; but when the going   72
is smooth and easy like this turn of words is, one speeds up   84
like a driver turning out to pass another car on a highway.   96
The trick lies in not speeding up or slowing down too much.   108

  1 | 2 | 3 | 4 | 5 | 6 | 7 | 8 | 9 | 10 | 11 | 12

51-C. Practice to achieve your improvement goal:

ACCURACY: The whole group of lines three times.

SPEED: Individually, each drill line three times.

SI 1.31—fairly easy

51-C. Improve control of A, B, C, D, E

5 aaa All aaa aid aaa alas aaa apart aaa salad aaa appeal aaa
6 bbb But fbf bit fbf blob fbf blurb fbf abbot fbf bubble bbb
7 ccc Can dcd cue dcd corn dcd clock dcd click dcd clinic ccc
8 ddd Did ddd dye ddd dude ddd dried ddd idled ddd muddle ddd
9 eee End ded eye ded heel ded elves ded tense ded eleven eee
10 When library books are due back, please take care that   12
they get back, because dedicated readers may be waiting for   24
their chance at them. Anyone can get a book back when due.   36

  1 | 2 | 3 | 4 | 5 | 6 | 7 | 8 | 9 | 10 | 11 | 12

51-D. Type to reach your skill-improvement goal:

ACCURACY: The whole group of lines three times.

SPEED: Each drill line, individually, three times.

SI 1.32—fairly easy

51-D. Improve control of F, G, H, I, J

11 fff For fff off fff buff fff fifth fff fifty fff affair fff
12 ggg Got fgf log fgf gong fgf going fgf soggy fgf groggy fgf
13 hhh Hot jhj the jhj high jhj which jhj hunch jhj higher jhj
14 iii Ink kik did kik Mimi kik visit kik mimic kik liquid kik
15 jjj Job jjj joy jjj just jjj major jjj jewel jjj justly jjj
16 Judge Joy ay have just as much fun going to the fifth   12
annual affair as Major Hughes. Fifty to fifty-five mimics,   24
I hear, are going to join a gang of kids and serve liquids.   36

  1 | 2 | 3 | 4 | 5 | 6 | 7 | 8 | 9 | 10 | 11 | 12

LINE: 60
TAB: 15
SPACING: SINGLE
DRILLS: THREE TIMES
GOAL: REVIEW PART
   SEVEN LEARNINGS
STRESS: EFFICIENCY

173-A. Each line three times, or half-minute writings, to get back your full typing pace. Repeat in Lesson 174.

173-A. Tune up on these review lines

1   The chairman of the panel may wish to sign the audit forms.
2   My black ax just zipped through the fine wood quite evenly.
3   Reports #10, #28, and #39 were much harder than #47 or #56.
    1 | 2 | 3 | 4 | 5 | 6 | 7 | 8 | 9 | 10 | 11 | 12

173-B. What's your goal?

ACCURACY: Lines 4-7 as a paragraph, three times.

SPEED: Type each line individually three times.

173-B. Boost skill by selective preview practice

4   abbreviation resulted United States follow three after body
5   punctuation distinct "close" option letter comma style form
6   expectation (except) pattern (line) common still block ends
7   salutation signature involve phrase commas looks other ones
    1 | 2 | 3 | 4 | 5 | 6 | 7 | 8 | 9 | 10 | 11 | 12

173-C. Sustain skill on production copy

Part 3. Letter Punctuation Styles

173-C. Change machine to 50-space line (lines will align), double spacing, 5-space tab indention.

Type one complete copy.

SI 1.44—upper normal

ALTERNATE PLAN:
1. Take a 5-minute timed writing, resting for 10 seconds after each minute.

2. Take a 5-minute timed writing without rests.

GOAL: To type 45 or more wam within 2 errors.

The punctuation used in the *body* of a letter involves no option; 16
the demands of proper English must be met. But in the punctuation 29
that follows the ends of the *display lines* above and below the letter 48
body, there *is* option; and it has resulted in three distinct styles for 63
use with such lines. 67

A. Standard Style. This is the one in most common use. It re- 88
quires the salutation to end in a colon, the closing phrase to end in 102
a comma; no other punctuation, except for the period after an abbre- 116
viation, is used to end or to "close" any of the letter parts that precede 131
or follow the body. 135

B. Open Style. In this pattern, no display line—not even a 154
salutation or a closing phrase—ends with a punctuation mark. The 167
lone exception is a line that ends with an abbreviation; it will have a 182
period after it. When a letter is written in this style, it has a clean, 196
modern look to it. 202

C. Closed Style. This design, once in wide use in this coun- 222
try and still in wide use in many other countries, requires some punc- 235
tuation at the end of every display line to "close" it. All the display 240
lines end with either a period or a comma except the salutation, which 254
ends with the colon. The comma is used to close each line of an inside 269
address (except the last line) and each line of a signature block (except 283
the last line); all other display lines must be closed with a final period. 299

   1 | 2 | 3 | 4 | 5 | 6 | 7 | 8 | 9 | 10 | 11 | 12 | 13 | 14

173/174-D. Apply skill to production assignments

Manuscript 60

BOUND REPORT (10)
Include page heading to identify this material as page 10

Manuscript 61

PREFACE
Use 169-C, typed on a 60-space line, double spaced, beginning on line 11

51-E. Improve control of K, L, M, N, O

```
17   kkk Key kkk eke kkk kick kkk knick kkk knack kkk knocks kkk
18   lll Lay lll all lll will lll level lll allot lll little lll
19   mmm Map jmj jam jmj maim jmj mimic jmj madam jmj moment mmm
20   nnn Nay jnj nag jnj nine jnj inner jnj anent jnj winnow nnn
21   ooo Oak lol own lol odor lol motor lol moron lol follow ooo
22   Oliver King may not like lemons or lemons may not like    12
him, but my dollars will take even money that Mr. King will   24
not balk at eating lemon meringue pie like my mother makes.   36
     1  |  2  |  3  |  4  |  5  |  6  |  7  |  8  |  9  |  10  |  11  |  12
```

51-F. Make an interim progress check

52-A. Learn to type on and center on a line

51-F. To confirm progress in Lesson 51 and to set your goal for Lesson 52, repeat 51-B, page 85.

52-A. The numbers within parentheses refer to the numbered machine parts that are shown on pages 2-5. Machines vary; so:

(1) Type a solid line of underscores; how much space, if any, shows between the line and aligning scale?

(2) Check whether variable spacer on your machine (the button in the left cylinder knob) must be pressed in or, on some models, pulled out to adjust line of writing.

(3) Determine how to adjust the ribbon control so that the ribbon is disengaged (to set it for stencil). A typical arrangement:

STEP 1. Adjust the paper to place the line in the position that a line of underscores would occupy.

To loosen the paper while you adjust it, use the paper release (24).

To turn the paper slightly up or down, turn the left cylinder knob while the palm of your left hand presses the variable spacer (43, the button in the left cylinder knob).

To test the position of the line, type one *light* underscore stroke with the ribbon-control lever (35) set for stencil (disengaged).

STEP 2. Determine how many spaces to indent the typing from the start of the line: set the carriage at the start of the line; tap the space bar once for each space the typed line will fill; then (counting strokes) continue spacing to the end of the line to find how many spaces remain to be divided around the name.

```
?  John Jones  ?
John Jones12345678
1234John Jones5678
```

PRACTICE. Draw 10 straight lines, varying from 30 to 40 strokes long, on a sheet of paper. Insert the paper and center your name on each line.

```
  Too Low
  Too High

 Just Right
```

52-B. Improve control of P, Q, R, S, T

```
23   ppp Pay ;p; pen ;p; prop ;p; upper ;p; paper ;p; prompt ppp
24   qqq Que aqa qui aqa quit aqa quell aqa queen aqa quaint qqq
25   rrr Roy frf rug frf roar frf error frf carry frf repair rrr
26   sss Sue sws sis sws loss sws sales sws issue sws system sss
27   ttt Tom ftf tot ftf mutt ftf title ftf total ftf static ttt

28   Roy stated that he thought aqua paper was pretty.  Sue     12
says statistics show that total sales of white paper do far   24
surpass aqua sales.  Queen plans to get six quires of aqua.   36
     1  |  2  |  3  |  4  |  5  |  6  |  7  |  8  |  9  |  10  |  11  |  12
```

Table 5

SOME CORRECT FORMS OF ENCLOSURE NOTATIONS 20

One Enclosure	More than One	Enumerated
Enclosure	2 Enclosures	Enclosures:
Enc.	2 Encs.	Cheques
Encl.	2 Enc.	Invoice
1 Enc.	Enc. 2	
1 Enclosure	Enclosures (2)	Enclosures—
Cheque Enclosed	Enclosures: 3 + 5	1. Cheque
Bill Enclosed	Enclosures—4	2. Bill

5 ← Typing Enclosure or 3 Enclosures is enough in most ← cases, but "It is important to identify enclosures if any is small, if any is valuable (as a cheque would be), or if someone other than the typist will seal and mail the letter."[10] The only time when an enclosure notation can be omitted is when a letter is formal (when the address is at the bottom).

N. The Post Script is an extra paragraph added at the very bottom of the letter and is treated as such. It is indented or is blocked as are the other paragraphs. The initials PS., PS:, P. S., or PS— are typed at the start of the paragraph.

O. The "cc" notation is typed under the enc notation to indicate to the addressee that carbon copies (hence "cc") have been sent to the persons indicated. Samples of styles:

cc Miss Hall   cc JJH   cc: Hall
cc Mr. Lewis   cc FJL   Lewis

P. The "bcc" Notation indicates to whom copies of the letter have been sent without the addressee's knowing it. "Blind carbon copies" (hence "bcc") are identified:

[Typist: Insert here the second and third sentences, para. 7, page 246, of the typewriting book.]

52-C. Improve control of U, V, W, X, Y, Z

29 uuu Use juj ups juj dual juj usual juj usury juj unused uuu
30 vvv Vow fvf vie fvf view fvf vivid fvf valve fvf velvet vvv
31 www Why sws two sws wavy sws which sws would sws wigwam www
32 xxx Six sxs box sxs next sxs taxis sxs index sxs extras xxx
33 yyy You jyj yet jyj year jyj yearn jyj yards jyj heyday yyy
34 zzz Zip aza zoo aza zone aza zeros aza azure aza zigzag zzz

35   Zimmy will amaze you, I know, with his unusually even,   12
speedy typing. Six or seven times every week, he types for   24
an extra hour or two to very even music, to improve rhythm.   36
    1 | 2 | 3 | 4 | 5 | 6 | 7 | 8 | 9 | 10 | 11 | 12

52-D. Type to your goal:
ACCURACY: The whole group of lines three times.

SPEED: Each drill line, individually, three times.

One-hand words:

"ed" words:

Double letters:

Alternate-hand words:

52-D. Speed up on downhill preview words

36 betters brash only zest seat upon were ever you at no be in
37 directed precede hailed raised failed pledge named tried ed
38 affectionate installed college recall issue guess good door
39 problem social worms right them duty than clan they own the

52-E. To measure your skill improvement, follow either of these two schedules: (1) Type paragraph 40 two times.

GOAL: To finish either copy within 5 or fewer minutes and with not more than 4 typing errors.

(2) Or, take two 5-minute writings on the article.

GOAL: 35 or more words a minute, within 4 errors. (Record the better score.)

In either case, use a tab-5 paragraph indention and double space the copy.

SI 1.34—nearly normal

IDEA: Use both paragraphs for stretching your skill, not for testing your skill:

(1) Take a 5-minute timing with a 10-second rest after each of the minutes; then,

(2) Take a 5-minute timing without rests but with the minutes called off, so that you can see whether or not you are staying on pace.

52-E. Measure your skill in sustained writing

40   When I was a college boy and a pledge to a fraternity,   12
the good brothers had a number of rules by which they tried   24
to acquaint us unworthy ones with the right paths of social   36
behavior. There was a rule, for example, that no one of us   48
worms, as we were affectionately named, should ever precede   60
one of our betters, and you can guess who were our betters,   72
through a doorway but rather were directed to open the door   84
and hold it open as a gesture of love and service. The one   96
who failed in this duty would be hailed before the tribunal   108
and instructed in manners with a justice and zest that went   120
at once to the heart, or the seat, of the problem. I still   132
tingle each time I hold the door open for my own fair lady.   144

41   Well, one day the college installed a lot of revolving   156
doors at its many entrances and exits. Can you imagine the   168
problem that this made for the fraternal clan? These doors   180
were very heavy, and it was next to impossible to push them   192
without going through them. If any of us worms had to open   204
the door by pushing it, he then had to precede his superior   216
through the doorway. Always a brash person, I was the worm   228
who raised the issue; and I spoke more eloquently about the   240
subject than a worm should, as I recall painfully.   250
    1 | 2 | 3 | 4 | 5 | 6 | 7 | 8 | 9 | 10 | 11 | 12

J. The <u>attention line</u>, is an extension of the inside ad- 20

dress, and is typed between the inside address and salutation. 32

It is always preceded and followed by ①blank line. It is usually 46

blocked left but may be centered, too. It may be arranged in 58

many different styles, as shown in Table 4, below. 68

× 13 mm # 71

Table 4 77

STYLES OF MODERN ATTENTION AND SUBJECT LINES 100
112

Subject Lines	Attention Lines	122
		133
ATTENTION: CREDIT MANAGER	SUBJECT: SPECIAL SALE	144
Attention: Credit Manager	Subject: Special Sale	172
Attention of the President	Subject——Special Order	200
Attention of the President	Subject——Special Order Sale	216
Attention Legal Department	Refer to File 158–6599	233
ATTENTION Mr. John Parsons Jack Dennis	RE: The Lewiston Case	243
Attention of Mr. Jack Dahl	In re Shaw vs. Shipley	260
		272

13 mm # 275

K. The <u>Subject Line</u> is a preview of the message and so 357

is typed between the salutation and the body. It may be cen- 369

tered; it may be blocked at the left. It may be arranged in 381

many different styles, as shown in Table 4 [Tell where it is]. 391

Since the purpose of an attention line is to direct 286
the letter to a particular person in the company, 297
the inclusion of this line does not change the saluta- 309
tion. The letter is <u>addressed</u> to the firm; there- 323
fore, the salutation must be <u>Gentlemen</u>.⑧ 337

L. The <u>Company Signature</u> is typed in all-capitals, a 414

double space below the complimentary closing. Illustrations 426

of its use are shown in Table 3, page 6. It is often left 438

out, but is sometimes required ". . . when the letter in- 447

volves an obligation of the company rather than the signer."⑨ 461

M. The Enclosure Notations is a signals, like the ones shown in 485

Table 5, next page, to remind both the sender and the receiver of a letter that 500

something is enclosed in the same envelope. The notation is 512

typed a or two lines below the reference initials. 521

Manuscript 58

BOUND REPORT (8)
Caution: You must
determine where to
end page 7 and to
start page 8; do
not forget heading
at top of page 8.

QUOTATION REMINDERS

1. A quotation taking
three or fewer lines of
typing is displayed in
quotation marks. Longer
quotations are not put
in quotation marks but
are displayed in single
spacing and indented 5
spaces on each margin.

2. Make and insert the
footnote for quotation
No. 8. It is from page
18 of the book by Gavin,
previously mentioned
(see page 261).

3. Make and insert the
footnote for quotation
No. 9. It is from page
97 of the book by Lloyd,
previously mentioned
(see pages 262, 263).

4. Ellipsis (. . .)
indicates omission.

Skill Drive

53-A. Tune up on these easy lines

1   paid firm born hand pair land burn busy form half soap sigh

2   Refer to a metric character as a symbol, not an abbreviation.

3   Did it happen on May 10, 1956; May 3, 1947; or May 1, 1928?

53-A. Set a smooth pace on line 1; then hold the pace on lines 2 and 3. Repeat this warmup in Lesson 54.

53-B. Measure and improve your skill

4   About the time when our parents were children, two out   12
of ten Canadian citizens lived in a city. The others lived   24
on farms or in small towns where most people lived in homes   36
with lawns, knew each other well, and enjoyed an atmosphere   48
of quiet calm. The picture has changed today; seven out of   60
ten now live in cities or close to them, not because cities   72
are better places in which to live but because there exists   84
in the urban centers something that mechanization has taken   96
from the farm and the forest: the chance to make a living.   108
    1 | 2 | 3 | 4 | 5 | 6 | 7 | 8 | 9 | 10 | 11 | 12

53-B. To define practice needs, type a double-spaced copy; then proofread it carefully. GOAL: To finish it in 3 minutes or less.

If you make 3 or more typing errors, your practice goal in Lesson 53 is ACCURACY.

If you make 2 or fewer typing errors, your goal is SPEED.

SI 1.37—normal

53-C. Improve control of sideway motions

5   AFA affix afar ARA arrow rain ATA attic data AGA again saga

6   LJL jural jell LUL lucid dull LYL slyly duly LHL lathe hall

7   ABA papal baby AVA avail vain ZGZ graze gaze QTQ quiet quit

8   LNL banal only LML balms melt PHP graph soph PYP happy pure

9   The photographer tried an hour to get the baby to look   12
happy and sit quietly. He finally got a dull photograph of   24
the baby gazing stupidly, slyly, at an array of jelly jars.   36
    1 | 2 | 3 | 4 | 5 | 6 | 7 | 8 | 9 | 10 | 11 | 12

53-C. Type to reach your practice goal, with special attention to keeping wrists from swinging in and out.

ACCURACY: The whole group of lines three times.

SPEED: Each drill line, individually, three times.

SI 1.54—difficult

53-D. Improve control of vertical motions

10   BTB baton tubs BRB bribe ribs CTC catch tact CRC crack rich

11   NYN money yank NUN nutty unit MYM maybe hymn MUM mummy bump

12   XEX vexed exit XWX waxen waxy ZEZ dozen maze BEB begin ebbs

13   NIN ninth nine NON north once MIM mimic rims MOM month some

14   Monty may bring a bunch of records to give as our door   12
prize on the ninth. At the next meeting, maybe someone can   24
bring us six extra boxes of candy or crackers or something.   36
    1 | 2 | 3 | 4 | 5 | 6 | 7 | 8 | 9 | 10 | 11 | 12

53-D. Type to reach your goal; keep hands quiet— don't let them bounce!

ACCURACY: The whole group of lines three times.

SPEED: Each drill line, individually, three times.

SI 1.30—fairly easy

Table 3

SOME CORRECT ARRANGEMENTS FOR CLOSING LINES

Cordially yours,	Yours very truly,
Vice-President	Vice-President, Research Personnel
Very sincerely yours,	Respectfully submitted,
Paul Todd, President	Secretary to Mr. Wilson
Yours very truly,	Sincerely yours,
THE KERR CORPORATION	DOWN CONSTRUCTION COMPANY
Harrison Dwyer	Richard Markham Graham
President	General Manager
Yours truly,	Very cordially yours,
THE INTERNATIONAL COMPANY	S T Y L E , L T D .
Parke Alexander	Mrs. Ruth Mann Osborne
Chairman of the Board	Advertising Department

TECHNICAL NOTES:

1. Underscore rules are often used to divide long tables and displays.

2. For equal space above and below a line, single space before typing it and double space after it.

3. To save space, leave only two blank lines in each signature space.

4. For fast production, just copy the indentions in Column 1 by visual inspection; but do tabulate to start of Column 2.

THE SUPPLEMENTAL LETTER PARTS

In the course of many years, the business letter has picked up a great many extra parts to serve particular purposes. None of these is essential for getting a message across to the addressee, but they do serve as aids to him, or to the writer, or to their secretaries. Table 2, on Page 3, lists eight supplemental letter parts.

The Reference Line is used in businesses where records are kept in numerical files or transactions are handled by a very large staff. It is a line, When reply-ing, Refer to, printed in the letterhead. The typist of an out-going letter types the correct file number alongside that reference guide. When replying to such a notation, the typist includes a subject line (in which he refers to the same reference file number) in his letter of response.

53-E. Type to reach your practice goal, with very special attention given to continuity—don't let the copy break your rhythm.

ACCURACY: The whole group of lines three times.

SPEED: Each drill line, individually, three times.

SI 1.32—fairly easy

53-E. Improve control of one-hand words

15 effect minion after knoll zest only fear pool gab him at no

16 limply agreed hilly wages lion were puny safe you bad up be

17 ✓ feared lumpy, extra union gate milk fast lily car hop as in

18 pinion accede pylon trace junk fees link rate joy was no we

19 dreads nylon, cases join; ease pill test holy set ink as in

20   In my opinion, we were in bad after you set up a union   12
rate on wages. We feared a million ill effects. I dreaded   24
a union fee. I gave in only after you set up better rates.   36

  1 | 2 | 3 | 4 | 5 | 6 | 7 | 8 | 9 | 10 | 11 | 12

53-F. Make an interim progress check

53-F. Repeat 53-B, page 88, to confirm your progress and to pinpoint goals for Lesson 54.

54-A. Using the aligning scale to align insertions is important not only for inserting a missing letter but also in all kinds of corrections of work and in the use of all kinds of fill-in business forms.

Different typewriters vary in the precision of the placement of the aligning scale; this is why it is so important to note closely the position of the scale on any machine you use.

54-A. Learn how to make typed insertions

The key to correct typed insertions is the alignment of your typing with your machine's aligning scale. Right now, type the alphabet on your machine and compare your typing and aligning scale with this illustration:

1. To align insertions *vertically*, you must know *exactly* how much space (if any) there is between the typing and the top of the aligning scale.

2. To align insertions horizontally, you must know *exactly* how nearly the markers on the scale come to the center of the letters (easiest to check:

i, l, m, I, T, period, colon).

PRACTICE 1. Type this name (with space left for the omitted letters) in four places on a sheet of paper:

M ss El a W ll amson

Remove the paper, reinsert it, and fill in the missing letters:

Wrong: Miss Ella Williamson
Right: Miss Ella Williamson

Use the variable spacer (in the left cylinder knob) for vertical adjustments of the paper. Use the paper release for horizontal adjustments.

PRACTICE 2. In four places on the paper, type FROM: and, under it, TO:. Remove the paper, reinsert and align it, and then type your name 2 or 3 spaces after each of the colons.

54-B. Improve control of double-letter words

54-B. Type to reach your goal, with special attention given to accenting second letter of the doubles as much as the first letter.

ACCURACY: Type the group of lines three times.

SPEED: Type each drill, individually, three times.

SI 1.42—normal

21 bb bubble cc accent dd middle ee needle ff suffer gg logger

22 ll bullet mm jammer nn dinner oo poodle pp dapper rr borrow

23 ✓ ss issues tt putter zz sizzle bb lubber cc accord dd puddle

24 ee keeper ff muffle gg rigger ll called mm hammer nn annoys

25 oo rooter pp supply rr mirror ss missed tt little zz puzzle

26   Bill Mazzle needs a bookkeeper and will see applicants   12
tomorrow. He will screen all who apply. He will arrange a   24
follow-up meeting for all who seem well fitted for the job.   36

  1 | 2 | 3 | 4 | 5 | 6 | 7 | 8 | 9 | 10 | 11 | 12

LINE: 60
TAB: 5
SPACING: SINGLE
DRILLS: THREE TIMES
GOAL: SUSTAIN SKILL
   IN STEADY TYPING
STRESS: EARNEST
   KEEP-GOING-NESS

171-A. Each line three times at a very steady, word-eating pace. Repeat 171-A in Lesson 172.

171-B. Three copies at least, plus as many more as may be required for you to produce at least one copy without error. Repeat in Lesson 172.

SI 1.03—VERY easy

171-C. Change machine to double spacing and check margins for 60-space line (lines will align) and a 5-space tab indention.

ACCURACY: Type each of the paragraphs once.

SPEED: Type any one of the paragraphs three or more consecutive times.

Repeat in Lesson 172.
SI 1.25—easy

171-D. Before resuming work on the Manual, you would find it helpful to review information about footnotes given on pages 115, 116, 120.

171-A. Tune up on these easy review lines

1 The men may fix their antique auto and go downtown with it.
2 Jack found the gravel camp six below zero quite a few days.
3 The 10's, 28's, 39's, 47's, and 56's make up pair patterns.

   1 | 2 | 3 | 4 | 5 | 6 | 7 | 8 | 9 | 10 | 11 | 12

171-B. Restore full skill on very easy material

4 The men quit their work to run down the dock and catch   12
the light lines we threw from the deck of the big ship. In   24
no time at all, the men on the dock had pulled in the light 36
lines and the thick ropes we had tied to them. The men got   48
the end of each rope looped over a post, and then we turned 60
to the deck engines to take up the slack and so pull us in. 72

   1 | 2 | 3 | 4 | 5 | 6 | 7 | 8 | 9 | 10 | 11 | 12

171-C. Sustain full skill on easy alphabetic paragraphs

5 One of the smartest girls I know is one who sat beside me when   14
I took a course in typing. She was not the fastest typist in our class,   28
and modesty will not let me say who it was that acquired this honor;   42
but it was she who turned out the most and best work. It happened,   56
over and over. While the rest of us were still analyzing the problem,   70
that young lady would be poking keys. No job was too complex for   83
her.   84

6 One day I asked her how she did it. I expected her to say she had   99
acquired a key to the problems, like the one an instructor gets, and   112
that she simply studied the key before coming to class each day. Or,   126
I thought, perhaps she would say that she had taken the same course   140
somewhere else, even using the same book; that would justify her   153
success. But I was wrong; her answer left me amazed at her coy   166
craftiness.   168

7 She paused before giving her reply, and I pressed with more ques-   182
tions. No, she did not have a machine at home nor one she could   195
borrow. No, she did not have an answer book. I must have looked   208
exasperated or something, for she turned on a suspicious but dazzling   222
smile and asked whether I felt it unjust to study the book and solve   236
the problems ahead of time. No, I did not. A light dawned. What   250
I mean, smart!   253

   1 | 2 | 3 | 4 | 5 | 6 | 7 | 8 | 9 | 10 | 11 | 12 | 13 | 14

171/172-D. Continue typing the Correspondence Manual

54-C. Type to reach your goal, with special attention to striking keys so briskly these key-jammers don't!

ACCURACY: Type the whole group three times.

SPEED: Type each drill, individually, three times.

SI 1.12—very easy

```
27   apricot island visit their when rich town man and for go is
28   bicycle profit vigor field dish down kept dog the but an to
29   bushels laughs right works land fish girl sit pay bid so by
30   rituals eighty turns roams with firm lake eye big men do he
31   auditor icicle goals shape body auto both fit cut aid of it
```

```
32   Did the men make a visit to the auto firm in the city,     12
or did they go to the firm at the lake? If they got to the     24
lake, Bob may pay for the auto and also land a fish for us.     36
```

```
1 | 2 | 3 | 4 | 5 | 6 | 7 | 8 | 9 | 10 | 11 | 12
```

54-D. Measure your skill in sustained writing

54-D. To measure your skill improvement, follow either schedule (use double spacing and a tab-5 indention):

(1) Type paragraph 33 twice. GOAL: To finish either copy within 5 minutes, with 4 or fewer typing mistakes.

(2) Or, take two 5-minute timings on the paragraphs; record your better score. GOAL: 35 or more words a minute, within 4 errors.

SI 1.31—fairly easy

```
33     What is the Postal code? The Postal code is comprised    12
of 6 characters. The code contains enough precise informa-     24
tion to direct your letter to a specific side of the street    36
and between two intersections. This code will speed up the     48
sorting of mail, especially when mail is sorted by machines    60
using optical scanners.                                        65

       One space separates the first three characters, called  77
the Area code, from the last three. The Area code in urban     89
areas describes an area approximately the size of 25 letter    101
carrier routes. The last three characters designate a very     113
small and clearly defined section within that area, such as    125
one side of a city block, an apartment, office building, or    137
organization which has a large volume of mail. In addition     149
they can specify a postal station or rural route or general    161
delivery. In rural areas, the Postal Code indicates a par-     173
ticular post office.                                           177

34     The inclusion and correct positioning of the Postal code 189
is an essential requirement in addressing Canadian mail. On    201
the letter it may appear either two spaces after the city and  213
province (on the same line) or, by itself, form the last line  225
of the inside address.                                         229

       The envelope, or outside address, should follow the same 241
form as the inside address of its letter. The Postal code      253
may be written either as the last line of the address or on    265
the same line as the city and province. In any case, the       277
Postal code must appear at least 19 mm (¾") from the bottom     289
edge of the envelope. Leave at least two character spaces       301
between the province and the Postal code.                      309
```

```
1 | 2 | 3 | 4 | 5 | 6 | 7 | 8 | 9 | 10 | 11 | 12
```

IDEA: To use the paragraphs for skill stretching instead of testing, (a) take a 5-minute writing; (b) type every line in which you made an error three times each; and (c) repeat the 5-minute timing to measure growth.

In a display like this, center longest line and align others with it.

Mr. Clark Hess, Manager	15
Toronto Fashion Company	22
Dr. Lawrence Coulter	28
Secretary–Treasurer	34
Miss Rowena G. Thompson 2 3	41
Manager, Victoria Hotel	48

The factor that determines in which position the title should be placed is the length of the lines, which should be kept as nearly equal as possible. Rowe and his coauthors say, "Use the position that best equalizes the lines of the address."[4]

   D. The Salutation is placed between the inside address and body. It is typed at the left margin, always preceded and followed by a blank line. It is almost always followed by the colon. One should capitalize only the first word, any title, and any noun; thus, *Dear Doctor Jones* vs. *My dear Doctor Jones.*

   E. The Body contains the message. It is most likely to be single spaced with a blank line between paragraphs. If a letter is very short (50 or fewer words) or if it is a report that is several pages long, it may be double spaced.

   F. The Complimentary Closing is the signing-off phrase. It begins at the left margin in some letter arrangements; but most commonly it begins at, or near, the center. It almost always ends with a comma. Only the first word is capitalized.

   G. The Signer's Identification, which is typed under the space left for the handwritten signature, may be the name, or the title (or department), or both, of the writer. Illustrations of various arrangements and various combinations of the signer's identification are given in Table 3, next page. [Page 265.]

   Three blank lines are ordinarily left for the penwritten signature, but some leeway is allowed; the space may be "up to 6 blank lines"[5] or "as few as 2 blank lines."[6]

   H. The Reference Initials include the initials of the letter dictator (unless the name appears under the signature) and those of the typist, separated by some kind of mark. The common forms are *DIC:TYP* and *DIC/typ* when both sets are used and *TYP* and *typ* when only the initials of the typist appear.

   The reference initials are typed at the left margin two lines below the identification of the signer but can be typed higher or lower when doing so will improve letter placement.[6] [Continues on page 265]

61	
74	
87	
97	
119	
132	
145	
160	
179	
198	
212	
226	
231	
257	
270	
285	
292	
318	
332	
346	
359	
365	
380	
395	
402	
426	
440	
452	
472	
481	
496	
510	
520	
526	

___

3. John L. Rowe, *et al., Gregg Typing, 191 Series, Book One* (Toronto: McGraw-Hill, 1965), page 112.   555 / 562

4. *Ibid.,* page 138.   6. *Loc. cit.* — *IBID*   576

5. Lloyd, *op. cit.,* page 57.   7. *Loc. cit.*   593

CAUTION!

1. Stop the page-4 text in time to get footnotes 3 and 4 on that page and still maintain the bottom margin of 6-9 lines.

2. Provide the proper heading for page 5, too.

Manuscript 55
BOUND REPORT (5)

IN THE FOOTNOTES:

1. "Et al." means "and others."

2. "Ibid." means "same book as in the preceding footnote" and "same page" unless a different page number is given.

3. "Op. cit." means "in the book by this author named in a previous (but not the preceding) footnote."

4. "Loc. cit." means "in the same place as the preceding footnote" (same book and same page).

5. Short footnotes may be typed beside or below one another, whichever is best for bottom margin.

LINE: 60
TAB: 5
SPACING: SINGLE
DRILLS: EACH THREE
  TIMES
GOAL: BOOST SKILL
  ESPECIALLY NUMBER
  CONTROL
STRESS: TOUCH
  CONTROL

55-A. Alternate line 1 and line 2, line 1 and line 3, etc. Repeat in Lesson 56.

55-B. To define practice goals, make two double-spaced copies of paragraph 4; proofread your work.

GOAL: To complete the two copies within 3 minutes, without looking up once.

Your goal in Lesson 55 is ACCURACY if you make 3 or more errors.

Your goal is SPEED if you make 2 or fewer errors.

SI 1.25—easy (if you know your number keys well!)

55-C. Type to reach your skill-improvement goal.

ACCURACY: The whole group of lines three times.

SPEED: Each drill line, individually, three times.

SI 1.15—easy IF

55-D. Type to reach your skill-improvement goal.

ACCURACY: Type the whole group three times.

SPEED: Type each drill, individually, three times.

SI 1.12—easy IF

55-E. Type to your goal.

ACCURACY: Alternate 15 and 16 three times.

SPEED: Type 15 and 16, individually, three times.

SI 1.04—very easy

SUGGESTION: For certain number-key control, focus practice on 3, 6, and 9 until they are as automatic as ABC. If you do this, the numbers will be easy.

55-A. Tune up on these easy lines

1   town them when form down dock firm with girl work both they

2   As metric symbols are not brief forms, no period is required.

3   I plan to study pages 10, 28, 39, 47, and 56 for that test.

55-B. Measure and improve number-typing skill

4   He expects a special group of 180 to 195 to attend the   12
June 17 meeting. About 43 of these are due from Vancouver,   24
37 to 46 from Dunnville, 28 or 29 from Louisville, 46 to 50   36
from Glenville, plus about 25 or 30 local members, as well.   48

  1 | 2 | 3 | 4 | 5 | 6 | 7 | 8 | 9 | 10 | 11 | 12

55-C. Improve control of 1, 2, 3, 4

5   111 a1a1a a1a The 11 teams played 11 games with 11 players.

6   222 s2s2s s2s The 22 men got 22 tickets for the 2:22 train.

7   333 d3d3d d3d The 33 boys had 33 books with 33 stamps each.

8   444 f4f4f f4f The 44 dogs had 44 collars with 44 gold tags.

9   Try to get Order No. 31 out on the 12:43 train. Then,   12
if you can, get Order No. 42 out on the next train at 3:42.   24

  1 | 2 | 3 | 4 | 5 | 6 | 7 | 8 | 9 | 10 | 11 | 12

55-D. Improve control of 5, 6, ½, ¼

10   555 f5f5f f5f The 55 men checked 55 references in 55 books.

11   $\frac{1}{2}\frac{1}{2}\frac{1}{2}$;$\frac{1}{2}$;$\frac{1}{2}$; ;$\frac{1}{2}$; The 9$\frac{1}{2}$ size sells 1$\frac{1}{2}$ times as many as the 8$\frac{1}{2}$.

12   $\frac{1}{4}\frac{1}{4}\frac{1}{4}$;$\frac{1}{2}$;$\frac{1}{4}$; ;$\frac{1}{4}$; The first $\frac{1}{4}$ includes $\frac{1}{4}$ as many as the last $\frac{1}{4}$.

13   666 j6j6j j6j The 66 tests were for 66 girls in 66 classes.

14   All 56 words can be seen in the top ¼ and ½ of sheets   12
of metric paper and in the bottom ¼ and ½ of imperial too.   24

  1 | 2 | 3 | 4 | 5 | 6 | 7 | 8 | 9 | 10 | 11 | 12

55-E. Regain stride on these easy paragraphs

15   My goal is to make a big profit when I go down to work   12
for the rich man by the lake. If so, then I may aid Jan if   24
he kept the bicycle of the neighbour girl down by Cal Lane.   36

  1 | 2 | 3 | 4 | 5 | 6 | 7 | 8 | 9 | 10 | 11 | 12

16   When Jack said he might take six scouts to the zoo, he   48
did not know they would be so quick to take him up on it at   60
this time. He should have known that most boys would be in   72
the mood to go on just such a trip at the drop of your hat.   84

  1 | 2 | 3 | 4 | 5 | 6 | 7 | 8 | 9 | 10 | 11 | 12

Manuscript 53
Table 51
BOUND REPORT (3)

Table 2

PARTS OF THE BUSINESS LETTER

Basic Parts	Supplemental Parts
A. Letterhead	I. Reference Line
B. Date Line	J. Attention Line
C. Inside Address	K. Subject Line
D. Salutation	L. Company Signature
E. Body	M. Enclosure Notation
F. Complimentary Closing	N. Postscript
G. Signer's Identification	O. "cc" Notation
H. Reference Initials	P. "bcc" Notation

TECHNICAL REMINDERS:

1. Leave 3 lines under table.

2. Leave TWO spaces after "A.," "B.," etc.

3. Italic printing is underscored when typed.

4. Any short display line is centered.

5. Footnote separation line is 50 mm long.

6. "Et al." in footnote means "and others" and is used when there are more than two authors.

7. In footnote, title of book is underscored but edition is not.

A. The Letterhead contains the name and address of the company, in print. Most letterheads are 44 mm (11 lines) deep, but they may be as shallow as 6 lines and as deep as 18 lines. When a letterhead is more than 12 lines deep, the date should be typed at least three lines below the bottom of the printing.

B. *The Date Line* contains the month, day, and year the letter is typed. The month is never abbreviated in a business letter; a comma always separates the day and year:

October 9, 1977

The armed forces and some government bureaus (and many persons who have served in those forces or bureaus) prefer the "military" arrangement, with the day before the month:

9 October 1977

In time, numeric dating may become recognized practice. Numeric dating expresses the date by means of numbers. For example, October 9, 1977, would be expressed as 1977 10 09.

C. *The Inside Address* includes the identity and address of the addressee. These are normally typed above the body of a business letter; but as one authority notes, "Placing the inside address at the bottom, which is correct arrangement when writing to a public official, makes a letter formal."[3]

When the business title of an addressee is used in addition to his name, the title may be placed after the name, or on a line by itself, or at the start of the next line:

[Continues on next page]

Manuscript 54
BOUND REPORT (4)

Display with quotation marks only a quotation that will fill three or fewer typewritten lines.

LINE: 60

56-A. Leave 3 spaces between the state abbreviation and zip code.

Set a tab for each state column. Leave 6 spaces between columns.

See p. 100 for list of American states and abbreviations.

56-A. Build speed on American Zip Codes

1	AL	35201	AK	99688	AZ	85625	AR	71701
2	CA	92077	CZ	29572	CO	80541	CT	06473
3	DE	19730	DC	20001	FL	32201	GA	30301
4	GU	96910	HI	96785	ID	83522	IL	61778
5	IN	46156	IA	50026	KS	66543	KY	40320
6	LA	70101	ME	04401	MD	21034	MA	01101
7	MI	48501	MN	55005	MS	39326	MO	63083
8	MT	59075	NE	68048	NV	89316	NH	03101
9	NJ	07101	NM	87519	NY	12015	NC	27046
10	ND	58264	OH	44301	OK	73101	OR	97044
11	PA	15201	PR	00101	RI	02901	SC	29301
12	SD	57622	TN	38101	TX	75165	UT	84084
13	VT	05101	VI	00801	VA	23803	WA	98351
14	WV	25301	WI	53027	WY	82622	U.S.A.	

56-B. Measure your skill in sustained writing

56-B. To measure you skill improvement, follow either schedule (double space and use a tab-5 indention):

(1) Type paragraph 15 two times. GOAL: To complete either copy in 5 minutes, with 4 or fewer errors.

(2) Using paragraphs 15 and 16, take two 5-minute timings. GOAL: 35 or more words a minute, within 4 errors. Then, record the better of the two scores.

SI 1.35—nearly normal

17   The ZIP numbers which must be used on mail to the U.S. 12
initially appeared early in 1963, when the U.S. Post Office 24
introduced a "Zoning Improvement Plan" to speed up delivery 36
of the mail. The plan of using five digits after the state 48
name caught on in the U.S., where the Department took pains 60
to "sell" the plan. Firms were requested to show their new 72
numbers on their letterheads and envelopes and reply cards, 84
and most firms made that adjustment when they got new ones. 96
The Post Office in each zone told the public what the local 108
zone number was to be and asked people to include it in the 120
return address on their letters and envelopes. So success- 132
ful was the promotion that most persons began using the new 145
numbers and have continued doing so up to the present time. 158

18   Writers were asked to type the names of the states out 170
in full or to use the new two-letter, all cap abbreviations 182
without periods. Writers were asked to leave space between 194
state and code. How much space? When pressed on this, the 206
Post Office said there should be no less than two spaces or 218
more than six spaces on a pica typewriter. Translated into 230
elite spacing, that would be not less than three spaces and 242
not more than seven spaces. Wanting to come up with a firm 254
and single recommendation that would fit all machines best, 266
the authors of this book selected three spaces as the right 278
number on which to standardize ZIP Codes on American mail. 289

SPECIAL NOTES

1. Listings are double indented (i.e., indented 10 spaces).   *must*
2. Periods after numbers and letters in listings and headings may be followed by either one or two spaces, uniformly. In this report, follow such periods by TWO spaces.
3. In a footnote, "ff" means "and following pages."

Manuscript 52

BOUND REPORT (2)
Shown: in elite
Paper: plain
SI: 1.48—fairly hard

line 7 CAPS

double space   *line 10*

100 and 200 words, he builds a placement plan that will serve all such   23
average letters; then he stretches shorter letters and telescopes the   37
longer ones to make them, too, fit in the space of an average letter.   51
To stretch a short letter, he may: 58

in 10
          1. Allow extra space after the date.   *Single space*   68
          2. Divide letter into more paragraphs.   79
       → 3. Insert a company signature line.   89
          4. Allow extra space for signature.   98
          5. Lower the reference lines.   107

To telescope a long letter into less space, he may: 118

          1. Allow less space after the date.   129
          2. Divide letter into fewer paragraphs.   139
          3. Edge lines farther into right margin.   150
          4. Possibly omit the company signature.   160
          5. Allow less space for the signature.   171
          6. Raise the reference lines.   179

The point is that he makes every possible letter fit into the space of   194
an average one. Only for letters under 75 words or over 225 words does   208
he adjust margins or alter the date line.   217

                                                                          218

Block CAPS
Part 2. Parts of a Letter   235

watch where table is
A business letter may have as many as 16 different parts,[1] listed   250
in Table 2, next page. It is rare, of course, that any letter contains   264
all the possible parts.   269

                                                                          270

NO CAPS
THE BASIC LETTER PARTS   275

Every business letter has eight parts that are so basic that the   289
letter would be incomplete or unusual if any were omitted. These parts   303
are listed in Column 1, Table 2, next page.   312
                                                                          318

15 underscores

_____
in 5 1. R. E. Gavin and W. A. Sabin, Reference Manual for Stenog-   344
raphers and Typists, Canadian Edition (Toronto: McGraw-Hill Ryerson,
1970), pages 197 ff.

Continuation Page of a Formal Manuscript

Leave 1 space after the first three characters in the code. Space twice between codes.

Codes are in geographical order from east to west.

56-C. Build speed in typing Canadian postal codes

Atlantic Postal Region

Newfoundland	1	A1C 4S5	A1B 1V5	A1C 2P5	A1E 3X2	A2A 1W9	A2N 1Z7	A2H 3V8
Nova Scotia	2	B4H 2X3	B2G 1Y5	B4V 1T3	B2X 1C4	B2W 1B2	B3B 1G7	B3H 1G9
Prince Edward Id.	3	C1A 5Z2	C1A 4R7	C1A 4M6	C1A 7B3	C1A 3G6	C1A 3Y9	C1A 4Z1
New Brunswick	4	E2Z 3X6	E3N 2Y9	E1N 1M6	E3V 1H3	E3Z 2W9	E3B 4J9	E1B 6L5

Quebec Postal Region

Quebec East	5	G0X 1N0	G8B 6C3	G2E 3G7	G7S 2V7	G7G 4G1	G7H 3R8	G6W 3B6
Montreal	6	H4W 2B1	H3P 2E5	H9R 3X5	H3Y 1G6	H2J 3P9	H1L 4X8	H3X 3N1
Quebec West	7	J2T 6N8	J6S 4G3	J3Z 1A1	J4R 1T3	J8P 6C5	J6E 4G5	J8L 1W9

Ontario Postal Region

Ontario East	8	K8N 1T5	K6V 5J6	K6H 1B6	K2B 5A6	K1R 6T2	K9J 3Z2	K7A 3T5
South Central	9	L0P 1B0	L6X 2G6	L9C 1K2	L3V 2Y6	L2M 1M8	L2R 2H6	L4J 1Z9
Toronto	10	M5H 1W8	M4X 1J3	M8W 4K7	M8X 1E3	M6N 3J3	M8V 2E4	M9L 2T2
Southwestern	11	N6G 2V7	N7T 7P8	N3Y 4R5	N5R 5C3	N5A 4Z5	N2C 1T9	N5W 4E9
Northwestern	12	P4N 7M6	P3C 2T4	P1B 4P8	P9A 2S4	P5A 2C7	P0X 1C0	P6B 2X9

Western Postal Region

Manitoba	13	R7B 0S7	R7A 4W6	R7N 2G5	R8A 0C7	R1N 1Z3	R1N 0X6	R1A 0W9
Saskatchewan	14	S9V 0M3	S6H 6K8	S9A 3K4	S4T 7A9	S7L 3R5	S3N 0G6	S9H 3X6
Alberta	15	T2V 1P9	T2M 1J2	T4V 2M9	T9H 3M5	T1J 3K5	T8A 2L3	T6K 0J5
British Columbia	16	V2P 4T9	V1C 2Z1	V4K 3A9	V9L 3Z8	V9S 4G3	V9Y 2T7	V5H 3Z5
Northwest Territories	17	X0E 0M0	X0C 0G0	X1A 2H5	X1A 1M7	X1A 2G4	X1A 1T7	X1A 1C6
Yukon Territory	18	Y1A 4N9	Y1A 2B5	Y1A 3G9	Y1A 4M3	Y1A 3Z7	Y1A 4H5	Y1A 1L7

56-D. Learn how to make corrections

56-D. SPECIAL NOTES.

(1) Erase only when your instructor directs or gives you permission to do so. Erasing: a crutch learners should avoid leaning upon!

(2) One erasure crumb can disable a machine; this is why it is so important the carriage be moved aside.

(3) Never moisten an eraser. A damp eraser "scags" paper.

(4) On an electric machine, you must temporarily turn the pressure regulator (26) to 0 before typing over any erasure you have made.

ERASING. Turn paper up so error is on top of cylinder. Move carriage to extreme left or right (use margin release, 15) so erasure grit *can't* fall into machine. Keep paper from slipping as you erase by pressing it against cylinder with fingertips (but don't touch the typing!). Use an *ink* eraser in light, up-and-down, oval motions while blowing lightly and dryly to puff away erasure grit. Then restore paper to typing position and type—*lightly!*—the correction.

SQUEEZING. If an extra letter must be inserted, move all letters in the word a half space to the *left*:

Method 1. Before each stroke, press and hold down the half-space key—if your machine has one. On some makes, the space bar can be held down to half-space the carriage.

Method 2. Before each stroke, press and hold down the backspace key at an estimated halfway-down depth.

Method 3. Before each stroke, press against the left end of the carriage, pushing it back a half space.

Method 4. If only the correction is to be typed, use the paper release and shift the paper itself.

SPREADING. To make a correction fill an extra space, move the word a half space to the *right*, using any of the methods of carriage control.

PRACTICE. Make three *exact* copies of lines 22 and 23.

19   The firs step in any operation iss to review all the steps.

20   The first step in any operation is to review all the steps.

REVIEW: Formal manuscript arrangement, pages 113-114
REVIEW: Ruled table arrangement, pages 139-140

Manuscript 51

Table 50

BOUND REPORT (1)
Shown: in pica
Paper: plain
Line: 60
Spacing: as shown
SI: 1.47—high normal

CORRESPONDENCE MANUAL

Part 1. Letter Placement

A letter should be so arranged that the margins serve as a white frame around the letter. In general, the arrangement should be in the same proportion as is the paper (longer than wide); the text centers within equal side margins. The bottom margin should be a little wider than either side margin.

Many plans for placement have been invented, but none is a set answer for all letters because the lengths of letters and sizes of letterheads vary so much. Table 1, below, shows the one plan that is used most widely; but even this plan is just a general guide and has to be adapted for many letters.

The veteran office typist does not use a formula. Knowing that a great majority of business letters contain between

Table 1

STANDARD LETTER-PLACEMENT PLAN

Letter Factor	Short	Average	Long
Words in the body	Under 100	100-200	Over 200
Position of date*	Line 15	Line 15	Line 15
Drop to address	5 lines	5 lines	5 lines
Length of line, pica	40 strokes	50 strokes	60 strokes
Length of line, elite	50 strokes	60 strokes	70 strokes

*On letterheads more than 12 lines deep, position the date three lines below the bottom of the letterhead printing.

First Page of a Formal Manuscript

Tables go at top or bottom of page, with a locational reference to them (such as "Table 1, below") in text.

Unit 10. Correspondence

LINE: 60
TAB: 5
SPACING: SINGLE
DRILLS: THREE TIMES
GOAL: LEARN NEW
   CORRESPONDENCE
   FORMS
STRESS: PREPLANNING

57-A. Lines 1-3 three or more times, with emphasis on pressureless effort. Repeat them in Lesson 58.

57-A. Tune up on these review lines

1   They may make a big profit if they work with the field men.

2   Symbols are always in the same form, even in a block title.

3   10 & 28 & 39 & 47 & 56 $10 and $28 and $39 and $47 and $56.

57-B. Instead of repeating lines individually, type all four lines as a group three times. Start slowly; speed up on repetitions.

57-B. Build skill on these preview words

4   AA answer BB blocked CC choice DD date EE prefer FF helpful

5   GG give HH which II like JJ judge KK pick LL letter MM most

6   NN one's OO others PP people QQ unique RR better SS persons

7   TT that UU use VV have WW what XX extreme YY yes ZZ bizarre

57-C. You should be able to type both paragraphs in 5 minutes or less, within 4 errors. See if you can!

If you have doubt about your speed, precede this effort by retyping line 1 three times. If you doubt your ability to meet the accuracy requirement, retype line 2 three times.

Swing quickly from this preliminary practice into the sustained typing.

SI 1.35—easy-normal

57-C. Build and measure skill in sustained writing

8   What is the best letter style? That question does not   12
have an answer, for preference in letter styles is a matter   24
of one's own taste. For example, some people like a letter   36
to be blocked; others may prefer it indented. Some like to   48
use a company name. Some prefer the date centered horizon-   60
tally. There is no way to judge what one form is the best,   72
but it is helpful to know what forms are most popular: the   84
blocked and semiblocked forms, the two of which are used in   96
around 95 percent of the letters typed in business offices.   108

9   The purpose of a letter might influence your choice of   120
style, too. For example, you might pick for an advertising   132
letter a bizarre form that would catch one's eye because it   144
is unique; but you would reject that same style for, say, a   156
letter of sympathy. Yes, these are extreme cases; but they   168
do show that the purpose of a letter might affect its form.   180

  1 | 2 | 3 | 4 | 5 | 6 | 7 | 8 | 9 | 10 | 11 | 12

57-D. The production word counts from here on will assume that you are using one or the other of these two positioning shortcuts.

Most letters today have the date at the right margin but the trend is to start it at the center.

57-D. Learn a shortcut for positioning a date line

In the letters you have typed this far, you have pivoted (backspaced from the right margin) to position the date. Slow, wasn't it! There are two popular shortcuts:

1. Estimate the starting point of the date, as many typists do. You have pivoted enough dates, now, to have good judgment. And, after all,

you can't go *far* wrong! The shortest date (May 1) takes 11 spaces; the longest (September 30) fills but 18.

2. Start the date at the center, thus aligning the date with the closing lines (it balances neatly). This method is very easy, very quick, and *the method you are to use* in the letters and cards in this part.

Unit 28. Manuscripts

LINE: 60
TAB: 5
SPACING: SINGLE
DRILLS: THREE TIMES
GOAL: SUSTAIN SKILL
  ON LONG MANUSCRIPT
STRESS: PRECISION

169-A. Tune up on these easy review lines

1 Kane kept the key so he may paint the shelf ivory and blue.
2 Paul reviewed the subject before giving Max and Kay a quiz.
3 Pages 10, 28, 39, 47, and 56 were most interesting to them.
   1 | 2 | 3 | 4 | 5 | 6 | 7 | 8 | 9 | 10 | 11 | 12

169-A. Each line three times. Use them to get your fingers flying! Repeat in Lesson 170.

169-B. Restore full skill on very easy material

4 If you put some small stones and one or two big stones   12
   in a bottle and shake it, the big ones will quickly rise to 24
   the top. Turn the bottle upside down and shake it, and the 36
   big stones are back at the top in no time flat. There is a   48
   moral in that story, and it has to do with life. When life   60
   is dull, no one rises; it takes a shake to find the leader.   72
   1 | 2 | 3 | 4 | 5 | 6 | 7 | 8 | 9 | 10 | 11 | 12

169-B. Three copies—one of which is errorless—or more until you do one that IS errorless. Repeat this in Lesson 170, too.

SI 1.10—very easy

169-C. Sustain skill on production material

PREFACE

This manual has been prepared to serve the writer as a sum-   13
mary of the technical details, large and small, involved in typing 25
business letters and formal reports. It is hoped that these pages   38
will serve as a reference source, as well.   47

Letters. Because so many different persons in so many different   64
kinds of work write letters for so many different reasons, it is natural 79
that there be, as there are, a great number of fine points, some of which 93
will pertain to all or most letters, but some of which concern only a 107
special few. Whether they concern a few or many letters, these   120
technical points are so many facts that the typist must have in mind. 134

Reports. Like letters, reports may be typed with many special   151
flairs or touches unique to the persons who prepare them; but, by and 165
large, there is a standard format for the formal report. The pages of 179
this handbook have been set up to illustrate the standard format,   192
complete with footnotes, quotations, tables, listings, headings of all 206
kinds, and so on, along with the right spacing—single, double, or   220
extra.   221

The authority for the statements in this manual is the textbook   235
by Lloyd, Rowe, and Winger: *Gregg Typewriting for Colleges*, Canadian 263
Edition, to which credit is herewith made.   275
1 | 2 | 3 | 4 | 5 | 6 | 7 | 8 | 9 | 10 | 11 | 12 | 13 | 14

169-C. Change machine to double spacing and check margins for 60-space line (lines will align) and a 5-space tab indention.

NOTE: words in italic print must be underscored.

Type two copies (one in Lesson 169, one in 170); repeat extra paragraphs, if necessary, until each is typed without error.

Or, take a 5-minute writing with a 10-second rest at the end of each minute; and then another 5-minute writing without rests. GOAL: To finish the selection within 6 minutes and 2 mistakes.

SI 1.45—upper normal

169/170-D. Apply skill to typing a Correspondence Manual

The production work of this unit is a 10-page Correspondence Manual. It will be easier to do if you precede it with the Learning Guide on workbook pages 337-338 and use the visual guide on workbook page 339.

57/58-E. Practice the production of postal cards

Study the illustrations and annotations below; then, using workbook pages 79-82 (or slips of paper 140 mm by 90 mm), type Cards 1-6. Once the machine is set, you should *easily* produce each card within 5 minutes, with no errors or with not more than 1 error.

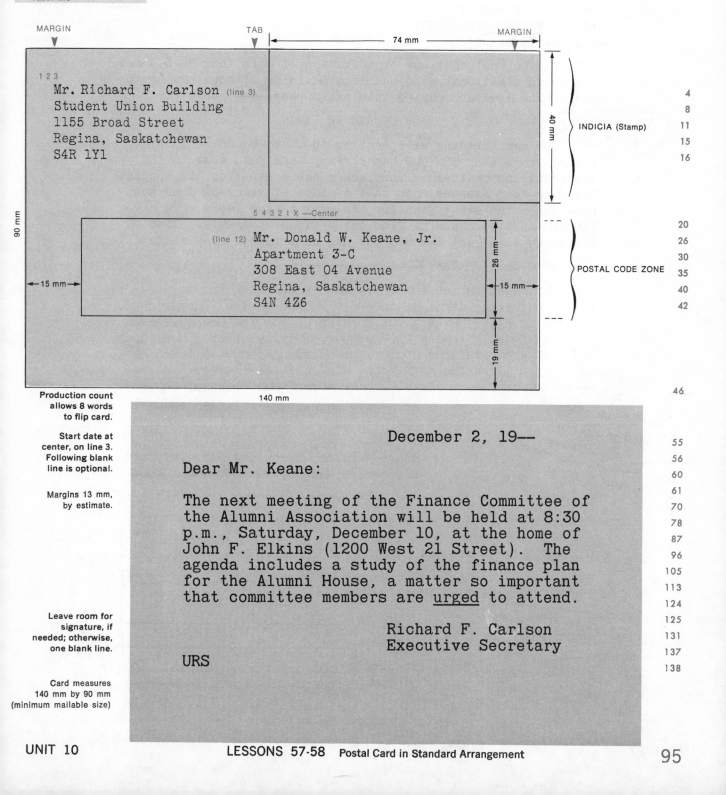

MARGIN   TAB   74 mm   MARGIN

1 2 3

Mr. Richard F. Carlson (line 3)
Student Union Building
1155 Broad Street
Regina, Saskatchewan
S4R 1Y1

40 mm   INDICIA (Stamp)   4 8 11 15 16

90 mm

5 4 3 2 1 X —Center

(line 12) Mr. Donald W. Keane, Jr.
Apartment 3-C
308 East 04 Avenue
Regina, Saskatchewan
S4N 4Z6

26 mm   POSTAL CODE ZONE   20 26 30 35 40 42

15 mm   15 mm   19 mm

140 mm   46

Production count
allows 8 words
to flip card.

Start date at
center, on line 3.
Following blank
line is optional.

Margins 13 mm,
by estimate.

December 2, 19--   55 56

Dear Mr. Keane: 60

61

The next meeting of the Finance Committee of   70
the Alumni Association will be held at 8:30   78
p.m., Saturday, December 10, at the home of   87
John F. Elkins (1200 West 21 Street). The   96
agenda includes a study of the finance plan   105
for the Alumni House, a matter so important   113
that committee members are urged to attend.   124

125

Richard F. Carlson   131
Executive Secretary   137

Leave room for
signature, if
needed; otherwise,
one blank line.

URS   138

Card measures
140 mm by 90 mm
(minimum mailable size)

Letter 83

SEMIBLOCKED LETTER
WITH REPLY COUPON
Paper: plain
Line: 60
SI: 1.51—fairly difficult

THE NATIONAL FEDERATION OF VETERANS

190 Somerset Street W.

Ottawa, Ontario K2P 0J4

Date

Dear fellow Member
of the National Federa-
tion of Veterans:

Do you feel that an our organization of more than 25 000 men
can build a National Headquarters Building without having to
get a bank loan and paying interest on borrowed money?

borrow money
from

OF COURSE WE CAN!

Our new building is going to cost us about $100 000. Of this
amount, more than $65 000 has already been paid over to the
architect and builders. This money was drawn from the special
Building Fund Account into which a share of Member's dues has
been deposited every year for the past twelve years. We have
$10 000 that we can draw from our National treasury. That
leaves us with just $25 000 that we must raise. Can we do it?

OF COURSE WE CAN!

Our Constitution forbids our raising dues, but it doesn't
forbid our going straight to every Member of the Federation
and asking him, "How's about anteing up for the Headquarters
Building Fund?" That's the purpose of this letter. How about
it? How about anteing up for the building fund? All you have
to do is fill in the form below and mail this letter back to
us with your cheque for a dollar or more. Can we count on you?

OF COURSE WE CAN!

Typist - Tell
Duplicating Dep't we
need 1 000 of these
by next Monday morning.
I will need to see the stencil
R.W.

Roger Wilkins, Executive Secretary and
Treasurer, Headquarters Building Fund

- -

National Federation of Veterans
190 Somerset Street West
Ottawa, Ontario K2P 0J4

Sure, you can count on ME! Here's my cheque for $ _____ for
The NFV Headquarters Building Fund.

OK as corrected
R.W.

Name _____

Street _____

City/Town, Province _____

Postal Code _____

Draft of a Solicitation Circular Letter

19
34
51
54
72
75
80
94
105
117
131
144
156
169
181
194
207
215
229
241
253
266
278
280
292
298
311
313
322
336
343
347
352
365
373
383
393

From: Richard F. Carlson | Student Union Building | 1155 10
Broad Street | Regina, Saskatchewan S4R 1Y1 | *To:* Reser- 22
vations Department | Washington Hotel | 120 Fifth Street | 32
Portland, Oregon 97236, U.S.A. | *Date* | Gentlemen: | I 58
should like to reserve four double rooms with bath, at $22 70
each, for a party of eight people for the weekend of Decem- 82
ber 14-16. We shall arrive about seven o'clock on Friday 94
evening and depart in midafternoon on Sunday. I should 107
appreciate your sending me a confirmation of this reserva- 119
tion. | ↓₃ | Richard F. Carlson | (*No initials*) 125

From: Richard F. Carlson | Student Union Building | 1155 10
Broad Street | Regina, Saskatchewan S4R 1Y1 | *To:* Mr. 22
Damon Struthers | Men's Suits Department | Stacy's Depart- 32
ment Store | 451 College Avenue | Regina, Saskatchewan S4N 54
0X1 | *Date* | Dear Mr. Struthers: | Thank you for letting me 61
know that the annual clearance sale of winter suits is sche- 73
duled for the first week in January. If you have any dark 85
blue or gray 37-Longs, I should be grateful if you could set 98
them aside for me. I shall stop in to look at them on the first 116
day of the sale. Thanks for remembering me! Dick Carlson 128
(*No initials*)

Duplicated fill-in cards
are often used for
acknowledgments. Front is
addressed as usual (but
no return address). This
side is filled in as is
shown: date at center,
salutation and initials
aligned at margin, and
amount centered in area.

ALUMNI ASSOCIATION - Student Union - Regina, Saskatchewan

December 3, 19--

Dear Mr. Kenilworth:

We should like to acknowledge your contribution of

$25.00

to the Alumni House Fund. We are confident that it
will not be long before we can begin construction.

Richard F. Carlson
Executive Secretary

URS

Card 4. Acknowledge a contribution of $25.00 by Mr. Charles S. Kenil-
worth | 1819 Atlin Avenue | Prince Rupert, British Columbia V8J 1E7. 56
Card 5. Acknowledge a contribution of $100.00 by Mr. Edwin G. Bern-
hardt | 5620 North 58 Street | Portland, Oregon, 97236 U.S.A. 57
Card 6. Acknowledge a contribution of $1000.00 by Mr. and Mrs. Fred
W. Miller | 1928 Hillcrest Drive | Swift Current, Saskatchewan | S9H 1P2. 58

Ruled Forms

LINE: 60 SPACES
TAB: 10, 25, 56
DRILLS: THREE TIMES
GOAL: SKILLFUL TYPING
  BETWEEN RULES
STRESS: EYES ON COPY

167-A. Each line three times, or two ½-minute timed writings on it. Repeat in Lesson 168.

167-A. Tune up on these review lines

1 The widow is kept busy with the field and turkeys she owns.
2 Jeff moved six dozen quilted coats at night by power truck.
3 The 56¢ and 47¢ toys sold before the 10¢, 28¢, or 39¢ ones.

    1 | 2 | 3 | 4 | 5 | 6 | 7 | 8 | 9 | 10 | 11 | 12

167-B. Change to double spacing and confirm tab stops: 10, 25, and 56 spaces from left margin.

Type each line, as shown, three times. Then take a 3-minute writing or type one complete copy; GOAL: an errorless copy within 3 minutes.

SI 1.33—fairly easy if you can manage tab and numbers wholly by touch

167-B. Sustain skill on production material

CONTRIBUTIONS TO THE HEADQUARTERS BUILDING FUND

Date	October 6, 19—	No. Contributors	4	7
Name	Address		Amount	8
Jason F Faucett	35 Craydon St West			15
	Arctic Red River N W T		5	22
Ruben L Edwards	138 Duquesne Rd			30
	Harrison Hot Springs B C		15	38
E I Marshall	560 Park Ave			44
	Harrison Hot Springs B C		25	52
Herman L Hess	476 Imperial Ave			59
	Fort Assiniboine Alta		10	67
	October 7, 19—			72
R E Clarke	10 Spruce St			78
	Fox Island River Nfld		25	86
John Jay Shane	9 Centennial Drive			94
	Lloydminster Sask T9V 1C5			101
Mark Platnick	729 E 13 St			107
	Pelican Rapids Man		10	114
Alvin C Corey	18 Breezewood Rd			121
	Round Lake Centre Ont		5	129
Max C McDuff	30 Pine Crest Ave			136
	Wellington Stn P E I		25	144
Carl F Leigh	159 Pitcairn St			151
	Ste-Marie-sur-Mer N B		5	159

Form 67
RULED REPORT FORMS
Forms: workbook 333
Directions: Prepare October 6 report and October 7 one separately
Style: space-saver abbreviating

Form 68
FILL-IN POSTAL CARDS
Cards: workbook 335
Directions: Prepare acknowledgment cards for the four cheques arriving October 6

167/168-C. Apply skill to production output

LINE: 60
TAB: 5
SPACING: SINGLE
DRILLS: THREE TIMES
GOAL: LEARN NEW
  CORRESPONDENCE
  TECHNICALITIES
STRESS: OUTPUT

59-A. Try to type these lines smoothly, as though keeping time to music. Repeat them in Lesson 60.

59-B. Type these lines the same as you would type a paragraph. Repeat this "paragraph" three times; speed up on repetitions.

59-C. You should be able to type both paragraphs within 5 minutes, with 4 or fewer errors. Can you?

If speed is a problem for you, retype line 1 three times before starting 59-C, to set a fast pace. But if accuracy is your problem, retype line 2 three times, for an intensive review of all the key reaches. Be sure to swing quickly from this preliminary practice to the sustained writing before the effect of the preliminary practice fades.

SI 1.37—normal

59-A. Tune up on these review lines

1 The goal of the rich man is to fix a bicycle for the girls.
2 I walked 4 km yesterday, 6 km today, and will soon do 9 km.
3 Look for boxes #10, #28, #39, and #47; then search for #56.

59-B. Build skill on these preview words

4 AA paragraph BB back CC casual DD indented EE each FF flash
5 GG zigzag HH have II lines JJ just KK look LL all MM common
6 NN penned OO tone PP experts QQ quite RR address SS message
7 TT that UU build VV have WW writer XX extra YY style ZZ zip

59-C. Measure and build skill in sustained writing

8   Back in the days when a letter had to be penned by the   12
writer, it was not usual to leave extra space between parts   24
of a letter; the writer had to use indentions instead. The   36
start of each paragraph had to be indented. The lines of a   48
return address, of an inside address, and of the close were   60
all set up as a series of indentions, just like steps. The   72
result was that letters seemed to have quite a zigzag look.   84

9   Letters got a new look when the typewriter came along.   96
Because it is a lot faster to block than to indent lines on   108
a machine, a letter today is not likely to have many inden-   120
tions. The experts say you can build a "tone" for a letter   132
by the number of indentions you do or do not inject in your   144
letter. Many indentions make a letter look conservative; a   156
few make it seem casual; having none at all gives a message   168
a streamlined zip that is the equivalent of a modern touch.   180

  1 | 2 | 3 | 4 | 5 | 6 | 7 | 8 | 9 | 10 | 11 | 12

Use the letterheads on workbook pages 85-94 for letters 17-21. If you have no workbook, use plain paper—but rule or type a line across the paper, 3 lines from the top, to simulate the depth of a letterhead. Line length: 50 pica; 60 elite.

59/60-D. Practice the production of letters

Type Letters 17-21, trying to finish each of these "average length" letters in 6 minutes, with 4 or fewer errors. Note that the letters feature these special display parts:

1. The attention line (page 98) precedes the salutation. It may be centered, but is usually blocked at the margin and underscored.

2. The subject line (page 100) follows the salutation. It may be typed at the margin, but is usually centered and underscored or all-capped.

3. A company signature is usually typed in all capitals a double space below (and aligned with) the complimentary closing. It is used when the letter involves an obligation of the company rather than of the signer.

4. A "cc" (*carbon copy*) *note* is added to the other reference symbols if someone gets a copy of the letter.

Form 64

MAILING LABELS

Forms: workbook 327

Directions: Address a label to each of the adjutants named on Form 61

To simulate sheet of labels, type hyphen row every six lines and divide page into thirds by vertical rulings.

Mr. Daniel F. Shapiro
NFV Post Adjutant
10, rue du Moulin
St-Anselme, Québec

Mr. Nathan S. Graham
NFV Post Adjutant
40 Sherbrooke Road
St-Prosper, Québec

Dr. Trayne W. Foster
883, rue des Bois
Ste-Agathe, Quebec
J8C 1J1

Mr. Clifford S. Atkinson
NFV Post Adjutant
P.O. Box 198
St-Jean-Port-Joli
Québec

Mr. J. Kenneth Reladio
NFV Post Adjutant
6, rue du Canon
St-Remi, Québec

Mr. Harrison R. Hall
NFV Post Adjutant
30, rue Saint-Jean
Ste-Thérèse-de-Gatineau
Québec

Addressing of Plain Labels on a Gummed, Perforated Sheet

Plain labels in sheets perforated for easy detachment are used for addressing packages, tubes, and oversize envelopes. Faster to address than are envelopes, the sheets are also used in mass mailings of envelopes for circulars, catalogues and the like.

The typist uses all the labels in the first column, then those in the second, then those in the third.

The typing begins on the second line below the perforation, two or three spaces from the edge, blocked and single spaced. The province is typed under the name of the city or town if there is not room after it.

Form 65

FILE-FOLDER LABELS

Forms: workbook 329

Directions: Prepare labels for folders for a geographic file of the data in Form 61

Chisholm, J. L.

File-Folder Label: Alphabetic

Manitoba, Brandon

File-Folder Label: Geographic

For identifying file folders, gummed labels are available in long rolls, perforated for easy detachment and grooved (narrow line in each illustration) for easy folding. The typing is begun three spaces from the left edge two lines below the groove, thus

leaving a full blank line of space between the groove and the typing.

To simulate a label roll, on every fourth line of a page type alternating lines of underscores ("grooves") and of periods ("perforations"); then slice the page into three equal strips.

Form 66

FILL-IN POSTAL CARDS

Forms: workbook 331

CARD 1. Baldwinton Post owes October post schedule and the finance statement for quarter that began on July 1.

CARD 2. Willowbrook Post is overdue with initiation report for the July 1 quarter and its building-fund pledge.

CARD 3. Holdfast Post owes its log of August activities and its building-fund pledge.

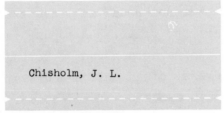

NATIONAL FEDERATION OF VETERANS

190 Somerset Street West

Ottawa, Ontario
K2P 0J4

October 5, 19--

Post Adjutant: This office has not yet received your—

___ Log of Post Activities for month of _____
__X__ Schedule of Post Activities for month of   October
___ Register of Members, quarter beginning _____
___ Initiation Report, quarter beginning _____
___ Statement of Finance, quarter beginning _____
__X__ Other   Post pledge for building fund

Please forward this information by return mail.

urs

OFFICE OF THE NATIONAL COMMANDER

Fill-in Notification Postal Card

JUDD-KANE, INC.
CABLE ADDRESS: JUDKANDEN

410 FREDERICK STREET • Brandon, Manitoba R7A 5K8 • 825-7500

December 4, 19--

4

8

Parke & Blake, Ltd.
5067 Wallace Avenue
Hope, British Columbia
V4M 1A1

12

16

20

22

Attention of the President

23

38

Gentlemen:

39

41

Thank you for the letter in which you describe the
financial problems that you are having and request
us to extend for two months the date on which your
final payment on our building contract will be due.

42

52

63

73

83

We are happy to make the extension you wish, and we
enclose with this letter an agreement to cover the
added time. You will note that it simply involves
your continuing for two more months the same rate
of interest you have been paying on your balance.

84

95

105

115

125

135

Our south-west area agent, Mr. Willis Crane, will
call you early next week to learn when you may wish
him to visit you and execute the papers. If there
is any help or counsel that he can provide, you may
be sure he will be happy to be of service to you.

136

146

157

167

177

188

189

Yours truly,

192

JUDD-KANE, INC.

193

197

200

Thomas J. Kane, Jr.
Executive Vice-President

205

211

212

urs
Enclosure
cc Mr. Judd
cc Mr. Crane

214

216

219

Business Letter in Blocked Style, with Attention Line,
Company Signature, and "cc" Notations

UNIT 10   LESSON 59

98

Form 61
MAILING LIST
Paper: workbook 325

165/166-D. Apply skill to production forms typing

Post (City)	Adjutant	Address	Postal Code
Brandon, Manitoba	John L. Chisholm	410 Frederick Street	R7A 5K8
Brantford, Ontario	Edward S. Venters	19 Meadow Road	N3R 3K9
Chilliwack, B.C.	John St. Vincent	229 Portage Avenue	V2P 3E7
Dartmouth, N.S.	~~Albert Fitzsimmons~~ *Charles W. Foreman*	306 Prince Albert Road	B2Y 1N2
Edmonton, Alberta	Maurice Hopkins	7206 158 Street	T5R 2B3
Flin Flon, Manitoba	C. C. Kenobski	26 Fifth Avenue East	R8A 0Z4
Fredericton, N.B.	Benjamin Wister	239 Highland Avenue	E3H 2S7
Kamloops, B.C.	~~Drew L. Gauthier~~ *Victor Mallette*	352 West Eighth Avenue	–
Kirkland Lake, Ont.	Kirby J. Anderson	5 Government Road West	P2N 2C9
London, Ontario	Martin Corwin, Jr.	11 Medway Crescent	N6G 2V7
Moncton, N.B.	Harold Naczynski	32 Grant Street	E1A 3R4
Ottawa, Ontario	~~Wilbur F. Carmody~~ *Prentice E. Clover*	190 Somerset Street West	K2P 0J4
Portage-la-Prairie, *Man.*	Barton D. Dixon	22 21st Street	R1N 2Z3
Regina, Saskatchewan	F. Randolph Carr (Dr.)	1155 Broad Street	S4R 1Y1
Prince ~~Albert~~ *Rupert*, B.C.	James K. Oksiutik	1819 Atlin Avenue	V8J 1E7
Saskatchewan	Louis van Polk	902 Temperance Street ~~148 Tunkannock Avenue~~	– S7N 0N4
Saskatoon, Sask.	Oliver R. Henderson	148 Central Avenue South ~~900 Caledonia Street~~	S9H 3E8
Swift Current, Sask.	Thomas Szymanski	1928 Hillcrest Drive	S9H 1P2
Thunder Bay, Ontario	Furston Lincoln	327 Mary Street West	P7E 4X9
Vancouver, B.C.	*Conrad Hunkley*	1039 8th Avenue West	V6H 1C3
Winnipeg, Manitoba	Paul F. Tremaine	5 Frank Street	R3N 1W1
Weyburn, Saskatchewan	*Franklin J. Kelly*	~~37 Peebles Street~~ 37 Bison Avenue N.E.	S4H 0H9

Forms 62-63
PLAIN INDEX CARDS
Paper: 5 x 3 cards or slips of paper
Directions: make (a) an annotated name file and (b) a geographic file of the Form 61 data

```
Chisholm, John L.
    410 Frederick Street
    Brandon, Manitoba
    R7A 5K8

    Adjutant, Brandon Post
```

Card for alphabetic name file, with annotation for further identification.

```
Manitoba, Brandon
    Mr. John L. Chisholm
    Adjutant, Brandon Post
    410 Frederick Street
    Brandon, Manitoba
    R7A 5K8
```

Geographic card (filed by province and city) used in circulation lists.

LEGEND

▭	POSTAL CODE BAND	between 19 mm and 45 mm from bottom edge
▯ (dashed)	MAILING ADDRESS ZONE	between 19 mm from bottom and 40 mm from top
▯ (dash-dot)	RETURN ADDRESS ZONE	between 45 mm from bottom and 74 mm from right edge
▨	INDICIA (Stamp) ZONE	between 40 mm from top and 74 mm from right edge
⋯	NO PRINTING ZONE	15 mm from outside edges (except top)

|← 74 mm →|

XXX Line 3, 3 spaces from left edge begin Return Address

40 mm

Line 12, 5 spaces left of centre begin Mailing Address

Line 13 for special envelope for P5 letterhead

←15mm→   ←15mm→

45 mm

19 mm

---

① Mr. Paul D. Sturbens
② 2901 Ocean Boulevard
   Victoria, British Columbia V9C 1B6

② REGISTERED

④ Attention: Mr. B.P. Gabrielle (line 10)

⑤ Cormack-Mawhrer Company

295 Parkhurst Drive

Fredericton, New Brunswick* E3B 2K2 ⑥

① Mr. Paul D. Sturbens
② 2901 Ocean Boulevard
   Victoria, British Columbia
   V9C 1B6

② AIR MAIL

③ Confidential

⑤ Cormack-Mawhrer Company
   295 Parkhurst Drive
④ Attention: Mr. B.P. Gabrielle FREDERICTON, New Brunswick*
   ⑥ E3B 2K2

ENVELOPE SIZES SUGGESTED
BY THE FEDERAL GOVERNMENT

No. 9   10.2 cm x 22.9 cm (for P4 letterhead)

No. 10   10.5 cm x 24.1 cm (for P4 letterhead)

No. *   11.4 cm x 14.6 cm

*Special envelope for P5 letterhead

The federal government has prescribed a minimum envelope size of 9 cm x 14 cm and a maximum size of 15.2 cm x 25.5 cm.

How Envelopes Are Addressed

1. Return address (if not already printed) begins on line 3, single spaced and blocked 3 strokes from the edge.
   NOTE: If you wish to align the return address with an attention line, start the return address 7 strokes from the left edge.
2. Special mail service or on-arrival instructions are typed 2 carriage returns below the return address. Postal directions have priority.
3. On-arrival instructions following a postal direction are double spaced below the postal direction.
4. Attention line must appear within the mailing address zone. This means on line 10 or below, 15 mm or 7 strokes from the left edge. The attention line may NOT appear as the last line or below the mailing address. The two common locations are illustrated.
5. Mailing address begins on line 12, 5 strokes left of the centre of the envelope, arranged in 3 double-spaced lines or in 4 or more single-spaced lines. In letters sent outside Canada, the country of destination is in all caps on a separate line.
6. Postal code MUST appear in the postal code zone. Always show the code as the last item of the address. Place the code on a line by itself at the bottom of the address. If this is not possible, because of addressing machine limitations, place the code at least 2 spaces after the province. The same postal code style should be used in both addresses on the envelope and on the letter. Do not use punctuation in or after the code. Do not underline the code.
* The *Canada Postal Guide* recommends the use of non-abbreviated addresses. Province and territory abbreviations *may* be used by large-volume mailers using addressing machines if there is not room for the complete address. New, two-letter abbreviations for this use appear on p. 100.

LINE: 60
SPACING: SINGLE
DRILLS: THREE TIMES
GOAL: LEARN MAIL
  ROOM TYPING
STRESS: EYES ON COPY

165-A. Lines three times without looking up once! Repeat in Lesson 166.

165-A. Tune up on these review lines

1 It is their turn to rid the chapel of the ornament problem.

2 Five "wizards" very quickly jumped in the box on the stage.

3 The outstanding cheques are for $5, $47, $39, $28, and $10.
  1 | 2 | 3 | 4 | 5 | 6 | 7 | 8 | 9 | 10 | 11 | 12

165-B. What's your goal?

ACCURACY: Type each group of lines like a paragraph, three times.

SPEED: Type each line individually three times.

165-B. Boost skill by selective preview practice

4 capitalization accountant secretaries quarterly junior copy

5 concentrating advertising grammatical worthless zigzag too;

6 transcribing corrections handwritten quotations select fact
  1 | 2 | 3 | 4 | 5 | 6 | 7 | 8 | 9 | 10 | 11 | 12

7 work with very much that are from his that is done in we do

8 must look fact that must not must one must be able to it is

165-C. Each paragraph two times, one of which must be perfect or contain not more than one error.

Use double spacing, a 70-space line (margins will align), and a tab indention of 5 spaces.

SI: 1.35—easy-normal

165-C. Boost skill on sustained alphabetic paragraphs

1 | 2 | 3 | 4 | 5 | 6 | 7 | 8 | 9 | 10 | 11 | 12 | 13 | 14

A lot of the typing that is done in a modern office is from copy   14
that is far from perfect. A copy expert in an advertising agency   27
may type from her own sketchy notes. A junior accountant may   39
prepare his quarterly reports from his own pencil work, complete   52
with corrections and erasures. The bill clerk types from handwritten 66
copy, too; while editors and their staff work with a stream of rough 80
drafts. And most secretaries spend many hours transcribing those   93
zigzag marks that are called shorthand. We do not work very much   106
with perfect copy matter.   111

ALTERNATE PLAN:

In Lesson 165, take a 3-minute writing with a 10-second rest after each minute; then follow up with a 3-minute writing without rests, trying to maintain the same pace. Goal: maximum speed with one or fewer mistakes.

In Lesson 166, repeat the same routine, using 5-minute efforts. Goal: maximum speed with two or fewer errors.

Now all this adds up to the simple fact that a typist must learn   125
how to think while he is typing. He must be able to make grammat- 138
ical corrections; he must be able to manage capitalization and   151
quotations, read rough drafts, catch and fix wrong dates and names, 164
think through problems of word division at the ends of lines—and   178
all this thinking must be done in a quick flash of good judgment.   191
These skills require practice; the place to get it is not on the job 204
but in the classroom. Asked to select which one of these skills is 218
most worth concentrating on, we should pick out the use of the warning 231
bell. The other skills are worthless if one must look up at the end of 244
every line of typing.   251

1 | 2 | 3 | 4 | 5 | 6 | 7 | 8 | 9 | 10 | 11 | 12 | 13 | 14

New Abbreviations for the Provinces and Territories of Canada

Province or Territory	New	Old
Alberta	AB	Alta.
British Columbia	BC	B.C.
Labrador	LB	....
Manitoba	MB	Man.
New Brunswick	NB	N.B.
Newfoundland	NF	Nfld.
Northwest Territories	NT	N.W.T.
Nova Scotia	NS	N.S.
Ontario	ON	Ont.
Prince Edward Island	PE	P.E.I.
Quebec	PQ	P.Q.
Saskatchewan	SK	Sask.
Yukon Territory	YT	Y.T.

American Zip Code

In an American address, type the ZIP code three spaces after the name of
the state. Either the full name of the state or the new two-letter, all-cap abbreviation, as follows, is used:

New State Abbreviations

	New	Old		New	Old
Alabama	AL	Ala.	Missouri	MO	Mo.
Alaska	AK	....	Montana	MT	Mont.
Arizona	AZ	Ariz.	Nebraska	NE	Nebr.
Arkansas	AR	Ark.	Nevada	NV	Nev.
California	CA	Calif.	New Hampshire	NH	N.H.
Canal Zone	CZ	C.Z.	New Jersey	NJ	N.J.
Colorado	CO	Colo.	New Mexico	NM	N. Mex.
Connecticut	CT	Conn.	New York	NY	N.Y.
Delaware	DE	Del.	North Carolina	NC	N.C.
District of Columbia	DC	D.C.	North Dakota	ND	N. Dak.
Florida	FL	Fla.	Ohio	OH	....
Georgia	GA	Ga.	Oklahoma	OK	Okla.
Guam	GU	....	Oregon	OR	Oreg.
Hawaii	HI	....	Pennsylvania	PA	Pa.
Idaho	ID	....	Puerto Rico	PR	P.R.
Illinois	IL	Ill.	Rhode Island	RI	R.I.
Indiana	IN	Ind.	South Carolina	SC	S.C.
Iowa	IA	....	South Dakota	SD	S. Dak.
Kansas	KS	Kans.	Tennessee	TN	Tenn.
Kentucky	KY	Ky.	Texas	TX	Tex.
Louisiana	LA	La.	Utah	UT	
Maine	ME	....	Vermont	VT	Vt.
Maryland	MD	Md.	Virgin Islands	VI	V.I.
Massachusetts	MA	Mass.	Virginia	VA	Va.
Michigan	MI	Mich.	Washington	WA	Wash.
Minnesota	MN	Minn.	West Virginia	WV	W. Va.
Mississippi	MS	Miss.	Wisconsin	WI	Wis.
			Wyoming	WY	Wyo.

To Chainfeed Envelopes and Cards . . .

After typing first envelope or card, roll it back until only 1.25 cm or so are showing. Insert next envelope or card *from the front*, placing its bottom edge between the first envelope or card and the cylinder. Turn cylinder to back out the first envelope or card and to draw the second into position. Continue "feeding" the envelopes or cards in this manner (from the *front*) until all are done. The completed envelopes or cards stack up on the paper table in the same sequence in which they were typed.

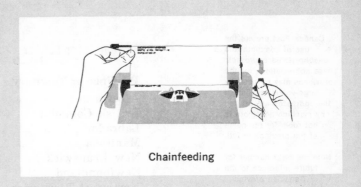

Chainfeeding

Form 59

PLAIN INDEX CARDS
Paper: use 12.5 x 7.5 cm cards or slips of paper
Directions: for each name on the Form 57 list, type a name and a geographic card

```
Stevens, Patrick K. (Dr.)

19 Meadow Road

Brantford, Ontario

N3R 3K9
```

Name file

```
Ontario, Brantford

    Stevens, Patrick K. (Dr.)
    19 Meadow Road
    Brantford, Ontario
    N3R 3K9
```

Geographic file

When typing on plain index cards:

1. Arrange the first line in index (filing) order. Omit *Mr., Ms.* and *Miss* but indicate all other personal titles (type them in parentheses).

2. Start in the third space of the second line.

3. Leave one blank line under the first (key) line. The other lines may be blocked or be indented, and either single or double spaced.

Form 60

FILL-IN INVOICES
Forms: workbook 323
Directions: for each name on the Form 57 list, prepare an appropriate invoice

Date the four invoices for the first of next month and figure the dues ($1.00 a month) to the end of the year. On each invoice, insert the amount of the dues and the total due.

NATIONAL FEDERATION OF VETERANS

190 SOMERSET STREET W.   OTTAWA, ONTARIO K2P 0J4

October 1, 19--

Dr. Patrick K. Stevens
19 Meadow Road
Brantford, Ontario

Initiation Fee $15.00

Membership Emblem 5.00

Dues until next December 31 . . . .   3.00

Total Amount Due $23.00

(Please return this statment with your remittance)

Fill-in printed invoice form

MARTIN MILLER & SONS

HEALY BUILDING

58 BROADVIEW AVENUE   TORONTO, ONTARIO   M4M 2EA

December 5, 19—

Mr. Alexander Kovacs
National Federation of
    Sales Executives
120 Countess Avenue
Portage-la-Prairie, Manitoba
R1N 0T2

Dear Mr. Kovacs:

SUBJECT: YOUR EASTERN TRIP

When I let our Eastern NFSE chapters know that you might be
willing to speak at one of their dinners if they could plan
their meetings to fit your trip schedule, their response was
wonderful.   Therefore, the following schedule has been set
up for you:

Date	City	Audience
May 30	Halifax	225
May 31	Sydney	150
June 1	Truro	160
June 2	Kentville	175
June 3	Moncton	100

If you approve this heavy schedule, Mr. Kovacs, we will move
at once to make proper arrangements for your transportation
and hotels.   I want you to know that we shall spread out the
welcome mat for you!

Cordially yours,

Humphrey N. Lambert
Area NFSE Chairman

urs
cc Chapter Presidents
cc Martin Miller, Jr.

Business Letter in Blocked Style, with Subject Line,
Tabulation Display, and "cc" Notation

Type the handwritten data on the workbook form, with the left margin stop set a space or two inside "Post" and a tab stop similarly after "Date." If you do not have the workbook form, copy the one shown here before inserting the data; make your form a full page (enough for ten names). List names alphabetically and type them in indexing sequence (last name first).

NATIONAL FEDERATION OF VETERANS

REPORT OF INITIATION OF NEW MEMBERS

Post *Lethbridge Alberta*   Initiation Date *October 1, 19—*   8

1. Name	Robert E. Perkins	Service	Navy	16
Address	103 Trinity Lane	Highest Rank	Petty Officer	22
	Lethbridge Alberta	Years in Service	6	27
	T1K 3W8	Present Work	Dept. Store Buyer	31
2. Name	J. Thomas Perkins	Service	Air Force	39
Address	103 Trinity Lane	Highest Rank	Warrant Officer	46
	Lethbridge Alberta	Years in Service	4	51
	T1K 3W8	Present Work	Lawyer	54
3. Name	Eugene L. Carr	Service	Army	60
Address	719 Cumberland Circle	Highest Rank	Lieutenant	69
	Lethbridge Alberta	Years in Service	3.5	74
	T1K 3Z5	Present Work	Owns Men's Store	78
4. Name	Oscar T. Moeller	Service	Air Force	86
Address	2311 Highland Avenue	Highest Rank	Lt. Colonel	93
	Lethbridge Alberta	Years in Service	3.5	99
	T1J 1C5	Present Work	Minister	102

Card holders, UP . . . when typing on cards or envelopes

Stevens, Patrick K. (Dr.)		
LAST NAME	FIRST NAME	MIDDLE NAME OR INITIAL

Post .... Brantford, Ontario
Initiation ... September 22, 19__
Address .... 19 Meadow Road
Brantford, Ontario
N3R 3K9

Service .... Navy (Medical Corps)
Rank ...... Commander
Years Service $3\frac{1}{2}$
Occupation Physician

Fill-in printed index card

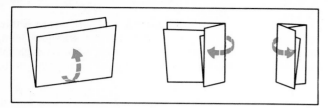

FOLDING A LETTER FOR A SMALL ENVELOPE

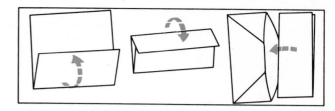

FOLDING A LETTER FOR A LARGE ENVELOPE

Letter 19

BLOCKED LETTER
Body: 131 words
Line: 50
Tab: center only
SI: 1.44—normal

Current Date | Mr. Marvin N. Maxwell | 28 Clare Crescent | 18
Saskatoon, Saskatchewan S1J 2P7 | Dear Mr. Maxwell: 27

SUBJECT: YOUR JOB APPLICATION 47

We have received and have noted with interest your letter of 60
application for a sales position with us. 69

At present we do not have a vacancy near Saskatoon, but we 82
do need a representative who would make his headquarters in or 94
near Melfort and cover the northern part of your province. If 107
you would like to be considered for this opening, please fill in and 121
mail back to us the enclosed application form. 130

I shall be in Saskatoon near the end of the month to attend a 144
convention; while I am there, I should be pleased to talk with 156
you. If you are qualified for and truly interested in the position, 170
we might be able to settle the matter then and arrange the em- 182
ployment details. | Sincerely yours, | MARTIN MILLER & SONS | 198
Humphrey N. Lambert | General Sales Manager | urs | En- 213
closure | cc Personnel Department 219

Letter 20

BLOCKED LETTER
Body: 133
SI: 1.48—fairly
difficult

Date | Dr. James Kendall | School of Commerce | Brock Uni- 17
versity | St. Catharines, Ontario | Dear Doctor Kendall: 30

SUBJECT: CONFERENCE PLANS 47

I am writing to confirm our telephone conversation about 59
your taking part in our March 14 conference. It is most grat- 71
ifying to know you will join us. 78

The audience will consist of 75 men who represent our com- 90
pany in the central provinces, plus 11 of our executives. These 104
men meet here in Toronto two times a year to learn about our 116
new products and to advance in their knowledge of professional 129
selling. 131

We should like you to lead a session, to last about one and a 144
half hours, on "How to Help the Retailer Expand His Business." 157
We shall reimburse you for all expenses, plus your $250 fee. 169

Let me say again that we are very glad you will be with us. We 183
look forward to your program. | Yours sincerely, | MARTIN 198
MILLER & SONS | Humphrey N. Lambert | General Sales Man- 212
ager | urs | cc Mr. John Miller 218

LINE: 60
TAB: 5
SPACING: SINGLE
DRILLS: THREE TIMES
GOAL: KEEP SKILL
  FROM LAGGING
STRESS: WRISTS,
  SHOULDERS, ARMS

163-A. Each line three times, smooth as music! Repeat in Lesson 164.

163-B. What's your goal?

ACCURACY: Type each group of lines like a paragraph, three times.

SPEED: Type each line individually three times. Repeat in Lesson 164.

163-C. Each paragraph two times, one of which must be perfect or contain not more than one error. SI 1.35—normal

ALTERNATE PLAN: Take 2-minute timings on each paragraph until you can complete each in 2 minutes with one or no error. Then (a) take one 5-minute timing to see how rapidly you can type within two errors, or (b) type the selection completely, to see how nearly you can complete it in 6 minutes with not more than two errors.

SPECIAL ASSIGNMENT: To review the rules of alphabetic indexing, do the Learning Guide on workbook pages 315-318.

163-A. Tune up on these review lines

1 The profit they make by it may pay for the downtown chapel.
2 I was quickly penalized five or six times by Major Higgins.
3 Please fill in blanks No. (10), (28), (39), (47), and (56).
   1 | 2 | 3 | 4 | 5 | 6 | 7 | 8 | 9 | 10 | 11 | 12

163-B. Boost skill by selective preview practice

4 professional alternated constantly questions amateur wonder
5 instructions telephones conference shrewdest realize novice
6 officemates interrupted executives notepaper respect reveal
   1 | 2 | 3 | 4 | 5 | 6 | 7 | 8 | 9 | 10 | 11 | 12
7 know what that they does not what the like to what he if it
8 will make will ever with the will not wish to sign of so he

163-C. Boost skill on sustained alphabetic paragraphs

9   The typical beginning worker does not like to ask many   12
questions. His is a normal fear: he does not want to seem   24
a novice; he does not wish to reveal what he does not know.   36
So he hopefully goes ahead with the tasks that are assigned   48
him, praying that all comes out well. He does not realize,   60
of course, that any error he makes just because he does not   72
know what he is to do next will make his officemates wonder   84
why in the world the newcomer didn't ask a question or two.   96
   1 | 2 | 3 | 4 | 5 | 6 | 7 | 8 | 9 | 10 | 11 | 12
10   To protect himself and at the same time to get clearly   108
in mind the exact details of a set of instructions, the new   120
worker should grab a pencil and jot down enough notes to be   132
certain he has every step itemized. If there is any detail   144
that is not clear, he should ask a question about it. What   156
the majority of young workers do not know is that they will   168
be interrupted constantly. Steps three, four, five are not   180
so easy when they are alternated with steps in another job!   192
   1 | 2 | 3 | 4 | 5 | 6 | 7 | 8 | 9 | 10 | 11 | 12
11   Jotting down notes or asking questions is not the sign   204
of an amateur but the mark of a professional. All the real   216
executives carry a pencil and notepaper in their pockets at   228
all times. They keep a pencil and pad by their telephones.   240
They never go to a conference without pen and pencil. They   252
are the shrewdest quiz masters and speediest answer writers   264
you will ever see in action. They have great respect for a   276
person who knows what to ask, and when to ask it, and asks!   288

163/164-D. Apply skill to production forms typing

ASSIGNMENTS	ARRANGEMENTS	SPECIAL INSTRUCTIONS	WORDS
Letter 21	Blocked form	Type the letter shown below (set tab stops for table before starting to type).	196
Letter 22	Blocked form	Type the letter below, but add JUNIOR EXECUTIVE (as a company signature).	202
✓ Letter 23	Blocked form	Type the letter below, but add <u>Attention Mr. Frank L. Klein.</u>	214
Letter 24	Blocked form	Type the letter below, but add SUBJECT: YOUR RATE INQUIRY.	215

Letter 21

BLOCKED LETTER
Shown: in elite
Paper: workbook
Body: 122 words
Tabs: 3 (center and table)
SI: 1.52—fairly difficult

December 10, 19—

4

8

Foote, Klein & Hughes, Ltd.
1300 Granville Street
Vancouver, British Columbia
V6Z 1M7

14
18
22
24
25

Gentlemen:

26
27

Thank you for your inquiry of December 5 concerning our rates
for space in JUNIOR EXECUTIVE magazine. We are enclosing our
standard rate card. You will note on it that the rates for
the space dimensions about which you specifically asked are
as follows:

39
51
63
75
78
79

Quarter page	$125.00
One-half page	235.00
Complete page	400.00

85
91
98
99

Worth noting also is the 10% discount that you earn for four
or more reservations in one calendar year. We allow the usual
15% agency fee, of course.

111
123
129
130

If you wish to reserve space in our February issue, which is
the next one going to press, we should have your reservation
(and copy, if it is to be set) not later than December 28.
Thank you for your inquiry.

142
154
166
172
173

Yours very truly,

179

182

J. Paul Prescott
Business Manager

187
192
193

urs
Enclosure

194
196

Business Letter in Blocked Style, with Table

Letter 82

ORDER-FORM LETTER
Paper: plain
Carbons: 3
Position: center
SI: 1.49—fairly hard

Prepare four copies of this order-form letter, centered vertically and horizontally: ~~the original to bear the fastened note to the Duplicating Department~~, two carbons for enclosing with Letters 81 and 82, and one carbon for Mr. Harris's Promotion Plans file. Indicate on his copy "cc's to Owen Johnson and Jim Blake; original to Duplicating on [date]."

Duplicating Department:
500 copies by 4:00 p.m. tomorrow, please.
F. G. H.

Judd-Kane, Inc.	*Fall* ~~Spring~~, 19—	10
410 Frederick Street		14
Brandon, Manitoba R7A 5K8	*Frank G. Harris*	19
ATTENTION OF ~~THE SALES MANAGER~~		39

Gentlemen: — 43

Please send me, *express* ~~postage~~ prepaid, the indicated quantities of the ~~the~~ following advertising aids for Judd-Kane Products: — 57, 67

Quantity	Item No.	(Description) *(center)*	
_____	WC7R	Large window cards in which a J-K radio may be ~~inset~~ *placed*. ~~Approx.~~ 1.2 m x 1.2 m	103, 109
_____	WC7T	Large window cards that may be used to frame a J-K television set. 1.5 m x 1.8 m	124, 133
_____	SC3R	Set cards to place beside a J-K radio. Hand on cards points to dials. 45 cm x 20 cm	148, 158
_____	SC3T	Set cards to place ~~atop~~ *on* a J-k television set. Hands point to push buttons. 60 cm x 40 cm	172, 183
_____	Nm5R	News mat, for use in advertising any ~~Judd Kane~~ *J-K* radio in newspaper. 7 cm x 7 cm	197, 206
_____	Nm5T	News mat, for use in advertising any J-K television *set* in newspapers. 12.5 cm x 7 cm	220, 231

I understand that these aids *will* come to me with~~no~~*out* charge and maybe used or not ~~be~~ used as I may prefer. — 245, 254

Send to: — 258
Person or Dept. .... — 271
Company Name .... — 285
 — 299
Street Address .... — 300
City, Province .... — 313

OK as corrected F. G. H.

Draft of an Order-Form Letter

Unit 11. Printed Forms

LINE: 60
TAB: 5
SPACING: SINGLE
DRILLS: THREE TIMES
GOAL: PRODUCE
   OFFICE MEMOS
STRESS: TOUCH
   OPERATION

63-A. Tune up on these review lines

63-A. Set an easy, steady pace on line 1; then try to maintain it on lines 2 and 3. Repeat in Lesson 64.

1   When is it the duty of the eight men to visit their island?
2   Express specific amounts in symbols rather than in writing.
3   10 28 39 47 56 we 23 up 70 out 975 wit 285 rue 473 yip 680.

63-B. Build skill via preview word practice

63-B. Type these preview lines as though they were a paragraph; then type the "paragraph" three times; speed up on repetitions.

4   AA any BB bills CC check DD don't EE need FF office GG good
5   HH help II its JJ adjust KK work LL likely MM memos NN many
6   OO once PP reports QQ quarter RR require SS less TT typists
7   UU cut VV involves WW whole XX example YY unlikely ZZ sizes

63-C. Build skill in sustained writing

63-C. Read the copy and silently rehearse reaches to the tabulator and the numbers; type a single-spaced copy (leaving a blank line between each of the paragraphs, of course) completely by touch and without pausing.

Or, take a 5-minute timing (with a short rest after every minute) in Lesson 63 and another 5-minute one (with no rests) in Lesson 64. GOAL: 35 or more words a minute, within 4 errors.

SI 1.35—nearly normal (if you indent by touch!)

One of the modern trends in office work is to use more   12
printed forms.   There are many good reasons for this trend: 24

1. One reason is the fact that our government requires   37
many reports, all of which must be prepared on exact forms.   49

2. A second is the fact that the forms are so designed   62
that the typist is unlikely to leave out or to misplace any   74
important details; thus, accuracy is helped to some extent.   86

3. One value of forms is the way they get rid of prob-   99
lems of placement and arrangement; you don't have to adjust   111
margins for memos or bills of different sizes, for example.   123

4. The use of forms reduces the need for adjusting the   136
typewriter, too.   Once a machine has its margin and its tab   148
stops set for a certain form, the typist can produce copies   160
of that form all day long without adjusting the typewriter.   172

5. Forms cut down the amount of typing required to say   185
what is to be said.   A check, for instance, is a whole mes-   197
sage boiled down to its essence, which involves less than a   209
quarter of what would have to be said in a complete letter.   221

6. Studies show that using forms for routine work cuts   234
costs, because they increase output, with a higher quality.   246

1 | 2 | 3 | 4 | 5 | 6 | 7 | 8 | 9 | 10 | 11 | 12

63/64-D. Learn to type interoffice memoranda

63-D. It might be a good idea for you to repeat the two alignment drills in Lesson 54-A on page 89.

Study the illustrations on the next two pages; then see how many of the assignments you can complete within the time limits suggested.

161-A. Each line three times. Repeat in 162.

161-A. Tune up on these review lines

1 Why not buy him the new cap and let him see you pay for it?

2 When did Professor Black give you a major quiz on the text?

3 The 10%, 28%, and 39% discounts remain; the 47% and 56% go.

   1 | 2 | 3 | 4 | 5 | 6 | 7 | 8 | 9 | 10 | 11 | 12

161-B. Change to double spacing and a 70-space line (lines will align).

Type each paragraph (the letter body) twice; one copy, at least, must be typed with 0 or 1 error.
SI: 1.29—easy

161-B. Sustain skill on production copy

This letter is to Mr. Owen Johnson, Manager, Meyer TV-Radio Store, 229 Portage 27
Avenue, Chilliwack, British Columbia V2P 3E7. Provide a bcc copy for the Dealer 36
Service Dept. OPENING LINES.

4 Dear Mr. Johnson: I apologize for the delay in replying to 13 50
your recent letter in which you inquired whether we would have 26 63
new display pieces for our dealers this fall; we were working on 39 76
the announcement about them when your letter reached my 50 87
desk, and so I held up a reply until I could have a copy for you. 63 100
Well, the copy is enclosed; check off what you want, just as you 75 114
did last year, and send it back to me. I invite your attention to 90 128
the third item on the list; it is new, and it is a honey that will 103 141
pull in the customers right off the sidewalk! Thank you again 116 155
for writing. I hope you get excellent sales results. CLOSING LINES. 126 191

  1 | 2 | 3 | 4 | 5 | 6 | 7 | 8 | 9 | 10 | 11 | 12

Letter 80

BLOCKED LETTER
Paper: workbook 311
Carbons: ?
Paragraphs: 3
Enclosure: Letter 84
Body: 119 words
SI: 1.36—easy-normal

This letter is to James N. Blake, Manager, Farm Park Music Store, 4273 105 Avenue, Edmonton, Alberta T6A 1A1. Provide a bcc copy for the Dealer Service Dept. 28
OPENING LINES. 34

5 Dear Jim: As I promised you at the convention in Medi- 138 47
cine Hat, I am sending to you an advance copy of the general 150 59
announcement about our new fall advertising aids, the one that 162 72
will be mailed out to the dealer list about the first of next month. 176 86
If you will send the list back to me by return mail, marked for 189 100
my attention, I will take steps to see that your requisition rea- 202 113
ches you in time for your big sale. The third item on the list is 216 126
the dandy I described at Medicine Hat. If there's any hitch, 228 140
Jim, don't hesitate to wire or call me collect; I am just as eager 242 153
as you are to see you sell a thousand of our sets! CLOSING LINES. 252 189

  1 | 2 | 3 | 4 | 5 | 6 | 7 | 8 | 9 | 10 | 11 | 12

Letter 81

BLOCKED LETTER
Paper: workbook 313
Carbons: ?
Paragraphs: ?
Enclosure: Letter 84
Body: 123 words
SI: 1.33—fairly easy

If you lack the workbook letterheads, use plain paper on which you show the depth of a letterhead by a ruled line or crease 9 lines from the top.

161/162-C. Apply skill in letter production

An interoffice memo is a message from one person to another in the same firm, usually typed on a form with printed "guides" (like *To* and *Date*).

1. The forms are either full size (P4) or half size (P5). Guide words may appear in any of many different arrangements.

2. Set left margin at the heading aligning point and right margin to equal the left (by estimate).

3. Begin insertions 2 or 3 spaces after the pertinent guides, aligned with them at the bottom.

4. Separate body and heading by 2 blank lines.

5. Ordinarily, use no salutation or closing.

6. Align the signature line (initials, name, or title, as writer prefers) with the date (set tab).

7. Use reference lines as you do in letters.

To: Margaret Norton   December 12, 19--
         Millinery Department

From: Frederick Lincoln
         Personnel Department

Subject: Promotion for Jean Louise Young

We are pleased to approve your recommendation that Miss Young be advanced to the position of Assistant Buyer and receive a salary increase of an additional $100 a month. The new position will become effective on January 2. Please extend our sincere congratulations to Miss Young.

                                              F. L.

urs
cc Payroll Department

Memos may also be typed on plain paper. LINE: 60. TAB: 10 (to align heading details). TOP MARGIN: 6 lines. DATE: Pivoted. SIGNATURE: Aligned with date (tab).

Form 4

INTEROFFICE MEMO
Shown: in pica
Form: in workbook
SI: 1.30—fairly easy

Interoffice Memorandum

TO:	N. P. Montclaire	DATE: December 12, 19---
	Bureau of Personnel	

FROM: Simon V. Johnston
         Vice-President

SUBJECT: Conference on New Kinds of Employment Tests 3

At some time in the near future, Nate, please try to set up a meeting at which you, Miss Benz, Mr. Clark, and I could spend an hour or two in conference with Dr. Mark Bjorgens, of Houlton College, to talk about the tests we give to job applicants.

Doctor Bjorgens has just wound up a long study on the values of some new kinds of tests for predicting the success of new office workers. From what I have been told, his findings should be of keen interest to us. We may ask him to review the tests we are now using.

                                   S. V. J.

urs

8
12
13
17
20
21
29
30
31
42
53
63
74
81
82
93
104
114
125
136
137
140
141
142

Standard Arrangement of an Interoffice Memorandum

Letter 77

BLOCKED LETTER
Paper: workbook 305
Carbons: two bcc's,
  two cc's, one file
Paragraphs: 3
Body: 119 words and
  attention line
SI: 1.40—normal

This letter is from Mr. Harris to Allied Carrier Group, Ltd., 1800 First Trust Building, 1448 | 20
Somerville Avenue, Winnipeg, Manitoba R3T 1C5, attention of Mr. J. T. Norge. Provide bcc | 45
copies for the Roswell Factory and Mr. Hodges. Provide cc copies for Mr. Kearn and Mr. | 49
Pierson. Identify the enclosure as "Silverman letter." Provide all missing elements. | 57

This letter is to confirm our telephone call about the three damaged | 74
TV sets delivered two days ago to the retail store of Silverman & | 88
Brothers, Ltd., Thunder Bay. Protection against this damage is our | 102
Policy No. 88-3617 with you. As you will note from the letter enclosed, | 117
we have asked the store to hold the damaged TV sets and the crates in | 131
which they arrived until your agent can pick them up. We are also ask- | 145
ing Mr. John Pierson, our own agent, to view these materials to see | 159
what change, if any, ought to be made in our crates. When you are | 173
ready to settle this case, please write our counsel, Mr. Ralph E. Kearn, | 188
at this address. CLOSING LINES. | 208

Letter 78

BLOCKED LETTER
Paper: workbook 307
Carbons: ?
Paragraphs: 3
Body: 149 words
SI: 1.36—easy-normal

This letter is to Mr. John F. Pierson, Field Service, Ltd., 327 Mary Street West, Thunder | 22
Bay, Ontario P7E 4K9. Provide bcc copies for Mr. Hodges and Mr. Kearn. Provide a cc copy | 24
for the Roswell Factory. Identify the enclosure letters. Because Pierson and Harris are | 39
friends, this is a "Dear Jack" letter. OPENING LINES. | 41

As you will see from the enclosed carbon copies, we have one more | 56
case of a damaged shipment to Silverman & Brothers, Ltd. — the | 68
third case in two years. If you can, Jack, fly that Apache of yours over | 84
to our factory in Nipigon, to see the exact steps used in crating our TV | 99
sets; then fly over for a look at the sets and crates at Silverman's | 113
before the Allied agent picks them up. I know this is a great deal of | 127
trouble for three little TV sets, but there may be more involved than | 141
meets the eye. I shall be most interested in what you may find out. | 156
Who is at fault? Our men at the factory, the truck driver, or someone | 170
at the store? Although I am very anxious for your report, Jack, take | 184
enough time to dig out the facts and tie them together for us. CLOSING. | 212

Letter 79

BLOCKED LETTER
Paper: workbook 309
Carbons: ?
Paragraphs: 3
Body: 51 words
SI: 1.46—fairly hard

This letter is to the addressee of Letter 78, page 244. Provide a bcc copy to Jeannette | 33
Rawlins, of Letter 74, with the annotation "Good! The kind man gave us a GO signal. Let's
move on the first newsletter, shall we?" Add a copy, including the bcc notation, to the
Letter 74 file. Provide all missing elements.

Thank you very much for your prompt reply to my letter of [*date of* | 50
Letter 74]. Thank you even more for giving permission for us to quote | 64
you in the newsletter we plan to publish soon for our dealers! I hope | 79
that I may have an early chance to repay your kindness. CLOSING LINES. | 117

INTEROFFICE MEMO

Date: December 13, 19--

From: Ewell Blackstone   Ext: 2182
Art Department

To: George McAdams   Floor: 5
Advertising Department

Subject: Art for the Maclean's Advertisement

     I am sorry to tell you that we sh___
be delayed at l___

     ___ in Maclean's.

Blackstone

urs

Memorandum

TO: Stephen R. Quinette   FROM: Inez C. Carpenter
Systems Division   Training Department

SUBJECT: Use of Printed Forms   DATE: December 12, 19--

     When I attended a recent meeting of the National Office
Management Association, I was amazed to learn that--

1. Most of the other large firms in the city use many
   more printed forms than we do.

2. The

                           I. C. C.

urs
cc Mr. Thompson

Interoffice memorandum forms appear in many sizes, arrangements, and styles; but the guide words make most of them "self-coaching."

Form 5
INTEROFFICE MEMO
Form: workbook (or
plain paper; see
page 105 example)
Goal: 5 minutes
SI: 1.43—normal

Memo to Paul W. Graham | Training Bureau | *From* Simon V. 15
Johnston | Vice-President | *on the subject of* Sending Someone to 24
Toronto Conference | I noted in an article in Junior Executive 45
magazine that the University of Toronto will conduct a con- 57
ference for a week this summer for directors of office training. It 71
seems to me that it might be wise for us to have you or a mem- 83
ber of your staff take part in this program. *New Paragraph.* 92
Please write to the University and obtain full details. When you 106
have them, please draft for me an estimate of what it would cost 119
for us to send someone. If possible, let me have your report well 132
before the first of March. | S. V. J. | urs | cc Mr. Montclaire 147

Form 6
INTEROFFICE MEMO
Form: workbook
Goal: 5 minutes
SI: 1.39—normal

Memo from George McAdams | *Extension* 2044 | Advertising 13
Department | *To* Ewell Blackstone | *Floor* 8 | Art Department 23
| *on the subject of* Art for the Maclean's Advertisement || Thank 37
you for letting me know about the delay in getting the art ready 52
for the special Maclean's campaign. I got in touch with the maga- 69
zine as soon as I received your note and found we could have an 79
extension of a week in the deadline. *New Paragraph.* Even so, we 90
shall have to move with dispatch in getting the art finished and 103
the plates made. I hope it will be possible for you and your staff 117
to place a high priority on the job for us. Thanks again for your 130
help. | McAdams | urs | cc Miss Patrick cc Mr. Benardo 144

Form 7
INTEROFFICE MEMO
Form: workbook
Goal: 10 minutes
SI: 1.36—normal

Memo to Inez C. Carpenter *of the* Training Department *from* 9
Stephen R. Quinette *of the* Systems Division *on the subject of* Use 19
of Printed Forms *dated today.* | You are correct in noting the 35
trend toward the increasing use of forms. There are many good 47
reasons for this trend: [*Continue with the six numbered para-* 52
graphs on page 104; arrange them in enumeration form, as on 294
page 80.] S. R. Q. | urs 298

Type "bcc" notation
after removing the
original and carbon
copies that are not
to carry this note.

bcc Roswell Factory Shipping Department
bcc Mr. Hodges—fourth complaint this week!

September 22, 19—

Mr. Marti
Silverman
388 Cumbe
Thunder B
P7A 4P8

Dear Mr. S

Thank you
the marrir
television
assure you

I am havir
you. Pleas
in which
you are v
Allied Ca
He will d
relieve yo

Again let
inconvenie
you wish

urs
cc Allied
cc Mr Pie

JUDD-KANE, INC.

CABLE ADDRESS: JUDKANDEN

1410 GLENARM STREET ● Brandon, Manitoba ● TABOR 5-7500

September 22, 19—

Mr. Martin T. Silverman
Silverman & Brothers, Ltd.
388 Cumberland Street N.
Thunder Bay, Ontario
P7A 4P8

Please retype on full-size stationery

Dear Mr. Silverman:

Thank you very much for ~~calling~~ bringing our attention to
the marring of the finish on three of the twelve
television sets that you recieved last week. I
assure you that your chagrin is matched by ours.

I am having three replacement sets expressed to
you. Please ~~return~~ keep the damaged sets and the boxes
in which they came, if you still have them, until
you are visited within a week or so by an agent of
Allied Carrier Group, which insures our shipments.
He will decide on the disposition of the sets and
relieve you of them.

Again let me say that we are sorry you have been
inconvenienced. If there is any further action
you wish us to make, please let ~~us~~ me know.

Very sincerely yours,

Frank G. Harris
Sales Manager

urs
cc Allied Carrier
cc Mr. Pierson

4
7
12
17
22
28
30
31
33
34
44
54
64
74
75
84
94
104
114
125
135
139
140
150
159
168
169
174
176
180
185
189
192

Letter 76

BLOCKED LETTER
Paper: workbook 303
Carbons: two cc's,
   two bcc's, one file
Body: 123 words
SI: 1.42—normal

LINE: 60
TAB: 5
SPACING: SINGLE
DRILLS: THREE TIMES
GOAL: PRODUCE
  INVOICES
STRESS: NUMBERS
  BY TOUCH

65-A. Tune up on these review lines

65-A. Set an easy, smooth pace on line 1; then try to hold the same pace on lines 2 and 3. Repeat this warmup in Lesson 66.

1 He paid the neighbor to make an ivory panel for the chapel.
2 Six or seven flashing new jet planes quickly zoomed by him.
3 He got 56 green ones @ .39; 47 blue @ .28; 10 purple @ .10.

65-B. Speed up on downhill preview words

65-B. Type lines 4-7 three times each: first, slowly and very evenly; then, steadily speeding up until you race across the line on your third typing of it.

4 glance, tricks forms ought make them with aid for the to be
5 weights sheets check judge gift then also yet the one if no
6 closing flinch would study know each time out all his or if
7 papers, typist whole first sure size that the aid may be on

65-C. Build skill in sustained writing

65-C. Read the copy; then type and retype each of the paragraphs until you can complete each one in 3 minutes, within 3 errors.

Or, take a 3-minute timing on each paragraph, followed by a 5-minute timing on the two together.

GOAL: 40 or more wam with 4 or fewer errors.

SI 1.24—easy (fine for increasing your speed!)

8 At first glance, some of the printed forms used in the   12
office might seem to be complex; but only a moment of study   24
is required to understand how to use most of them, for most   36
forms are simply letters. Take a bill, a cheque, or a memo   48
or a telegram, for instance; each is just a letter with the   60
greeting and closing left out. Once you realize this fact,   72
forms begin to make sense. You can also see from this fact   84
how much time forms save; if you had to type a whole letter   96
instead of fill in a form each time you prepared a telegram   108
or bill or cheque, you would'nt get a quarter as much done.   120
9 One more aid that pays its way by saving time and that   132
is part of the equipment to be found in all desks is carbon   144
paper. If no one knew of carbon sheets, so that the typist   156

If you can maintain the standard "waltz" tempo of 3 strokes a second, your speed is 36 words a minute!

had to write one at a time all the extra copies of business   168
papers, and then someone came up with carbon paper as a new   180
thing, you sure would judge it to be the finest gift of all   192
time. Far from flinching from the use of carbons, a typist   204
ought to bless the lovely stuff and learn all the tricks of   216
using it. Yet few typists know much about the many colors,   228
sizes, and weights in which this magic aid may be obtained.   240

   1 | 2 | 3 | 4 | 5 | 6 | 7 | 8 | 9 | 10 | 11 | 12

65/66-D. Learn to type invoices and telegrams

If you do not have the workbook forms, perhaps you can rule some like those shown on page 108.

Study the illustrations on the next two pages; then see how many of the assignments you can complete within 5 minutes and 4 errors each.

LINE: 60
TAB: 5
SPACING: SINGLE
GOALS: BUILD SKILL,
   MASTER "BCC"
STRESS: STROKING FOR
   CARBON COPIES

159-A. Each line three
or more times. Repeat
fully in Lesson 160.

159-A. Tune up on these review lines

1   You may ask her for the old oak box she had him get for us.

2   James lazily picked the big onyx rings off the woven quilt.

3   The five maple boards measured 10", 28", 39", 47", and 56".
   1 | 2 | 3 | 4 | 5 | 6 | 7 | 8 | 9 | 10 | 11 | 12

159-B. Change to double
spacing. Confirm margin
settings for a 60-space
line (copy aligns if you
observe bell correctly).

Type each paragraph one
or more times—until it
is typed with no or only
one error. You may wish
to divide this practice
between 159 and 160.

SI 1.37—normal, average

159-B. Extend skill on copy of normal difficulty
   1 | 2 | 3 | 4 | 5 | 6 | 7 | 8 | 9 | 10 | 11 | 12 | 13 | 14

4   There are two kinds of carbon copy notations, and they are used   14
so frequently that the typist should know of both.   24

5   The first is the one that is typed below the reference symbols to   39
assure the addressee that other persons involved in the matter at   53
hand have been informed. If Mr. Harris is writing to Mr. Dole to   66
tell him that Mr. White will make an adjustment in a bill, Mr. Dole   79
will be reassured if he sees the expected "cc Mr. White" note at the   93
foot of the letter.   97

6   The second kind of note is the one that is made when a copy of a   112
letter is to go to a third party without the fact being told to the ad-   126
dressee of the letter. For example, if a customer writes you an angry   141
letter, you might answer him gently but hustle a copy of his letter   154
and of yours to your local agent with the request that he check into   168
the matter. Or, again, suppose your firm is worried about a flaw in   182
one of its products; you might have been asked to relay to some   195
department copies of all the correspondence about the item.   207

TOP OF PAGE:

bcc Accounting
bcc Miss Carr
bcc Mr. French

7   When a copy is to be sent without the knowledge of the addressee,   222
the fact should not be shown on the original, of course, but has to be   236
written on the copy itself and on the file copy. When the typist   249
finishes the letter and removes it from his machine, he peels off the   263
original copy and any others on which the notation is not to appear;   277
then he puts the rest of the carbon pack back into the machine and   291
types the notation at the left margin, about an inch from the top of   304
the paper. The notation consists of the letters "bcc"—blind carbon   318
copy—and the name of the department or person to whom the copy   331
is to be sent; if several copies are to be distributed, the letter may have   346
both "cc" and "bcc" notes.   353
   1 | 2 | 3 | 4 | 5 | 6 | 7 | 8 | 9 | 10 | 11 | 12 | 13 | 14

BOTTOM OF PAGE:

cc Mr. Jones
cc Miss Smith
cc Lima Office

If you lack the workbook
letterheads, use plain
paper on which you show
the depth of a letterhead
by a ruled line or crease
9 lines from the top.

159/160-C. Apply skill to an integrated letter series

An invoice is a list of the charges for one delivery of goods or services, usually typed on a form with printed guide words for positioning heading details and ruled lines for positioning the columns.

1. Invoices come in an infinite variety of sizes, designs, and arrangements.

2. Number columns are aligned at the right, 2 or 3 spaces before the end of their column areas.

3. Word columns are aligned at the left, 2 or 3 spaces after the start of their column areas.

4. The left margin is set at the first column. Tab stops are set for additional columns.

5. To the extent possible, heading entries are aligned at the margin or tab stops of the body.

6. The words *Amount Due* are aligned (tab stop) at the start of the printed word, *Descriptions*.

7. The typist is responsible for *all* details.

```
            MEREDITH TYPING SERVICE
  4115 Elgin Street, Vancouver, British Columbia V5V 4R3

To:     Mr. Chester L. Harris        December 14, 19--
        1039 West Eighth Avenue
        Vancouver 10, British Columbia

Subject:  Invoice for Materials Delivered Herewith

        Chapter I of thesis:
  12    Pages of straight copy @ .30            3.60
   6    Pages involving unique display @ .50    3.00
   2    Pages involving tables @ .50            1.00
  40    Pages of carbon copies @ .05            2.00

        AMOUNT DUE                              9.60
```

Invoices may also be typed in memo style on plain paper. Return address is centered (not typed after From). LINE: 60. TABS: 10 and 56. TOP MARGIN: 3 lines. DATE: pivoted.

MEREDITH TYPING SERVICE

4115 ELGIN STREET, VANCOUVER, BRITISH COLUMBIA V5V 4R3

TO: Mr. Chester L. Harris
      1039 West Eighth Avenue
      Vancouver 10, British Columbia

DATE: December 14, 19--   INVOICE

QUANTITY	DESCRIPTIONS	UNIT PRICE	AMOUNT
	Chapter II of thesis		
14	Pages of straight copy	.30	4.20
6	Pages including tables	.50	3.00
40	Pages of carbon copies	.05	2.00
	Chapter III of thesis		
24	Pages of straight copy	.30	7.20
2	Pages including tables	.50	1.00
52	Pages of carbon copies	.05	2.60
	AMOUNT DUE		20.00
	3% SALES TAX		.60
	TOTAL AMOUNT DUE		20.60

STANDARD INVOICE FORM

The bottom two lines would be omitted if no taxes were involved.

Prepare another invoice to Mr. Harris, above; compute all amounts. For Chapter IV of thesis: 30 Pages of straight copy @ .30 | 6 Pages including tables @ .50 | 72 Pages of carbon copies @ .05 || For Chapter V of thesis: 19 Pages of straight copy @ .30 | 13 Pages including tables @ .50 | 64 Pages of carbon copies @ .05. Check the "Amount Due" carefully and add on the 3% sales tax. The "Total Amount Due" should come to $31.93.

25
35
54
81
89
104
119
121

UNITED APPLIANCES COMPANY   LINE 6

1851 Lorne Avenue   LINE 8

Saskatoon, Saskatchewan   S7H 1Y5   LINE 10

December 21, 19—

C O P Y

Mr. Frank G. Harris
Sales Manager
Judd-Kane, Inc.
1410 Frederick Street
Brandon, Manitoba   R7A 5K8

Dear Mr. Harris:

This is not the usual kind of letter in which
a dealer writes to protest about something. To the
contrary, it is a letter of appreciation.

We have now been handling Judd-Kane television
and radio sets for almost exactly one year. In that
time we have sold more than a thousand J-K products.
At no time have we had to wait for deliveries. At
no time have we suffered either loss or inconvenience
from shipping damages. At all times your firm moved
promptly and effectively to serve our needs.

So, this is just a quiet note to let you know
that at least one of your dealers truly appreciates
the service that Judd-Kane gives its dealers. It's
a real privilege, we feel, to carry the J-K sign on
our door and to represent you in Saskatoon.

Yours very sincerely,

UNITED APPLIANCES COMPANY

(SIGNED)

E. L. Houston, Manager

FTT/urs

Exact Copy of an Incoming Semiblocked Letter

Typist makes exact, line-for-line copy (even including errors, if any), adding
only the parts (shown here in color) that identify it as a copy, not original.

Form 10

INVOICE
Form: workbook (or
plain paper, as
shown on page 108)

Form 11

INVOICE
Form: workbook

Prepare an invoice of the Manufacturers Institute to the J. F. Belton Company | 333 River Drive | Moose Jaw, Saskatchewan | S6H 6K4 for the following items: 21 (copies of) Rafael: Production Tooling @ 4.50 = 94.50 | 1 (copy of) Rafael: PT Instructor's Manual @ 5.50 = 5.50 | 70 Benkley: Modern Plant Safety @ 2.50 = 175.00 | 1 Benkley: MPS Instructor's Manual @ 3.50 = 3.50 | AMOUNT DUE = 278.50 | 10% MEMBER'S DISCOUNT = 27.85 | TOTAL AMOUNT DUE = 250.65.

Prepare another invoice of the Manufacturers Institute to Training Department | Condon & Willhite, Ltd. | 2700 Connaught Avenue | Halifax, Nova Scotia B3L 2Z7 | for the following (compute all amounts): 10 Stephens: Dredges and Drills @ 4:00 | 1 Stephens: DD Instructor's Manual @ 7.50 | 20 Rafael: Production Tooling @ 4.50 | 1 Rafael: PT Instructor's Manual @ 5.50 | 1 Rafael: PT Filmstrip (Set) @ 65.00 | Compute AMOUNT DUE | Indicate 10% MEMBER'S DISCOUNT | TOTAL AMOUNT DUE should be 187.20.

Telegram **Télégramme**	

send this message subject to the terms on back
dépêche à expédier aux conditions énoncées au verso

10:30 Dec. 15, 19--

To: Dr. Robert Rafael, School of Business
McGill University,
Montreal, Quebec, H1G 3J9

Editorial board has authorized new edition of your book.
How soon can we have manuscript?

Donald Bideaux
Manufacturers' Institute

check mots		full rate plein tarif	X	night letter lettre de nuit	tolls cout
charge account no numéro de compte	4583	cash number numéro de caisse			
sender's name nom de l'expéditeur	Manufacturers' Institute				
address and telephone adresse, téléphone	151 Grange Ave., Toronto, M5T 1C8 300-5411				

Telegram 1. Full rate | *from* Manufacturers Institute | New Toronto, Ontario, *current date* | *to* Mr. Herbert F. Lewis | Starrett Engineering Co. | 15300 Euclid Avenue | Akron, OH, 44301, U.S.A. | Pleased to accept your invitation to speak at May 9 convention. Thanks for the privilege. | Donald Bideaux | Manufacturers Institute | urs
Telegram 2. Full rate | *from* Manufacturers Institute | New Toronto, Ontario, *current date* | *to* Dr. Maurice Trethaway School of Business | University of Manitoba | Winnipeg, Manitoba R2X 1K6 | New Simpson edition delayed until May 1. Shall we fill order with present edition? | Donald Bideaux | Manufacturers Institute | urs

Forms 12-13

TELEGRAMS
Forms: workbook
Style: as illustrated

NOTE: Attach to each letter all the materials to be enclosed with it.

Letter 72

BLOCKED LETTER
Paper: workbook 297*
Paragraphs: 3
Carbons: file and
   letter 74 enclosure
Body: 113 words
Enclosures: original
   of Letter 76
SI: 1.45—average

*Or plain paper on which you rule or crease a line across the page 1½ inches from the top to represent the depth of a letterhead.

Letter 73

BLOCKED LETTER
Paper: workbook 299
Paragraphs: 5
Carbons: file only
Body: 181 words
Enclosures: copies of
   Letters 73, 76
SI: 1.40—average

Mr. Harris prefers numbered paragraphs to be displayed as shown on page 80.

Letter 74

BLOCKED LETTER
Paper: workbook 301
Paragraphs: 3
Carbons: file only
Body: 82 words
SI: 1.34—easy-normal

Mr. Harris permits use of company signature when it helps letter placement.

Your employer is Frank G. Harris, sales manager of Judd-Kane, Inc. He prefers the blocked form (see page 206). This letter is to Mr. E. L. Houston, Manager, United Appliances Company, 1851 Lorne Avenue, Saskatoon, Saskatchewan S7H 1Y5. Provide all missing elements. | 11
| 28
| 44

Last December you were kind enough to send us a fine letter concerning the services that Judd-Kane had extended to you during your first year as a Judd-Kane agency; I am enclosing a copy of your letter on the chance you may not have one at hand. If you still feel as enthusiastic about our services as you did when you sent that letter, we should like your permission to quote your last sentence in one of a series of promotion newsletters that we are planning to develop as an additional service to our dealer network. We should be very happy, Mr. Houston, to receive a letter of permission from you. CLOSING LINES. | 58 71 85 100 114 127 141 156 183

This letter is to Miss Jeannette Rawlins, Graham-Jacobs Agency, 200 Spruce Avenue, Victoria, British Columbia V8T 2S1. OPENING LINES. | 21 | 31

Thank you very much for bringing us up to date on the status of the plans you are developing for our campaign to recruit more dealers in the western provinces. Let me answer the questions you raised: (1) While there are a few details that I should like to discuss with you, the general plan has the full approval of our Executive Committee. (2) I have reviewed a number of recent letters from our dealers to find one with a good "quotable quote" that might be suitable for your purpose. I am enclosing a copy of it. I have written to my correspondent to ask his permission for us to quote him; I am enclosing a copy of this letter. (3) Yes, I think we are ready to establish a schedule for putting the campaign in action; I should appreciate your suggesting one that would fit the design of your campaign. I expect to be in St. Louis in about two weeks. Do you think we could meet at your office then and iron out the final details of the campaign? CLOSING LINES. | 44 58 74 89 101 118 132 147 162 178 192 208 222 235 253

This letter, to be issued over your signature as "assistant to Mr. Harris," is to Reservations Manager, Victoria-Vancouver Hotel, 415 Michigan Street, Victoria, British Columbia V8V 1R8. OPENING LINES. | 19 | 36 | 39

Please make a reservation for Mr. Frank G. Harris, sales manager of this firm. Mr. Harris would like a single room, with either shower or bath, for five nights beginning [*insert date of second Sunday from now*]. He will arrive by air late in the day and is willing to make a deposit to assure that a room is held for him. Please let us have a confirmation of this reservation and let us know whether you wish us to make a deposit on the room. CLOSING LINES. | 53 68 80 92 107 120 138

LINE: 60
TAB: 5 AND CENTER
SPACING: SINGLE
DRILLS: THREE TIMES
GOAL: REVIEW FORMS
   AND LETTERS
STRESS: VIGOR

Review

67-A. See whether you can type lines 1-3 four times in a minute. Repeat these lines in Lesson 68, too.

67-A. Tune up on these review lines

1 When did she go to the man and pay for the Oak Lake island?

2 We acquire jerky habits from having typed exercises lazily.

3 10 28 39 47 56 we 23 rot 495 pew 032 toy 596 rip 480 up 70.

67-B. The vertical lines are simply to guide you in recognizing phrases; don't pause when you come to one. Start slowly and speed up on repetitions.

67-B. Speed up on fluent preview phrases

4 with this long list this work know that been more been true

5 you the and the has not for you for the and for and for you

6 of your to know of most to work we are to our of the in the

7 list of true of most of give us you to may we and if one of

67-C. Take five 1-minute writings, with a pause after each minute; then take a straight 5-minute writing (with no rests). Try to equal the score you made in Lesson 65-C.

Or, type a copy of this letter, trying to finish it within 5 minutes and with 4 or fewer errors.

Note that the letter is shown here on a 55-space line; when you type it, however, use a 50- or 60-space line (whichever is correct for an average letter on your machine).

67-C. Sustain your skill in production typing

8   *Current date*   4

Mr. Chester L. Harris   8
1039 8th Avenue West   12
Vancouver, British Columbia   V6H 1C3   17
                                                                23
Dear Mr. Harris:
                                                                27
              SUBJECT: END OF THE JOB!
                                                                44
With this letter we are sending you the final parts of
your thesis: the last two chapters and the long list   56
of readings. We are also enclosing an invoice for this   67
work, which brings your balance to $45.   78
                                                                86
We should like you to know that typing this material has
been more than "just one more job" to our group of typ-   99
ists. All of us have found your writing to be extremely   109
interesting, a fact that has not been true of most of   121
the theses that we've typed in the past.   132
                                                                140
We are grateful to you for the many kind things you have
said about our work. May we quote from one of your let-   152
ters when next we compete for a contract? Please give   163
us permission, Mr. Harris; and give us also a chance to   174
work for and with you once more.   186
                                                                192
                    Very sincerely yours,   199
                    MEREDITH TYPING SERVICE
                                                                206

                                                                209

                    Jean I. Meredith   213

urs   215
Enclosures   217

Letter 25

BLOCKED LETTER
Paper: workbook
Body: 146 words
SI: 1.35—the easy
   side of normal

NOTE: Reference initials (like "urs") may be typed either in small letters, as shown, or in all caps.

LINE: 60
TAB: 5
SPACING: SINGLE
GOALS: STABILIZE
  SKILL; MAKE COPIES
STRESS: SHARP,
  MULTICOPY STROKING

Unit 26. Correspondence

157-A. Tune up on these review lines

157-A. Each line three
or more times. Repeat
fully in Lesson 158.

1 Rod can use the new car and let Dad fix the old one for me.

2 Working quietly, Max alphabetized the census of vital jobs.

3 Pair patterns are typed like this: 10 & 28 & 39 & 47 & 56.

  1 | 2 | 3 | 4 | 5 | 6 | 7 | 8 | 9 | 10 | 11 | 12

157-B. Sustain skill on copy of normal difficulty

157-B. Change to double
spacing. Confirm margin
settings for a 60-space
line (copy aligns if you
observe bell correctly).

Type paragraphs 4 and 5
in Lesson 157, paragraphs
6 and 7 in Lesson 158.
Repeat each paragraph
until it is typed with no
or with only one error.

SI 1.42—normal, average.

  1 | 2 | 3 | 4 | 5 | 6 | 7 | 8 | 9 | 10 | 11 | 12 | 13 | 14

4 When a man has more mail to handle than he can manage, he hires   14
someone to help him with it. He expects to decide what is to be said   28
in each letter and then, having said it, to leave to the person he hired   42
the responsibility of doing whatever else has to be done to complete   56
the communication.   60

5 The boss assumes that his helper will check the dates, names,   76
addresses, amounts, times, and the like. He assumes that the helper   89
will provide the salutation and the closing phrase, or correct the ones   104
dictated if they are incorrect. He assumes that the helper will divide   118
the letter body into proper paragraphs, will give appropriate display   132
to subject and attention lines and body quotations or tables, and   145
will handle the carbon copies. These are what he is paid to do.   158

Thumbnail letter index:

6 Making and handling the copies is more of a chore than one might   174
at first anticipate. To start with, there should be a copy for the files;   189
and this copy must bear a complete record of the distribution of all   203
copies of the letter. If the firm is large enough to be departmentalized,   218
a copy may be needed for another department. If the letter concerns   231
a third person, perhaps he should receive a copy. The typist must   245
plan his carbons with care lest he not have enough. A wise typist   258
always makes a spare copy or two, to play safe!   268

7 Sometimes the employer may wish to send someone a copy of a   282
letter he has received; he tells his secretary so. In large firms, the   296
secretary can make the copy in a second or two on a photocopying   309
machine. But if there is no machine, or if the one in that office is out   324
of order or is reserved for the work of someone else, then the helper   338
must know not only how to type the copy but also how to show it is   352
a copy and not the original letter. Sometimes the employer wishes to   366
send just part of a letter, copied from an incoming one, to another   379
department for a follow-up; the typist must know how a transfer   392
sheet is used for such purposes. The typist has to be very expert in   406
working with many kinds of copies.   413

  1 | 2 | 3 | 4 | 5 | 6 | 7 | 8 | 9 | 10 | 11 | 12 | 13 | 14

ALTERNATE PLAN

1. Take a 3- or 5-minute
writing. Type a full line
of each word you missed.

2. Type three times each
all the lines you typed
in the timed effort, plus
one more line of copy.

3. Repeat the first step
to see whether you cover
all the practiced copy
in the same time but with
no additional errors.

Carbon paper has a dull side and a glossy side that does the work.	Put glossy side against the paper on which the copy is to be made.	Check: You must have one more sheet of paper than of carbon paper.	Use both hands to get pack behind roll. You can see glossy sides.	Hold pack in left hand; turn roll with right. Dull sides show in front.

67/68-D. Apply your skill in a production review

Type Letter 26 (page 110) and Forms 14-16 below, each with one carbon. Time your work. GOAL: At least 35 words a minute production speed from time when machine is adjusted and paper is inserted, ready to type.

Form 14

INVOICE
Form: workbook (or plain paper, as shown on page 108)
Note: compute all extension figures

Invoice to Mr. Chester L. Harris ⎮ 1039 8th Avenue West ⎮   9
Vancouver, British Columbia V6H 1L3 *for the following:*   29
Chapter IX of thesis: ⎮ 22 Pages of straight copy @ .30 ⎮ 3   46
Pages including tables @ .50 ⎮ 50 Pages of carbon copies @   66
.05 ⎮ Chapter X of thesis: ⎮ 10 Pages of straight copy @   83
.30 ⎮ 4 Pages including tables @ .50 ⎮ 8 Pages of biblio-   102
graphy @ .50 ⎮ 44 Pages of carbon copies @ .05 ⎮⎮ AMOUNT   128
DUE ⎮ 3% SALE TAX ⎮ TOTAL AMOUNT DUE 22.45   133

Memo to MTS Production Staff ⎮ MTS Service Staff ⎮ *From* Jean I.   7
Meredith ⎮ Manager ⎮ *on the subject of* The Next Big Job ⎮ *Date.*   24

We have just been notified that we have been awarded the   38
big contract to prepare eight training manuals for the Air Force   51
Base in Rockcliffe, Ontario. The manuscript will begin to   62
flow to us on or about March 1 and will provide a sufficient   75
volume to keep us on full production for at least two months.   87

Form 15

INTEROFFICE MEMO
Form: workbook (or plain paper, as shown on page 105)

Between now and March 1, therefore, we will wish to clean   100
up any small jobs that came to us but had to be deferred while   113
we were concentrating on the Harris job. We will also wish to   126
have all the equipment serviced; the Air Force job will consist   139
of our preparing many thousand Duplimat masters for offset   151
reproduction, and for this we need machines to be in perfect-   163
plus condition. ⎮ J. I. M. ⎮ urs   172

Day-letter telegram from Meredith Typing Service ⎮ Vancou-   13
ver, B.C., *date* ⎮ *to* Senior Training Officer ⎮ Rockcliffe RCAF   29
Base ⎮ Rockcliffe, Ontario ⎮   34

Form 16

TELEGRAM
Form: workbook
Caution: note that this is a day letter and not full rate

We look forward with pleasure to beginning work on Air   46
Force contract AFT17/64A-H on March 1. Suggest your repre-   58
sentative make first delivery of manuscript in person to set up   71
style manual for production. ⎮ Jean I. Meredith ⎮ Meredith   85
Typing Service ⎮ urs   90

156-B. Two copies with eyes rigidly on the copy or a 3-minute writing.

If you make two or more errors, your goal should be accuracy; fewer than two, the goal is speed.

156-A. Repeat the tune-up on page 241

156-B. Measure your skill on a technical paragraph

23   The men asked for a 15% increase across the board, but   12
they settled—if that is the word—for a 10% one. My raise   24
was for $22.50 a week, bringing me from $250.00 to $272.50,   36
which increased my annual salary to $14 170. After all the   48
deductions were out—about 28%—my take-home pay was $9 919   60

   1 | 2 | 3 | 4 | 5 | 6 | 7 | 8 | 9 | 10 | 11 | 12

156-C-D-E Pattern:

ACCURACY: The one-line drills alternately three times (plus once more if you missed the symbol in 156-B), then the three-line paragraph twice.

SPEED: Each one-line drill twice (plus once more if you missed the symbol in 156-B), then the paragraph three times very steadily.

156-C. Improve control of the $ key

24   fff f4f f44 f4$ f$$ fff f4f f44 f4$ f$$ $4 $44 $444 $44.44.
25   They asked for $10 and $28 and $39 and $47 and $56 at once.
26   The 1903 dollar was $1,500 in 1962 and went up $30 one   12
year later, to $1,530. The 1898 mintings varied greatly in   24
cost after 1950: $300, $10, $6, $7, $38, and $350 in 1964.   36

   1 | 2 | 3 | 4 | 5 | 6 | 7 | 8 | 9 | 10 | 11 | 12

156-D. Improve control of % key

27   fff f5f f55 f5% f%% fff f5f f55 f5% f%% 5% 55% 555% 55.55%.
28   Our daily totals went from 10% to 28% to 39% to 47% to 56%.
29   My decision: freshmen, 15%; sophomores, 20%; juniors,   12
30%; and seniors, 35%. As it turned out, freshmen got 20%;   24
sophomores, 30%; and juniors and seniors received 25% each.   36

   1 | 2 | 3 | 4 | 5 | 6 | 7 | 8 | 9 | 10 | 11 | 12

156-E. Improve control of the hyphen key

30   ;;; ;-; ;— ;;; ;-; ;— ;;; ;-; ;— ;;; ;-; ;— ;;; ;-; ;—
31   These are some prefixes: for-, com-, pre-, con-, and mis-.
32   My in-laws own a sock-manufacturing firm; they concen-   12
trate on off-color two-tone patterns, like green-yellow and   24
orange-brown, or pink-red against slate-gray, and the like.   36

   1 | 2 | 3 | 4 | 5 | 6 | 7 | 8 | 9 | 10 | 11 | 12

156-F. Regain fluency by typing "we 23" combinations

33 we 23 22 21 two 529 528 527 rip 480 479 478 put 075 074 073
34 it 85 84 83 our 974 973 972 wet 235 234 233 eye 363 362 361
35 to 59 58 57 woo 299 298 297 rut 475 474 473 pie 083 082 081
36 up 70 69 68 rye 463 462 461 pep 030 029 028 too 599 598 597

   1 | 2 | 3 | 4 | 5 | 6 | 7 | 8 | 9 | 10 | 11 | 12

156-G. Repeat 156-B to measure your progress

LINE: 60
TAB: 5
SPACING: SINGLE
GOAL: HOLD PACE ON
REVISED COPY
STRESS: ATTENTIVENESS

Unit 12. Manuscripts

69-A. Tune up on these review lines

1 To make it to town, I paid a neighbor to sit with the girl.

2 Symbols never change, even when part of block-letter titles.

3 Type 1 and 2 and 3 and 4 and 5 and 6 and 7 and 8 [Continue to 50]

| 1 | 2 | 3 | 4 | 5 | 6 | 7 | 8 | 9 | 10 | 11 | 12 |

69-B. Learn how revisions are indicated

These are the markings used by writers, editors, and typists to indicate changes in all kinds of typed work when revising it for final retyping:

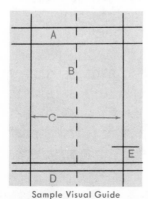

^	Insert word	and the
—	Omit word	and so it
~~	No, don't omit	and so it
\	Omit stroke	and sob the
/	Make letter small	And so the
=	Make capital	it may not
≡	Make all capitals	It may not
→	Move as indicated	and so the
//	Line up, even up	and so the
=	Line up, even up	TO: Mr. A.
SS	Use single spacing ...	and so the
~	Turn around	and the so
ds	Use double spacing ...	and so the
=	Insert a hyphen	red tipped
5	Indent 5 spaces	It may not

#	Insert a space	and so the
|	Insert a space	and so the
⌒	Omit space	the a. m.
—	Underscore this	It may be
⊙	Move as shown	it is not
⌒	Join to word	in search
—	Change word	and if it
o	Make into period	or to it.
◯	Don't abbreviate	Dr. Wilson
◯	Spell it out	1 or 2 who
¶	New paragraph	We can try
∨	Raise above line	Hale, says
+#	More space here	It may not
−#	Less space here	It may not
2#	2 linespaces here	It may not

69-C. Sustain a steady rate on revised material

69/70-D. Produce a two-page report (unbound form)

69-A. Each line three times or for a minute each. Repeat all three drills when you do Lesson 70.

69-B. To reinforce your mastery of the use and interpretation of these "rough draft" revision marks, do the exercises on workbook pages 115-6.

69-C. Read the material on page 113 carefully, to be sure you can read it as fluently as would be the case if it were not in rough-draft form.

Then, beginning with paragraph 1, either copy all the material (GOAL: To finish in 7 minutes within 4 errors) or take a 5-minute writing on it (GOAL: 35 or more wam, within 4 mistakes).

SI 1.40—normal

69-D. A ready-made visual guide appears in your workbook, page 117; use it for the production work in Lessons 69-74.

A visual guide is, of course, a summary of margin rules; compare the directions for this visual guide with rules given on pages 113-114.

A visual guide doesn't save much time on short reports, but saves time and assures consistency through a long report.

Sample Visual Guide

Study the technical information on pages 113-114; then type the material (make all the indicated revisions) as a formal, academic, two-page report.

It will be easier for you if you first make a "visual guide" on a plain sheet of P4 paper:

A. Draw heavy lines 6 and 12 lines from the top.

B. Draw heavy centering line in the middle.

C. Draw margin lines for a 60-stroke writing line.

D. Draw heavy lines 9 and 6 lines from the foot.

E. Draw a short warning line 6 lines above (D).

Place this guide under the paper on which you will type; the lines will show through to guide you.

155-A. Three times each. Repeat in Lesson 156.

155-A. Tune up on these easy review lines
Both the firm and city own half the lake and half the land.
Jo's brain is taxed with a very fine quiz on black pigment.
Type 1 and 2 and 3 and 4 and 5 and 6 and 7 and 8 [Continue to 50]

155-B. Two copies with eyes rigidly on copy, or a 3-minute writing.

155-B. Measure your skill on a technical paragraph
In the United States of America, the silver dollar was
certified in April, 1792. The first one was minted in 1794
and weighed 416 grains of silver, 892.4 fine. Not one dollar was minted during 1804 & 1836, 1873 & 1878, 1904 & 1921
and after 1935. In all, five mints made 855,661,153 coins.

1 | 2 | 3 | 4 | 5 | 6 | 7 | 8 | 9 | 10 | 11 | 12

155-C. Each line three times, plus twice more if the number is one which you mistyped in 155-B, plus twice more if you or anyone else catches you raising your eyes as you type each drill.

155-C. Improve control on individual number keys
aa 11 Of 111 teams, 11 were great, 11 poor, and 11 average.
ss 22 The 22 boys brought 22 gloves, 22 balls, and 22 bats.
dd 33 They gave me 33 boxes of the 33 kinds of No. 33 tape.
ff 44 Bingo game No. 44 had 44 players and paid 44 dollars.
ff 55 Car 55 comes out of the 55th Division on 55th Street.

1 | 2 | 3 | 4 | 5 | 6 | 7 | 8 | 9 | 10 | 11 | 12

;; 00 Figures like 010, 0010, and 00010 are just simply 10.
ll 99 When adding 9, 99, and 999, the sum can't be a 9,999.
kk 88 Club 88, on 88th, has 88 members paying 88 per month.
jj 77 No. 7 showed 77 times for No. 77 and for 777 dollars.
jj 66 I drove on Route 66 for 66 miles at 66 miles an hour.

155-D. If your allover basic need is for surer ACCURACY, type the three lines, as a paragraph, three times. But if your need is for SPEED, type each line three times.

155-D. Increase fluency by typing "we 23" combinations
we 23 24 25 two 529 530 531 rip 480 481 482 put 075 076 077
it 85 86 87 our 974 975 976 wet 235 236 237 eye 363 364 365
or 94 95 96 woo 299 300 301 rut 475 476 477 pie 083 084 085

155-E. Type two copies, earnestly trying to type at a steady, unbroken pace with your eyes kept rigidly on the copy.

155-E. Strengthen skill on cumulative-count groups
6701 8202 6303 7204 8705 9606 2707 1008 7409 8510 9311 8212
7613 6714 7015 6116 1017 5618 4919 3920 2821 1622 1723 1624
9725 8626 6727 5028 4729 3930 2831 7632 6733 6534 7435 1036
8737 1938 6739 9340 8241 7742 9843 9044 5645 4046 3947 2848
8049 3850 4851 2852 9453 5954 8955 9356 9857 9958 9059 4860

155-F. Repeat 155-B to measure your progress

FORMAL MANUSCRIPTS

A Report for Typing I
By John E. Lake

The standard rules for typing a formal manuscript, such
as a term paper, are illustrated on this *and* the next page.

THE SPACING TO USE

Single space all special displays, such as headings that
take 2 lines, quotations that *will* fill more than two
typed lines, foot notes, listings, and so forth.

Double space the body of the manuscript unless there is
a special reason for single spacing it (such as the need for
saving space in filing or saving materials in duplicating).

Triple space (that is, leave 2 blank lines) after the
heading of any page and before any major sub-heading.

Quadruple space (leave three blank lines) to seperate a
table from the adjacent body of the manuscript.

THE MARGINS TO USE

The top margin should be 5 cm deep on *the* first page and
2.5 cm deep on the other pages. So, typing will begin on
Line 13 of the first page and *on* Line 7 of all *other* pages.

The bottom margin should be at least 2.5 cm deep and
may be up to 3.8 cm deep. If the last page *of a manuscript* is short,
the bottom margin will, of course, be deeper.

69-C

12   53

24   65

25   66

29   70

46   87

58   99

67   108

84   125

97   138

108 149

125 166

135 176

154 195

163 204

164 205

168 209

187 228

199 240

211 252

229 270

244 285

253 294

| 1 | 2 | 3 | 4 | 5 | 6 | 7 | 8 | 9 | 10 | 11 | 12 |

Page 1 of a 2-Page Unbound Manuscript

GOAL: SAME AS
IN LESSON 153

154-A. Repeat the 153-A tune-up on page 238

154-B. Type to your goal.

ACCURACY: Lines 17-20
(as a paragraph) four
times; and lines 21-24
(as a paragraph) twice.

SPEED: Lines 17-20 two
times each; lines 21-24
four fast times each.

154-B. Increase skill through selective sentence practice

17 Clyde fixed quaint puzzles to give to John, Mark, and Webb.
18 Vick's big squad of experts clearly won three major prizes.
19 Jacques was amazed by Vi's skill and fixed her a good part.
20 Five or six big Zero planes sent by Mac to GHQ were junked.

  1 | 2 | 3 | 4 | 5 | 6 | 7 | 8 | 9 | 10 | 11 | 12

21 Both the town and city may make the firm fix both big oaks.
22 They got paid for both the corn and fish but kept the hams.
23 Dick got both the land and auto but paid for half the lake.
24 When the busy man paid the men, the city got keys for them.

154-C. Type to your goal.

ACCURACY: Type entire
selection two times.

SPEED: Type individual
paragraphs twice each.

ALTERNATE PLAN: Take
1-minute writings on
paragraph 25 until you
set a new speed record
without error; then do
similarly on each of the
other paragraphs until
you equal on each the
paragraph 25 record.

154-C. Sustain skill on developmental paragraphs

25 Each time we plan to get out of town and buy some   11
house out where no one else is, I think of the old man   22
I know who had the same wish as we; each time he moved   33
out, the town caught up with him.   SI 1.00—very easy   40

26 The day that most dads dread most is the day when   11   51
junior is old enough to drive a car. On that day, one   22   62
man groaned, his son became tall enough to drive a car   33   73
but too short to pay for the gas.   SI 1.10—easy   40   80

27 If you live near a main road that leads to a lake   11   91
or seashore, you can tell when summer has come: Count   22 102
the autos that have a boat in tow. They swish by like   33 113
an avalanche of hopeful sunshine.   SI 1.20—easy   40 120

28 Loyalty to a team is a great thing, but I noticed   11 131
just recently that the sport screaming loudest for the   22 142
head of the coach of a losing team was the guy who had   33 153
cheered loudest in its victories.   SI 1.30—fairly easy 40 160

  1 | 2 | 3 | 4 | 5 | 6 | 7 | 8 | 9 | 10 | 11

154-D. Type to your goal.

ACCURACY: Lines 29-31, as
a paragraph, four times;
lines 32-34 two times.

SPEED: Lines 29-31 two
times each, lines 32-34
four fast times each.

154-D. Strengthen skill by selective preview practice

29 harvesting nostrils crystal secured packed vapor steam drum
30 distillery planting extract growers you're stews piped tank
31 lucrative condenser pungent sunripe tramps acres mowed cars

  1 | 2 | 3 | 4 | 5 | 6 | 7 | 8 | 9 | 10 | 11 | 12

32 just like |must find |that are |for the |is not |but it is |as if
33 that flow |from this |will you |all the |or add |and if it |or so
34 will find |that they |when the |and for |if you |are by it |to us

**154-E. To measure your
progress over 153-B, take
a 5-minute writing from
page 239, starting at the
top of column 2; or copy
its first two paragraphs.**

154-E. Measure your progress

5

    The <u>side margins</u> should permit a 60-stroke line of writing   24

(60 spaces pica, 70 spaces elite), centered ~~in~~ the ~~report~~ *if* *manuscript* is   37

not to be bound in a note book or binder but moved 6 mm   49

to the right (giving a left margin of 3.8 cm and right   62

margin of 2.5 cm) if the manuscript is to be so bound.   ▼?   73

74

THE PLACEMENT OF <u>H</u>eadings   79

    The <u>page-1 heading lines</u> should be centered, the title   101

in all caps and other lines in capital and small letters.   112

¶ <u>Major subheadings</u> may be blocked at the margin (in which case   133

they are called "sideheadings") or be centered; They may be   145

typed in all caps, as in this manuscript, or be underscored.   157

    <u>paragraph headings</u> are indented and underscored.   175

    The <u>page number</u> is omitted on page 1; On other pages, it   187

is typed on line 7 at the right margin, with or ~~without~~ the   199

word "page," and is followed by ②blank lines~~paces~~.   209

LINE: 60
TAB: 5
SPACING: SINGLE
GOAL: USE FOOTNOTES
STRESS: THE DETAILS

Footnotes

71-A. Each drill for a minute or three times. Repeat in Lesson 72.

71-A. Tune up on these lines

1   The two old men set out the big red box and the boy saw it.

2   Type four-figure numbers either as 1000 cm or 1 000 cm now.

3   Type 1 for 2 for 3 for 4 for 5 for 6 for 7 for 8   [Continue to 50]

   1 | 2 | 3 | 4 | 5 | 6 | 7 | 8 | 9 | 10 | 11 | 12

71-B. Beginning with first paragraph, type the revised material on page 115 (GOAL: To finish in 8 minutes with 4 or less errors) or take 5-minute timing on it (GOAL: 35 or more wam within 4 or fewer mistakes). SI 1.60—difficult

71-B. Sustain a steady rate on revised material

71/72-C. Produce a two-page report (bound form)

Study the information on pages 115-116; then type a correct copy as a 2-page *bound report* (so: 3.8 cm left margin and 2.5 cm right margin).

To end lines evenly, LINE: 60, TAB: 5.
Use double spacing. SI: 1.25—easy

1 | 2 | 3 | 4 | 5 | 6 | 7 | 8   1 | 2 | 3 | 4 | 5 | 6 | 7 | 8

MINTING GOLD FROM OIL

The next time you delight in the flavor 9
of peppermint, put in a word for Oregon, 17
won't you? It is likely that the mint you 26
enjoy came from there, because more mint 34
is raised in Oregon than anywhere else. 42
It just happens that Oregon, with its 50
rich soil and its frequent but light rains, 59
is one of the few places in the country 67
where mint can be grown as a crop, just as 75
other parts of the country grow sugar beets 84
or corn or what have you. For a long time, 93
mint was raised only in the middle valley 101
of the state; but now you can see and sniff 110
those green, beautiful fields all over the 119
state. 120

CULTIVATION

The mint plants are set out in the field 130
in rows some 60 cm apart, which allows 139
room for cultivating even when the plants 147
have grown into bushes about 45 cm in 155
height. Mint has to be cared for like a 164
baby, for it is subject to many diseases, 172
most of which make the mint plant wilt; 180
and once a mint field has become diseas- 188
ed, it will be many years before the acre- 197
age will again produce a good and pure 205
crop. To ripen, the plants must have a 214
hot summer sun precisely like the one 223
that Oregon has on tap every summer. 229

Weeds are a bit of a minor problem, or 239
used to be, for they thrive on the same 247
things that mint needs; but someone found 256
that geese do not like mint but do enjoy 264
the kinds of weeds and grass that grow in 272
mint fields; so the sight of a flock of geese, 282
busy at the task of weeding out a field for 291
a farmer, is a common and welcome one 298
throughout the state. 303

PROCESSING

When it is sunripe and mature, the mint 313
crop is mowed, just like hay, and dried 321
for two or three days. Then it is fed into 330
a machine that chops the plants into little 338
pieces and flows them into trucks that are 347
tank cars. To pack the mint hay solidly in 356
the tank, teams of young workers tramp, 364
tramp, tramp the flow of hay until the tank 373
is packed full. 376

Off goes the tank truck to the mint 385
distillery. There a cover is secured on the 394
tank and live steam is piped into it for 402
about an hour and a half, cooking the hay. 411
The mint stews in the steam; a vapor of 419
mint oil and steam rises and is drawn 427
through a condenser, which separates the 435
water and mint oil. The mint oil that flows 444
into storage drums is as clear as crystal 452
and so pungent that it makes your nostrils 461
quiver even if you're a good 0.80 km 470
from the distillery. 473

THE FINANCIAL PICTURE

There is not a mint of money in mint 483
growing, but it's still a lucrative busi- 492
ness for the top growers. One tonne of 500
mint hay is the produce of some 1.2 ha. 509
A drum of oil is the extract of about 518
three tonnes of hay. A drum is worth 526
about two thousand dollars. This means 535
a mint farmer can earn about two hund- 543
red dollars per hectare, but from that he 551
must take all the cost of planting and 560
raising and harvesting the crop. Even so, 568
there is a profit in a normal year; and if 577
you are able to count your hectares by 585
the hundreds, you will find you have 593
struck oil, the golden kind, straight from 602
the Oregon mint. 606

Manuscript 13
Manuscript 14

2-PAGE REPORT
IN BOUND FORM
Shown: in elite
Paper: plain
Visual guide: work-
   book page 118
SI: 1.58—difficult

To provide 3.8 cm left margin and 2.5 cm right margin—
1. Use the visual guide on workbook page 118; or
2. Set stops for 60-stroke line and then shift them 3 spaces to right; or
3. Set stops for 60-stroke line and then shift paper guide 6 mm to left.

FOOTNOTES IN MANUSCRIPTS

71-C
15
16
30
41

A Report for Typing I
By A. J. Wilson 3

71-B

The principal rules for typing footnotes in manuscripts are shown
and explained on this and the next page. The works of Hutchinson,[1] of
Gavin and Sabin,[2] and of others are authority for the statements
that will be made in this brief report. 3

14   58
29   73
44   88
50   94

51   95

Purposes of Footnotes

64   108

1. Footnotes are used to identify references mentioned in the body
of the manuscript; for example, the footnotes on this page identify
the two references in the first paragraph.

78   122
92   136
101   145

2. Footnotes are used to give the source of of a quotation that is
cited in the manuscript. Examples: Footnotes 3 and 5.

113   157
124   168

3. Footnotes are used for an explanations of something mentioned
in the body. Example: Footnote 4. 3

138   182
146   190

147   191

Styling of Footnotes

159   203

4. If a footnote refers to a book, the data are arranged as shown
in the footnotes in this report: authorship, title, publishing source
and date, and exact page if it is needed. 1

173   217
187   231
196   240

_____ 2

202   246

1. Lois Hutchinson, Standard Handbook for Secretaries, Eighth
Edition (New York: McGraw-Hill, 1969).

230   274
238   282

239   283

2. Ruth E. Gavin and William A. Sabin, Reference Manual for
Stenographers and Typists, (Toronto: McGraw-Hill Ryerson, 1970).

261   305
285   329

1 | 2 | 3 | 4 | 5 | 6 | 7 | 8 | 9 | 10 | 11 | 12 | 13 | 14

Page 1 of a 2-Page Bound Manuscript, with Footnotes

Table 48

Boxed
Double Space on
top half of P4
page. Include
special note.

UNITS PERMITTED FOR USE WITH SI

Quantity	Name of Unit	Symbol
Time	second	s*
	minute	min
	hour	h
	day	d
	year	a

*A base unit in SI

Table 49

Boxed
Single Space on
bottom half of
same page.

SOME SI DERIVED UNITS
Having Special Names

Quantity	Name of Unit	Symbol
Frequency	hertz	Hz
Force	newton	N
Pressure, Stress	pascal	Pa
Energy, Work Quantity of heat	joule	J
Power	watt	W
Electric charge	coulomb	C

5

5. Each footnote is set up as a separate, single-spaced paragraph,   20

preceded by a blank line and indented five spaces.   30

6. Foot notes must be clearly separated from the body, or text, of   44

a manuscript.   One book states: 51

Indent quotations
of three or more
lines 5 spaces
on each side

> Separate the footnote from the text by a line of under-   65
> scores 5 cm long. Single space before typing the line   78
> and double space after typing it in order to leave one blank   91
> space above and below.[3]   99

7. If the last page of the manuscript is short, ~~insert~~ extra space   113

above the separation line to make sure that the footnotes will appear   127

just above the *proper* ~~appropriate~~ bottom margin.   135

136

Numbering of Footnotes   149

8.   The references in a manuscript should be numbered in sequence.   164

The footnote *for a reference* is given the identical number and must appear on the same   181

page as the references.

9. The number in the body must be superior[4] and follow, without a   201

a space, the reference or ~~the~~ punctuation mark following ~~it~~.   212

[10. The number in a footnote may be superior, "without any space   225

following it," 5 or may be in ordinary enumeration form as shown in this   240

report 6.

To know how much
space to leave here,
read paragraph 7.   *underscored period*

"Et al." means "and others."
"Op. cit." means "the book
already mentioned."   248

3. Alan C. Lloyd, et al., Gregg Typewriting for Colleges, Second   272
Canadian Edition (McGraw-Hill Ryerson, 1978), page 116.   284

285

4. A "superior" number is one raised above the line ~~by holding the~~   297
~~cylinder-turned part way while you type the number key.~~   297

298

5. Gavin and Sabin, op. cit., page 237.   311

312

6. Lloyd, op. cit., page 116.   322

underscore period

Page 2 of 2-Page Bound Manuscript, with Footnotes

152-C. Metric tables

SI is comprised of seven base units and two supplementary units. From these units, we can derive all other measurements in SI. Derived units are expressed in terms of the base and/or supplementary units.

Although most of our measurement functions can be performed without a knowledge of the structure of SI, we should have some familiarity with the names and symbols of its units. For a quick reference to the foundation of SI, type the following tables and include them in your SI reference manual.

Table 46
Boxed
Single Space on top half of P4 page. Include special note.

SI BASE UNIT TABLE

Quantity	Name of Unit	Symbol
Length	metre	m
Mass	kilogram*	kg
Time	second	s
Electric current	ampere	A
Thermodynamic temperature	kelvin	K
Amount of substance	mole	mol
Luminous intensity	candela	cd

* The only base unit which contains a prefix

Table 47
Boxed
Double Space on bottom half of same page.

SI SUPPLEMENTARY UNIT TABLE

Quantity	Name of Unit	Symbol
Plane angle	radian	rad
Solid angle	steradian	sr

Typing style guide for SI and metric symbols   *Review*

A common international language of measurement is most desirable. SI is a truly universal metric system; therefore, it is essential that a typist note and conform to these precise international symbols and style instructions.

1. Type the symbols in upright, roman type regardless of the type used in the rest of the text.
   The upright m *represents metre, but the slanted m may represent mass.*

2. Type the symbols in lower case, unless the unit is derived from a person's name. cm for centimetre, but °C for Celsius.

3. Use symbols rather than units when writing specific amounts.
   It was 1 m between windows.
   Exceptions: a) Litre is symbolized by the capital L to avoid confusion with number 1.
   b) The unit may be used when the number with it *must* be in words.
   One metre was the distance between windows.

4. When no number is used, the unit should be spelled out.
   I think it was kilograms.

5. Leave a full space between a number and a symbol.
   23 kg   Exception: 20°C

6. Do not pluralize a symbol because the plural form is the same as the singular.   3 mL of vanilla

7. Use a period after a symbol *only* when the symbol ends a sentence.
   1 kg of corn, but The corn measured 1 kg.

8. Type a zero before the decimal marker with a number whose value is less than one.   0.37 mg

9. Use a decimal rather than a fraction to express partial units.
   10.5 kg

10. Use an exponent to express square and cubic units.
    3 m^2 and 5 m^3

11. Round off commonly used values rather than express them in precise figures.   It is 100 km from Vancouver to Victoria.

12. Use a space, not a comma, between groups of 3 digits to the left and right of the decimal marker.   53 000.214 956
    Exception: The space is unnecessary if there are only 4 digits to the left or right of the decimal marker. Use consistent spacing, however, when such numerals occur in a table with others having a greater numbers of digits.

13. Use the solidus (/) to indicate *per* between two SI symbols. 50 km/h

14. Do not use a dot or decimal as a multiplication symbol between numerals.   2 x 3

SPELLING AND PRONUNCIATION

1. Note that *metre* with or without a prefix is spelled *re*.

2. To ensure that prefixes keep their identity when pronounced, we should say them with the accent on the first syllable — *centi*metre, *kilo*gram. Therefore, to be consistent, we should also pronounce *kilo*metre with the same accent.

A trademark is often a picture, symbol, word, mark, or
figure used to make some product stand out from all others.
At first, pictures or symbols were used because most people
could not read or write. Do you recall the barber pole and
its red and white stripes? You really did not have to know
how to read to know what it meant. The pole served as sign
of the fact that one seeking a barber could find him there.

In the early days, goods were purchased because of the
worker's reputation. If the craftsman was skilled with the
tools of his trade, he did not have to affix a tag or label
to the product he had made; folks knew him and knew that an
item he had made was good. But as others began to make and
offer similar products, each man applied some kind of mark,
as a sign that the product was his and that he stood by it.

So long as firms were small and the buyers lived near,
control was not too much of a problem. But as machine–made
goods appeared and as the markets grew, customers would ask
for brands. At first, a man had to prove in court that his
was the first product of that nature so branded. Now, laws
permit anyone to register a trademark at the patent office.
This step taken, no such mark can be used on similar goods.

The stories of how makers first came to pick their own
trademarks would be fun to read. A study of the first ones
would show a trend toward pictures and common names; a very
good case in point is the popular cough drop that has never
had its whiskers trimmed. Some firms have created words to
depict their wares, and the public has added many a special
nickname. Symbols are becoming very popular as trademarks.

Many of our brands have been shown for decades without
basic changes in design. On the other hand, one large firm
just made its sixth change in four years. One popular mark
resulted from a schoolboy contest fifty years ago which led
to national favor. Still another has made such good use of
color and design that the mark is displayed on every box of
this item. A study of trademarks should be <u>most</u> rewarding!

SI 1.20—
easy

SI 1.25—
easy

SI 1.30—
fairly easy

SI 1.35—
fairly easy

SI 1.40—
normal

12
24
36
48
60
72
84
96
108
120
132
144
156
168
12   180
24   192
36   204
48   216
60   228
72   240
84   252
96   264
108 276
120 288
132 300
144 312
156 324
168 336
180 348
192 360
204 372
216 384
228 396
240 408
254 422

1 | 2 | 3 | 4 | 5 | 6 | 7 | 8 | 9 | 10 | 11 | 12

Apply your skill in a production review

Forms 17-18

INVOICES
Review: pages 108-109
Goal: within 4 minutes and 3 errors
Forms: workbook (or on plain paper as shown on page 108)

Letter 26

BLOCKED LETTER
Review: pages 97-100
Goal: within 6 minutes and 4 errors
Body: 152 words
Paper: letterhead
Tab: center only
SI: 1.44—normal

**Manuscript 15
Manuscript 16**

PAGE 1 OF REPORT
Review: pages 112-116
Goal: a copy within 8 minutes, 6 errors
Copy 1: arrange as page 1 of UNBOUND report; may use the visual guide on workbook page 117
Copy 2: arrange as page 1 of a BOUND report and under-score sideheadings instead of all caps; use visual guide, workbook page 118
SI: 1.48—fairly difficult

Prepare the following invoices from the Manufacturers Institute:

1. No. 26173 to Mr. Clarence J. Markham | Training Department | Shreveport Sugar, Ltd. | 1600 Clark Street | Vancouver, British Columbia *for the following:* 10 (*copies of*) Benkley: Modern Plant Safety @ 2.50 = 25.00 | 1 (*copy of*) Benkley: MPS Instructor's Manual @ 3.50 = 3.50 | 1 (*set of*) Benkley: MPS Filmstrip (Set) @ 36.00 = 36.00 | AMOUNT DUE = 64.50 | 10% MEMBER'S DISCOUNT = 6.45 | TOTAL AMOUNT DUE = 58.05

2. No. 26174 to Training Division | Nucleonics Corporation | 121 Belmont Avenue | Pointe-Claire, Québec H9R 2P7 | *for the following (compute all amounts):* 20 Rafael: Production Tooling @ 4.50 | 1 Rafael: PT Instructor's Manual @ 5.50 | 20 Gavelin: Cost Estimating @ 4.00 | 1 Gavelin: CE Instructor's Manual @ 5.00 | 20 Poe: Production Reporting @ 1.25 | 1 Poe: PR Course Outline @ 2.00 | *Compute* AMOUNT DUE | *Indicate* 10% MEMBER'S DISCOUNT | TOTAL AMOUNT DUE *should be* $186.75

Following exactly the directions in the boxes, see whether you can turn out the production assignments within the cited time and error limits.

HOW TO MAKE A CORRECTION

The purpose of this report is to review the techniques involved in erasing and correcting errors in typed work.

TO ERASE ON THE ORIGINAL COPY

Turn the paper so that the point of correction will be on the top of the cylinder; move the carriage to one side, far enough for eraser grit to fall outside the machine.

Press the paper against the roller with the free hand, to prevent slippage; then, blowing lightly to puff away all eraser grit and using a typewriter (ink) eraser with a sharp point or edge, erase each letter that is to be deleted.

TO ERASE ON THE CARBON COPIES

Use a soft (pencil) eraser; erase the carbon copies one at a time, starting at the top and ending at the bottom. To keep the erasing on any page from marking the next, use a stiff card; before erasing on a page, insert the card under the paper at the point of correction, between the paper which is to be erased and the following sheet of carbon paper.

Double space all but the footnote

1. The procedures outlined in this report are explained in great detail by Ruth E. Gavin and William A. Sabin in Reference Manual for Stenographers and Typists, Canadian Edition (McGraw-Hill Ryerson, 1970), pp. 190-2.

UNIT 12   LESSON 74   118

Skill Drive
Metric Tables

LINE: 60
TAB: 5
SPACING: SINGLE
DRILLS: THREE TIMES
GOAL: BOOST SKILL
STRESS: KEEPING HANDS
AND WRISTS QUIET

Unit 25. Skill Development

151-A. Each line three times, or a half-minute timing on each line. Repeat in Lesson 152.

151-A. Tune up on these review lines

1   Henry works with me and pays for the auto with the profits.

2   Mr. Pix was quick to admit frankly he gave Buzz the jewels.

3   Models 1028, 1039, 1047, and 1056 are all new for the year.

   1 | 2 | 3 | 4 | 5 | 6 | 7 | 8 | 9 | 10 | 11 | 12

151-B. If you make more than 2 errors, your goal in Lessons 151-152 is ACCURACY. If you make 2 or fewer errors, your goal should be SPEED.

151-B. Inventory your present skill

Take a 5-minute writing on page 236 (or copy the first two paragraphs; you should be able to complete them both in 4 minutes) to determine your practice goal for Lessons 151-152 and establish your present rate. The paragraphs are loaded with combinations like those drilled below.

Table 45

Ruled
Double space, P4

151-C. Type the following metric table

EVERYDAY METRIC UNITS
Symbol and Value

Quantity	Unit	Symbol	Value
Area	square kilometre	km^2	1 km^2 = 100 ha
	hectare**	ha	1 ha = 10 000 m^2
	square metre	m^2	1 m^2 = 100 dm^2 = 10 000 cm^2
	square decimetre*	dm^2	1 dm^2 = 100 cm^2
	square centimetre	cm^2	
Length	kilometre	km	1 km = 1000 m
	metre	m	1 m = 10 dm = 100 cm
	decimetre*	dm	1 dm = 10 cm
	centimetre	cm	1 cm = 10 mm
	millimetre	mm	
Mass	tonne**	t	1 t = 1000 kg
	kilogram	kg	1 kg = 100 g
	gram	g	1 g = 1000 mg
	milligram*		
Volume	cubic metre	m^3	1 m^3 = 1000 dm^3
	cubic decimetre*	dm^3	1 dm^3 = 1000 cm^3
	cubic centimetre	cm^3	
	kilolitre*	kL	1 kL = 1000 L
	litre**	L	1 L = 1000 ml
	millilitre	mL	
Temperature	degree Celsius**	°C	0°C = water's freezing point
			100°C = water's boiling point

*Less common but useful in illustrating the prefix and its value in relation to the other units in this category.

**Permitted non-SI units

Progress Test on Part Three

Test 3

Test 3-A

5-MINUTE WRITING
ON PARAGRAPHS
Paper: workbook page
125, or plain paper
Line: 60
Tab: paragraph 5
Spacing: double
Start: machine set,
carriage at margin
Grade: box below
SI: 1.39—normal

5-MINUTE SPEED
WITHIN 4 ERRORS*
45-up wam . . . . . . A
40-44 wam . . . . . . B
30-39 wam C
25-29 wam . . . . . . D
* If more than 4 errors
are made, compute the
speed on what is typed
before the fifth error.

Test 3-B

Letter 27

5-MINUTE WRITING
ON BLOCKED LETTER
Paper: workbook page
126 or plain paper
Tab: center only
Start: carriage set
at center tab
Body: 148 words
Grading: box above
SI: 1.39—normal

If preferred, Tests 3-B,
3-C, and 3-D may each be
typed on plain paper
(time: 15 minutes each,
maximum). Test 3-C
should then be arranged
in memo form (see
page 108), on a 70-space
line, with tabs in 9, 20,
54, and 64. Omit the
column headings. Check
each paper for penalties
and grade it on the
adjacent grading scale.

	A	B
Please send the following letter to Mr. Gerald Jordan,	12	12
Acme Drill Company, 38 Weston Street, Sault Ste. Marie, On-	24	21
tario P6C 5W9. At the appropriate point, center and type	36	23
in all capitals the subject line: Please Settle Your Bill.	48	41
Dear Mr. Jordan: We were pleased to extend to you the	60	53
rare privilege of buying from us on credit, although it has	72	65
long been our policy to require the payment of all invoices	84	77
in ten days. As you can see from the date on the duplicate	96	89
bill that I have enclosed, more than nine weeks have passed	108	101
since we delivered to you the merchandise that you ordered.	120	113
In all those many weeks, you have made no payment. We	132	126
do not like to press the matter, Mr. Jordan, but we feel it	144	138
is only fair for us to ask you to settle this bill at once.	156	150
The only way by which we can continue to offer the low	168	163
prices for which we are well known is to avoid the expenses	180	175
of a credit department. Mr. Jordan, we trust that you will	192	187
repay our courtesy by sending us your cheque very promptly.	204	199
Now, assure Mr. Jordan that we are sincerely his. Put	216	204
in our company name, Nelson Hardware Company, above my name	228	214
and title, Carlton Zoerner, general sales manager, plus the	240	224
usual initials and anything else that may need to be added.	252	227

1 | 2 | 3 | 4 | 5 | 6 | 7 | 8 | 9 | 10 | 11 | 12

PENALTY SCALE

—3 for each major error (top margin, line length, line-spacing,
general correctness of form, etc.)
—2 for each minor error (blocking, aligning, centering, indenting, etc., of individual parts of the job)
—1 for each typographical error

GRADING SCALE

0-1 PENALTY	. . . .	A
2-3 PENALTY	. . . .	B
4-6 PENALTY	. . . .	C
7-8 PENALTY	. . . .	D

7 METRIC UNITS TABLES • LETTER COPIES
RECORDS FORMS • 10-PAGE MANUAL

Test 3-C

Form 19

**5-MINUTE WRITING
ON AN INVOICE**
Form: workbook page 127
Spacing: single, with
  groupings as shown
Start: machine set;
  carriage positioned
  to type the address
Grade: box below

Invoice: Acme Drill Company 383 Weston Street Sault-Ste-Marie, Ontario   14
Special: Type DUPLICATE *before* Invoice *and use* October 28, 19-- *date.*   29

QUANTITY	CAT. NO.	DESCRIPTION	UNIT PRICE	AMOUNT	
50	PD14	Electric power drills	4.00	200.00	45
50	PD399	Electric power drills	5.00	250.00	58
50	PD422	Electric power drills	6.00	300.00	71
100	WHO12	Hoses, 8 000 x 25 mm, plastic	2.00	200.00	85
50	WHO38	Hoses, 12 000 x 19 mm, plastic	3.00	150.00	99
25	WHO50	Hoses, 15 000 x 16 mm, plastic	3.00	75.00	113
50	PDB11	Drill bits, kit sizes	.80	40.00	127
50	PDB32	Drill bits, kit sizes	1.00	50.00	140
100	PDB66	Drill bits, kit sizes	1.25	125.00	152
200	EX125	Electric cords, 1.5 m	.10	20.00	166
150	EX135	Electric cords, 2 m	.12	18.00	178
100	EX160	Electric cords, 2.5 m	.20	20.00	190
		AMOUNT DUE		1,448.00	200
		DELIVERY		47.00	208
		TOTAL AMOUNT DUE		1,495.00	219

**5-MINUTE SPEED
WITHIN 4 ERRORS***
  45-up wam . . . . . . A
  40-44 wam . . . . . . B
  30-39 wam C
  25-29 wam . . . . . . D
* If more than 4 errors
are made, compute the
speed on what is typed
before the fifth error.

SHORT CUTS FOR USE IN FOOTNOTES   *double space
all body but
not footnotes*   18

center → A Report for Typing I   34

center → By J. N. Strong   45

When a full *complete* book reference is cited *given* in a footnote, much   61
data must be given *cited*: the author or authors; the title of the   73
book, under scored or in capitals; the city, publishers, and   85
data of publication, typed in parentheses; and the page.[1]   98
ENTER THE SHORTCUTS   103

But footnotes may be shortened, when especially the very same   115
data are repeated, by using these 4 abbreviations:[2]   128

Loc. cit. means "Exactly as in the preceding footnote."   143

Ibid. means "same as the preceding footnote, but on a   157
different page, which is—." It is followed by a number.   168

Op. Cit. means "as in the previous footnote relating to   183
—the same authorship." It is preceded by the last name   194
of the author or authors and is followed by a page number.   206

Et al. means "and others" and is used only *when* if there are   220
three or more authors. Note that it is typed after the name   232
of the first author in place of the other authors names.[3]   245

        250
    1. John L. Rowe, et al., Gregg Typing, 191 Series Book 2   278
Canadian edn. (McGraw-Hill Ryerson, 1966), Page 246.   287

    2. Ibid., page 247.   295

    3. Loc. cit.   302

Test 3-D

Manuscript 17

**5-MINUTE WRITING ON
UNBOUND MANUSCRIPT**
Form: workbook page 128
Style: arrange as the
  first page of a long
  UNBOUND manuscript
Start: carriage set
  at center tab
Grade: box above
SI: 1.42—normal

Test 6-D

Manuscript 50

5-MINUTE WRITING
ON AN AGREEMENT
Paper: workbook 288
or plain, ruled
Spacing: double
Start: machine set,
carriage centered
Grade: box, page 231

If preferred, Tests 6-B, 6-C, and 6-D may be typed completely (maximum time for each: 15 minutes) and then be graded on this penalty basis:

PENALTY SCALE

—3 for each major error (top margin, line length, line-spacing, general correctness of form, etc.)
—2 for each minor error (blocking, aligning, centering, indenting, etc., of individual parts of the job)
—1 for each typographical error

GRADING SCALE

0-1 PENALTY . . . . A
2-3 PENALTY . . . . B
4-6 PENALTY C
7-8 PENALTY . . . . D

top margin: 6 line spaces

A G R E E M E N T

THIS CONTRACT made and concluded this *use next Monday* eleventh day of June, 1977, by and between the Charinge Precision Corporation, of 315 Fourth Street, Bowmanville, Ontario, party of the first part, and Charles L. Ferguson, *P. Clark* *402 Cochran Road* *Port Coquitlam, British Columbia* 2828 Ruskin Street, Fort Garry, Manitoba, party of the second part.

Article 1. Services. The said party of the second part covenants and agrees to and with the party of the first part, to furnish his services *exclusively* to the said party of the first part as *advertising manager* special demonstrator and representative for the period of one year, or twelve (12) calendar months, beginning *(start this beginning next month)* July 1, 1969, and expiring *(date this a year later)* June 30, 1970; and the said party of the second part covenants and agrees to perform faithfully all duties incident to such employment.

Article 2. Wages. And the said party of the first part covenants and agrees to pay the said party of the second part, for the same, the sum of *twelve* seven thousand two hundred dollars ($7 200.00), *$12 000.00* as follows: The sum of *one thousand* eight hundred dollars ($800.00) *$1 000.00* on July 31, 1977, *(use end of next month)* and an equal sum on the last day of each succeeding calendar month until the period of one year shall have expired. *2# here*

IN WITNESS WHEREOF, the parties to this Contract have hereunto set their hands the day and year first above written.

_____ *center*

Charles L. Ferguson
P. Clark

_____

Witness to Signature *center*

Bryant Gaynor, Vice-President

_____

Witness to Signature

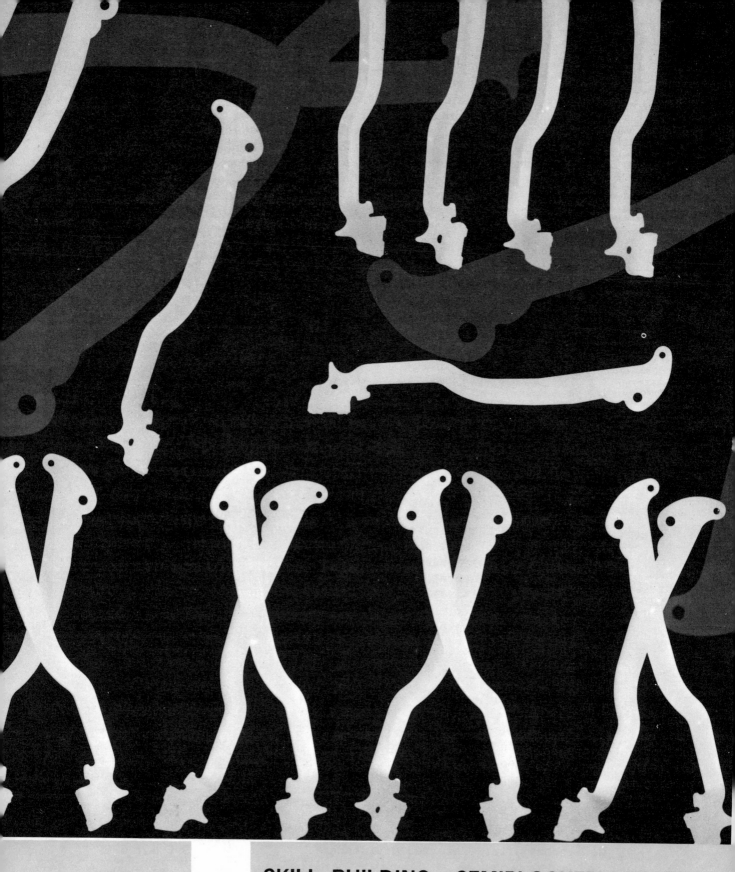

4 SKILL BUILDING • SEMIBLOCKED LETTERS
DISPLAY TABLES AND MANUSCRIPTS

Test 6-B

Letter 71

10-MINUTE WRITING
ON 2-PAGE LETTER
Paper: workbook 285
Style: blocked
Body: 400 words
Start: machine set,
  carriage at date
Grade: box, page 231
SI: 1.38—normal

SPECIAL DIRECTIONS: Type a copy of the "Mr. Wilson" letter, page 231, altering the salutation, wording, and closing as may be necessary, so that it is from Bryant L. Gaynor, Advertising Director, to Charles P. Clarke, 402 Cochran Road, Port Coquitlam, British Columbia. Insert a subject line, centered in all capitals: *Welcome to the Family!* If you use plain paper, type a line 15 lines from the top, clear across the page, to represent the depth of a first-page letterhead. The 6-B word count includes appropriate allowances for the inside address and other opening lines (40), second-page heading (26), and letter closing (22).

Test 6-C

Table 44

5-MINUTE WRITING ON
A FINANCIAL REPORT
Paper: workbook 287
Line: 70 spaces (not
  65, as shown below)
Start: machine set,
  carriage at center
Grade: box, page 231

STATEMENT OF OPERATIONS			14
For Nine Months Ended September 30, 19—			41
			43
Operating revenues		$77 763 296	63
Operating expenses:			68
Cost of materials	$25 135 401		80
Cost of services purchased	20 434 964		92
Maintenance of services	5 229 245		104
Amortization of conversion costs	199 697		116
Provision for depreciation	3 576 652		128
Federal income taxes	3 563 300		140
Other taxes	9 222 607		152
Total operating expenses		67 361 866	169
Operating income		$10 401 430	183
Other income		305 112	201
Gross income		$10 706 542	214
Nonoperational deductions:			221
Interest on long-term debt	$ 2 943 225		233
Miscellaneous other deductions	306 990		250
Total nonoperational deductions		3 250 215	267
Net income		$ 7 456 327	281
Dividends on preferred stock		618 751	299
Net income after preferred dividends ...		$ 6 837 576	312
Earnings per share of common stock		$1.34	335

Unit 13. Skill Development

LINE: 60
TAB: 5
SPACING: SINGLE
DRILLS: THREE TIMES
GOAL: BOOST SKILL
STRESS: LOW WRISTS

76-A. Each line three times very evenly (or a 1-minute timing on each). Repeat in Lesson 77. Keep the wrists low.

76-A. Tune up on these reach-review lines

1 late dusk into dark long file jets came call eyes full size
2 Gary won five more prizes but quietly junked the xylophone.
3 Alll J777 S222 K888 D333 L999 F444 J666 F555 K800 S200 L900
   1 | 2 | 3 | 4 | 5 | 6 | 7 | 8 | 9 | 10 | 11 | 12

76-B. To define practice goals, type a double-spaced copy (GOAL: To type it in 3 minutes). Proofread carefully.

If you make 4 or more errors, your Lesson 76 goal is ACCURACY. If you make 3 or fewer errors, it is SPEED.

SI 1.24—easy

76-B. Measure and improve your skill

4 As the late dusk slowly faded into dark, Squadron Five   12
steamed on and on, a long file of shapes along the horizon.   24
Somewhere above us was the air escort; we heard the distant   36
whine of the jets above the throb of our own engines. From   48
the ship ahead came a gleam, a flicker, a signal to call up   60
extra hands and eyes for the night watch. The darkness was   72
tense, for it was a full job just to keep in station within   84
a squadron of such size. The con officer studied the radar   96
box on the bridge, waiting for the exact second of the next   108
quarter hour, when he must change course so as to zig or to   120
zag in cadence with the other blobs of light on the screen.   132
   1 | 2 | 3 | 4 | 5 | 6 | 7 | 8 | 9 | 10 | 11 | 12

76-C. Type to your goal.

ACCURACY: The whole group of drills three times.

SPEED: Each drill, individually, three times.

SI 1.05—very easy

76-C. Improve control of A, B, C, D

5 A Alma Alan Alamo aAa gala papa salad aAa alas aria canal A
6 B Bobo Baby Bobby fBf bomb blob blurb fBf bleb blab abbot B
7 C Coca Cola Chuck dCd crow cork clock dCd tick city check C
8 D Dude Dody Daddy dDd dyed odds dried dDd duds died dandy D
9 Dude hailed a cab and dashed back to the dark cabin on   12
the back beach. The dry sand squeaked as he raced from the   24
cab to the back door of the cabin. He called out to Chuck.   36
   1 | 2 | 3 | 4 | 5 | 6 | 7 | 8 | 9 | 10 | 11 | 12

76-D. Type to your goal.

ACCURACY: The whole group three times.

SPEED: Each drill three times.

SI 1.21—easy

76-D. Improve control of E, F, G, H, I

10 E Erne Edie Ethel dEd else jeep eerie dEd even meet level E
11 F Fifi Effy Guffy fFf buff doff fluff fFf tiff muff offer F
12 G Gene Gigi Gregg fGf gang gong going fGf glug grog aging G
13 H Hale Hope Heath jHj hash hath shush jHj hush hand hunch H
14 I Inez Ibis India kIk kiwi into livid kIk irks tips limit I
15 The eighteen fire rangers came by a night flight to be   12
with us by eight in the morning, to help fight the nine big   24
fires in the heights. They were mighty efficient fighters.   36
   1 | 2 | 3 | 4 | 5 | 6 | 7 | 8 | 9 | 10 | 11 | 12

Progress Test on Part Six

1 | 2 | 3 | 4 | 5 | 6 | 7 | 8 | 9 | 10 | 11 | 12 | 13

	6-A	6-B

Dear Mr. Wilson: We are pleased to learn that you have accepted our offer and that you will be joining our staff on the first of next month. We know that you have a big contribution to make to our sales effort, and all of us here in the home office will be pleased to meet you again and to welcome you to a desk in our Advertising Department.

We have made a few plans for your first weeks with us. You will start, of course, by becoming familiar with the company organization, getting to know the persons with whom you will work, and learning all you can about our products and our services. The first two days, you will report to Personnel for the regular orientation program in which you will learn a great deal not only about the company but also about all our employee policies—vacations, paydays, insurances, and so on.

Then, after you have been at your own desk long enough to become familiar with the duties that will be yours, you will spend two weeks making calls with one of our local salesmen. You will meet customers and hear the questions they raise. You will see what features of our products interest them and why. You will have a chance to visit some workrooms of our present customers and to see how these customers use our products; you will see what our merchandising problems are. And, you will learn much about the kinds of service we give our customers.

Our plans indicate that you will be busy with training for quite some time before you come to grips with your main duties. We believe that the training can be completed, however, several weeks before the time when our next promotion campaign, which will be your first major assignment, must get rolling. Thus, you will have opportunity to get acquainted with all aspects of the job before you start the campaign.

I am enclosing a contract for your position, Mr. Wilson. Please note that it covers all the elements that we talked about. We should like to have it back soon. If you would like help in your search for your new home, all of us here would be pleased to help. Let me state once again, Mr. Wilson, that we are pleased to have you join us. All of us are looking forward to your working with us. Yours very truly,   [START OVER]

6-A	6-B
13	49
25	61
38	74
51	87
64	100
70	106
83	120
96	133
109	146
122	159
134	171
148	185
160	197
169	206
181	219
195	233
208	246
220	258
233	271
246	284
258	296
270	308
280	318
293	332
306	345
319	358
331	370
344	383
357	396
364	403
377	442
390	455
403	468
416	481
429	494
442	507
448	531

1 | 2 | 3 | 4 | 5 | 6 | 7 | 8 | 9 | 10 | 11 | 12 | 13

76-E. Improve control of J, K, L, M

76-E. Type to your goal.

ACCURACY: The whole group of lines three times.

SPEED: Each drill, individually, three times.

SI 1.28—fairly easy

16 J John Jojo Jerry jJj jury joys judge jJj jade just rajah J
17 K Kirk Kate Kenny kKk kink kick knock kKk kind bake knack K
18 L Lola Lois Lloyd lLl tall bill shall lLl dull toll allow L
19 M Mimi Emma Mammy jMj maim mums mimic jMj mama mums mamma M

20 Judge Kellock sent Jake Lamont to jail for a month for   12
taking money from the Lake James Motel last July. Old Jake   24
claimed Judge Kellock and the jurors had made unjust jokes.   36

　　1 | 2 | 3 | 4 | 5 | 6 | 7 | 8 | 9 | 10 | 11 | 12

76-F. Make an interim progress check

76-F. To confirm your progress in Lesson 76, type a double-spaced copy of paragraphs 21 and 22 (GOAL: Within 3 minutes, 3 errors) OR take one 3-minute writing (GOAL: 40 or more words a minute within 3 errors).

If you make 4 or more errors, your goal for Lesson 77 must be for ACCURACY. Otherwise, your goal is SPEED.

SI 1.32—fairly easy

SI Metric
See p. 117 for Metric Typing Style Guide

21 When we see in a newspaper a picture that, the caption   12
says, was taken by a camera from a jet flying a dozen or so   24
miles above the earth, most of us gape and marvel. For one   36
quick moment we think of one of the sad shots we have taken   48
with a box Brownie at only 3 m, then we wonder what kind of   60
mystic camera can photo an area of 260 km² in only one shot.   72

22 Compared to what the shutterbug has, the aerial camera   84
seems to be a mystic tool, indeed. Its lens is so powerful   96
that even tiny details can be registered from kilometres up.   108
In a test, an airplane took photos of a city from 12 km up;   120
one photo was so remarkably clear that it showed a man in a   132
backyard, rocking in a rocking chair as he read his papers.   144

　　1 | 2 | 3 | 4 | 5 | 6 | 7 | 8 | 9 | 10 | 11 | 12

77-A. Improve control of N, O, P, Q

77-A. Type to your goal.

ACCURACY: The whole group of lines three times.

SPEED: Each drill, individually, three times.

SI 1.27—fairly easy

23 N Mann Anne Ronny jNj none inns sunny jNj nine nuns inner N
24 O Oreo Olaf Orono lOl oboe cool solos lOl took foot odors O
25 P Paul Pepe Peppy ;P; prop pups happy ;P; plop pipe paper P
26 Q Quen Quad Queen aQa quit quid pique aQa quip quay quilt Q

27 On our Quebec trip we popped aboard a quaint old ship,   12
the Norse Queen, anchored on the quay. We poked around it,   24
quite happy, for a quiet noon hour and departed for Quebec.   36

　　1 | 2 | 3 | 4 | 5 | 6 | 7 | 8 | 9 | 10 | 11 | 12

77-B. Improve control of R, S, T, U, V

77-B. Type to your goal.

ACCURACY: The whole group of lines three times.

SPEED: Each drill, individually, three times.

SI 1.18—easy

28 R Ruth Raul Kerry fRf roar errs marry fRf purr burr error R
29 S Sirs Tess Susan sSs less sues socks sSs uses sits loses S
30 T Tora Etta Dotty fTf that trot truth fTf toot tote trout T
31 U Ulla Judy Trudy jUj used rule usual jUj tour true usury U
32 V Vera Vick David fVf very veil vivid fVf view even never V

33 Rusty never did trust Vic to touch our TV set while he   12
was a star student in his TV course; but after Vic wound up   24
his study, Rusty loved to have him visit us and our TV set.   36

　　1 | 2 | 3 | 4 | 5 | 6 | 7 | 8 | 9 | 10 | 11 | 12

Please double space

top margin 12 line-spaces

A G R E E M E N T — *Center between rules*

THIS AGREEMENT, made the fifth day of June, 19--, by and between The Dwyer Construction Company, a corporation under the laws of the province of Ontario, located at 1938 Mills Road, Port Perry, Ontario, hereinafter called The Contractor, and The Black-Gray Company, 139 Commissioners Street, Peterborough, Ontario, hereinafter called The Owner.

WITNESSETH that the contractor and Owner, in consideration of the stipulations hereinafter named and made a part hereof, agree as follows:

Article 1. Scope of Work. The Contractor agrees to furnish all the materials and to perform all the works indicated on the drawings and described in the Specifications, entitled "Specifications, with Accompanying Drawings, Describing Materials to be Used and Labors to Be Performed in Constructing an Extension to the GARAGE of the Black-Gray Company at 135-137 Commissioners Street, Peterborough, Ontario", prepared by Mortimer L. Bell, 20 Sloane St., Fenelon Falls, Ontario, and referred to and acting as Architect in this Agreement, the General Conditions of the Contract, the Specifications, and the Drawings. *and referred to as such*

Article 2. Time for Completion. Work which is to be performed under this contract shall be commenced as soon as is possible after the signing of this agreement.

2# →

Page 1 of 8

Top margin 9 line-spaces

10 Article 8. The Contract Documents. The General Conditions of the Contract, the Specifications and Drawings, together with this Agreement, constitute the Contract, and are considered as much a part of the contract as if herein given.

2#

IN WITNESS WHEREOF, the parties hereto have executed this Agreement, the day and year first above written.

2#

FOR THE BLACK-GRAY COMPANY   FOR DWYER CONSTRUCTION COMPANY

3#

_____   _____
Executive Vice-President   President

3#

_____   _____
Witness for the Owner   Witness for the Contractor

2#

Page 8 of 8

77-C. Type to your goal.

ACCURACY: The group of lines three times.

SPEED: Each drill, individually, three times.

SI 1.44—normal

77-C. Improve control of W, X, Y, Z

34 W Will Owen Twila sWs wows whew which sWs away when where W
35 X Next Taxi X—ray sXs axis foxy sixes sXs axle oxen taxes X
36 Y Your Yule Daily jYj days many shyly jYj year duly slyly Y
37 Z Zola Zero Dizzy aZa hazy doze fizzy aZa zone zoom dozen Z

38   Citizens are always unhappy to pay taxes; yet you must   12
realize that a city the size of Wentz has extra expenses to   24
meet, which you pay by taxes and not by quizzing the mayor.   36
  1 | 2 | 3 | 4 | 5 | 6 | 7 | 8 | 9 | 10 | 11 | 12

77-D. By reviewing the paragraphs typed in Lessons 76-77, select the five keys causing you the most trouble. Repeat, twice each, the drills for those keys.

77-D. Spot-check your weakest controls

77-E. Type to your goal.

ACCURACY: The group of lines three times.

SPEED: Each drill, individually, three times.

77-E. Confirm control on preview words

39 AA faces BB budgets CC chief DD desks EE executive FF false
40 GG agree HH high II item JJ junior KK desk LL tell MM small
41 NN only OO one's PP group QQ squirm RR trim SS such TT trim
42 UU bureau VV every WW wreathes XX except YY young ZZ sizzle

77-F. To measure your progress, follow either of these two schedules:

1. Type a complete copy of these paragraphs. GOAL: To do so within 6 minutes and 4 errors.

2. Take two 5-minute timings on the article (GOAL: 35 or more wam within 3 errors). Then, record the better score of the two on the chart on workbook page 131.

SI 1.32—fairly easy

77-F. Measure your skill in sustained writing

43   The bigger any organization is, the more meetings that   12
the men and women in the executive group must attend. This   24
is uniquely true in the business world. If you run a small   36
firm and are the one and only executive, you do not have to   48
go to any meetings at all; but if you are head of a depart—   60
ment or chief of a bureau, you must attend a dozen meetings   72
a month. At such meetings, all will agree that budgets and   84
salaries and sales are not high enough and that the expense   96
items of personnel and service costs must be trimmed in all   108
the major departments, except one's own, in the whole firm.   120

44   Once in a long, long while, a scheduled meeting has to   132
be postponed; this is the moment when you learn whether you   144
are a junior or a senior executive: No one tells the young   156
juniors that the meeting is called off, and so they show up   168
after all; they sizzle in their chairs for a while and then   180
squirm all the way back to their own desks, furious despite   192
a false smile that wreathes their faces. Once this happens   204
to you, and it will, you will make it a firm rule that your   216
secretary must confirm every meeting before you hike to it.   228
  1 | 2 | 3 | 4 | 5 | 6 | 7 | 8 | 9 | 10 | 11 | 12

SPECIAL REMINDER: If you make more errors in any timed writing than are cited as a goal, compute the speed on the basis of what you type before exceeding the error limit. For example, if the goal is "within 3 errors" and you make 4 or more, compute the speed on what you finished before making the fourth mistake.

Tables 41-43

FINANCIAL REPORTS
Paper: full, plain
Spacing: as shown
Position: center

From the letter below, lift the *Comparative Financial Results, January Through May* (modify the column headings) and type it in three styles:
TABLE 40. With *no* leaders after column 1. Review page 211.
TABLE 41. With *close* leaders, on a 50-space line. Review page 212.
TABLE 42. With *open* leaders, on a 60-space line. Review page 215.

Letter 70

BLOCKED LETTER WITH
FINANCIAL STATEMENT
Shown: in elite
Paper: workbook 279
Line: 60

June 5, 19—   3

7

TO OUR SHAREHOLDERS: 11

12

There are shown below the financial results of our operation for the   26
five months ended May 31, with the corresponding figures for the same   40
five months of last year: 45

	This Year	Last Year
Gross Revenue	$34 559 388	$32 984 787
Operating Expenses	29 653 710	27 402 135
Net Income before Federal Income Taxes	$ 4 905 678	$ 5 582 652
Estimated Federal Income Taxes	2 616 667	3 005 247
Net Income	$ 2 289 011	$ 2 577 405
Earnings per Share (880,000 Shares)	2.60	2.93

In first column, note irregular linespacing, to keep the spacing consistent in the money columns.

Although the earnings figure is lower for the first five months than it   188
was last year, the operating expenses include several appropriations for   202
activities that will continue throughout the year. Accordingly, there   217
is reason to expect that earnings for the year will be equal, or nearly   231
equal, to the record earnings that we enjoyed last year.   243

244

Very truly yours,   251

255

Chairman of the Board   262

267

Some executives wish their names to be typed in the reference position:

Vincent Young/URS

LINE: 60
TAB: 5
SPACING: SINGLE
DRILLS: AS DIRECTED
GOAL: RAISE SPEED,
  IMPROVE TECHNIQUE
STRESS: PURPOSE

78-A. Tune up on these reach-review lines

78-A. Lines three times or ask someone to pace you by typing line 1 while you type 2 and 3 in even cadence. Do again in Lesson 79.

1 that just like this line when goal type make hazy rate grow
2 He quickly trained a dozen brown foxes to jump over a gate.
3 Al Al J7 J7 S2 S2 K8 K8 D3 D3 L9 L9 F4 F4 :0 :0 F5 F5 J6 J6
   1 | 2 | 3 | 4 | 5 | 6 | 7 | 8 | 9 | 10 | 11 | 12

78-B. Measure and improve your skill

78-B. To define practice goals, type a double-spaced copy (GOAL: To finish within 3 errors and 3 minutes). Check your work carefully.

If you make 4 or more errors, your Lesson 78 goal is ACCURACY.

If you make 3 or fewer errors, goal is SPEED.

SI 1.36—normal

4 How quickly should the typist improve skill in typing?   12
It depends on the typist. Oh, the machine matters; and the   24
numbers of hours of practice matters; and the material that   36
is used matters; but how much these things matter is rather   48
hazy. The major thing that marks the rate of growth of the   60
expert typist is what brainpower is invested in the effort.   72

5 For example, just copying a line of drill, even a half   84
dozen copies, will not benefit your typing. It is when you   96
study a drill to see what it is for, when you set your goal   108
for squeezing out the practice juice, and when you type the   120
drill over and over until you make your goal that you grow.   132
   1 | 2 | 3 | 4 | 5 | 6 | 7 | 8 | 9 | 10 | 11 | 12

78-C. Eliminate all hesitation on the space bar

78-C-D-E. In each set, type toward your goal.

ACCURACY: Each group, like a paragraph, once for each error in 78-B (but at least three times).

SPEED: Each line once for each error in 78-B (but at least three times).

6 and dog gun not the elm may yes sow who our run nip pen nor
7 rue end dot two old due elf fly yen new way yet tub bar row
8 The U. S. A. has the U. S. N. and the U. S. M. C. together.

78-D. Eliminate all hesitation on one-hand words

9   hilly free join seat mill get oil saw pun car hum far my at
10 waste noon dear upon rate my; wax hip act mop bad pin as on
11 pylon fast only race hill was you far him see up; set in be

78-E. Eliminate all hesitation on double-letter words

POINT TO CONFIRM: Between your body and the machine there is a handspan of space.

12 wall less seem mass seek keep puff fill loss soon need dill
13 still loose error rooms sleet toddy yells snoop polls sassy
14 sizzle essays summer rubbed dinner really yellow wheel loop

78-F. Now speed up, on very easy copy, for a minute

78-F. Type paragraph 15 three times (GOAL: A perfect copy within 1 minute) or take three 1-minute timings to see how rapidly you can type without an error.

SI 1.00—very easy

15 If you wish to see your speed rate go up and up, first   12
you must give the speed a big push through the use of lines   24
like these, so full of short words that you will be sure to   36
type them at a high speed, like a race you run down a hill.   48
   1 | 2 | 3 | 4 | 5 | 6 | 7 | 8 | 9 | 10 | 11 | 12

To end lines evenly:
LINE: 70   TAB: 5
SI: 1.33—fairly easy

148-C. Sustain skill on easy, fluent paragraphs

| 1 | 2 | 3 | 4 | 5 | 6 | 7 | 8 |

In a day and age when most of our men 9
of science are looking far beyond the skies 17
into the heavens of space, it is interesting 26
to know that other men of science are 34
looking in the opposite direction, down 42
into the earth itself, to see what our world 51
is made of. Men already know more about 59
the space that surrounds our globe than 67
they do about what is in it. We know how 76
to hurtle a mortal hundreds of kilo- 84
metres into space; but the deepest hole 92
we have made in the earth is one oil well 101
only 8 km deep, and the deepest mining 110
shaft is but 3.2 km deep. 112

There is much speculation about the 121
nature of the globe on which we live, most 130
of it based on where the echoes of earth- 138
quakes show up, plus what has been learned 147
from the study of volcanoes, all of which, 155
taken together, is something less than what 164
you could learn about the elephant by 172
studying a flea bite on the tip of its tail. 181
We know the earth is not a solid chunk of 189
rock, for example, because quake echoes 197
do not run through the globe the way they 206
would through a solid rock. We know, 213
similarly, that there must be liquid and 221
heat and tremendous pressure under our 229
shoes, for volcanic action and lava require 238
these. Putting such scant evidences to- 246
gether, the scientists built a theory. 254

The current thought is that the earth 263
is an iron ball surrounded by three lay- 272
ers or shells, each made up of a different 280
material. The iron ball, known as the in- 288
ner core, has a thickness of about 2400 296
km. Around this ball lies the outer core, 305

| 1 | 2 | 3 | 4 | 5 | 6 | 7 | 8 |

a mixture of nickel and iron so hot and 313
under such pressure that it is liquid. Ac- 321
cording to the geologists, the thickness 329
of this layer is about 2200 km. 337

The next layer is the big one, called the 345
mantle, which is about 2800 km thick. 353
The mantel is made of basalt, the lava 362
rock. Judging from the heat of running 370
lava, the mantle must have a minimum 378
temperature of 2700°C. Basalt is so heavy, 386
while in the oozing stage, that mere gra- 394
nite practically sails on its surface. 404

The final layer of the earth is the out- 414
side, known as the crust, made up of a 422
thin skin of light rocks, if you do not 430
mind thinking of the Rockies and Alps 438
and other granite mountains as being 445
light. The depth of this skin ranges from 454
4.8 km, under some parts of oceans, to as 462
much as 64 km in the highest and deepest 470
parts of many continents. 472

Now, to get to the point of the matter, 480
what the scientists hope to do is learn 488
whether their speculation is right. To 496
this end, a project has been started by 504
the National Science Foundation to lo- 512
cate one of those thin places where it may 520
occur within 3 to 5 km from the surface 528
of the sea; and having located it, to drill 536
through this crust at sea bottom into the 544
mantle with a pipe drill that is 5 cm or 7.6 552
cm across and 11 km long, or more! There 559
will be a dazzling triumph when the first 567
mantle rock comes within the reach of the 575
hand of Science. To think of it puts per- 583
spective on our own efforts, does it not? 591

[START OVER]

| 1 | 2 | 3 | 4 | 5 | 6 | 7 | 8 |

148/149-D. Review the production problems of this part

78-G. Each sentence two times; then a complete copy (GOAL: Within 2 minutes and 2 errors) or a 2-minute timing. (GOAL: Highest speed within 2 mistakes). SI 1.00—very easy

78-H. Repeat 78-B to confirm your progress in Lesson 78 and set goals for Lesson 79.

If you make 4 or more errors, your goal for Lesson 79 must be ACCURACY. Otherwise your goal is SPEED.

16 Both men said they would like to make the trip for us.   12
She lost those keys and found them when she looked in here.   24
You will hear from him when he gets down to the lake shore.   36
She said that she did not wish to work with them this year.   48

17 If he wants to see us, please tell him to let us know.   60
I said that we might hear from them by the end of the week.   72
The men do as well as they can with the time they have off.   84
The six men took the old boat down to the side of the lake.   96

1 | 2 | 3 | 4 | 5 | 6 | 7 | 8 | 9 | 10 | 11 | 12

78-H. Make an interim progress check

79-A. Renew your new speed on common words

79-A. Type to your goal.

ACCURACY: The group of lines three times.

SPEED: Each drill, individually, three times.

18 days feel just call here deal came file help keep came fill
19 give knew hear high back does find glad know bank done pace
20 hold last gone been five good home come each hope left bill
21 coal girl lent half goal land paid down form both keys hand

1 | 2 | 3 | 4 | 5 | 6 | 7 | 8 | 9 | 10 | 11 | 12

79-B. Hold your new speed on easy copy for 5 minutes

79-B. Type two copies (GOAL: A copy within 5 minutes, 3 errors).

Or, a 1-minute timing on each paragraph and a 5-minute writing on the whole selection (GOAL: Highest speed within three errors).

SI 1.00—very easy

22 If you wish to see your speed rate go up and up, first   12
you must give the speed a big push through the use of lines   24
like these, so full of short words that you will be sure to   36
type them at a high speed, like a race you run down a hill.   48

23 Once you get the feel of the new rate for a short time   60
on a few smooth drill lines of short words, you should then   72
move on to what you know the next step must be: to keep up   84
the new speed for more time and on more lines of new words.   96

24 When you first start to type at a new speed, you sense   108
that you are not sure of some of the keys you hit; but when   120
you have typed a lot of lines of speed words, you feel much   132
less ill at ease with the new pace; you get the feel of it.   144

25 Now you know, of course, that the speed you have built   156
is one that you can hold just on lines that are full of the   168
kind of words you have found in the smooth drills; what you   180
do next is to shift to drills with more long or hard words.   192

26 This does not mean that you should turn to drills that   204
are full of long and hard words; it means that you now must   216
turn to drills with a few of them, then to drills with more   228
of them, and then to lines with a fair share of such words.   240

1 | 2 | 3 | 4 | 5 | 6 | 7 | 8 | 9 | 10 | 11 | 12

PROFESSIONAL HINT:

When typing very easy copy like this, don't press for speed (let the ease of the copy bring the speed) but rather press for a steady, unabating pace that is as even as you can hold on the copy.

Top margin 6 line-spaces

2 # here

Mrs. Pavlue reported that the material for the mailing to *Wallace* delaers was now on press and than an investment of $970 would be lost if the mailing were not made. Mr. Perkins pointed out that calcenning space in <u>Premium</u> would bring our year's space in that magazine under the minimum for the special reates that we have been enjoying. Miss Clarke reported that nearly all mechanicals, art work, and engravings have already been made for our present advertising schedule and would have to be done over, at an estimated cost of $1500, if the space dimensions were reduced in our advertisements in other magazines. The committee decided to eliminate spcae in the next *three* issues of <u>Premium</u>, with Mr. Perkins demurring, *Wallace*

Respectfully submitted,

3-5 spaces

Marguerite Powell, Secretary

Distribution:
    Vice-Presidents
    Committee Members
    Permanent File

LINE: 60
SPACING: SINGLE
DRILLS: THREE EACH
GOAL: APPLY SKILL
  IN REVIEW
STRESS: ACCURACY

148-A. Each line three times or two ½-minute timings on each line. Repeat in Lesson 149.

148-A. Tune up on these review lines

1   Those girls think their dress sales might bring extra cash.
2   Jacqueline was glad her family took five or six big prizes.
3   we 23 **22 23 24** it 85 **84 85 86** to 59 **58 59 60** ur 74 **73 74 75**
     1 | 2 | 3 | 4 | 5 | 6 | 7 | 8 | 9 | 10 | 11 | 12

148-B. Type to goal. ACCURACY: Each set three times, as a paragraph. SPEED: Each line three times, successively.

148-B. Increase skill on selective preview drills

4   AA age BB bit CC core DD down EE earth FF far GG get HH hot
5   II oil JJ just KK rock LL lava MM may NN one OO most PP pit
6   QQ quake RR our SS is TT two UU run VV five WW we ZZ dazzle

7   earthquake tremendous direction volcanoes opposite surround
8   science require deepest mixture mortal hurtle theory liquid
9   shaft chunk globe layer crust flea bite big one of it do so

148-C. Same routine as in 144-C, page 219.

79-C. Type paragraph 27 three times (GOAL: To finish it within 1 minute and 1 error) or take two 2-minute races on it (GOAL: To equal your best 79-B speed, but within 2 errors).

SI 1.14—easy

79-D. Type to your goal.

ACCURACY: The whole group three times.

SPEED: Each drill, three times.

79-E. Type paragraph 31 three times (GOAL: To finish it within 1 minute and 1 error) or take two 2-minute races on it (GOAL: To equal your best 79-C speed, but within 2 errors).

SI 1.28—fairly easy

79-F. To measure your progress, follow either of these two schedules:

1. Type a complete copy of these paragraphs. (GOAL: To do so within 6 minutes, 4 errors).

2. Take two 5-minute timings on the article (GOAL: 40 or more wam within 3 errors). Then record the better score of the two on the chart on workbook page 131.

SI 1.37—normal

79-C. Hold your new speed on slightly harder copy

27 When you work on lines that are just a bit harder than 12
the copy on which you built your new speed, you have to put 24
pressure on yourself to keep up the pace, even though to do 36
so may mean that you may have to risk a couple more errors. 48

1 | 2 | 3 | 4 | 5 | 6 | 7 | 8 | 9 | 10 | 11 | 12

79-D. Stabilize your rhythm on these quiet-hand drills

28 all led ask tea ill dad ail red if; fed pal lad old lea was
29 desk risk sold tall told tusk will gold held leak mask fold
30 rocks leaks scold sells speak tiles rules males ricks pleas

79-E. Hold your new speed on still harder copy

31 You should not expect to equal the new speed the first 12
time you tackle a harder selection. If you did achieve the 24
proper feel for the new pace, however, you should find that 36
you accomplish it on the second or third time that you try. 48

1 | 2 | 3 | 4 | 5 | 6 | 7 | 8 | 9 | 10 | 11 | 12

79-F. Now measure your skill on normal, sustained typing

32 When speaking of speed building, it would not be right 12
to overlook the matter of accuracy; speed without accuracy, 24
of course, is worth nothing at all. It takes a half minute 36
to erase on an original and about a quarter minute or so to 48
erase on each carbon. If you are typing something with two 60
carbon copies, it takes just a little more than a minute to 72
make a correction; so you can recognize why making an error 84
a minute would give you exactly a zero, or less, in output. 96

33 There are four major elements that solve the questions 108
about accuracy. First of all, you must intend to type with 120
few or no errors; you must make a conscious effort to avoid 132
running down the hill so fast that you trip. Secondly, you 144
must maintain good posture; if you squirm around and change 156
posture, so that you also change the angle at which fingers 168
jump up and down the keyboard steps, then the errors occur. 180
Thirdly, you need exact control of the keys; the importance 192
of this is confirmed by the great number of drills you have 204
noted in this book. Finally, you must be sure that you use 216
easy copy when you drive to increase speed; only when a new 228
rate has been achieved should you then turn to normal copy. 240

1 | 2 | 3 | 4 | 5 | 6 | 7 | 8 | 9 | 10 | 11 | 12

PROFESSIONAL HINT:

Drill lines 28-30 are especially useful. Each line is of same-length words and therefore a fine aid for rhythm. Each word results in your hands' return to the home-key position; so the drills are fine practice for retaining the home-key position, for keeping the wrists low, and for keeping the hands very quiet.

We are to th foundation cannot meet your requirement.

These minutes illustrate the correct arrangement for minutes; they are usually single spaced to save space in the permanent file of minutes. These minutes also show the proper sequence for reporting what transpired, whether or not events took place in the order that is shown.

top margin
12 line-spaces

Of the Advertising Committee

MINUTES OF THE MONTHLY MEETING

May 18, 19--

margin: 9 line spaces

indent

margin: 6 line spaces

ATTENDANCE

The regular monthly meeting of the Advertising Committee was held in the office of Mr. Larimore, Advertising Director, who presided at the meeting. The following were present:

put names in 2 columns

Mr. J. Carty	Mr. Fisher	Miss Powell
Miss Clarke	Mr. Larimore	Mr. Stark
Miss Clooney	Mrs. Pavlu	Mr. Wallace
	Mr. Perkins	

The meeting began at 14:00 and adjourned at 16:00.

OLD BUSINESS

The secretary

Miss Powell read the minutes of the last meeting. They were approved as read.

Mr. Stark reported that the show-case cards which that had been prepared for dealer's use had have proved notable successful. His follow-up survey among 250 dealers indicated:

Dealers wanting additional cards 230 (92%)
Dealers using the cards 180 (72%)
Dealers reporting sales increases 215 (86%)

NEW BUSINESS

Mr. Larimore reported that the Department has been directed to curtail its advertising expenditures by $2,500.00 for the coming quarter. Discussion hinged on these three possibilities:

1. Eliminate ion of the June Mailing to dealers; and/or
2. Elimination of the space in _Premium_ magazine; or
3. Reduction of space in all magazine ads.

9 to 12 line spaces bottom margin

(CONTINUED ON NEXT PAGE.)

Skill Drive

80-A. Tune up on these reach-review lines

80-A. Each line three times or for 1 minute. Stress steady, even stroking. Repeat in Lesson 81.

1   The profit they make by their fight may pay for the chapel.
2   Jasper quietly viewed the fox, zebra, kangaroo, and camels.
3   A161 J767 S262 K868 D363 L969 F464 :060 F464 J666 S234 L987

     1 | 2 | 3 | 4 | 5 | 6 | 7 | 8 | 9 | 10 | 11 | 12

80-B. Measure your skill on these numeric sentences

80-B. Type a complete copy (GOAL: Within 3 minutes and 3 errors) or take a 3-minute timing (GOAL: Highest speed within 3 errors).

If you make 4 or more errors, your Lesson 80 goal is ACCURACY.

If you make 3 or fewer errors, goal is SPEED.

4   I phoned rooms 10, 28, 39, and 47 before he called room 56.
5   Did the Halls move to 1028 39th Street or 3947 56th Street?
6   Read pages 10 and 28, then 39 and 47, and finally page 156.
7   Ask for 10 to 28 men, 39 to 47 women, and 56 boys or girls.
8   We put guests in rooms 10, 28, 39, and 47, then in room 56.
9   The dates on pages 10, 28, and 39 match those on 47 and 56.
10   We emptied boxes 10, 28, and 39; box 47 still has 156 left.
11   Is the room 10 by 28, 10 by 39, 10 by 47, or 10 by 56 feet?

     1 | 2 | 3 | 4 | 5 | 6 | 7 | 8 | 9 | 10 | 11 | 12

80-C. Strengthen your control of number keys

80-C. Preliminary step: Put a light pencil mark before each line in 4-11 in which you made any error in 80-B. For each number incorrectly typed in 80-B, put a mark in front of the matching number drill in 12-21.

ACCURACY: (1) Type three copies of each drill, 4-21, before which you have put a pencil mark. (2) Type a complete copy of drills 4-21.

SPEED: (1) Type a copy of each drill in 4-21 before which you have a mark; then (2) type drills 4-21, each line typed twice as a consecutive pair.

SI (Metric) See p. 117 for spacing with 4-digit or more numbers

12   l a q l a q l a l or l and 11 and 111 and l 111 and 11 111.
       l a q l Albert said that 111 is l less than l 111, I think.

13   2 s w 2 s w 2 s 2 or 2 and 22 and 222 and 2 222 and 22 222.
       2 s w 2 Steven said that 222 is 2 less than 2 222, I think.

14   3 d e 3 d e 3 d 3 or 3 and 33 and 333 and 3 333 and 33 333.
       3 d e 3 Deidre said that 333 is 3 less than 3 333, I think.

15   4 f r 4 f r 4 f 4 or 4 and 44 and 444 and 4 444 and 44 444.
       4 f r 4 Flavia said that 444 is 4 less than 4 444, I think.

16   5 f 5 f 5 f 5 f 5 or 5 and 55 and 555 and 5 555 and 55 555.
       5 f 5 5 Foster said that 555 is 5 less than 5 555, I think.

17   6 j y 6 j y 6 j 6 or 6 and 66 and 666 and 6 666 and 66 666.
       6 j y 6 Johnny said that 666 is 6 less than 6 666, I think.

18   7 j u 7 j u 7 j 7 or 7 and 77 and 777 and 7 777 and 77 777.
       7 j u 7 Joanne said that 777 is 7 less than 7 777, I think.

19   8 k i 8 k i 8 k 8 or 8 and 88 and 888 and 8 888 and 88 888.
       8 k i 8 Kathie said that 888 is 8 less than 8 888, I think.

20   9 l o 9 l o 9 l 9 or 9 and 99 and 999 and 9 999 and 99 999.
       9 l o 9 Leslie said that 999 is 9 less than 9 999, I think.

21   0 ; p 0 ; p 0 ; 0 or 0 and 10 and 100 and 1 000 and 10 000.
       0 ; p 0 Philip said that 100 is 0 less than 1 000, I think.

80-D. Measure your progress in controlling numbers

80-D. Repeat 80-B to measure your progress.

Manuscript 45

RESOLUTION

Paper: plain
Spacing: double
Line: 60
Position: center

JOHN HERBERT KAUFMANN

WHEREAS John (H.) Kaurmann is retiring from his ~~post~~ position

as Secretary-Treasurer of this firm, having served it and his

associates for more than (35) years; and

WHEREAS, he devoted all his skill and knowledge
to the development and expansion of this company,
its products, its services, its facilities, and its
staff, to the end that today this company is the
largest and most successful in its field of
business enterprise; and

WHEREAS he has given generously of himself in the

encouragement, inspiration, and ~~assistance~~ of ~~everyone~~ all those who

were
~~was~~ fortunate enough to work with him personally, to the end

this
that virtually all the Executives of ~~his~~ company have, in

schooled
effect, been ~~taught~~ by this wise and gentle teacher; and

Whereas he has proved himself a generous leader, a

thoughtful and warm associate, and a man endowed as much with

open-ness of heart and hand as with ~~a spirit of justice and~~

wisdom, so that his name is a legend in this industry and ~~so~~

that he is loved for what he is even more than for what he

has done: Therefore, be it ~~hereby~~

RESOLVED, That the Officers, the Members of the

Board of Directors, and the Entire Personnel of The Hayes

devotion
Manufacturing Company do commend, for his ~~dedication~~ to them

unstinting
and his loyalty, JOHN HERBERT KAUFMANN

and leadership
in their behalf

center, triple
space below

Manuscript 46

RESOLUTION

Paper: plain
Spacing: single
Line: 50
Position: center

81-A. Measure your skill in technical typing

22 There are three sure keys to expert typing of numbers: 12

    1. Type <u>many</u> numbers (this is why there are so many of   26
them in the production jobs and drill groups in this book).   38

    2. Force yourself <u>always</u> to use correct fingering (the   52
"we 23" and other basic drills are designed for this need).   64

    3. Automatize the numbers in pairs for use as pegs for   76
quick control of the numeral keys (this is the objective of   88
drills like "10 and 28 and 39 and 47 and 56" in this book).   100

1 | 2 | 3 | 4 | 5 | 6 | 7 | 8 | 9 | 10 | 11 | 12

81-B. Practice the punctuation symbol keys

23M   k8k k'k k8k k'k That isn't Bob's dog.   I'm sure it's Joe's.
23E   ;'; ;'; ;'; ;'; That isn't Bob's dog.   I'm sure it's Joe's.

24M   s2s s"s s2s s"s I said, "Hey, there."   He growled, "Hello."
24E   ;'; ;"; ;'; ;"; I said, "Hey, there."   He growled, "Hello."

25   ;-; ;-; ;-; ;-; My in-laws are the stay-away-from-you type.
26   191 1(1 ;0; ;); Tell them (1) what, (2) why, and (3) where.

27M   j6j j_j j6j j_j Well, I <u>told</u> him to read <u>Ask the West Wind</u>.
27E   ;-; ;_; ;-; ;_; Well, I <u>told</u> him to read <u>Ask the West Wind</u>.

81-C. Speed up your typing of numbers

28   wet 235 tie 583 rye 463 pet 035 you 697 owe 923 wit 285 285

29   tow 592 rip 480 roe 493 our 974 pie 083 yet 635 too 599 599

30   ire 843 pup 070 ere 343 ewe 323 toe 593 eye 363 yew 632 632

31   weep 2330 tour 5974 type 5603 pity 0856 wept 2305 rope 4903

32   riot 4895 pipe 0803 wore 2943 your 6974 wire 2843 toot 5995

33   wiry 2846 true 5473 poor 0994 rout 4975 prow 0492 trip 5480

81-D. Drill on typing solid, cumulative numbers

34   1601 1602 1603 1604 1605 1606 1607 1608 1609 1610 1611 1612

35   1513 1514 1515 1516 1517 1518 1519 1520 1521 1522 1523 1524

36   1925 1926 1927 1928 1929 1930 1931 1932 1933 1934 1935 1936

81-E. Remeasure your skill in technical typing

37   When our club was at 39 28th Street, it was called the   12
"3928 Club."   Now that we've moved to 47 56th Street, it is   24
called the "4756 Club."   The club is growing since we moved   36
(last June 10), for 100 to 110 <u>more</u> men have now joined us.   50

1 | 2 | 3 | 4 | 5 | 6 | 7 | 8 | 9 | 10 | 11 | 12

81-A. Type a complete copy (GOAL: To finish within 3 minutes and 3 errors) or take one 3-minute writing on it (GOAL: Highest speed within 3 errors).

SI 1.39—normal, if you are master of top row

NOTE: In this book, word counts credit you with triple strokes for each underscored word and 5 strokes for each use of the tabulator mechanism (as, in indenting).

81-B. "M" drills are for manual machines; "E," for electrics.

Each drill twice plus once more if you erred on the related symbol key when typing 81-A.

81-C. In all "we 23" drills, the word cues you to the fingering of the next number.

1. Each line twice.
2. Repeat lines 28-33 twice more, omitting all the "cue words."

81-D. Type the lines as a paragraph; type the paragraph twice (GOAL: To finish in 1 minute and within 1 mistake).

81-E. Type the paragraph twice without stopping. GOAL: To surpass your pretest score in 81-A.

Or, take one 3-minute writing on the paragraph (GOAL: Highest score within 3 errors).

SI 1.17—fairly easy

146-C. Type one copy in
Lesson 146 and another
in Lesson 147; or, take
these practice steps:

1. Read the material.

2. Practice the three
hardest words you see
in each paragraph.

3. Take a 5-minute timed
writing with a 10-second
rest after each minute.

4. Practice words with
which you had trouble.

5. Take a final 5-minute
writing without rests.

GOAL: Maximum speed
within 3-error limit.

SI 1.25—easy if you can
respond to warning bell!

146-C. Stretch your skill on easy straight copy

The error into which most of us fall is in thinking that we will   14
get a new lease on life whenever we decide to do so. We coast along,   28
telling ourselves that, when our big chance comes along, one worth an   42
effort, we will then stretch and make good. There is no mistake that   56
is worse than this. Once you get the habit of coasting, it's too bad   70
for you. The habit gets you and keeps you coasting; and there's only   84
one direction you can coast. To build muscles, you have to use them.   98

Ambition is seldom wholly dead in any of us; most of us long for   112
the good things that are out of our reach at the moment. But the way   126
to get them is not to give up and let go; rather, it's to take a leaf   140
from the story of the old warrior whose son complained that his spear   154
was too short. The boy's father said, "Then step closer to the foe."   168

All this is worth talking about because you will soon be in your   182
first position; and the work in any first position is usually so easy   196
for you, since no one expects much of you as a beginner, that you can   210
get the idea that you can relax on the job and stop growing. If that   224
happens, you start coasting, which takes you back down the hills that   238
you climbed to get where you are. If your work is easy, then that is   252
the time to push, and push hard while the pushing is easy. Don't let   266
yourself coast nor stand still; get your muscles ready for the climb.   281

The climb is not easy, which is a good thing for you; if it were   295
easy, the ladder would be full of people ahead of you. Sometimes the   309
ladder of advancement shakes and trembles, and you with it; some-   321
times the rungs seem mighty far apart. But it's when the stretching   335
is the hardest and the climbing the toughest that your strength and   349
will and heart enable you to reach the next rung that others could not   363
attain. The relaxing and coasting is for those who lack the drive to   377
succeed.   379

146/147-D. Apply skill to legal-styled typing—perhaps

Such legal-*looking* touches as deep indentions, all-caps, vertical rules, and so on, are often used in other manuscripts (whether or not legality is involved) for the sake of dramatic formality. The following minutes and resolution are illustrations. Alternative assignments may, however, be more helpful to you:

DEVELOPMENTAL SKILL DRILL

If increasing speed or accuracy is more important, repeat the drills on pages 125-127.

SUSTAINED PRODUCTION OUTPUT

If maintaining steady production is more important, produce a magazine article on "What's What about Horizontal Centering" (pages 194, 197) for a journal that uses a 45-space line, 3-space paragraph indention, and subheadings that are centered and underscored.

Suggestion: Make three
carbon copies of each
of these manuscripts.

LINE: 60
TAB: 5 AND CENTER
SPACING: SINGLE
DRILLS: AS DIRECTED
GOAL: PRODUCTION OF
   CORRESPONDENCE
STRESS: CONTINUITY

Unit 14. Correspondence

82-A. Tune up on these review lines

82-A. Lines three or more times or a 1-minute timing on each line. Repeat in Lesson 83.

1 They got a giant of a man to make the panel for the chapel.
2 Jumping quickly from the taxi, Hazel brushed a woven chair.
3 He called "10," then "28," then "39," then "47," then "56."
   1 | 2 | 3 | 4 | 5 | 6 | 7 | 8 | 9 | 10 | 11 | 12

82-B. Boost skill on these preview words

82-B. For speed boost, each line three times. For accuracy boost, the group of lines three times. Try to hold a steady pace, speeding up a little on each line.

4 particularly conference products familiar plastic thank wax
5 combination scheduling pamphlet hallways covering about two
6 application durability described designed traffic which one
7 protective properties engineers airtight familiar heavy but

82-C. Build skill on production material

82-C. Type a double-spaced copy, line for line (GOAL: To finish within 5 minutes and 3 errors) or take one 5-minute writing on it (GOAL: At least 40 wam within 3 errors).

SI 1.38—normal

If time permits, take a 5-minute writing in Lesson 82, with a 10-second rest at the end of each minute; then repeat in Lesson 83, without any pauses.

8 Dear Mr. Jeffers: 4

   Thank you for your inquiry about Floor Guard, our   15
   fine new kind of protective floor covering. I enclose   26
   a pamphlet that describes this new product, which is a   37
   combination of liquid plastic and wax, with the finest   48
   properties of each: the ease of application and shine   59
   of wax and the high durability of strong plastic film.   70

9 Although Floor Guard was designed to serve in the   81
   home, particularly in the kitchen and in hallways that   92
   bear heavy traffic, there is no reason why Floor Guard   103
   should not be used in the case that you described; the   114
   wax won't yellow, and the plastic is an airtight bond.   125

10 One of our engineers is scheduling a trip to your   136
   city in about two weeks. He is familiar not only with   147
   Floor Guard but also with our other floor products; if   158
   you would like him to visit you for a conference about   169
   your problem, please tell us within the next few days.   180

                              Sincerely yours,   185
   TAB ➤ TAB ➤
   1 | 2 | 3 | 4 | 5 | 6 | 7 | 8 | 9 | 10 | 11

82/83-D. Practice the production of semiblocked letters

Analyze the arrangement of the letter on page 131; then type it and the letters assigned on page 132. GOAL: To type each letter within 6 minutes, with 3 or fewer errors.

LETTER GUIDE

Date 15
Address .. 20
—100 .... 4"
100-200 ... 5"
200+ .... 6"

Manuscript 44

POWER OF ATTORNEY
Paper: plain, ruled
Spacing: double
Position: centered
vertically

Remember: Double
line should fall
15 spaces from
left; single line,
5 spaces from right.

POWER OF ATTORNEY

please double space & center

TS ← 2#

KNOW ALL MEN BY THESE PRESENCE:

That I, HAROLD L. KINGSTON, of the town of Essex,
in the county of Essex, Gentleman, do hereby constitute and
appoint Bob P. Kingston, of the City of Toronto, Physician,
my true and lawful Attorney for me, and in my name, place,
and stead, and for my sole use and benefit:

To sell all my real estate wherever situated at such
time or times and either by public auction or private sale,
and upon such terms and conditions as my *said* attorney shall think
fit, with liberty to buy in at any such sale as aforesaid,
and also to execute to the purchasers of the said lands such
deeds of grant, conveyances, or assurances as may be required, and also to give effectual receipts for the purchase
moneys of the said lands, and such receipts shall exempt the
person or persons paying such moneys from all responsibility
of seeing to the application thereof.

IN WITNESS WHEREOF I have hereunto set my hand and seal
this fourth day of January, 19--. 2↓

center this line   2#
SIGNED, SEALED AND DELIVERED in the presence of 2↓
_____ and _____

← *make equal* →

LINE: 60
SPACING: SINGLE
GOAL: MORE ABOUT
  LEGAL TYPING
DRILLS: THREE TIMES
STRESS: CONTINUITY

LESSONS
146–147
Legal Styling

146-A. Type lines 2, 3
in cadence with someone
who sets a sharp, even
pace on the first line.
Or, each three times.

146-A. Tune up on these review lines

1 Did you see the big new axe her dad had her get out for me?
2 Queen Judy gave my boy an exciting gold prize for his work.
3 Give us a quick report on (10), (28), (39), (47), and (56).

   1 | 2 | 3 | 4 | 5 | 6 | 7 | 8 | 9 | 10 | 11 | 12

146-B. Type to your goal.

ACCURACY: Each pair
three times, as a
paragraph.

SPEED: Each line three
times successively.

In all cases, emphasize
smooth, continuous work.

146-B. Increase skill on patterned preview drills

4 coasting thinking climbing relaxing growing pushing talking
5 Sometimes Ambition Don't There Once All But The To If We Or
6 so. you. are. them. this. good. easy. short. coast.
7 position; coasting; effort, rather, still; "then" easy; go;
8 beginner warrior attain still; effort error hills fall; too
9 usually happens telling succeed ladder good, will, soon all

SEMIBLOCKED LETTER STYLE

Letter 28

SEMIBLOCKED LETTER
Shown: in pica
Body: 152 words
Line: 50
Tab: 5 and center
Paper: letterhead
SI: 1.44—normal

January 4, 19-- ↓5   4

                                                            8

Miss Lee Anne Sloane   12
The Graham Company   16
47 Court Street North   21
Thunder Bay, Ontario   P7A 4T5   25
                                                          26
Dear Miss Sloane: 29
                                                          30
     I am happy to answer your questions about the   41
details of our letter patterns. The answers are,   51
I believe, illustrated by this letter.   59
                                                          60
     This is a semiblocked letter, which is simply   74
a blocked letter with the paragraphs indented. As   84
a rule, indentions are for five spaces; but it is   94
not uncommon to indent ten or even more spaces.   104
                                                         105
     In this letter style, the date line is typed   115
either to end at the right margin or, as shown in   125
this letter, to start at the center; and the group   135
of closing lines is blocked at the center, too.   145
                                                         146
     This letter also shows how and where a typist   156
indicates that something is enclosed with the   166
letter: To serve as a reminder to the typist and the   177
addressee, Enclosure or Enclosures is typed on the   194
line below the reference initials.   202
                                                         203
                          Sincerely yours, ↓4   207

Address a woman Ms.
unless Mrs. is either
typed as shown here or   210
included parenthetically in
the penned signature.

                          Mrs. Ruth Leeds Murphy   216
                          Training Department   221
                                                         222
urs
Enclosure   224

Business Letter in Semiblocked Style

If you take a timed writing on
production copy and end with an
incomplete line, count 1 word
credit for each 5 strokes and
for each use of the tabulator
in that final incomplete line.

Continuation page has 9-line top margin (so start on line 10). Top margin is deep because legal papers are bound together at the top.

IN WITNESS WHEREOF, the said parties have hereunto set

their hands and seals.

SIGNED, SEALED AND DELIVERED)
In the presence of)
)
)
)
)

Final page number is typed a triple space under body, not at bottom of the page.

Page 2 of 2

Form 56

BILL OF SALE
Form: workbook 277
Data: Manuscript 42

Form 55

BILL OF SALE
Form: workbook 275
Data: as shown

Bill of Sale

This Indenture

made the twenty-seventh - - - - - day of November - - - - - - 1977

Between John Allan Zabrowski, of the City of Toronto, in the County of York, Industrial Designer - - - - - - - - - - - - - - - - hereinafter called the Bargainor of the First Part and Robert Remington and Sons, of the City of Toronto, in the County of York, Manufacturers - - - - - - hereinafter called the Bargainees of the Second Part

WHEREAS the Bargainor is - - - possessed of the goods, chattels and effects hereinafter set forth, described and enumerated, and has - - contracted and agreed with the Bargainees for the absolute Sale to them - - - thereof, for the sum of Two Thousand ($2 000.00) - Dollars

NOW THIS INDENTURE WITNESSETH, that in pursuance of the said Agreement, and in consideration of the sum of Two Thousand ($2 000.00) - - - - Dollars of lawful money of Canada, paid by the said Bargainees - to the said Bargainor -- at or before the sealing and delivery of these presents (the receipt whereof is hereby acknowledged), the said Bargainor-- does - bargain, sell, assign, transfer and set over unto the said Bargainees, their - - executors, administrators, successors and assigns his design and working model of a typewriter. - - - - - - - - - - - - - - - - -

TO HOLD the said hereinbefore assigned goods, chattels and effects and every of them and every part thereof, and all the right, title and interest of the said Bargainor-- therein and thereto, unto and to the use of the said Bargainees .

AND the said Bargainor - does - hereby, for himself, his - - - - - - executors, administrators, successors and assigns, covenant, promise and agree with the said Bargainees, their - - - - - - - - - executors, administrators, successors and assigns, in manner following, that is to say: THAT the said Bargainor is - - now rightfully and absolutely possessed of and entitled to the said hereby assigned goods, chattels and effects and every of them, and every part thereof.

IN WITNESS WHEREOF, the said parties have hereunto set their hands and seals.

_____   _____

SIGNED, SEALED AND DELIVERED In the presence of

_____

Legal Document on Fill-in Printed Form (Reduced)

Current Date | Dr. Edward L. Prall | Dean of Instruction | The | 17
Park Place School | Huntsville, Ontario | Dear Dean Prall: | 30

Thank you for your letter inquiring about the training pro- | 43
gram we have developed for new employees. I am pleased to tell | 56
you about its three phases. | 62

For the first week, each new employee learns about the com- | 76
pany, its policies, and its products. | 84

In the second week, each new employee studies the style | 97
manual used by all our office employees. This concerns our let- | 110
ter style, the forms used to requisition supplies, telephoning, | 123
and so on. | 125

During the next few weeks, the new employees work in a pro- | 139
duction pool from which they are sent to cover the desks of | 151
absent workers or help with rush assignments. As we have va- | 163
cancies, then, the trainees are ready for quick placement. | 175

We are quite pleased with the success of this training pro- | 188
gram, Dean Prall. We should be happy to have you visit us and | 201
observe the program. | Sincerely yours, | Mrs. Ruth Leeds | 220
Murphy | Training Department | *Initials?* | 228

Current Date | Mr. C. W. Vance | Vance Service Centre | 26 | 17
East Street | Wawa, Ontario | P1C 7K7 | Dear Mr. Vance: | 30

Your letter asking about our new Floor Guard protective | 43
floor covering arrived on the same day that we mailed to you | 55
and all our other dealers a complete report on this wonderful | 67
new product. On the chance that your copy is delayed, | 78
however, let me answer the questions you asked in your letter. | 91

Yes, our advertising campaign for Floor Guard will begin | 105
next month in the national magazines. | 112

No, we did not authorize the article you saw in Runyon's | 126
column; because his comments echo what we say in our first | 138
ads, we guess that one of the magazines tipped him off about | 150
our advertisement. | 154

Yes, Floor Guard is in full production, ready to deliver to | 167
dealers who rush their orders to us. Window display units and | 180
store banners will go out with the first Floor Guard shipment to | 193
each dealer. | [*Complimentary Closing:*] Get your order in! | 203
Howard T. Blackstone | District Sales Manager | *Initials?* | 217

Current Date | Mr. Kenneth M. Jeffers | Supervising Engineer | | 17
Hotel Mann Lodge | Torbay, Newfoundland | Dear Mr. Jeffers: | 29

[*The body and closing of this letter are on page 130.*] Howard | 233
T. Blackstone | District Sales Manager | urs | Enclosure | 246

B I L L   O F   S A L E

THIS INDENTURE made in duplicate the fifth day of

September, 19___

BETWEEN: FRANK C. SPENCER, of the City of Toronto, in the Coun-

ty of York, Merchant, hereinafter called the Bargainor

OF THE FIRST PART,

and   MORTON CRANE, of the said City of Toronto, Publisher,

hereinafter called the Bargainee, OF THE SECOND PART.

NOW THIS INDENTURE WITNESSETH that, in consideration

of the sum of One Thousand Dollars ($1 000.00) paid by the Bar-

gainee to the Bargainor at or before the sealing and delivery of

these presents (the receipt whereof is hereby acknowledged), the

Bargainor doth bargain, sell, and assign unto the Bargainee:

Three Oak Office Desks; Two Underwood Typewriters; One
Steel Safe; One Oak Card-Index File; One Four-Section
Steel Letter File; One Oak Bookcase.

TO HOLD the said hereinbefore assigned goods and chat-

tels, and all the right, title, and interest of the Bargainor

thereto and therein, unto, and to the use of the Bargainee.

AND the Bargainor doth hereby for himself, his execu-

tors, and administrators, covenant with the Bargainee, his exe-

cutors, and assigns, that the Bargainor is now rightfully and

absolutely possessed of the said goods and chattels.

Page 1 of 2

(CONTINUED ON NEXT PAGE)

Legal Document on Ruled Stationery (Reduced)

Stationery is P4 or longer. Margin stops are set a space or two inside double rule
15 spaces from left and single rule 5 spaces from right edge.

LINE: 60
TAB: 5 AND CENTER
SPACING: SINGLE
DRILLS: AS DIRECTED
GOAL: SPEEDUP IN
    PRODUCTION
STRESS: POSTURE

84-A. Each line three or more times (or 1-minute timing on each line).

Repeat in Lesson 85.

84-A. Tune up on these review lines

1 The name of the firm they own is to the right of the forms.
2 Six jumbo elephants quickly moved the wagon from the blaze.
3 The sum of "47" and "56" is more than "10," "28," and "39."
   1 | 2 | 3 | 4 | 5 | 6 | 7 | 8 | 9 | 10 | 11 | 12

84-B. For speed boost, each line three times; or, for an accuracy boost, the group of lines three times. Start each line slowly and evenly, and gradually accelerate.

84-B. Boost skill on these preview words

4 toastmaster Saturday whether consult annual honor hope that
5 invitation sincerely evening Council should voice find time
6 selection designate schedule helping please today then will
7 earnestly committee selected banquet notify heard know sure

84-C. Type a double-spaced copy, line for line (GOAL: To finish within 5 minutes and 3 errors or take one 5-minute writing on it). (GOAL: At least 40 wam, within 3 errors).

SI 1.29—fairly easy

84-C. Build skill on production material

8 Dear Judge Young: 4

I am writing to confirm that the annual dinner to   15
honor our "Man of the Year" will be held on a Saturday   26
evening in April and to ask you whether we might count   37
on your helping the Council, as you did in each of the   48
past six years, by serving as the banquet toastmaster.   59

If time permits, take a 5-minute writing in Lesson 84, with a 10-second rest at the end of each minute; repeat in Lesson 85, without any pauses.

9   As a member of the selection committee, you know,   70
of course, that Fred Hughes is The Man; I have written   81
to him today to notify him and to ask him to designate   92
the date of the banquet. As soon as I have heard from   103
him, which should be within a few days, I shall inform   114
you of the date he has selected; then you will be able   125
to consult your own schedule and let us know for sure.   136

PROFESSIONAL HINT:

Whenever you can, precede the start of a timed writing by special drilling, as:

(1) To sharpen your concentration, type a line or two backwards.

(2) To reduce errors, practice any unique stroking combinations (like the quotation marks in paragraph 8).

(3) To increase speed, race through two or three copies of a very easy sentence, like line 1.

10   The invitation to serve as toastmaster comes from   147
all of us on the committee, of course. But please let   158
me add my own voice: busy though you are, I earnestly   169
hope that you can find the time to help us once again.   180
                    Yours very sincerely,   186
   1 | 2 | 3 | 4 | 5 | 6 | 7 | 8 | 9 | 10 | 11

84/85-D. Practice the production of semiblocked letters

Study the arrangement of Letter 33; then see whether you can type it and Letters 34-36 within 6 minutes and 3 errors each.

To end lines evenly:
LINE: 70 spaces
INDENTIONS: 10 spaces
SI: 1.30—fairly easy

Most of us have great respect for the law, for we feel that it is complex and full of fine points that might trip us in some way. As a result, there is a tradition, or what amounts to one, that legal typing is very hard. Nothing could be further from the truth. Legal jobs are quite easy to type, much easier, come to think of it, than a majority of the jobs that are typed day in and day out in the office.

After all, such documents are nothing more or less than the routine kind of manuscript with some fancy touches to impress people. One such touch is the flair of indenting paragraphs ten spaces rather than the standard five spaces. One more such flair is the antiquated wording that is used time and again, such as "executors and heirs and assigns forever." A wise typist just smiles, knowing that such terms become easy to type when they are typed often enough. After a while, the typist learns how to zip off such turns of words in nothing flat.

An extra legal touch in most provinces is using vertical lines to show you where to set the margin stops. The lines are in color in most cases, giving a bright but stern and official look to the papers on which they appear. What is typed on the paper is supposed to stay between the ruled lines without touching either of them; so the smart typist adjusts the margin stops so they will be a space or two inside the lines, and that is that. When you realize how much time is saved by such guides, you can't help but wish we had them for letters, too!

One more unique thing in typing legal documents is that the pages are bound at the top instead of at the side, which means that a continuation page must have three additional line spaces at the top; so you leave nine blank lines at the top of such pages instead of the six lines that you leave on the continuation pages of manuscripts and reports. In law offices, covers are made for legal documents that have many pages. The covers are trimmed a little larger than the size of the paper, and the upper 1.2 cm is folded over; the typed pages are jounced into the pocket thus made, and the entire packet is fastened by two or three staples.

But the splendor of this lavish treatment of manuscripts is dimming. One can find most of these papers in printed form at a dime a dozen in any stationery shop, and one just inserts a few words here and there on the form. Gone are the rows of shouting capitals. Gone are the deep bows at the starts of the paragraphs. Gone are the firm but colorful rules that fenced in the majestic words. And to replace them, what have we? We have a printed form, a form full of holes and gaps in which we insert a word, a name, a date, an amount. We do not even display these things; we put each as near the start of its space as we can, then dump in stuttering hyphens to fill up any extra room. A fine day it is, when a document is no more challenging than a bill!

14
28
41
55
69
83
97
112
126
139
153
167
181
195
209
223
237
251
265
279
293
308
322
336
350
364
378
392
406
420
434
448
462
476
490
504
518
532
546
560
574
588
602

Dear Mr. Jones:

    Thank you for r
than we had expected

KNOW ALL MEN BY THES
    That I, Ro

Concord, Merrimack C

part, for and in con

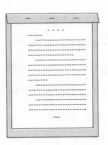

o the said part ies -of the
  I do for me and my --
the said part ies -of the :
invention ------------
dministrators and assigns,

hereunto set my - hand -
1 the year one thousand nir

Letter 32

SEMIBLOCKED LETTER
IN FORMAL DISPLAY
Shown: in elite
Body: 170 words
Line: 50
Tab: 5 and center
Paper: letterhead
SI: 1.43—normal

V BC Victoria Business Council

120 Monona Avenue • Victoria, British Columbia

February 9, 19— ↓5   4

5 lines

8

Dear Mr. Hughes: 12

                                                   13

Each spring the members of the Victoria Business Council   25
select and honor at a dinner the member of the Legislature   37
who has done the most to promote the growth of business in   48
our area. I am privileged to inform you that you have been   61
awarded this honor for this year. We should like to invite   73
you to attend and to speak at the dinner in your honor.   84

                                                   85
We should like to hold the dinner on a Saturday evening   97
in April. If you would let us know which date would be most 109
convenient for you, we could then proceed to make the arrange- 121
ments for the dinner.   126

                                                   127
Will you help us keep this news confidential? From past   139
years you probably know that we seek to withhold the news of 152
our selection until the moment it is announced at the dinner. 164
Only the selection committee and a few of those involved in   176
the dinner program will know who is our "Man of the Year."   188

                                                   189
                    Yours very sincerely, ↓4   197

                                                   200

              Executive Secretary ↓3 or 4   (at least 3   206
                                              lines)   207
                                                   208
Fred Hughes, Esquire   213
Member of the Legislative Assembly   218
Parliament Buildings   223
Victoria, British Columbia   227
V8V 1X4   228

Use no reference
symbols when an
address is typed
below the letter.

Typing the address at the
bottom of any letter makes
it "formal" or "official."
Letters to dignitaries are
given this special display.

Formal or Official Letter in Semiblocked Style

LINE: 60
SPACING: SINGLE
GOAL: LEARN ABOUT
LEGAL TYPING
DRILLS: THREE TIMES
STRESS: WARINESS IN
PRODUCTION

Unit 24. Manuscripts

144-A. Tune up on these review lines

144-A. Type lines 2, 3
in cadence with someone
who sets a crisp but
even pace on line 1;
then, exchange roles.

1 Sue said that they will have your gray suit back next week.
2 Vick did put a dozen tiny jugs from Iraq on the waxy table.
3 Type page 10 or 28, page 39 or 47, and page 56 or 100, Joe.

   1 | 2 | 3 | 4 | 5 | 6 | 7 | 8 | 9 | 10 | 11 | 12

144-B. Build skill on selective preview drills

144-B. Type to your need.

ACCURACY: Lines 4-7 like
a paragraph three times;
lines 8-11, twice; then
lines 4-7 once more.

SPEED: Type each line, 4
through 11, three times.

In all cases, emphasize
the elimination of arm,
elbow, and hand motion;
stress finger action.

4 paragraphs result papers easier truth heirs hard how for   2-3
5 blanks, black; small, hands, canal lack fans can and man   2-1
6 supposed further either appear people flair just are way   2-3
7 between become bounce unique worn upon more come ten now   1-3

8 very hard|less than|with some|than most|form that will   4&4
9 and his|the law|zip off|the use|off the|you can|but for   3&3
10 is too|by the|to one|is the|in any|on the|all of|if you   2&3
11 of us|of it|is to|up to|to be|to it|to do so|if it is so   2&2

144-C. Build skill on easy alphabetic paragraphs

144-C. Make a complete
copy of page 220, doing
half of it in Lesson 144
and half in Lesson 145.
Or, follow these steps:

1. Read the material.

2. Practice the three
hardest words you see
in each paragraph, 1-3.

3. Take a 5-minute timed
writing with a 10-second
rest after each minute.

4. Practice words with
which you have trouble.

5. Take a final 5-minute
writing without rests.

In Lesson 145, use these
steps on paragraphs 4-5.

SI 1.30—fairly easy

For surer understanding
of legal typing, do the
special learning guide
on workbook pages 273-4.

The paragraphs are on the next page. Note that you are to use a 70-space line for it and (in preparation for the legal documents that follow) a *10-space* paragraph indention. The selection is long enough that, if you wish, you could test your skill on a 7- or 10-minute writing—the kind you would be given in an employment test.

144/145-D. Apply skill to legal typing—perhaps

The legality of a document is based on its contents and signatories, not on how it is typed; but certain conventions have been established which must be observed by typists:

1. Documents are equally legal whether typed in full or on a form.

2. Erasures on *key* details, such as names and amounts and dates, are forbidden in most states (the page must be retyped or be initialed by all signers of the document).

3. The mechanical elements are illustrated and discussed on the next three pages; study them analytically.

The legal-typing assignments on pages 221-222 are interesting and valuable experiences, but it is possible that alternative practice may be more helpful to your growth:

DEVELOPMENT SKILL DRILL

If you cannot yet type 40 wam for 5 minutes with 3 or fewer errors, you may wish to omit the legal assignments and repeat the sequence of skill drills on pages 122-124.

SUSTAINED MANUSCRIPT TYPING

Or, you may wish to substitute for the legal typing the production of a magazine article by you, "What's What about Carbon Paper" (pages 158 and 161), for a magazine that uses a 45-stroke line and 3-space paragraph indentions (review page 150).

Current Date | Dear Judge Young: | [*The body and closing of this letter are on page 133*] | Yours very sincerely, | Executive Secretary ↓ 3 or 4 | His Honour Judge J. Young | County Law Courts | 850 Burdett Avenue | Victoria, British Columbia | V8W 1B3

202
214
226
237

Current Date | Dear Mr. Blaine: | The Victoria Business Council, which is a civic group in this city, wishes to ask and to urge you to support House Bill 3301. This is the bill that would give the owners of retail stores the right, such as owners of factories now have, for an early tax write-off for new equipment.

16
30
42
55
68

As you may know, the Victoria Business Council is made up of top management of nearly 400 Victoria firms (only a quarter of which are retail outlets) which employ some 18,500 persons. The members of the Council believe firmly not only that this bill is fair and just but also that it is long overdue.

79
91
104
116
127

Mr. Blaine, our whole city would benefit from tax relief for our retail stores, for it would save some stores and encourage others to modernize, thus helping all the supporting trades and bringing new life to our downtown business center. We urge you to do all you can to support H. B. 3301 and bring its benefits to your constituents. | Respectfully yours, | VICTORIA BUSINESS COUNCIL | Executive Secretary | Paul S. Blaine, Esquire | Member of Parliament | The House of Commons, Ottawa, Ontario | *Initials?*

142
154
167
179
191
209
225
236
242

Current Date | Mr. Harvey F. Hall, Manager | The Hilton Motor Lodge | 211 Atkins Road | Victoria, British Columbia V9B 2Z9 | Dear Mr. Hall:

16
27
31

The Victoria Business Council plans to hold its annual spring banquet on some Saturday evening in April. We estimate that attendance will be between 200 and 250 persons and that the affair will run from 18:00 to 22:00.

44
56
68
78

Please let us know for what Saturday evenings, if any, your main ballroom could be reserved for us and what menus can be offered at $7.50 and $10.00 per plate.

92
104
112

Please phone or write us so that we may hear from you not later than the first of next month. | Sincerely yours, | Executive Secretary | MJB | urs

126
146
149

Current Date | Mr. Fairleigh Lee Graham | Manager, Victoria Hotel | 153 Elford Street | Victoria, British Columbia | V8R 3X8 Dear Mr. Graham: [*Prepare the same message.*]

16
28
150

Table 40

LEADER TABLE, BOXED
Center exact copy, P4
paper sideways in
machine. Available
lines: 51

DISTRIBUTION OF SALES INCOME

(Prepared by the Department of Research and Statistics)

How Our Sales Dollar Was Distributed	This Year		Last Year	
	Amount	Ratio	Amount	Ratio
Materials, Services from Others	$512 236 000	54.2%	$456 367 000	53.8%
Wages, Salaries	298 289 000	31.6%	281 769 000	33.2%
Pensions, Social Security, Insurance, Other Benefits	19 938 000	2.1%	18 470 000	2.2%
Depreciation, Amortization	17 314 000	1.8%	15 174 000	1.8%
Interest on Long-Term Debts	4 875 000	.5%	4 595 000	.5%
Taxes on Income and Property	47 772 000	5.0%	41 657 000	4.9%
Dividends Declared for the Year	22 052 000	2.3%	19,963,000	2.3%
Extra Dividend Last Quarter	4 284 000	.5%	—	—
Reinvested in the Business	18 480 000	2.0%	10 769 000	1.3%
TOTALS	$945 240 000	100.0%	$848 764 000	100.0%

For review of
"boxed" table,
turn to pages
142 and 143.

LINE: 60
TAB: 5
SPACING: SINGLE
DRILLS: AS DIRECTED
GOAL: SPEEDUP IN
   LETTER TYPING
STRESS: DETAILS

86-A. Each line twice; then repeat three more times whichever one fits your objective. Repeat in Lesson 87.

86-B. For speed boost, each line three times; or, for an accuracy boost, the solid group, like a paragraph, three times. Type without pausing.

86-C. Type a double-spaced copy (GOAL: To finish within a limit of 5 minutes and 3 errors) or take one 5-minute writing to see whether you can type 40 or more wam, with 3 or fewer errors.

SI 1.30—fairly easy

Letter typing requires so much attention to detail that you might be tempted to cut your pace; these paragraphs should help to restore your best momentum.

86-D. Special notes: To give you a broad review of the display of feature lines in a letter, Letter 38 is shown with far more different displays than you are likely to see in a business letter. Rarely is an attention line used in a letter with a subject line.

If you were to make a carbon of each letter, you could mark up the carbon with reminders about the arrangement for the next letter.

86-A. Tune up on these review lines

1 If the men do their work by six, they may go to the social.

2 Hal was quick to give us extra pizza and juice for my boys.

3 I need number signs for: (10), (28), (39), (47), and (56).

   1 | 2 | 3 | 4 | 5 | 6 | 7 | 8 | 9 | 10 | 11 | 12

86-B. Revive speed on fluent preview phrases

4 his use of the|than it is to|or how they|one of the|what to

5 will always be|how they will|and if they|just a bit|when he

6 in the same way|in the world|who has the|is the one|most of

   1 | 2 | 3 | 4 | 5 | 6 | 7 | 8 | 9 | 10 | 11 | 12

86-C. Sustain speed on fluent paragraph material

7   One of the most difficult things in the world for most   12
of us is to be consistent, yet the habit of being so is the   24
jewel in the crown of success. He who is consistent is the   36
person who has the respect of his fellow citizens, for they   48
know what to expect of him, right or wrong. The people who   60
do not always act the same way are the ones of whom most of   72
us are suspicious; our not being able quite to predict what   84
they will do or how they will act or what decision they may   96
make leaves us wary and just a bit uncomfortable with them.   108

8   The knack of being consistent is more important to the   120
typist than it is to most people. When one is grinding out   132
page after page of a long report, for example, the touch of   144
quality comes from the use of the same margins and the same   156
heading style on each page. When one is turning out tables   168
that summarize what the department has just done this month   180
or quarter, they must match the style and design of reports   192
of prior periods in order that the same data will always be   204
found at a glance at the same point. And what is accuracy,   216
you know, but always hitting the same keys in the same way?   228

   1 | 2 | 3 | 4 | 5 | 6 | 7 | 8 | 9 | 10 | 11 | 12

86/87-D. Produce a summary project of display letters

Type as a four-page project on plain paper or workbook pages 155-158 the four versions of Letter 38, as directed on page 137. The table in the letter is to be centered with 6 spaces between columns; preset a tab stop for each column. Use a 60-space line for each letter.

LINE: 60
TAB: 5, 10, 30, 42
SPACING: SINGLE
GOAL: AUTHORITATIVE
PRODUCTION OUTPUT
STRESS: WARINESS

142-A. To develop a skill momentum that will carry through the production, take two 1-minute timings on each sentence.

NOTE: Italicized words must be underscored when they are typed.

142-B. If you have not yet reached 50 or more wam within 3 errors for 5 minutes, use 140-B on page 213 and the steps at the foot of the page. Otherwise, these steps:

1. Analyze this letter.

2. Practice every line containing any numbers.

3. Take a 5-minute timed writing with a 10-second rest after each minute, or type a copy with a rest for each paragraph.

4. Take a 5-minute timed writing or type one copy without pausing to rest.

GOAL: 50 or more wam, with 3 or fewer errors.

SI 1.44—normal

Table 39

PIVOT-LEADER DRILL
Paper: half sheets P5
Copies: make three
Leaders: open
Spacing: double
Line: 40, 60, 50

Letter 69

BLOCKED LETTER WITH LEADERED TABULATION
Paper: workbook 271
Line: 60, as shown
Body: 180 words
SI: 1.44—normal

UNIT 23

142-A. Tune up on these review lines

1 The men held a social to pay for their visit to the chapel.

2 The expert quickly noted five bad jewels among the zircons.

3 Report *Monday* on Sections (10), (28), (39), (47), and (56).

  1 | 2 | 3 | 4 | 5 | 6 | 7 | 8 | 9 | 10 | 11 | 12

142-B. Sustain skill on production copy

Current Date

Mr. and Mrs. J. W. Swensen
Apartment 9-J West
35 Bowring Place
St. John's, Newfoundland   A1E 3P4
(Salutation)

We are always happy to reply to questions from stockholders. Our report for our operations in the last quarter, which is being printed now and will be mailed in about two weeks, will show that our Net Earnings are $5.04 a share, which is better than average for the time of year. These are the figures:

Gross Revenue	$55 999 275.00
Net Income before Federal Income Taxes	9 339 180.00
Estimated Fed. Income Taxes	4 905 227.00
Net Income	4 433 953.00
Earnings per share	5.04

We expect a strong increase in our sales for the next quarter, for we shall be launching Vita-shine, the fine new product we have been working on for more than two years; if Vita-shine lives up to our forecasts, which are based on a very careful market survey, our sales and profits will show sharp gains, putting us far ahead of any previous margin we have enjoyed.

We trust that this information is what you wished. If there are other details that you would like to have, we should be happy to send them to you.

                    Yours very truly,

                    Orville L. Mitchell
                    Aide to the president

urs

142-C. Apply skill to leadered production problems

ASSIGNMENTS	ARRANGEMENTS	SPECIAL DIRECTIONS	WORDS
Letter 37	Semiblocked, in business display	Use 60-space line. Copy as shown but indent paragraphs 15 spaces and omit the subject line.	236
Letter 38	Semiblocked, in business display	Use 60-space line. Copy as shown, with paragraphs indented 10 spaces; but omit attention line.	237
Letter 39	Semiblocked, in formal display, as on page 134	Use 60-space line, date at right margin. Convert attention line to first line of inside address, with "Dear Mr." salutation. Omit subject line and indent paragraphs only 5 spaces.	225
Letter 40	Blocked, as shown on page 98	Use 60-space line, paragraphs NOT indented. Omit subject line and the company signature.	232

February 11, 19-- ↓5

4

8

Canadian Speakers Bureau
1250 Cannon Street East
Hamilton, Ontario L8H 1V3

13

18

24

Attention of Mr. Clark T. Krane

43

Gentlemen:

47

SUBJECT: TRIP FOR DOCTOR MAHR

67

We are pleased to report that we have been able to make final plans with four Kiwanis groups for the East Coast trip of your client, Dr. Charles Mahr:

79

91

99

Letter 37
Table 13
SEMIBLOCKED LETTER
Paper: letterhead
Body: 141 words
SI: 1.43—normal

May 6	Saint John	106
May 7	Fredericton	113
May 8	(Travel)	119
May 9	Charlottetown	126
May 10	(Travel)	132
May 11	Dartmouth	138

As we said in our prior letter, the Kiwanis groups will pay all of Doctor Mahr's expenses and his speaker's fee of $150 each time he gives his "Give Him a Break" talk.

150

163

174

We hope that you will let us know at once that the plans meet with your and Doctor Mahr's approval in order that we may complete the contract with Kiwanis. Please tell us, also, whether Doctor Mahr would like our help in making his hotel and his travel arrangements for the trip.

186

199

211

223

232

Yours very truly,

240

THE EAST COAST LYCEUM

248

251

The College Division

259

MFS/urs
cc Kiwanis Clubs

260

264

Semiblocked Business Letter with Special Features

the vertical spacing of each half, adding or deleting blank lines so as to make both halves end evenly.

4. Divide the heading lines to embrace both pages. The section on the first page is pivoted from the right margin; the section on the second page begins with the left margin.

5. Use the same length of line on each half; if necessary, spread the data to fill the line. The display on each page *may* be centered, but the total display will look better if the margins are narrower on the sides where the pages will adjoin.

6. Tape the pages together on the *back* side, fastening them with two or three strips of tape.

LINE

14 Acme Corporation

15
16 SHEET

17
18 December 31, 19--

19
20
21
22
23 Legal Reserve for Life and Annuity
24   Contracts $302 514 963.00

Table 38
BALANCE SHEET
(PAGE 2 OF 2)
Line: 60, with 2.5 cm
    left margin
Leaders: open

LIABILITIES

25
26 Reserve for Disability Policies 2 257 617.00

27
28 Reserve for Epidemics and
29   Mortality Fluctuations 2 500 000.00

30
31 Reserve for Investment Fluctuations 5 000 000.00

32
33 Reserve for Policy Claims in
34   Process of Adjustment 1 459 619.00

35
36 Gross Premiums and Interest Paid
37   in Advance 1 768 036.00

38
39 Taxes Accrued but Not Yet Due 2 078 495.00

40
41 Agents' Bond Deposits (Field Employees) . .   683 764.21

42
43 Commissions Accrued to Agents,
44   and Miscellaneous Items 936 106.60

45
46 Total Liabilities Other Than
47   Capital and Surplus $319 198 600.81

48
49 Capital and Surplus 28 667 592.10

50
51 TOTAL LIABILITIES $347 866 192.91

52

Unit 15. Tabulation

LINE: 60
TAB: EVERY 9 SPACES
SPACING: SINGLE
DRILLS: THREE TIMES
GOAL: MASTER
    RULED TABLES
STRESS: EFFICIENCIES

88-A. Maintain perfect rhythm—including the tabulating in line 2—if you possibly can.

88-A. Tune up on these review lines

1 cab ade fag ham aim jar kay lax pan oat qua was vat tap zag

2 one   six   two   ten   two   six   eight

3 Flight 47 leaves at 10:28, while Flight 56 leaves at 10:39.

88-B. To gain speed, type each line three times. To gain accuracy, type the group of lines, as a paragraph, three times. Try for rhythm without trying to speed up.

88-B. Sustain rhythm on these preview words

4 horizontal centering shortcut writing crease let's even six

5 adjustment backspace checking someone anyhow quite back out

6 arithmetic advancing vertical realize square paper once for

88-C. In Lesson 88, type one complete copy, being sure to type as evenly as you can and to rest after finishing each paragraph. Then, in Lesson 89, warm up by typing, three times each, every line in which you had an error the first time you copied this; and type four copies of the last paragraph (GOAL: To type the four copies in 5 minutes, with not more than 3 errors, without looking up even once!).

Or, take a 5-minute writing in Lesson 88, with a 10-second pause after each minute; and take a 5-minute timing without rests in Lesson 89 (GOAL: 40 or more wam, within 3 errors).

Use double spacing, a 5-space paragraph tab indention, and listen for the bell. If you respond correctly to the bell, all lines will end even at the margin.

SI 1.31—fairly easy

88-C. Sustain speed on fluent alphabetic paragraphs

7   Just about the time that we think we know all there is to   12
know about our work, along will come someone with a fine   23
shortcut that is new to us. I ran into such a plan five or six   36
months ago. It is a plan for taking the arithmetic out of verti-   48
cal centering. What you have to do is to back down from the   60
center of the paper, just like we back up from the middle of the   73
paper for horizontal centering. You will not quite realize how   86
easy it is until you try it for yourself.   95

8   But first you have to learn how to locate the vertical center   108
of the paper when it is in the machine. Let's learn to do this   121
right now. Fold a sheet of paper from bottom to top and crease   134
it horizontally. Next, open and insert this sheet in the machine,   147
advancing the paper until the top and bottom come even when   159
you press them back against the paper table, the way you do   171
anyhow when you are checking that the paper is straight. Now,   184
count how many lines you must turn up the paper to bring the   196
crease to the writing point; this will be four to six lines. Re-   208
member the number. From here on you can insert paper and   220
advance it until the bottom and top square up, then make the   232
adjustment of the extra lines, whose number you know, to get   244
to the exact vertical center.   250

9   Now you can guess how the plan works. You insert your   262
paper to its exact center; then, looking at the lines to be   274
centered, back out the page one line for every two lines of space   287
the copy will require, just as you backspace once for each pair   300
of spaces when you center something horizontally.   310

1 | 2 | 3 | 4 | 5 | 6 | 7 | 8 | 9 | 10 | 11 | 12 | 13

"Open" or "spread" leaders (alternate periods and spaces) are slower to type than "close" leaders (page 212) but look better when a table includes many blank lines between the typed lines.

Begin the first leader line with one space (note below the space between *Loans* and the first period). Note whether the periods fall in the odd- or even-number spaces on the scale; use this fact when you start each subsequent leader line. You will often need to space twice at the start of a leader (see the two spaces after *Owned* in the sixth leader) to enable you to keep all the periods aligned.

NOTES ON TYPING TWO-PAGE TABLES

1. Two-page tables are usually planned so that the two pages may be taped in adjacent positions.

2. Divide the data into equal or logical halves.

3. Use the same top margin on both pages. Check

Table 37

BALANCE SHEET
(PAGE 1 OF 2)
Line: 60, with 2.5 cm
right margin
Leaders: open

The Providence—		14
BALANCE		16
For the Year Ending		18
ASSETS		21
Real Estate Loans	$162 587 305.68	23
Bonds Owned:		24
Government Bonds	$45 507 650.33	26
Railroad Bonds	4 508 135.65	27
Public Utility Bonds . .	62 449 231.34	28
Industrial Bonds	26 878 473.54	29
Total Bonds Owned	139 343 490.86	31
Stocks Owned (Basic Industries with Dividend Records)	13 129 036.89	34
Policy Loans Made to Policyholders	11 862 942.16	36
Net Unpaid and Deferred Premiums (Being Collected)	7 099 713.61	39
Cash in Banks and Offices	6 340 534.93	41
Real Estate Owned (Including Home Office Building)	5 980 846.78	44
Interest Due and Accrued on Bonds and Mortgages	1 412 662.00	47
Collateral Loans (First Mortgages Only) . .	109 660.00	49
TOTAL ASSETS	$347 866 192.91	51

Review, on page 66, the basic steps in typing a table and, on page 69, the procedure for a table that includes column headings.

NOTES: When a table has an averages or totals line: (1) underscore the columns concerned; (2) precede the line by 1 blank line; (3) type the word *Average* [or *Total*, whichever is appropriate] in all capitals at the left edge of the table; and (4) if the line includes a $ sign, align it with the one above it.

PRACTICE. Type Table 14. GOAL: To be ready within 3 minutes and to type a copy within 3 minutes and 3 errors.

Line		Words
1	ADVERTISING RATIOS	11
2		12
3	January, 19—	21
4		22
5		23
6	Insertion Number of Cost per	41
7	Order No. Readers Thousand	58
8		59
9	4 534 2 000 000 $4.00	68
10	4 535 1 550 000 3.50	77
11	4 536 675 000 3.75	83
12	4 537 1 125 000 4.00	89
13	4 538 1 725 000 4.25	95
14	4 539 1 265 000 6.00	109
15		110
16	AVERAGE 1 390 000 $4.25	118

Table 14

OPEN TABLE
Paper: full sheet

As Table 15 illustrates, tables are often prepared with ruled lines of underscores to separate the parts of the table. Note that: (1) *one* blank line is left above and below each ruled line; (2) column heads are *not* underscored; but (3) in other regards a ruled table is arranged just like an open-form table.

Two helpful cautions: (1) Complete all machine adjustments and compute the top margin *before* inserting the paper; and (2) be sure to extend the rules to the full width of the table.

PRACTICE. Type Table 15. GOAL: To be ready within 3 minutes and to type a copy within 3 minutes and 3 errors.

Line		Words
	ADVERTISING RATIOS	11
		12
	January, 19—	21
	————————————————	29
		30
	Insertion Number of Cost per	38
	Order No. Readers Thousand	45
	————————————————	53
		54
10	4 534 2 000 000 $4.00	63
11	4 535 1 550 000 3.50	72
12	4 536 675 000 3.75	78
13	4 537 1 125 000 4.00	84
14	4 538 1 725 000 4.25	90
15	4 539 1 265 000 6.00	96
16	————————————————	108
17		109
18	AVERAGE 1 390 000 $4.25	116
19	————————————————	124

Table 15

RULED TABLE
Paper: full sheet

89-F. Produce tables (next page) in ruled form

Table 36

BALANCE SHEET
WITH LEADERS
Shown: in elite
Line: 60 spaces

The Providence-Acme Corporation

B A L A N C E   S H E E T

For the Year Ending December 31, 19--

To facilitate your copying, paper-clip to the page a line guide (envelope or paper) you can slide down the page as you begin each line.

A S S E T S

Real Estate Loans...........................	$162 587 305.68
Bonds Owned:	
Government Bonds	$45 507 650.33
Railroad Bonds	4 508 135.65
Public Utility Bonds	62 449 231.34
Industrial Bonds	26 878 473.54
Total Bonds Owned	139 343 490.86
Stocks Owned (Basic Industries	
with Dividend Records)	13 129 036.89
Policy Loans Made to Policyholders	11 862 942.16
Net Unpaid and Deferred Premiums	
(Being Collected)	7 099 713.61
Cash in Banks and Offices	6 340 534.93
Real Estate Owned (Including	
Home Office Building)	5 980 846.78
Interest Due and Accrued	
on Bonds and Mortgages	1 412 662.00
Collateral Loans (First Mortgages Only) ...	109 660.00
TOTAL ASSETS	$347 866 192.91

Leaders carried through column area end evenly with the column.

Long items are doubled up if fewer than 3 leaders would be left. Basis of doubling up is clarity for the reader.

Principal totals in a balance sheet are preceded and followed by one blank linespace.

L I A B I L I T I E S

Legal Reserve for Life and Annuity	
Contracts	$302 514 963.00
Reserve for Disability Policies	2 257 617.00
Reserve for Epidemics and	
Mortality Fluctuations	2 500 000.00
Reserve for Investment Fluctuations	5 000 000.00
Reserve for Policy Claims in	
Process of Adjustment	1 459 619.00
Gross Premiums and Interest Paid	
in Advance	1 768 036.00
Taxes Accrued but Not Yet Due	2 078 495.00
Agents' Bond Deposits (Field Employees) ...	683 754.21
Commissions Accrued to Agents,	
and Miscellaneous Items	936 106.60
Total Liabilities Other Than	
Capital and Surplus	$319 198 590.81
Capital and Surplus	28 667 602.10
TOTAL LIABILITIES	$347 866 192.91

Consistent steps of any size (2, 3, 5, 10, etc.) may be used for runover lines.

Capitalization and phrasing patterns are optional, but they must be consistent.

Table 16
RULED TABLE
Paper: full sheet

SPECIAL NOTES:
1. Arrangement here is alphabetic.
2. $ signs at bottom and top must align.
3. One blank line precedes and follows each underscore line.

Block →

AMENDED SALES QUOTAS

Fourth Quarter, 19—

Name	Quota	Headquarters
Allerton, Fred	$ 7 500	Halifax
Cox, Francis	9 000	Edmonton
Farley, Harold	6 000	Regina
Jordan, Thomas	8 000	Moncton
Maxwell, Joe	6 500	Montreal
Paulson, Henry	7 500	Lindsay
Teacher, Leo	8 000	Vancouver
TOTAL	$52 000	

52
53
64
72
79
87
97
105
115
124
125
132
141

(handwritten: must be as long as Vancouver)

Table 17
RULED TABLE
Paper: full sheet

Arrangement here is by sales amounts.

REPORT OF SALES

Fourth Quarter, 19—

Rank	Name	Sales	Quota
1	Jordan, Thomas	$10 000	$ 8 000
2	Cox, Francis	8 500	9 000
3	Paulson, Henry	6 750	7 500
4	Teacher, Leo	6 000	8 000
5	Maxwell, Joe	5 200	6 500
6	Farley, Harold	4 980	6 000
7	Allerton, Fred	4 500	7 500
TOTAL	. . . .	$45 930	$52 000

9
10
23
33
43
52
61
70
80
90
100
109
118
128
140
149

Table 18
RULED TABLE
Paper: full sheet

Arrangement here is by percentages. The percent sign must be repeated; it is not omitted as the $ sign usually is.

ANALYSIS OF SALES PERFORMANCE

Fourth Quarter, 19—

Rank	Name	Quota	Sales	Ratio
1	Jordan, Thomas	$ 8 000	$10 000	125%
2	Cox, Francis	9 000	8 500	94%
3	Paulson, Henry	7 500	6 750	90%
4	Farley, Harold	6 000	4 980	83%
5	Maxwell, Joe	6 500	5 200	80%
6	Teacher, Leo	8 000	6 000	75%
7	Allerton, Fred	7 500	4 500	60%
TOTAL	. . . .	$52 000	$45 930	87%

18
32
41
52
61
74
85
96
107
117
128
139
148
160
169

(handwritten: must be as long as longest word)

LINE: 60
TAB: 5
SPACING: DOUBLE
GOAL: MASTERY OF
    LEADERED TABLES
STRESS: PERSONAL
    EFFICIENCY

LESSONS

140–141

Finance Tables

140-A. Whisk through each line three times.

140-B. These alphabetic paragraphs are fluent and easy (SI 1.22), just the thing to enable you to withstand the "drag" effect of the leadered tables you are typing.

GOAL: You ought to be able to complete each paragraph within 2 minutes and 1 error.

Before you type each table in Lessons 140 and 141, type at least one of these paragraphs within 1 error; attach the paragraph to the table to show you have paid your premium on your "skill insurance."

SI 1.22—easy

140-A. Repeat the warmup on page 210, then—

140-B. Revive typing fluency on this easy copy

1 | 2 | 3 | 4 | 5 | 6 | 7 | 8 | 9 | 10 | 11 | 12

1   When I take a business trip, I stay in good hotels. I 12
do not like to stay in private homes. Now and then someone 24
will urge me to stay at his home; but I know that the offer 36
is likely to be just a show of goodwill and that the friend 48
is holding his breath, not quite sure how he can explain to 60
his wife the importance of having this guest. I always let 72
my host off the hook at once, for I am by no means eager to 84
forego a long shower and half hour of reading before I turn 96
out the light and curl up for a long sleep. No, thank you. 108

2   When you stay at a hotel, you can do as you wish. You 120
can order up a late snack, take a quick nap if you have the 132
urge to do so, repack the luggage, walk around in your bare 144
feet, write a report, or read all night if the book is that 156
good. You can make a phone call home to see whether Junior 168
brought home his report card. If you prefer, you can relax 180
as long as you wish in a tub or snooze through a TV program 192
or two that you cannot get at home. By contrast, what's it 204
like when you get trapped into staying all night in a home? 216

3   In the first place, you have trouble finding the home. 228
Your host cannot take you, of course, because he has to zip 240
home ahead of you. If he lives in town, it is in an apart- 252
ment that your taxi driver cannot locate. If he lives in a 264
suburb, which is quite likely, the train he suggests is one 276
that, it turns out, runs just on Sundays. So you catch the 288
bus; and, of course, the directions he gave you for getting 300
from the station do not serve to get you from the bus stop. 312
When you do arrive, the host has hopefully given up on you. 324

NOTE: These paragraphs are also excellent for increasing your skill:

1. Read the material.

2. Practice the three hardest words you see in each paragraph.

3. Take a 5-minute timed writing with a 10-second rest after each minute.

4. Practice words with which you had trouble.

5. Take a final 5-minute writing, without rests.

4   The family has eaten, of course; but it is no trouble, 336
no trouble at all, to fix up something for you. So you eat 348
cold food that squelches such appetite as you brought along 360
while the family sits there and watches each jiggle of your 372
fork. Then your hostess, after a suspiciously long session 384
of dishwashing, packs the little ones off to bed. But they 396
do not fall asleep; they have been shuffled to create a bed 408
vacancy. Thus you waste all evening, trying resolutely not 420
to think of the lazy ease you would be enjoying in a hotel. 432

1 | 2 | 3 | 4 | 5 | 6 | 7 | 8 | 9 | 10 | 11 | 12

140/141-C. Apply typing skill to financial statements

Boxed Tables

LINE: 60
TABS: EVERY 9 SPACES
SPACING: SINGLE
DRILLS: THREE TIMES
GOAL: LEARN TO TYPE
  BOXED TABLES
STRESS: TOUCH
  TABULATION

90-A. Maintain perfect rhythm—including the tabulating in line 2—if you possibly can.

90-A. Tune up on these review lines

1   eat ice vex few bye jet keg elm row pen que set ode the zoo

2    $10 $28 $39 $47 $56 $10 $1000

3   We had 1 039 employees in 1947 and 2 847 employees in 1956.

90-B. To gain speed, type each line three or more times. To gain accuracy, type the group of lines (like a paragraph) three times.

90-B. Maintain rhythm on these preview words

4   model plane being seize every ahead prize quest tasks quota

5   true test drug shop jugs desk keep beat only dull need dare

6   job day new lab fix try way who one not can for old any par

90-C. In Lesson 90, first take a 2-minute writing or make one copy of paragraph 7 (SI 1.13—very easy), trying to complete it in 2 minutes. Then, practice paragraph 8 (SI 1.28—fairly easy) in the same manner; and, finally, practice paragraph 9 (SI 1.44—normal) similarly.

Then, in Lesson 91, take a 5-minute timing on the three paragraphs together or make one copy, trying to finish it in 6 minutes or less.

SI 1.27 allover—fairly easy when practiced.

Use double spacing, a 50-space line, and the usual tab-5 indention.

90-C. Sustain speed on fluent alphabetic paragraphs

7   Much of the work in any kind of job is about   10
the same, day in and day out. This is as true in   20
the clouds where you test a new model of a plane,   30
or in a lab where you work with a new drug, or in   40
a shop where you design new ways to fix up broken   50
jugs as it is at an office desk. The way to keep   60
from being bored is to seize every chance to beat   70
the record, to try the unique, and to find better   80
ways to do all the things you have to do somehow.   90

8   The only sure way to get ahead in most kinds   100
of work is to gain a reputation for doing good or   110
better work. If you are the only person who does   120
a certain job, no one knows whether you deserve a   130
prize or not. Only in the routine tasks that you   140
do in common with other people can what you do be   150
compared. Only in these things can others recog-   160
nize that your work excels. If you want success,   170
your quest should be for skill in doing the dull.   180

9   But there is one hazard about which most new   190
workers have to be cautioned, and that is the old   200
danger that the new worker does not know what has   210
already been tried and rejected by the older mem-   220
bers of the firm. A quota of natural mistakes in   230
judgment is permitted to any newcomer; but trying   240
to tell more experienced workers what they should   250
be doing is not included in the newcomer's quota.   260
One has to reach par before he dare coach others.   270

   1 | 2 | 3 | 4 | 5 | 6 | 7 | 8 | 9 | 10

Tables 32-33
RECONCILIATION
WITH LEADERS
1. Single spaced on
   60-space line
2. Double spaced on
   56-space line

Jos. Cooper & Sons
BANK RECONCILIATION STATEMENT
Month Ending April 30, 19—

Open space at
start and end
of leader line

Bank balance, March 31	$10 722.58
Deposit, April 4	2 750.00
Deposit, April 11	2 750.00
Deposit, April 18	2 750.00
Deposit, April 25	3 000.00
Total deposits and balance	$21 972.58
Cheques cleared since March 31	$ 9 633.75
Cheque Apl4 outstanding	525.25
Cheque Apl78 outstanding	100.00
Total cheques drawn	10 259.00
Corrected bank balance	$11 713.58
Chequebook balance	$11 713.58

Leaders end at
same point

To arrange table
on an assigned
length of line,
pivot from right
to set tabs for
money columns*

These are "close" or "solid" leaders;
compare with "open" ones, page 215

$10 722.58 $21 972.58

* Tab stops help only in locating the
first entry in each money column.
The other entries and leaders are
aligned visually—you have to look.

Tables 34-35
INCOME STATEMENT
WITH LEADERS
1. May, 60 spaces,
   single spaced
2. June, 56 spaces,
   double spaced

Lincoln & Packer, Ltd.
INCOME STATEMENT
For the Month Ending May 31, 19--

Compare with
Table 30 for
capitalization
and phrasing.

SALES		$27 453.28	$26 943.35
COST OF MERCHANDISE			
Starting inventory	$15 267.00		$12 613.50
Inventory purchases	8 476.50		18 732.90
Total available	$23 743.50		$31 346.40
Closing inventory	12 613.50		19 290.60
Cost of merchandise sold		11 130.00	12 055.80
GROSS PROFIT ON SALES		$16 323.28	$14 887.55
EXPENSES			
Selling expense	$ 5 425.85		$ 5 109.20
Rent expense	2 500.00		2 500.00
Heat and light	620.43		481.30
Depreciation of equipment	1 000.00		1 000.00
Total expenses		9 546.28	9 090.50
NET PROFIT, BEFORE TAXES		$ 6 777.00	$ 5 797.05

use this

— June 30

13
14
33
34
49
58
59
65
74
83
84
98
106
113
121
129
136
145

Table 19

RULED TABLE
Paper: full, plain
Spacing: single

In ruled table, lines are typed as underscores.

National Motor Company

POSITION IN THE AUTO INDUSTRY

(In Thousands of Units)

Year	Industry	Number We Made	Percent We Made
1955	6666	1555	23.2%
1957	5433	1166	21.4%
1959	4312	1003	23.3%
1961	6117	1541	25.2%
1963	5559	1688	30.4%
1965	7908	2238	28.3%

90-D. Produce tables in "boxed" form

A *boxed* table is one with both vertical and horizontal ruled lines. The lines divide the columns and headings but do not close in the sides. The typist types the table as usual, *omitting all the rules but leaving space for them,* and then draws the lines by pen or pencil and ruler. Fine points:

1. The horizontal lines should extend 3 strokes beyond the two sides of the typed table.

2. The vertical lines should be centered within the 6 blank spaces left between the columns.

3. It is acceptable to type the horizontal lines and draw the vertical ones; but it is preferable to draw all the lines so they match each other.

Compare Tables 19 and 20. They are to be done alike except that all the rules in Table 20 are to be drawn in after the table has been typed.

Table 20

BOXED TABLE
Paper: full, plain
Spacing: single

In boxed table, lines are drawn after the table has been typed.

National Motor Company

POSITION IN THE AUTO INDUSTRY

(In Thousands of Units)

Year	Industry	Number We Made	Percent We Made
1955	6666	1555	23.2%
1957	5433	1166	21.4%
1959	4312	1003	23.3%
1961	6117	1541	25.2%
1963	5559	1688	30.4%
1965	7908	2238	28.3%

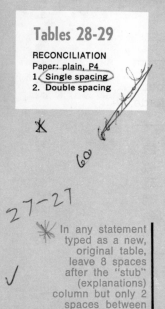

Tables 28-29

RECONCILIATION
Paper: plain, P4
1. Single spacing
2. Double spacing

In any statement typed as a new, original table, leave 8 spaces after the "stub" (explanations) column but only 2 spaces between money columns.

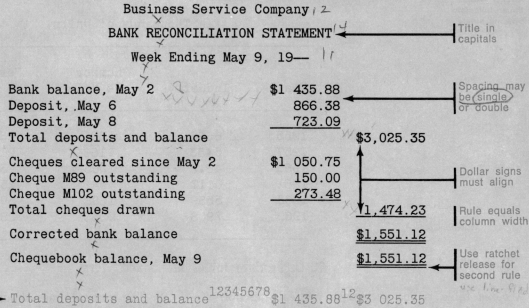

Center

Business Service Company

BANK RECONCILIATION STATEMENT

Week Ending May 9, 19—

Bank balance, May 2	$1 435.88	
Deposit, May 6	866.38	
Deposit, May 8	723.09	
Total deposits and balance		$3,025.35
Cheques cleared since May 2	$1 050.75	
Cheque M89 outstanding	150.00	
Cheque M102 outstanding	273.48	
Total cheques drawn		1,474.23
Corrected bank balance		$1,551.12
Chequebook balance, May 9		$1,551.12

Title in capitals

Spacing may be single or double

Dollar signs must align

Rule equals column width

Use ratchet release for second rule

Total deposits and balance 12345678 $1 435.88 12 $3 025.35

Before typing Tables 28-31, read 138-C carefully—doing so can save you much time, particularly in Table 31.

Tables 30-31

INCOME STATEMENT
1. February
2. March

The Winslow-Halpin Company

INCOME STATEMENT

Month Ending February 28, 19--

	February	March 31
SALES	$48 431	$49 651
DEDUCT COST OF MERCHANDISE SOLD:		
Merchandise Inventory, February 1	$16 401	$16 512
Merchandise Purchases	35 208	33 147
Total Available for Sale	$51 609	$49 659
Merchandise Inventory, February 28	16 512	14 185
Total Cost of Merchandise Sold	35 097	35 474
GROSS PROFITS ON SALES	$13 334	$14 177
DEDUCT EXPENSES:		
Selling Expense	$ 4 131	$ 4 273
Rent Expense	1 024	1 194
Heat and Light	261	273
Depreciation of Equipment	500	480
Total Expenses	5 916	6 220
NET PROFIT, BEFORE TAXES	$ 7 418	$ 7 957

A *braced* heading identifies and is centered above two or more columns (example: *Men Employees* in Table 21). Technical fine points:

1. Omit the braced heading (but leave appropriate space for it) until the line under the braced heading has been typed; then, turn back the paper and carefully insert the braced heading.

2. Easiest way to center the braced heading over its columns: count the spaces in the columns' area (including the spaces between the columns) and the spaces in the braced heading; then, from the start of the first column, indent the braced heading half the difference in the two counts (drop any fraction). Thus, *Men Employees* (13) takes 6 spaces less than *Number*+6+*Percent* (19) and so is indented 3 spaces from the start of the *Number* column.

3. Use of a braced heading in a table requires the use of the *boxed*-table arrangement.

Table 21

BOXED TABLE WITH
BRACED HEADINGS

Table 1

SUMMARY OF OFFICE EMPLOYEES

Year	Men Employees		Women Employees		Total
	Number	Percent	Number	Percent	
1940	32	40.0%	48	60.0%	80
1945	35	38.8%	55	61.2%	90
1950	40	38.1%	65	61.9%	105
1955	40	32.0%	85	68.0%	125
1960	45	31.2%	99	68.8%	144
1965	37	38.1%	60	61.9%	97

Note that the number of a table, if it has one, is centered above the title line.

Table 22

BOXED TABLE
METRIC SYMBOLS

SYMBOL TABLE FOR COMMONLY USED PREFIXES

Prefix	Meaning	Symbol	Multiplier
mega	one million	M	1 000 000
kilo	one thousand	k	1 000
hecto	one hundred	h	100
deca	ten	da	10
deci	one tenth of a	d	0.1
centi	one hundredth of a	c	0.01
milli	one thousandth of a	m	0.001
micro	one millionth of a	μ	0.000 001

LINE: 60
SPACING: SINGLE
DRILLS: THREE EACH
GOAL: MASTERY OF
  LEADERED TABLES
STRESS: PRECISION

Unit 23. Tabulation

138-A. Lines three or more times; type lines 2 and 3 in cadence with someone who sets even pace by typing line 1. Then, reverse roles.

138-A. Tune up on these review lines

1 They will seek some more work when they have done your job.

2 The banquet speaker, James Boxell, analyzed a few carvings.

3 we 23 25 27 29 ow 92 94 96 98 to 59 57 55 53 up 70 68 66 64

    1 | 2 | 3 | 4 | 5 | 6 | 7 | 8 | 9 | 10 | 11 | 12

138-B. Target on goal.

ACCURACY: Three copies of lines 4-6 as though they were a paragraph.

SPEED: Three copies of each, consecutively.

138-B. Increase skill on an acceleration preview

4 backspacing example, easiest columns tables size you get it

5 explanation whatever squared special method type not six or

6 statements financial quarter project hazard sign the end of

138-C. Adjust machine: 50-space line, double spacing, and a tab-5.

Type one complete copy in Lesson 138; repeat in Lesson 139. GOAL: a copy in six minutes or less, with three or fewer typing errors.

Or, take one 5-minute writing, with a short rest after each minute, in Lesson 138; and one similar writing, but without any rests, as a Lesson 139 follow-up.

SI 1.29—fairly easy

138-C. Sustain skill on technical, alphabetic paragraphs

7   Of all the forms of tables, the ones easiest   10
to set up are financial statements. They are al-   20
ways in the same form, month after month, quarter   30
after quarter. The right way to set up a new one   40
is to copy the old one; that is, you get from the   50
files the last statement of the same type, insert   60
it in the machine, and set up your margin and tab   70
stops by eye. If there is none to copy, however,   80
you can plan it just as you would any other kind,   90
size, or form of table: simply backspace to cen-   100
ter it. There is even a special method, based on   110
the fact that the explanations column can be wide   120
or narrow, as you may wish. You set your margins   130
for whatever line length you wish; you pivot from   140
the right margin, backspacing through your amount   150
columns and setting tab stops for them. Then you   160
use whatever space is left for your first column.   170

8   There are some things you must keep in mind.   180
For example, all dollar marks in a column must be   190
squared up; and you might forget that the longest   200
number, which makes the dollar sign project most,   210
may be the one at the bottom of the column. Note   220
that you do not put six spaces between columns in   230
a statement; instead, put two spaces between your   240
money columns and eight spaces between the state-   250
ment column and the following money column. When   260
you type lines of leaders, watch one more hazard: 270
you must not forget to leave one blank space both   280
at the start and at the end of a line of leaders.   290

  1 | 2 | 3 | 4 | 5 | 6 | 7 | 8 | 9 | 10

SPECIAL NOTE: On pages 267-270 of your workbook is a powerhouse of drills to strengthen your grip of the keyboard. If the numbers in the tables on the following pages give you trouble, concentrate on workbook page 269!

LINE: 60
TAB: EVERY 9 SPACES
SPACING: SINGLE
GOAL: REVIEW TABLE
   PRODUCTION
STRESS: ATTENTION
   TO DETAILS

92-A. Each drill three or more times. Do the special extra-spacing drill (No. 3) wholly by touch, alternating the pair of lines.

92-B. For an accuracy gain, type the drills four times as a paragraph; for a speed gain, type each line four times.

92-C. Type a complete copy (GOAL: Finish it within 6 minutes and within 3 errors).

Or, in Lesson 92, take a 5-minute timing with a 10-second rest after each minute; and, then, in Lesson 93, take a 5-minute writing with no pauses to rest.

Adjust the machine for double spacing, a 55-space line, and a 5-space tab indention.

SI 1.33—fairly easy

92-A. Tune up on these lines

1 aid ice jig kin rip sir wit zip bit fix him via qui oil yip

2 I asked discounts of 47% and 56% but got 10%, 28%, and 39%.

3
| 100 | 280 | 390 | 470 | 560 | 100 | 10.00 |
| 47 | 56 | 39 | 28 | 10 | 1000 | 100.00 |

92-B. Regain rhythm on these fluent preview words

4 which table often three first model which shown other lines

5 must know this form when they have many most will have been

6 can use the one for its use and can set off any but has not

7 is to be if we to do so or is he to do or be to us am or by

92-C. Sustain your rate on this fairly easy copy

8 It is not often that the typist has to select the
style in which to arrange a table, for the patterns to
be used are usually determined by the character of the
table or the occasion for its use; but the typist must
know any table can be set up in at least three styles,
which are shown by the three model tables that follow.

9 First of all, the table can be set up in the open
form; this form requires no ruled lines other than the
underscores that set off the column headings and total
lines if and when they are used. This style is picked
for very short tables and for tables in letter bodies.

10 Second, the table can be displayed in ruled form,
which uses horizontal lines of underscores to mark off
the main parts of the table. This is the normal style
for use in tables in formal papers and reports and for
tables that are wide or have many very narrow columns.

11 Third, the boxed form can be used for this table;
in this form the columns and headings and footings are
set apart by both vertical and horizontal lines, which
most commonly are drawn on the table after it has been
typed. This form is the one that must be used where a
braced column heading is involved or when a table will
be very long or has many columns or is fairly complex.

11 | 22 | 33 | 44 | 55 | 66 | 77 | 88 | 99 | 110 | 121 | 132 | 143 | 154 | 165 | 176 | 187 | 198 | 209 | 220 | 231 | 242 | 253

1 | 2 | 3 | 4 | 5 | 6 | 7 | 8 | 9 | 10 | 11

Manuscript 18

CENTERED DISPLAY
Paper: workbook
   page 161 or plain
Directions: center
   a double-spaced copy
   of 92-C on the full
   page. Entitle it
   THREE WAYS TO
   TYPE ANY TABLE

92/93-D. Produce a project that reviews table styles

Using workbook pages 161-164 or four sheets of plain paper, center Manuscript 18 and Tables 23-25 according to the directions. GOAL: To complete each of the four assignments within 7 minutes and 4 errors.

Letter 66

BLOCKED TWO-PAGE
BUSINESS LETTER

Paper: standard, with 15
line-space deep letterhead,
on workbook page 263
Paragraphs: 6
Body: 308 words
SI: 1.38—average

Mr. Nelson B. Pierce, Director of Re- 13
search, Pearson and Pierce, Ltd., 829 St. 21
George Street, Moncton, New Brunswick 29
E1C 1V8 (*Salutation*) SUBJECT: RE- 49
QUEST FOR YOUR REPORT 53

It is our hope that you will soon be able 63
to finish the study you are making of our 71
garage operation and to let us have your 79
report. A number of recent developments 87
have occurred which make it urgent that 95
we have your report soon; here are four: 104

First, there has been no decrease in the 113
number of complaints that we are getting 121
from our customers; if anything, we note 129
a slight increase in the number. We do not 138
dare delay action very much longer. Second, 148
our loss from the operation of the garage 157
is still mounting; again, we feel we must 165
take some action. Even as we wait for 173
your report and findings, our balance 180
sheet gets worse and worse. 186

Third, the workmen at the garage have 195
become more and more apprehensive about 203
the work of your team and of the possible 211
results of their study. Rumors of every kind 220
are flying, as you would imagine. The men 229
are showing the strain. We lost a foreman 238
last week, and today a group of six work- 246
men began talking about quitting. Fourth, 255
the agent of the firm that has sounded us 264
out about buying the property tells us that 272
his customer seems to have lost interest and 281
is looking at several other garages. The 290
agent may or may not be trying to force 298
us to a lower figure, but his pressure does 307
enter the story. 310

We would not wish you to neglect any 343
part of the study which is vital, of course; 352

but the members of the board and com- 359
pany officers are no less eager to learn 367
your findings than are the men in the 375
garage. All of us hope, therefore, that you 384
will find it practical to give us your report 393
within the next three weeks and will tell 401
us when we may expect to receive it. 409
(*Complimentary closing*) 414

GRISTMEYER BROTHERS Senior Vice-Pres- 428
ident, JKE:URS 431

Letter 67

BLOCKED TWO-PAGE
BUSINESS LETTER

Paper: P5, on workbook
page 265
Paragraphs: 5
Body: 254 words
SI: 1.37—average

Repeat the same letter, with these modifications:
(1) Delete the *fourth* reason given in the letter and
change the ending of the first paragraph to "here
are three:"; (2) change the inside address by deleting
Mr. Pierce's name and title, and make the corresponding changes in the salutation and closing.

✓

Letter 68

BLOCKED LETTER

Paper: P5 on workbook
page 265
Paragraphs: 3
Body: 85 words
SI: 1.34—fairly easy

Miss Dorrie Anne Barr, whose address 14
you have [Letter 65]. (*Salutation*) 29

Thank you for replying so promptly to 38
my request for permission to tell about 46
your fire fighting with Flameproof Fabrics. 55
We do understand and honor your reasons 64
for not wishing your name or that of your 72
firm to be linked to the story. We assure 81
you that such use as we may make of the 89
incident will involve no names. We are 98
grateful to you for reporting the matter to 106
us; if we can repay your favor in the future, 116
please let us do so. (*Complimentary closing,* 125
etc.) 138

Table 23

OPEN TABLE
Paper: workbook
page 162 or plain
Special: double
space the body

Table 3

AGES OF OFFICE EMPLOYEES

Range	Men	Women	Total
To 25	43	150	193
26-35	70	68	138
36-45	53	81	134
46-55	39	69	108
56-65	22	38	60
66 up	2	6	8
TOTAL	229	412	641

Table 24

RULED TABLE
Paper: workbook
page 163 or plain
Special: insert
today's date as a
subtitle line

Table 3

AGES OF OFFICE EMPLOYEES

Range	Men	Women	Total
To 25	43	150	193
26-35	70	68	138
36-45	53	81	134
46-55	39	69	108
56-65	22	38	60
66 up	2	6	8
TOTAL	229	412	641

Table 25

BOXED TABLE WITH
BRACED HEADINGS
Paper: workbook
page 164 or plain
Special: condense
table as shown*

* Condense this table
in these two ways:
1. For each ruled line
double space instead
of triple spacing (as
you did in Table 21).
2. Instead of leaving
the standard 6 spaces
between columns, leave
only 4 spaces.

Table 3

AGES OF OFFICE EMPLOYEES

Range	Men		Women	
	No.	Percent	No.	Percent
To 25	43	18.8%	150	36.4%
26-35	70	30.6%	68	16.5%
36-45	53	23.1%	81	19.7%
46-55	39	17.0%	69	16.7%
56-65	22	9.6%	38	9.2%
66 up	2	0.9%	6	1.5%
TOTAL	229	100.0%	412	100.0%

136/137-D. Learn and apply rules about letter technicalities

LETTER SALUTATIONS *capitalize & underscore*

indent 5 *go back to margin*

1. Use the last name of the addressee if it is known, preceded by *Dear* and a title, thus:

Dear Mr. Lench:	Dear Prof. Grant:
Dear Miss Barr:	Dear Doctor Hall:

tab this

2. Whenever a letter is addressed to a firm or department instead of to a person by name or title, and always after an attention line, use *Gentlemen:*.

3. If a letter is addressed to a person by a business title (as, *Personnel Director*) without the use of a name, use *Dear Madam/Sir:* as the salutation.

4. Use a first name (as, *Dear Jack:*) only when it is dictated or was used in previous letters.

5. Plural salutations are quite acceptable:

Dear Mr. and Mrs. Jones: (both)
Dear Mr. and Mrs. Jones: (either)
Dear Miss Hall and Mr. Williams:
Dear Committee Members:
Dear Friends: or *Ladies and Gentlemen:*

6. Professional titles like *Doctor, Professor,* and *Captain* may be spelled out or abbreviated.

LETTER COMPLIMENTARY CLOSINGS

7. A closing means the same no matter in what sequence words appear or whether *very* is used. Thus, *Cordially yours, Very cordially yours,* and *Yours very cordially,* all mean the same.

8. Use a "truly" closing (*a*) whenever a letter is frosty or formal and (*b*) whenever *Gentlemen, Dear Madam:* or *Dear Sir:* is used as the salutation.

9. Use a "cordially" or "sincerely" closing if the letter is casual, friendly, or sales-slanted *and* if the addressee is named in the salutation.

10. Use a "respectfully" closing in a letter to anyone to whom great respect is due, such as a churchman, public official, or elderly person.

11. Use an informal closing (like *See you soon!*) only when it is specifically dictated.

12. In case of doubt, use a "truly" closing.

LETTER PARAGRAPHING

13. Letters should have at least two paragraphs.
14. Paragraphs should reflect the letter parts.
15. No paragraph should exceed ten lines.

Letter 64 ✓

BLOCKED LETTER
Paper: P5,
workbook 261
Body: 101 words
Paragraphs: 3
SI: 1.39—normal

This letter is to Mr. John K. Lench *of* Young & Wilde, Ltd., *whose address is* 4422 Yorkton Street *in* Digby, Nova Scotia. (*Salutation*)   15 / 27

Your inquiry about the use of Flameproof Fabrics for drapes in a business office has been forwarded from our Digby branch. Flameproof Fabrics were developed to meet the need of offices for a drape material that would conform to Fire Code standards for buildings that were to be insured as fireproof structures. You will find, on page 11 of the enclosed booklet, precise details on the resistance value of each of our four grades of Flameproof Fabrics. If you need a statement to show to your insurance agent, the branch at which you made the purchase will issue one to you. (*Complimentary closing*)   40 / 55 / 69 / 83 / 98 / 112 / 126 / 140 / 150

From Paul F. Clarke, Jr., Service Manager. (*Reference lines*)   164

Letter 65 ⌄

BLOCKED LETTER
Paper: P5,
workbook 261
Body: 110 words
Paragraphs: 3
SI: 1.34—fairly easy

This letter is to Miss Dorrie Anne Barr, *at* 805 Sixth Avenue N.W., Moose Jaw, Saskatchewan S6H 4A3. (*Salutation*)   16 / 29

Thank you for all those kind things you said about our Flameproof Fabrics in the letter you wrote us on May 12. Although we have received letters in the past which gave tribute to the colors and patterns built into our fabrics, we have never before received one that described so vividly how a drape was torn down and used to smother a fire that had started. Miss Barr, you certainly thought quickly! Your letter was so novel that it has been shown to most of our executive staff, all of whom wondered whether you might permit us to tell your story in our advertising. May we have your permission?   43 / 59 / 73 / 87 / 101 / 117 / 131 / 144 / 153

Close in the same way you did Letter 66.   170

Unit 16. Manuscripts

News Releases

LINE: 60
TAB: 5
SPACING: SINGLE
GOAL: LEARN ABOUT
NEWS RELEASES
STRESS: FULL POWER
IN PRODUCTION

94-A. Lines three times. If possible, have a classmate type line 1 to set a cadence for you to match while typing lines 2 and 3.

94-A. Tune up on these review lines

1 oar zoo box quo cod boy woe son fog mop how vox oil oak jot

2 If the SHIFT LOCK is depressed, New York IS typed NEW YORK.

3 On March 10, 1928 and 1939; and on April 28, 1947 and 1956.

94-B. To gain speed, type each line three or more times. To gain accuracy, type the group of lines (like a paragraph) three times.

94-B. Stabilize rhythm on these preview words

4 large first steps would could green prize sound quite short

5 made fine then wish must find what kind will sell best when

6 new one for box let use you buy out to do so or if it is so

94-C. Type two complete copies (one in Lesson 94, one in Lesson 95). GOAL: To finish each copy within 5 minutes and within 3 errors.

Or, take a 5-minute writing in Lesson 94 with 10-second rests after each minute; then, take a 5-minute writing in Lesson 95 without rests. GOAL: 40 or more wam with 3 or fewer errors.

Use double spacing, a 5-space indention.

SI 1.20—easy (good for increasing speed)

94-C. Sustain speed on fluent alphabetic paragraphs

7 If you made a fine new product that you wished to sell   12
to the public at large, one of your first steps would be to   24
find what kind of package for your product would appeal the   36
most to your customers. If you learned that you could sell   48
it best in a green cake box with a prize thrown in for good   60
measure, you would use a green cake box with a prize, would   72
you not? Your sound judgment would require that you do so.   84

8   That theme is quite important to the typist. When you   96
type a manuscript that you hope to have published, the work 108
you turn out is the product; and the person who receives it 120
and reads it and passes judgment on it is, let us hope, the 132
customer. If you really do wish to sell your product, then 144
you must find out in what kind of package he is most likely 156
to buy your product. An editor of a magazine, for example, 168
is more likely to buy your article or one you type for your 180
employer if it is typed with wide margins; so of course you 192
use a short line. You know: green cake box, with a prize. 204

1 | 2 | 3 | 4 | 5 | 6 | 7 | 8 | 9 | 10 | 11 | 12

If you do not have the news releases on workbook pages 165 and 167, type only Manuscripts 19 and 22, arranging both like Manuscript 19.

94/95-D. Apply your skill to producing news releases

Review the use of revision symbols, page 112; then, type the news releases that follow. GOAL: Each within 7 minutes and 3 errors.

LINE: 60
TAB: 5
SPACING: SINGLE
DRILLS: THREE EACH
GOAL: MASTER LETTER
 TECHNICALITIES
STRESS: ATTENTION
 TO FINE DETAILS

136-A. Each line three times or two ½-minute timings on each line. Repeat in Lesson 137.

136-A. Tune up on these review lines

1　The two men who had had the car got the gas and oil for us.
2　Jack's man found exactly a quarter in the woven zipper bag.
3　we 23 22 21 20 to 59 58 57 56 or 94 93 92 91 it 85 84 83 82
　　 1 | 2 | 3 | 4 | 5 | 6 | 7 | 8 | 9 | 10 | 11 | 12

136-B. Type to your goal.

ACCURACY: Three copies of lines 4-7 as though they were a paragraph.

SPEED: Three copies of each line consecutively.

136-B. Increase skill on an acceleration preview

4　paragraphs graciously sentences question, proposal message:
5　factors typical writing obvious divide finale allows single
6　break serve parts first right when must that each will then
7　how may two has try the out and now but any ten it is so be

136-C. Change to double spacing. Follow steps:

1. Read the material.

2. Practice the rapid insertion of an extra line, followed by the all-capital sideheadings.

3. Take a 5-minute timed writing, pausing for a 10-second rest after each minute; or type one copy, pausing to rest after every 5 or 6 full lines.

4. Take a 5-minute timed writing, without pauses; or type a copy without pausing a single time.

GOAL: To finish the copy within 5 minutes and with 3 or fewer errors.

SI 1.28—fairly easy

136-C. Sustain skill on fairly easy production copy

8　　When the typist must decide how to break a letter into　　12
paragraphs, two factors may be counted on to act as guides.　　24

OUTLINE OF THE LETTER　　29
　　The typical letter has three parts. Try to divide the　　41
letter so that each of these parts stands out very clearly.　　53
　　The first part tells who is writing the letter, why it　　65
is written, and how it happens to be written right now; but　　77
a typist can, of course, leave out things that are obvious.　　89
　　The second part is the main message: the details, the　　101
facts of the matter, the proposal, the question, and so on.　　113
　　The third part is the grand finale in which the writer　　125
explains what action is expected of the reader to date, and　　137
then bows out as graciously as the tone of the note allows.　　149

LENGTH OF A PARAGRAPH　　155
　　The second clue to the typist is the hope that he will　　167
be able to keep his paragraphs down to eight or fewer lines　　179
of typing; ten lines is a top limit for a single paragraph.　　191
　　It is easy to keep the first and last parts within the　　203
desired number of lines; each of these parts is a paragraph　　215
that will contain only one or two sentences, in most cases.　　227
If there is a problem, and there may not be, it will appear　　239
in the middle part of the letter, where the writer may have　　251
more to say than can be set within ten lines. In that case　　263
simply divide the part into two or more smaller paragraphs.　　275
　　 1 | 2 | 3 | 4 | 5 | 6 | 7 | 8 | 9 | 10 | 11 | 12

SPECIAL:
From now on, you will need to divide letters into their paragraphs and to provide missing salutations and closing phrases. So, read 136-C and 136-D very closely; and, then, reinforce your knowledge by doing the Learning Guide given on workbook pages 259-260.

N E W S   R E L E A S E

From James M. Donald
Press Syndicate
390 West 44 Street
New York, New York   10036

Release February 17, 19--

A TYPIST CAN WRECK A NEWS RELEASE

DATELINE

NEW YORK CITY, Feb. 17--Many a publicity ~~writer~~ expert works up
a fine press release ~~release~~ only to have his typist spoil any
chance of its getting ~~any~~ attention on an editor's desk, for
how a news release looks is just as ~~more~~ important ~~than~~ as what it says.

That is what James M. Donald, ~~distinguished~~ chief wire
editor for the Press Syndicate, told members of the New York
Publicity club at their annual luncheon for news~~hawks~~ editors, which
was attended by 200 publicists at the ~~Savoy Plaza~~ Hilton Statler today.

"We Editors receive news releases by the ~~dozen~~ score in every
mail," he said, "telling us about the great talent of a stage
star or the unsurpassed merits of some new dog food. We ought
to read each hand-out with great care, I know. But an editor
is so ~~lazy~~ busy that he is likely to use first whichever release
will require the least change and so can be put on the press
or on the wire circuit ~~most~~ easily. If you are ~~savvy~~ wise, you'll
make your releases easy for the editors to use." ~~he said~~.

Donald gave ~~seven~~ six guides for "easy to use" releases:

1. In the heading, indicate who vouches for the facts.

2. Give a clear title, telling the story in one glance.

3. Start the story with a date line: city and date.

4. Be sure the typing is correct. ~~If we spot an error, we~~ Errors make editors
wonder whether the release is reliable.

5. Use a 50- or 60-stroke line of typing, never longer.

6. Keep the story down to one page if you can. ~~We like double~~ Double
spacing is fine; ~~but~~ if you must single space, then do so.

Draft of a News Release
(arranged as it would be typed or duplicated on plain or colored paper)

United Cooperative Association

1243 Keane Street • Georgetown, Ontario

May 4, 19—

Mr. Edward L. Kingsport
The J. K. Hauser Company
7376 Grant Avenue
Moncton, New Brunswick E1A 3R4

Dear Mr. Kingsport:

We should like to invite an estimate for production
of 10,000 copies of our next price list. A copy of
our present list is enclosed to illustrate the size
and mechanical features of the publication.

We shall have the manuscript and pictures ready for
the new price list by the first of June. We require
delivery of the new edition prior to September 15.
We assure prompt handling of all proofs. Your cost
estimate should include the costs for all printing,
composition, engraving, paper, and delivery to us.

We hope that you will let us know that we may look
forward to receiving an estimate from you within a
week or ten days.

Sincerely yours,

Albert A. Arden
Advertising Manager

urs
Enclosure

THE DARRIS COMPANY

367 NORTH DRIVE, WINNIPEG, MANITOBA R3T 0A1

May 4, 19—

Mr. Edward L. Kingsport
The J. K. Hauser Company
7376 Grant Avenue
Moncton, New Brunswick E1A 3R4

Dear Mr. Kingsport:

We should like to invite an estimate for production
of 10,000 copies of our next price list. A copy of
our present list is enclosed to illustrate the size
and mechanical features of the publication.

We shall have the manuscript and pictures ready for
the new price list by the first of June. We require
delivery of the new edition prior to September 15.
We assure prompt handling of all proofs. Your cost
estimate should include the costs for all printing,
composition, engraving, paper, and delivery to us.

We hope that you will let us know that we may look
forward to receiving an estimate from you within a
week or ten days.

Sincerely yours,

Albert A. Arden
Advertising Manager

urs
Enclosure

CHARINGE

PRECISION CORPORATION
INDUSTRIAL DEVELOPMENT DEPARTMENT

22 COLE AVENUE
BOWMANVILLE, ONTARIO, L1G 1X9

May 4, 19—

Mr. Edward L. Kingsport
The J. K. Hauser Company
7376 Grant Avenue
Moncton, New Brunswick E1A 3R4

Dear Mr. Kingsport:

We should like to invite an estimate for production
of 10,000 copies of our next price list. A copy of
our present list is enclosed to illustrate the size
and mechanical features of the publication.

We shall have the manuscript and pictures ready for
the new price list by the first of June. We require
delivery of the new edition prior to September 15.
We assure prompt handling of all proofs. Your cost
estimate should include the costs for all printing,
composition, engraving, paper, and delivery to us.

We hope that you will let us know that we may look
forward to receiving an estimate from you within a
week or ten days.

Sincerely yours,

Albert A. Arden
Advertising Manager

urs
Enclosure

Canadian Paper Company
SAINT JOHN, NEW BRUNSWICK

111 BRITAIN STREET E2L 1X3
Vancouver - Montreal - Saint John

Mr. Edward L. Kingsport
The J. K. Hauser Company
7376 Grant Avenue
Moncton, New Brunswick
E1A 3R4

May 4, 19—

Dear Mr. Kingsport:

We should like to invite an estimate for production
of 10,000 copies of our next price list. A copy of
our present list is enclosed to illustrate the size
and mechanical features of the publication.

We shall have the manuscript and pictures ready for
the new price list by the first of June. We require
delivery of the new edition prior to September 15.
We assure prompt handling of all proofs. Your cost
estimate should include the costs for all printing,
composition, engraving, paper, and delivery to us.

We hope that you will let us know that we may look
forward to receiving an estimate from you within a
week or ten days.

Sincerely yours,

Albert A. Arden
Advertising Manager

urs
Enclosure

LETTER 60: A4 (European) stationery . . . 29.7 cm by 21 cm . . . accommodates letters on 40-, 50-, 60-stroke line, like standard stationery, but center is 2 strokes left . . . date on line 15 . . . address 8 lines lower.

LETTER 61: LEFT-WEIGHTED standard P4 stationery . . . 21.5 cm x 28 cm . . . center is moved 5 strokes to right, but otherwise placement is standard: 40-, 50-, 60-stroke line, with date on line 15 and address begun 5 lines lower.

LETTER 62: DEEP-LETTERHEAD standard P4 stationery . . . 21.5 cm x 28 cm . . . letterhead more than 12 linespaces deep . . . uses 40-, 50-, 60-stroke line . . . date goes at right, 3 lines below letterhead . . . address only 3 lines below.

LETTER 63: Standard WINDOW stationery . . . for use with window envelope . . . center address in cornered area . . . placement otherwise normal: date on line 15, salutation on line 25 (as though address were in normal position).

NEWS RELEASE

MARTIN MILLER and SONS
58 BROADVIEW STREET
TORONTO, ONTARIO M4M 2E4

RELEASE: February 18, 19—

FROM: William V. Miller ▼ 3

Manuscript 20

NEWS RELEASE
Shown: in elite
Form: workbook
Spacing: double
SI: 1.47—fairly difficult

NEW USE OF COLOR INCREASE*S* PRODUCTION RATES ▼ 3

TORONTO, ~~Ontario~~ *Ont.*, Feb. 18—Painting the work~~ing~~ spaces in offices and factories ~~with~~ the right color can ~~bring about~~ *result in* much higher production rates, according to the results of a practical test ~~which has just been~~ *recently* completed by the Research department of Martin Miller & Sons, of this city.

"Using the bright color," said Richard Miller, director of the MM&S research *program*, "does not make the machinery go ~~any~~ faster or the mechanics work any harder. ~~But~~ *#* But the right color reduces eye strain; and ~~that~~ *this* means much less fatigue, and fewer accidents, and a lessening of tension ~~in~~ *among* workers. ~~Boosts~~ *Increases* in production rates are a natural result."

The ~~test~~ of "color dynamics" was made in several departments of the Clover Mills Company, Amherstburg, Ontario. The results credited color with reducing absenteeism by hundreds of hours and *with* allover production ~~boosts~~ *increases* of 7 per cent in the factory and 9% in the offices.

The color is applied to walls, to machinery, and to work areas,— ~~including~~ *even* floors. The plan tested at Clover reduced ~~inside~~ *from outside* glare and, at the same time, provided eye-rest areas that lessened eye strain and the tensions to which ~~this~~ *it* usually leads. The paints used, especially manufactured (for the purpose by MM&S), ~~is~~ *are* nonreflective and gloss free.

Draft of a News Release
(arranged as it would be typed or duplicated on a news release form)

Manuscript 21	Retype Manuscript 19 on a	**Manuscript 22**	Retype Manuscript 20 on plain
NEWS RELEASE	news release form (workbook). Use single spacing.	NEWS RELEASE	paper, as shown on page 147. Use double spacing.

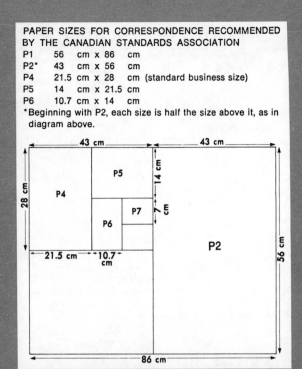

LETTER 59: P5 stationery . . . 14 cm x 21.5 cm . . . accommodates up to 125 words on 40-stroke line only . . . longer letters require second page . . . date goes on line 9 or 10 . . . address begins 4 lines below the date.

Letters 59-63

BLOCKED LETTERS ON PROBLEM STATIONERY
Body: 120 words
SI: 1.42—normal

SPECIAL DIRECTIONS: Type this letter five times—three times on the different styles and once on each of the P4, P5, and A4 sizes—all illustrated above and on page 206. Use workbook pages 253-258 or plain paper on which you mark lines to simulate the proportions and arrangements of the six letterheads.

Mr. E. L. Kingsport | J. K. Hauser Company | 32 Grant Street | 18
Moncton, New Brunswick E1A 3R4 | Dear Mr. Kingsport: | 30

    Thank you for sending us so quickly your estimate for producing 10,000 copies of our price list. We are more than pleased by the promptness with which you replied.   43 / 56 / 64

    We are equally pleased by the figures you supplied, but they are so much lower than we had anticipated that we wonder whether you might have left out some cost factor. There is no mention, for example, of our use of a second color; is it included in the press charges, or is it an oversight?   77 / 88 / 101 / 114 / 123

    We are ready to accept your bid but feel you should have a chance to confirm it or correct it before we issue a contract on it. May we expect to hear from you soon?   136 / 149 / 158

    Sincerely yours, | Albert A. Arden | Advertising Manager | urs   175

1 | 2 | 3 | 4 | 5 | 6 | 7 | 8 | 9 | 10 | 11 | 12 | 13

Publishing

96-A. Tune up on these review lines

1 buzz vous quit must jury crux sunk cuff pour laud huge lure
2 we 23 up 70 or 94 et 35 pi 08 to 59 it 85 ow 92 ep 30 we 23
3 Names of "stores" (like Morgan's) have to be "capitalized."

96-A. Lines three times. If possible, have a classmate type line 1 to set a cadence for you to match as you type lines 2 and 3.

96-B. Stabilize rhythm on these preview words

4 guide sheet which heavy lines zones other place under quick
5 this task each time mark that will type same page sure that
6 one for all who odd job use off and any set all you can new

96-B. To gain speed, type each line three or more times, speeding up as you repeat it. To gain in accuracy, type the whole group of lines three or more times, trying to hold your pace constant.

96-C. Sustain speed on fluent alphabetic paragraphs

7 One of the best tricks of the typing trade, a trick to   12
be recommended for all who frequently have to type some odd   24
kind of typing task, is the use of a visual guide. This is   36
just a sheet of paper on which you draw heavy lines to mark   48
off the margin zones, center point, and any other factor in   60
the arrangement of that odd task. Then, each time you must   72
do that task, you simply place the guide under the paper on   84
which you will type; the lines show through to guide you as   96
you set the margins, and so on, for doing that special job.   108

8 For example, suppose that the man for whom you work is   120
the author of a column in a journal or a magazine. All the   132
manuscripts you type for him should be set up alike, always   144
with the same margins, same display of headings, same posi-   156
tion for page numbers, and so on. Rather than try to memo-   168
rize the settings, design a visual guide that shows all the   180
details; then you can be ready to type a new installment in   192
one quick minute or less, sure that the form is consistent.   204

1 | 2 | 3 | 4 | 5 | 6 | 7 | 8 | 9 | 10 | 11 | 12

96-C. Type two complete copies, one in Lesson 96 and one in Lesson 97. GOAL: To finish a copy within 5 minutes and within 3 errors. Or, take a 5-minute writing in Lesson 96 with a 10-second rest after each minute; and, take a 5-minute timing in Lesson 97 with no rest after each minute. GOAL: 40 or more words a minute within 3 or fewer errors.

SI 1.28—fairly easy

96-D. Apply your skill to typing publication manuscripts

Analyze closely the assignments on the next two pages; then, type them. GOAL: To type Manuscripts 23-24 within 5 minutes and 3 errors each, and Manuscript 25 within 10 minutes and 5 errors.

IDEA: For experience, why not make a visual guide for Manuscripts 23-24 or Manuscript 25, or both? Doing so will make typing easier.

134-A. Lines three times or two ½-minute timings on each line. Repeat in Lesson 135, as well.

134-A. Tune up on these easy review lines

1 He paid the widow for the enamel emblem he got for his pal.

2 Jack quietly gave some dog owners most of his prize boxers.

3 we 23 24 25 26 up 70 71 72 73 or 94 95 96 97 it 85 86 87 88

    1 | 2 | 3 | 4 | 5 | 6 | 7 | 8 | 9 | 10 | 11 | 12

134-B. Type to your goal.

ACCURACY: Three copies of lines 4-7 as though they were a paragraph.

SPEED: Three copies of each line consecutively.

134-B. Increase skill on metric matter

4 Refer to metric characters as symbols, not abbreviations.

5 Leave a space between the figure and the following symbol.

6 In numbers of less than 1 a zero must be used, as in 0.251.

7 Square centimetres are expressed as follows: 4 cm^2, 8 cm^2.

134-C. METRIC COPY
Change to double spacing; follow steps:

1. Scan the material.

2. Take a 5-minute timed writing, pausing for a 10-second rest after each minute; or, type one copy, pausing to rest after you finish each paragraph.

3. Take a 5-minute timed writing, without rests; or, type a copy without pausing for any rests.

GOAL: To finish the copy within 5 minutes and with 3 or fewer errors.

SI: 1.33—fairly easy

134-C. Increase skill in sustained writing

8 It is important for the typist to realize that metric 12
symbols are just that, and not abbreviations for the metric 24
term written in full. As an example, the symbol for kilo- 36
metre is km and no period is necessary. Of course, as you 48
know, all sentences end with a period; therefore, if a symbol 60
happens to be the last word in the sentence, if will be fol- 72
lowed by a period. Metric terms are written in full unless 84
they are preceded by a figure. If they are preceded by a 96
figure, the symbol must be used. If the figure is written in 108
full, the metric term is likewise written in full; however, 120
it is preferable to use the figures. For the plural form the 132
symbol remains the same. 137

9 One character space on the typewriter is left between the 149
figure and the symbol, except in the case of degrees Celsius, 161
where no space is left. In numbers of less than one, a zero 173
is placed to the left of the decimal marker. To type the 185
symbol for degrees or other exponents, the typist simply uses 197
the cylinder knob to turn the cylinder back one-half line. 209
Refer often to the metric guide in this text to be sure of the 221
metric symbols. Think metric, and your function as a typist 233
will come easily. 236

    1 | 2 | 3 | 4 | 5 | 6 | 7 | 8 | 9 | 10 | 11 | 12

134-D. The six letters will make a booklet if you use workbook pages 253-258 or paper marked and cut to simulate the illustrated stationery.

134/135-D. Learn how to tailor letters to stationery
Read the next two pages; then type the problem letter correctly for each of the six letterheads described. GOAL: to produce each copy within 4 minutes and 3 errors after the machine is adjusted.

MANUSCRIPTS WITH SALESMANSHIP   18

19

By Kenneth B. Willhite   34

Formerly, Associate Editor   52

Today's Secretary   71

72

(44 Lines of 40 Spaces)   88

90

THE TYPING of a manuscript can help or   99

hinder its publication. An editor is a   107

busy person who reads many manuscripts,   115

many more than he can publish. It is   123

(Continue in column one, below.)

natural that he should be prejudiced in   8
favor of material that looks as though he   16
had written it himself.   21

There lies the secret of selling any maga-   31
zine article: Convince the editor that the   39
article was written especially for him by   48
one who knows his magazine.   54

56

IT IS NOT enough to tell the editor that   64
such is the case. The typist must prove the   73
point by the form of the manuscript. It   81
must look professional. My advice: 89

1. Type the article with the same length   98
of line as that used in the columns of the   107
magazine. Type 10 lines from a copy of the   116
magazine. Determine the average line   141
length—and use it. Do not exceed that   149
line length by more than two spaces on any   158
one line.   160

2. Precede the page number on every   168
page by the author's name.   174

3. Indicate how many lines your manu-   182
script will fill in the magazine.   189

4. Double space the manuscript. If it   198
divides into sections, like this one does,   207
type a number sign in the middle of the   215
blank line, to indicate "insert 1 blank line."   225
It counts as a whole line.   230

5. Use only P4 paper.   238

6. Use touches of the magazine's own   247
style. If it uses sideheads, use them; if it   256
uses short paragraphs, use them; if it uses   265
footnotes, so should you. If it—whatever   274
it does, so should you.   279

281

MY, WHAT a lot of trouble! Yes, but not   289
as much trouble as it is to write an article   298
and have it rejected because it did not look   307
professional—did not seem to belong in the   316
magazine.   318

(END)   323

Continuation pages of a magazine manuscript:
A. Use same line length as on page 1.
B. Type heading (author's last name, a dash, and the page number) on line 7 at the right margin.
C. Triple space before resuming the text.

Mr. John Reed Carr
Page 2
May 3, 19—

328
329
332
334
346
358
365
366
378
401
413
426
427
439
447
448
453
455
459
464
465
466

7. The page—2 heading is begun on line 7, leaving 6 lines in the top margin. Two blank lines are left between the heading and the material that follows it.

8. The second page of an interoffice memo addressed to one or two persons is given a heading like that of a letter; but if there are more addressees, give the subject of the message (as, Personnel Order No. 8) instead of listing all the names.

I hope that this information resolves your problem, Mr. Carr. Is there any other help I can offer?

Yours very sincerely,

William R. Rice
Training Consultant

urs

Second Page of a Two-Page Business Letter in Blocked Form

Letter 57

LETTER, PAGE TWO
Paper: plain
Words: 113

Arrange the page-2 material above in the alternate form shown in the illustration below.

Mr. John Reed Carr   Page 2   May 3, 19—

7. The page—2 heading is begun on line 7, leaving 6 lines in the top margin. Two blank lines are left between the heading and the material that follows it.

8. The second page of an interoffice memo addressed to one or two persons is given a heading like that of a letter; but if there are more addressees, give the subject of the message (as, Personnel Order No. 8) instead of listing all the names.

I hope that this information resolves your problem, Mr. Carr. Is there any other help I can offer?

Yours very sincerely,

William R. Rice
Training Consultant

urs

Page-2 letter heading, alternate style

Letter 58

MEMO, PAGE TWO
Paper: plain
Words: 90

Arrange the material above (delete closing paragraph) as page 2 of a memo, as illustrated below.

Personnel Order No. 8
Page 2
May 3, 19—

7. The page—2 heading is begun on line 7, leaving 6 lines in the top margin. Two blank lines are left between the heading and the material that follows it.

8. The second page of an interoffice memo addressed to one or two persons is given a heading like that of a letter; but if there are more addressees, give the subject of the message (as, Personnel Order No. 8) instead of listing all the names.

William R. Rice

urs

Page 2 of a memo, with subject heading line

Manuscript 25
BOOK MANUSCRIPT
Shown: elite draft
Paper: plain
Carbon copies: 1
Tab: 5, 10
SI: 1.44—fairly difficult

NOTES ABOUT BOOK MANUSCRIPTS
1. They are typed in standard "bound manuscript" form. Review page 114.
2. Listings are single spaced and "double indented" 10 spaces.
3. The title of the book or chapter is identified in a "running head," typed in all-caps at the left margin, on a line with the page number.

AUTHORS GUIDE   Page 21

but whether to use st, d, th, etc., after street numbers will depend on

local preference; they are omitted more and more.

2#

17. Most Common Uses of Capitals:

We apply some rules about the use of capitals so often that we do not

even think of ~~their being~~ *them as* rules. Every ~~writer~~ *author* knows, ~~we trust~~, to use

a capital letter—

> Indent
> 10 spaces.

        1)   to start a proper name.
        2)   to start any sentence.
        3)   to start a direct quotation.
        4)   to start each line in an outline or poem.

The first rule is used ~~the~~ most often, for there are so many different

~~different~~ kinds of names. We must use a capital for names of—

> In material to be
> published, italic
> type is indicated
> by underscoring.

        1)   deity, like <u>God</u> and <u>Holy Spirit</u>.
        2)   people, like <u>Joe Brown</u> and <u>Ann Smith</u>.
        3)   geographic places, like <u>Parry Sound</u>.
        4)   companies, like <u>Hudson's Bay Company</u>.
   5   6)   trade names, like <u>Ivory Soap</u> and <u>Wheaties</u>.
   6   7)   days of the week; months; holidays.

Any word substituted for a name begins with a capital, too; like <u>Windy</u>

<u>City</u> for <u>Chicago</u>, <u>Honest Abe</u> for <u>Lincoln</u>, etc.

     One rule that is often ~~forgotten~~ *overlooked* is this: Use capitals for family

titles that are used as names but are <u>not</u> preceded by a possessive pro-

noun. Thus: "My aunt ~~will~~ *would* be glad to tell Mother, but I shall ask

Father to speak to my mother first."

     When a title is used with a name in a sentence, capitalize the title

if it precedes the name <u>but not if it follows the name</u>. Thus: "There is

Professor Toth with Tom Lake, mayor of our town." Exceptions: <u>Always</u>

capitalize the title of any high government official, *such* as: "Mr. Reed, Sec-

retary of Commerce."

Draft of a Manuscript for a Book

UNIT 16   LESSON 97

Two-Page Letter
IN THE VERY, VERY FLEXIBLE
Blocked Style

Letter 56

TWO PAGES, BLOCKED
Shown: in pica
Paper: workbook 251
SI: 1.33—fairly easy

May 3, 19—   4

                                                        8

Mr. John Reed Carr   12
Director of Training   16
Parke and Wells, Ltd.   21
91, chemin de la Reine—Marie   25
Notre—Dame—du—Lac, Québec   31
                                                        32
Dear Mr. Carr: 35
                                                        36
This two—page letter illustrates the guidelines for letters   49
that take more than one page: 55
                                                        56
1. The line length and top margin are the same as for a long 69
letter. The typist uses a 60-space line of writing; types the   81
date on line 15 or 2 lines below the letterhead, whichever   93
is lower; and drops 5 lines to begin the inside address.   104
                                                        105
2. The bottom margin of page 1 should be 7 or 8 lines deep,   117
so that it will be slightly broader than either side margin;   129
but it can be as many as 10 lines deep or as few as 5.   141
                                                        142
3. At least two lines of a paragraph should be typed at the   154
foot of page 1 and at the top of page 2. If a paragraph has   166
three lines, they should all appear on one or the other page. 179
                                                        180
4. Page 1 is typed on a letterhead; page 2 is typed on plain 192
paper of the same quality as that used for the letterhead.   204
                                                        205
5. Page 2 and each additional page should have a heading so   217
complete that it would identify the page if it were detached   229
from the rest of the letter. The heading should include the   242
name of the addressee, the page number, and the date.   253
                                                        254
6. The usual arrangement of the page—2 heading is to arrange 266
the name, page number, and date in three lines blocked at the 278
left margin. The three items may, however, be displayed in   300
one line across the page, with the name at the left, the date 313
at the right, and the page number centered between them.   324

First Page of a Two-Page Business Letter in Blocked Form

LINE: 60
SPACING: SINGLE
GOAL: REVIEW PART
  FOUR TECHNICALITIES
STRESS: FOLLOWING
  DIRECTIONS EXACTLY

98-A. Copy each line for a full minute. Repeat in Lesson 99.

98-A. Tune up on these review lines

1 Let the two men get out the box and rip off the lid for us.
2 busy city edgy fray hazy joys quay yank yelp wavy waxy yams
3 Use the quotation (") for inches: 10", 28", 39", 47", 56".

98-B. To gain speed, each line three or more times. To gain accuracy, the group of lines (like a paragraph) three times.

98-B. Boost Accuracy on these preview words

4 AA paces BB about CC cares DD dictation EE speed FF offices
5 GG good HH thing II time JJ judge KK talk LL slow MM matter
6 NN number OO short PP speak QQ frequently RR rapid SS story
7 TT tenth UU unless VV very WW who XX exact YY you ZZ zigzag

98-C. Type a complete copy in each lesson (GOAL: To finish it within 5 minutes and within 3 errors).

Or, take a 5-minute timing in Lesson 98 with a 10-second rest after each minute; then, in Lesson 99, take another 5-minute timing, this time with no end-of-minute rest. GOAL: 40 or more words a minute within 3 or fewer typing errors.

Adjust the machine for double spacing, a 50-space line, and a 5-space tab indention.

SI 1.42—normal

98-C. Sustain your rate on alphabetic paragraphs

8 One of the topics frequently talked about by   10
all who work in offices is the rate of dictation.   20
Most dictators think they speak at a modest pace,   30
while most secretaries say that the dictators ac-   40
tually talk much faster than they realize. It is   50
hard to judge the exact speed of dictation unless   60
you have, and use, special devices to measure it.   70

9 A short time ago, a man who cares about this   80
matter made such a machine and measured the speed   90
of dictation as it was going on in a great number   100
of offices. When he analyzed the results, he had   110
quite a good picture of dictation and the jolting   120
news that no one has such a thing as an "average"   130
rate of expressing oneself. The speaking varies.   140

10 He suggests that dictators use four paces of   150
speaking. About a sixth of the dictation is very   160
slow, about half is fairly fast, about a third is   170
fluent, and about a tenth is very rapid. He also   180
found that there is no routine pattern; dictation   190
speed is jumbled. It zigzags from fast to rapid,   200
from slow to extreme speed. It is quite a story.   210

1 | 2 | 3 | 4 | 5 | 6 | 7 | 8 | 9 | 10

98/99-D. Review the production work of Part Four

Type the four assignments indicated on the next page, preceding each by the indicated review. GOAL: To do each within 10 minutes and 3 errors.

This review will get you completely ready for the end-of-part test in Lesson 100.

LINE: 50
TAB: 5
SPACING: SINGLE, BUT
  DOUBLE IN 132-C
GOAL: APPLY SKILL TO
  TWO-PAGE LETTERS
STRESS: CONTINUITY
DRILLS: THREE EACH

Unit 22. Correspondence

132-A. Recall skill by taking two ½-minute timings on each line. Repeat in Lesson 133

132-A. Tune up on these easy review lines

1 The man who got the job said you did not want it.
2 Quietly pack the crate with five dozen gum boxes.
3 Take 10 and 28 and 39 from 47 and 56 to get what?

   1 | 2 | 3 | 4 | 5 | 6 | 7 | 8 | 9 | 10

132-B. Increase skill on an acceleration preview

132-B. Type to your goal:

ACCURACY: Three copies of lines 4-7 as though they were a paragraph.

SPEED: Three copies of each line, consecutively.

4 justify squeeze second signer person chance extra
5 sheet paper dozen trap; let's most fall long page
6 more pack does into each look now and one two any
7 has who one the his get had our or so it if to us

132-C. Sustain skill on alphabetic paragraphs

132-C. Steps to take for developmental effort:

1. Scan the copy, just to see what it says.

2. Select the hardest line in each paragraph; type them three times.

3. Take a 5-minute timed writing, pausing for a 10-second rest after each minute; or, type one copy, pausing to rest after you finish each paragraph.

4. Take a 5-minute timed writing, without rests; or, type one copy, without pausing for any rests.

GOAL: To finish the copy within 5 minutes and with 3 or fewer errors.

SI 1.34—fairly easy

8 Most of us fall into the trap, now and then,   10
of trying to squeeze on one page a letter that is   20
long enough to justify using two pages. Somehow,   30
we begrudge the extra sheet of paper or the dozen   40
or so seconds involved in inserting one more pack   50
of paper and typing a heading on the second page.   60

9 Well, let us not fall into any trap; rather,   70
let's look for each chance to stretch our letters   80
into two pages. Think of the person who gets the   90
letter. In one hand he holds a letter that is so   100
filled that the signer had to squeeze his name to   110
get it in. In the other hand he holds our letter   120
that has generous margin space and that runs over   130
to an extra page. Which letter will impress him,   140
will please him, will make him feel that the sub-   150
ject of the letter merits his thoughtful reading?   160

10 "When I see a letter that is squeezed," said   170
a business acquaintance of mine, "I get a feeling   180
that the writer is going to put a squeeze on me."   190
This is mere hokum, of course; but it does reveal   200
that the allover appearance of a letter does make   210
a general impression that can prejudice, for good   220
or for bad, the mind of the reader even before he   230
starts to read. The investment of an extra page,   240
plus a few seconds, can pay rich dividends to us.   250

   1 | 2 | 3 | 4 | 5 | 6 | 7 | 8 | 9 | 10

132/133-D. Apply skill to two-page letters

132-D. Type Letter 57 on workbook page 251. Use plain paper for the continuation pages.

Study Letter 57 carefully, then type it and Letters 58-59.

Letter 41

SEMIBLOCKED LETTER
Body: 157
Paper: letterhead
Review: page 131
Tab: 5, center
SI: 1.59—difficult

Editor, Executive Weekly | 505 Elm Street | Edmonton, Alberta | Dear Sir:

Most of your readers are, I know, executives who have secretaries and who give dictation regularly. I believe that your readers might be interested in an article that discusses the dictation rates and habits of dictators and ends with a number of suggestions for increasing dictation skill.

I have prepared such an article. I enclose the first part and a table from the manuscript. The entire article includes 438 lines and four tables. The article is based on a fine study conducted a few years ago at the University of Waterloo by Dr. H. H. Green and on several recent studies that confirm his findings and enlarge on them to some degree.

I should appreciate learning from you whether you would wish me to submit the entire manuscript for your review.

Yours very truly, | Thomas Swartz | English Department | *Initials?* | *Other reference notations?*

| 19 |
| 24 |
| 37 |
| 50 |
| 62 |
| 75 |
| 84 |
| 99 |
| 111 |
| 124 |
| 137 |
| 150 |
| 157 |
| 171 |
| 181 |
| 201 |
| 203 |

Table 26

RULED TABLE
Paper: plain
Spacing: double
Review: page 139

EVERY DICTATOR'S CHANGES OF PACE			
Dictator's Manner	Dictation Pattern	Percent of Time	
Groping	Very slow	15.0%	
Thoughtful	Steady	45.0%	
Confident	Fluent	30.0%	
Sprinting	Very fast	10.0%	
TOTAL	-------	100.0%	

| 19 |
| 27 |
| 36 |
| 43 |
| 51 |
| 60 |
| 67 |
| 73 |
| 80 |
| 89 |
| 98 |
| 105 |

Using the page-1 heading shown below and a 40-space line, type 98-C as a magazine article. Use plain paper. Make 1 carbon copy of each page.

HOW BUSINESSPEOPLE DICTATE
By Thomas Swartz
Laurentian University
Sudbury, Ontario

Using a 60-space line (shifted to the right to provide space for inserting the page in a three-ring binder) and double spacing, type 98-C as *Page 43* of a book on *Executive Dictation*. Use plain paper. Make 1 carbon copy of the page. NOTE: Between the first and second paragraph, insert an underscored sideheading, *Study of Dictators' Rate of Speaking.*

Numeric dating

Numeric dating is not part of SI. However, it is related to SI in that it involves measurement — the measurement of time. In numeric dating, the year, month, and day are recorded totally in numbers. They appear in descending order of magnitude. For example, March 31, 1977, is expressed as 1977 03 31. There are four digits in the year and two digits each for the month and day. Note that there is a space between the year, month, and day. Alternatives to this spacing are: 1977-03-31 and 19770331.

Table 28

NUMERIC DATING
Open
Single space
Bottom half of page

PRODUCTION COUNT ADJUSTMENT
FOR NUMERIC DATING

Subtract from Count	Months	Number of Digits in the Day	
		1-digit day	2-digit day
0	May	*	*
	June-July	*	
1	January-April	*	*
	June-July		*
	August	*	
	October	*	*
2	August		*
	September	*	
	November-December	*	*
3	September		*

Numeric dating. Use the dates given in the letters of Lessons 132-133 as practice in converting to numeric dating.

Use this simple chart to help you adjust the production count for numeric dating. It is only a matter of subtracting from one to three words from the current production count.

The 24 h clock

Paper: P4
double space

Going metric does not mean that we necessarily use the 24 h clock. However, we already use it in travel schedules for trains, buses, and planes. It will become more commonly used in the everyday business world.

Times in the day are expressed by four digits, beginning at midnight with 00:00 (zero hours). The first two digits stand for the number of hours since midnight; the second two represent the number of minutes in the last hour. A colon separates each pair of digits. Times in the day are shown as follows:

Table 29

24 h CLOCK
Open
Double space, P4
Type the dividing
line. Allow space
for the bottom note
as well. Give the
table an appropriate
title

Usual Method	24 h Clock
12:00 p.m. (midnight)	00:00 or 24:00
4:30 a.m.	04:30
11:55 a.m.	11:55
12:00 a.m. (noon)	12:00
1:30 p.m.	13:30*
7:05 p.m.	19:05
11:30 p.m.	23:30

*It's easy. To get afternoon and evening times, simply add 12:00 to the usual expression of time — 1:30 p.m. is 12:00 + 1:30 = 13:30.

Progress Test on Part Four

Test 4

		4-B
N E W S R E L E A S E	From William L. Miller	10
	Martin Miller & Sons	16
	58 Broadview Street	20
	Toronto, Ontario M4M 2E4	26
	Release February 22, 19—	32
		34
	PAINT FIRM TO OPEN SCHOOL	50
		52
	TORONTO, Ont., Feb. 22—	58

	4-A	
The first special school for engineers to be	10	68
trained in how to use color to help production in	20	78
plants and offices will open here within the next	30	88
six weeks. The new school will be sponsored by a	40	98
local paint firm that has set the pace in the new	50	108
field of color dynamics. Head of the school will	60	118
be the company's color expert, Dr. Lauren Martin.	70	128
Announcement of plans for the new school was	80	138
made by Martin Miller, head of the firm of Martin	90	148
Miller & Sons, who pointed out that the company's	100	158
research in the use of color not only had created	110	168
a new field of study but also had led to requests	120	178
for experts who could serve as color consultants.	130	188
Only by setting up the new school could the local	140	198
firm assure its patrons the counsel they request.	150	208
All enrolled for the training will be put on	160	218
the MM&S payroll in return for a pledge to remain	170	228
with the firm for two years. They must be twenty	180	238
or older, must be single, and must have completed	190	248
two or more years of college. The training is to	200	258
be a six-month program in the "color kitchens" of	210	268
the firm's new plant in the suburbs of this city.	220	278

1 | 2 | 3 | 4 | 5 | 6 | 7 | 8 | 9 | 10

LINE: 60
TAB: 5
SPACING: SINGLE
DRILLS: THREE TIMES
STRESS: KEEPING
 EYES ON THE COPY
GOAL: BOOST SKILL
 ON THE TOP ROW

130-A. Each line three times, or a half-minute writing on each line. Repeat in Lesson 131.

130-A. Tune up on these reach-review lines

1 The rifleman got eight big ducks at the lake for the girls.
2 Five or six new jet planes quickly zoomed by the big tower.
3 The 10's and 56's are harder to type than 28's, 39's, 47's.

| 1 | 2 | 3 | 4 | 5 | 6 | 7 | 8 | 9 | 10 | 11 | 12 |

130-B. Measure your skill on this technical paragraph

130-B. Type one copy in 2 minutes or less time. If you make more than 2 errors, your goal is accuracy; 2 or fewer, your goal is speed.

When you proofread, make a list of every number you mistype.

SI 1.41—normal, with all digits and letters

4 The Post Office Department of each region includes 250   12
zones, with 250 zone branches.   Each region has 148 special   24
men trained to handle lost parcels and 63 more who are kept   36
busy with dead letters.   The 1976 annual report showed that   48
22.737 478 letters and 906 437 packages had been delivered.   60
These figures scored quite a jump, about 8.83 percent, over   72
those of 1960, which had been exactly the same as for 1955.   84

| 1 | 2 | 3 | 4 | 5 | 6 | 7 | 8 | 9 | 10 | 11 | 12 |

130-C. Improve your control of the number keys

130-C. Type to your goal:

ACCURACY: The lines as a group three times, then repeat once more lines that concentrate on a number you missed.

SPEED: Each line three times, plus once more if it concentrates on a number key you missed.

5 3 9 33 39 93 99 333 339 393 399 933 939 993 999 3939 9393
6 2 8 22 28 82 88 222 228 282 288 822 828 882 888 2828 8282
7 4 7 44 47 74 77 444 447 474 477 744 747 774 777 4747 7474
8 5 6 55 56 65 66 555 556 565 566 655 656 665 666 5656 6565
9 1 0 00 01 10 11 001 010 011 100 101 110 111 101 1010 1110

130-D. Improve fluency in typing numbers

130-D. Type to your goal:

ACCURACY: The group of lines three times.

SPEED: Each line three times consecutively.

10 we 23 24 25 26 27 28 up 70 71 72 73 74 or 94 95 96 97 98 99
11 ow 92 93 94 95 96 97 it 85 86 87 88 89 ye 63 64 65 66 67 68
12 wet 235 236 237 238 tie 583 584 585 586 rip 480 481 482 483
13 out 975 976 977 978 ere 343 344 345 346 wry 246 247 248 249

130-E. Speed up with pair-pattern sentences

130-E. Type to your goal as you did in 130-D.

14 You should be able to type 10, 28, 39, 47, and 56 fluently.
15 Cars 10 and 28 raced at 1:00; Cars 39 and 47 raced at 1:56.
16 Joe sold 1028 clips, 3947 pens, and 5610 tablets yesterday.
17 They won the games 56 to 47, then 39 to 28, then 100 to 56.
18 I filled Order No. 1028, Order No. 3947, and Order No. 566.

| 1 | 2 | 3 | 4 | 5 | 6 | 7 | 8 | 9 | 10 | 11 | 12 |

130-F. Precede retyping the paragraph in 130-B by typing twice every line in which you made an error the first time.

130-F. Repeat 130-B to measure your progress

—3 for each major error (top margin, line length, line-spacing, general correctness of form, etc.)

—2 for each minor error (blocking, aligning, centering, indenting, etc., of individual parts of the job)

—1 for each typographical error

0-1 PENALTY .... A

2-3 PENALTY .... B

4-6 PENALTY C

7-8 PENALTY .... D

if it is not feasible for you to do Tests B-C-D as timed writings, then type each task separately and fully (10-minute limit on each) and grade your work on the adjacent scales.

Test 4-C

Letter 42

5-MINUTE WRITING ON SEMIBLOCKED LETTER
Paper: workbook page 179 or plain paper
Body: 166 words
Start: machine set, carriage centered
Grade: box below
SI: 1.41—normal

5-MINUTE SPEED WITHIN 3 ERRORS*

45-up wam ...... A
40-44 wam ...... B
30-39 wam C
25-29 wam ...... D
* If more than 3 errors are made, compute the speed on what is typed before the fourth error.

Test 4-D

Table 27

5-MINUTE WRITING ON A RULED TABLE
Paper: workbook page 180 or plain paper
Start: machine set, carriage centered
Grade: box above

Today's date | Pelham Assurance Company | 19 Meadow   15
Boulevard | Lethbridge, Alberta T1H 4R3 | Gentlemen: 25

We believe that it is time for a review of the insurance rates   40
that we are paying you in behalf of our six main plants.   51

The contract rates we now pay were set in 1964 on the basis of   66
our accident record for a period of four years that began in   78
January, 1960. An earnest campaign for safety since that time   91
has slashed the number of accidents and the extent of damage so   103
much that we feel a lower rate is due us.   112

I have enclosed a table that gives the accident figures for   126
the six factories that are covered under our contract with you.   139
All the accidents that have involved damages are, of course, al-   152
ready in your own records. The details are a matter of record,   164
which we shall be pleased to place at your disposal.   175

We hope that you will ask your underwriters to study our   189
rates and that we may expect a reduction in the rates by the   201
start of the next quarter. | Yours truly, | J. D. SPEIRS & COM-   219
PANY, LTD. | C. D. Ferry, Treasurer | *reference notations?*   235

AVERAGE NUMBER ACCIDENTS **PER MONTH**   21

J. D. Speirs & Company, Ltd.   39
                                                                50

# Factory Locations	1950 to 1959	1960 to 1969	1970 to Date	
Elfros, Saskatchewan	18.3	16.5	10.8 ~~12.4~~	98
Lavington, (B. C.)	12.4	10.3	8.7 ~~9.2~~	108
Manitowaning, Ontario	31.7	24.6	18.7 ~~20.8~~	119
Medicine Hat, Alberta	15.0	12.1	10.3 ~~10.9~~	129
Montgomery, Alberta	9.1	6.4 ~~6.5~~	6.3 ~~6.5~~	139
Winnipeg, Manitoba	....	4.5	3.4 ~~3.8~~	149
				162
~~TOTALS~~ AVERAGES	17.3	12.4	9.7 ~~10.6~~	169

56
65
75
86

182

Triple space and start over   192

129-A. Increase skill via weighted sentences

19 You were off base, in my opinion, when you gave Lou a pony.
20 Philip drove my car carefully uphill but sloppily downhill.
21 Dad gave Molly a fat pumpkin at breakfast, as a funny joke.

  1 | 2 | 3 | 4 | 5 | 6 | 7 | 8 | 9 | 10 | 11 | 12

22 Joe's squad never quits until their sales reach their goal.
23 How soon will your boys come back here from that long trip?
24 Why did the boy cut the top off the new box you got for us?

129-B. Concentrate via a half-space centering drill

To type a character in half-space position, (1) set the carriage at the following full space; (2) press the left end of the carriage until the printing-point indicator is at half position; then, (3) tap the appropriate key with the free right hand.

Practice on this numbers exercise and then copy the adjacent display.

```
ONE
FOUR
THREE
FIVE
ELEVEN
```

```
THE
FOUR
MINSTRELS
APPEAR
NIGHTLY

DON'T
MISS
THEIR SHOW
TONIGHT!
```

129-C. Increase skill on patterned word drills

25 ages hymn sags jump drag kink fads look grab hulk drag junk
26 quart plump sweat plunk eases hilly reset phony tread jolly
27 crazed limply extras oniony exceeds opinion dredger million

  1 | 2 | 3 | 4 | 5 | 6 | 7 | 8 | 9 | 10 | 11 | 12

28 quantity element island panel girls quake blend shake works
29 sight ivory tight bland fight chair eight furor right cocoa
30 also both city dusk end, fuel goal hand isle jams keys name
31 oaks pair quay risk such tick urns vial when six, flay doz.

129-D. Increase skill on patterned sentences

32 Why did Professor Black give you a quiz on the major taxes?
33 Bill gave a quick jump as the zebra and lynx fought wildly.
34 Jacqueline was very glad the day her film took a prize box.

  1 | 2 | 3 | 4 | 5 | 6 | 7 | 8 | 9 | 10 | 11 | 12

35 Keith may wish to make oak handles for the six giant signs.
36 She is so busy with big problems that she might not aid us.
37 If the girl makes a sign for them, it is their duty to pay.

129-E. Measure your skill improvement

Type the last two paragraphs on page 197 (or take a 5-minute timing on the last three paragraphs) to measure your improvement.

129-A. Type to your goal. ACCURACY: each line two times, then repeat lines 19-21 two more times. SPEED: each line two times; then, repeat lines 22-24 two more times. Don't let the one-hand runs in 19-21 make you break rhythm, and don't let the rhythm of 22-24 speed you up so much that you make a lot of errors!

129-B. These drills would be very easy to do on a machine with a half-space key; but you might not always have a machine with such a key—so "do it the hard way," as it is described here. Half-spacing is worth the effort only when the display is brief or the paper is very important. See paragraph 5, page 197.

129-C. Type to your goal. ACCURACY: type the seven lines, as though they were a paragraph, three times. SPEED: type each twice, then repeat lines 28-31 twice more each. Don't let the one-hand words in 25-27 make you slow down or sway, and don't let the ease of the alternate-hand words in 28-31 speed you up so much you jam your keys!

129-D. Type to your goal. ACCURACY: type the three alphabetic sentences in 32-34 three times each and the alternate-hand sentences twice. SPEED: all lines twice, and then repeat 35-37 twice more.

129-E. GOAL: Maximum speed within 3 errors. Remember to listen for the end-of-line bell.

5 SKILL BUILDING • LETTER STYLING •
BILLING, PAYROLL FORMS • DISPLAYS

Lines end evenly
on a 70-space line.
See also page 194.

COUNTING

METHOD

LESSON 1 2 3 4
ASSIGNMENT
LESSON
ASSIGNMENT

THREE

SHORTCUTS

40   50

| 1 | 2 | 3 | 4 | 5 | 6 | 7 | 8 | 9 | 10 | 11 | 12 | 13 | 14 |

Most of the times when you must center something, you can do the 14
centering with the backspace key or the space bar; but there are some 28
occasions when you will find it easier, in the long run, to count the 42
characters and spaces in the problem and solve it by easy arithmetic. 56

If a column heading is four spaces narrower than its column, for 70
example, you do not have to use the backspace key or the space bar to 84
determine that the heading should be indented two spaces; in any such 98
situation, it is easier to count the spaces and split whatever is the 112
difference than it is to avoid the simple bit of arithmetic involved. 126

With so much centering to be done even in routine work, it is no 140
surprise that typists have invented shortcuts and rules of thumb that 154
speed up the task of centering in some cases. Here are some of them. 168

The most common aid to centering is adjusting the paper guide so 182
the center of the paper will fall at a point that is easy to remember 196
and is easy to locate. If you are one of those who has set the paper 210
guide so that the center of your paper will fall at 50, you would not 224
even know that this is a shortcut. But there are millions of typists 238
who still set the paper guide to align with zero on the linescale, so 252
that the midpoint of their paper falls at an odd number like 42 or 43 266
or 51, which do not appear as numbers on the scale and so are readily 280
confused with 37 and 38 and 49, and which are difficult to add to and 294
subtract from when planning margins. Using 50 or 60 as the centering 308
point is a great deal surer and faster; so it is a shortcut, you see. 322

SALES   ESTIMATED
BUDGET EXPENSES

SALES   ESTIMATED
BUDGET EXPENSES

HALF
SPACE

SALES   ESTIMATED
BUDGET EXPENSES

One of the awkward problems is what to do with a two-line column 336
heading when one line is only one space shorter than the other. Now, 350
if each line is centered separately, sometimes the left-over space is 364
on one side and sometimes it is on the other, depending on the number 378
of strokes in the two lines; but most typists now ignore this trivial 392
difference, saving time by centering the longer one and then blocking 406
the shorter line with the start of the longer one. Worth mentioning, 420
however, is the fact that some machines now have a half-space key for 434
use if the work must be dressed up. If you hold down this key as you 448
tap a letter key, the letter appears half a space to the right. This 462
key permits exact centering that is grand to see but very slow to do. 476

Allocation
--$1 000--
 2 500

Allocations
 $1 000
---2 500---

SI 1.34—easy normal

In a similar vein, typists now use the dollar sign as a flexible 490
point in centering a money column under its heading. If counting the 504
dollar sign as a part of the column width will make centering easier, 518
then count it; otherwise, do not count the dollar sign in the column. 532
This is a shortcut that will save time in every money table you type! 546

| 1 | 2 | 3 | 4 | 5 | 6 | 7 | 8 | 9 | 10 | 11 | 12 | 13 | 14 |

Unit 17. Skill Development

LINE: 60
TAB: 5
SPACING: SINGLE
DRILLS: THREE TIMES
STRESS: CORRECT
TECHNIQUES
GOAL: BOOST SKILL

101-A. Lines three or more times, or a half-minute writing on each line.

101-B. Proofread your work carefully, to set your Lesson 101 goal: If you make 4 or more errors, your goal is ACCURACY. Type each set of drills like a paragraph three times and once more if assigned. If you make three or fewer errors, your goal is SPEED. Type each drill three consecutive times, plus an additional time if so indicated.

101-C. Type as directed in 101-B. Add an extra repetition if you had any raised capitals in the 101-B writing.

101-D. Type as directed in 101-B. Add an extra repetition if you left out a word in 101-B.

101-E. Type as directed in 101-B. Add an extra repetition if you find any very light or very dark letters in 101-B.

101-F. Type as directed in 101-B. Add an extra repetition if you made any error in, or jammed keys in, a one-hand word in the 101-B copy.

101-G. To confirm your progress, repeat 101-B.

101-A. Tune up on these reach-review lines
If it is their turn to go, they may find the work cut down.
The six zebras very quickly jumped out of the winter glare.
He assigned us pages 10, 28, 39, 47, and 56 for our lesson.
　1　|　2　|　3　|　4　|　5　|　6　|　7　|　8　|　9　|　10　|　11　|　12

101-B. Inventory your operating techniques
Type the first four paragraphs on 101-H (or take a 5-minute writing on it), pressing your skill to its utmost: type rapidly but with good control, relentlessly keeping eyes on the copy and forcing yourself to continue the way you would if you worked in an office and if your employer gave you five minutes to get the job done!

101-C. Improve your capital-shifting technique
Ted Lou Red Ima Dan Joe Sam Lil Eve Jim Cal Kip Val Ina Wes
Alf Ken Don Kay Rue Ned Wyn May Bob Yve Guy Hal Bud Pam Son
Dana Nora Stan John Carl Lila Fred Mike Sara Joel Drew Hope
Ruth Mary Alan Jack Cora Paul Vick Pats Dora Hank Will Oren
Joe told Bob, Tom, and Red to bring Peg, Jen, Eve, and Gay.
We elected Bill Hamm, Anne Toll, Lynn Rodd, and Bobby Gill.
They drove to Norval, Hamilton, Buffalo, and Niagara Falls.
　1　|　2　|　3　|　4　|　5　|　6　|　7　|　8　|　9　|　10　|　11　|　12

101-D. Improve your eyes-on-copy technique
down. cut work the find may they go, to turn their is it If
.eralg retniw eht fo tuo depmuj ylkciuq yrev sarbez xis ehT
H— qu-ckl- tr—ned a d-z-n br-wn f-x-s t- j-mp -v-r a g-te.

101-E. Improve the evenness of your stroking
one some knows what end long would work big like sheet with
had five typed each out need times both who made which side
ink thin stock more wax used pound make six four eight know

101-F. Improve control of one-hand words
My case was deferred after John agreed on greater tax fees.
In my opinion, Lynn was dazed after severe stress in water.
Phillip was my best pupil after we defeated Joplin in polo.
You gave Johnny a great scare after you faced a grave test.

101-G. Measure your progress in sustained writing

LINE: 70
TAB: 5
SPACING: SINGLE
DRILLS: THREE TIMES
STRESS: ELBOWS IN
  AND WRISTS DOWN
GOAL: BOOST SKILL,
  IMPROVE CENTERING

128-A. Each line three times, or a half-minute writing on each line. Repeat in Lesson 129.

128-B. If you make 3 or more errors, your goal in Lessons 128-129 is ACCURACY; otherwise your goal is SPEED.

128-C. Type to your goal. ACCURACY: The group of lines three times. SPEED: Each line three times. Try to avoid pausing at the thin vertical lines.

128-D. Clear tabs. Set one every 13 spaces. Copy the "typewritten" lines; then, center under each word the entry given in regular print. Use the arithmetic method (paragraph 2, page 197), ignoring all fractions.

128-E. Type to your goal, just as you did in 128-C. Type slowly (even lazily) the first time through, but then speed up; hold rhythm constant, even.

128-F. Type three lines consisting of 20, 19, and 18 underscores and repeat a triple space below; then, center the names of the months as shown, above and below.

128-G. Type to your goal. ACCURACY: The group of lines three times. SPEED: Each line three times. Don't pause; keep going as smoothly as you can!

128-A. Tune up on these reach-review lines

1 She said that Kent told them both that they must work hard.
2 Jim knew the buzzing talk could vex my quiet old professor.
3 The pair patterns of 10, 28, 39, 47, and 56 will total 180.

   1 | 2 | 3 | 4 | 5 | 6 | 7 | 8 | 9 | 10 | 11 | 12

128-B. Inventory your present rate of skill

Type the first three paragraphs on page 197 (or take a 5-minute writing on the page), pressing your skill to its utmost—as though you were in a speed-and-accuracy contest and were ahead of the others.

128-C. Increase skill on runs of two-letter words

4 report on it which of us have to do when it is to one of us
5 expect to be since it is much as we have to be at see if it
6 wonder if it would he be sent to us most of it is can it be

128-D. Concentrate via a special centering drill

EXPENSE	AMOUNTS	MANAGER	BUREAUS	PERCENT
10%	10.00	Jones	Eastern	19.1%
DIVISION	LOSS	NUMBERS	PROFIT	TOTAL
Budget	$1 000	41 200	(None)*	381.14
BRANCHES	SALES	TERRITORY	DATE DUE	RESULTS
Chicago	$1 477	Southern	May 2	-137

128-E. Increase skill on runs of three-letter words

10 filled the one think you are which may not went out for the
11 looked for his tried the new since the one must ask him why
12 better for our which our men write out the will you get our

128-F. Concentrate via a special centering drill

January	February	March
April	May	June
July	August	September
October	November	December

128-G. Build skill on one-hand-run preview words

15 difference remember however shorter easier faster only fact
16 characters millions dressed similar spaces common easy case
17 separately subtract readily awkward column locate link bars
18 determines planning exactly started simple center sets upon

128-H. Repeat 128-B to measure your pro

WHAT'S WHAT ABOUT CARBON PAPER

No one knows who invented carbon 7
sheets, for the event happened long ago, 15
even before the typewriter was invented; 23
but whoever it was deserves to be honored 32
by a big monument in the middle of Wall 40
Street or some other business street. 47

Can you imagine what office work would 57
be like with no carbon paper? On the aver- 65
age, business uses five copies of what- 73
ever is typed; if each copy had to be typed 82
separately, business would need five times 90
as many typists, which would be the end of 99
business, or typists, or both. Out of honest 108
respect to the person who made office work 117
possible through his invention, let's review 126
what we ought to know about it. 134

QUALITY IN CARBONS

A carbon paper is a sheet of thin, strong 145
paper coated on one side with a solution of 154
ink and wax. The quality of the sheet 161
depends on the quality of the paper and 169
coatings. 172

The thickness, or weight, of the paper 182
used in carbons is one factor to check. The 191
thinner the sheet is, the more copies you 199
can make at one typing, but the sooner the 207
sheet wears out. If you normally make from 216
four to seven copies, as most typists do, 225
then you should stock the middle weight of 233
carbon, the six pound. If you commonly 241
make more copies than seven, then you use 250
a thinner weight, such as the four pound; 258
or, if you normally make four or fewer 266
copies of what you type, then you would 274
get more value from heavier paper, such as 282
the eight pound. But, six pound is almost 291
standard. 293

A second main factor of carbon paper 302
that every typist should know is the hard- 310

ness, or finish, of the coating. In general, 320
a hard finish gives more uses of the carbon 328
sheet; but each copy is lighter. On the other 338
hand, a soft finish gives darker copies; but 347
the sheet cannot be used as often. If you 355
have a noiseless machine or a light touch, 364
you ought to use a soft finish. If you have 373
an electric machine or a heavy touch, then 381
you should use a hard finish. For normal of- 390
fice work on a manual machine, the best 398
finish is medium. 402

PLUS EXTRA FEATURES

Putting together what you have just 411
noted about finish and weight, you can 419
understand why most orders for boxes of 427
carbon sheets seem to be for "a medium 435
six, if you please." 439

But, makers of carbon papers are always 449
looking for new ways to make their prod- 459
uct better than that made by others; as a 465
result, some brands feature things that 473
others do not. 477

You can get carbon paper, for example, 486
that is given a special coat that will 494
prevent curling. You can get carbon 501
sheets with clipped corners, for easy sepa- 510
ration of a sheaf of papers and carbons. 518
You can get carbons edged in white, for 526
clean handling; and some carbons even 534
have a line count printed on the white edge, 543
so you know how far you are from the 551
bottom. All such features increase the price 560
of carbon paper, of course; but they are 568
worth the extra few pennies. 574

But, whether or not you use carbon 583
paper with such plus features, be sure to 591
include a word of thanks to the person who 600
began it all, the next time you reach for a 608
medium six.   [START OVER] 611

THE LATEST VERSION OF THE METRIC SYSTEM--SI

SI is the international abbreviation for the official French name | 14

Le Système International d'Unités or The International System of Units. | 28

In 1960 The International System of Units was established to re- | 42

place all former versions of metric systems and measurement in order to | 56

provide a universal, global system. The nations worldwide are making a | 70

change to SI. Some countries are changing to SI from another metric | 83

system; others are updating their metric practices to conform to SI. | 96

Because of the increasing volume of world trade, it is distinctly advan- | 114

tageous to have a worldwide system of measurement. | 126

Canada, too, has decided to convert from the imperial system of | 144

measurement to SI. Not only is Canada's economy heavily reliant on | 157

foreign trade but also most of the countries with whom Canada trades | 170

have either used the metric system for a long time or are converting to | 184

SI. | 185

Although no deadline has been established for Canada's full con- | 199

version, the Commission for Metric Conversion, formed in June 1971, has | 213

set certain target dates for metric usage. For example, the news media | 227

have announced the temperature in degrees Celsius since April 1, 1975. | 241

Since September 1, 1975, the weather forecasts have been given in milli- | 255

metres, centimetres and metres. And September 1977 was the target date | 279

to convert provincial highway signs to metric speeds and distances. | 292

SI is simple—much simpler than the imperial system. There is no | 306

consistent characteristic of the imperial system. However, the number 10 | 320

is the main characteristic of the metric system. The convenience of the | 334

decimal system along with the focus on 10 and multiples of ten make it | 347

easier to compute in the metric system than in the imperial system. | 360

It has been said that the metric system "makes it 10 times easier, | 374

100 times faster, 1000 times better." | 382

102-A. Set your practice goals for Lesson 102

102-A. Continue same goal and practice plan you used in Lesson 101:

ACCURACY: Consider each set of drills a paragraph; type the paragraph three times.

SPEED: Type each line three times consecutively.

Review the errors you made in Lesson 101 to see which of the following mistakes you made *two or more* times (indicate by light checkmark).

☐ Misstroke on bottom-row key   ☐ Misstroke on the space bar
☐ Misstroke on home-row key   ☐ Misstroke on an adjacent key,
☐ Misstroke on third-row key   like typing *w* for *e*, or *n* for *m*

102-B. Improve control on bottom-row keys

102-B. Type as directed in 102-A. Add an extra repetition if you had 2 or more bottom-row errors in your Lesson 101 work.

21   azaza ;/;/; sxsxs l.l.l dcdcd k,k,k fvfvf jmjmj fbfbf jnjnj
22   lazy, hazy, daze, maze, dozen vixen next, fixes mixes main.
23   f.o.b. c.o.d. a.m. blame bane cane vane came name balm calm
24   cab, dab, gab, jab, lab, nab, mob, sob, cob, nob, fox, fix.

102-C. Improve control on home-row keys

102-C. Type as directed in 102-A. Add an extra repetition if you had 2 or more home-row errors in your Lesson 101 work.

25   lad load road clad glad glade all gall call ball hall shall
26   ash dash hash mash lash flash ale gale kale dale hale shale
27   alk balk talk walk calk chalk ask bask cask mask task flask
28   ade fade jade made wade spade ail hail jail mail sail snail

102-D. Improve control on third-row keys

102-D. Type as directed in 102-A. Add an extra repetition if you had 2 or more third-row errors in your Lesson 101 work.

29   aqaqa ;p;p; swsws lolol deded kikik frfrf jujuj ftftf jyjyj
30   quirt quilt quits quips quirk apply apple paper piper papas
31   fully gully dully sully truly power tower lower bower cower
32   scows shows slows snows stows tried fried cried pried shied

102-E. Improve control on the space bar

102-E. Type as directed in 102-A. Add an extra repetition if you had 2 or more space-bar errors in your Lesson 101 work.

33   a b c d e f g h i j k l m n o p q r s t u v w x y z . , ; ?
34   thinner recent trial less see element typing guest they yes
35   Mr. J. D. said the C. O. D. shipment got here about 2 P. M.

102-F. Improve control on adjacent keys

102-F. Type as directed in 102-A. Add an extra repetition if you had 2 or more errors involving adjacent keys in your typing in Lesson 101.

36   EWE ewer fewer ERE here beret RTR trim earth UYU yule buyer
37   UIU ruin juice IOI join prior OPO rope spout ASA sash basal
38   SDS aids sides DFD daft doffs FGF gaff flags JHJ jury rajah
39   JKJ jack jokes KLK balk ankle CVC cave civic NMN mint enemy

102-G. Restore momentum on easy sentences

102-G. Type as directed in 102-A. Focus on even, rhythmic typing. Do not push hard for speed; let the ease and evenness of the copy boost your rate.

40   You know that they will help them when they need some help.
41   The last plan that they said they made does seem very fine.
42   We may ask the new man for the big dog she got for her son.
43   He and the boy got the car and had the two men fix the top.

   1 | 2 | 3 | 4 | 5 | 6 | 7 | 8 | 9 | 10 | 11 | 12

102-H. Confirm your progress in sustained writing

102-H. Type final four paragraphs of 101-H, or take another 5-minute writing on page 158.

HORIZONTAL CENTERING

Lines end evenly
on a 70-space line.
See also page 197.

Of all the techniques that help a typist turn out a lot of work, 14
especially when the work involves any display, the most useful one is 28
centering; this technique is also the one that you will find the most 42
dangerous, for nothing stands out so clearly as the mark of an office 56
amateur as a word or line that should be centered but is not. Expert 70
centering, therefore, is an art that merits a great deal of practice. 84

BACKSPACING
METHOD

CENTERING
ᴟᴟᴟᴟ

The standard steps by which a typist may center a line or a word 98
horizontally are, of course, well known: You set the carriage at the 112
midpoint of the paper, you press the backspace key once for every two 126
characters or spaces in what you must center, and thus you attain the 140
starting point for typing the line or word. The one caution you must 154
exercise is what you do when you have a single letter left over after 168
backspacing for the pairs: You must not backspace for such a letter. 182

Once in a while the words to be centered must also be spread; in 196
instances of this nature, you separate letters by one blank space and 210
separate words by three blank spaces. To center such a line, you may 224
proceed in the basic way if you wish, calling off a space after every 238
character that you name in calling the pairs of strokes for which you 252
backspace; but it will dawn on you that naming the space each time is 266
unnecessary, and after that you will use the shortcut: You will just 280
backspace once for each stroke, except the last letter, that the line 294
normally would fill if it were not spread. The last letter has to be 308
excepted, for it's not followed by the space it needs to make a pair. 322

THE MENU
ᴟᴟᴟᴟᴟ
THE MENU

SPACE BAR
METHOD

JOHN HALE 123456

123 JOHN HALE 456

But there is another way to center which is very useful and will 336
sometimes work better than the basic way. What you do is to set your 350
carriage at the beginning of the space in which you are to center the 364
material; tap the space bar once for each stroke in the words you are 378
centering; and continue tapping the space bar to the end of the space 392
available, counting the strokes to see how many spaces are left over. 406
Dividing your leftovers in half tells you how much the copy has to be 420
indented if it is to be centered within the space you have available. 434

John Hale

This method may be used on many occasions. It is efficient, for 448
example, if you must center a heading or title between two margins of 462
unequal width, or a column within a ruled space, or a title below the 476
typewritten name at the end of a letter, or names below the rules for 490
signatures on a legal paper, and so on. If your backspace key is not 504
operating correctly, you can always use this method as a reserve one. 518

NAME
John Hale
Tom Smith

AFFIDAVIT

John Hale
Vice-President

SI 1.35—easy-normal

LINE: 60
TAB: 5
SPACING: SINGLE
DRILLS: THREE TIMES
STRESS: WRISTS KEPT
   CLOSE TOGETHER
GOAL: BOOST SKILL

103-A. Lines three times or a 1-minute sprint on each line. Be sure to repeat these in Lesson 104.

103-A. Tune up on these reach-review lines

1 The profit of eighty bushels of corn may pay for the panel.
2 Max worked quietly, alphabetizing the cards for vital jobs.
3 See pages 28, 39, and 47 in Manual No. 1056 for new models.

  1 | 2 | 3 | 4 | 5 | 6 | 7 | 8 | 9 | 10 | 11 | 12

103-B. Type first third of 103-H, on next page (or, take a 5-minute writing on it) to set your practice goals: ACCURACY, if you make over 3 errors; SPEED if you make 3 or fewer.

103-B. Confirm your present level of skill

103-C. Boost your rate on rhythmic one-line sentences

103-C. Each couplet three times (for accuracy) or each line three times (for speed). Or, take 1-minute timings on couplets (for accuracy) or lines (for speed).

SI 1.08—very easy

4 He may yet see how the two men dug out the old log for him.
5 An old man may ask you how you got the red cap she had hid.

6 The boys know that they must read more when they come here.
7 Why must they stay here when they like your home much more?

8 Your older folks often speak about their never being tired.
9 Jake hoped these women would stamp these brown forms first.

  1 | 2 | 3 | 4 | 5 | 6 | 7 | 8 | 9 | 10 | 11 | 12

103-D. Sustain the new rate on an alphabetic paragraph

103-D. Type three copies (or three 2-minute writings), pausing to type correctly a line of each word mistyped in preceding effort.

SI 1.25—fairly easy

10   The person who wishes to get ahead in the world has to   12
realize that he is going to be compared. He will be judged   24
not so much by what he does that others do not do as by how   36
much better he does the things that the others also do. He   48
must excel in those common, frequent things that provide an   60
honest yardstick by which all may be measured and compared.   72

  1 | 2 | 3 | 4 | 5 | 6 | 7 | 8 | 9 | 10 | 11 | 12

103-E. Sharpen your concentration ability

103-E. The triplet three times (for accuracy) or each line three times (for speed). Or, take half-minute timings.

11 captain edward harris is now major edward harris.
12 there are mr. and mrs. frank toll, of pittsburgh.
13 tom carr invited lou pyle to visit bob at easter.

  1 | 2 | 3 | 4 | 5 | 6 | 7 | 8 | 9 | 10

Capitalize six words in each line.

103-F. Practice patterned preview words

103-F. The foursome three times (for accuracy) or each line three times (to focus on speed).

14 illustrate between appeal button called press need good all
15 normally treeing offices attack common sheet worry toss off
16 creases in my extra on up great only tree jump save you few
17 problem handle shake turns works such make snap both end it

103-G. Type the second third of 103-H (or a 5-minute writing) to confirm your progress.

103-G. Measure your progress in sustained writing

LINE: 60
SPACING: SINGLE

Build skill and confidence in number typing for numeric dating, the 24 h clock, and spacing with metric symbols.

126-A. Type each line twice, trying to type at a steady, unbroken pace with your eyes kept rigidly on the copy. Repeat lines 1 and 3.

126-A. Numeric dating

1   1975 12 31, 1976 01 01, 1977 09 29, 1977 02 28, 1978 04 01, 1978 12 25
2   1975-12-31, 1976-01-01, 1977-09-29, 1977-02-28, 1978-04-01, 1978-12-25
3   1979 06 07, 1969 07 21, 1980 08 18, 1990 10 16, 2000 01 01, 1945 11 11
4   1979-06-07, 1969-07-21, 1980-08-18, 1990-10-16, 2000-01-01, 1945-11-11

126-B. If your basic need is for surer ACCURACY, type the 6 lines as a paragraph twice. But if your need is for SPEED, type each line twice.

126-B. The 24-hour clock

5   01 00; 01 31; 02 00; 02 35; 03 00; 03 42; 04 00; 04 45; 05 00.   05 55.
6   12 00; 12 30; 11 00; 11 42; 10 00; 10 30; 09 00; 09 05; 08 00.   08 23.
7   00 00; 24 00; 12 00; 07 00; 07 10; 06 00; 06 08; 05 00; 05 12.   04 00.
8   13 00; 13 30; 14 00; 14 15; 15 00; 15 45; 16.00; 16 50; 17 00.   17 05.
9   18 00; 18 10; 19 00; 19 55; 20 00; 20 08; 21 00; 21 53; 22 00.   22 20.
10 23 00; 23 55; 24 00; 00 00; 07 43; 10 22; 01 16; 13 42; 12 00.   24 00.

126-C-D-E. Three copies of steady typing with your eyes rigidly on the copy.

126-C. Spacing optional.   Close the space in 4-digit numbers.

11 1213 4468 4110 3234 2930 4030 3050; 6692 3847 2039 3856 2056 3620 2051
12 8170 1860 2639 4958 5867 6736 5820; 1111 2222 3333 4444 9999 6565 6464

126-D. Numbers with more than 4 digits left of the decimal marker

13 100 000.50, 879 123.00, 389 888.50, 229 212.00, 384 567.00, 203 000.54
14 690 323.57, 339 290.59, 482 482.12, 131 220.56, 190 013.01, 125 025.67

126-E. Numbers whose value is less than 1

15 0.56 0.75 0.23 0.50 0.78 0.94 0.98 0.96 2.29 0.28 0.56 0.86 0.37 0.325
16 0.932 0.788 0.357 0.387 0.258 0.903 0.860 0.235 0.553 0.525 0.355 0.09

126-F. Double spacing. Type through once at an even pace. Keep eyes on copy and left hand on home row while turning the cylinder a half linespace toward you to type the exponents. Repeat lines 17-20 three times, building speed and accuracy.

126-F. Numbers and symbols

17 0.1 mm, 35 cm, 100 m, 135 km, 450 km, 50 km/h, 80 km/h, 100 km/h, 9 mm
18 2 mm2, 45 cm2, 9 dm2 10.5 m2, 40.5 ha, 7 km2, 19 000 km2, 5 mm2, 4 km2
19 3 cm3, 3.5 dm3, 73 m3, 32 ml, 12 kl, 34 cm3, 78 dm3, 6 m3, 9 ml, 63 kl
20 69 t, 30 kg, 357.5 g, 21.2 mg, 14.1 mg, 137 g, 82 kg, 3.75 t, 7g, 7 mg

126-G. Type line 21 three times to build skill in using the ° key or the o in a superior position. Type lines 22-26 as a paragraph three times. Goal: To type the temperatures with no hesitation.

126-G. Temperatures

21 ° 0°C, 20°C, 25°C, 30°C, 37°C, 40°C, 100°C, -10°C, -20°C, -30°C, -40°C
22 Water freezes at 0°C; water boils at 100°C; a heat wave comes at 40°C.
23 Normal room temperature is 20°C, with normal body temperature at 37°C.
24 At 30°C we are in swimming. At 40°C we are having quite a heat wave!!
25 We bake cookies at 200°C. We go skating on the pond at -10°C or more.
26 It's a cold winter day at -20°C. It's a very, very cold day at -40°C.

1 | 2 | 3 | 4 | 5 | 6 | 7 | 8 | 9 | 10 | 11 | 12 | 13 | 14

WHAT'S WHAT ABOUT CARBON PAPER, Continued

1 | 2 | 3 | 4 | 5 | 6 | 7 | 8

CHALLENGE TO CARBONS

There is one main worry for the spirit of   9
the inventor of carbon paper. This is the   18
thought that science may come forth with   26
some easy way to make extra copies with-   34
out using carbons, a problem in which   42
science is making some headway.   48

To illustrate: In most large offices there   58
is already a copying machine; if you need a   67
few more copies of a typed page, you slip   75
the page and some special copying paper   83
into the machine, push a button, and reach   92
for the copy that the device turns out in   101
a few seconds at a cost of a few cents.   109

Along another line of attack, science has   119
come up with chemical coatings for paper.   128
As you type on one sheet, you press the   136
chemical from the back of that page onto   144
and into the chemical on the front of the   152
next page; the result is a copy of what you   161
typed. The method works like magic but   169
is costly, and erasures are next to impos-   177
sible. Such paper is called NCR since it   186
makes a copy with "No Carbon Required."   194

SNAP-OUT CARBON PACKS

But what gain has been made in the ef-   203
fort to eliminate carbon paper has been   211
more than balanced by the great gains for   220
using a lot more of it, particularly through   229
snap-outs.   231

A snap-out is a ready-made carbon pack.   241
When you have used one, you hold it at the   250
bound end and snap your wrist; like magic,   259
the papers and carbons separate, or "snap   267
out." You toss away the used carbons;   275
that is how cheap they are.   281

Snap-outs come in all sizes. They come   291
both plain and with printing on some or   299
all papers. The papers may be any color,   307

1 | 2 | 3 | 4 | 5 | 6 | 7 | 8

in any sequence, you might wish. The pack   316
may be as lean as two pages or as thick   324
as a dozen, whatever you wish to order.   332
And order them people do! There are a   340
number of companies now that do nothing   348
but print snap-outs to order. Their ap-   356
peal is obvious: They are easy and clean   364
to handle and save a great deal of time   372
for the typist, and they give perfect align-   381
ment on any snap-outs that are a printed   389
form.   390

CARBON-PAPER EFFICIENCIES

Despite the trend toward using snap-   399
outs, most typists will have frequent use   408
for individual sheets of carbon paper and   416
need to know the common efficiencies in   424
their use. For example, always insert a   432
carbon pack slowly, to prevent the pages   440
from slithering; and always press the paper   449
release a time or two, to avoid creasing or   458
treeing the carbon paper.   463

Typists who use single sheets of car-   473
bon paper normally cut off the corners of   481
the sheets; then, to separate papers from   489
carbons, the typist holds the pack at one   498
corner as he shakes the pack gently; the   507
carbon sheets slide out easily. Typists   515
should turn carbons, top to bottom, for   523
each reuse.   526

To insert a thick carbon pack, first insert   537
a sheet of paper and run it up until only   545
an inch remains on the paper table; if you   554
put the carbon pack between the paper and   562
the cylinder, the pack will go in easily.   571
Some typists like to insert the paper   578
slightly, then to interleaf their carbons.   587

Using carbon paper is part of every   596
good typist's job.   600

[START OVER]

1 | 2 | 3 | 4 | 5 | 6 | 7 | 8

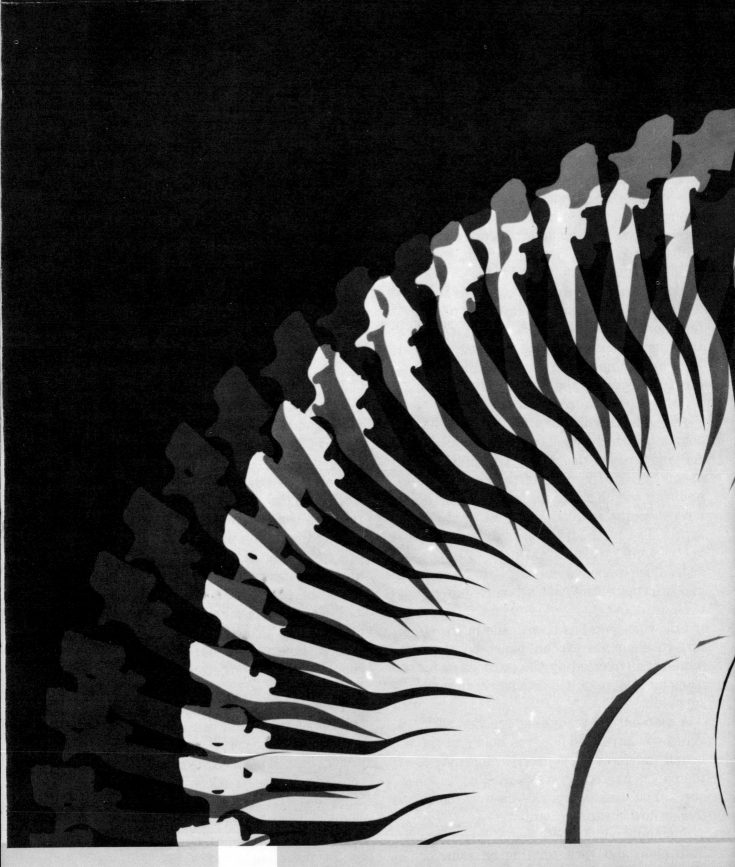

6 METRIC SKILL BUILDING • PROBLEM LETTERS •
FINANCIAL TABLES • LEGAL PAPERS

104-A. Your goal for Lesson 104 should be ACCURACY if you make 4 or more errors; be sure to type sets of drills as paragraphs.

Your goal is SPEED if you make 3 or fewer errors; repeat drill lines individually.

104-A. Inventory your keyboard control

Without pausing, type seven copies of the alphabetic sentence below; then, check your work to find in which controls you erred *two or more* times:

☐ First finger, left hand   ☐ First finger, right hand
☐ Second finger, left hand   ☐ Second finger, right hand
☐ Third finger, left hand   ☐ Third finger, right hand
☐ Fourth finger, left hand   ☐ Fourth finger, right hand

18   Jeff quickly amazed the audience by giving six new reports.

104-B. Strengthen control of your forefingers

104-B-C-D-E. Type each set of lines (accuracy) or separate lines (speed) once for every whole 10 words a minute you typed in your last long timed writing. (Example: if you typed 37 wam, do these drills three times.)

When you finish 104-E, repeat two times (on one line) each half-line drill for the fingers you checked off in 104-A.

LEFT HAND   RIGHT HAND
19   frf fry fret frog fruit front|juj jut jury just judge jumpy
20   ftf aft tuft heft shaft after|jyj joy July duty jiffy juicy
21   fgf fag gaff guff foggy fight|jhj hub hunt hurt truth hurry
22   fbf fib buff flub bluff abaft|jnj Jan junk June funny runty
23   fvf vat five give favor fiver|jmj jam jump hums tummy gummy

104-C. Strengthen control of your second fingers

24   deded dee deed feed reed heed|kikik kid kind kick dike like
25   dcdcd cod dock duct cold cord|k,k,k ok, ink, irk, kip, ilk,
26   dedcd ace cede deck dice peck|kik,k pi, phi, chi, psi, Ali,

104-D. Strengthen control of your third fingers

27   swsws sew sews news swam wows|lolol low loll roll cool wool
28   sxsxs sex axes oxes exit next|l.l.l lb. Col. bbl. Del. Ill.
29   swsxs wax waxy wash taxi swab|lol.l so. too. ago. woo. Leo.

104-E. Strengthen control of your small fingers

30   aqaqa qua aqua quit quip quay|;p;p; pep prop pulp prep pump
31   azaza zag lazy hazy jazz raze|;/;/; a/b four/five nor/never
32   aqaza equalize quiz quizzical|;p;/; up; prep/prop step/stop

104-F. Now regain stride on easy paragraphs

104-F. Each paragraph two times (or, take a 1-minute timing on it).

GOALS: To set a record on very easy paragraph 33 (SI 1.00) with 1 or no error; then, to do equally well on easy paragraph 34 (SI 1.16) and on fairly easy paragraph 35 (SI 1.32).

33   Of all the things that tell a thief that a home has no   12
one there and so is ripe for a raid, it seems that the main   24
clue is on the steps out front: the milk you did not stop.   36

34   To learn more about the way that hearing works, a team   12
is making a study of the bat, which the team thinks is able   24
to see in the dark with its ears rather than with its eyes.   36

35   In case you are annoyed by the imperative ring of your   12
home telephone, you can have a chime installed, one you can   24
adjust to any pitch or volume that you just happen to like.   36

   1 | 2 | 3 | 4 | 5 | 6 | 7 | 8 | 9 | 10 | 11 | 12

104-G. Confirm your progress in sustained writing

PENALTY SCALE

—3 for each major error (top margin, line length, line-spacing, general correctness of form, etc.)
—2 for each minor error (blocking, aligning, centering, indenting, etc., of individual parts of the job)
—1 for each typographical error

GRADING SCALE

0-1 PENALTY .... A
2-3 PENALTY .... B
4-6 PENALTY C
7-8 PENALTY .... D

Test 5-C
Letter 55

SEMIBLOCKED LETTER WITH SPECIAL DISPLAY
Paper: workbook 243
Body (with postscript): 184 words, plus centered subject line
Tab: paragraph 10,
Date, closing: as in Illus. 10, page 172
Start: machine set, carriage at the date
Grade: box below
SI: 1.43—normal

5-MINUTE SPEED WITHIN 3 ERRORS*

50-up wam ...... A
45-49 wam ...... B
35-44 wam C
30-34 wam ...... D

* If more than 3 errors are made, compute the speed on what is typed before the fourth error.

Test 5-D
Forms 50-54

5-MINUTE TIMING ON PAYROLL VOUCHER CHEQUES
Forms: workbook 244-246
Start: machine set, form inserted to first entry
Grade, errorless copies:
5 forms done .... A
4 forms done .... B
3 forms done C
2 forms done .... D

Ms. Jeanette F. Baur | Weston's Department Store | 13   19
McTague Street | Guelph, Ontario, Canada N1H 2A7 | Dear   31
Ms. Baur: | [*subject line:*] IT'S TIME TO PLAN FOR HAWAII! | 52

    Are you going to be one of the 1 000 members of the National   66
Retail League who come to Hawaii for the convention in August?   79
We hope you are! Hawaii is beautiful at any time of the year, but   92
in August it simply shines with flowers and sunlight and splashing   105
whitecaps off Waikiki—a perfect place for holidays, and a perfect   119
place for conventions, also.   125

    If you wish to be at The Lanai Waikiki, where your conven-   138
tion is to be held, you need to reserve your room long in advance.   152
Hawaii is a busy place in the summer, with few rooms available   165
(with a view of Diamond Head, that is!). We should be pleased to   178
reserve one for you now, if you wish; the enclosed leaflet gives   191
you the details about room sizes, the rates, the deposit, and so   204
on.   Cordially yours,   218

               THE LANAI WAIKIKI   242
               Ruth Soong Ki, Reservations   263

Notations   266

    P. S. Most visitors who come here find Hawaii so lovely   279
that they stay over for a longer holiday. Should you decide to do   293
so, we should be pleased to assure you the same low rates you will   306
enjoy during your convention stay.   313

    1 | 2 | 3 | 4 | 5 | 6 | 7 | 8 | 9 | 10 | 11 | 12 | 13

PAYROLL REGISTER

NO.	NAME	TOTAL TAX EXEMPTIONS	GROSS PAY	DEDUCTIONS									NET PAY	
				INCOME TAX		C.P.P.		U.I.		MISC.		TOTAL		
1	Caswell, Robert G.	2091	193	80	33	35	2	93	3	19			39	47	154	33
2	Fordyce, J. Elliott	2081	206	40	37	40	3	16	3	40	1	87	47	66	158	74
3	Gordon, Elizabeth D.	2091	225	30	43	55	3	50	3	72			53	27	172	03
4	Klein, Mark L.	4705	197	25	19	35	3	60	3	26	1	87	29	05	168	20
5	Preston, Henry K.	3921	242	60	36	65	3	91	4	00			47	26	195	34
6																
7																
8																
9																
10																

Use above data for payroll voucher cheques J162-J166 for these five persons.

LINE: 60
TAB: 5
SPACING: SINGLE
GOAL: NUMBER
 CONTROL
STRESS: EYES ON COPY
DRILLS: AS DIRECTED

105-A. Each line three or more times—press for smooth, steady typing. Repeat in Lesson 106.

105-A. Tune up on these reach-review lines

1 Rickey did not wish to pay the usual duty for the fur pelt.
2 My fine black ax just zipped through the wood quite evenly.
3 3 and 6 and 9 and 12 and 15 and 18 and 21 and 22 [Continue to 60]

105-B. As a pretest, type a copy without pausing or looking up once. Proofread. For each number that you type incorrectly, put a light pencil mark before the matching drill in lines 5-14.

SI 1.42—normal, with all digits and letters

105-B. Measure your skill on this numeric paragraph

4 John's company now has 56 stores, located in 30 cities 12
in the West. They employ 147 girls and 138 men, or a total 24
of 285 workers, in these stores. The various products they 36
sell are supplied by some 90 different firms, located in 26 48
states. These figures are pretty exciting when you realize 60
that this unique firm did not get into business until 1947. 72

1 | 2 | 3 | 4 | 5 | 6 | 7 | 8 | 9 | 10 | 11 | 12

105-C. Each line three times, plus an additional time if the drill is for a number that you typed incorrectly in 105-B.

When you finish typing drill 14, check your work (lines 5-14) very carefully: If there is any drill for which you have not typed at least one perfect copy, retype that drill until you do have a perfect copy.

105-C. Improve your control of the number keys

5 11 a1a Of the 111 men, 11 were too tall, 11 were too short.
6 22 s2s Each of the 22 men got 2 copies of the 22-page book.
7 33 d3d The 33 boys in Camp 3 got 3 daily meals for 33 days.
8 44 f4f Of the 4444 men, 444 bought seats on the 4:44 train.
9 55 f5f The 55 men in Squadron 5 had accrued 55 days' leave.
10 66 j6j Project 666 was done by 66 men in each of 6 classes.
11 77 j7j They need 77 coats, 77 hats, and 77 kits in Camp 77.
12 88 k8k The 8th Group bought 888 boxes of No. 88 ammunition.
13 99 l9l You will never get 9999 by adding 99 and 99 and 999.
14 00; 0; They saw 10 or more on Islands No. 10, 100, and 110.

105-D. Type each line three times, with at least one perfect copy of it. Do not type the underscores.

105-D. Increase fluency in typing numbers

15 we 23 23 23 wey 236 236 236 tip 580 580 580 our 974 974 974
16 up 70 70 70 you 697 697 697 wit 285 285 285 ire 843 843 843
17 or 94 94 94 yet 635 635 635 rip 480 480 480 owe 923 923 923
18 to 59 59 59 wry 246 246 246 put 075 075 075 tie 583 583 583

1 | 2 | 3 | 4 | 5 | 6 | 7 | 8 | 9 | 10 | 11 | 12

105-E. Type each line three times, with at least one perfect copy of it.

105-E. Speed up with pair-pattern numbers

19 She scored 28, 39, 47, 56, and 100 on that series of tests.
20 Trunk No. 10 is in Room 47, No. 28 in 56, and No. 39 in 10.
21 Check in closets 10, 28, and 56 for boxes number 39 and 47.

1 | 2 | 3 | 4 | 5 | 6 | 7 | 8 | 9 | 10 | 11 | 12

105-F. Repeat 105-B.

105-F. Confirm your progress in number control

Progress Test on Part Five

POLICY ON REPETITION OF ADS

    The experts in the field of advertising find that
one question comes up time and again: Is it better to
repeat a good advertisement or to keep showing new ads
to the public? Our committee was asked to see whether
there is a reply to this question which would apply to
the basic products that we promote in our advertising.

RESEARCH

    We found that a great many studies have been made
on this subject. We were able to review nine studies.
We regret to report that no study deals with a problem
quite like ours; each is concerned with some one phase
of the problem, and in no case is that phase quite the
same as any of those we face in our promotion program.

    But put together, the studies add up to some help
for us. There is an interesting study on the best use
of color, for example. There is one on the space size
and two on the page position. There are other studies
dealing with the special problems of special products,
but there is none dealing with our repetition problem.

RECOMMENDATIONS

    On the basis of our own researches and experience
in recent years, we should like to suggest that future
displays for our main products include these features:

    1. Let us standardize on the color that we use in
all ads that involve the use of color; the color to be
selected should also be used in our product packaging.

    2. Let us design and use a uniform signature line
for all our ads, no matter where they appear, in order
that we may pound home our name and our new trademark.

    In other regards (including when to repeat an ad,
when to write a new one, and so on), we feel that members of the promotion team should be left a free hand.

    Harold Harms (Sales); Martha Holder (Production);
George Blane (Promotion); John Hess (Agency), Chairman

1 | 2 | 3 | 4 | 5 | 6 | 7 | 8 | 9 | 10 | 11

106-A. Measure your skill on a paragraph with symbols

106-A. As a pretest, type a copy without pausing or looking up once. Proofread. For each symbol that you typed incorrectly, put a light pencil mark before the matching drill in lines 24-28.

SI 1.36—normal

22   If you use a dash to show a break in thought, like "We   12
know——well, we think——we passed the test," make the dash of   26
two hyphens without a space before, between, or after them.   38

23   But when you wish to use a dash to indicate a span, as   52
in "about 10 – 20% off" or "about 10-20% off," use a single   64
hyphen, either with one space on each side of it or with no   76
space on either side of it; "about 10——20%" would be wrong.   88

    1 | 2 | 3 | 4 | 5 | 6 | 7 | 8 | 9 | 10 | 11 | 12

106-B. Improve mastery of these symbol keys

106-B. Each line three times, plus an extra time if the drill is for a symbol you got wrong in the pretest.

The "M" lines are for manual typists; the "E" lines are for the electric machines.

24M   k8k k'k ⎫
24E   ;'; ;';⎬ It's a good day, isn't it? John's dad won a prize!

25   ;p- ;-; My in-laws are cordial——well, reasonably so——to me.

26M   j6j j_j ⎫
26E   ;-; ;_;⎬ Stop reading The Call of the Wild and listen to me!

27   f5f f%f It may be typed 10% to 28%, or 10 – 28%, or 10-28%.

28M   s2s s"s ⎫
28E   ;'; ;";⎬ "Well," he said, "so long." We begged, "Don't go!"

106-C. Increase fluency in typing numbers

106-C. Type each line three times, with at least one perfect copy of it. Do not type the underscores.

Note that this drill differs from 105-D.

29   we 23 24 25 wey 236 237 238 tip 580 581 582 our 974 975 976
30   up 70 71 72 you 697 698 699 wit 285 286 287 ire 843 844 845
31   or 94 95 96 yet 635 636 637 rip 480 481 482 owe 923 924 925
32   to 59 60 61 wry 246 247 248 put 075 076 077 tie 583 584 585

    1 | 2 | 3 | 4 | 5 | 6 | 7 | 8 | 9 | 10 | 11 | 12

106-D. Regain stride on an easy paragraph

106-D. Type three copies (or take three one-minute writings), with this GOAL: To finish a copy within 1 minute and no errors whatsoever!

SI 1.11—very easy

33   I stood by the door of the cabin and looked at a vista   12
that seemed to stretch on and up to the rim of the world, a   24
deep cut of a valley that the snow had made as white as the   36
finest piece of china you may ever have held in your hands.   48

    1 | 2 | 3 | 4 | 5 | 6 | 7 | 8 | 9 | 10 | 11 | 12

106-E. Confirm and push your progress

106-E. As a post-test, make two attempts to complete this loaded paragraph within 2 minutes, with only 2 or fewer errors. Note that the word count gives triple credit for underscored words.

SI 1.59—difficult

34   "If you've a series of words to be underscored," Ralph   12
said, "underscore them solidly unless there is some special   27
reason why they must be stressed separately. For 90-95% of   41
the cases, you'll type the line with no breaks for spaces."   54

    I asked, "What about marks of punctuation?"   64

    He said, "You will——of course——underscore them if they   76
occur in a solid group; in other cases, it doesn't matter."   88

    1 | 2 | 3 | 4 | 5 | 6 | 7 | 8 | 9 | 10 | 11 | 12

Applicant: RACHEL E. JORDAN

Address: 10 Denlow Boulevard
                Don Mills, Ontario   M3B 1P2

Telephone: 416-821-4526

Applying for: Junior Accountant

Date: March 21, 19—

A. PERSONAL DATA
    1. Age: 22. I was born March 3, 19—.
    2. Height: 175 cm Mass: 72 kg
    3. Health: Excellent.
    4. Marital status: Single, but engaged.
    5. Residence: Live with parents.

B. PERTINENT EXPERIENCE RECORD
    1. Maintained storekeeper records and payroll records
        for father's business, for 1½ years.
    2. Was cashier at Carson's (Toronto) on Saturdays and
        some evenings during last year of high school.
    3. Was bookkeeper for a Junior Achievement Group during
        my first year at Central City College.

C. EDUCATIONAL RECORD
    1. Graduated from Don Mills High School, May 29, 19—,
        after completing a college-preparatory course.
    2. Will graduate from Central College on June 3, after
        completing the two-year accounting program.
    3. Academic and skill achievement—
        a. Accounting: 15 semester hours, honor grades.
        b. Business machines: Can use all calculators.
        c. Typewriting: 60 words a minute (10-minute test).
        d. Filing and Systems: Completed 50-hour course.
    4. Have ranked on Dean's list throughout college program.
    5. Extracurricular activities—
        a. Served as business manager for college newspaper.
        b. Treasurer of my church's Youth Group.

D. REFERENCES
    1. Dr. John K. Shapiro, Dean of Men, Central College,
        6 Victoria Boulevard, Toronto, Ontario   M6M 2C1.
    2. Mr. Richard Forbes, Manager, Men's Suit Department,
        Carson's, 4 Selkirk Street, Toronto, Ontario   M4J 1T4
    3. Mr. Adam Gerhold, Director, Don Mills Youth Guild,
        4 Medical Court, Scarborough, Ontario   M1K 5A4

Pages 237-238 of your workbook are a replica of a genuine employment
application form. Fill it in completely with your personal data, as though
you were applying for an office job.

LINE: 50
TAB: 5, CENTER
SPACING: SINGLE
GOAL: LEARN ABOUT
LETTER DESIGNS
DRILLS: 3 EACH
STRESS: APPLY FULL
SKILL TO LETTERS

107-A. Tune up on these easy review lines

107-A. Recall skill by taking two ½-minute timings on each line. Repeat in Lesson 108.

1 Jip has two men who can fix the old car you have.
2 He quickly extinguished the most dangerous blaze.
3 It began at 10:28 in Room 47, was in 56 by 10:39.

   | 1 | 2 | 3 | 4 | 5 | 6 | 7 | 8 | 9 | 10

107-B. Build skill via developmental sustained writing

107-B. Steps to take:

1. Scan the copy, just to see what is said.

2. Select the hardest word in each line and type a line of it.

3. Take a 5-minute timed writing, pausing for a 10-second rest at the end of each minute. Or, type a copy, pausing to rest after you complete each paragraph.

4. Take a 5-minute timed writing without rests. Or, type a copy without pausing a single time. GOAL: Best possible rate within 3-error ceiling.

SI 1.43—normal

4   FOREWORD

AT FIRST THOUGHT, it might seem desirable for all   10
letters to be standardized, to be arranged alike.   20
Certainly it would make the production of letters   30
quite easy for the typist. Imagine: No problems   40
in placement, in line lengths, in the arrangement   50
of the inside address and closing, in any of many   60
other points of form that now concern the typist.   70
                                                           71
     But the plain truth is that no one wants the   81
letters to look exactly like those of other writ-   91
ers. Like a football player who wishes a uniform   101
like that of his teammates but wants a number all   111
his own, each writer wants his letters to be like   121
other letters in general, but in some way unique.   131
                                                          132
     And so business letters appear in many forms   142
that, like the football uniforms, are quite alike   152
and yet can be distinguished by some unique point   162
of arrangement. These forms are called "styles."   172
Two styles, the blocked and the semiblocked, bear   182
the burden of traffic in nine out of ten letters;   192
and other styles share the remaining tenth. As a   202
review and a guide, the following pages present a   212
gallery of the modern styles of business letters.   222

Insert day's date   Pivot your name

   | 1 | 2 | 3 | 4 | 5 | 6 | 7 | 8 | 9 | 10

Manuscript 29

CENTERED FOREWORD
Paper: workbook page
183 or plain paper
Spacing: single
Arrangement: unbound
SI: 1.43—normal

Note: If you use plain paper for the letters, draw or type a line 1½ inches from the top, to represent the depth of a letterhead. Then, type in the blank letterhead space the caption that appears on the model illustration of the style you are to use in each letter.

107/108-C. Become an expert in letter design

Center Manuscript 29 on plain paper or on workbook page 183; then type Letters 44-47 on plain paper or workbook pages 185-192. Work carefully, for these five assignments may be used as the start of a *Letter Styles Book* that you can develop from the assignments in Unit 18.

LINE: 60
TAB: CENTER
SPACING: SINGLE
DRILLS: THREE TIMES
GOAL: PRACTICE ON
  APPLICATION PAPERS
STRESS: LOW WRISTS

123-A. Each line three times—consecutively, for a speed increase; but alternately, for a gain in your accuracy. Repeat in Lesson 124.

123-B. Note the changes in the letter. Adjust margins to make them suitable for a "long" letter. Skim the letter and type, three times, each capitalized word and each number. Insert clean paper, dropping to the proper starting line. Then follow one of these two routines:

1. See whether you can produce a correct copy of the letter within 6 minutes and 3 errors. You may try twice. If you succeed, lo! you have typed Letter 55.

2. Take two 5-minute timings, trying for 46 or more words a minute within 3 errors. Save your papers; you may be able to count one as your letter 55!

SI 1.50—fairly hard, especially in the form of a rough draft copy!

Letter 54

PERSONAL-BUSINESS
BLOCKED LETTER
Paper: plain, full
Body: 187 words (and an attention line)
Review: page 61
Caution: line length shown is not right for pica or elite!

UNIT 20

123-A. Tune up on these review lines

1 It is your turn to shape the emblem and pay the man for it.

2 John very quietly picked the six razors from the woven bag.

3 The checks outstanding are for $10, $28, $39, $47, and $56.

1 | 2 | 3 | 4 | 5 | 6 | 7 | 8 | 9 | 10 | 11 | 12

123-B. Sustain your skill on production copy

4

10 DENLOW BOULEVARD

Don Mills   ~~Richmond Hill, Ontario~~   5

Today's date   ~~March 22, 19~~ ......   11 / 15

16

~~The National Company~~ Martin + Stevens Ltd,   21

~~250 Queen Victoria Avenue,~~ 4652 College Street   24

Toronto, Ontario   M6G 1B8   30

ATTENTION OF THE PERSONNEL DEPARTMENT   38

Gentlemen: 42

junior accountant

I should like to apply for the position of ~~secretary~~,   55

as advertised in this morning's ~~Gazette~~, Times.   65

I was pleased to see your advertisement. I was among   77

the group of seniors from Central College conducted   87

on a tour of your offices a few weeks ago; ever since   98

then, I have hoped that a vacancy might occur for   108

which I might qualify. I shall graduate ~~on May 30~~ June 3;   118

my class schedule, however, is such that I could work   129

afternoons from now until that date.   137

For this vacancy, you require someone who is both in-   148

terested in the work and qualified for it. The fact   159

an accounting

that I am ~~a secretarial~~ major at Central College is   169

evidence of my interest in this work and the training   180

that I can bring to it.   185

With this letter I enclose a personal data sheet that   197

gives my qualifications in more detail. Won't you   207

please review it? If you will be kind enough to ~~tell~~   217

~~me on the enclosed postal card~~ when I might be given   230

a personal interview, I shall be grateful for the op-   241

portunity to apply for the position in person.   250

telephone me at 821-4526.

to let me know

Sincerely yours,   256

Rachel E. Jordan
~~Pauline W. Lambert~~   262

2 Enclosures   264

1. FULL-BLOCKED STYLE . . . so efficient it seems youthful, aggressive . . . every line starts at left margin . . . shown here with a subject line, too . . . and "open" punctuation (no salutation colon, no closing comma).

2. SIMPLIFIED FULL-BLOCKED . . . efficiency expert's dream: no insincere salutation or complimentary closing . . . no indentions . . . open punctuation . . . display of what reader wants most to know: what? from whom?

Letter 44   **45**

Date | Mr. Charles T. Elkins | 36 Greenwood Drive | Summer-   18   **18**
side, Prince Edward Island C1N 4S6 | Dear Mr. Elkins   27   **23**

Subject: Reference for John Walcutt   50   **30**

Mr. John Walcutt has given us your name, Mr. Elkins, as that   63   **44**
of someone who can attest his character and experience in store   76   **57**
management. We are considering him for the post of assistant   88   **69**
manager of the branch store we will open in your city next month.   101   **83**
Might you be kind enough to advise us?   109   **91**

1. Does Mr. Walcutt have the character required for handling   124   **106**
large amounts of cash?   129   **110**

2. Does Mr. Walcutt have the ability to direct the work of   144   **125**
nine or ten other persons?   149   **130**

3. Does Mr. Walcutt have the creative touch and the strong   164   **145**
sense of duty that are so important in running a large store?   178   **158**

If you will answer these questions, Mr. Elkins, and the few   191   **171**
others asked on the enclosed printed form, we shall be most   203   **183**
grateful to you. Your statements will, of course, be held in strict   216   **197**
confidence.   219   **200**

Sincerely yours | J. Walt Flynn | Personnel Manager | urs | 233   **211**
Enclosure   235   **213**

1 | 2 | 3 | 4 | 5 | 6 | 7 | 8 | 9 | 10 | 11 | 12 | 13

Manuscript 39

DISPLAY REPORT
Placement: center
Paper: plain, full
Line: 72 spaces
Tab: in 3, 39, 42
Shown: in elite

For added mastery of the rules
for number expression, use the
Learning Guide, workbook 235.

THE EXPRESSION OF NUMBERS

A Summary by Your Name

WRITE IN WORDS—

a. Ten and the numbers below it:
   The plane has four jet engines.
   I found five dogs and two cats.

b. Round numbers, in general:
   About ten thousand should vote.
   I expect nearly twelve hundred.

c. Numbers that start a sentence:
   Twenty-eight players took part.
   Two hundred twelve were needed.

d. Indefinite amounts of money:
   They gave thousands of dollars.
   He had several hundred dollars.

e. Numbers that are ordinals:
   It is their second anniversary.
   It's his twenty-first birthday.

f. Ages and years, when general:
   He must be seventeen years old.
   He worked here for eight years.

g. Names of centuries, decades:
   Back in the nineteenth century.
   He told about the gay nineties.

h. Street names, ten and below:
   The store is near Fifth Avenue.
   She lives at 191 Second Avenue.

i. Time, informal and o'clock:
   Come over about quarter to ten.
   My plane leaves at ten o'clock.

j. Military, political divisions:
   With the Forty-second Regiment.
   The Fortieth Election District.

WRITE IN FIGURES—

a. Exact numbers above ten:
   The airplane had 36 passengers.
   He has 367 or 368 Irish stamps.

b. Round numbers in advertising:
   We have sold over 10 000 books.
   We get nearly 500 orders a day.

c. Numbers in a series:
   Get 8 bags, 4 boxes, 28 crates.
   I saw 6 men, 11 boys, 14 women.

d. Exact amounts of money:
   They gave $1500 for the school.
   He had neither $1500 nor $2500.

e. Numbers used with percentages:
   No discount is over 10 percent.
   Sales: shoes, 16%; coats, 14%.

f. Ages and years, when exact:
   John is 17 years 11 months old.
   He worked 21 years and 3 weeks.

g. Graduation, historical years:
   He belongs to the class of '56.
   The fine spirit of '76 and '98.

h. Street names above ten:*
   The store is near 188th Street.
   He lives at 919 East 22 Street.

i. Time with minutes, a.m., p.m.:
   I expect Ralph at 9:45 tonight.
   The plane departs at 10:35 p.m.

j. Dimensions and measurements:
   The back room is 4 m by 7.5 m
   The pail holds 3 L of liquid.

---

* Whether to use st, d, rd, or th after street-name numbers (like 22
  Street) depends on local preference. More and more businessmen prefer not to use them, particularly when a word separates the building
  and street numbers, as in 919 East 22 Street or 199 South 147 Avenue.

Illustration of a Display Report

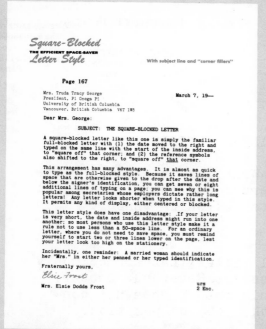

3. SQUARE-BLOCKED . . . greatest space-saver, can get an extra hundred words on page . . . for date is lowered to square up top right corner . . . and reference symbols are moved up and over to square off bottom right corner.

4. SEMIBLOCKED . . . the restrained, cordial look that top executives like . . . shown here with an attention line . . . deep 10-space paragraph indentation, just for distinctiveness . . . and carbon-copy notations, too.

Letter 45

SQUARE-BLOCKED LETTER
Paper: workbook page 189, or plain paper
Body: 170 words
Punctuation: standard
Directions: arrange like Letter 3 above
SI: 1.34—normal

Letter 46

SEMIBLOCKED LETTER
Paper: workbook page 191, or plain paper
Body: 170 words
Punctuation: standard
Directions: arrange like Letter 4 above
SI: 1.34—normal

October 13, 198-

	Letter 46	47
Date │ Employees Credit Union │ The Lehigh Corporation │ 1800		18
Lansdowne Street │ Campbellton, New Brunswick E3N 2L6 │ *In*	34	28
Letter 46: SUBJECT: CREDIT UNION STOCKS *but in Letter 47:* ATTEN-	38	34
TION HOWARD KLING │ Gentlemen:	57	49
At the suggestion of the League of Credit Unions, to which your	71	64
group belongs, we have made a survey to learn to what extent the	84	77
funds of credit unions are now invested in stocks.	95	88
The survey has been completed. A report has been published as a	109	103
64-page booklet. If you wish, one of our staff members will bring	122	116
you copies of this report and discuss its details with you.	134	128
Our findings show that, of the 320 groups that took part in the	148	143
survey, 274 groups now hold stocks and 30 more groups are plan-	160	155
ning to purchase them; thus, 304 of the 320 groups, or 95 percent of	174	169
them, will hold stocks by the end of this year.	184	179
The complete report indicates what stocks have been bought and	198	193
what stocks will be purchased, according to the present plans of	211	206
the 320 groups in the study. If you would like us to help you	223	219
review the report and shape a plan of future action, just return	236	232
the card that is enclosed. │ Yours very truly, │ Robert E. Splane │	252	252
Vice-President │ *reference symbols?*	261	259

1 │ 2 │ 3 │ 4 │ 5 │ 6 │ 7 │ 8 │ 9 │ 10 │ 11 │ 12 │ 13

Manuscript 37   Paper: plain
                     Shown: in pica
COMMITTEE REPORT   Tab: 5, center
IN SINGLE SPACING   SI: 1.53—fairly
Placement: center   difficult

Manuscript 38   Arrange same material
                     as a double-spaced,
COMMITTEE REPORT   two-page report; see
IN DOUBLE SPACING   pages 115-116 again.
Placement: formula   Paper: plain

PERSONAL TITLES IN BUSINESS LETTERS

The committee appointed by Mr. Wilhelms to study the use of personal titles in business letters found that the subject is amply treated in many sources, most of which concur.

DEFINITION

This report deals with personal titles that are commonly used in business letters, like Professor, Reverend, Doctor, Dean, Miss, Mr., Mrs., Ms., etc. This report does not concern social letters or titles of rank, job, or position.

FINDINGS

— 1. A personal title of some kind should always be used before a pesonal name that occurs in any part of a business letter other than in the signer's typed identification, which most often does not include a personal title.

2. Three titles, Mr., Mrs., Ms., are always abbreviated.

3. In addresses, personal titles other than Mr., Mrs. and Ms. are written in full only when the last name is given alone, with neither a first name nor an initial; if either is given, the title is abbreviated (if it is one that can be).

4. In a salutation, personal titles other than Mr., Mrs., and Ms. may be either abbreviated or typed in full, as a writer may prefer. The trend is toward the short form.

5. In the body, personal titles other than Mr., Mrs., and Ms. should be abbreviated if either a first name or initial is given with the last name; if neither is given, the title may be abbreviated or typed in full, as the writer may prefer.

6. In the typed signature, a man does not indicate his personal title unless his first name could be confused with that of a woman. An unmarried woman does not indicate Miss or Ms. unless her first name could be confused with that of a man. A married woman may (and some authorities say should) have the personal title, Mrs., typed before her name.

                    Thomas F. Allerton
                    Virginia Saxon
Chairman's name may Your Name, Chairman
be first, last, or
in alphabetic order.

21
23
36
48
59
61
63
77
92
104
116
118
120
132
145
157
166
179
197
209
222
233
252
264
274
291
303
315
327
349
361
375
387
401
411
418
423
429

Illustration of a Committee Report, Single Spaced

LINE: 60
TAB: 5
SPACING: SINGLE
DRILLS: THREE EACH
GOAL: LEARN MORE
    LETTER DESIGNS
STRESS: SKILL WITH
    AGGRESSIVENESS

109-A. Tune up on these review lines

109-A. Recall skill by taking two ½-minute timings on each line. Repeat in Lesson 108.

1   They may end the big fight by the lake by the usual signal.

2   Jack quietly moved up front and seized the big ball of wax.

3   On April 10, 1928, their firm moved to 3947 East 56 Street.

   1 | 2 | 3 | 4 | 5 | 6 | 7 | 8 | 9 | 10 | 11 | 12

109-B. Build skill via developmental sustained typing

109-B. Steps to take:

1. Scan the copy; solve the revision markings.*

2. Select a hard word in each line; practice it.

3. Take a 5-minute timed writing, pausing for a few-seconds rest at the end of each minute. Or, type one copy, pausing to rest when you finish typing each paragraph.

4. Take a 5-minute timed writing without a rest. Or, type a copy without pausing even one time.

SI 1.29—fairly easy, if you know revision marks.

4   If you have to answer a letter which is signed by Jean   12
Holt White, should you send your answer to Mr. Smith, or to   24
Miss Smith, or Mrs. Smith? Unless you happened to see that   36
the handwriting clearly is that of man, there is no way out   48
of your dilemma; the person who puts you in such a spot is   60
is discourteous. When writing to stranger, it is the height   72
of bad taste not to clearly show what title one should use.   84

A married woman is expected to show her Mrs. either (in   96
parenthesis) as part of her penned signature or, without the   108
parenteses) in the typed name line under her handwriting. A   120
lady who shows no Mrs. is, or may be assumed to be, a Miss.   132

Should the Mr. or Miss never be typed? Yes, whenever   144
the sex of the name is mistakeable. The name Marion, as an   156
example, is as often given to a boy as to a girl; a stranger   168
could not know. The bearer of any such name, man or woman,   180
has to indicate the Mr. or Miss; and these are shown in the   192
same way which Mrs. is shown: in or under the signature, it.   204

Such rules do not apply, of curse, to any person who is   216
a Notable or to letters betwixt people who know each other.   228

   1 | 2 | 3 | 4 | 5 | 6 | 7 | 8 | 9 | 10 | 11 | 12

Manuscript 30

CENTERED DISPLAY
Paper: plain
Spacing: double
Line: 60 spaces
Heading: "The Title of Your Name"
SI: 1.29—fairly easy

109/110-C. Continue production of letters in new designs

Type Letters 48-51 on plain paper or workbook pages 193-200, then type Manuscript 30 (entitle it *The Title of Your Name*) on a plain sheet for possible inclusion at the end of your *Letter Style Book*. Note that the new styles in these letters require *very* careful attention to your consistent use of the tabulator.

* Uncertain of meanings of the revision marks? Then review, on page 112, the table that explains these markings.

UNIT 18

LESSONS 109-110

Reports

LINE: 60
TAB: 5
SPACING: DOUBLE
DRILLS: THREE EACH
GOAL: APPLY SKILL
  TO TYPED REPORTS
STRESS: EYES ON COPY

121-A. Each line three times, or take a half-minute writing on each. GOAL: Flawless rhythm. Repeat in Lesson 122.

121-A. Tune up on these review lines

1 He may wish to visit the rock chapel with us on the eighth.

2 Vicky placed a dozen jugs from Iraq on the waxy table tops.

3 Discounts of 10%, 28%, 39%, 47%, and 56% are quite unusual.

   1 | 2 | 3 | 4 | 5 | 6 | 7 | 8 | 9 | 10 | 11 | 12

121-B. To increase your progress, follow either of these schedules.

1. Read the copy, type a full line of each of a half dozen words that are worth prepracticing. Then, type a copy of each paragraph; GOAL: To complete either within 3 minutes and 2 errors.

2. Read the copy, type a full line of each of a half dozen words that merit prepracticing, and then take two 5-minute writings, the first with rest after each minute and the second with full fluency but no rests. GOAL: 46 or more words a minute within 3 errors.

SI 1.31—fairly easy

121-B. Boost skill on fluent alphabetic paragraphs

4   It is said that each worker supports a dozen or so who   12
live on the circulation of his money. There is the man who   24
sells him his clothing, the one who delivers his groceries,   36
the one who fixes his shoes, the boy who cuts his lawn, the   48
teacher who instructs his children, and all the many others   60
to whom his earnings are relayed. If his income stops, be-   72
cause his hands are no longer purchased for farm or forest,   84
for mine or mill, all these others feel the pinch, too; the   96
worker who leaves is a leak in the local economy. If other 108
workers leave with him, those who exist on serving them are 120
not long in following; and thus the leak may quickly become 132
a break, and the break a flood that sweeps into our cities. 144

5   Now, cities are big and they grow fast; but there is a 156
limit to how rapidly they can expand before they feel grow- 168
ing pains. All our cities are suffering adjustments today. 180
People are moving in faster than new homes can be built for 192
them; so they must crowd into smaller quarters or move to a 204
suburb. People bring their cars, too, faster than the city 216
can widen streets to bear them or make places to park them. 228
People also bring their children with them, faster than the 240
city can build schools to seat them or parks in which these 252
new city citizens may play and let off their animal energy. 264
The problems are huge, but so are the talents and resources 276
that a city can join in firm efforts to solve its problems. 288

   1 | 2 | 3 | 4 | 5 | 6 | 7 | 8 | 9 | 10 | 11 | 12

If you have wondered how many carbons you could produce at one time, or if you have wanted to type a duplicating stencil or master, Manuscript 39 would be a good one to use—it merits multicopy production!

121/122-C. Apply skill to production typing

Manuscripts 37-39 require the longest sustained effort yet; GOAL: See whether you can finish each within 12 minutes and 4 errors.

Indented
THE ULTRACONSERVATIVE
Letter Style With 5-space indentations and closed punctuation

March 8, 19—

Mr. Harold V. Faunce,
28 Forest Avenue,
Paris, Ontario N3L 3L2
Dear Mr. Faunce:

This letter illustrates the indented form, as you see by a glance at the inside address and the closing lines. In each of these groups, the lines are tab-indented in steps of five spaces; and the paragraphs are each tab-indented five spaces, too.

One care to be exercised when you use indented letter form is to make sure that none of the final lines projects into the right margin; you must start the complimentary closing far enough to the left to assure that there is room for all the closing lines.

This letter also illustrates the "closed" form of punctuation: Each of the displayed opening and closing lines is "closed" by a punctuation mark.

Neither the indented arrangement nor "closed" punctuation pattern is commonly used in the United States, but they are both very popular (especially when used together) in Mexico, Canada, and Europe.

Yours very sincerely,
INTERNATIONAL SUPPLY COMPANY,
George Heard Chalmers,
Training Director.

urs.
Enclosures (3).

Indented
SPECIAL SPACE EATER
Letter Style With double spacing and standard punctuation

March 8, 19—

single space { Miss June R. Zane
2831 Browning Avenue
Collingwood, Ontario L9Y 2V8

Dear Miss Zane:

The indented style is one of the few that may be typed in either single or double spacing. The double-spaced form, therefore, is convenient when you have a short letter that must be stretched.

When you plan the placement of a double-spaced letter, you must remember that it will stretch out to twice its single-spaced length. This letter of 83 words, double spaced, occupies as much space as would a single-spaced letter of 166 words.

Cordially yours,
Herman I. Smith
District Manager

HIS/urs
cc Chicago Office

---

5. INDENTED STYLE . . . conservative, or European, look . . . has even, five-space indentation steps . . . shown here with closed punctuation (each heading and closing line is "closed" by some kind of punctuation mark).

6. DOUBLE-SPACED INDENTED . . . great letter-stretcher . . . permits even a brief message to look man-size . . . often used for simple acknowledgments . . . typist must remember to double body-length estimate for placement.

---

closed

Letter 48 **49**

Letter 47 ✓

INDENTED LETTER
Paper: workbook page 193 or plain paper
Body: 106 words
Spacing: single
Punctuation: closed
Directions: arrange like Letter 5 above
SI: 1.39—normal

LETTER 48 | *Date* | Lynch and Forbes, Ltd | 22, rue de Bois | Joli-   18   · ·
ette, Québec J6E 4E9 | Attention of the Personnel Department   52   · ·

Gentlemen: You will recall that a young man on your staff came   68   **38**
to our school to meet and talk with several of our seniors just be-   81   **51**
fore their graduation last year. As a result, your firm was able to   95   **65**
obtain a number of fine young employees.   104   **74**

Do you wish to conduct a similar schedule of interviews this   118   **88**
spring? If you do, please fill in and return to us by May 1 the   131   **101**
planning form that accompanies this letter.   140   **110**

You will note that the planning form asks you to choose two alter-   155   **125**
nate dates; we hope that having a choice will help us reduce the   168   **138**
number of conflicts in appointments. | Yours very truly,   183   **153**

COLLEGE OF COMMERCE | Dean of Women | SEV:URS | *Others?*   208   **165**
1 | 2 | 3 | 4 | 5 | 6 | 7 | 8 | 9 | 10 | 11 | 12 | 13

Letter 48 ✓

INDENTED LETTER
Paper: workbook page 195 or plain paper
Body: 106 words
Spacing: double
Punctuation: standard
Directions: arrange like Letter 6 above
SI: 1.39—normal

LETTER 49 | *Let's send a copy of that letter also to* Davis & Wilson, Ltd.   11
| *They're down on* la Roquette, *too, at* 318, *same city and so on.* | *I*   22
should like to see how the letter would look in double *spacing, with*
ordinary, standard *punctuation. I am afraid the letter might stretch*
out a great deal, so omit the attention *line and our school name.*

Center each line (B - G   C O M P A N Y   C A F E T E R I A

Menu for Thursday, March ~~1120~~ *1# 2#*

APPETIZERS *1#*

Tomato Soup or Clam Chowder (cup) .... .75
Fresh orange or Grapefruit Juice .... .50

LUNCHEON PLATES

Salmon Salad with French Dressing, Cucumber Slices,
    Tomato quarters, and Potato Waffles 1.35
Stuffed Braised Ribs of Beef, Jumbo Pears and Carrots,
    ~~Cold Slaw~~, and Mashed Potatoes 1.85
    Coleslaw

SANDWICHES *2# 1#*

Grilled Canadian Cheese, with tomato Slices 1.00
Tomato, Lettuce, and Bacon (on Rolls) .... .90
Chipped Ham Saute on Large Bun *or on toast* 1.25
Swiss Cheese and Tomato on Fresh rye Bread 1.35

DESSERTS *2# 1#*

Chocolate or Butterscotch Sundae on Chocolate Ice Cream .1.00
Apple, Cherry, Banana Cream, ~~and~~ *or* Peach Pie .... .90
Chocolate layer or Angel Food Cakes .... .95

BEVERAGES *2# 1#*

Milk (Individual Carton) .... .26
Hot Tea or Coffee .... .30

SCHEDULE FOR WINDSOR TRIP
March 21-23, *year*

MONDAY	March 21	*416*	
8:00	~~You will~~ leave Toronto on Flight AC~~214~~		Confirmed
10:15	~~You~~ arrive Windsor, ~~are~~ met by Mr. Graham		Assumed
11:00	*4#* Register ~~for room~~ at Book-Cadillac *Hotel*		Confirmed
11:45	Luncheon with Mr. Montrose, ~~of~~ Ford Motors		Confirmed
14:00	Appointment with Mr. Young, Fordyce Valve		Tentative
18:00	Dinner at ~~the~~ hotel with ~~Doctor~~. Sampson		Confirmed
TUESDAY	March 22 *+#*		
09:00	Appointment with Mr. Stahl, Oldsmobile, ~~GM~~		Promised
10:15	Appointment with ~~Fred~~ *Mr.* Reed, ~~of~~ Pontiac, ~~GM~~		Tentative *confirmed*
11:45	Luncheon with Mrs. Flower, of Ford-Mercury		~~Tentative~~
14:00	Appointment with Mr. Milton, Fisher Body		Unconfirmed
19:00	Dinner ~~for and~~ with Dr. and Mrs. Pfeiffer		Tentative
Wednesday	March 23 *+#*		
08:50	Leave Windsor on AC 57 for Toronto		Confirmed
09:45	Arrive Malton, return to office		Confirmed

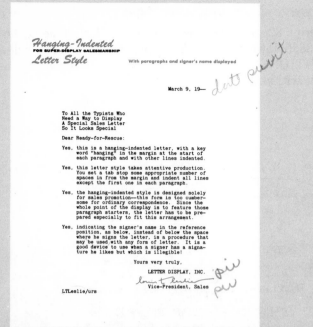

Hanging-Indented
FOR SUPER-DISPLAY SALESMANSHIP
Letter Style   With paragraphs and signer's name displayed

March 9, 19—   *don't print*

```
To All the Typists Who
Need a Way to Display
A Special Sales Letter
So It Looks Special

Dear Ready-for-Rescue:

Yes, this is a hanging-indented letter, with a key
     word "hanging" in the margin at the start of
     each paragraph and with other lines indented.

Yes, this letter style takes attentive production.
     You set a tab stop some appropriate number of
     spaces in from the margin and indent all lines
     except the first one in each paragraph.

Yes, the hanging-indented style is designed solely
     for sales promotion—this form is too cumber-
     some for ordinary correspondence.  Since the
     whole point of the display is to feature those
     paragraph starters, the letter has to be pre-
     pared especially to fit this arrangement.

Yes, indicating the signer's name in the reference
     position, as below, instead of below the space
     where he signs the letter, is a procedure that
     may be used with any form of letter.  It is a
     good device to use when a signer has a signa-
     ture he likes but which is illegible!

                    Yours very truly,

                    LETTER DISPLAY, INC.

                    Vice-President, Sales

LTLeslie/urs
```

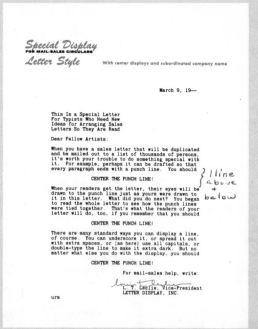

Special Display
FOR MAIL-SALES CIRCULARS
Letter Style   With center displays and subordinated company name

March 9, 19—

```
This Is a Special Letter
For Typists Who Need New
Ideas for Arranging Sales
Letters So They Are Read

Dear Fellow Artists:

When you have a sales letter that will be duplicated
and be mailed out to a list of thousands of persons,
it's worth your trouble to do something special with
it.  For example, perhaps it can be drafted so that
every paragraph ends with a punch line.  You should

                CENTER THE PUNCH LINE!

When your readers get the letter, their eyes will be
drawn to the punch line just as yours were drawn to
it in this letter.  What did you do next?  You began
to read the whole letter to see how the punch lines
were tied together.  That's what the readers of your
letter will do, too, if you remember that you should

                CENTER THE PUNCH LINE!

There are many standard ways you can display a line,
of course.  You can underscore it, or spread it out
with extra spaces, or (as here) use all capitals, or
double-type the line to make it extra dark.  But no
matter what else you do with the display, you should

                CENTER THE PUNCH LINE!

                For mail-sales help, write:

                L. T. Leslie, Vice-President
                LETTER DISPLAY, INC.

urs
```
1 line above + below

7. HANGING-INDENTED . . . for razzle-dazzle sales letters with catch-words "hanging" in left margin . . . all body lines are indented except the first in each paragraph . . . shown here with signer's name in reference position.

8. DISPLAY BLOCKED . . . another mail-sales design . . . hinges on use of paragraph-ending "punch lines" . . . shown here with company name under signer's title . . . Note here and in No. 7 the bizarre "inside address" form.

Letter 49

HANGING-INDENTED LETTER ✓
Paper: workbook page 197 or plain paper
Body: 143 words
Directions: arrange like Letter 7 above
SI: 1.37—normal

50

Letter 50 ✓ *60*

DISPLAY BLOCKED LETTER
Paper: workbook page 199 or plain paper
Body: 143 words
Directions: arrange like Letter 8 above
SI: 1.37—normal

Here's a sales letter I've written to mail to all the seniors of the local colleges. Would it look better in hanging-indented form or in center-display form? I don't know; draft it both ways, please. And, to make reading easy, use a short line— say, a 50-space line. Better experiment a bit, first!

	Letter 50	51
Date | To Every Young Person | Who Wants to Become | A	18	18
Business Executive | Dear Ambitious Friend:	26	26
If you could serve as apprentice to anyone whom you might	41	39
pick, whom would you pick? The errand boy? Of course not!	55	52
You would select some top businessperson, one who could show	69	64
you what an executive is. If you want to pick a person like that,	84	83
you must do something about it! *punch line*	87	92
If you want to work with an executive, you must be able to do	102	105
something that will make him/her want you as apprentice. Do	116	118
you possess secretarial or accounting skills? If you have know-	131	132
ledge or skills to sell, you can do something about it!	146	157
If you want to do something about it, see us. Our business is	161	170
helping top executives find the assistants they need. It does not	175	184
cost you anything—they pay us to find you. Now's the time to	190	197
do something about it! | Visit: | WHITE COLLARS, INC. | Richard	210	225
F. Benkley | District Manager | *reference symbols?*	226	233

1 | 2 | 3 | 4 | 5 | 6 | 7 | 8 | 9 | 10 | 11 | 12 | 13

119/120-D. Apply your skill to production typing

After typing Manuscript 32, page 182, as a quick recall of basic centering, type Manuscripts 33-36, following closely the helpful directions. You will need to look up often; CAUTION: *be careful not to omit any lines!* Your GOAL: To finish each manuscript within 10 minutes and 3 errors.

Manuscript 33

DISPLAY PROGRAM
Paper: plain, full
Spacing: double, extra
  line between "days"
Line: 51 spaces
Tab: center, 52
Caution: pivot lines
  with speakers' names

C O N F E R E N C E   P R O G R A M

Always put 3 spaces between spread-out words. Review page 10.

March 8-12, (year)   1#   2#

Monday: PUBLIC RELATIONS AND ADVERTISING
            Discussion Led by Harvey P. May   ←PIVOT

Tuesday: INCENTIVE WAGE PROBLEMS
            Discussion led by Emil H. *Hale* Bender

WEDNESDAY Morning: USING SALESMEN'S REPORTS M
            Discussion Led by William J. Noran

Wednesday afternoon: Luncheon and Excursion

Thursday: ADMINISTERING JOB EVALUATIONS
            Discussion Led by Joseph *K.* Strong

Friday: OUR WORK-SIMPLIFICATION PROGRAM
            Discussion Led by John Z. Duncan

Manuscript 34

DISPLAY PROGRAM
Paper: plain, full
Spacing: single
Line: 61 spaces
Tab: 10, center, 62
elite

THE B-G FOUNDER'S DAY FESTIVAL

Center each line   Saturday, March 13
            at)
            The Golden Bridge Club   2#

BANQUET .... 6:30 to 8:30 ←PIVOT
            A once-in-a-lifetime *big* charcoal-grilled   1#
10#→ steak dinner, complete from soup to nuts,
            speaking of which reminds me *us* to mention—— 2#

THE SPEAKERS/.................................. 8:30 to 9:00
            Toastmaster Harold Freeman is bringing his *an*   1#
            alarm clock to make sure that no speakers
            talk more than ⑤ minutes; we want to—— 2#

TRIP "THE LIGHT FANTASTIC" .... 9 10:00 to 12:30
            The music is that of Dave Elliott and his   1#
            famous band, with vocals by Dora Deevers.

LINE: 60
SPACING: SINGLE
DRILLS: THREE EACH
GOAL: COMPLETE
STYLE MANUAL
STRESS: COMPLETE
TOUCH OPERATION

111-A. Recall skill by typing lines 2 and 3 in cadence with someone who types only line 1.

111-A. Tune up on these review lines

1 They will find some more work when they have done your job.
2 The banquet speaker, James Carvings, analyzed a few hoaxes.
3 They have been at 3947 East 56 Street since April 10, 1928.

  1 | 2 | 3 | 4 | 5 | 6 | 7 | 8 | 9 | 10 | 11 | 12

111-B. Readjust machine for double spacing, 50-space line, 5-space tab indention. Then follow this practice routine:

1. Scan the copy to be sure you can read it.

2. Select and practice any half-dozen words.

3. Take a 5-minute timed writing, pausing for a few-seconds rest at the end of each minute. (Or, type one copy, pausing to rest when you finish typing each paragraph.)

4. Take a 5-minute timed writing without a rest. (Or, type a copy without pausing even one time.)

SI 1.42—normal, if you can read the writing!

111-B. Sustain your skill on handwritten copy

4   Judging whether a letter is long or short or 10
average is a problem to the novice, but it is not 20
one to the experienced office typist. Except for 30
a few very short or very long letters, the expert 40
treats all letters as average ones, trusting that 50
he will be able to stretch or squeeze the closing 60
lines enough to balance the letter placement. In 70
most cases he can do so, too, simply by adjusting 80
the signature space from the standard three lines 90
of open space to as few as two or as many as six. 100

5   The notations at the end of the letter are a 110
point of easy expanding and squeezing. These may 120
begin as high as level with the identification of 130
the signer or may begin two or three lines below; 140
and these lines may be single spaced, to conserve 150
space, or be double spaced, to spread the letter. 160
The enclosure notation is very useful in juggling 170
letter length, for the items to be enclosed might 180
or might not be listed, depending on space needs. 190
Almost any letter other than one that's very long 200
or very short can be treated as "average" length. 210

  1 | 2 | 3 | 4 | 5 | 6 | 7 | 8 | 9 | 10

Manuscript 31

CENTERED DISPLAY
Paper: plain
Spacing: double
Line: 50 spaces
Heading: "Letter Placement"
SI: 1.42—normal

NOTE: 111-B will double block on a 50-space line. When you type it as Manuscript 31, copy from either the writing or your 111-B copy of it.

111/112-C. Continue production of letters in new designs

Type Letters 52-53 on plain paper or workbook pages 201 and 203, then type Manuscript 31 (entitle it *Letter Placement*) by centering it on a full page. Then assemble your complete *Letter Style Book*.

UNIT 18   LESSONS 111-112

Unit 20. Manuscripts

LINE: 50
TAB: 5
SPACING: DOUBLE
DRILLS: THREE EACH
GOAL: APPLY PIVOTING TO MANUSCRIPT WORK
STRESS: POSTURE

119-A. Each line three times, or take a half-minute writing on it. GOAL: No hesitations.

119-A. Tune up on these review lines

1 Why did you not get the new job you said you got?
2 Quickly pack the box with five dozen modern jugs.
3 Price these items at 10¢, 28¢, 39¢, 47¢, and 56¢.

    1 | 2 | 3 | 4 | 5 | 6 | 7 | 8 | 9 | 10

119-B. A complete copy within 5 minutes and 3 errors, plus a retyping three times of any line you type with an error.

Or, take two 5-minute writings; the first with a rest at the end of each minute, the second with no rests at all. GOAL: 45 or more words a minute within 3 or fewer typing mistakes.

SI 1.32—fairly easy

119-B. Boost skill on fluent alphabetic paragraphs

4   The person who wants to get ahead on the job   10
has to learn how to use common sense. It is fine   20
to know and to be able to quote the rules, but it   30
is better to know when the exact rule ought to be   40
set aside. You have to analyze the situation. A   50
report can be set up in manuscript style, for ex-   60
ample; but if you have to duplicate it, you might   70
be smarter to use single spacing so that you will   80
get the report on fewer stencil or master sheets.   90

5   On the other hand, the saving of paper might   100
not be as important as making a better impression   110
on the executives to whom you will send copies of   120
the report; you must use your judgment. You must   130
choose between the quick shortcuts and the longer   140
methods that give a more attractive product. You   150
must realize that there is a right time for each.   160

6   Good judgment in such matters might not come   170
until you have risked a few mistakes. You should   180
repeat some of your jobs, when time permits, try-   190
ing to arrange them in a different way, or trying   200
to fit them on a smaller size of paper, or taking   210
other liberties with the exact directions. True,   220
you must be quick to do what you are told to do--   230
but you must nurture your judgment skill as well.   240

    1 | 2 | 3 | 4 | 5 | 6 | 7 | 8 | 9 | 10

Manuscript 32

BASIC DISPLAY
Paper: plain
Spacing: double
Placement: center
Title: "Rules Versus Judgment"
SI: 1.32—fairly easy

Review pivoting, page 56; then, type the two exercises shown here: center the title, then align the other lines with the start and end of the centered title. Note leaders. Each row of periods has a space before and after it, and all rows end at an identical point.

119-C. Review the technique of backspace pivoting

PRACTICE 1

THE HIGHWAY CAVALIER

Chapter	Page
I	1
II	37
III	89
IV	166

PRACTICE 2

THE MYSTERY OF THE GLOVE

Chapter	Page
I. We Buy It............	1
II. We Lose It...........	59
III. It Shows Up.........	138
IV. It Is Taken...........	203

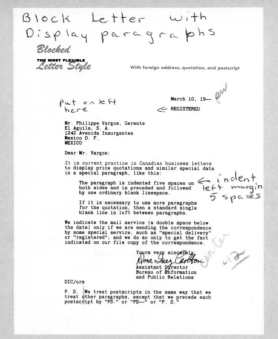

Block Letter with Display paragraphs

Blocked
THE MOST FLEXIBLE
Letter Style — With foreign address, quotation, and postscript

put on left here

March 10, 19—

← REGISTERED

Mr. Philippe Vargos, Gerente
El Aguila, S. A.
1242 Avenida Insurgentes
Mexico D. F.
MEXICO

Dear Mr. Vargos:

It is current practice in Canadian business letters
to display price quotations and similar special data
in a special paragraph, like this:

    The paragraph is indented five spaces on ← indent left margin 5 spaces
    both sides and is preceded and followed
    by one ordinary blank linespace.

    If it is necessary to use more paragraphs
    for the quotation, then a standard single
    blank line is left between paragraphs.

We indicate the mail service (a double space below
the date) only if we are sending the correspondence
by some special service, such as "special delivery"
or "registered"; and we do so only to get the fact
indicated on our file copy of the correspondence.

    Yours very sincerely,

    Nora Ines Carlson

    Assistant Director
    Bureau of Information
    and Public Relations

DIC/urs

P. S. We treat postscripts in the same way that we
treat other paragraphs, except that we precede each
postscript by "PS:" or "PS—" or "P. S."

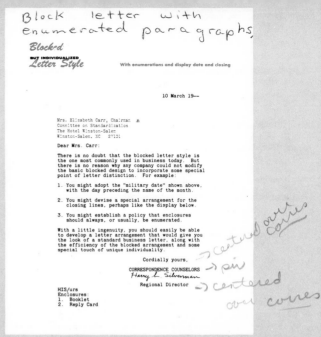

Block letter with enumerated paragraphs.

Block'd
BUT INDIVIDUALIZED
Letter Style — With enumerations and display date and closing

10 March 19—

Mrs. Elizabeth Carr, Chairman
Committee on Standardization
The Hotel Winston-Salem
Winston-Salem, NC 27101

Dear Mrs. Carr:

There is no doubt that the blocked letter style is
the one most commonly used in business today. But
there is no reason why any company could not modify
the basic blocked design to incorporate some special
point of letter distinction. For example:

1. You might adopt the "military date" shown above,
   with the day preceding the name of the month.

2. You might devise a special arrangement for the
   closing lines, perhaps like the display below.

3. You might establish a policy that enclosures
   should always, or usually, be enumerated.

With a little ingenuity, you should easily be able
to develop a letter arrangement that would give you
the look of a standard business letter, along with
the efficiency of the blocked arrangement and some
special touch of unique individuality.

      Cordially yours,

      CORRESPONDENCE COUNSELORS

      Harry L. Silverman

      Regional Director

HIS/urs
Enclosures:
1. Booklet
2. Reply Card

→ centred over corres
→ pin
→ centered over corres

9. BLOCKED LETTER . . . shown here with mail-service reminder under date . . . foreign address, country name on separate, all-capped line . . . set-off paragraphs . . . long signer's identification . . . and a postscript.

10. BLOCKED LETTER . . . most nearly "standard" form but often individualized by, as here: inverting date into armed-services style . . . centering closing lines on one another . . . listing enclosures in an enumeration.

Letter 51

BLOCKED LETTER
Paper: workbook page
  201 or plain paper
Body: 182 (with P.S.)
Line: 60 spaces
Directions: arrange
  like Letter 9 above
SI: 1.48—high-normal

Letter 52

BLOCKED LETTER
Paper: workbook page
  203 or plain paper
Body: 160 words
Line: 60 spaces
Directions: arrange
  like Letter 10 above
SI: 1.43—normal

Letter 52   53

Date | OVERSEAS AIRMAIL | Dr. and Mrs. Foster T. West | Arabian	18
American Oil Company | Abu Hadriya Refinery | SAUDI ARABIA	29
We have found the large home you wanted. I am enclosing six	48 56
photographs and a floor plan. Here are the main details:	60 69
The house has ten rooms—four bedrooms (and three baths)	74 83
upstairs, four rooms (and powder room) on the first floor, and	88 96
a utility room and a playroom (and lavatory) in the basement—	101 100
and a double garage.	106 114
The house is five years old and in very good condition. It	120 127
has thermostat controls both for heating (oil) and for air-	132 141
conditioning, although the latter has never been installed. The	146 151
house will need to be painted (about $1,500).	157 165
The asking price is $80 000, but I believe we could get	172 179
the home for about $72 500. It has a mortgage; the pur-	185 186
chase could be financed with 20 percent down.	192 199
This home seems to come close to the description you gave in de-	206 213
fining what you wished. Other realtors are looking at it, too; so	219 229
we should move swiftly if you wish to purchase it. | What is your	235 244
pleasure? | David D. Davis Agent | urs | Enclosures | P. S.	250 249
Since you may be on your way to Canada now, I am writing to	264
you also at your Canadian address.	270
LETTER 53 | *Address Dr. and Mrs. West* | at 3211 Charlottetown	17
Drive, | Summerside, Prince Edward Island. | *Delete the postscript.* |	25
Enumerate the enclosures. | *Number the three display paragraphs.*	44

JUNIPER SALES SPECIALTY COMPANY
3399 LAWRENCE AVENUE

VANCOUVER, BRITISH COLUMBIA   March 19, 19 --   No. 2118

1-785
266

PAY TO THE ORDER OF William Zaner $ 318.50

Three hundred eighteen and 50/100 - - - - - - - - - - -DOLLARS

JUNIPER SALES SPECIALTY COMPANY

TORONTO-DOMINION BANK
VANCOUVER, B. C.

AUTHORIZED SIGNATURE

DETACH AND RETAIN THIS STATEMENT   THE ATTACHED CHECK IS IN PAYMENT OF ITEMS DESCRIBED BELOW
                                          IF NOT CORRECT PLEASE NOTIFY US PROMPTLY. NO RECEIPT DESIRED

Payment of expenses on trip to Vancouver, March 1-7, 19—

Mr. William Zaner

411 West Packer Street

Green Bay, Wisconsin   54301

U.S.A.

VOUCHER CHEQUE is regular cheque with detachable
stub (on any side) for address and explanation.

$ 625.85 _____   _____ March 19, 19--

Thirty days - - - - - - - - - - - - - - - - - -*after date* we *promise to pay to*

the order of Juniper Sales Specialty Company - - - - - - - - - - - - - - - -

Six hundred twenty-five and 85/100 - - - - - - - - - - - - - - - - *Dollars*

at Toronto-Dominion Bank, Vancouver, British Columbia - - - - - - - - - - -

Value received   RODGERS WHOLESALE COMPANY

No. 183 ___ *Due* April 18, 19-- _____   _____

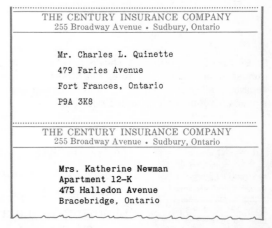

THE CENTURY INSURANCE COMPANY   *Sudbury, Ontario*

March 19, 19---

Dear Mr. Quinette:

We have received your request for a copy of:

"How Much Insurance Should I Have?"

We are sending it today, with our compliments. We hope that it will
prove to be of interest and value and that we may have the pleasure of
serving you again.

SERVICE MANAGER

urs

FILL-IN CARD has insertions that are
aligned vertically and horizontally.

THE CENTURY INSURANCE COMPANY
255 Broadway Avenue • Sudbury, Ontario

Mr. Charles L. Quinette

479 Faries Avenue

Fort Frances, Ontario

P9A 3K8

THE CENTURY INSURANCE COMPANY
255 Broadway Avenue • Sudbury, Ontario

Mrs. Katherine Newman
Apartment 12-K
475 Halledon Avenue
Bracebridge, Ontario

LABELS . . . block the addresses, use
single spacing for more than 3 lines.

Forms 44-45

PROMISSORY NOTES
Forms: workbook 233

Forms 46-47
Cards 7-8

ACKNOWLEDGMENT
CARDS
Forms: workbook 221

Form 48

SHIPMENT LABELS
Forms: workbook 233

FORM 44. *Promissory Note No. 183:* The Rodgers Wholesale Company promises to pay $625.85 to the order of the Juniper Sales Specialty Company, at the Toronto-Dominion Bank, Vancouver, 30 days from today.

FORM 45. *Promissory Note No. 184:* The Ford-Bart Corporation promises to pay $900.00 to the order of the Juniper Sales Specialty Company, at the Bank of Nova Scotia, Trail, British Columbia, 60 days from today.

FORM 46 / CARD 7. Acknowledge a request for "How Much Insurance Should I Have?" from Mr. Charles L. Quinette, 479 Faries Avenue, Fort Frances, Ontario, P9A 3K8.

FORM 47 / CARD 8. Acknowledge a request for "A College Education for Your Child!" from Mrs. Katherine Newman, Apartment 12-K, 475 Halledon Avenue, Bracebridge, Ontario.

LABEL NO. 1. To Mr. Quinette, address above.
LABEL NO. 2. To Mrs. Newman, address above.
LABEL NO. 3. To Dr. Edward Svensen, Central City Hospital, 3618 North Ridgewood Avenue, St. James, Manitoba.
LABEL NO. 4. To M. [Monsieur] Joseph-Pierre Poirier, 1800, rue Royale, Ste-Anne-de-Beaupré, Québec.

LINE: 60
TAB: 5
SPACING: SINGLE
DRILLS: THREE EACH
GOAL: INTELLIGENT
WORK ON FORMS
STRESS: NUMBERS
ONLY BY TOUCH

Unit 19. Printed Forms

113-A. Each line three times, holding on lines 2 and 3 the high pace you set on easy line 1. Repeat in Lesson 114.

113-A. Tune up on these review lines

1 I am to go to work for the audit firm by the eighth of May.

2 Beckwith just managed to verify his extremely popular quiz.

3 Pages 10, 28, 39, 47, and 56 were most interesting to them.

   1 | 2 | 3 | 4 | 5 | 6 | 7 | 8 | 9 | 10 | 11 | 12

113-B. Each line three times, for speed gain; or the whole group of lines three times, for gain in accuracy, too. Type steadily; do not pause at vertical bars.

113-B. Regain fluency on these easy phrases

4 who will |firm that |each part |they use |all the |but it |is the

5 the form |that most |have once |that you |who use |one of |if you

6 and then |that save |time will |form for |day and |set up |to use

   1 | 2 | 3 | 4 | 5 | 6 | 7 | 8 | 9 | 10 | 11 | 12

113-C. Type a complete copy in Lesson 113 and another in Lesson 114; GOAL: Finish the copy within 6 minutes, with 3 or fewer errors.

Or, take one 5-minute writing in Lesson 113, with a 10-second rest after each minute; and one 5-minute writing in Lesson 114 without pausing for any rest. GOAL: 45 or more words a minute within 3 or fewer typing errors.

Use double spacing and 5-space tab indention.

SI 1.29—fairly easy

113-C. Hold stride on fairly easy alphabetic paragraphs

7 One of the most thriving kinds of business in this day   12
and age is the business of designing business forms. True,   24
almost all stationers have standard forms on their shelves;   36
but it is true, too, that most big firms bring in an expert   48
who will analyze all the forms they use and then design new   60
ones that are easier to use and that save time for the per-   72
sons who use them. You would not suppose a firm that sells   84
jars of medicine would use the same billhead as a firm that   96
sells steel axles. In the same sense, the requisition form   108
for office supplies would not serve the needs of a factory.   120

8 Each form is organized on principles that good typists   132
should know. Here are some examples: All forms should use   144
standard typewriter spacing; you should never have to shift   156
a tab stop, squeeze a number, or adjust the variable spacer   168
after you have once set up the machine. A form should have   180
guide words or signals to show what should be typed in each   192
part of the form; you should not have to guess. Every form   204
must resemble a letter; that is, you should be able to type   216
the entries on the form in almost exactly the same sequence   228
that you would if you were typing them in a regular letter.   240

   1 | 2 | 3 | 4 | 5 | 6 | 7 | 8 | 9 | 10 | 11 | 12

113/114-D. Apply production skill to billing forms

If you lack workbook forms, type Lesson 113-114 assignments either in typed memo form (see page 108) or as blocked business letters, with all the data given in proper, complete sentence form.

Study the six illustrations that follow; then, type Forms 20-31 on workbook pages 207-218. Although these tasks are varied, they are so easy you should type them without error easily in five minutes each.

LINE: 60
TAB: 5
SPACING: SINGLE
DRILLS: THREE EACH
GOAL: CONFIDENT
   FORM PRODUCTION
STRESS: GO-POWER

117-A. Recall skill by half-minute writings on each line. Repeat these drills in Lesson 118.

117-A. Tune up on these review lines

1 Their men wish to blame me for both of their big work jams.
2 Rex amazed Jack by pointing quickly to five of the answers.
3 The data on pages 10, 28, and 39 are repeated on 47 and 56.

    1 | 2 | 3 | 4 | 5 | 6 | 7 | 8 | 9 | 10 | 11 | 12

117-B. Each three times (consecutively, for a speed gain; alternately, for an accuracy gain).

117-B. Sharpen your control of capitals

4 Wisconsin Terrific Packer Street Sales Zaner Green Dear Bay
5 Enclosure Manager William Alfred Stahl Sales Yours Bill But

117-C. Adjust machine for double spacing and copy line for line.

1. Scan the copy.

2. Make an exact copy in each lesson, trying to complete it within 5 minutes and 3 errors. Or, take a 5-minute writing twice—once with a rest after each minute and, then, once without any such rests. GOAL: Maximum speed within 3-error limit.

SI 1.32—fairly easy

117-C. Increase your skill on production copy

	(C)	(D)
6 Good morning. Please take this letter to William | 11 | 10 |
Zaner, at 411 West Packer Street, Green Bay, Wisconsin | 22 | 21 |
54301, U.S.A. Dear Bill: | 26 | 25 |

    When we have an account to settle, all we need to   37 36
do is issue a voucher cheque; we need not even write a   48 47
letter, because the stub on the cheque indicates fully   59 59
what payment we are making. I have been informed that   70 70
one of the reasons we use such cheques is to eliminate   81 81
the need for having a letter of explanation.   92 92

    But when a speaker has come the distance that you   103 103
did and has performed the service that you did for our   114 114
sales staff, he deserves a letter, too, that tells him   125 125
that he was terrific; so this is why I am writing you.   136 136

    Bill, you were terrific. <u>Terrific!</u>   148 148

    The cheque for your expenses is enclosed together   159 159
with a voucher that reminds you what the money is for;   170 170
the stub does not say you were terrific, but you were.   181 181

    Yours very sincerely, and the usual Alfred Stahl,   192 195
Sales Manager; be certain that you <u>do</u> make out and en-   204 197
close the voucher cheque. If you forgot it after what   215 200
I have said about it, he would never let <u>me</u> forget it!   227 · · ·

    1 | 2 | 3 | 4 | 5 | 6 | 7 | 8 | 9 | 10 | 11

117/118-D. Apply your skill to production typing

FORM 42. *Voucher Cheque No. 2118.* Pay $318.50 to Mr. Zaner for "Payment of expenses on trip to Vancouver, March 1-7, 19—."

FORM 43. *Voucher Cheque No. 2119.* Pay $150.00 to yourself for "Payment for services as technical advisor, March 6, 19—."

Letter 53
FULL-BLOCKED LETTER
Review: page 166
Paper: workbook 229
Punctuation: open
Body: 141 words
SI: 1.34—near-normal

Forms 42-43
VOUCHER CHEQUES
Forms: workbook 231
Illustration: page 181

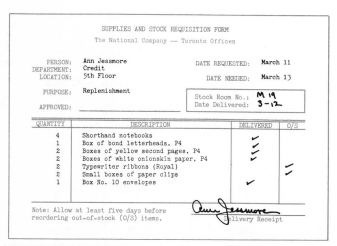

SUPPLIES AND STOCK REQUISITION FORM

The National Company — Toronto Offices

PERSON: Ann Jessmore
DEPARTMENT: Credit
LOCATION: 5th Floor

DATE REQUESTED: March 11

DATE NEEDED: March 13

PURPOSE: Replenishment

APPROVED: _____

Stock Room No.: M 19
Date Delivered: 3-12

QUANTITY	DESCRIPTION	DELIVERED	O/S
4	Shorthand notebooks		
1	Box of bond letterheads, P4	✓	
2	Boxes of yellow second pages, P4	✓	
2	Boxes of white onionskin paper, P4	✓	
2	Typewriter ribbons (Royal)		✓
2	Small boxes of paper clips		✓
1	Box No. 10 envelopes	✓	

Note: Allow at least five days before reordering out-of-stock (O/S) items.

Ann Jessmore
Delivery Receipt

STOCK REQUISITION is used to draw everyday supplies from a storeroom. Forms vary (depending on company inventory control) and may be either printed or (above) duplicated.

Purchase Requisition No. 2516

The National Company • 250 Queen Victoria Avenue • Toronto, Ontario M4J 1E8

DEPARTMENT: Sales Promotion
LOCATION: Room 416
PERSON: T. M. Winters

DATE OF REQUEST: 19— 11 03
DATE WANTED: 19— 01 04

REASON: Office furnishings for new employee

APPROVALS: *TMW.*   *Ellwood Perkins*
Signature of Department Head   Other Signature Required

QUANTITY	DESCRIPTION	SUGGESTED PURCHASE SOURCE
2	Steel file cabinets, 2-drawer, gray	MM&Sons
1	Steel desk, executive, gray	58 Broadview Street
1	Steel desk chair, executive, gray	Toronto, Ontario
2	Steel chairs, guest, arm, gray	M4M 2E4

PURCHASING DEPARTMENT INFORMATION

Ordered from: Martin Miller & Sons
58 Broadview Street
Toronto, Ontario M4M 2E4

Purchase Order Number: 6377
Date Ordered: 19— 3 12
Date Received: 19— 3 28

do not touch lines

PURCHASE REQUISITION is used to ask Purchasing Department to buy something, such as replacement of warehouse stock (above), furniture, and so on. Forms are usually printed.

Forms 20-21

STOCK REQUISITIONS
Forms: workbook 207
Directions: arrange
as shown above, left

FORM 20. Ann Jessmore, a Credit Department secretary, 5th Floor, needs these desk replenishments by next Friday: . . . 4 shorthand notebooks . . . 1 box of bond letterheads . . . 2 boxes of yellow second pages . . . 2 boxes of white onionskin paper . . . 2 typewriter ribbons (Royal) . . . 2 small boxes of paper clips . . . 1 box No. 10 envelopes.   11 32 47 61 73

FORM 21. John Deer, Shipping Department, 1st Floor, needs (by Monday of next week) routine replenishment of: . . . 6 rolls No. 14 twine . . . 5 000 shipping tags (12 cm x 7 cm, oaktag) . . . 300 No. 7 cardboard cartons . . . 200 No. 11 cardboard cartons . . . 5 rolls No. 17H (heavy duty) stapler wire . . . 10 rolls 7 cm paper binding tape.   19 32 47 61 73

Forms 22-23

PURCHASE REQUISITIONS
Forms: workbook 209
Directions: arrange
as shown above, right

FORM 22. Mr. T. M. Winters, head of Sales Promotion, Room 416, wants office furnishings for a new employee, due the first of next month: . . . 2 steel file cabinets, 4 drawer, standard width, in gray . . . a steel desk, executive type, in gray . . . a steel desk chair, executive type, in gray . . . and two steel guest chairs, with armrests on them, in gray.   15 25 43 55 63

Mr. Winter suggests that these be purchased from Martin Miller & Sons, at 58 Broadview Street, Toronto, Ontario M4A 2E4.   66 77

FORM 23. Mr. Aloysius Vincent, Stores-Supplies Department, 18th Street Annex, needs to replenish his paper stocks by the first of next month: . . . 500 boxes NatCo letterheads, P4 . . . 100 boxes NatCo letterheads, P4 . . . 300 boxes NatCo No. 10 envelopes (500 per box), third class (open-end flap) . . . 300 boxes NatCo No. 10 envelopes (500 per box), first class (standard flap) . . . 100 boxes NatCo No. 9 envelopes (500 per box), first class (standard flap).   12 24 42 57 72 88 102

Mr. Vincent mentions that these items are all available under Contract 61-332 with Walsh & Weir, Printers, of Peterborough.   104 114

An earnings record is kept for each employee. It must match corresponding payroll registers and is brought up to date at end of each payroll period.

EARNINGS RECORD OF **Benjamin F. CROSLEY**
NAME

ADDRESS **134 Confederation Drive** SOCIAL INSURANCE NO. **144-603-928**

Huntsville, Ontario POA 3K2 MARRIED **X** SINGLE

TELEPHONE **131-2208** TOTAL INCOME TAX EXEMPTIONS **$2 300.00**

| DATE PERIOD ENDED | AMOUNT EARNED | DEDUCTIONS | | | | NET PAY |
		INCOME TAX	C.P.P.	GROUP INS.	MISC.	
1/14	246 20	30 91	3 48	2 46	18 75	190 60
1/28	246 20	30 91	3 48	2 46		209 35
2-11	246 20	30 91	3 48	2 46	18 75	190 60
2-25	246 20	30 91	3 48	2 46		209 35
3-11	246 20	30 91	3 48	2 46	18 75	190 60
3-25	246 20	30 91	3 48	2 46		209 35

Forms 37-38 ✓

EARNINGS RECORDS
Forms: workbook 225
Copy 1: Mr. Crosley
Copy 2: Mr. Danderson

FORM 38. For the same six payroll periods as in Form 37, prepare the earnings record of Frederick L. Danderson, who lives at 908 North Elm Street in Huntsville P0A 4K9. His phone is 131-7736. His Social Insurance number is 273-384-707. He is married and his income tax exemptions total $2 600.00. As he has no miscellaneous deductions, each line of his record will read the same: Date ... Amount Earned, $218.40 ... Income Tax Withheld, $18.90 ... C.P.P., $3.48 ... Group Insurance, $1.14 ... Net Pay: $193.88.

T-4 Income Tax form is summary of employee's earnings record and tax withholdings for the previous calendar year.

Revenue Canada Taxation Revenu Canada Impôt **STATEMENT OF REMUNERATION PAID**
ÉTAT DE LA RÉMUNÉRATION PAYÉE

T4-1976
Supplementary–Supplémentaire

• For District Taxation Office
• Pour le bureau de district d'impôt

1

EMPLOYEE - EMPLOYÉ:
SURNAME FIRST (in capital letters), USUAL FIRST NAME AND INITIALS AND FULL ADDRESS
NOM DE FAMILLE D'ABORD (en capitales), PRÉNOM USUEL ET INITIALES ET ADRESSE COMPLÈTE

CROSLEY, Benjamin F.
134 Confederation Drive,
HUNTSVILLE, Ontario
POA 3K2

(A) PROVINCE OF EMPLOYMENT PROVINCE D'EMPLOI	(B) SOCIAL INSURANCE NUMBER Nº D'ASSURANCE SOCIALE	(N)	EMPLOYEE NO Nº DE L'EMPLOYÉ
Ontario	144 : 603 : 928		N/A

NAME AND ADDRESS OF EMPLOYER - NOM ET ADRESSE DE L'EMPLOYEUR

LEROY ELECTRIC COMPANY
7 Shipley Road,
Huntsville, Ontario POA 4K6

(C) TOTAL EARNINGS BEFORE DEDUCTIONS	(D) EMPLOYEE'S PENSION CONTRIBUTION CANADA PLAN / QUEBEC PLAN	(E) U.I. PREMIUM	(F) REGISTERED PENSION PLAN CONTRIBUTION	(G) INCOME TAX DEDUCTED	(H) U.I. INSURABLE EARNINGS	(I) C.P.P. CONTRIBUTORY EARNINGS	(J) EXEMPT C.P.P./Q.P.P. / U.I.
$6400 : 00	$82 : 80	$46 : 00	nil	$872 : 30	$2900 : 00	nil	CPP
GAINS TOTAUX AVANT DÉDUCTIONS	DU CANADA / DU QUÉBEC COTISATION DE PENSION (EMPLOYÉ)	PRIME D'A.-C.	CONTRIBUTIONS RÉGIME ENREGISTRÉ DE PENSIONS	IMPÔT SUR LE REVENU DÉDUIT	GAINS COTISABLES A.-C.	GAINS COTISABLES POUR R.P.C.	R.P.C./R.R.Q. / A.-C. EXONÉRATION

BOX (C) AMOUNT INCLUDES ANY AMOUNTS IN BOXES (H), (I), (K) AND (L) LE MONTANT DE LA CASE (C) COMPREND TOUS MONTANTS FIGURANT AUX CASES (H), (I), (K) ET (L)	(K) TAXABLE ALLOWANCES AND BENEFITS	(L) COMMISSIONS	(M) PENSION PLAN REGISTRATION NUMBER	If different from Box (C) S'ils sont différents de la Case (C)
	nil	nil		
	ALLOCATIONS ET PRESTATIONS IMPOSABLES	COMMISSIONS	Nº D'ENREGISTREMENT DU RÉGIME DE PENSIONS	

FORM 40. Prepare the T-4 form for Mr. Danderson (Form 38). His figures should read: $5 680.00 ... $82.80 ... $608.10. ...

FORM 41. Prepare the T-4 form for a fellow employee of Mr. Danderson's, Stephen L. Parkleigh, whose Social Insurance number is 088-364-414. He lives at 1392 South Oak Street, in Huntsville P0A 5K5. His figures: $6 000.00 ... $82.80 ... $844.10.

Forms 39-41 ✓

T-4 INCOME TAX FORMS
Forms: workbook 227
Copy 1: Mr. Crosley
Copy 2: Mr. Danderson
Copy 3: Mr. Parkleigh

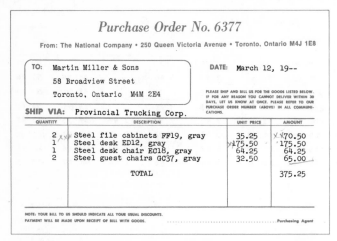

Purchase Order No. 6377

From: The National Company • 250 Queen Victoria Avenue • Toronto, Ontario M4J 1E8

TO: Martin Miller & Sons
58 Broadview Street
Toronto, Ontario M4M 2E4

DATE: March 12, 19--

PLEASE SHIP AND BILL US FOR THE GOODS LISTED BELOW. IF FOR ANY REASON YOU CANNOT DELIVER WITHIN 30 DAYS, LET US KNOW AT ONCE. PLEASE REFER TO OUR PURCHASE ORDER NUMBER (ABOVE) IN ALL COMMUNICATIONS.

SHIP VIA: Provincial Trucking Corp.

QUANTITY	DESCRIPTION	UNIT PRICE	AMOUNT
2	Steel file cabinets FF19, gray	35.25	70.50
1	Steel desk ED12, gray	175.50	175.50
1	Steel desk chair EC18, gray	64.25	64.25
2	Steel guest chairs GC37, gray	32.50	65.00
	TOTAL		375.25

NOTE: YOUR BILL TO US SHOULD INDICATE ALL YOUR USUAL DISCOUNTS. PAYMENT WILL BE MADE UPON RECEIPT OF BILL WITH GOODS.
.................................Purchasing Agent

MARTIN MILLER & SONS
58 BROADVIEW STREET   TORONTO, ONTARIO   M4M 2E4

INVOICE

CUSTOMER'S ORDER NO. 6377   DATE March 26, 19--   3122

SOLD TO   SHIP TO
The National Company
250 Queen Victoria Avenue,
Toronto 18, Ontario   M4J 1E8

SHIPPED VIA   Collect Provincial Trucking Corp.

QUANTITY	DESCRIPTION	CAT. NO.	UNIT PRICE	TOTAL
2	Steel file cabinets	FF19	35 25	70 50
1	Steel desk	ED12	175 50	175 50
1	Steel desk chair	EC18	64 25	64 25
3	Steel guest chairs	GC37	32 50	97 50
	TOTAL			407 75
	LESS 10% TRADE DISCOUNT			40 77
	TOTAL AMOUNT DUE			366 98

PURCHASE ORDER is an official order form from a Purchasing Department to any outside supplier of goods or services. It may be any size from half page (above) to many pages.

INVOICE is a form, different in different businesses, for listing the charges for one delivery of services or goods. Omission of decimals (above) is emerging trend.

FORM 24. Martin Miller & Sons [58 Broadview Street, Toronto, Ontario M4M 2E4], please ship via Provincial Trucking Corp. the following: . . . two steel file cabinets FF19, gray @ $35.25 . . . a steel desk ED12, gray @ $175.50 . . . a steel desk chair EC18, gray @ $64.25. Please double-check the total.   16 24 41 61 78

FORM 25. Walsh & Weir, Printers [220 Murray Street, Peterborough, Ontario R9H 2S8], please ship via C&C Express, Inc., the following items, priced by our Contract 61-332: . . . 500 boxes P4 NatCo letterheads @ $2.75 . . . 100 boxes P4 NatCo letterheads @ $2.63 . . . 300 boxes NatCo No. 10 envelopes (500 per box), third class (open-end flap) @ $3.15 . . . 300 boxes NatCo No. 10 envelopes (500 per box), first class (standard flap) @ $3.50. Confirm the total.   17 31 41 62 76 95 112 133

FORM 26. Invoice No. 3122 from Martin Miller & Sons to The National Company [250 Queen Victoria Avenue, Toronto, Ontario M4J 1E8] for a shipment, collect via Provincial Trucking Corp, for: . . . two steel file cabinets, catalogue FF19 @ $35.25, for $70.50 . . . one steel desk, catalogue ED12 @ $175.50, for $175.50 . . . one steel desk chair, catalogue EC18 @ $64.25, for $64.25 . . . and 3 steel guest chairs, catalogue GC37 @ $32.50, for $97.50. Total bill, $407.75, less 10% trade discount $40.77, for the total amount due: $366.98.   12 25 39 51 65 79 100 109

FORM 27. Invoice No. M-321 from Walsh & Weir, Printers, to The National Company [250 Queen Victoria Avenue, Toronto, Ontario M4J 1E8] for a collect shipment via C&C Express, Inc.: [*Compute extensions*] 500 boxes P4 NatCo letterheads @ $2.75 . . . 100 boxes P4 NatCo letterheads @ $2.63 . . . 300 boxes NatCo No. 10 envelopes, third class @ $3.15 . . . 300 boxes NatCo No. 10 envelopes, first class @ $3.50 . . . 100 Boxes NatCo No. 10 envelopes, first class @ $2.75. Add 5 percent sales tax.   1 21 30 50 67 84 104 130

NO.	NAME	TOTAL TAX EXEMP-TIONS	GROSS PAY	DEDUCTIONS								TOTAL		NET PAY	
				INCOME TAX		C.P.P.		GROUP INSURANCE		MISC.					
1	Bobbitt, Robert C.	2 600	189 50	16	45	3	48		80			20	73	168	77
2	Devine, William J.	1 300	178 90	26	06	3	48	1	80			31	34	147	56
3	Harrison, Joanne C.	1 000	236 30	45	01	3	48		50			48	99	187	31
4	Johnson, Charles K.	2 300	207 10	23	39	3	48	2	18			29	05	178	05
5	Masters, Helene L.	1 000	194 60	33	00	3	48		83	1	94	39	25	155	35
6	Norton, V. Russell	1 000	184 20	30	29	3	48	1	50			35	27	148	93
7	Romanoff, Jerome	1 550	203 80	29	89	3	48		57	1	94	35	88	167	92
8	Thomas, Robert G.	1 000	195 40	33	35	3	48	1	50	1	94	40	27	155	13
9															
10															

Form 34

PAYROLL REGISTER
Form: workbook 221

In some companies the permanent payroll register is a typed copy of a draft that is first made in handwriting from employees' timecards and related records.

1. When typing *between* a series of horizontal lines, center (approximately, by estimate) the typing vertically between the pairs of lines.

2. When typing amounts in a column with a vertical line to separate dollars from cents, adjust the paper so the decimal (which is *not* typed) would, if typed, fall exactly on the separation line.

[Most forms are designed for elite spacing; on a pica machine you will need to adjust the carriage, retarding it by hand, in order to insert some cents figures correctly in the space assigned them.]

3. When typing *on* a single ruled line, adjust the paper so the line is in the underscore position.

4. When typing amounts after a $ sign, position the figures so close to the $ sign that no figure could be inserted between the $ and the number.

5. To fill in a line with leaders, use hyphens and spaces alternately.

Forms 35-36

VOUCHER CHEQUES
Form: workbook 223
Copy 1: Cheque for
  Robert G. Thomas
Copy 2: Cheque for
  Jerome Romanoff

A payroll cheque is usually (as here) a "voucher cheque" with a stub on which may be explained the origin of the amount of the cheque (copied from a payroll register or a similar payroll record).

MARTIN MILLER & SONS
58 BROADVIEW ST., TORONTO, ONT. M4M 2E4

4-2
310

No. M-221

Name   V. Russell Norton   DATE March 26, 1978

DETACH AND RETAIN

GROSS PAY	DEDUCTIONS					NET PAY
	Income Tax	C.P.P.	Group Ins.	Misc.	Total	
175.40	26.65	3.48	1.50		31.63	143.77

MARTIN MILLER & SONS
58 BROADVIEW ST., TORONTO, ONT. M4M 2E4   No. M-221

Payroll Cheque

DATE March 26   19 78

PAY TO THE
ORDER OF   V. Russell Norton $ 143.77

One hundred forty-three and 77/100 - - - - - - - - - - - - - - - - - - DOLLARS

Payable at
THE ROYAL BANK OF CANADA
  Yonge & Bloor Branch
  Toronto, Ontario M4W 2L7

CREDIT MEMORANDUM is a fairly standard form used to let a customer know that a change has been made (usually but not always in his favor) in his account balance.

STATEMENT OF ACCOUNT is a periodic (usually monthly) summary of transactions with a customer, showing charges and credits and the cumulative balance right up to date.

Forms 28-29

CREDIT MEMOS
Forms: workbook 215
Directions: arrange
as shown above, left

FORM 28. Martin Miller & Sons issues Credit Memorandum No. 2435 to The National Company [250 Queen Victoria Avenue, Toronto, Ontario M4J 1E8] to correct error in shipment covered by Invoice No. 3122: For 1 steel guest chair in excess of order @ $32.50 for a total of $32.50. From this amount, however, must be deducted the 10 percent [$3.25] trade discount; then to the amount must be added the allowance for the two-way delivery charges for the chair [$2.60].

FORM 29. Walsh & Weir, Printers issues Credit Memorandum No. 1421 to National [address above] to correct a shortage in the shipment for which Invoice No. M-321 had been issued: For 200 boxes P4 NatCo letterheads, shortage in delivery, @ $2.75. Include 5 percent tax refund, too.

Forms 30-31

MONTHLY STATEMENTS
Forms: workbook 217
Directions: arrange
as shown above, right

FORM 30. Monthly statement from Martin Miller & Sons recapitulates the firm's transactions with The National Company for March:

Mar 1 Brought forward (from February)	......		130 00
Mar 5 Payment on account (credit)	......	95 00	35 00
Mar 19 Invoice No. 2913 (charge)	255 05	......	290 05
Mar 23 Payment on account (credit)	......	35 00	255 05
Mar 26 Invoice No. 3122 (charge)	366 98	......	622 03
Mar 28 Credit Memo No. 2435 (credit)	......	31 85	590 18
Mar 29 Payment on account (credit)	......	255 05	335 13

FORM 31. Monthly statement from Walsh & Weir, Printers recapitulates the firm's transactions with The National Company for March:

Mar 1 Brought forward (from February)	......		000 00
Mar 26 Invoice No. M-321 (charge)	4025 24	......	4025 24
Mar 27 Payment on account (credit)	......	3000 00	?
Mar 28 Credit Memo No. 1421 (credit)	......	566 50	?

LINE: 60
SPACING: SINGLE
DRILLS: THREE EACH
GOAL: LEARN TO TYPE
ON RULED FORMS
STRESS: TOUCH
CONTROL ON
NUMBERS

115-A. Recall skill by half-minute writings on each line. Repeat these lines in Lesson 116.

115-A. Tune up on these review lines

1 She may wish to pay them if and when they go to work for us.

2 To jeopardize and hit six of the brigades, we moved quickly.

3 She assigned pages *10, 28, 39, 47, and 56* for the next week.

  1 | 2 | 3 | 4 | 5 | 6 | 7 | 8 | 9 | 10 | 11 | 12

115-B. Readjust machine for double spacing, 50-space line, and tabs at 10 and 20. Then, steps:

1. Scan the copy, to be sure you can read it, and note use of tabulator.

2. Select and practice any half-dozen words

3. Take a 5-minute timed writing, pausing for a few-seconds rest at the end of each minute. (Or, type one copy, pausing to rest at each "double-double" spacing point.)

4. Take a 5-minute timed writing without pauses. (Or, type a copy without pausing even one time.) SI 1.40—normal, if you can tabulate by touch!

115-B. Sustain your skill on production copy

4 Date: *March 16, 19—*   6

To: John K. Speare, Head, Payroll Section   16

From: Ruth N. North, Personnel   23

Subject: Adding New Employee to the Payroll ↴4   33
                                                                    34

5 The following has been processed by Personnel and   44

may now be added to the payroll.   Data you need: ↴4   54
                                                                    55
6 Full name: *Mr. Ralph Dale Carr*   63

Local address: *1321 West Sixth Avenue*   72

Phone: *392-4141*   77

Soc. Ins. No.:   *343-286-102*   84

No. dependents: *Self and one*   91

Savings bonds: *$50 per month*   98

Section assigned: *Stores and Supply*   107

Effective date: *March 24, 19—*   115

Starting rate: *$5200 per year*   ↴4   122
                                                                   123
7 If there are other data you need, the file of this   133

new employee will be available in this department. ↴4   144

                 Holly Anne Graham   151
                 For Ruth N. North   157

Forms 32-33

FILL-IN MEMORANDUMS
Paper: workbook page 219 or plain paper
Copy 1: data shown here
Copy 2: your personal data, as a $130-a-week secretary in Sales

If you lack workbook forms, type the Lesson 115-116 assignments as memos or as tables, to the extent that they can be so arranged.

115-C. Learn to type payroll forms

The payroll forms used in different businesses vary considerably both in their arrangement and in the extent to which they *are* typewritten. Typical *typewriting* problems involved in typing on such forms include:

p211-212

312 (
314
316